lucille

Ludovic
Debeurme

Top Shelf Productions
Atlanta / Portland

Je remercie — My thanks
Cécile
Boris, Linda, et Ilaria

Lucille au fond des Bois

(Deep in the Woods)

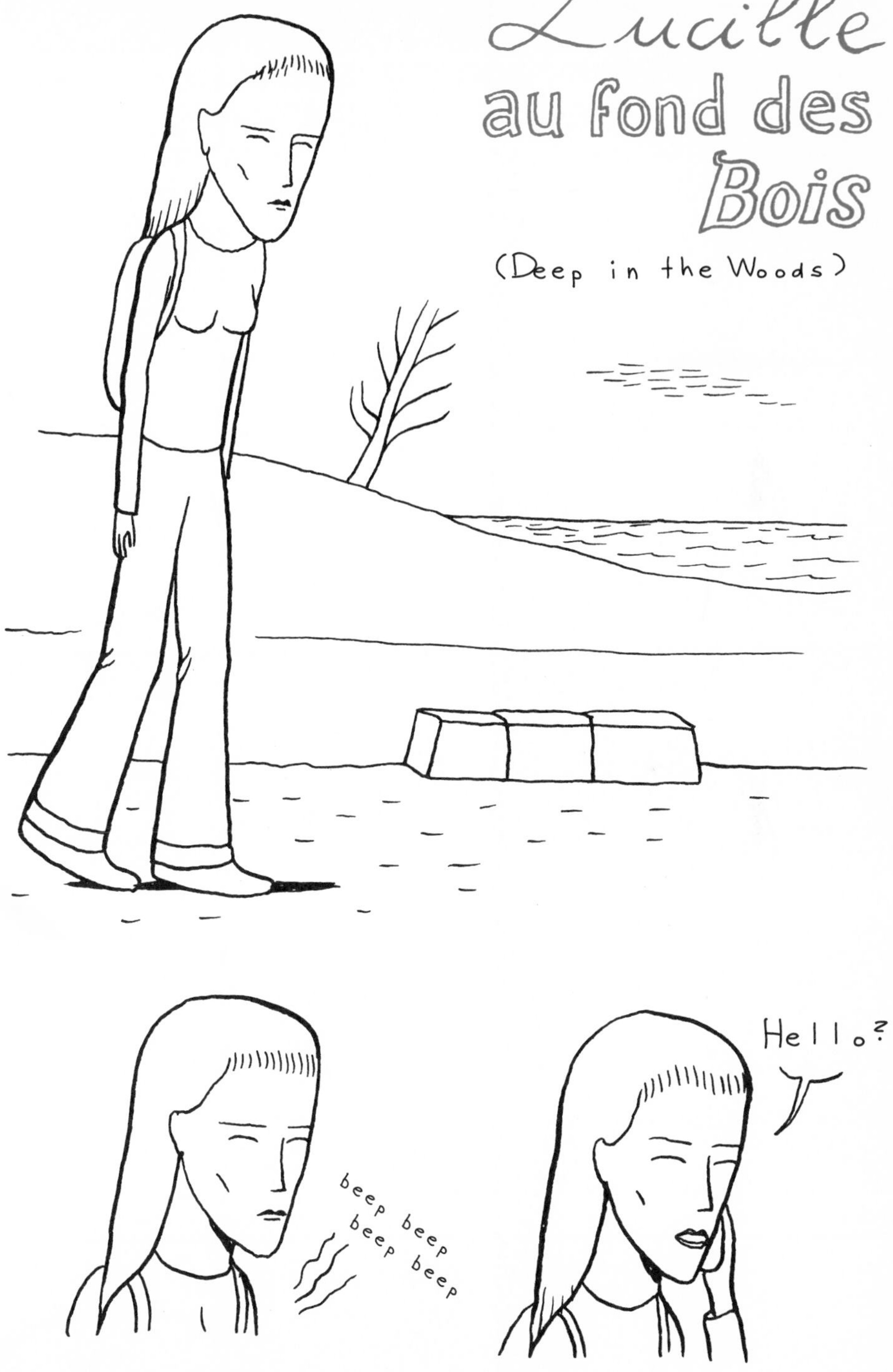

beep beep
beep beep
Hello?

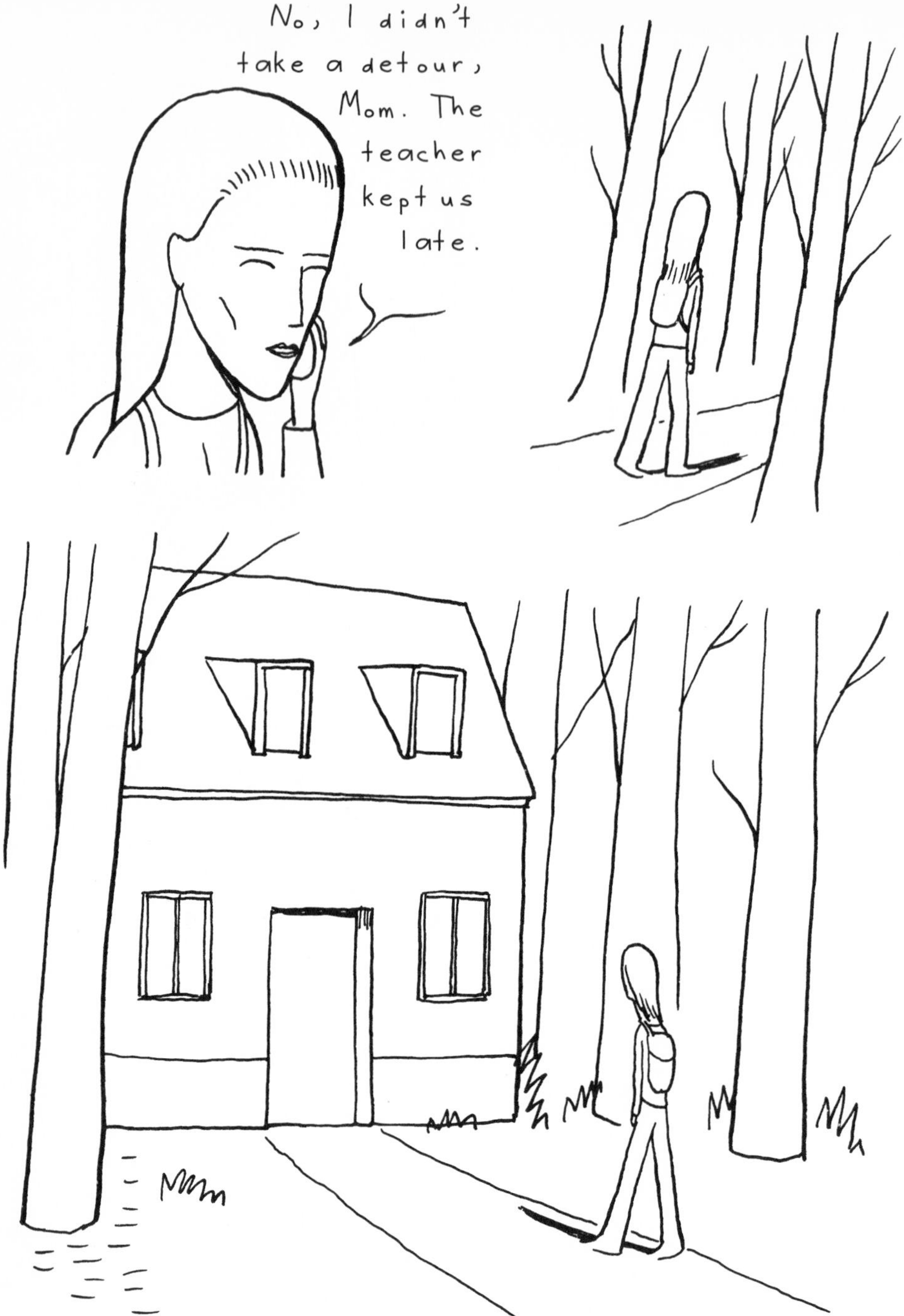
No, I didn't take a detour, Mom. The teacher kept us late.

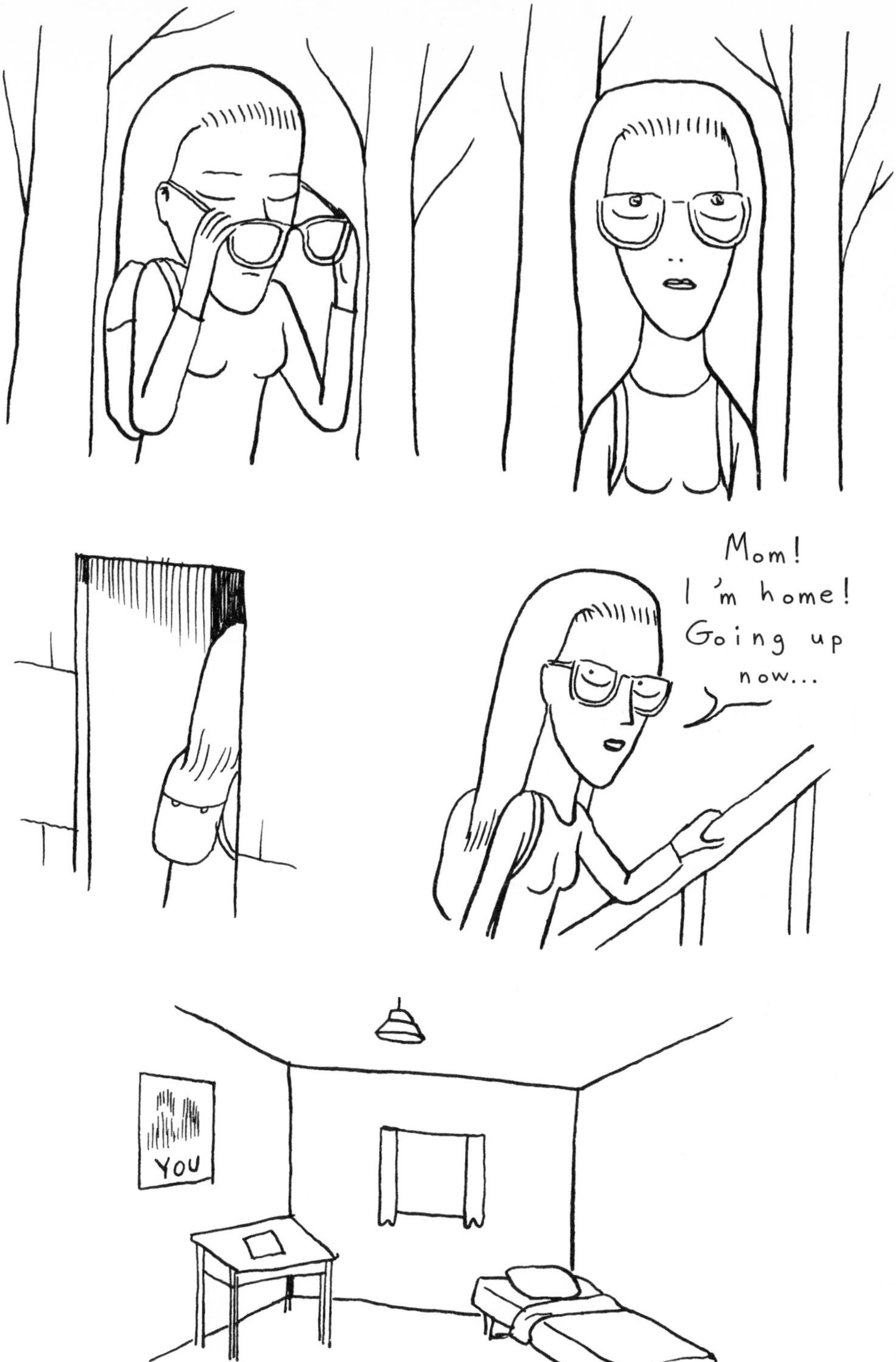
Mom! I'm home! Going up now...
YOU

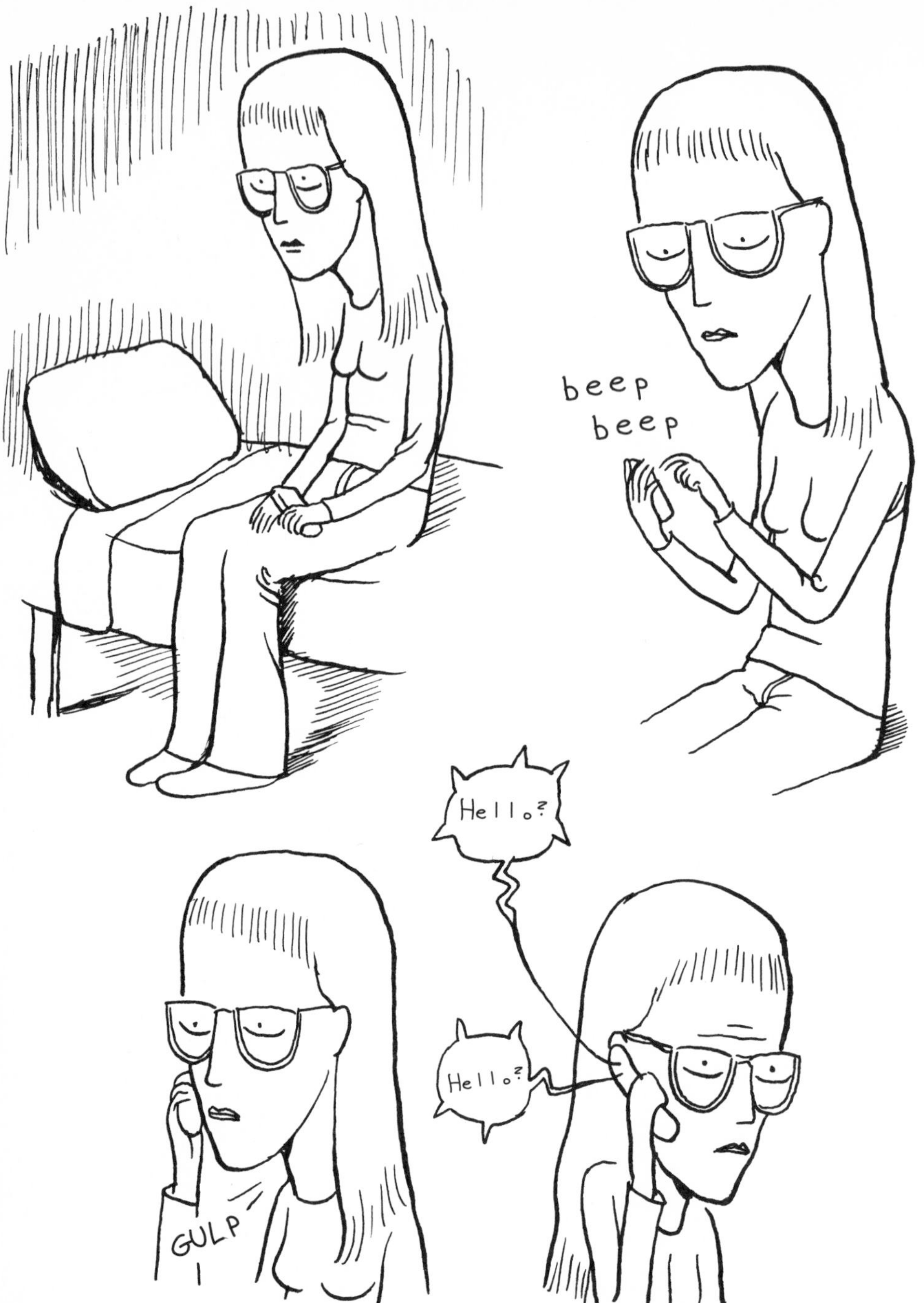
beep beep
Hello?
GULP
Hello?

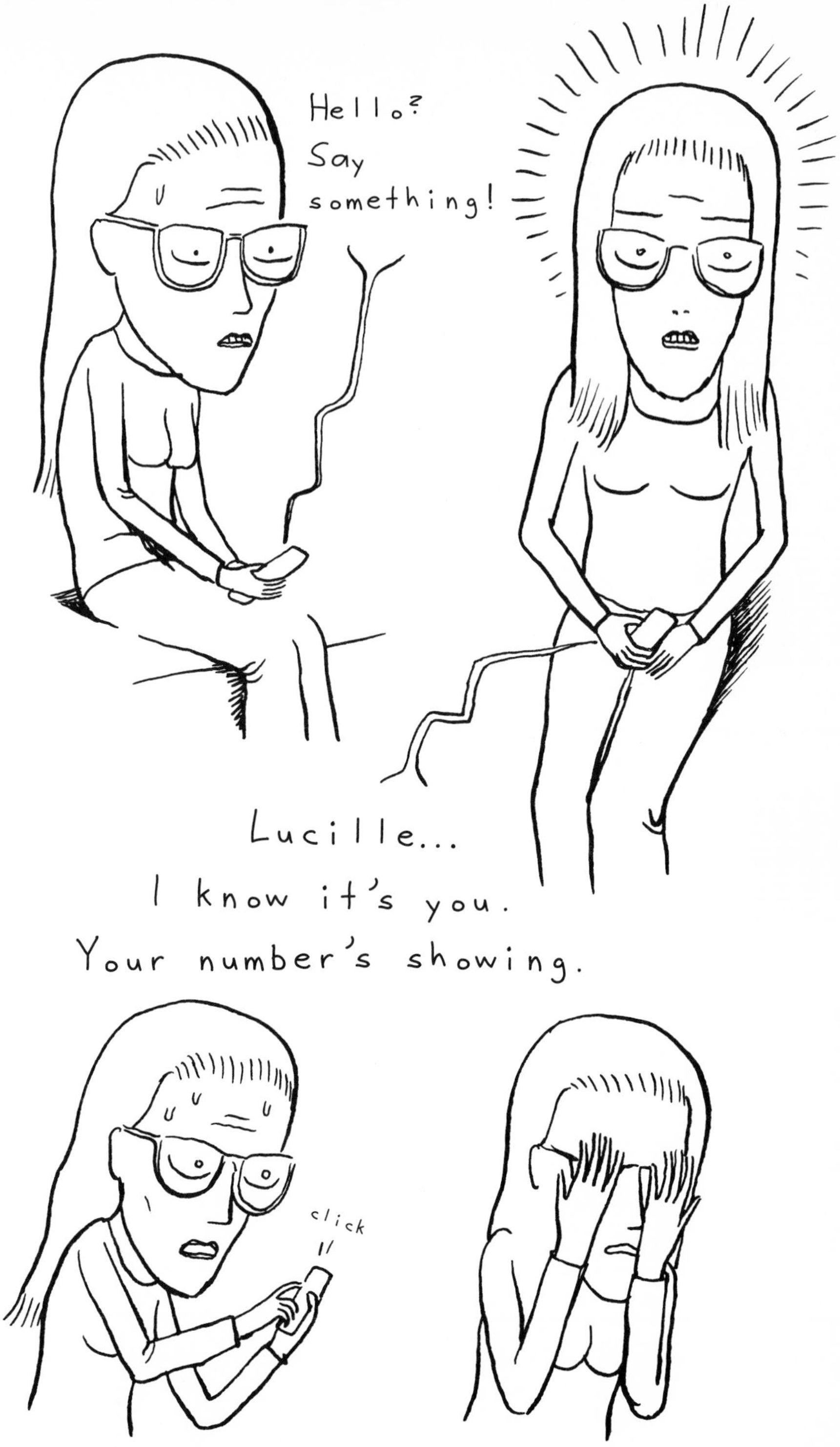

Hello?
Say something!
Lucille...
I know it's you.
Your number's showing.
click

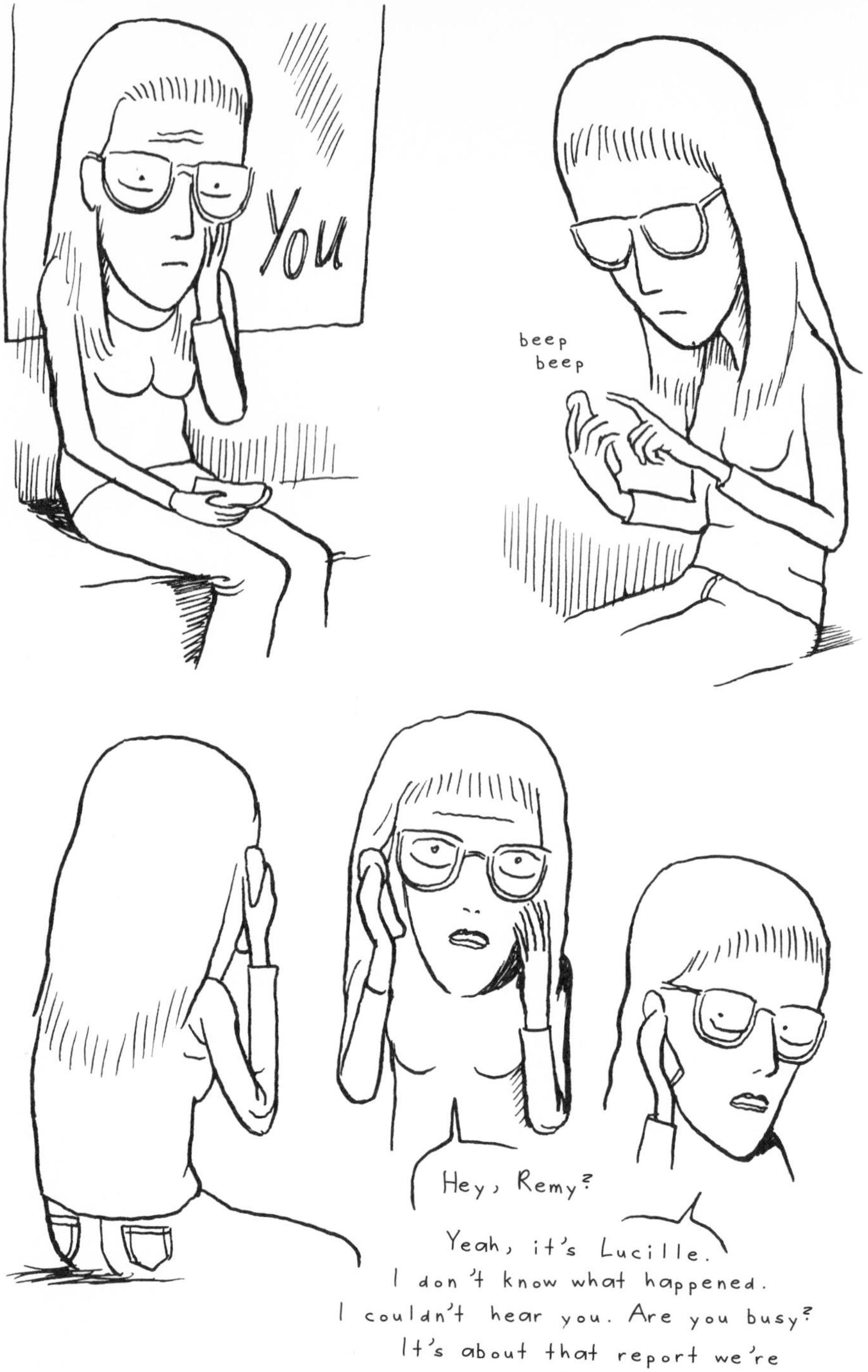
You
beep beep
Hey, Remy?
Yeah, it's Lucille. I don't know what happened. I couldn't hear you. Are you busy? It's about that report we're supposed to do together...maybe we could...uh...meet up...to...get started?

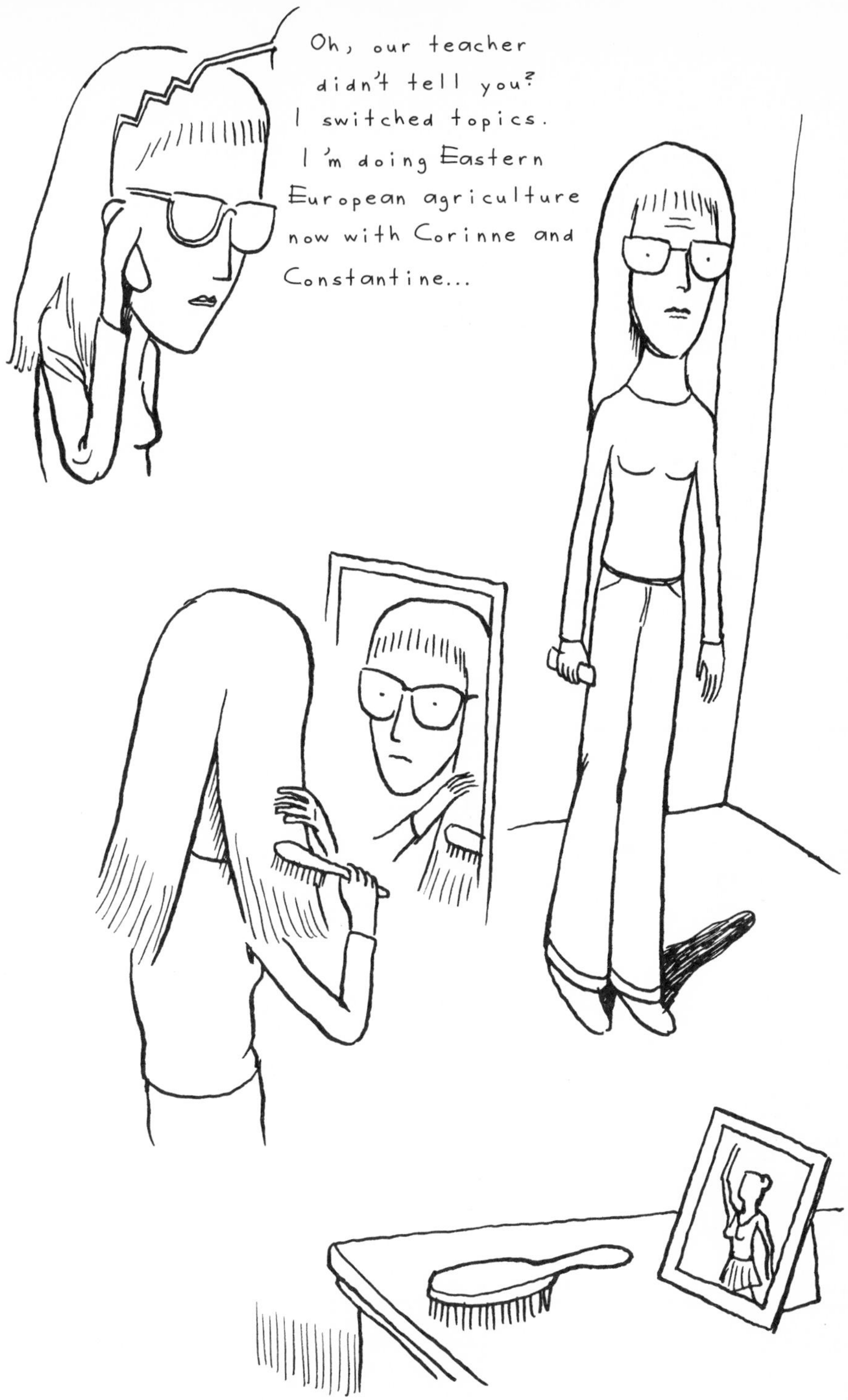
Oh, our teacher didn't tell you? I switched topics. I'm doing Eastern European agriculture now with Corinne and Constantine...

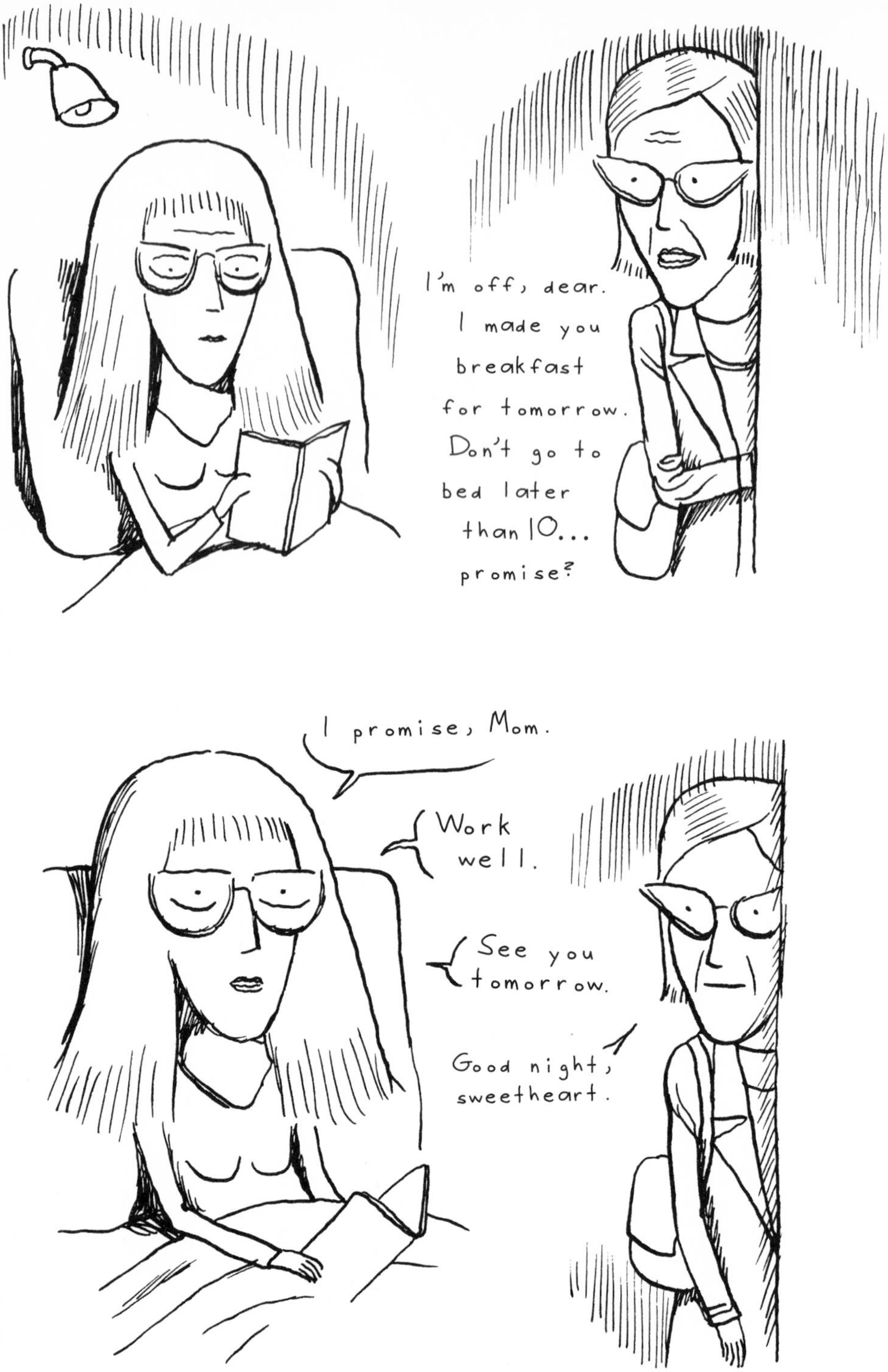
I'm off, dear. I made you breakfast for tomorrow. Don't go to bed later than 10... promise?
I promise, Mom.
Work well.
See you tomorrow.
Good night, sweetheart.

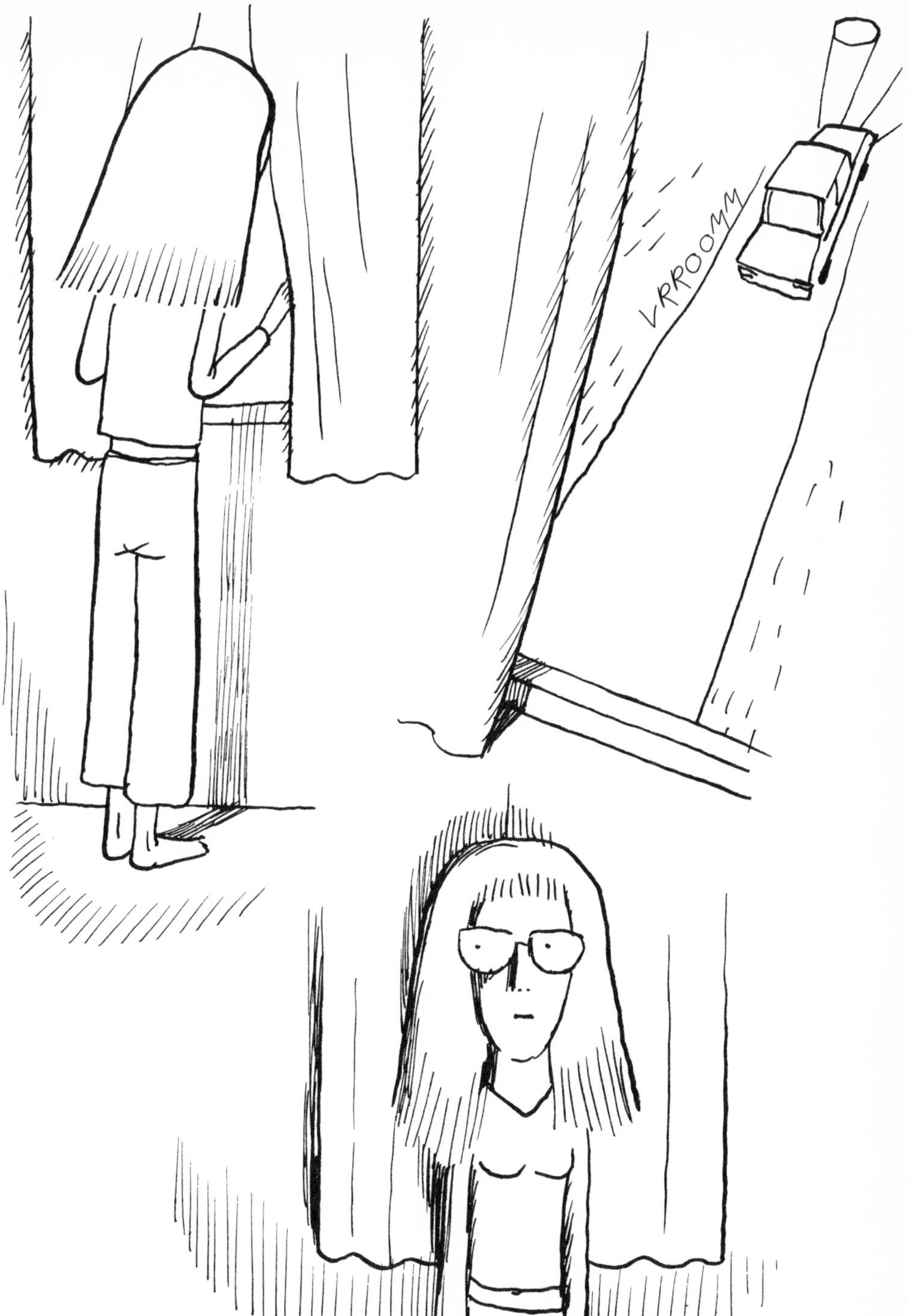
VRROOMM

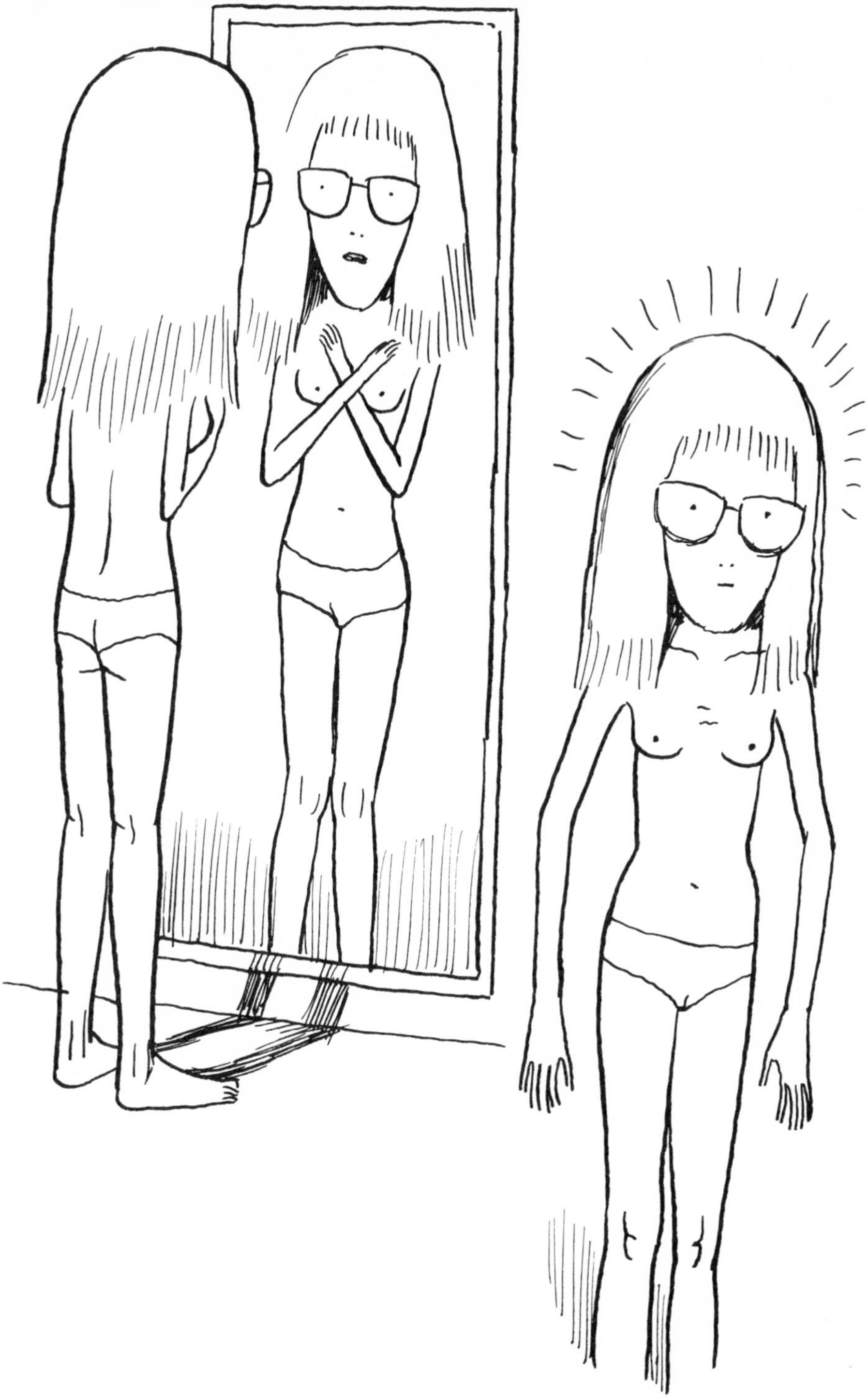

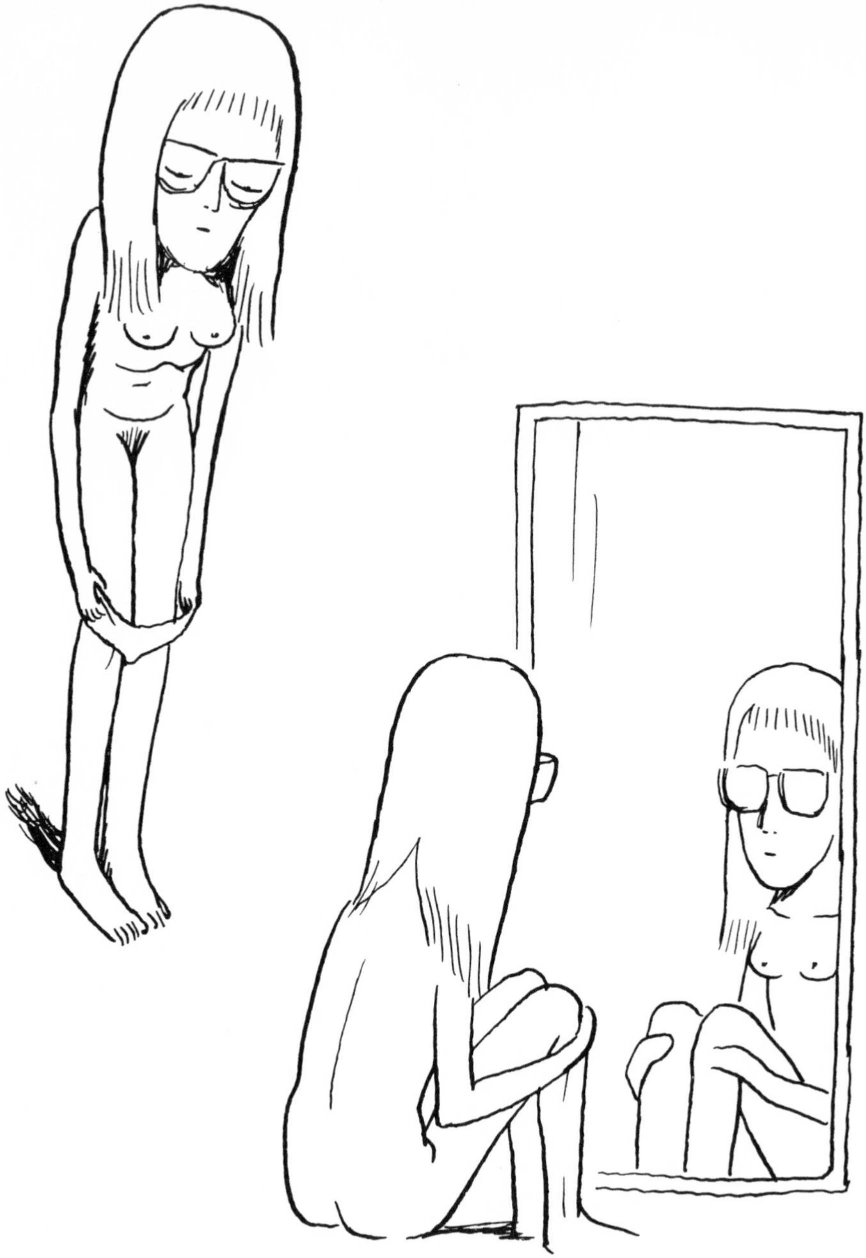

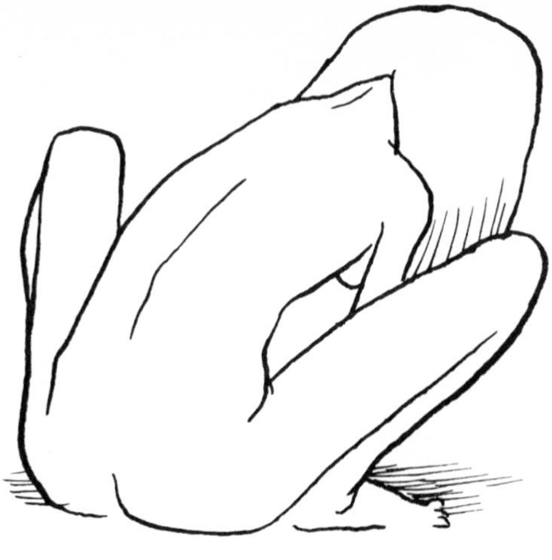

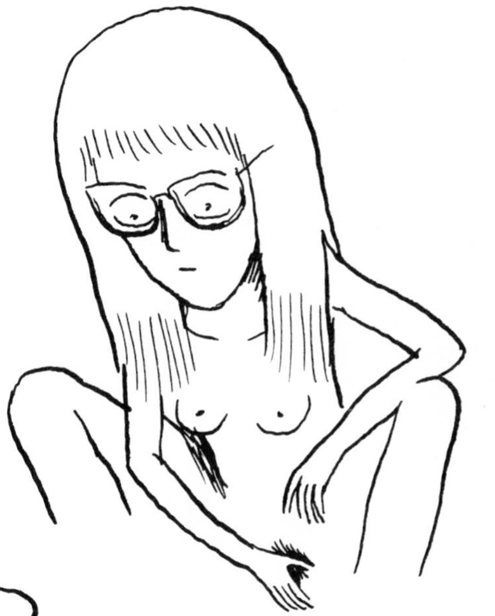

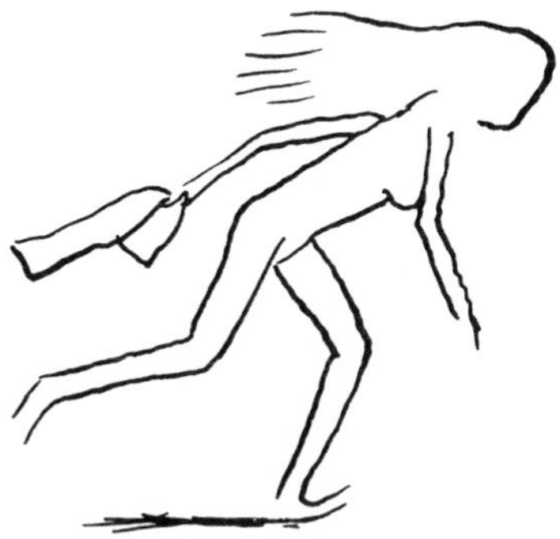

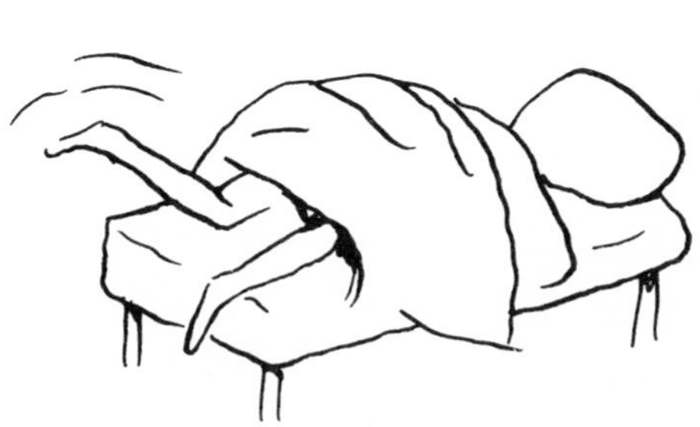

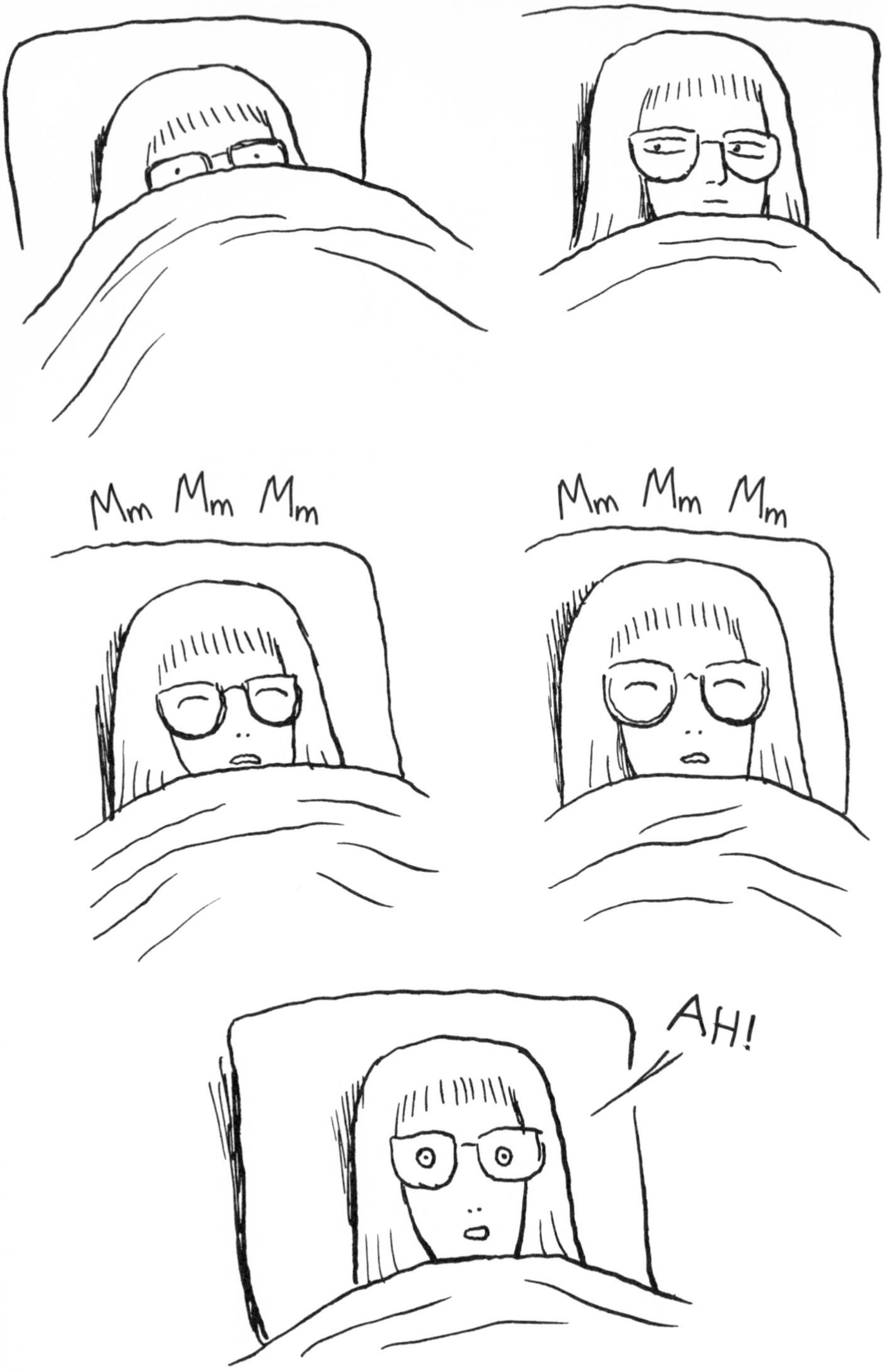
Mm Mm Mm
Mm Mm Mm
AH!

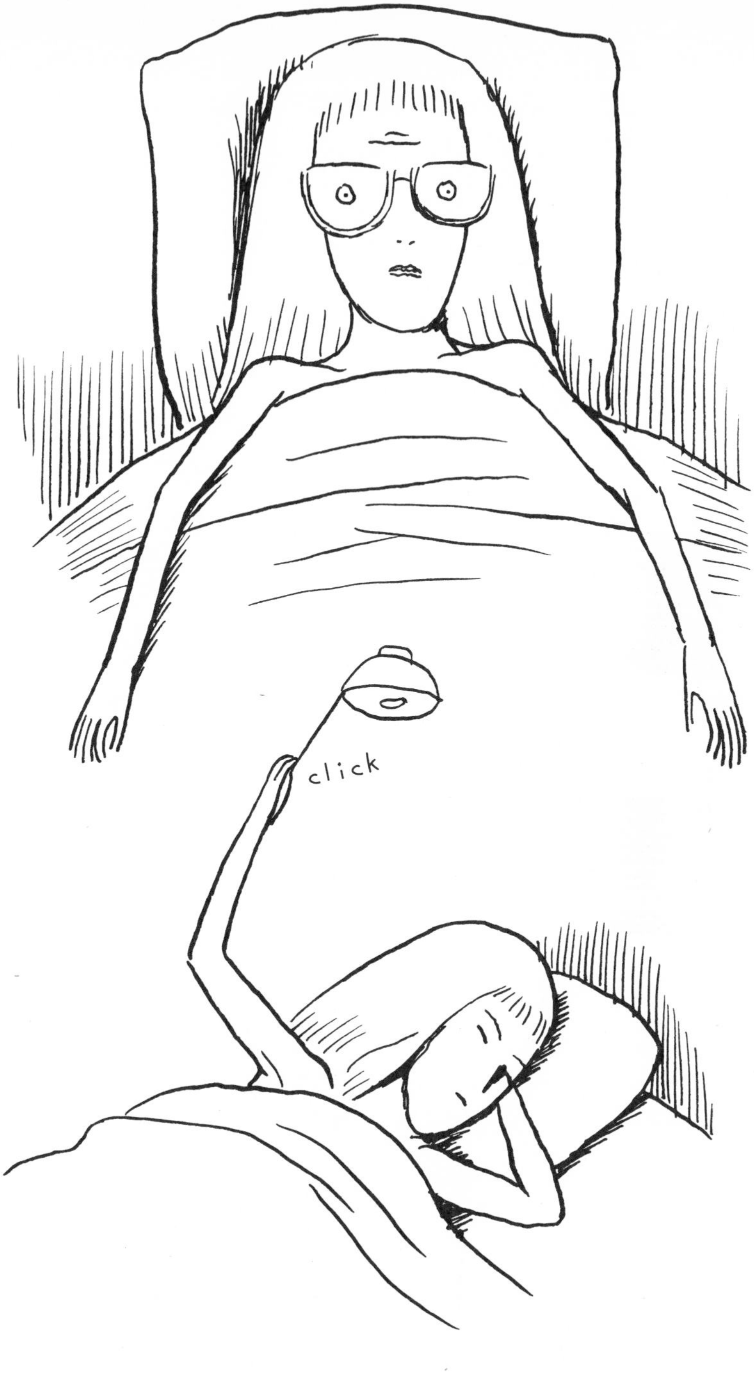
click

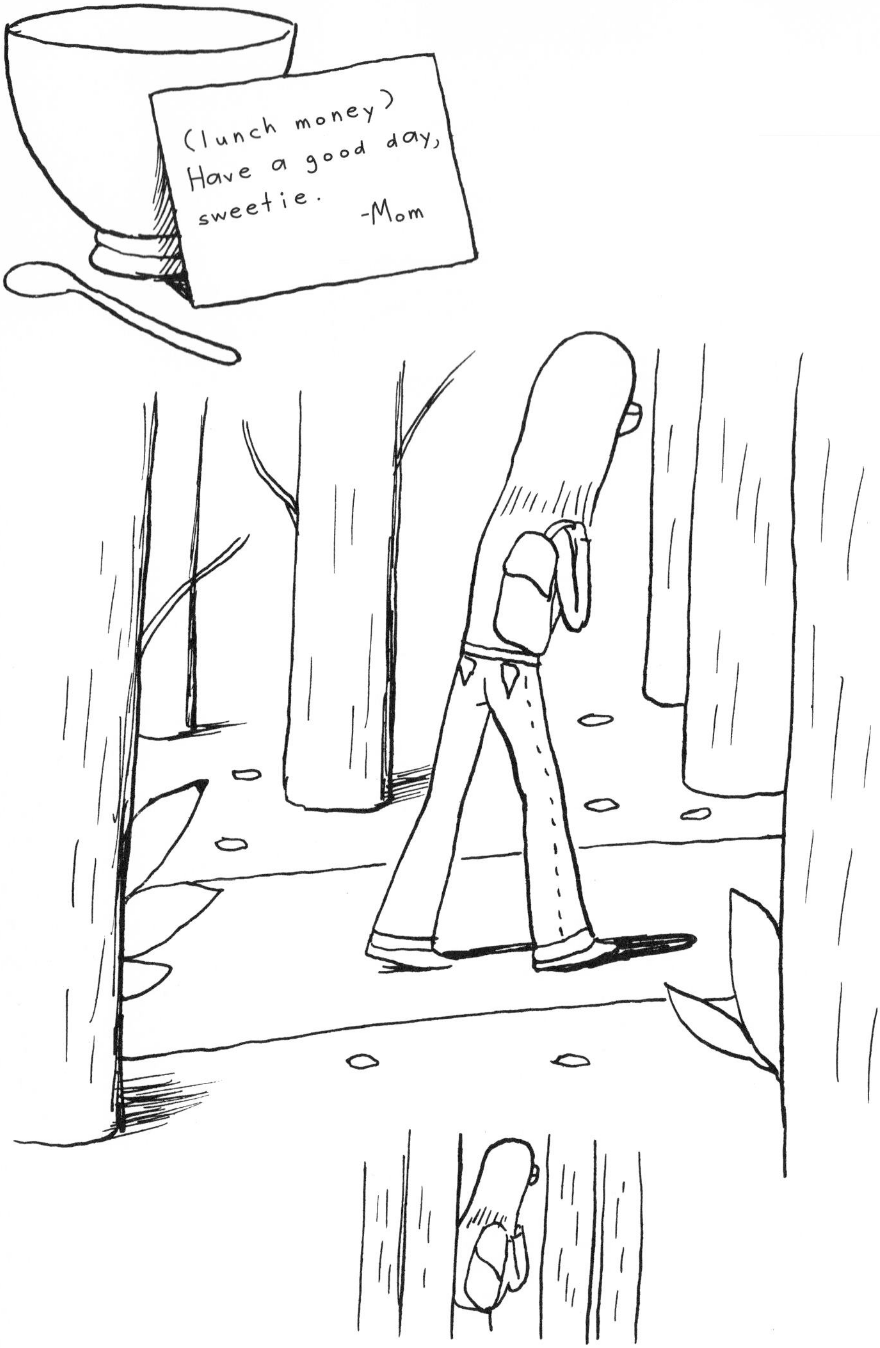
(lunch money)
Have a good day,
sweetie.
-Mom

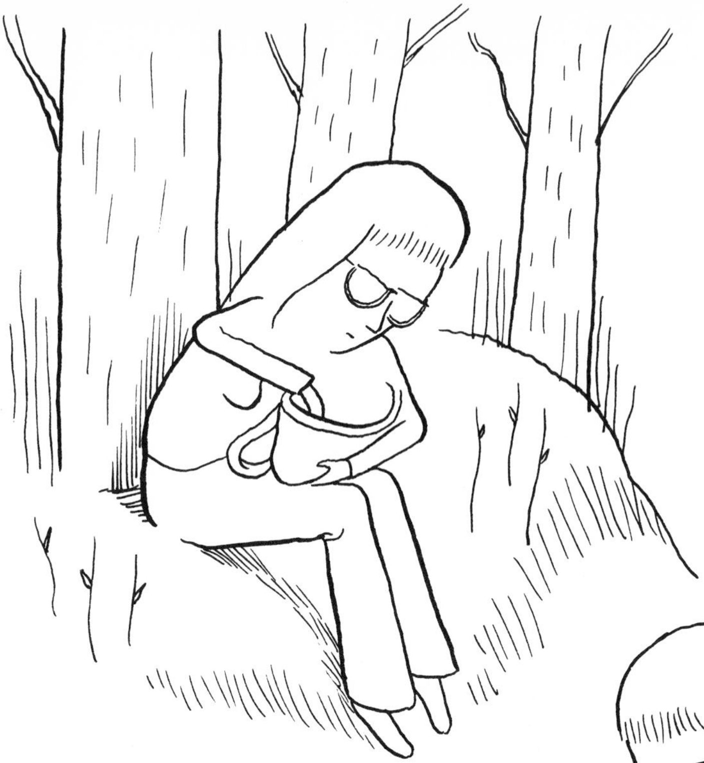

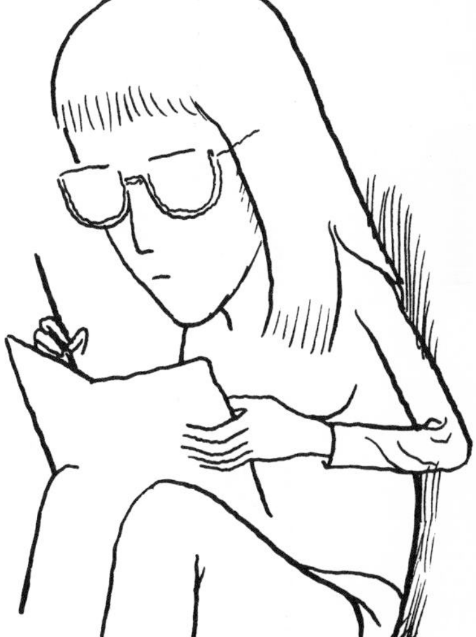

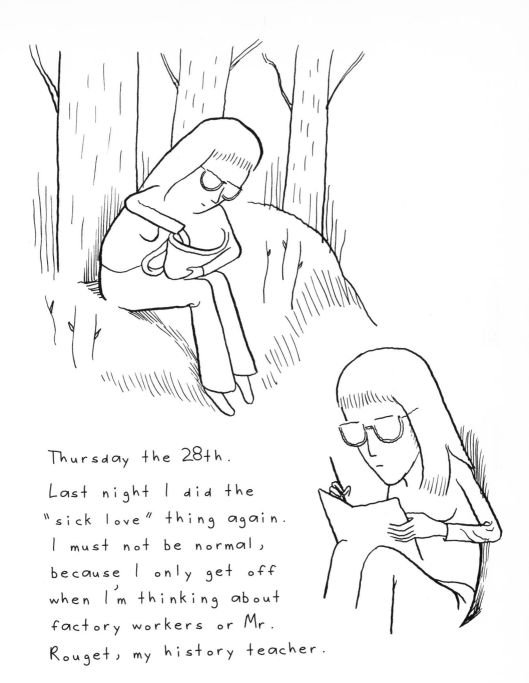

Thursday the 28th.

Last night I did the "sick love" thing again. I must not be normal, because I only get off when I'm thinking about factory workers or Mr. Rouget, my history teacher.

That disgusting fat pig.

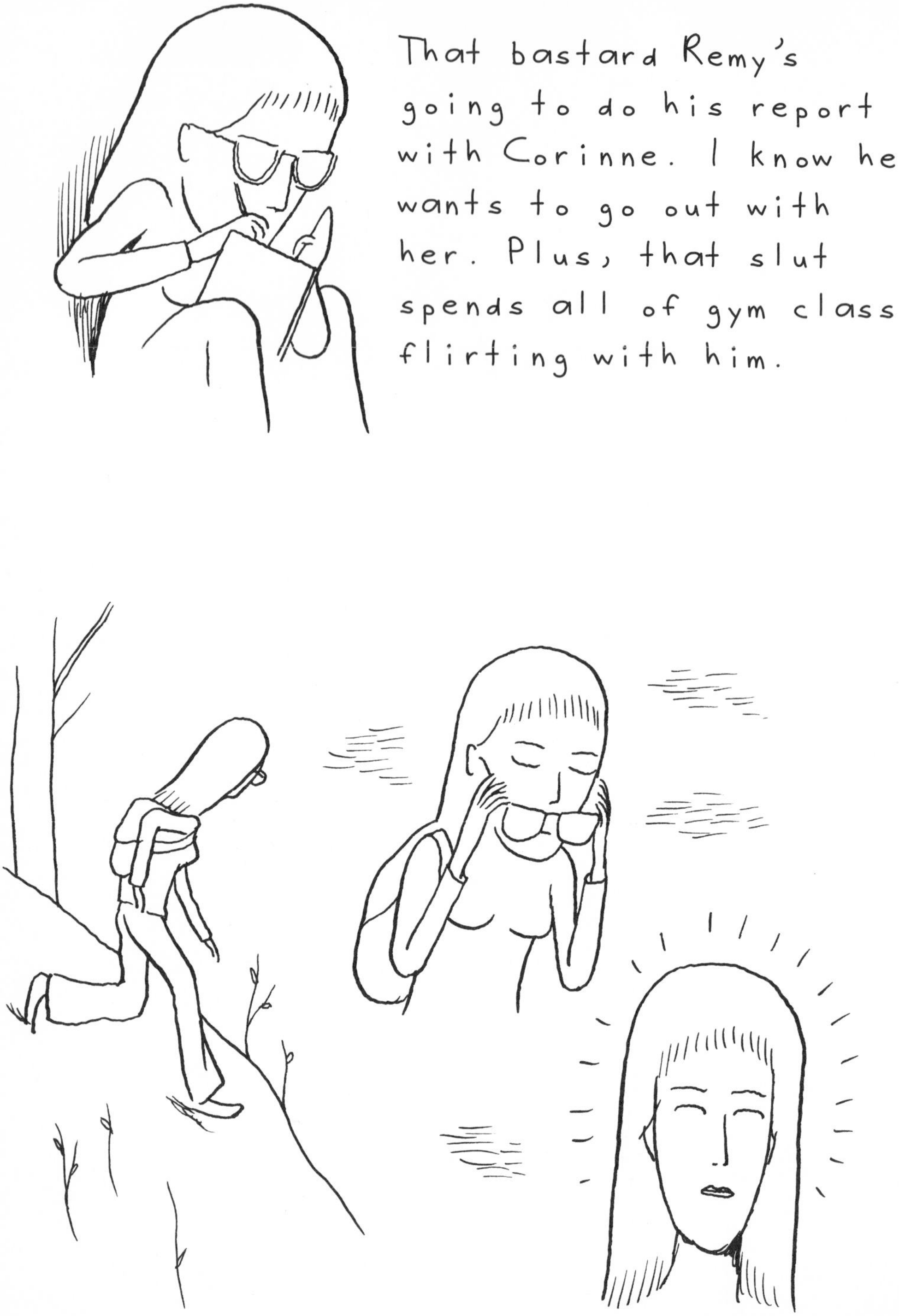
That bastard Remy's going to do his report with Corinne. I know he wants to go out with her. Plus, that slut spends all of gym class flirting with him.

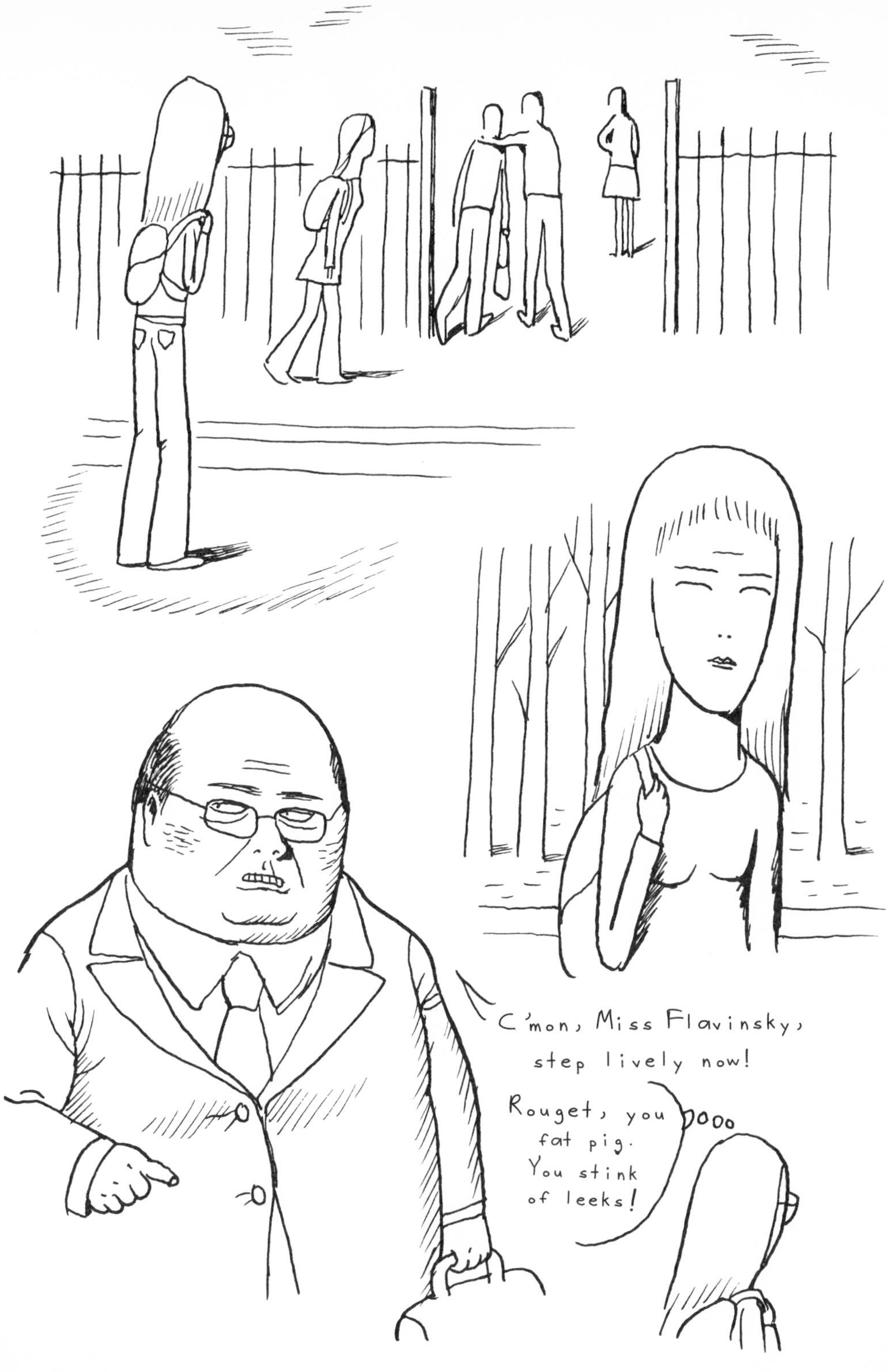
C'mon, Miss Flavinsky, step lively now!
Rouget, you fat pig. You stink of leeks!
Oooo

Arthur de Nulle Part
(Arthur from Nowhere)

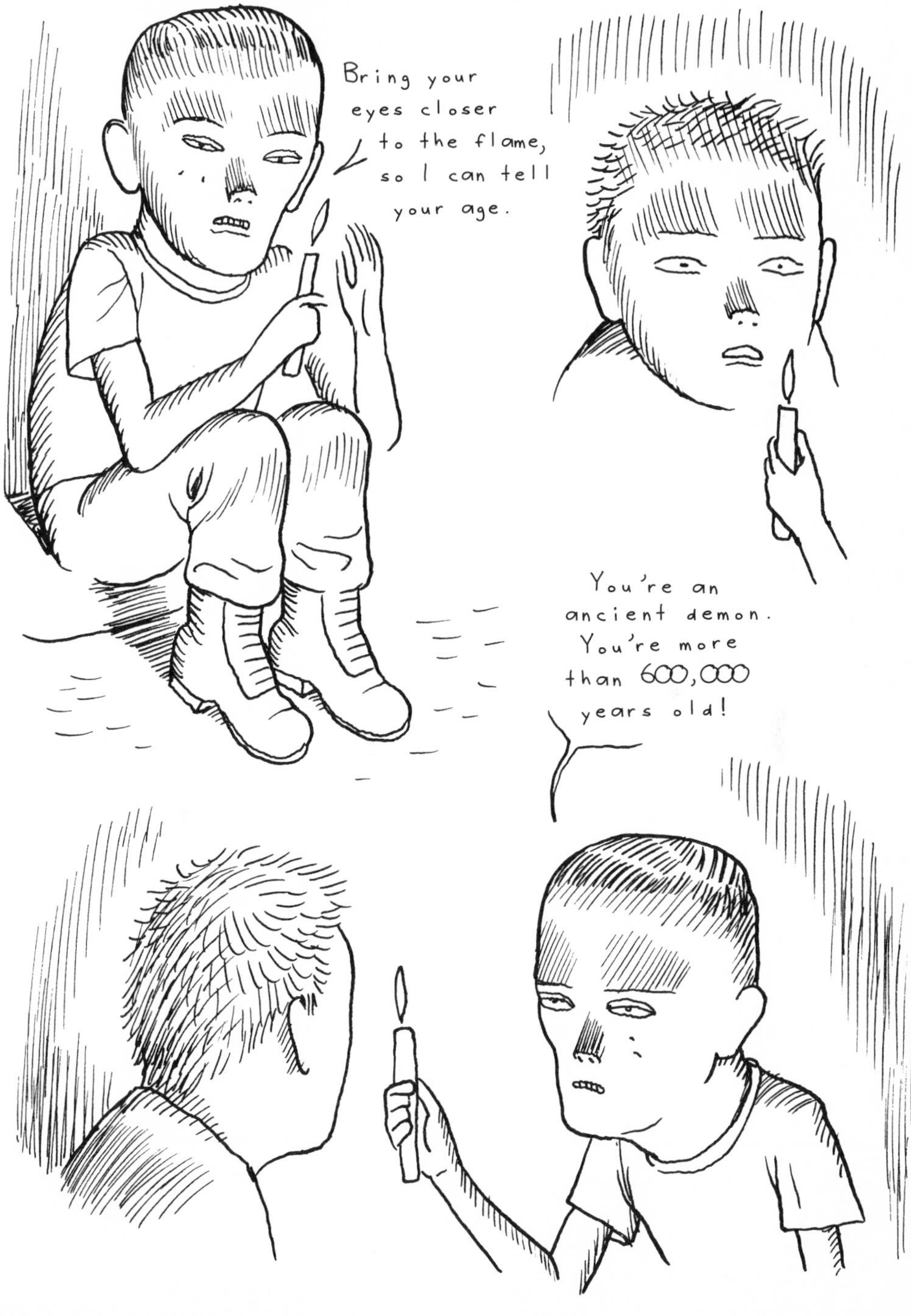
Bring your eyes closer to the flame, so I can tell your age.
You're an ancient demon. You're more than 600,000 years old!

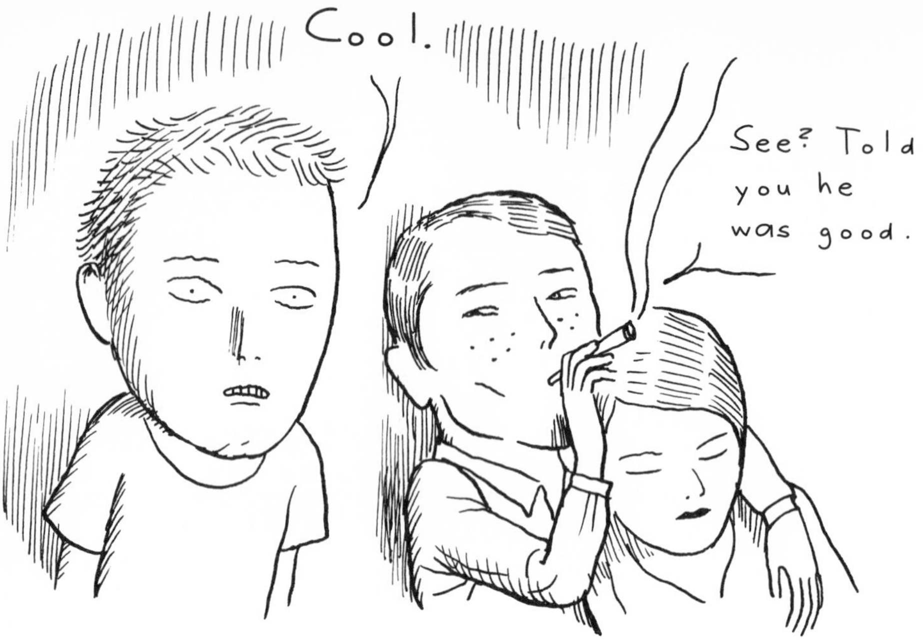

Cool.
See? Told you he was good.

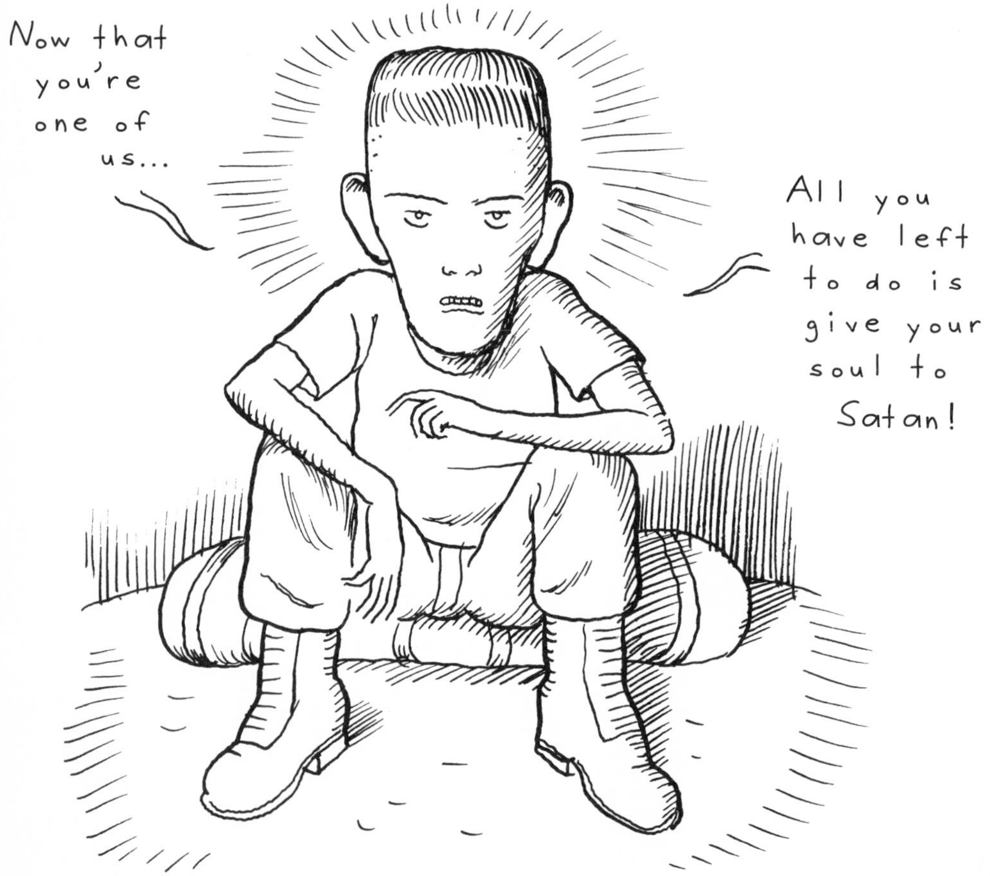

Now that you're one of us...
All you have left to do is give your soul to Satan!

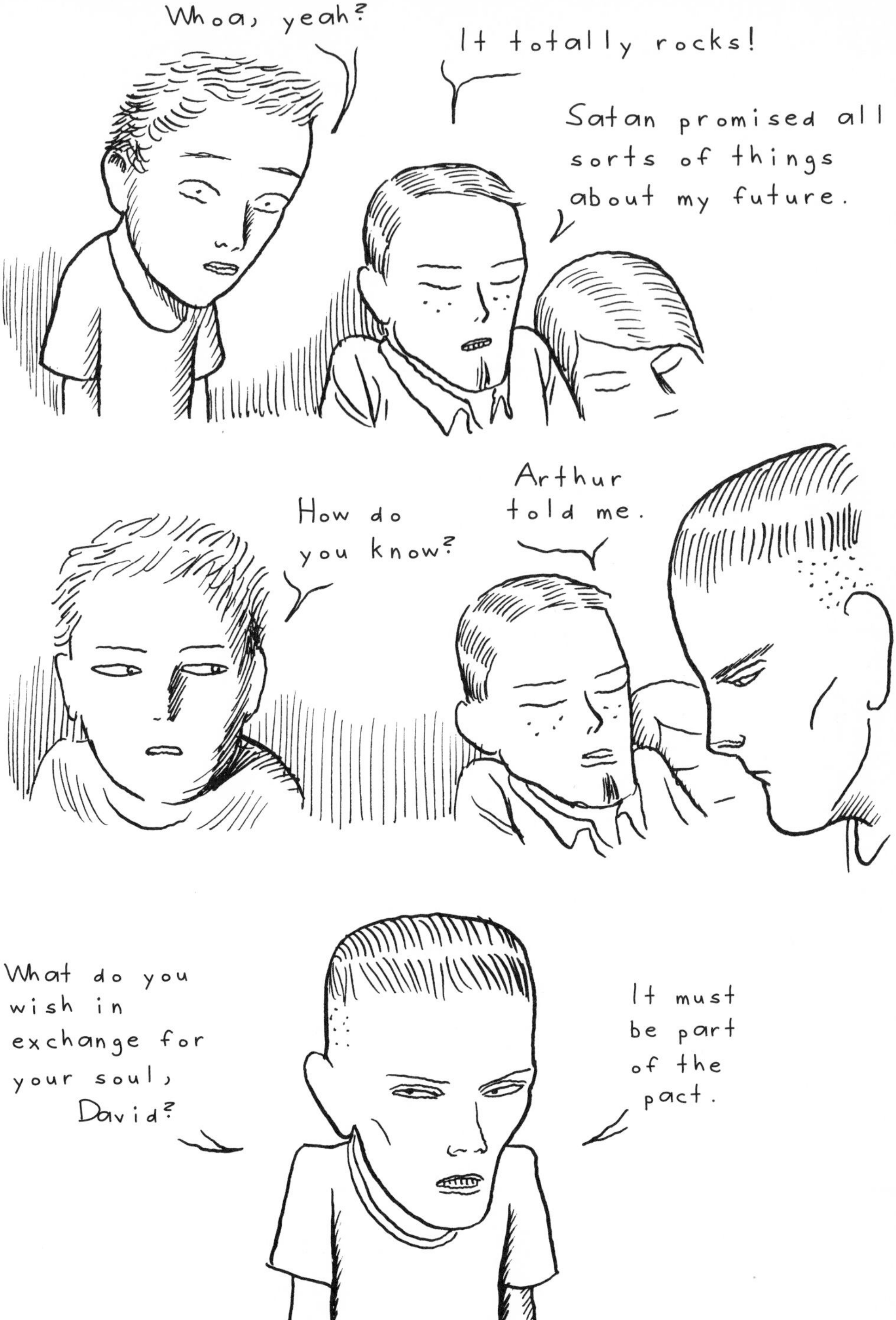
Whoa, yeah?
It totally rocks!
Satan promised all sorts of things about my future.
How do you know?
Arthur told me.
What do you wish in exchange for your soul, David?
It must be part of the pact.

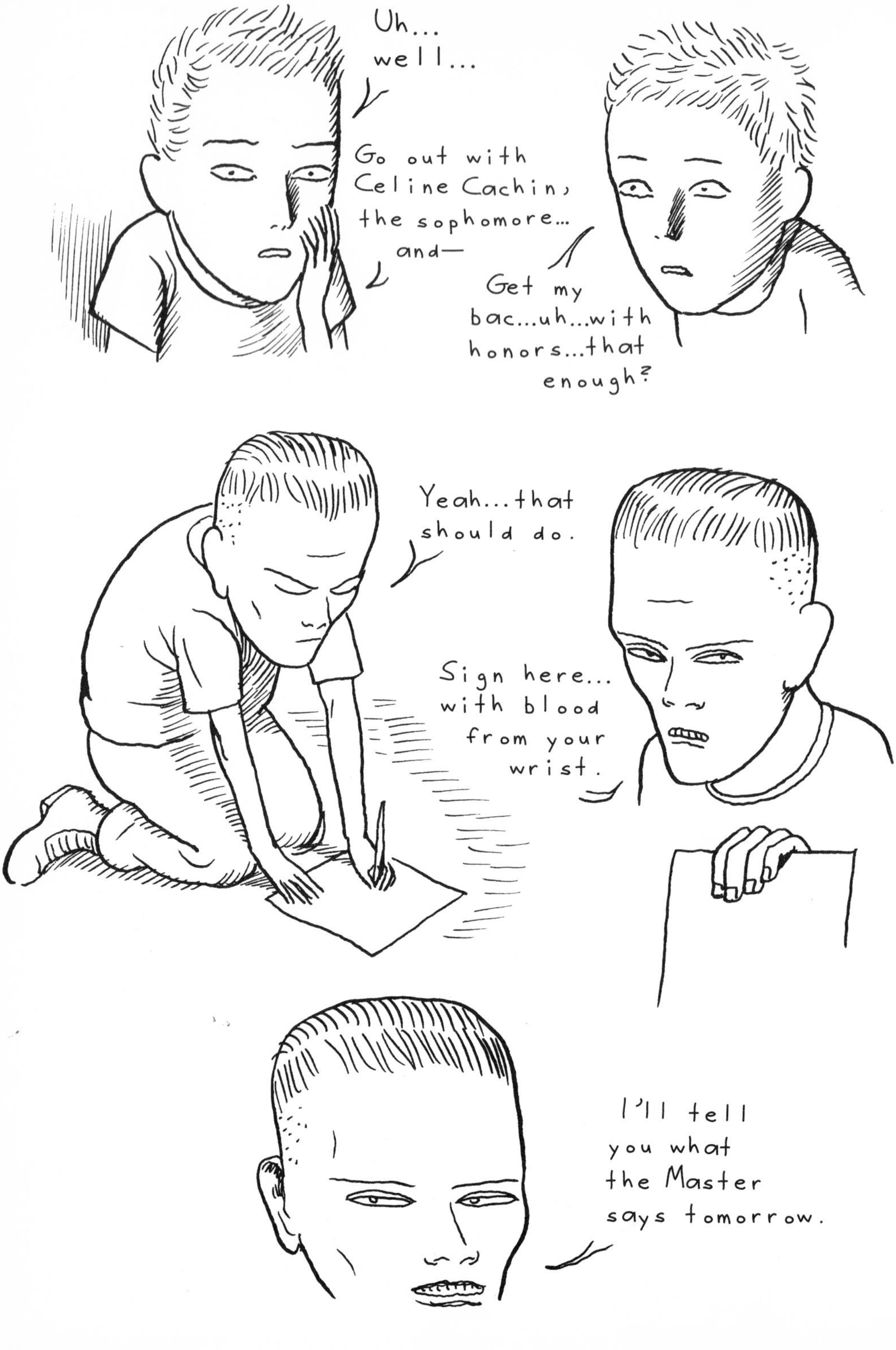
Uh... well...
Go out with Celine Cachin, the sophomore... and—
Get my bac...uh...with honors...that enough?
Yeah...that should do.
Sign here... with blood from your wrist.
I'll tell you what the Master says tomorrow.

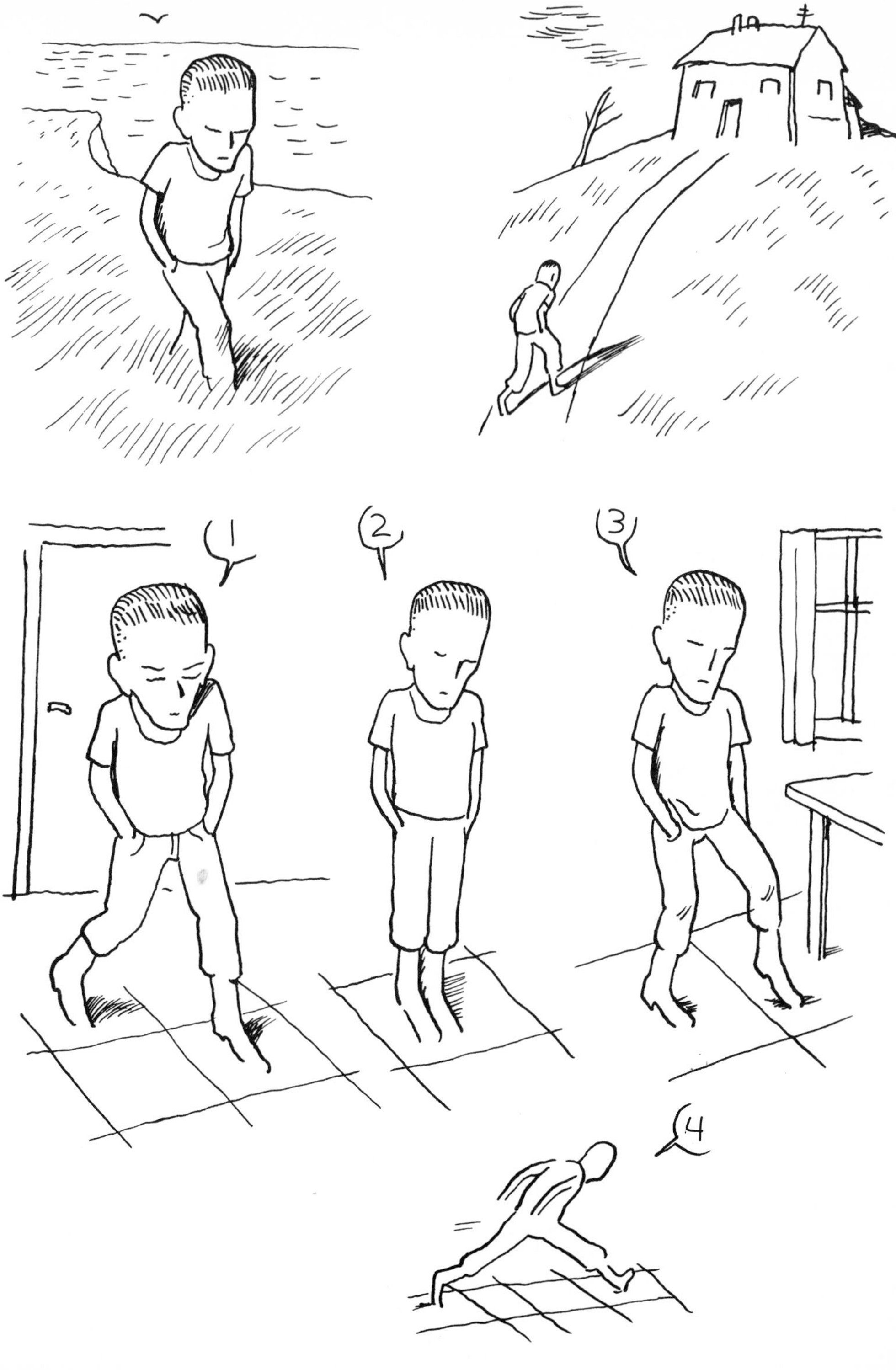
1
2
3
4

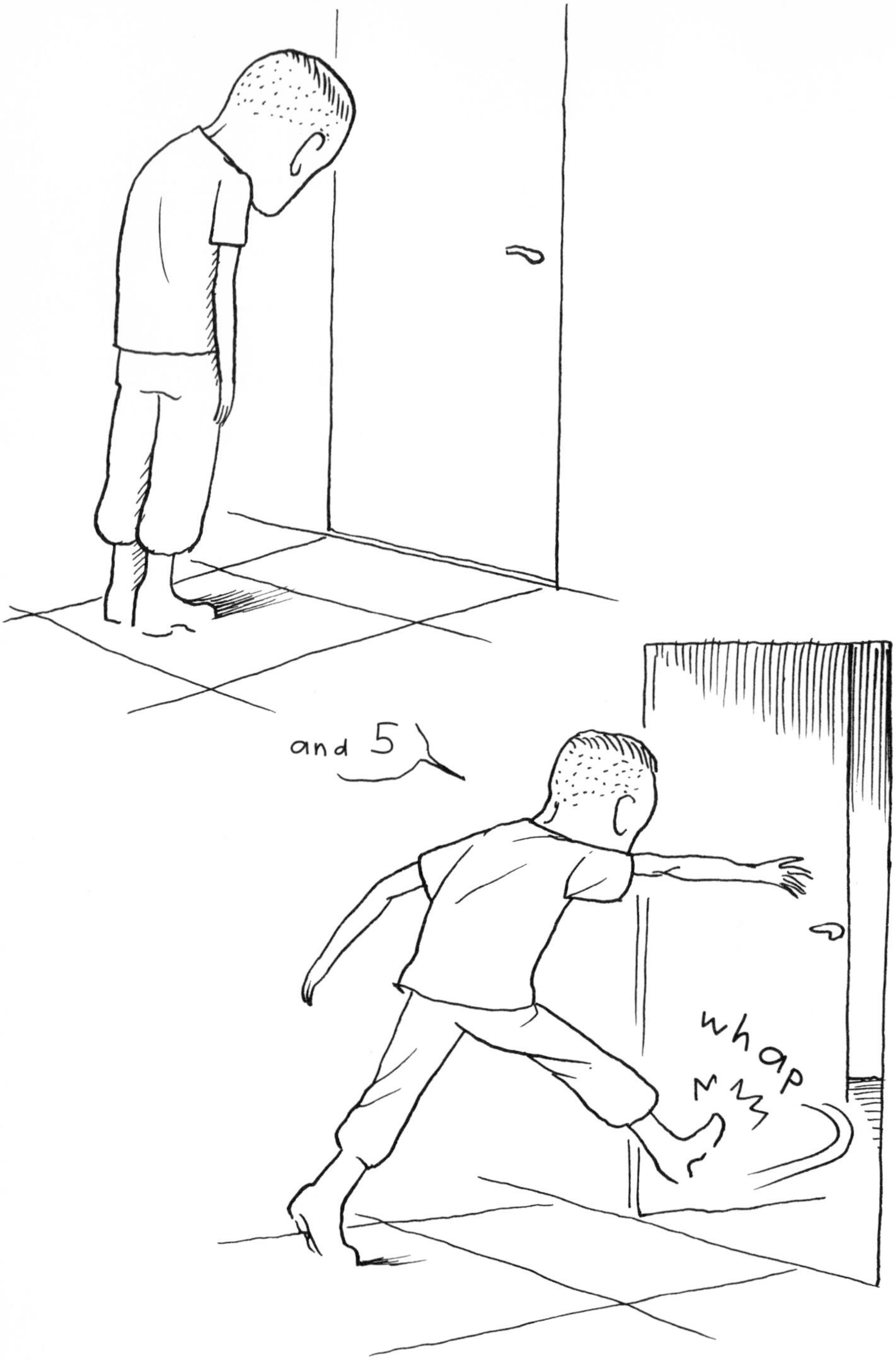
and 5
whap

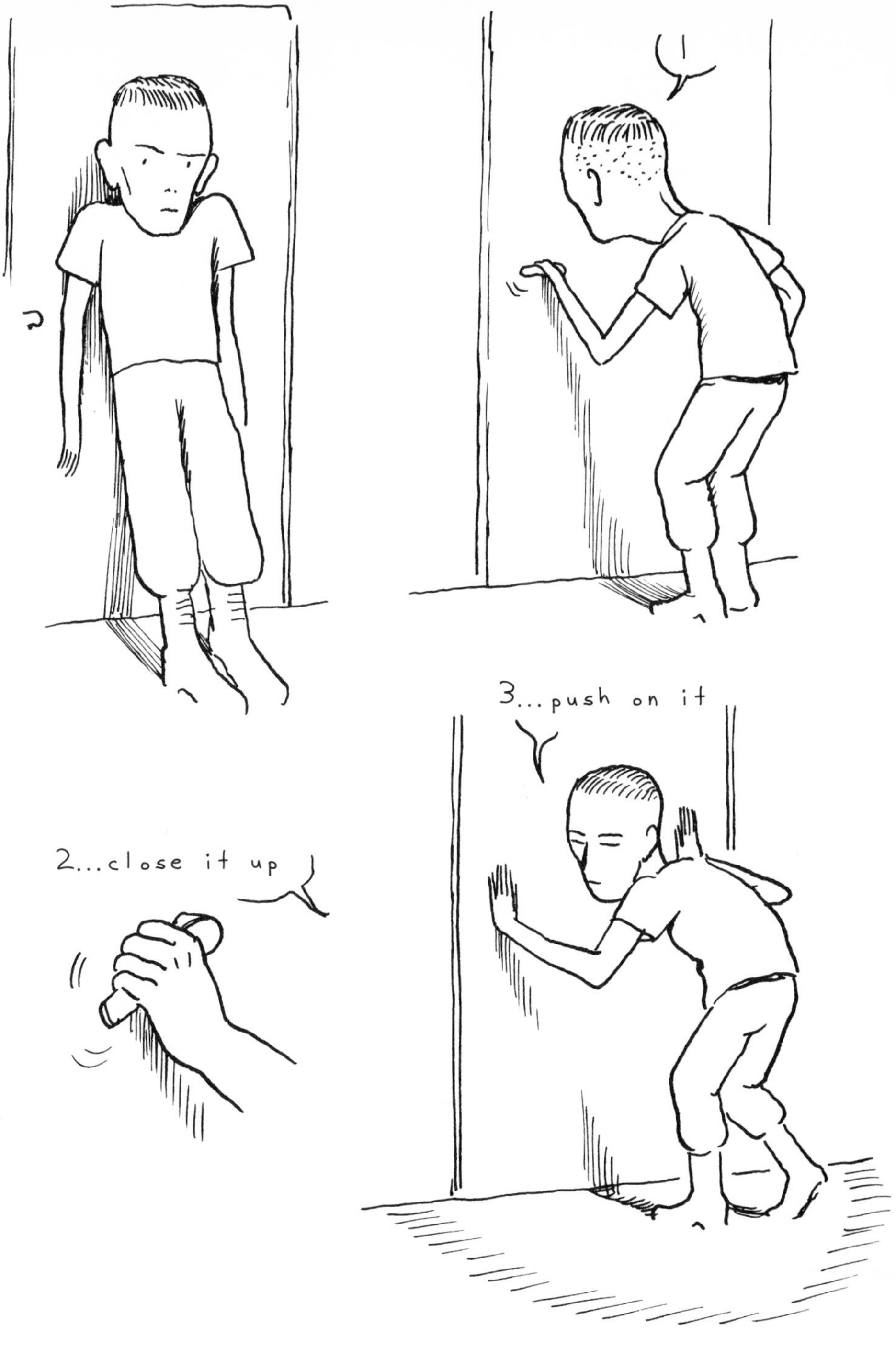
2...close it up
3...push on it

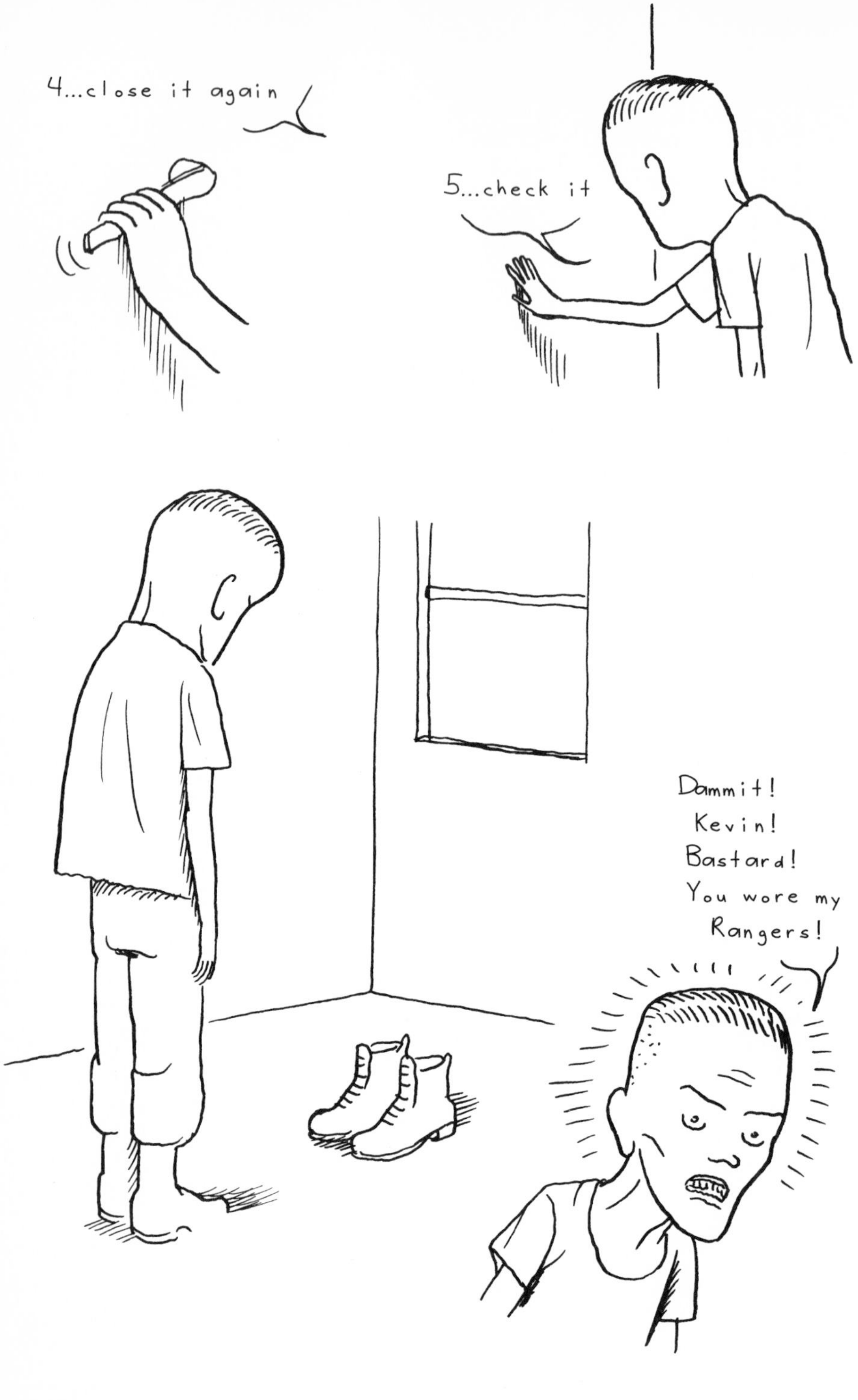
4...close it again
5...check it
Dammit!
Kevin!
Bastard!
You wore my Rangers!

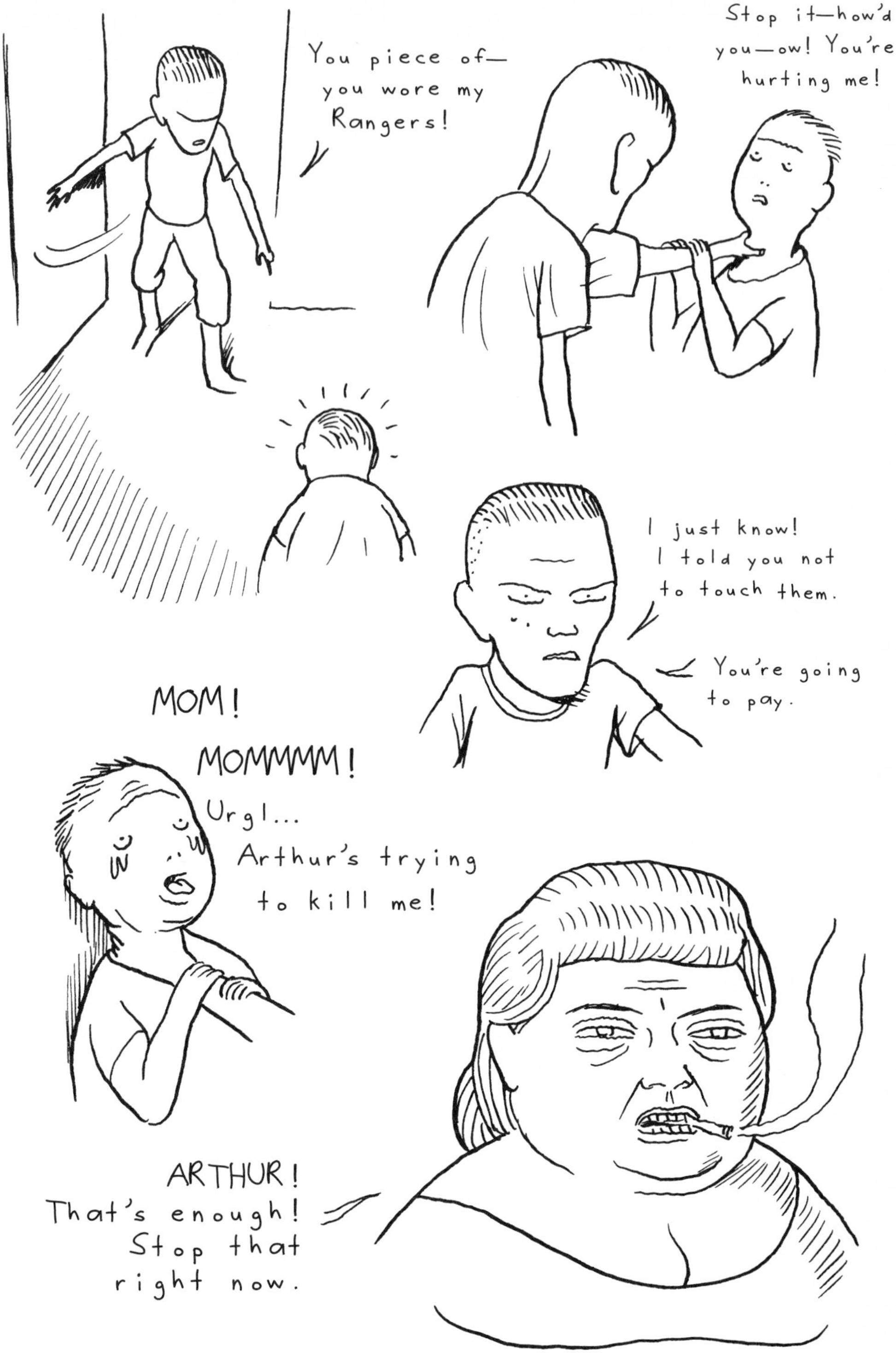
You piece of— you wore my Rangers!
Stop it—how'd you—ow! You're hurting me!
I just know! I told you not to touch them.
You're going to pay.
MOM!
MOMMMM!
Urgl... Arthur's trying to kill me!
ARTHUR! That's enough! Stop that right now.

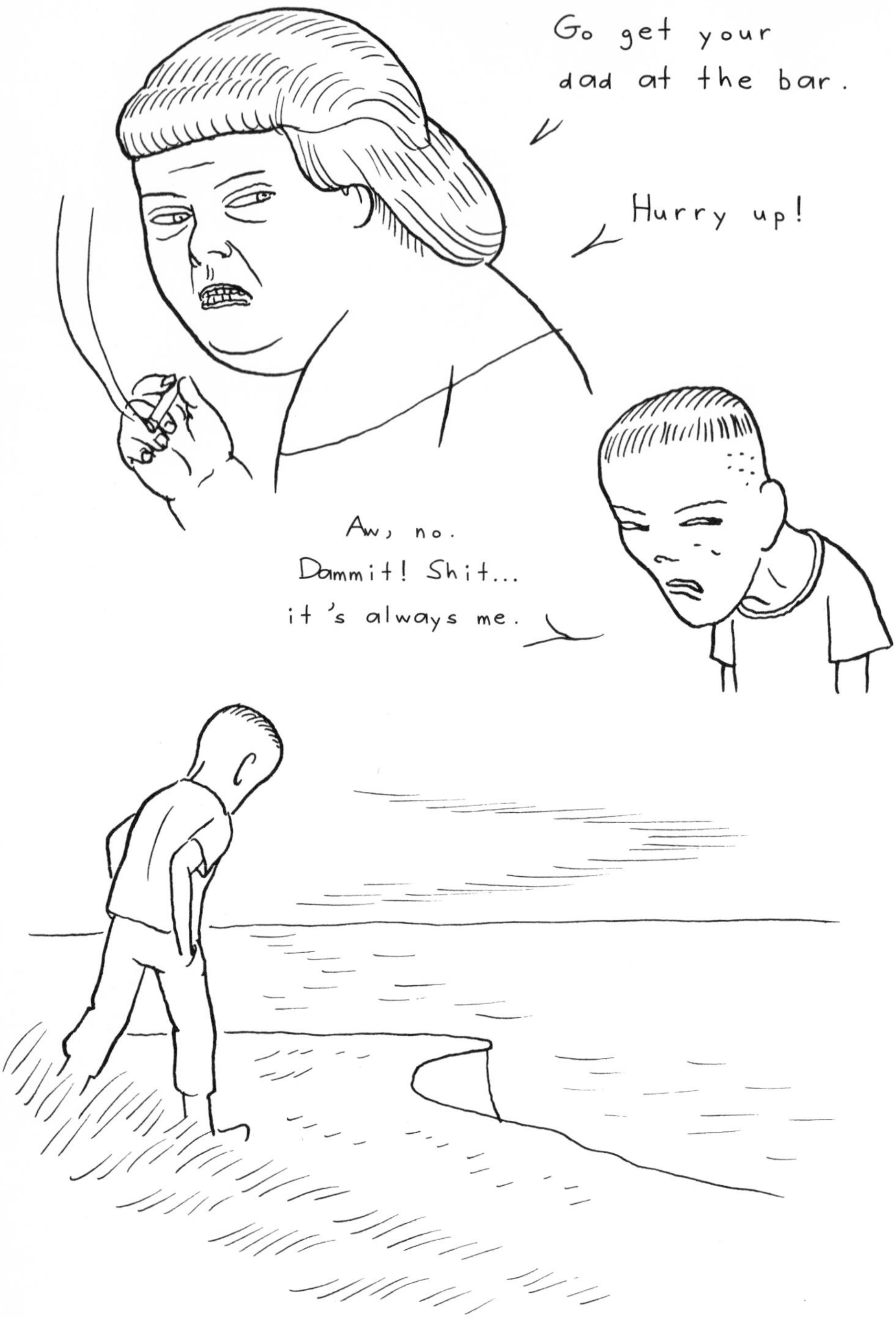
Go get your dad at the bar.
Hurry up!
Aw, no.
Dammit! Shit...
it's always me.

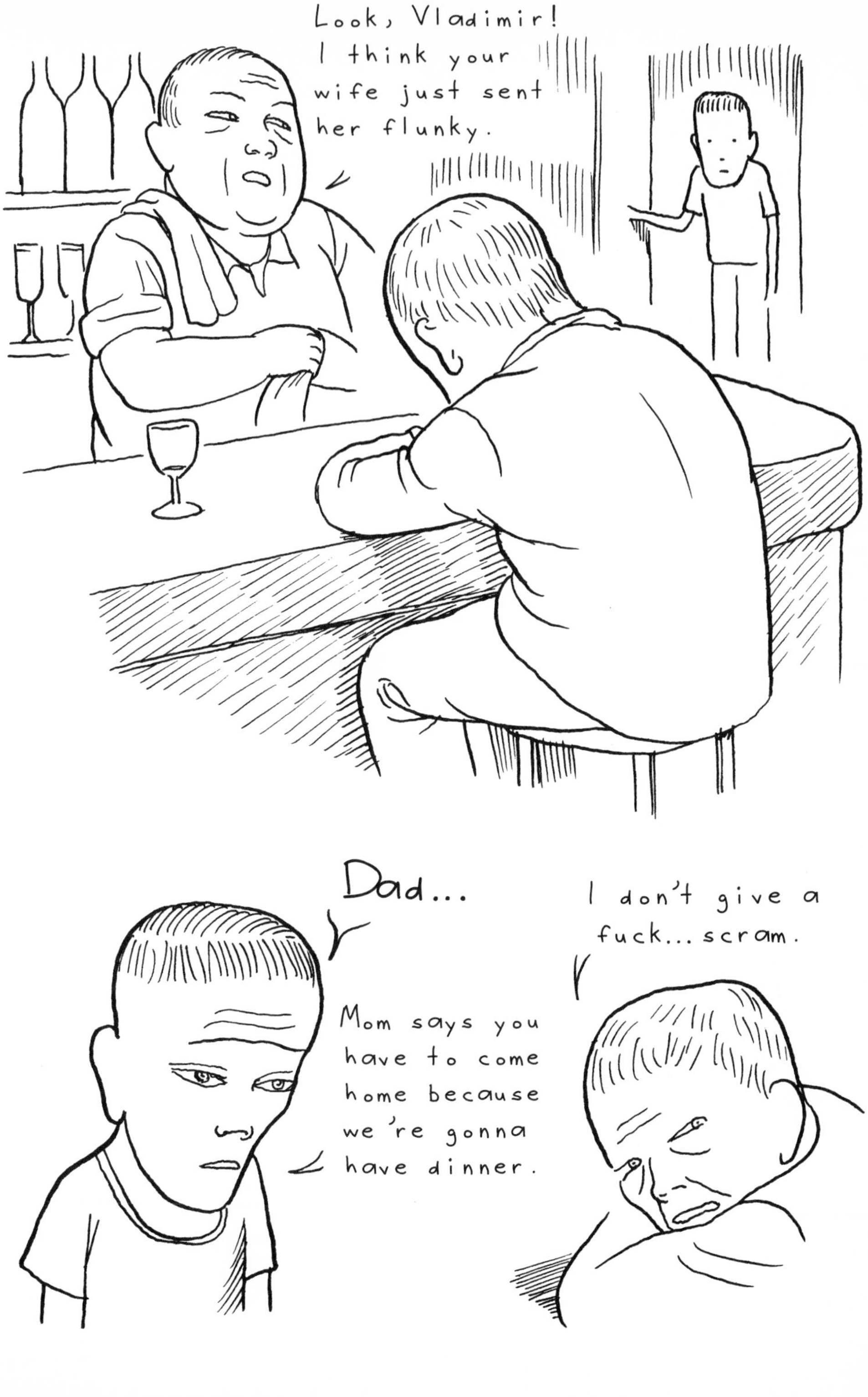
Look, Vladimir! I think your wife just sent her flunky.
Dad...
Mom says you have to come home because we're gonna have dinner.
I don't give a fuck... scram.

Son...remember this: a man must never forget where he's from. Hear me, son? Never forget where you're from.

Yeah, dad.

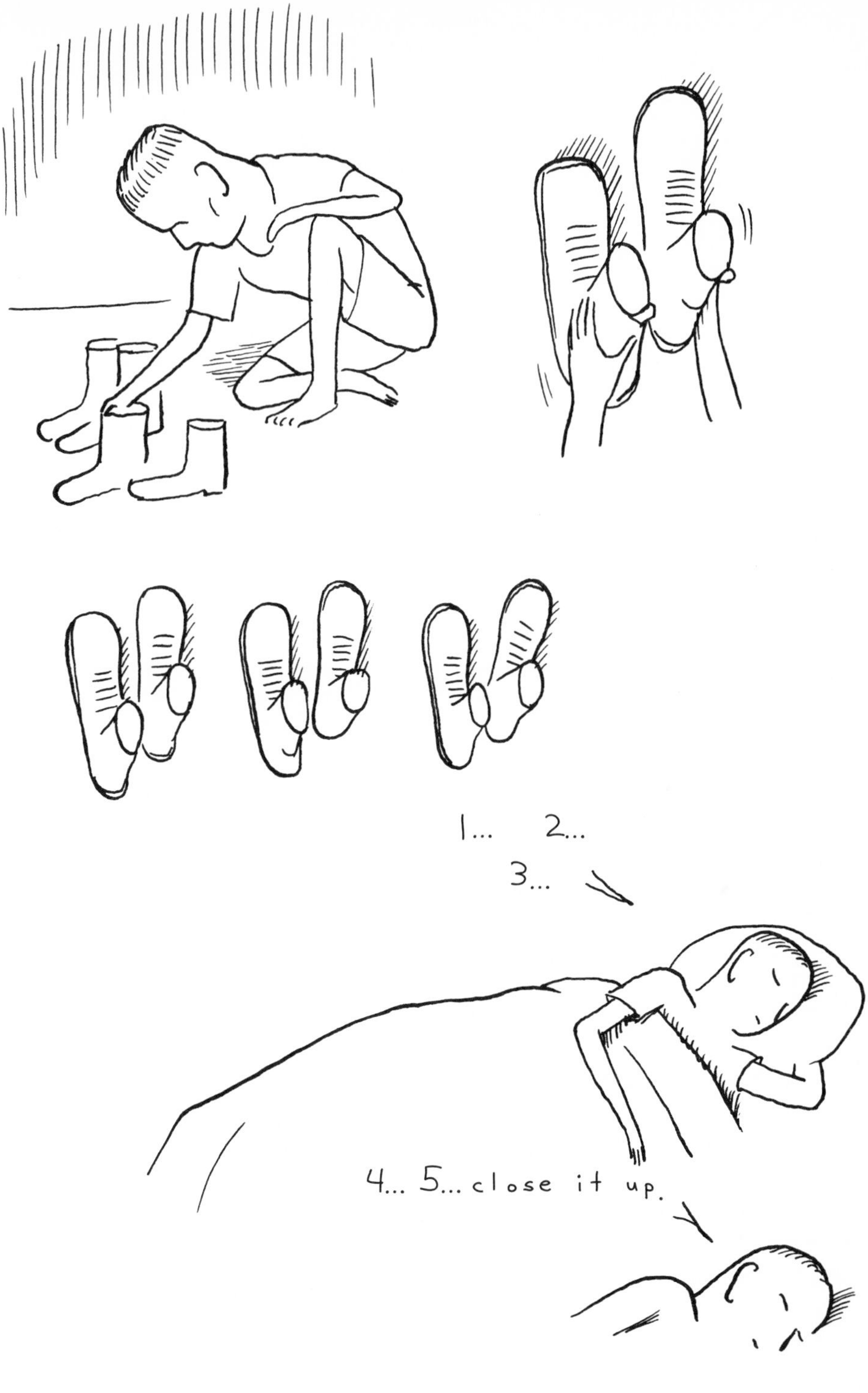
1... 2...
3...
4... 5... close it up.

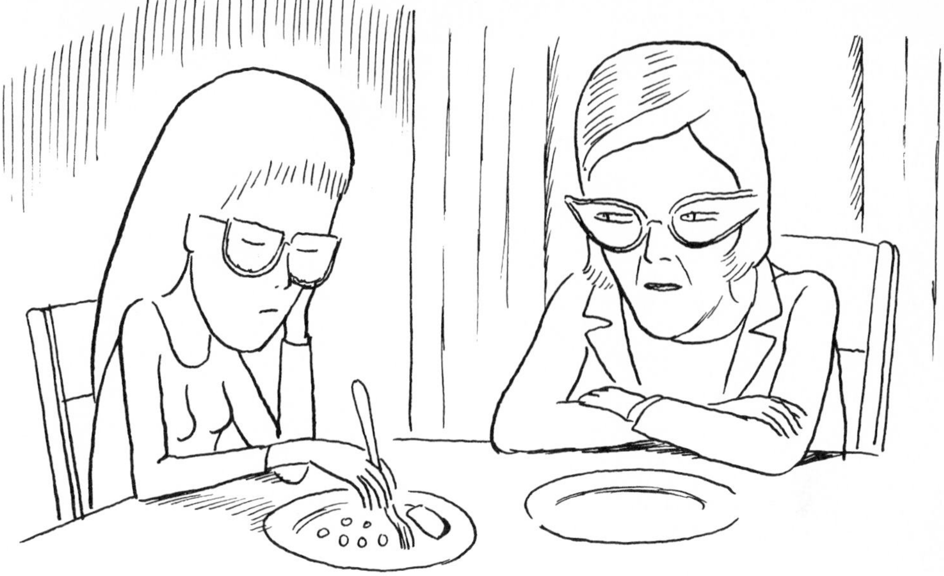

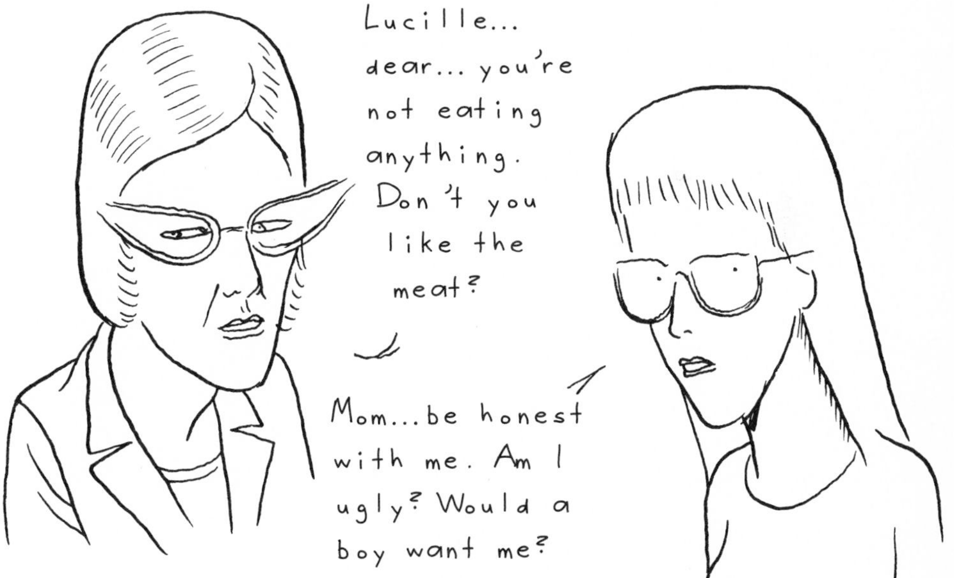
Lucille... dear... you're not eating anything. Don't you like the meat?
Mom... be honest with me. Am I ugly? Would a boy want me?

Princesse des Bois

(Princess of the Woods)

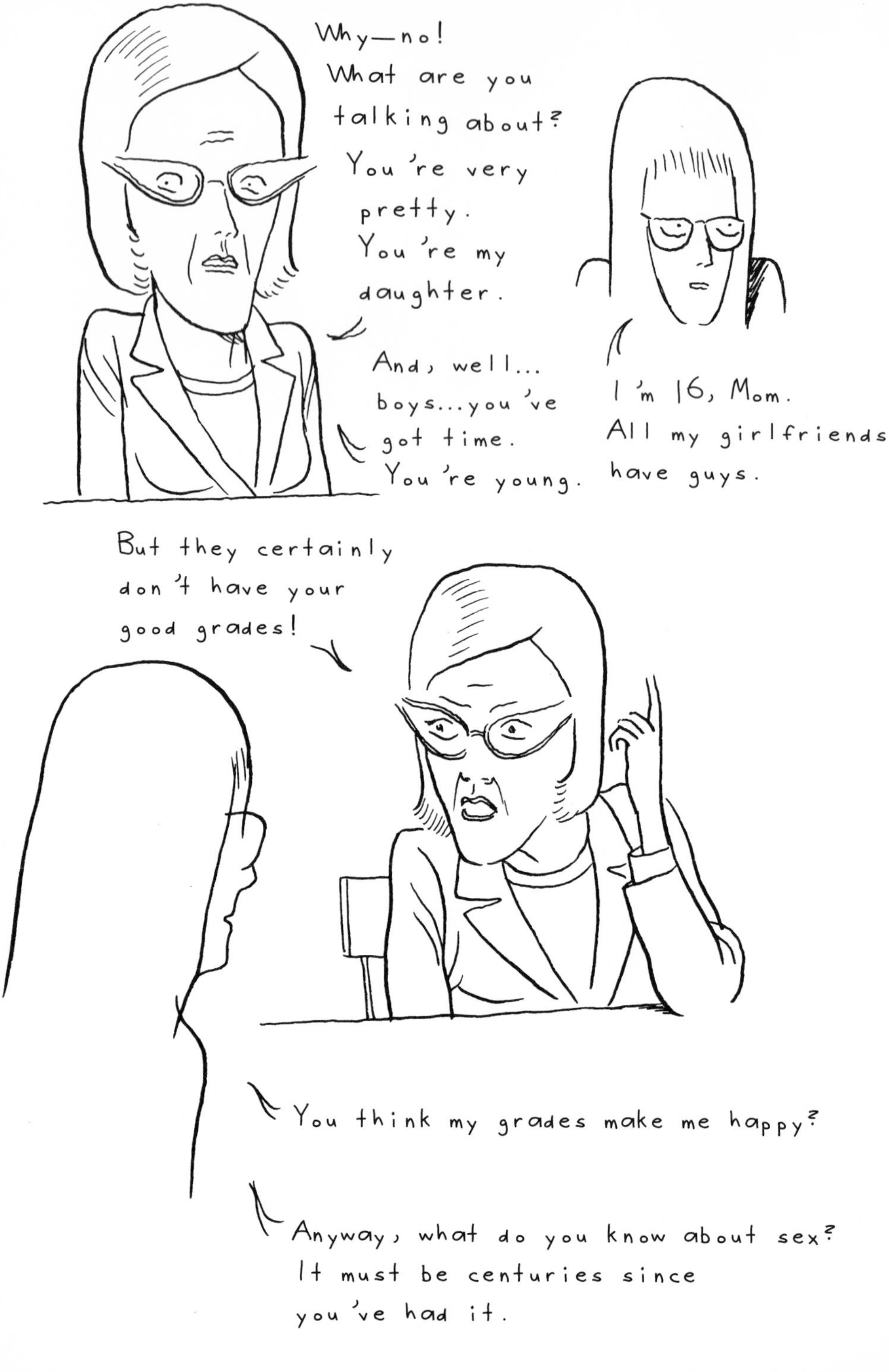
Why—no! What are you talking about? You're very pretty. You're my daughter.
And, well... boys...you've got time. You're young.
I'm 16, Mom. All my girlfriends have guys.
But they certainly don't have your good grades!
You think my grades make me happy?
Anyway, what do you know about sex? It must be centuries since you've had it.

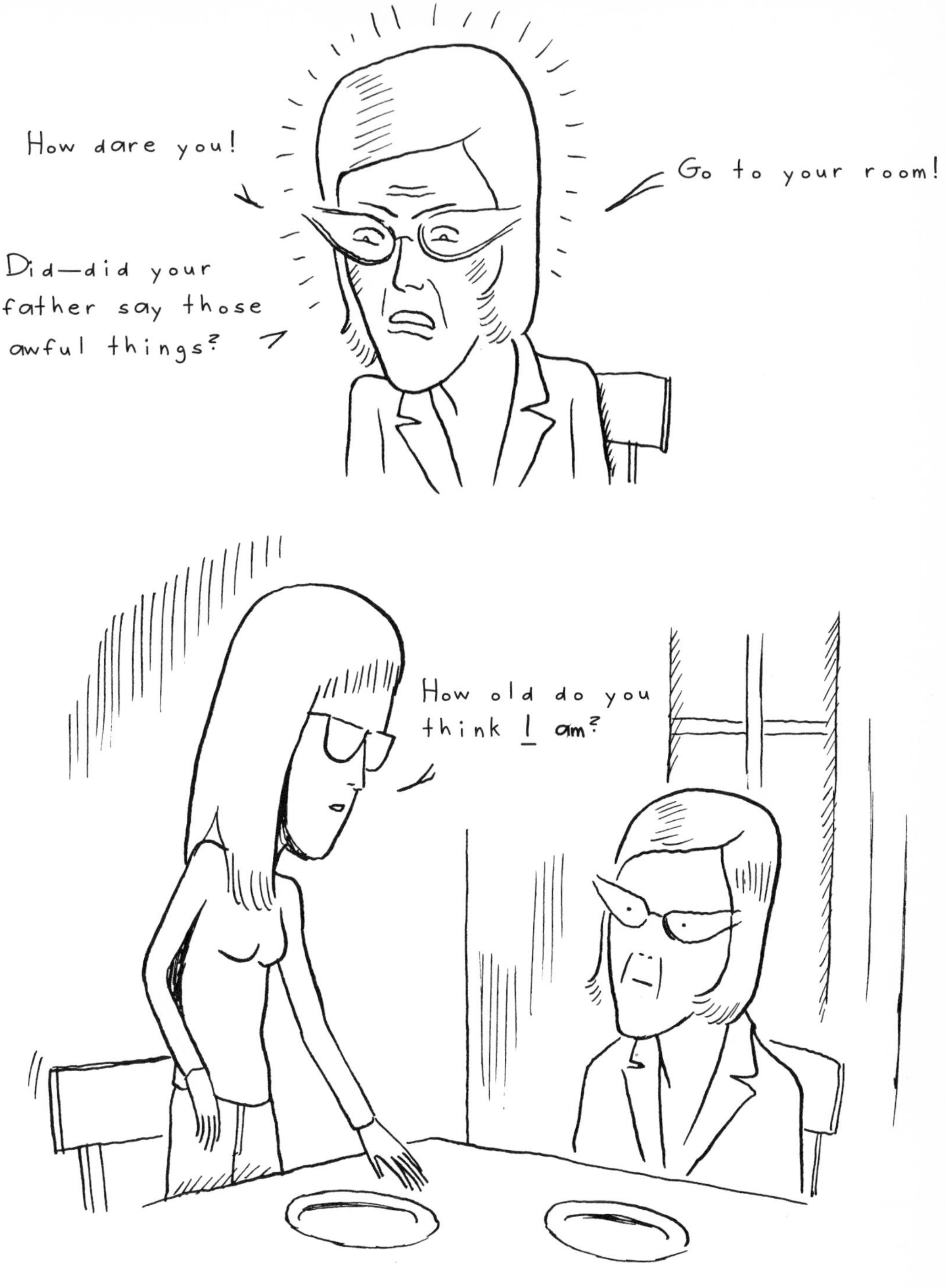
How dare you!
Did—did your father say those awful things?
Go to your room!
How old do you think I am?

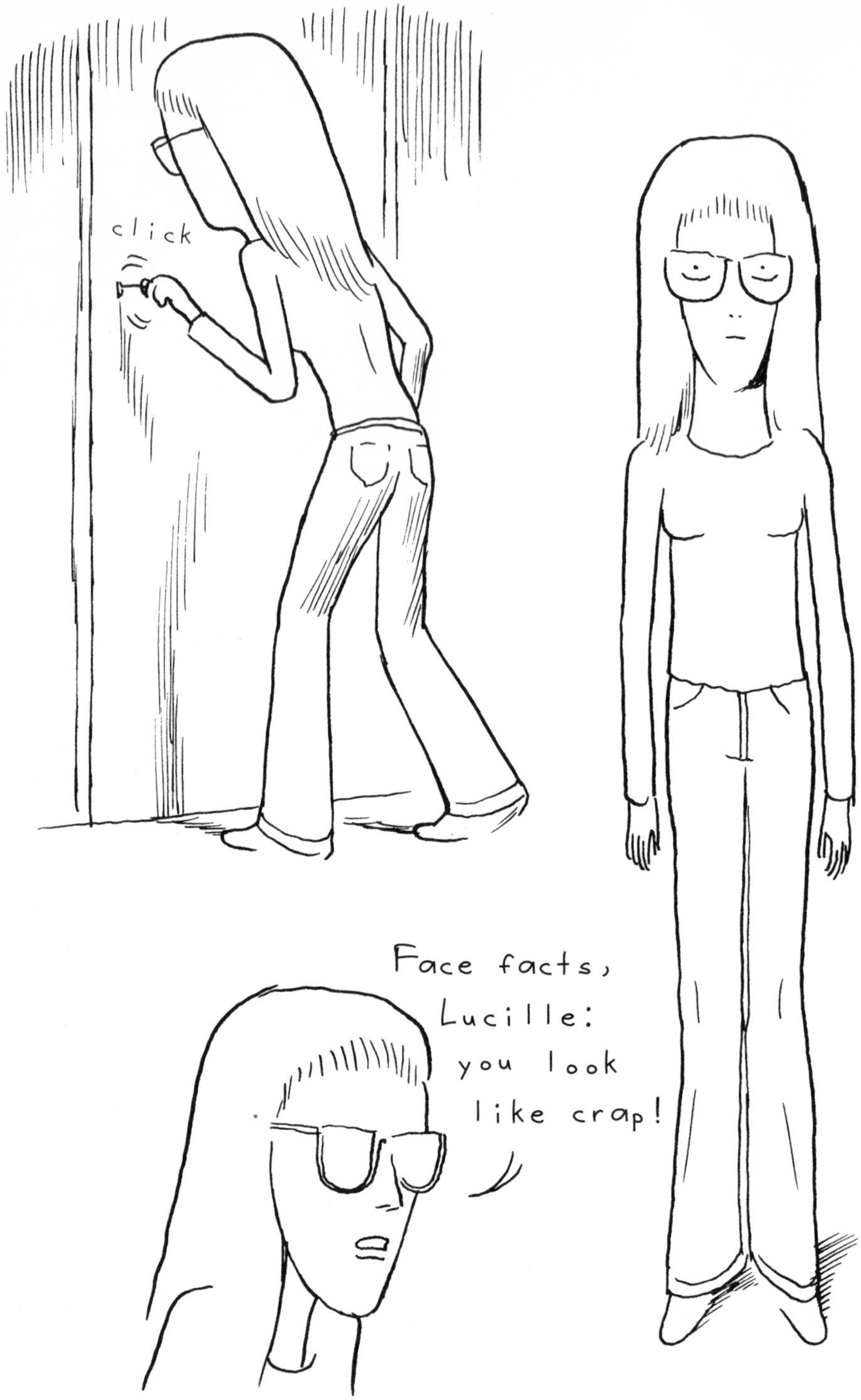
click
Face facts, Lucille: you look like crap!

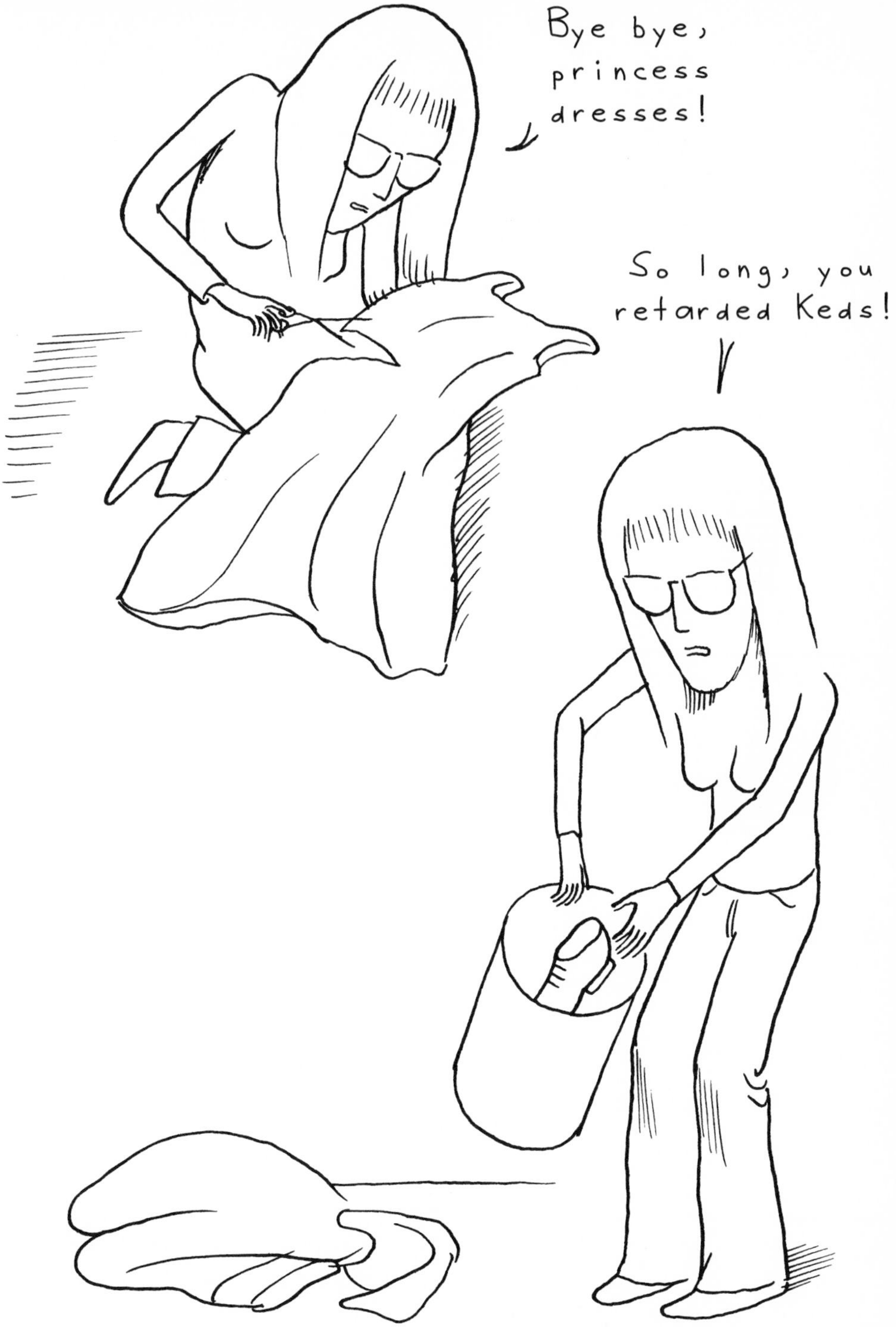
Bye bye, princess dresses!
So long, you retarded Keds!

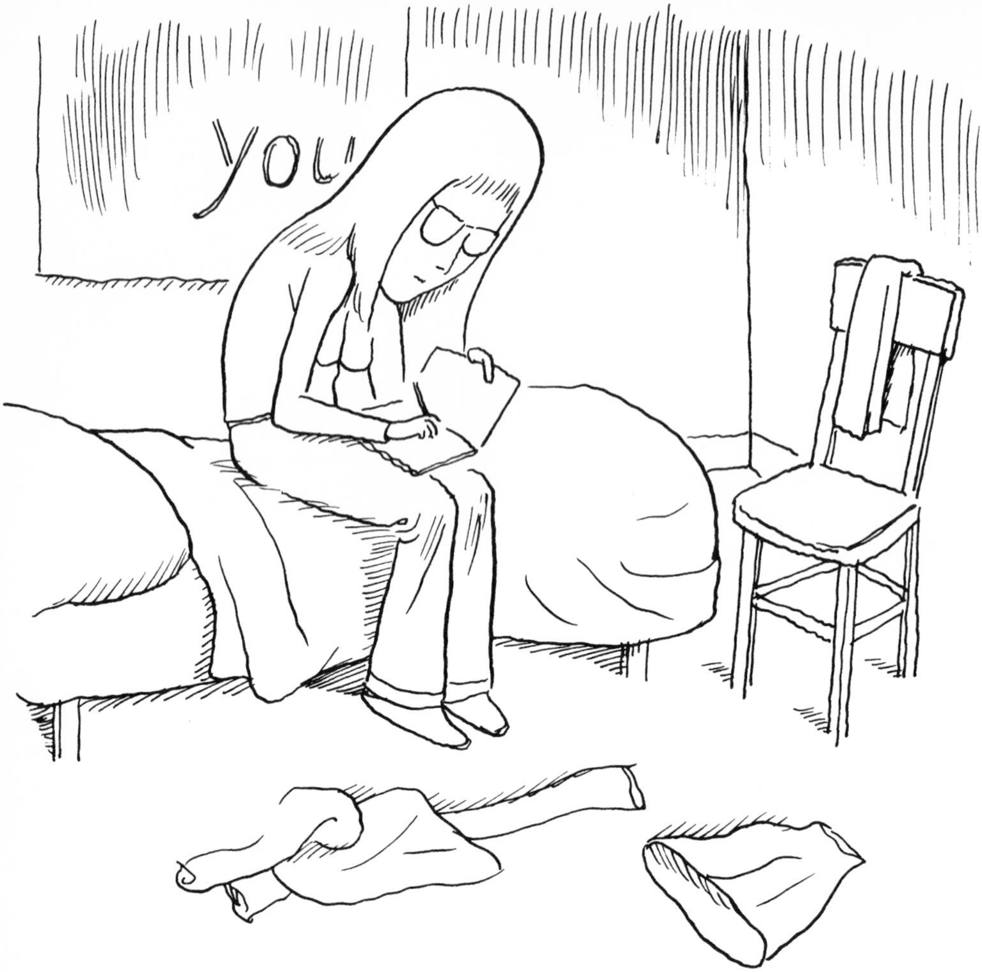
YOU

Why do guys only care about our asses?
Actually, I don't know if that's all
they really care about...but I know
they're on the list, way up top.
Is all I care about their dicks?
I've never actually seen one for real...

SCORIES de L'ENFER

(Slag from Hell)

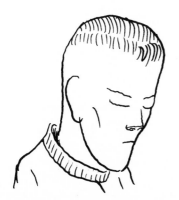

Uh...David wants to know about his future.

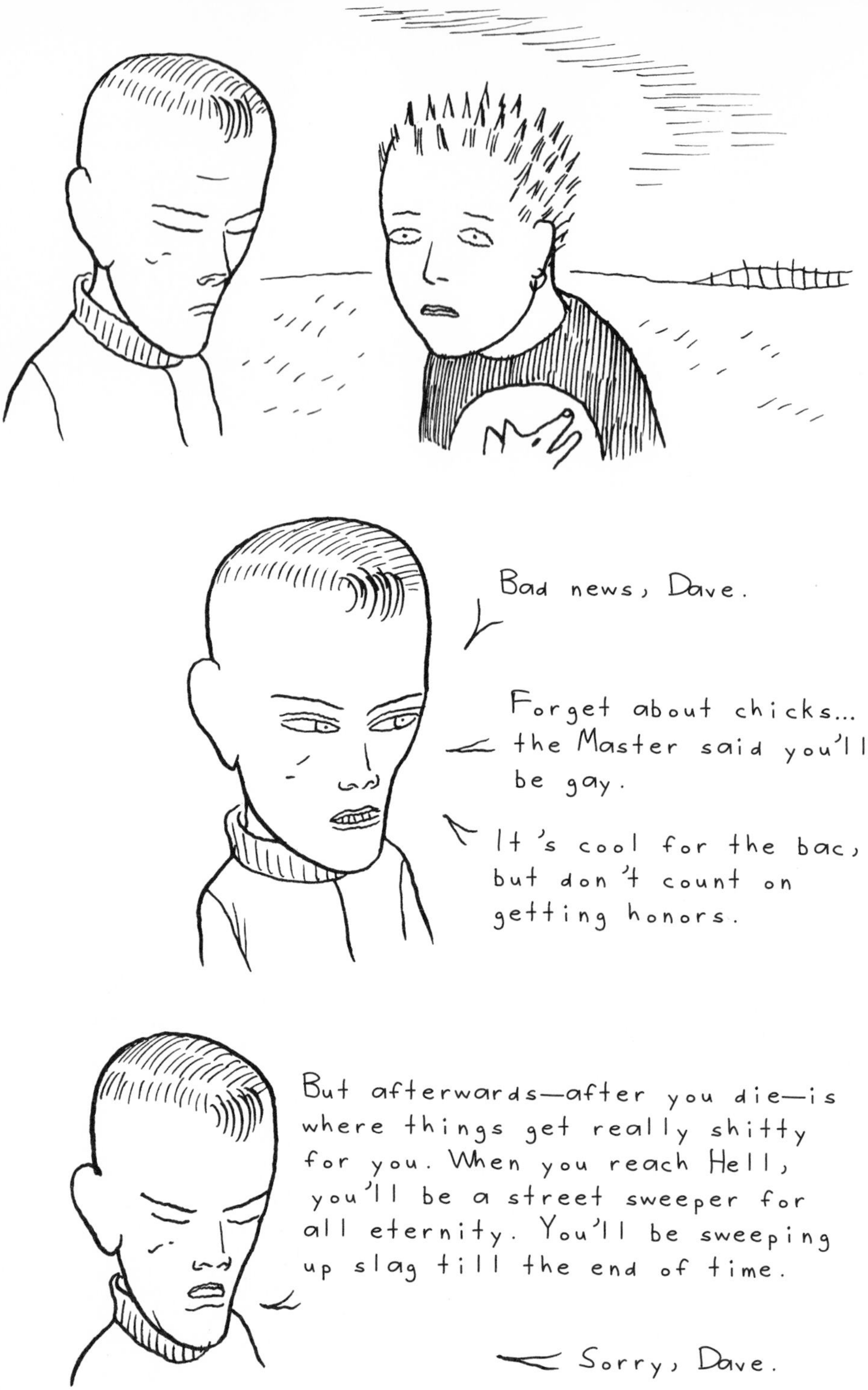

Bad news, Dave.
Forget about chicks... the Master said you'll be gay.
It's cool for the bac, but don't count on getting honors.
But afterwards—after you die—is where things get really shitty for you. When you reach Hell, you'll be a street sweeper for all eternity. You'll be sweeping up slag till the end of time.
Sorry, Dave.

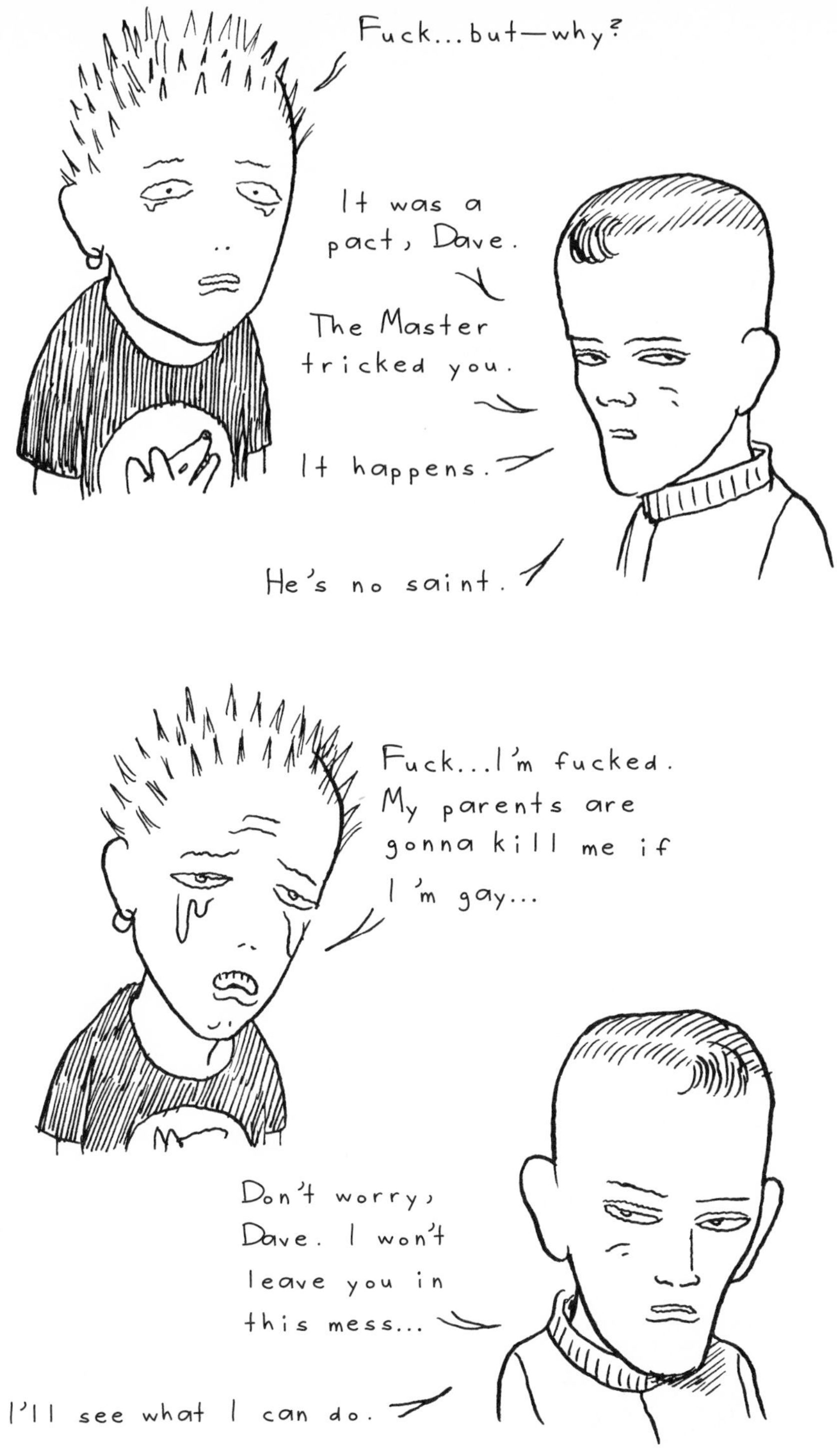
Fuck...but—why?
It was a pact, Dave.
The Master tricked you.
It happens.
He's no saint.
Fuck...I'm fucked. My parents are gonna kill me if I'm gay...
Don't worry, Dave. I won't leave you in this mess...
I'll see what I can do.

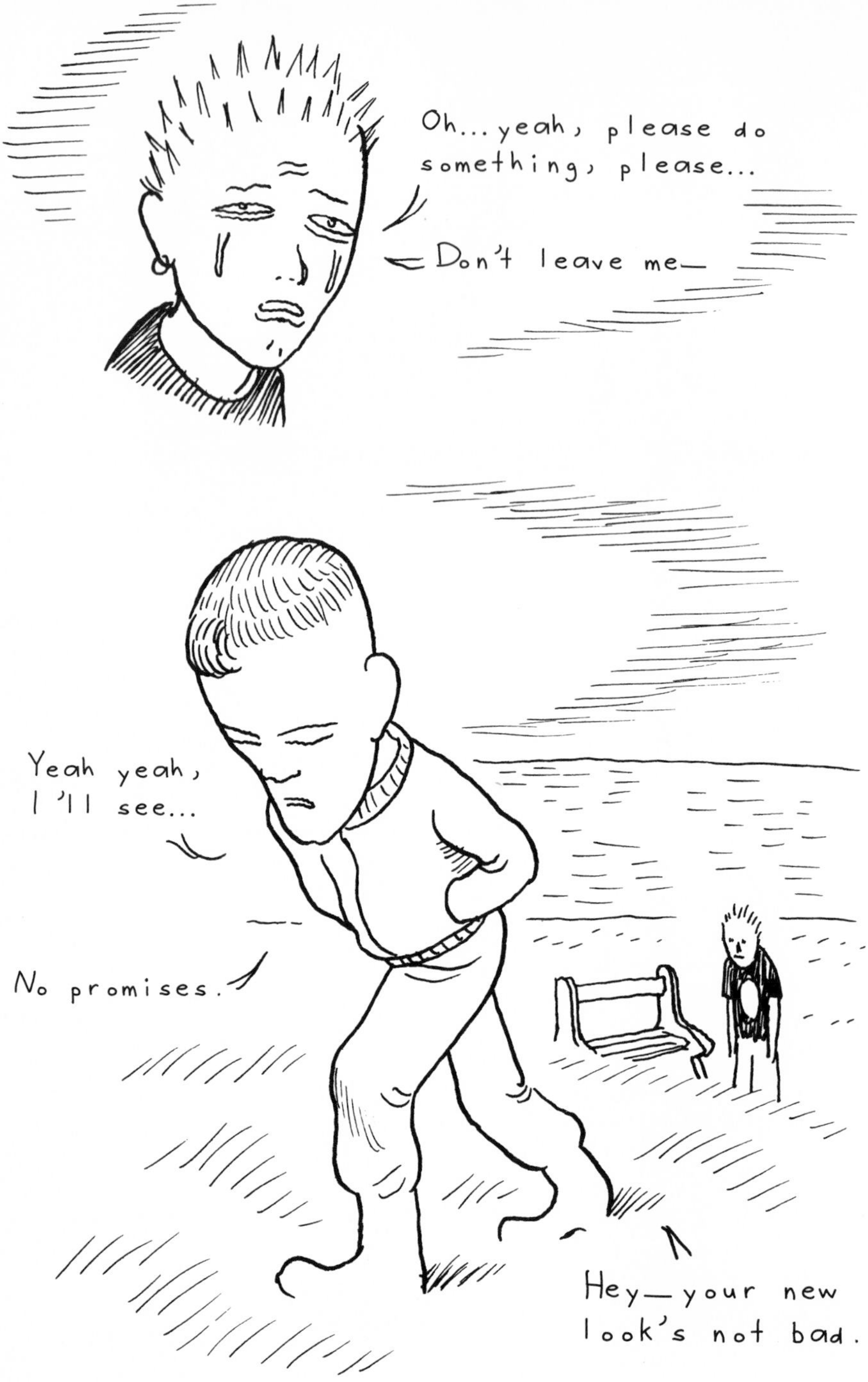

Oh... yeah, please do something, please...
Don't leave me—
Yeah yeah, I'll see...
No promises.
Hey— your new look's not bad.

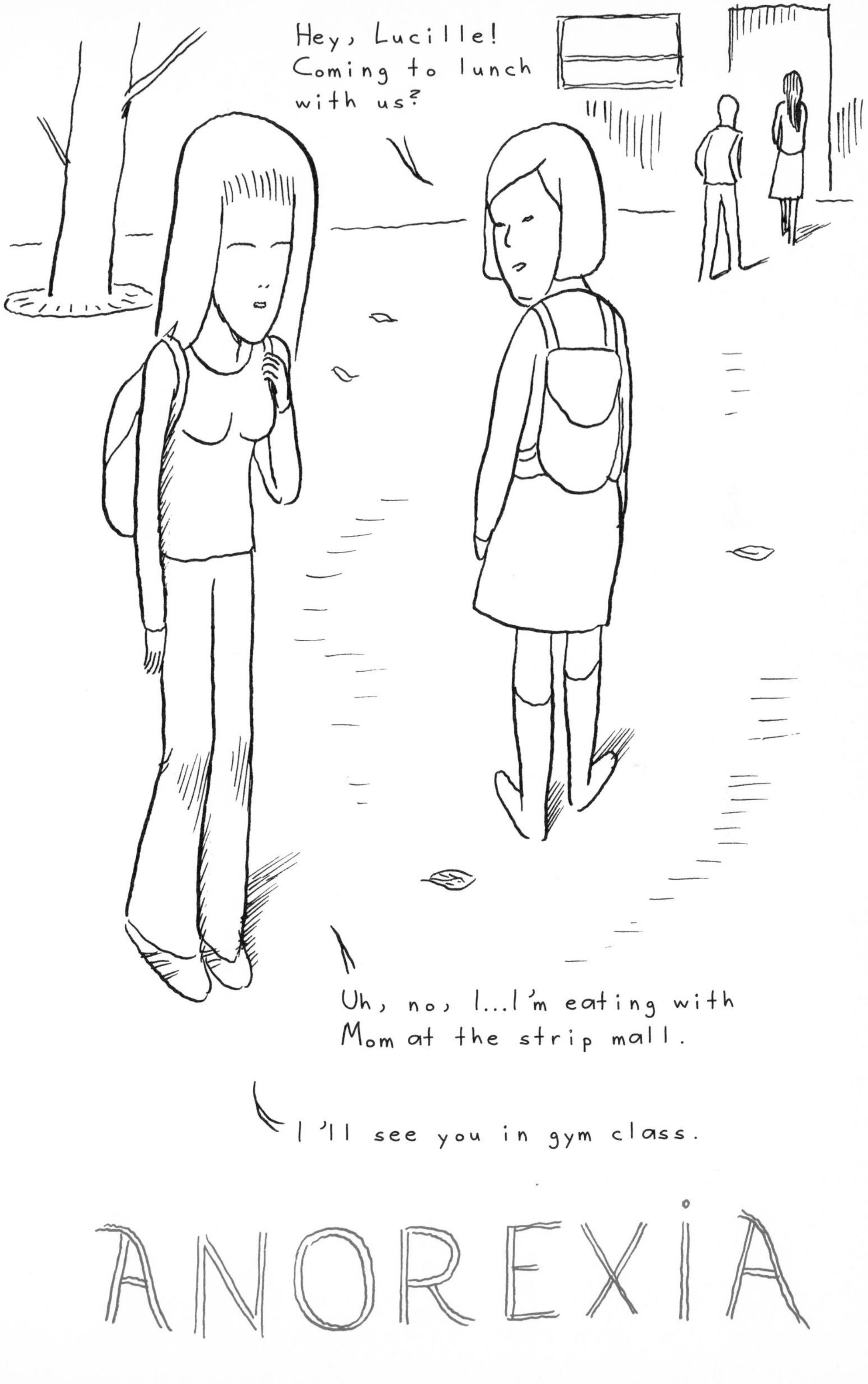
Hey, Lucille! Coming to lunch with us?
Uh, no, I...I'm eating with Mom at the strip mall.
I'll see you in gym class.
ANOREXIA

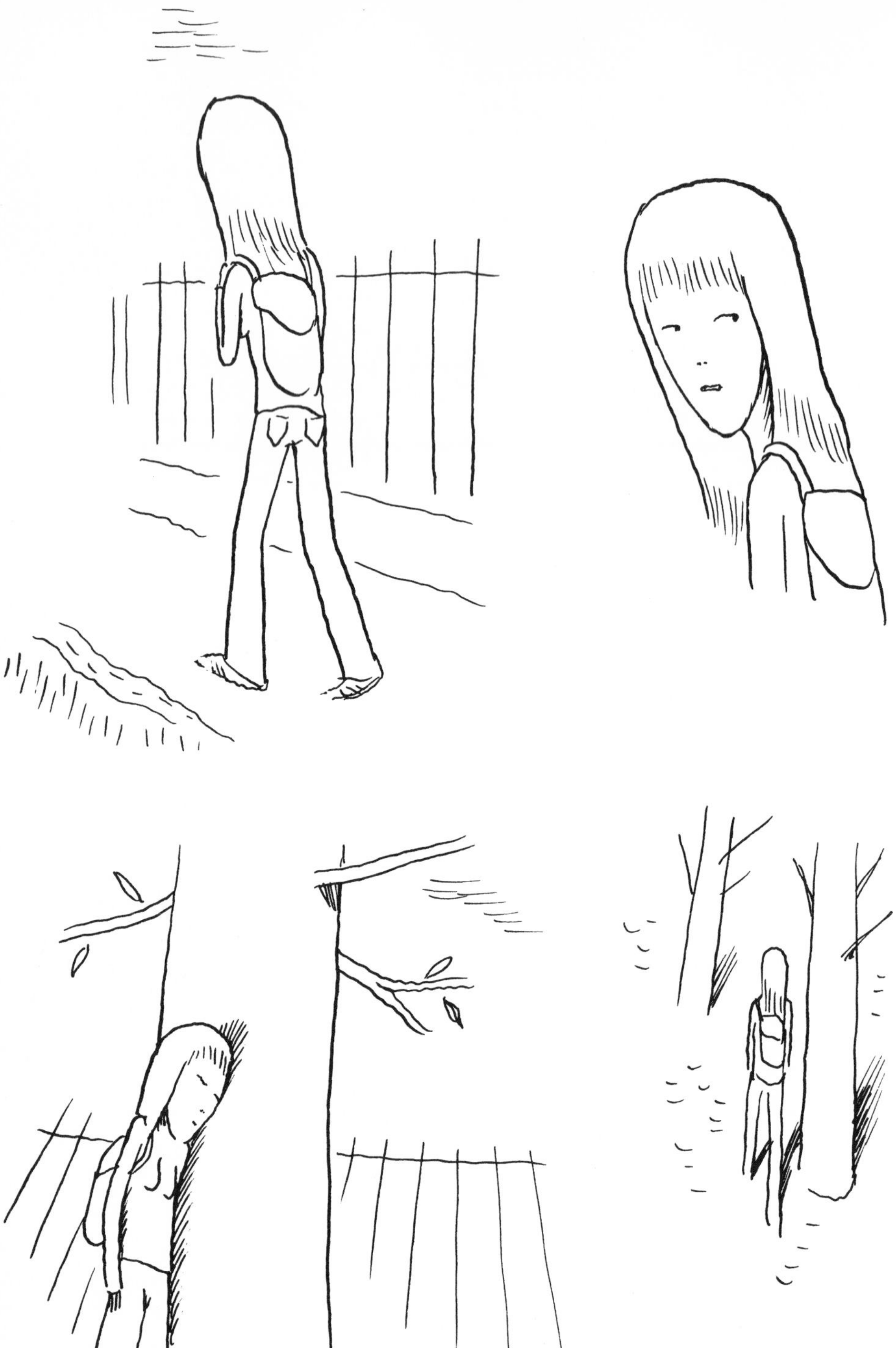

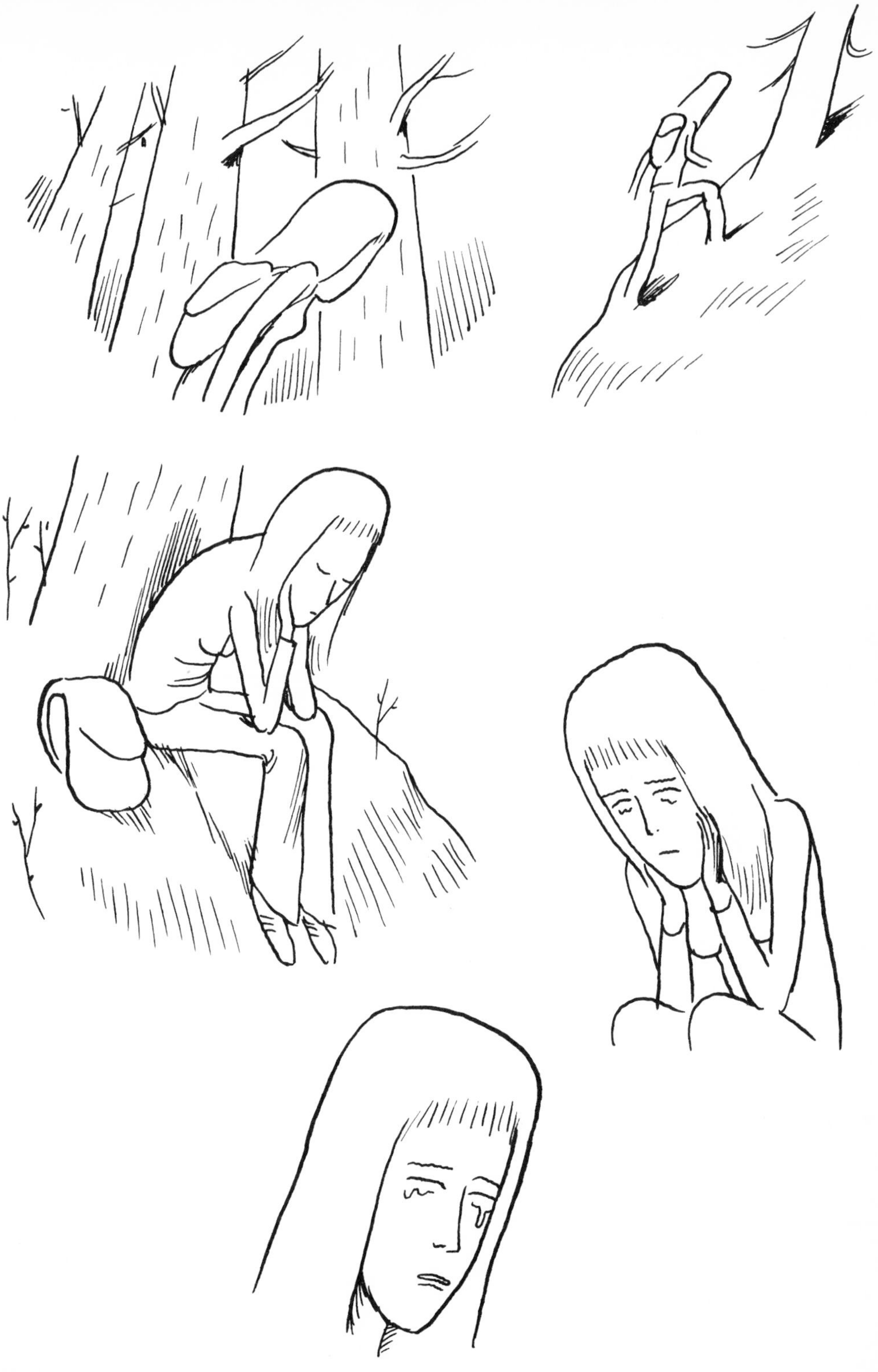

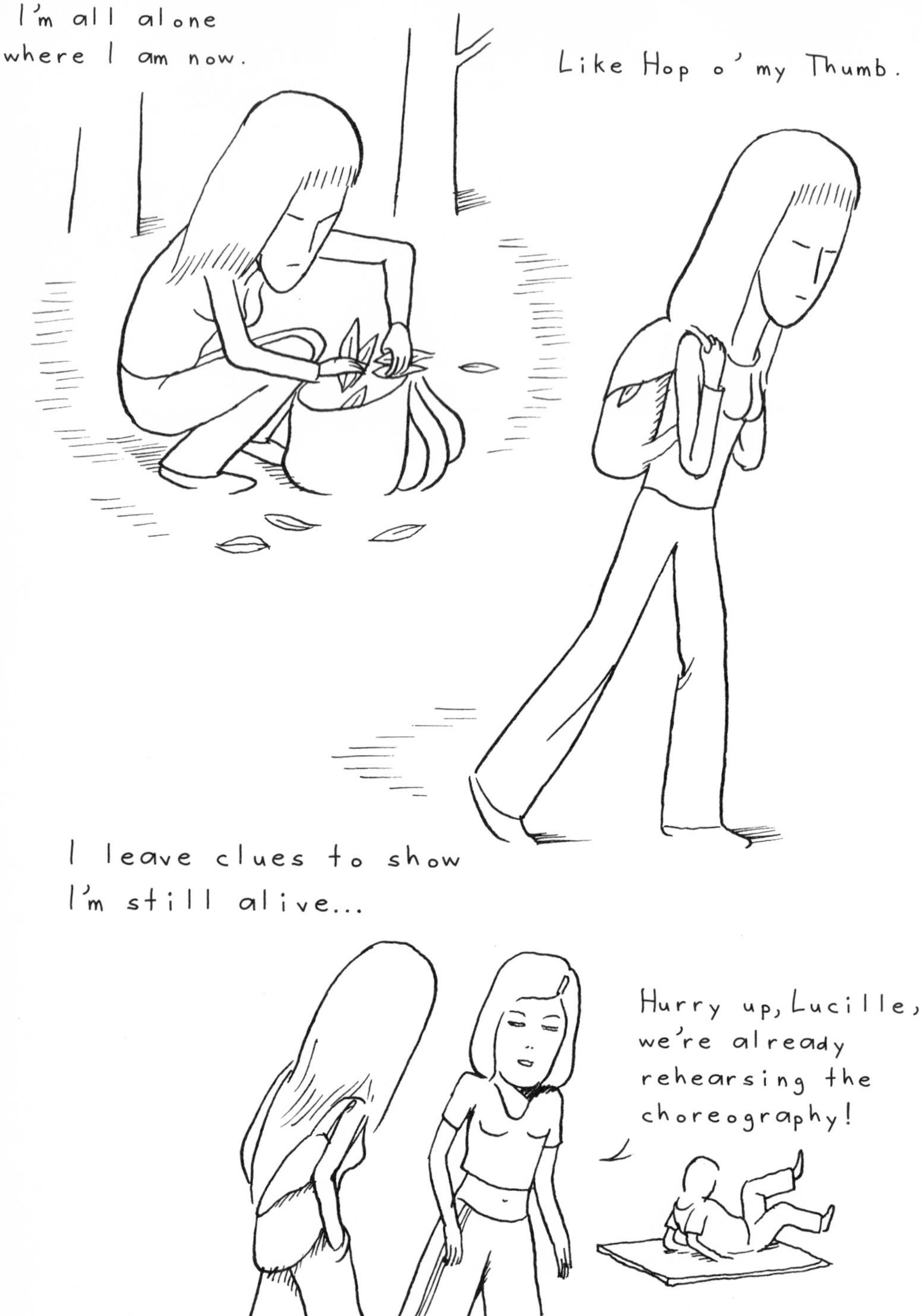
I'm all alone where I am now.
Like Hop o' my Thumb.
I leave clues to show I'm still alive...
Hurry up, Lucille, we're already rehearsing the choreography!

So they'll finally see there are no trees at the strip mall...So I won't have to hear them at the next rehearsal saying:

Hey, Lucille! Me and the girls thought it'd be more fun—I mean, sexier—if we did the last dance of the year in miniskirts.

I can't tell them that I hate myself...my body... and even worse in a skirt.

Why don't they understand?
Why can't they see?

I don't need to lie anymore. I don't spend lunch
in the woods anymore.
For two weeks now, I haven't even been to school.
My mom thinks I'm doing it to piss her off.
That it's just a phase.

She thinks she knows what I have better than I do.

I don't know anything about what's happening to me...

I don't love life anymore. I think. But I've never been really good at that.

Remy called to check up on me. That made me happy. I almost wanted to invite him over, if I didn't look like an alien. Right, and there was Rouget, too. Worried not to see me in class anymore. Rouget... what a fat pig. But it was nice of him, anyway.

Le Nom du Père

(The Name of the Father)

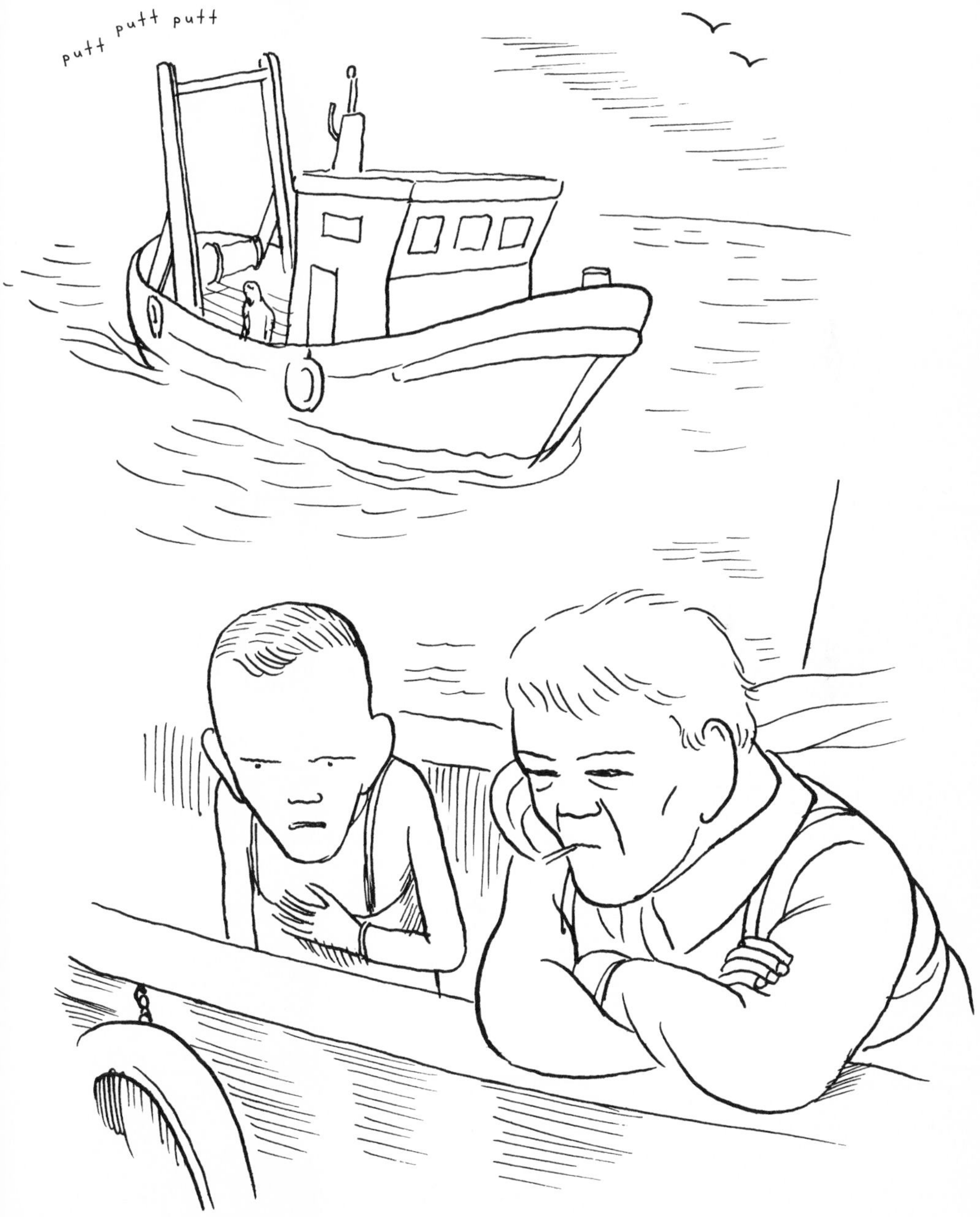
putt putt putt

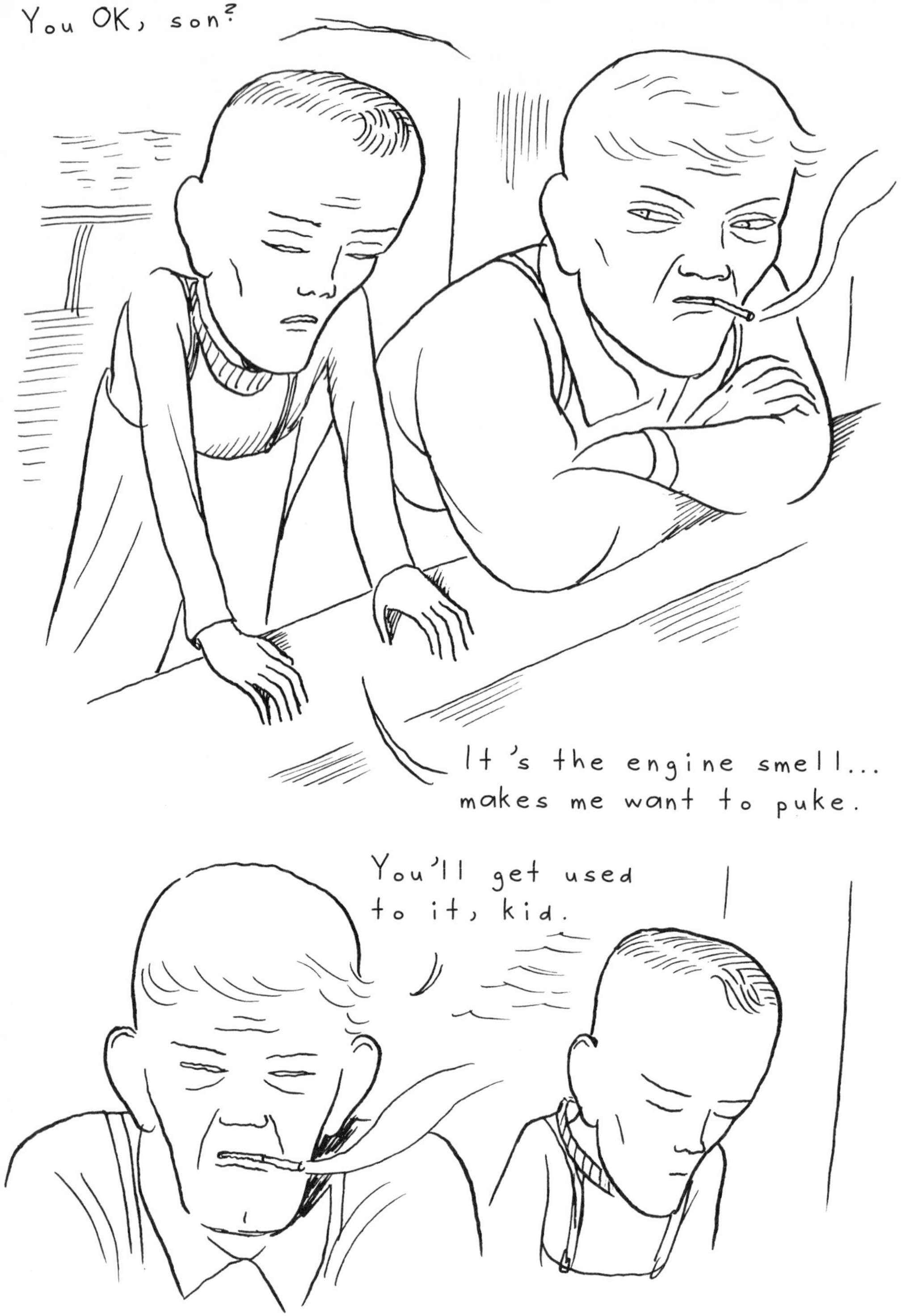
You OK, son?
It's the engine smell... makes me want to puke.
You'll get used to it, kid.

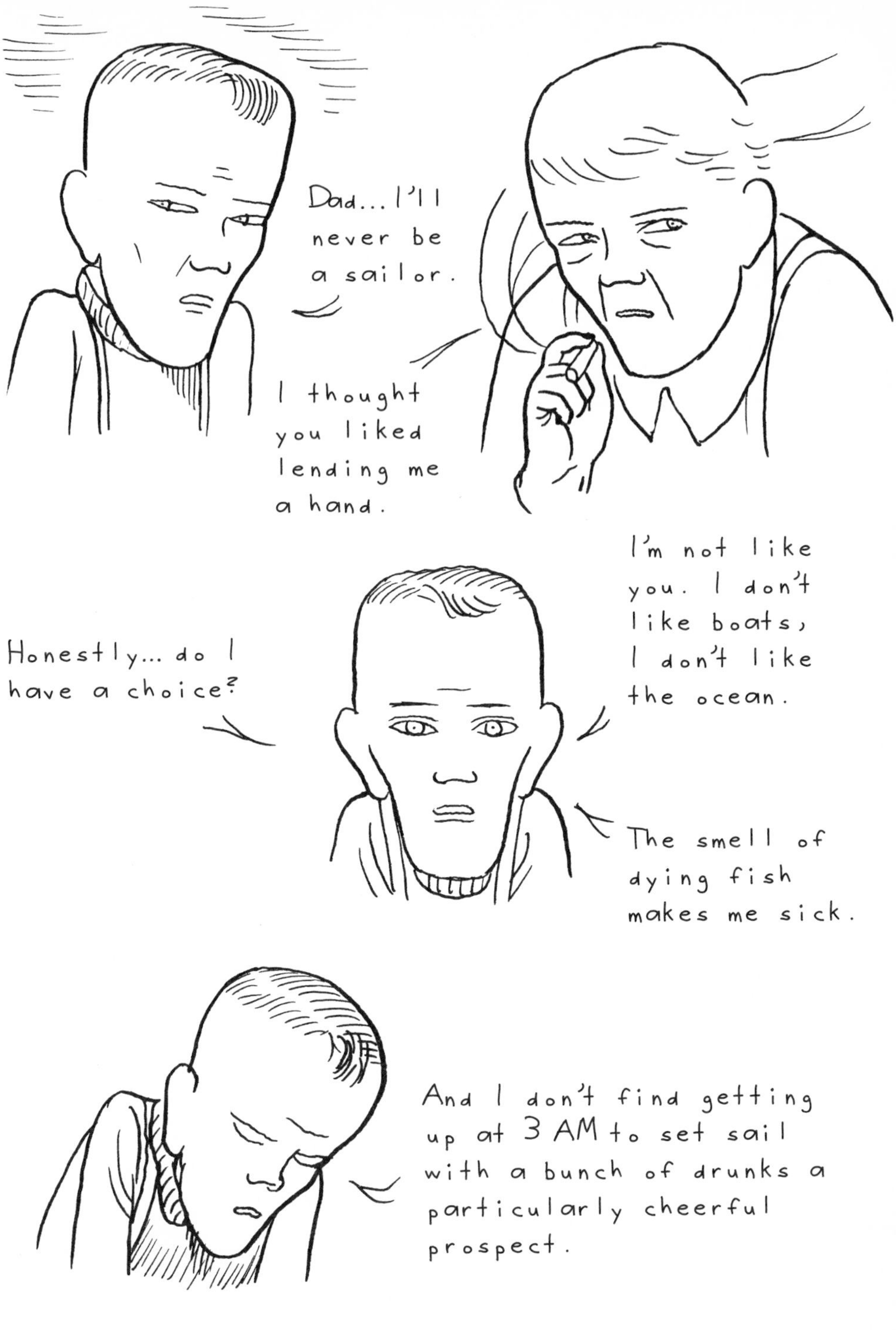
Dad... I'll never be a sailor.
I thought you liked lending me a hand.
Honestly... do I have a choice?
I'm not like you. I don't like boats, I don't like the ocean.
The smell of dying fish makes me sick.
And I don't find getting up at 3 AM to set sail with a bunch of drunks a particularly cheerful prospect.

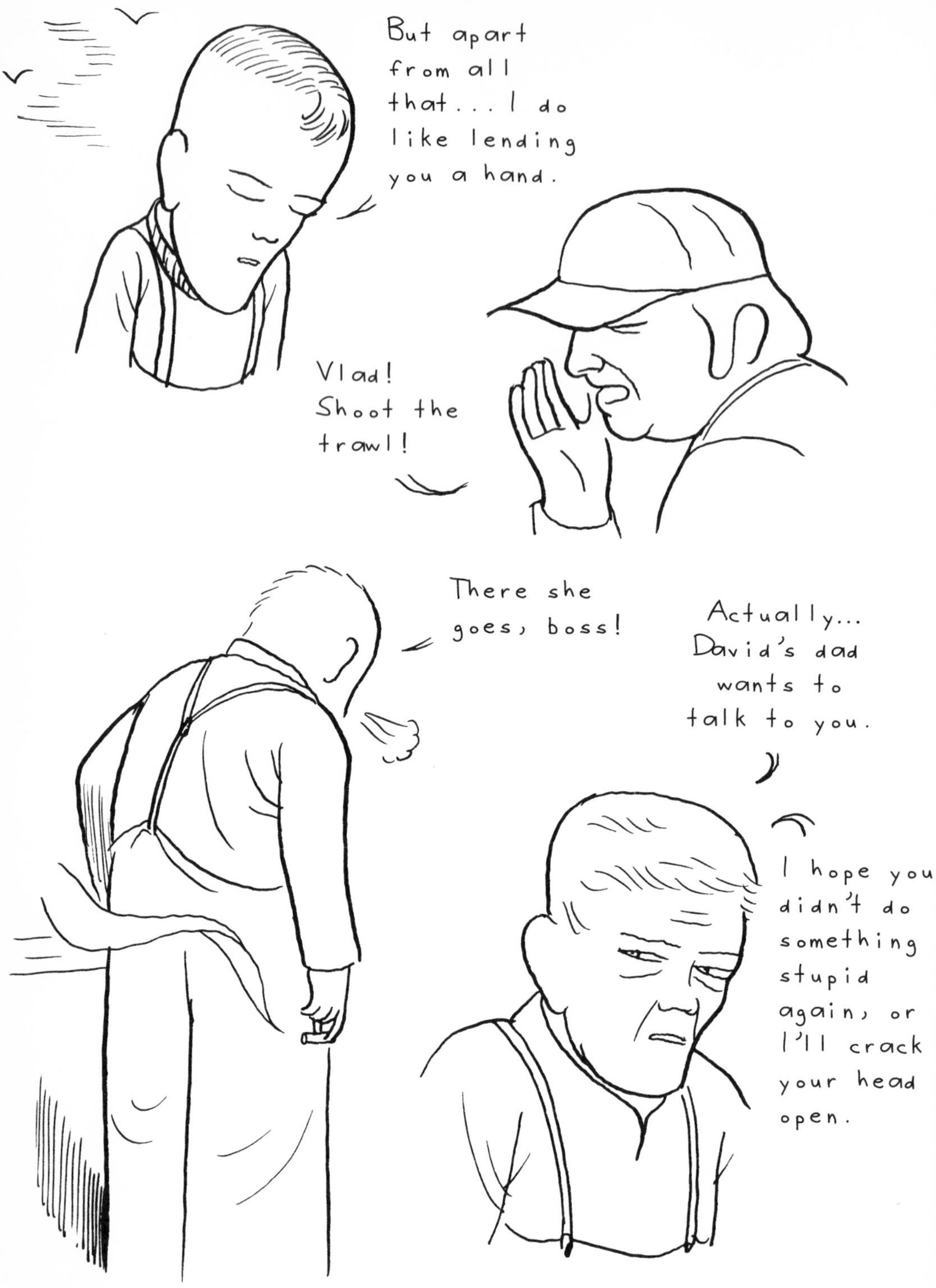
But apart from all that... I do like lending you a hand.
Vlad! Shoot the trawl!
There she goes, boss!
Actually... David's dad wants to talk to you.
I hope you didn't do something stupid again, or I'll crack your head open.

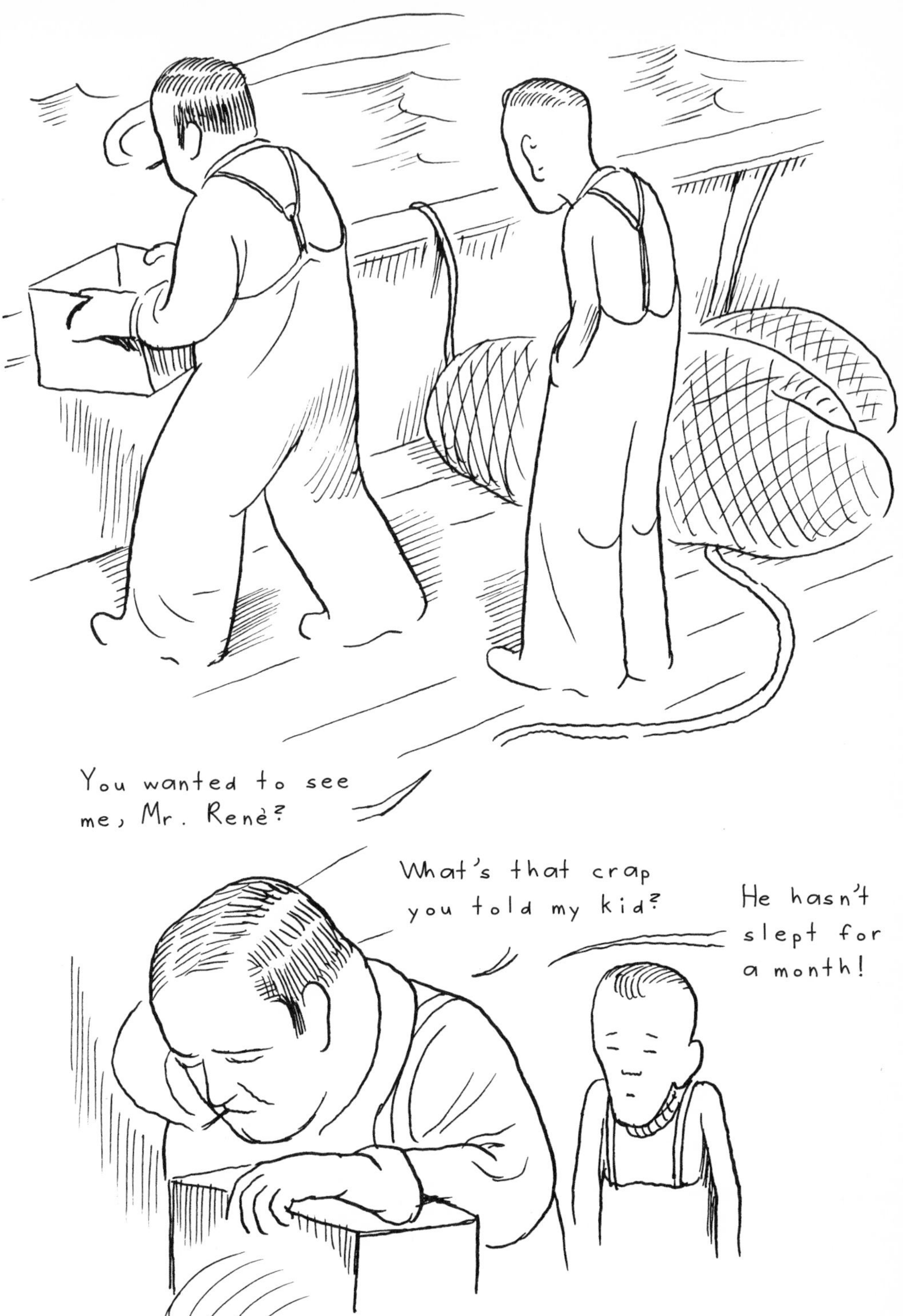
You wanted to see me, Mr. René?
What's that crap you told my kid?
He hasn't slept for a month!

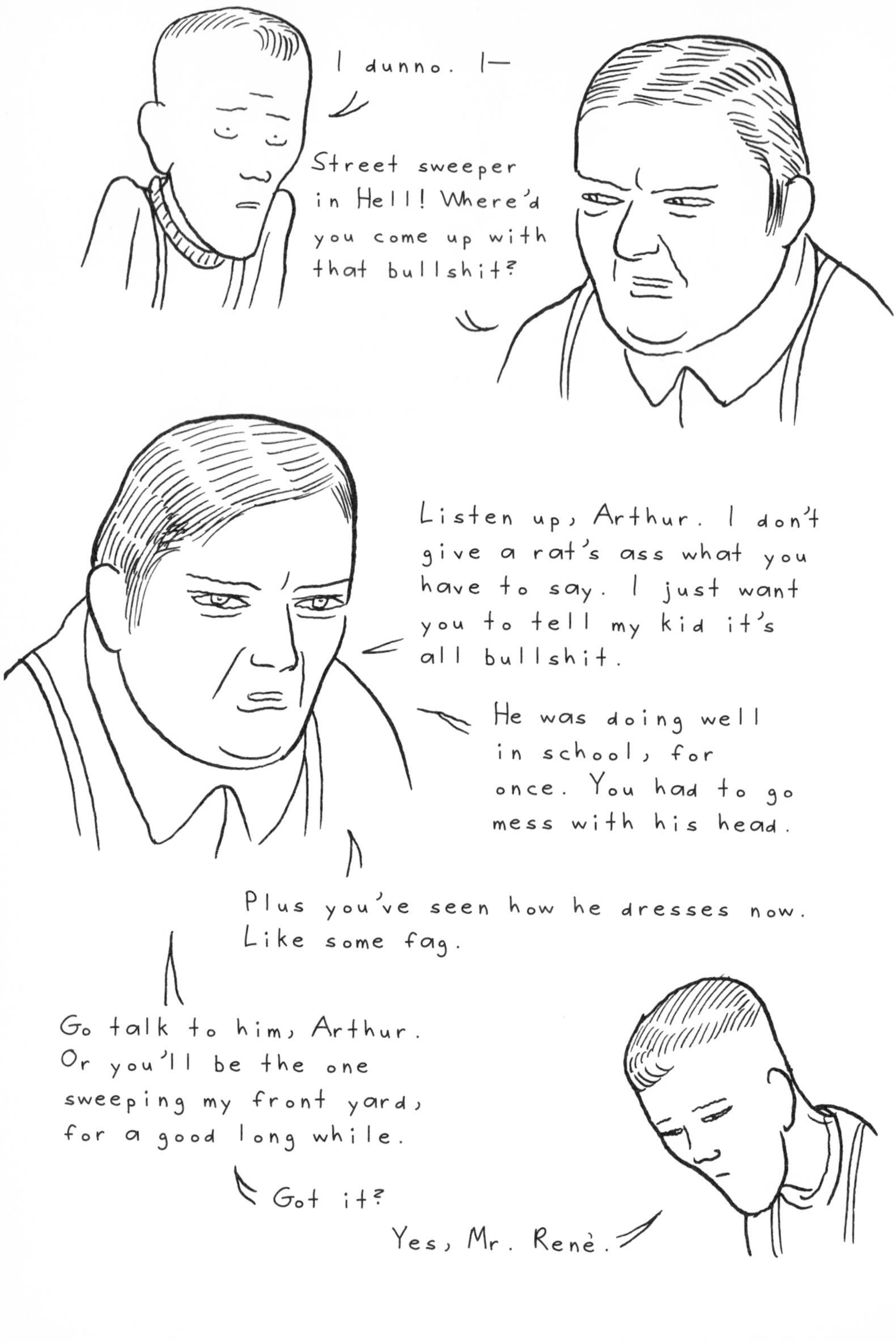
I dunno. I—
Street sweeper in Hell! Where'd you come up with that bullshit?
Listen up, Arthur. I don't give a rat's ass what you have to say. I just want you to tell my kid it's all bullshit.
He was doing well in school, for once. You had to go mess with his head.
Plus you've seen how he dresses now. Like some fag.
Go talk to him, Arthur. Or you'll be the one sweeping my front yard, for a good long while.
Got it?
Yes, Mr. René.

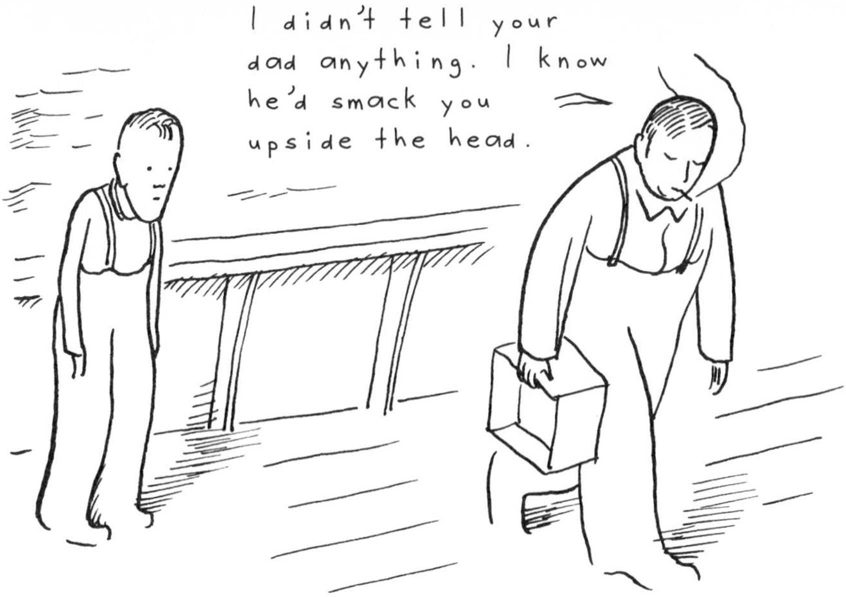
I didn't tell your dad anything. I know he'd smack you upside the head.

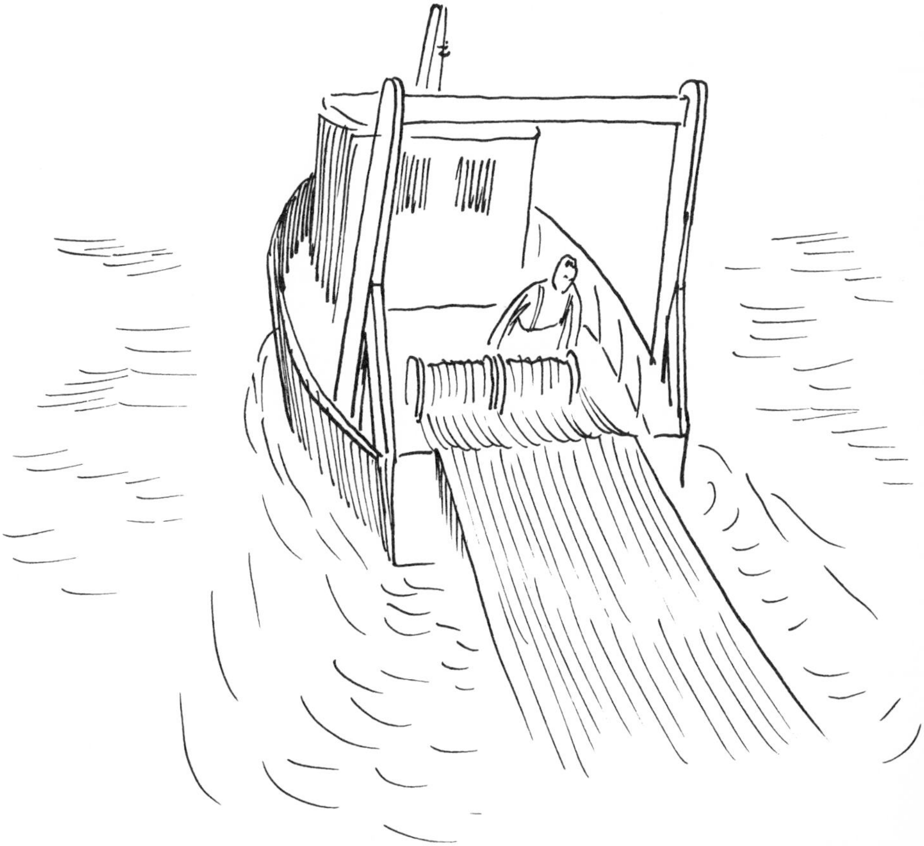

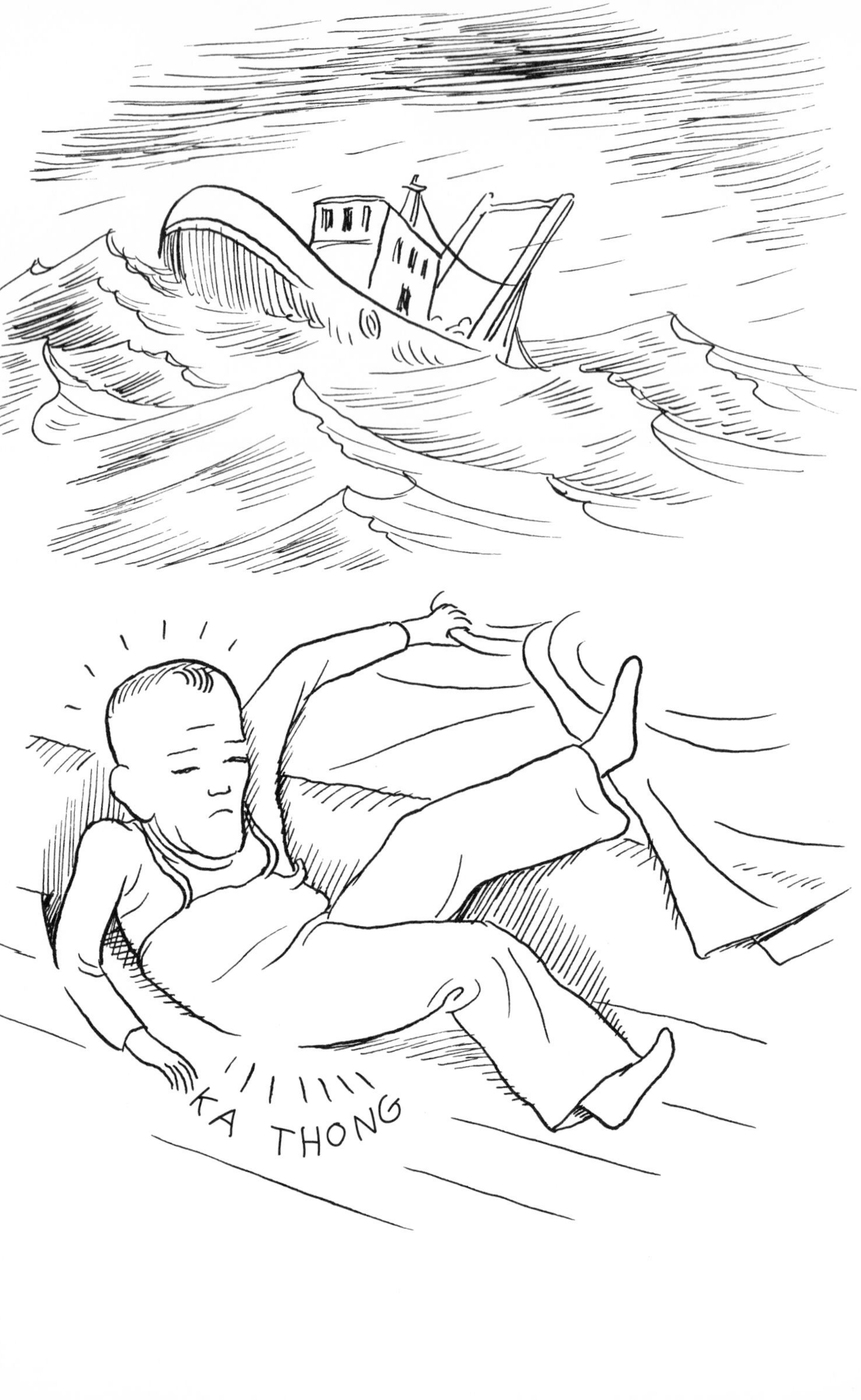
KA THONG

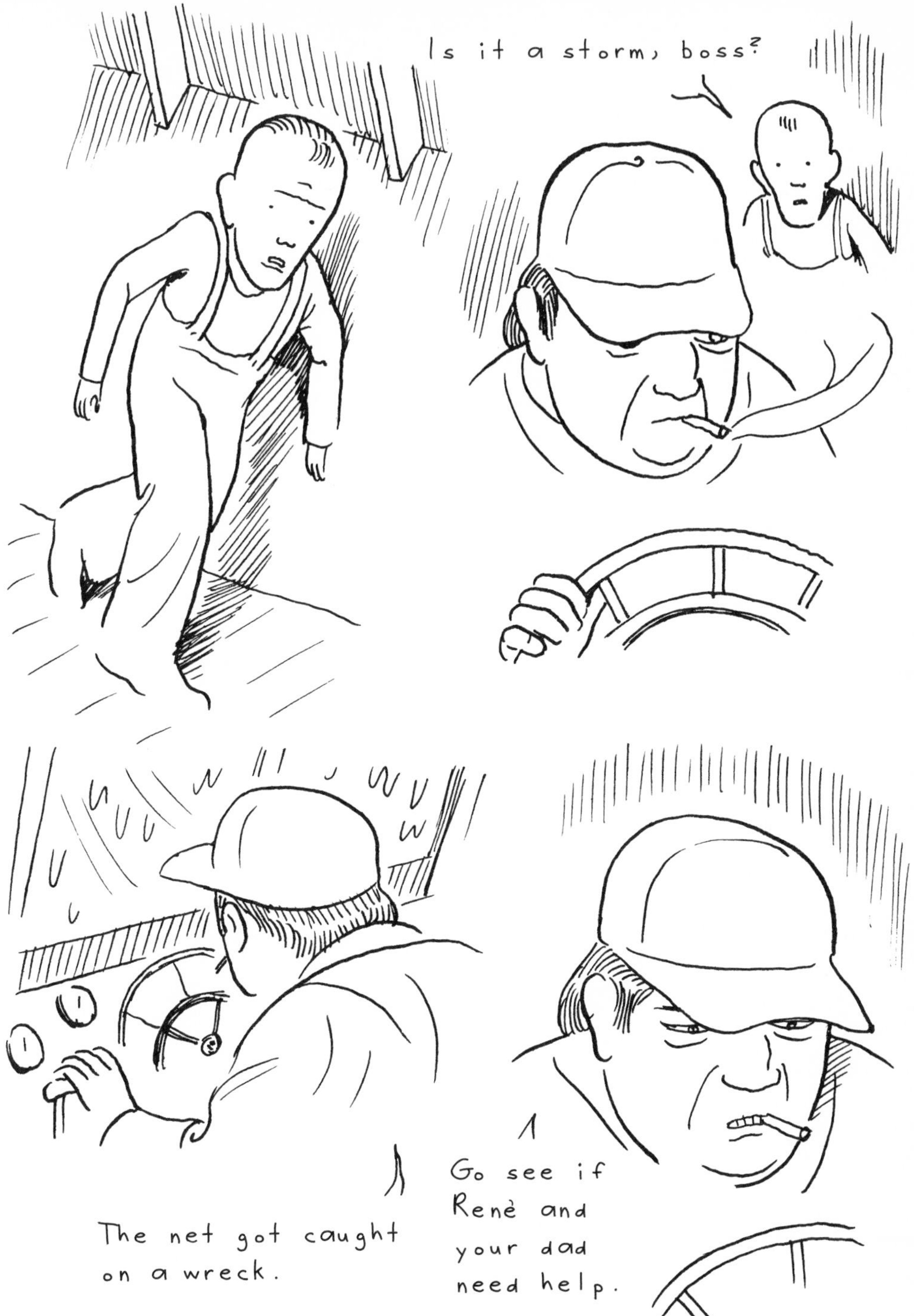
Is it a storm, boss?
The net got caught on a wreck.
Go see if René and your dad need help.

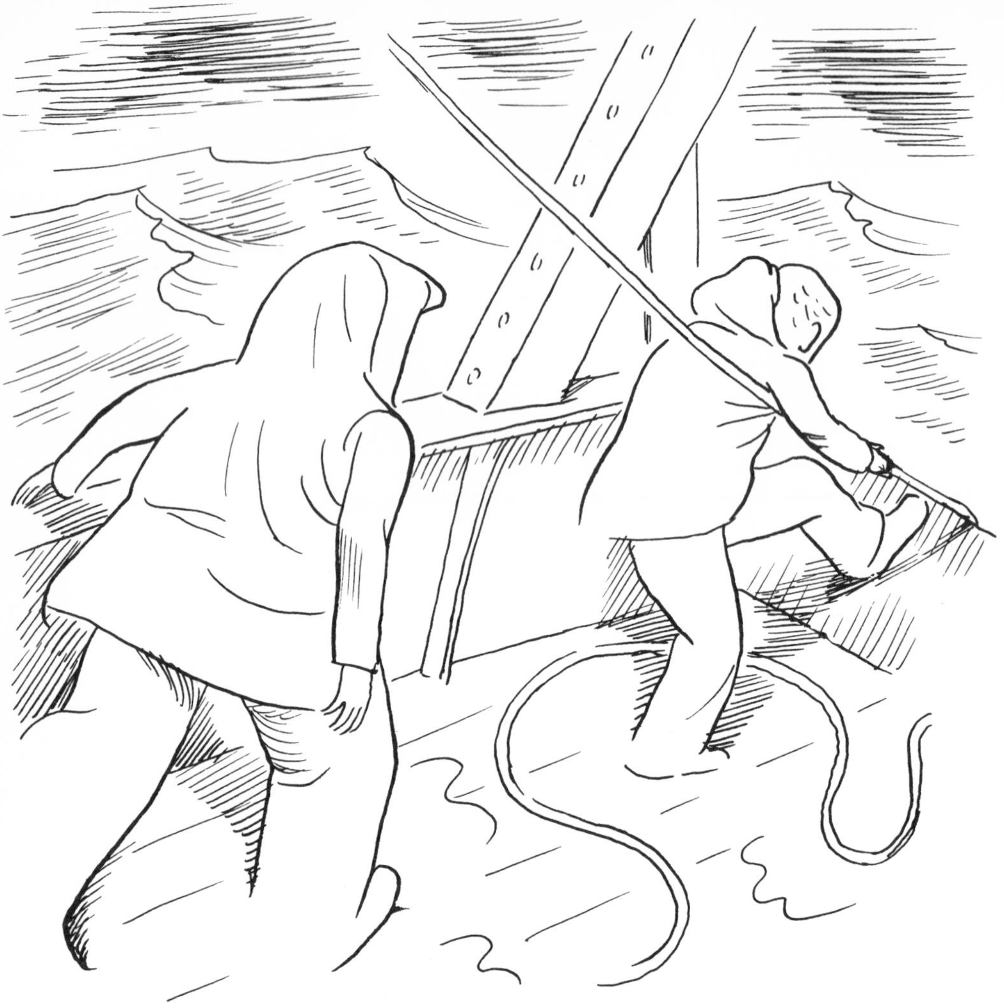

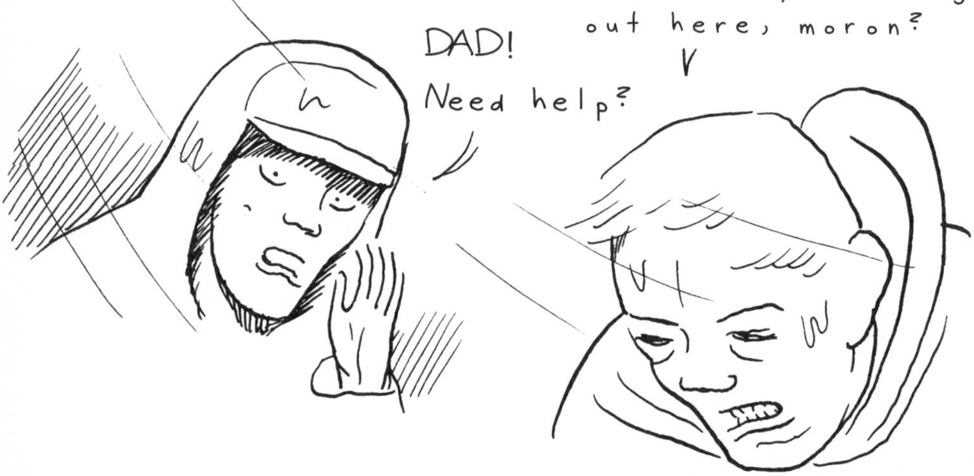
DAD!
Need help?
What are you doing out here, moron?

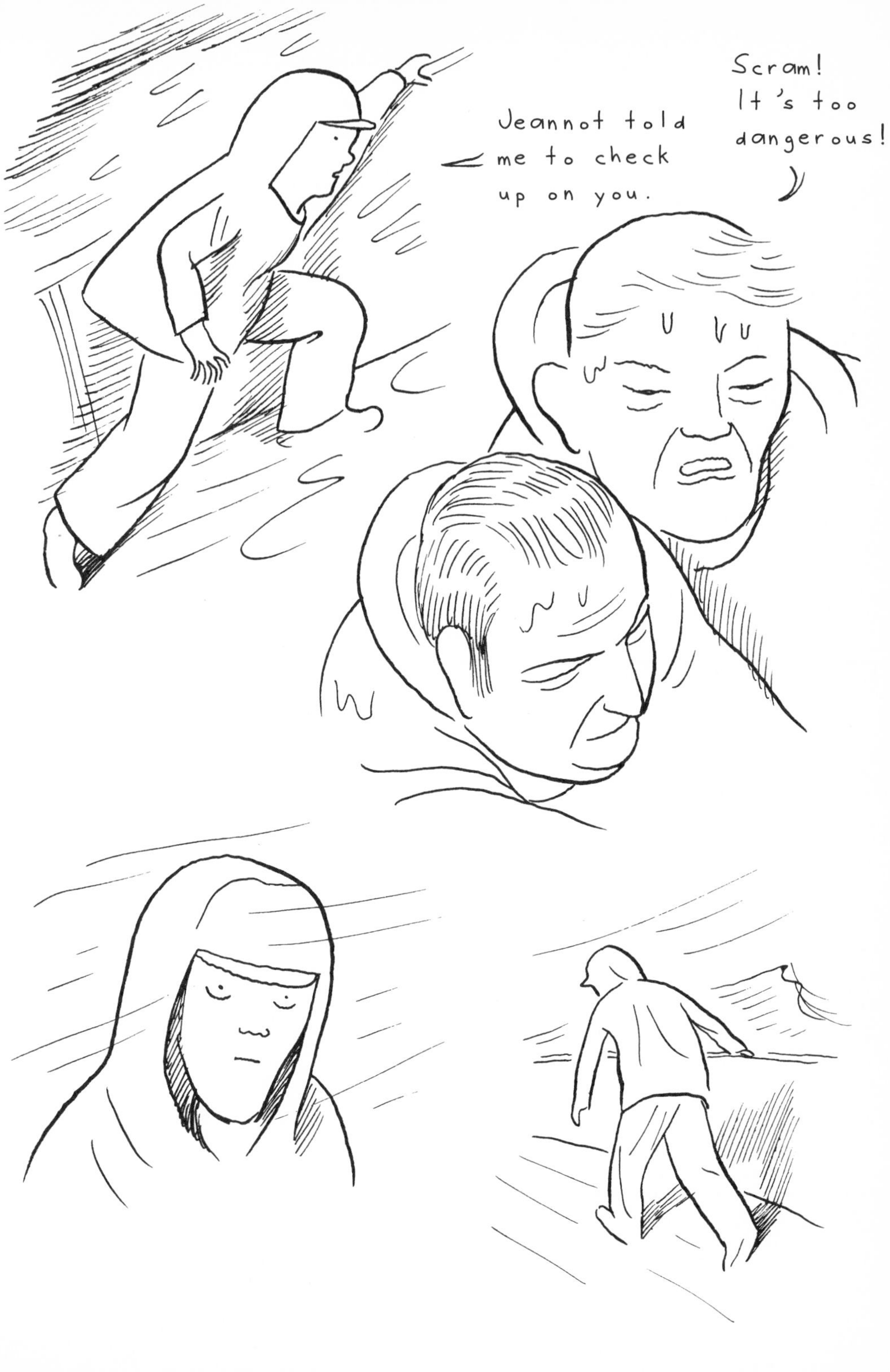
Jeannot told me to check up on you.
Scram! It's too dangerous!

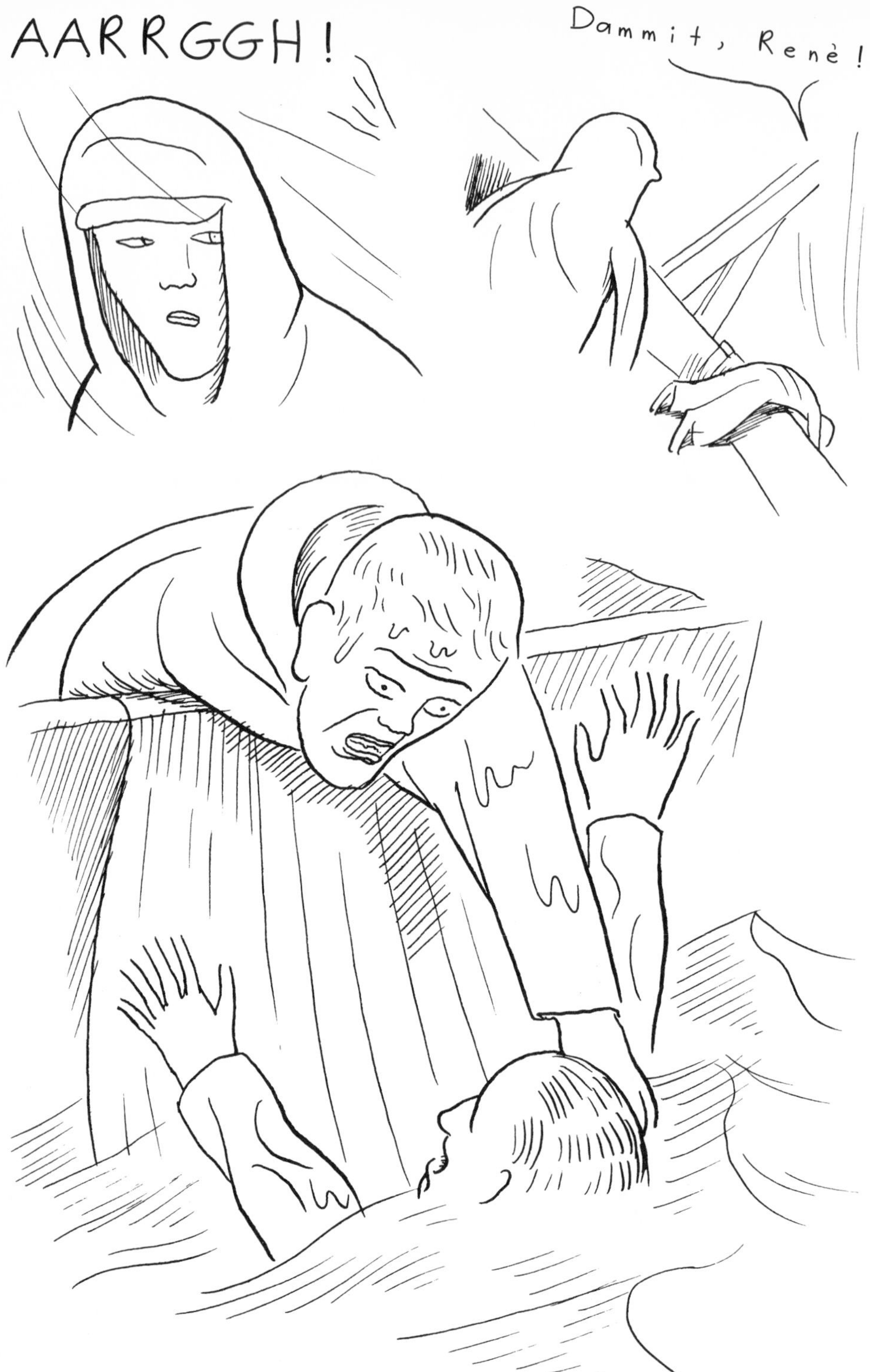
AARRGGH!
Dammit, Renè!

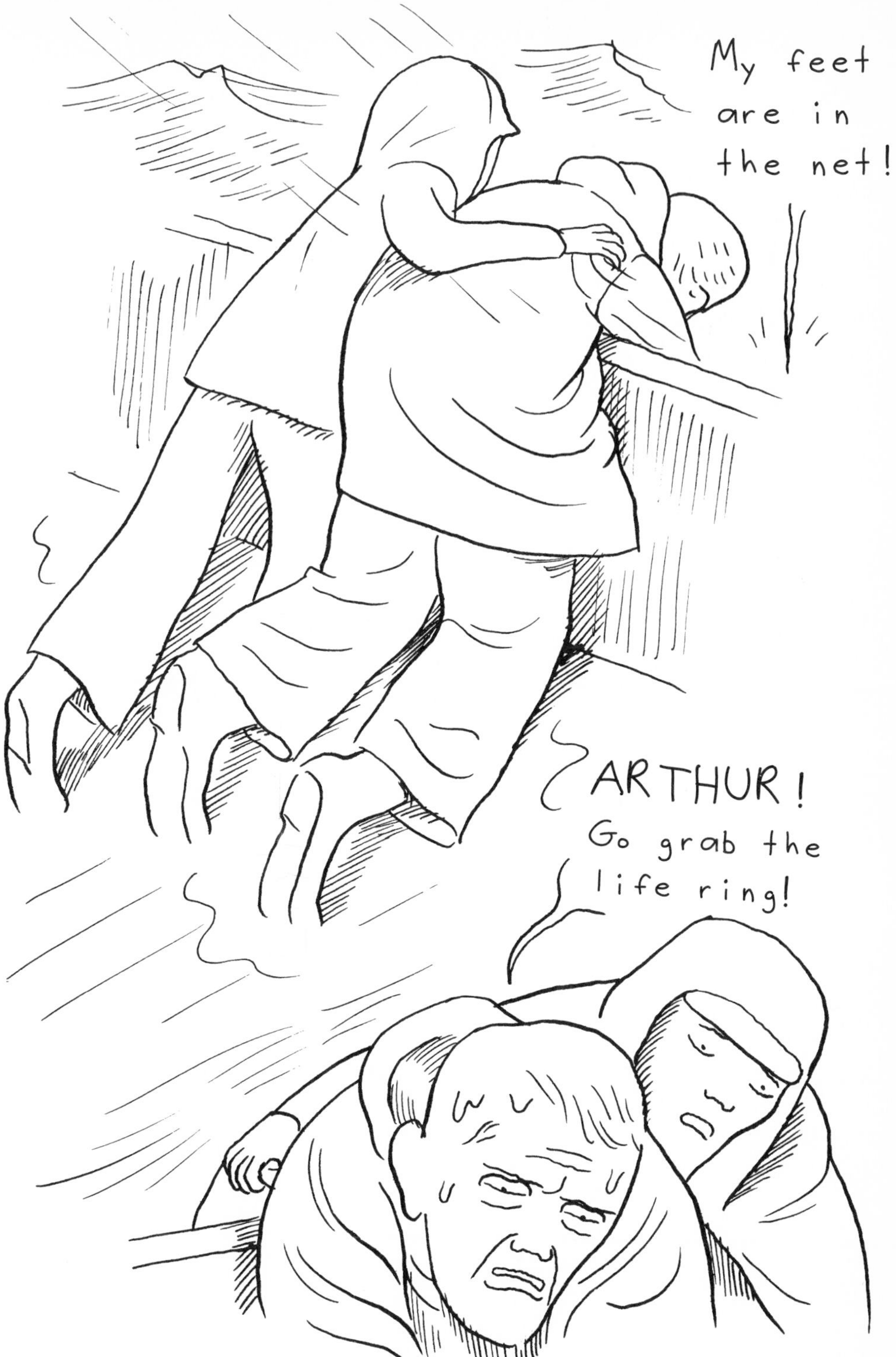
My feet are in the net!
ARTHUR! Go grab the life ring!

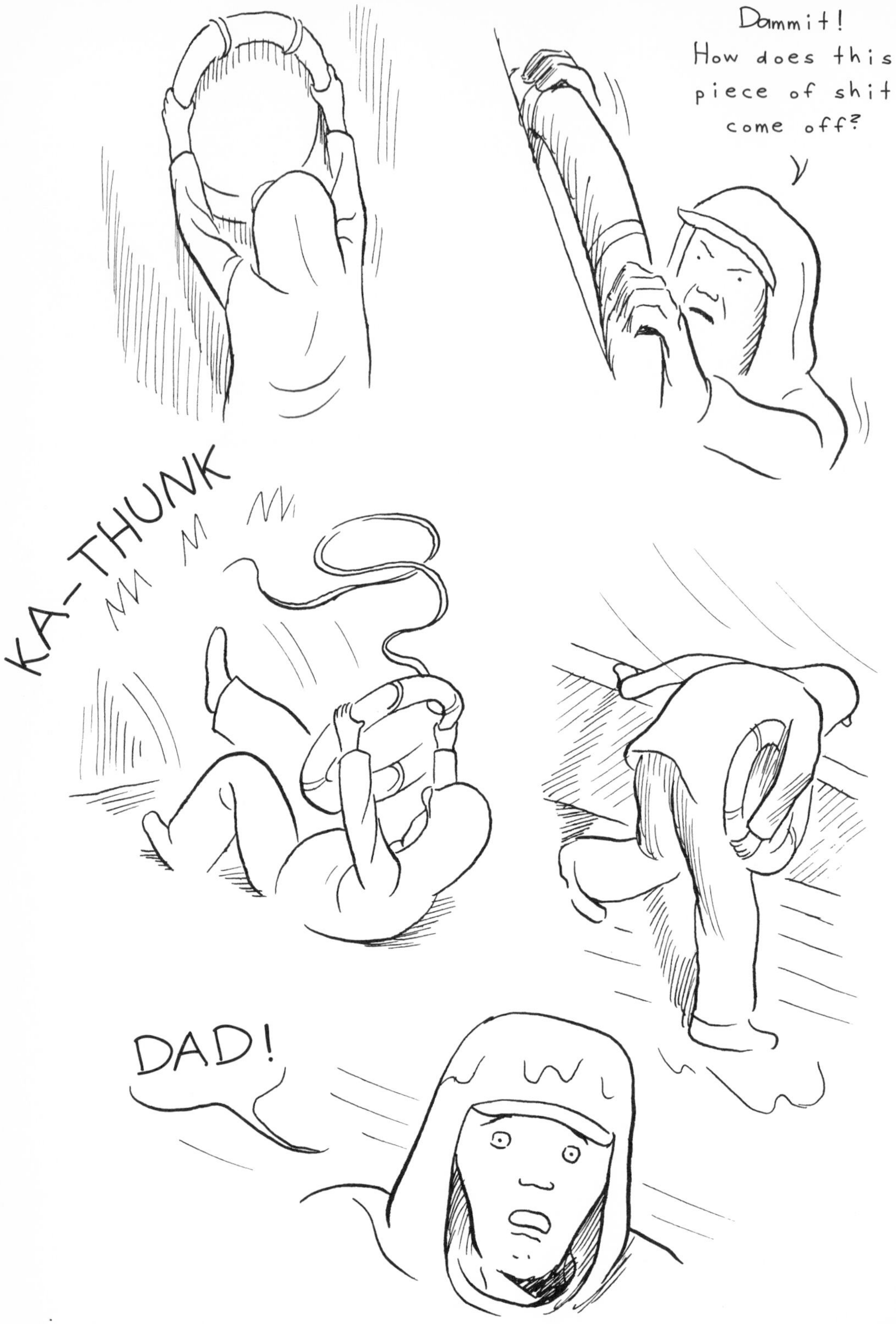
Dammit! How does this piece of shit come off?
KA-THUNK
DAD!

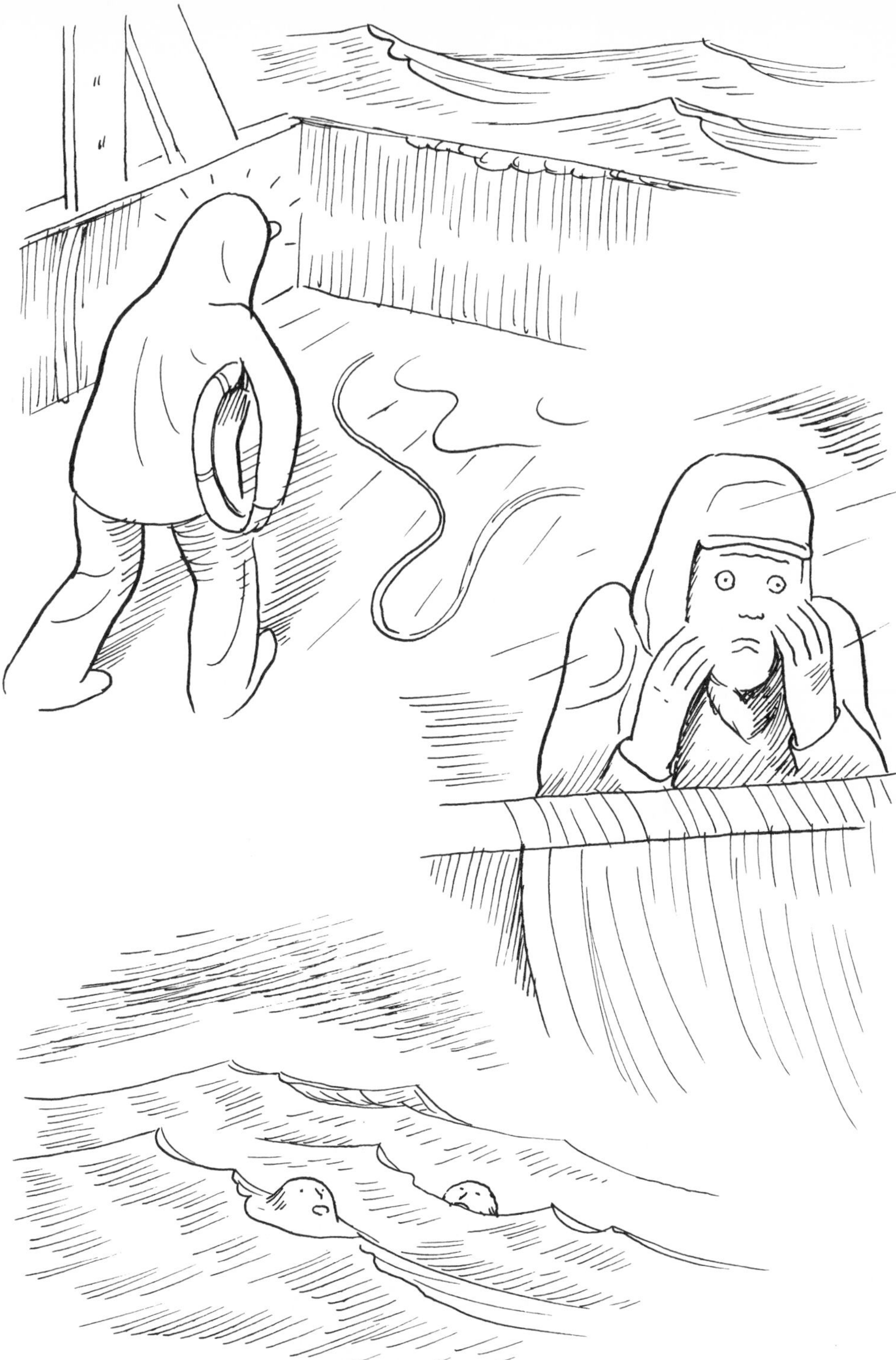

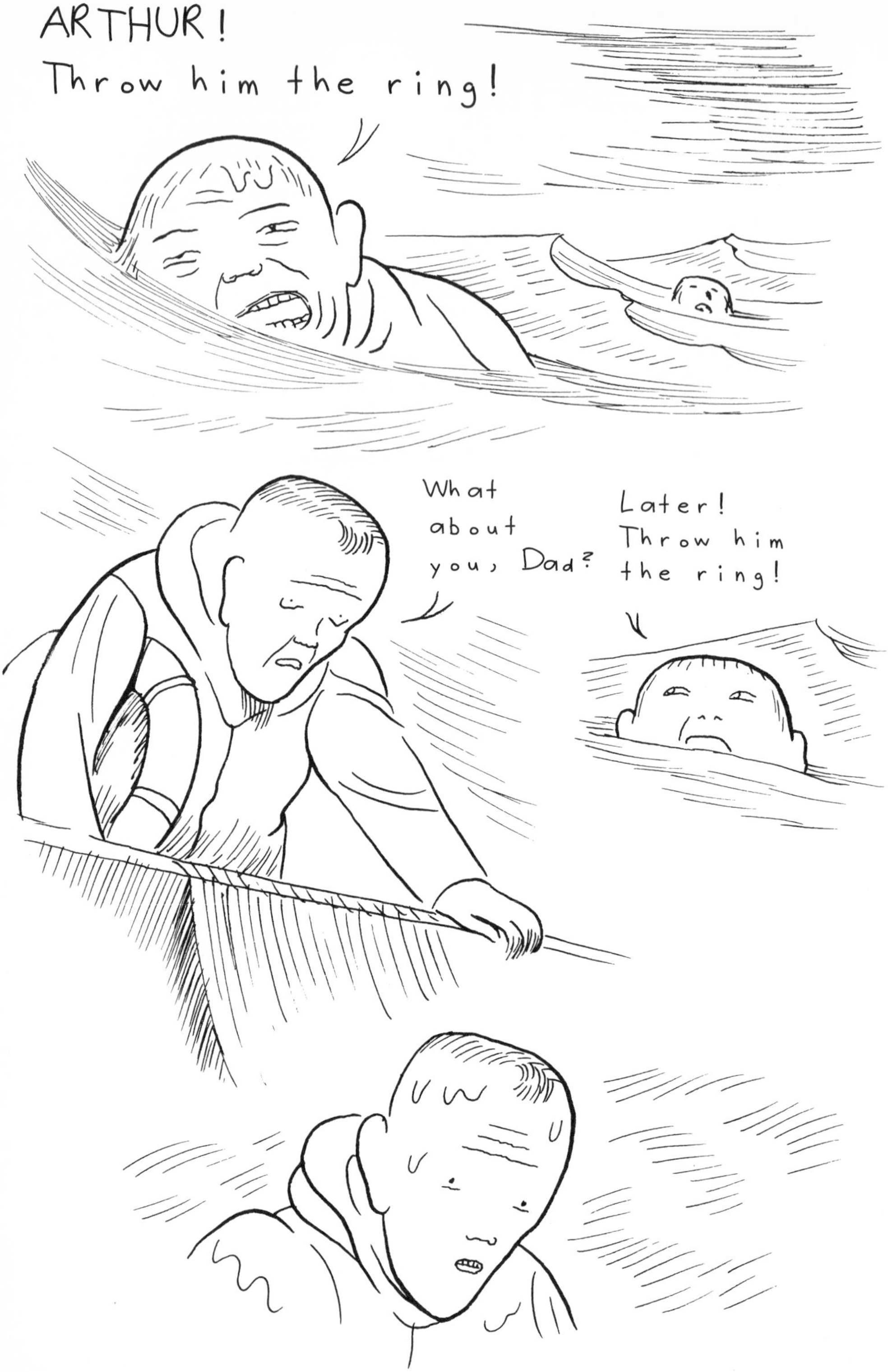
ARTHUR! Throw him the ring!
What about you, Dad?
Later! Throw him the ring!

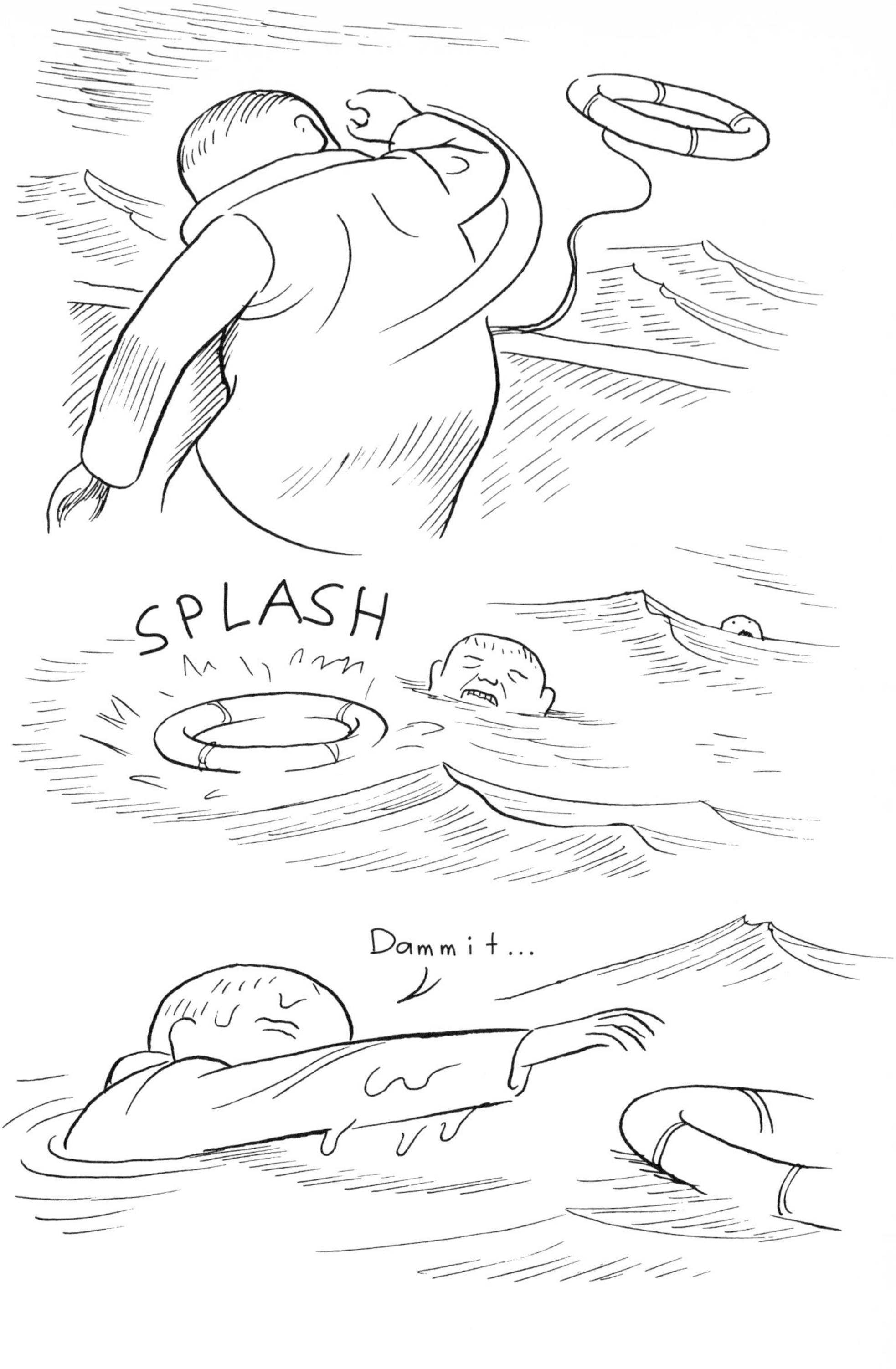
SPLASH
Dammit...

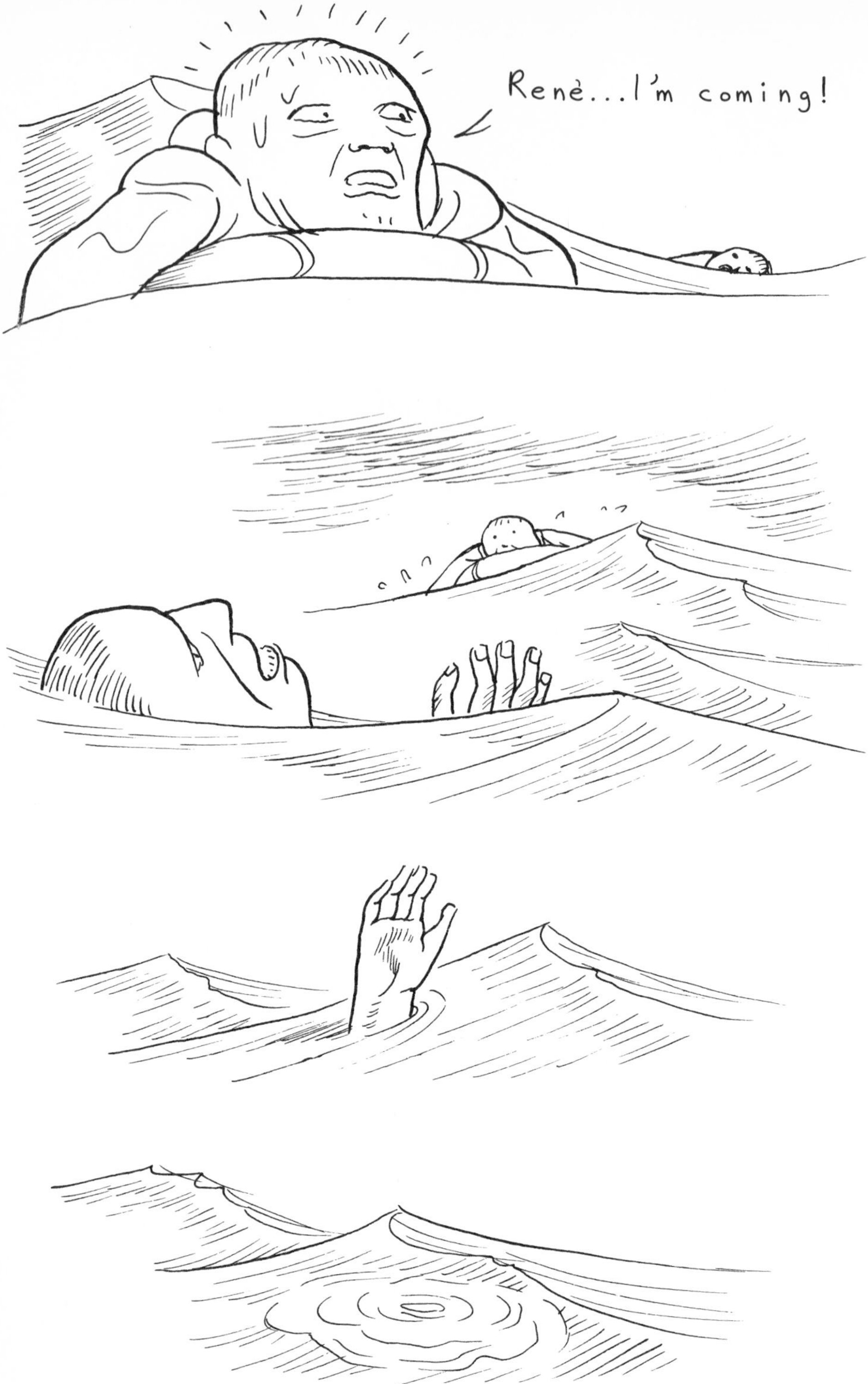
René...I'm coming!

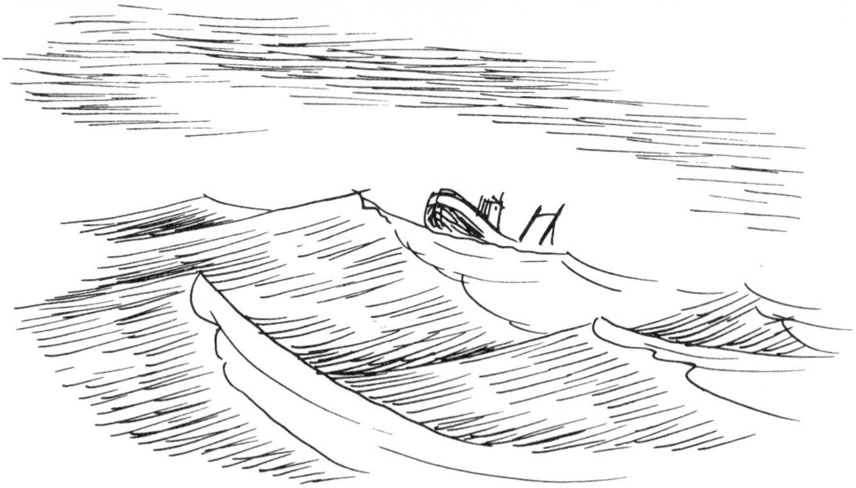

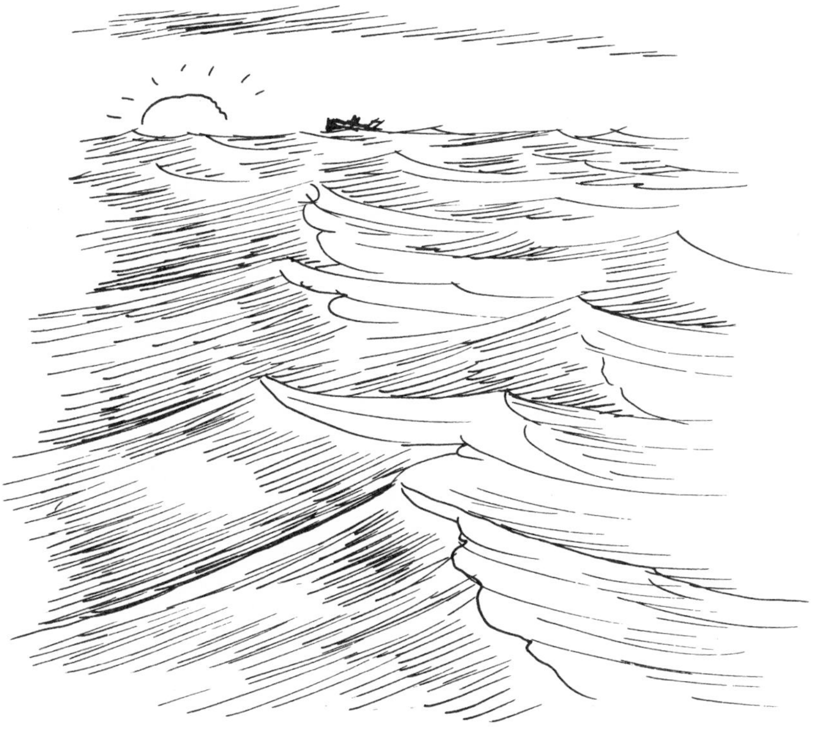

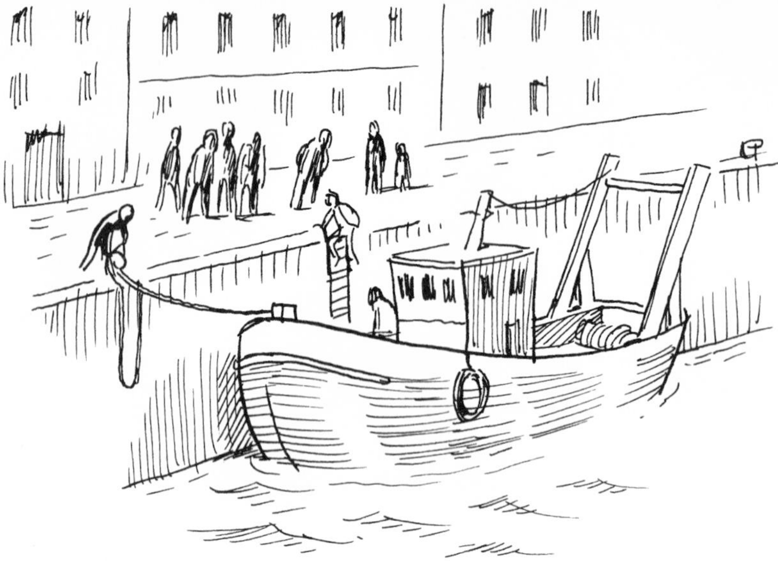

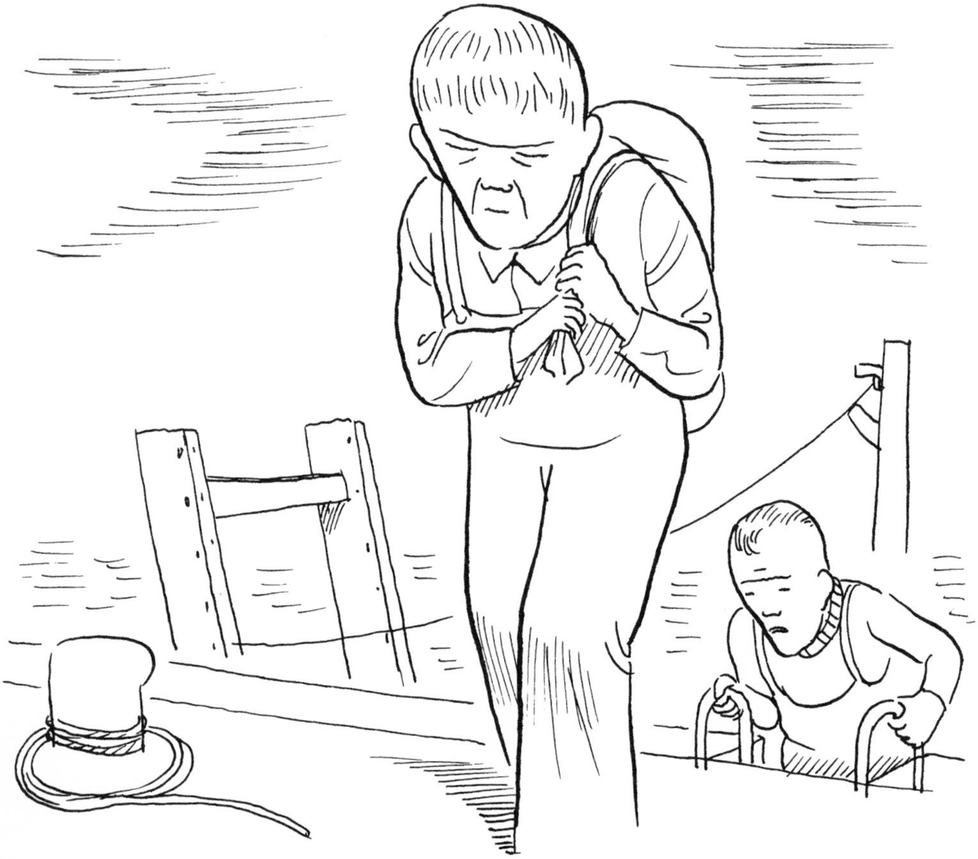

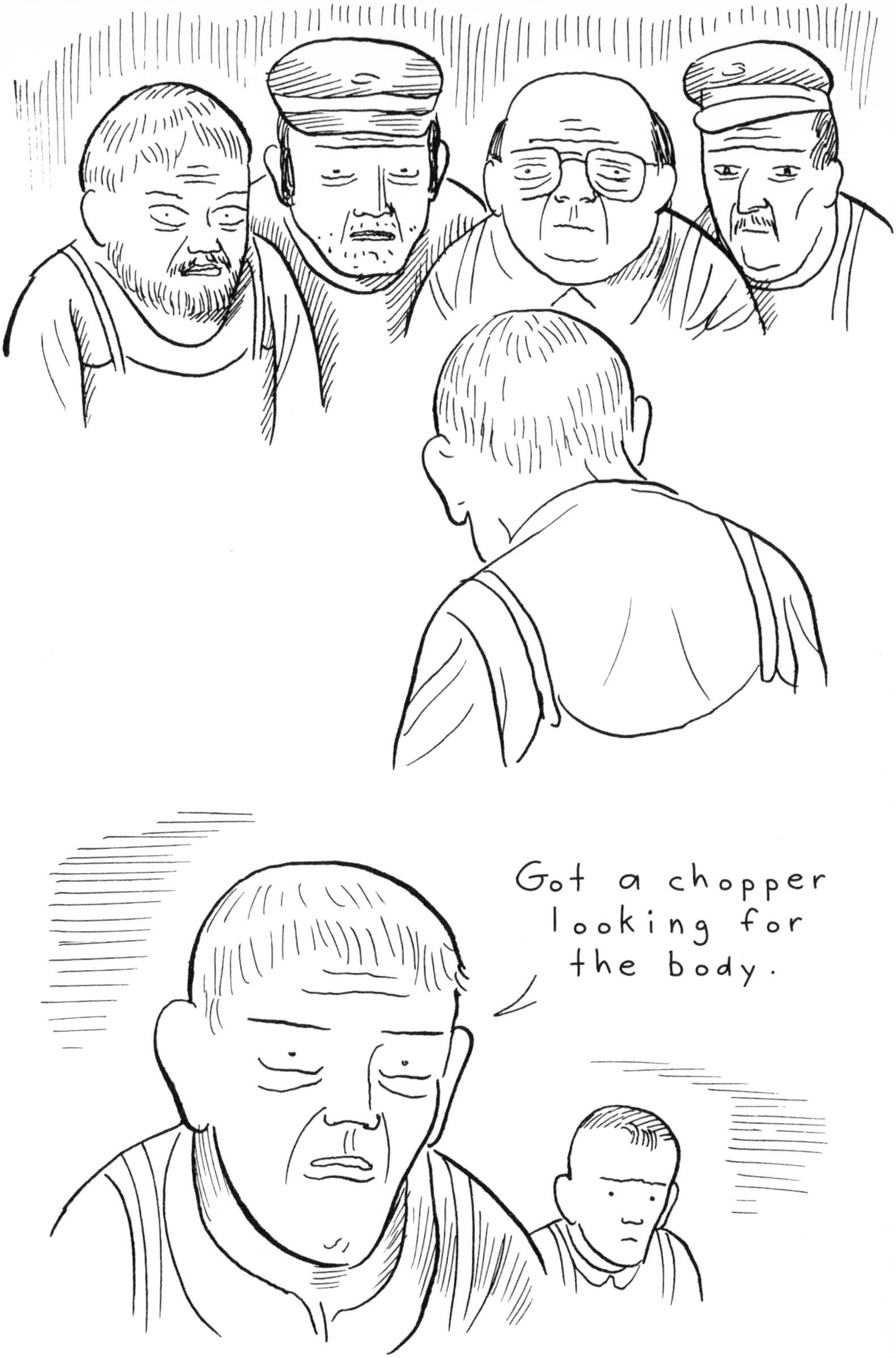
Got a chopper looking for the body.

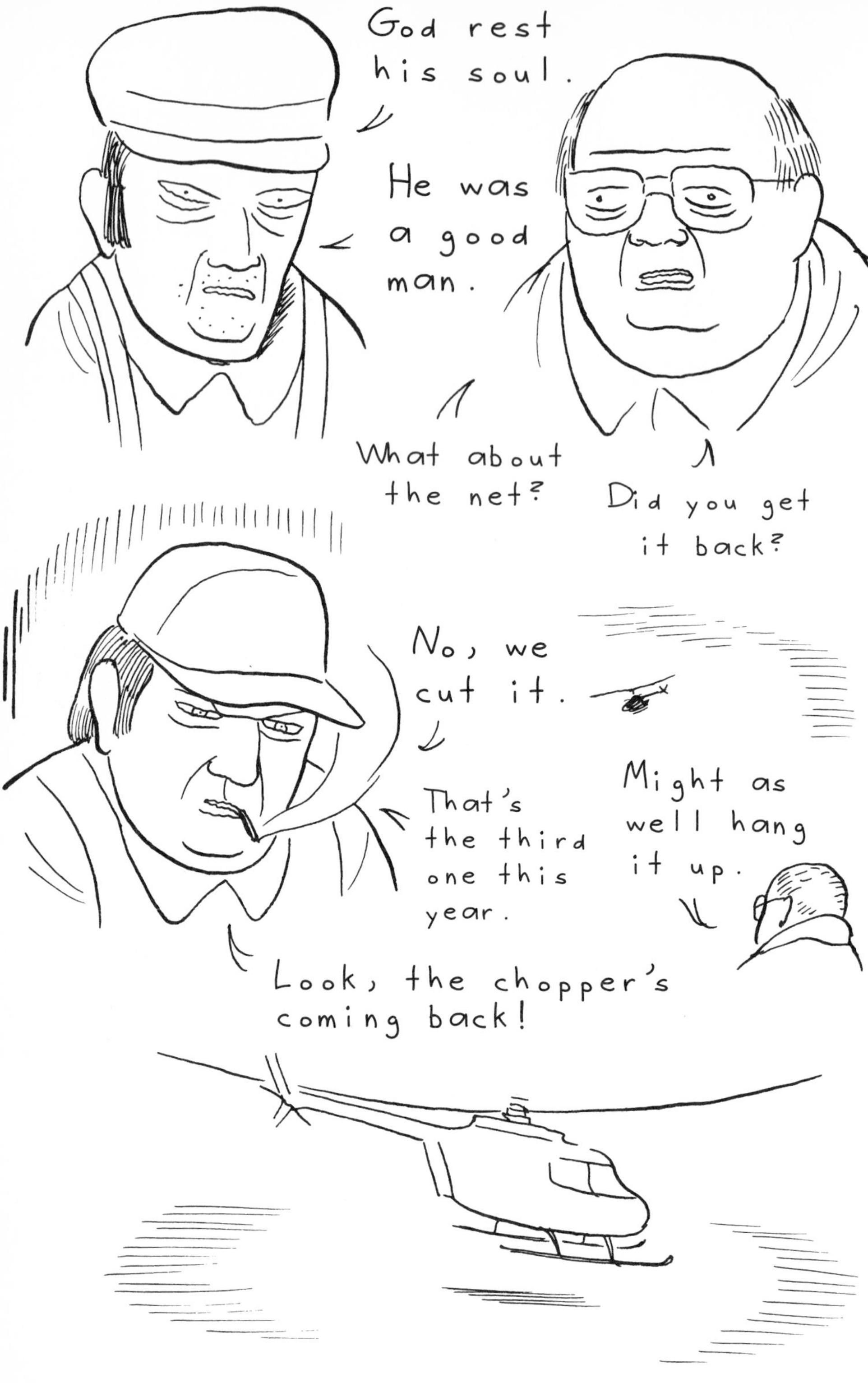
God rest his soul.
He was a good man.
What about the net?
Did you get it back?
No, we cut it.
That's the third one this year.
Might as well hang it up.
Look, the chopper's coming back!

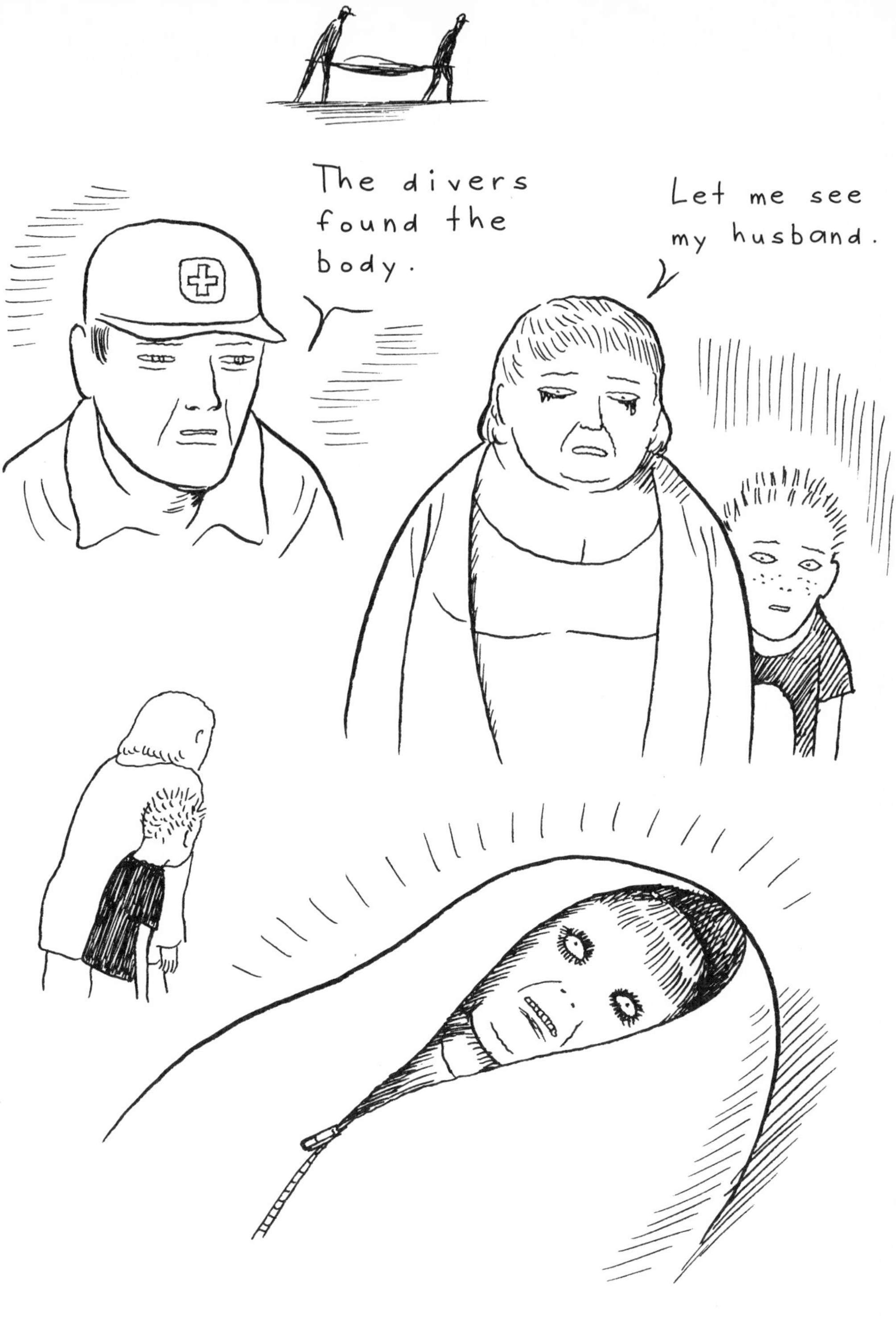
The divers found the body.
Let me see my husband.

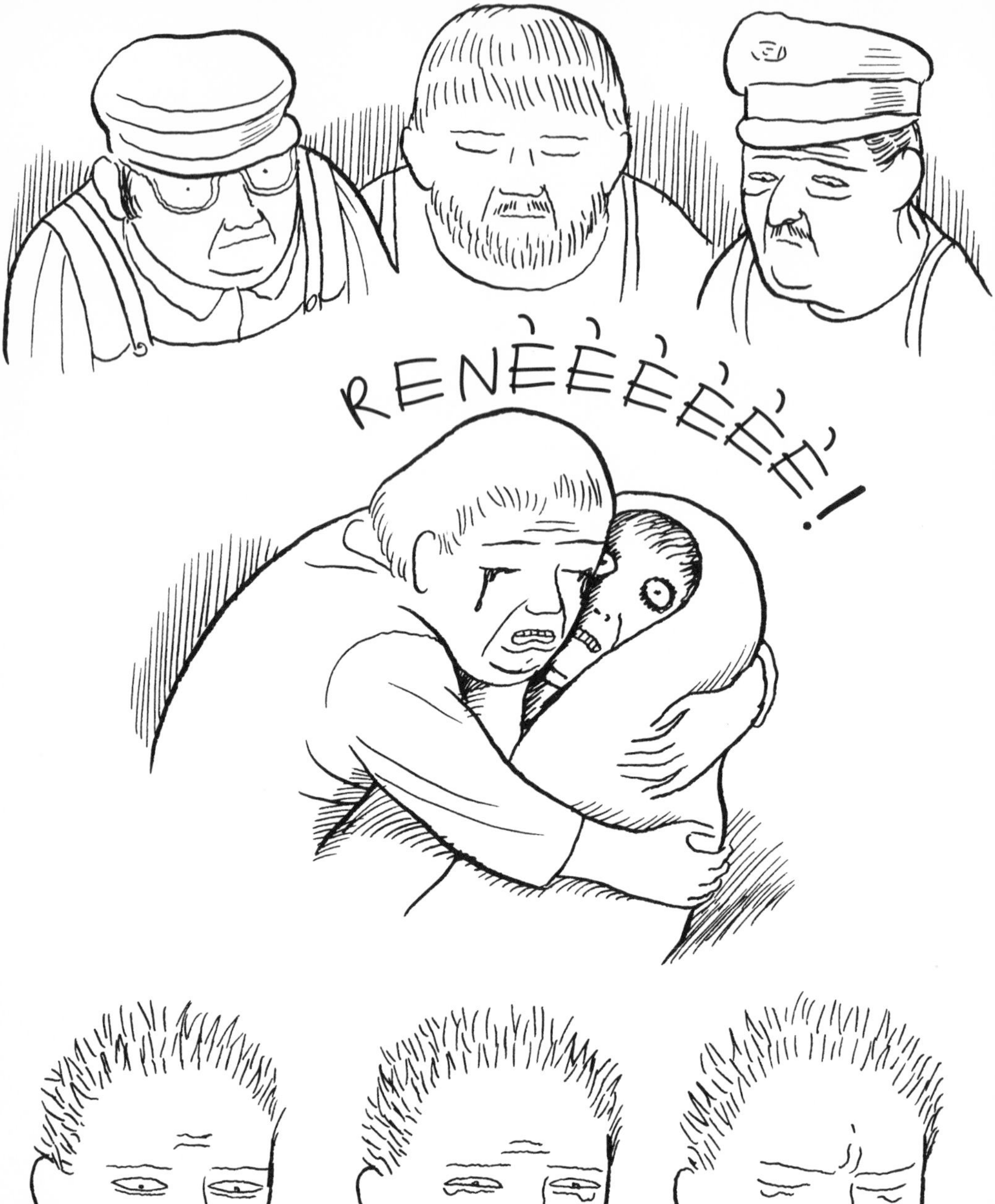
RENÈÈÈÈÈÈ!

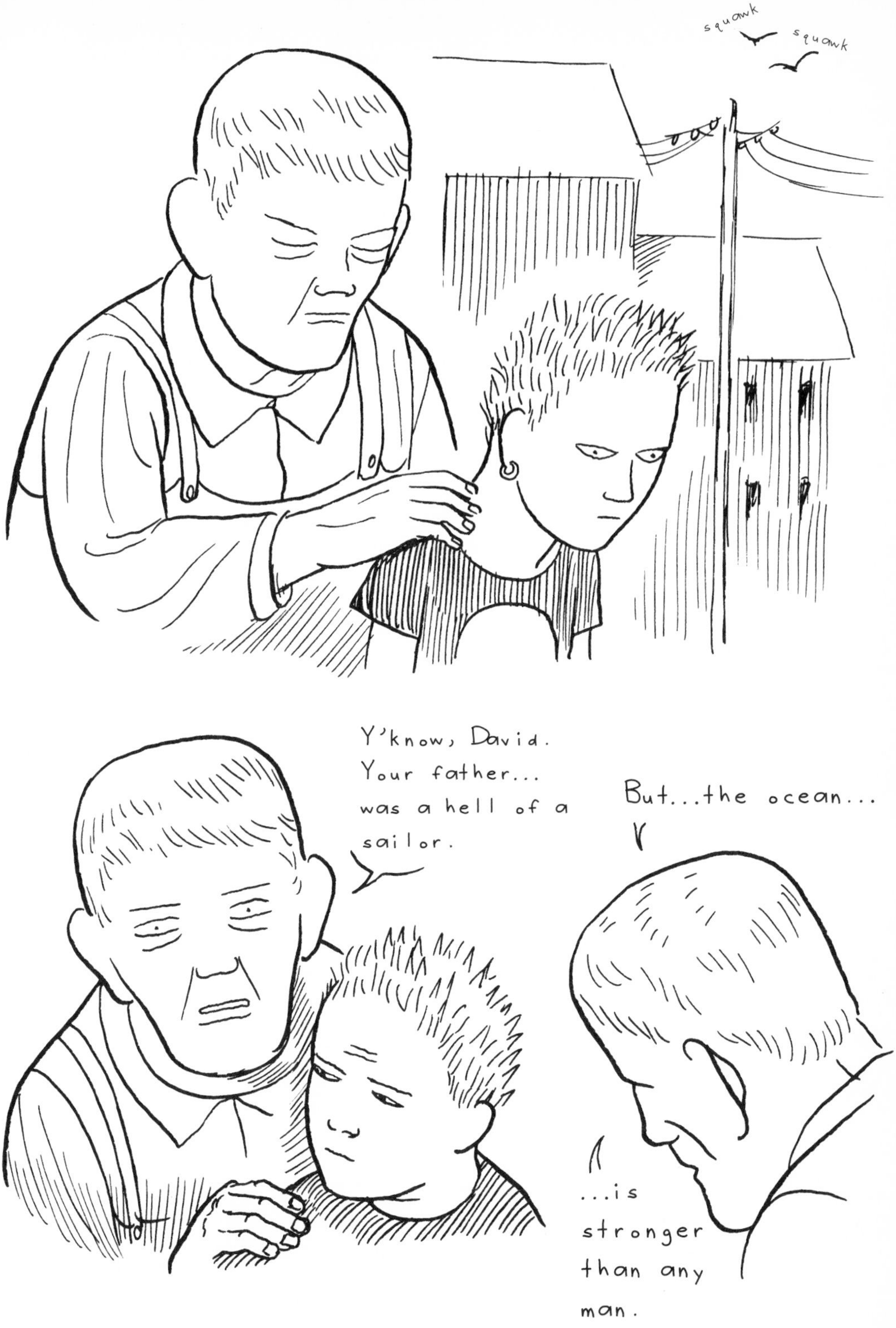
squawk
squawk
Y'know, David. Your father... was a hell of a sailor.
But...the ocean...
...is stronger than any man.

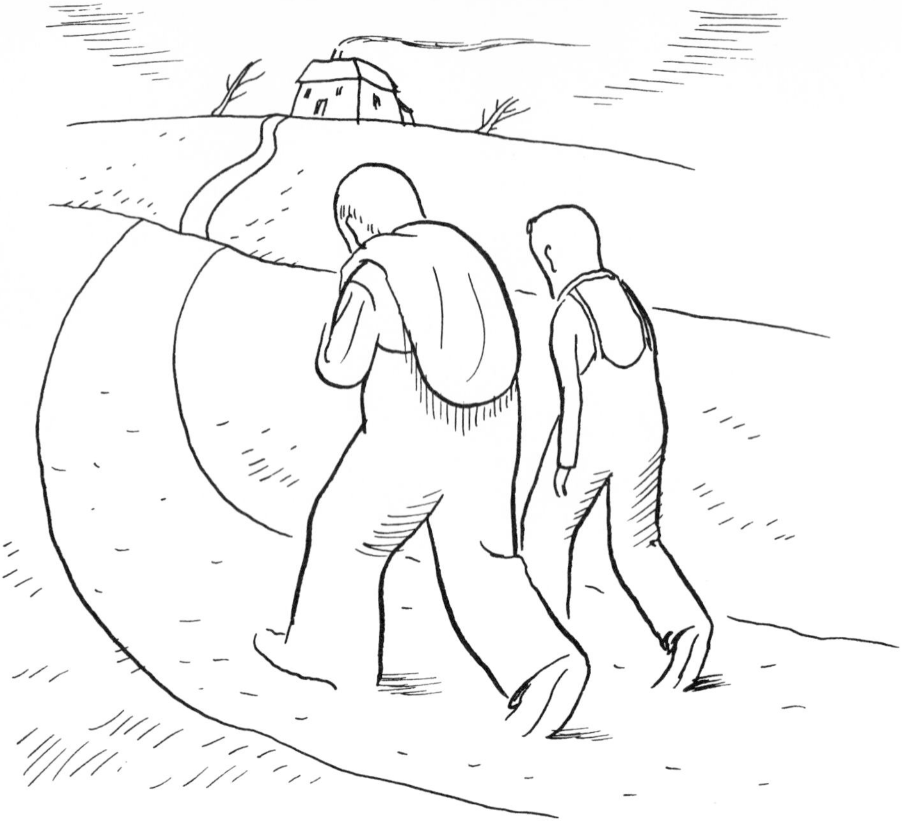
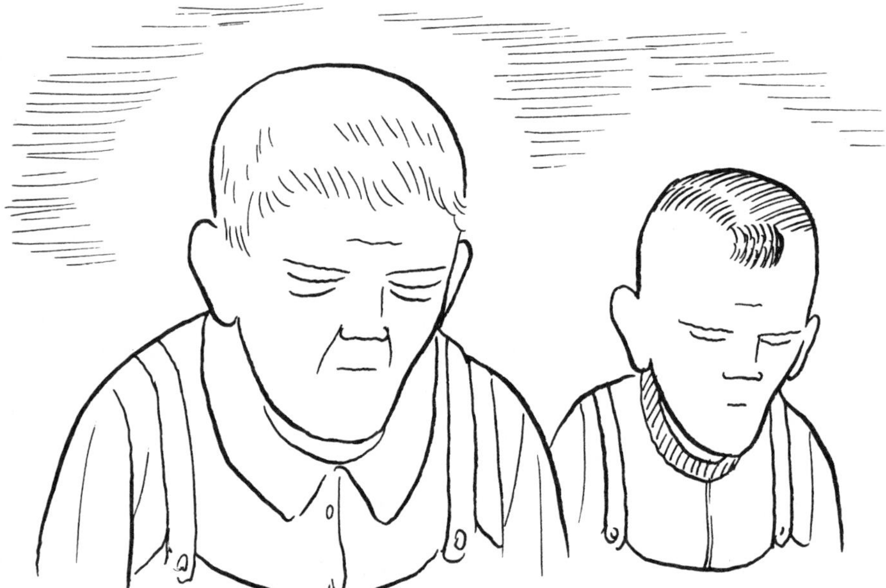

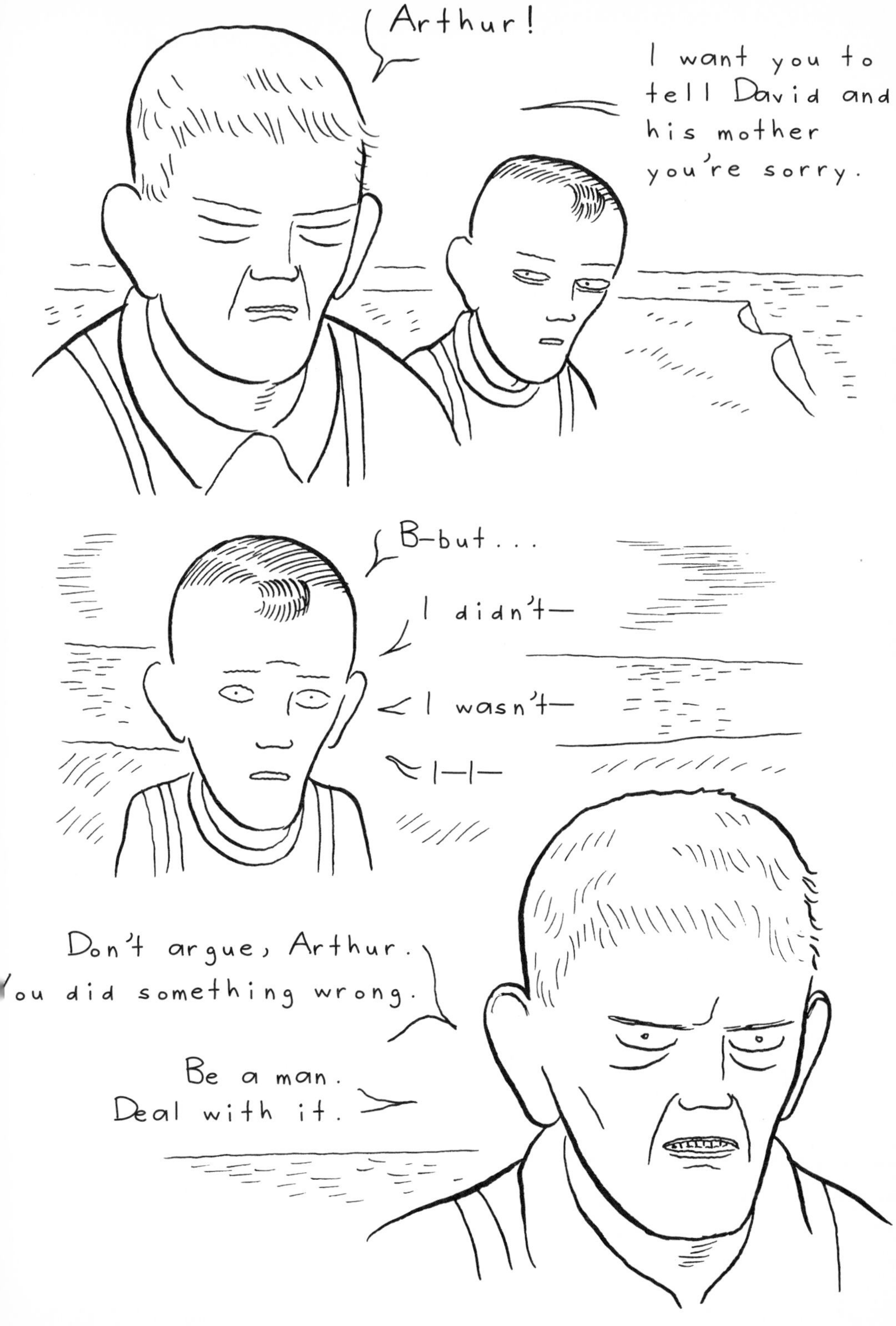
Arthur!
I want you to tell David and his mother you're sorry.
B-but...
I didn't—
I wasn't—
I-I—
Don't argue, Arthur. You did something wrong.
Be a man. Deal with it.

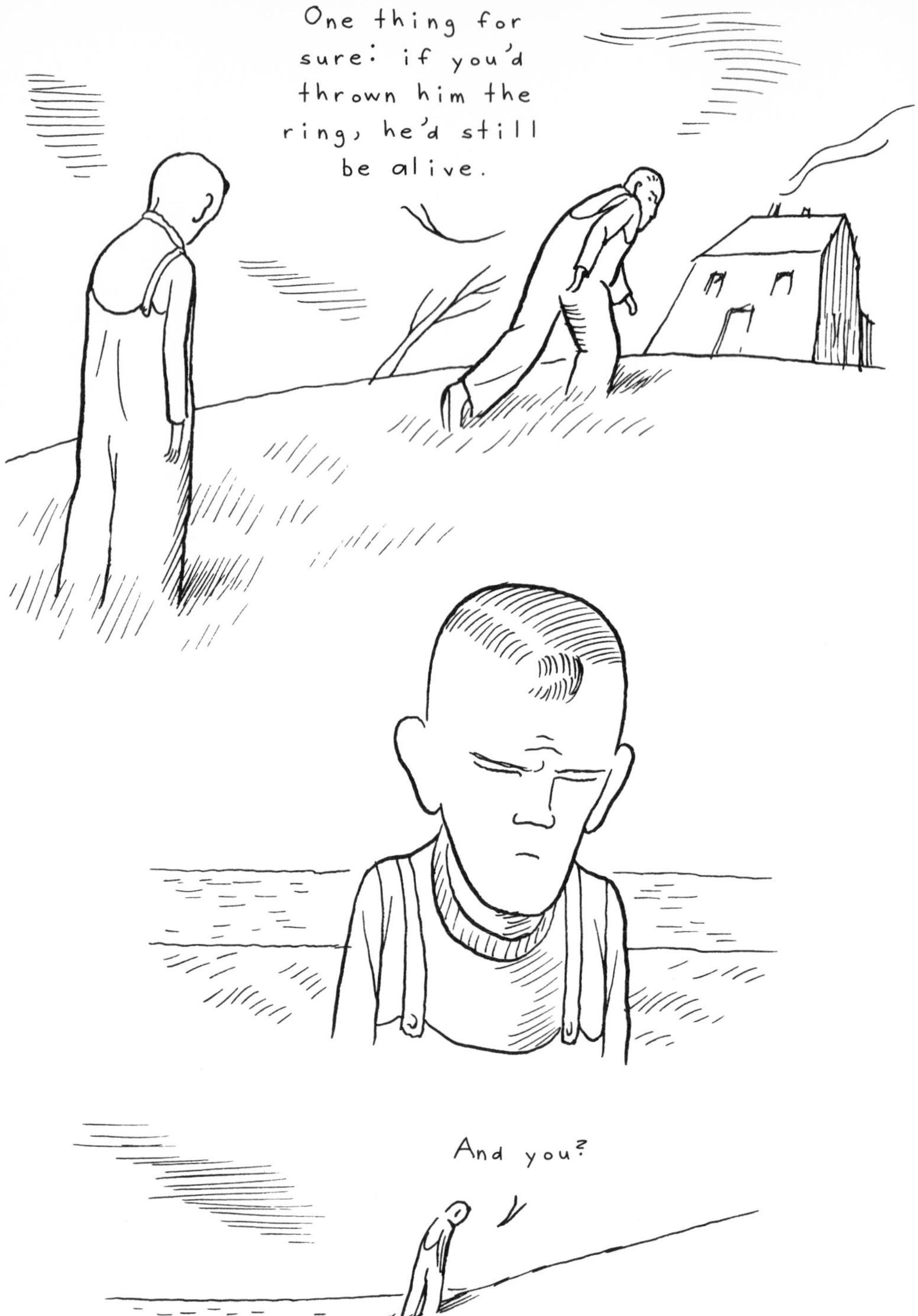
One thing for sure: if you'd thrown him the ring, he'd still be alive.
And you?

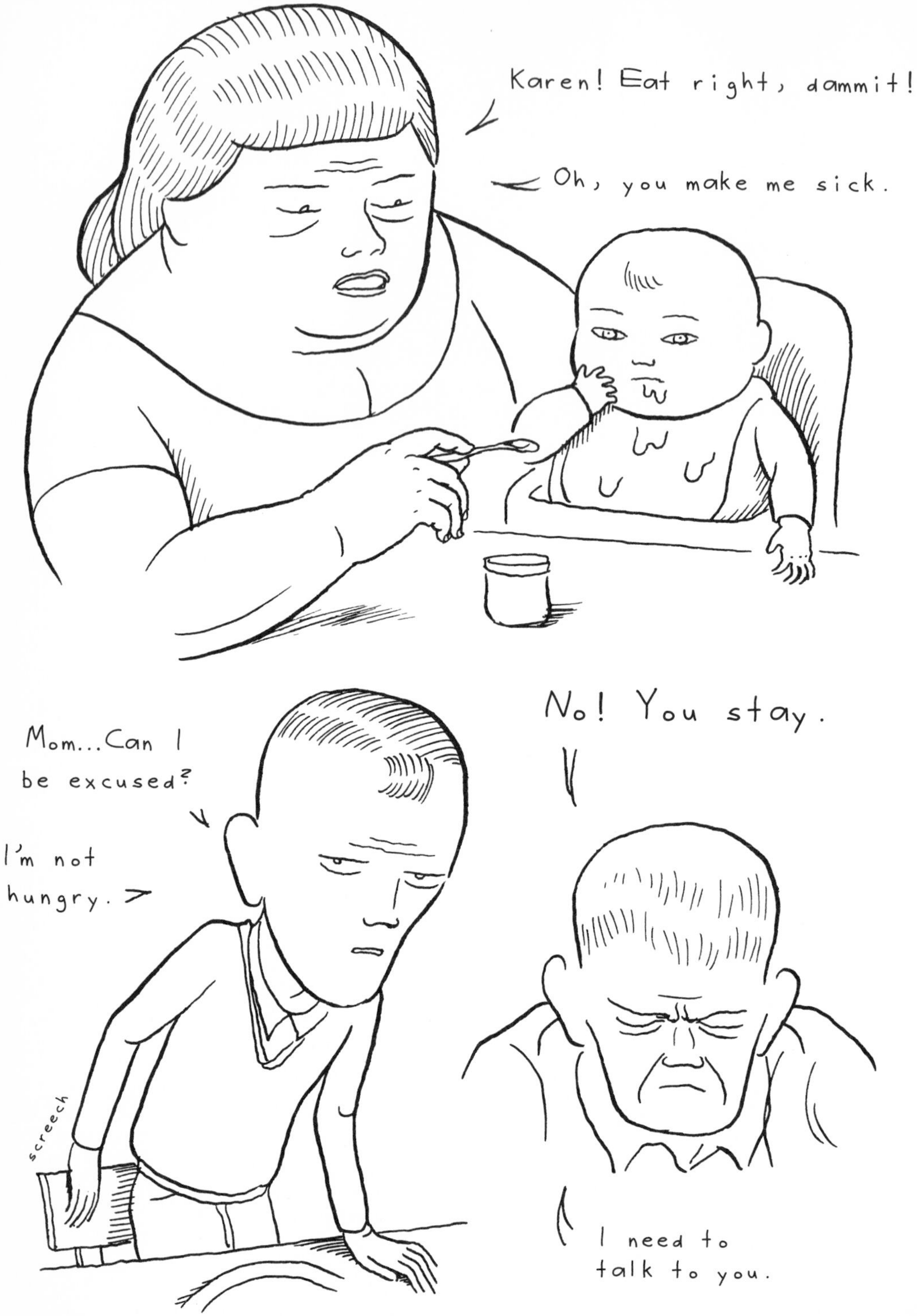
Karen! Eat right, dammit!
Oh, you make me sick.
Mom...Can I be excused?
I'm not hungry.
No! You stay.
I need to talk to you.
screech

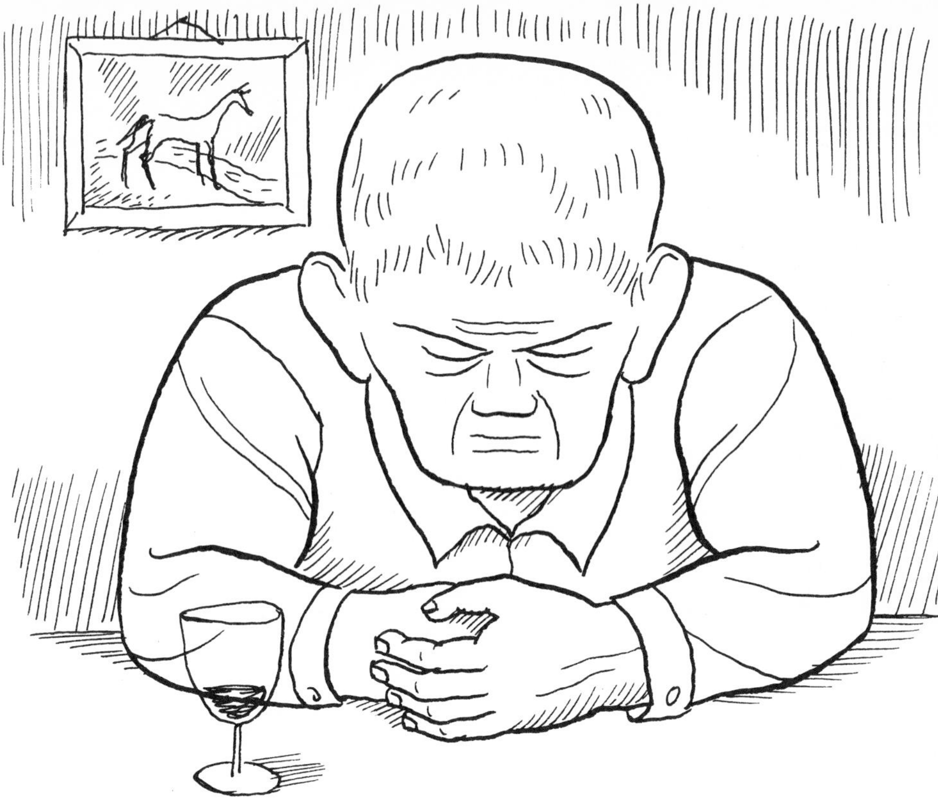

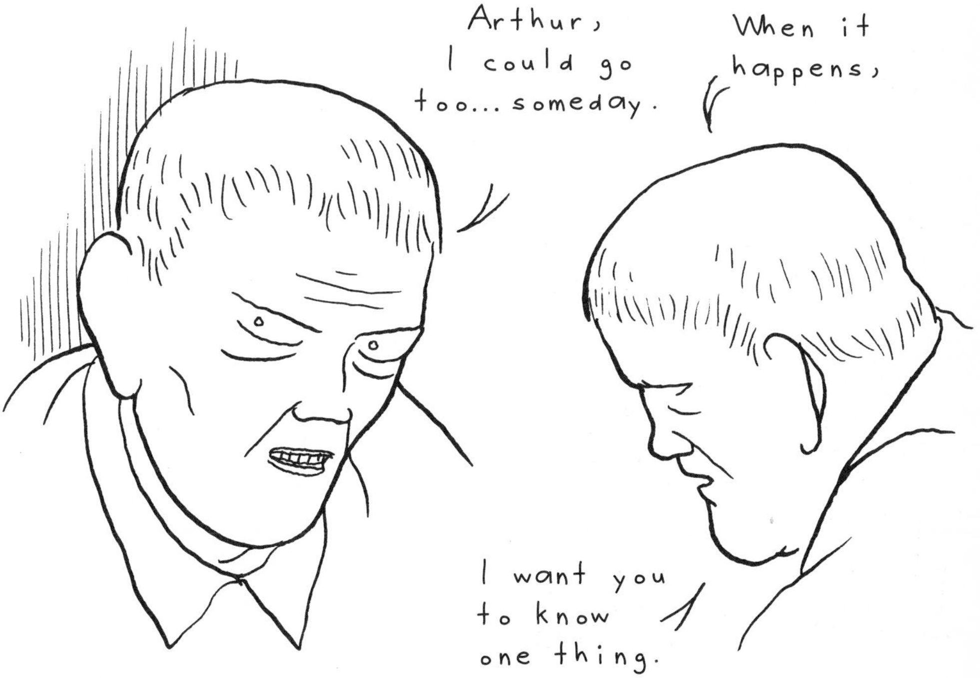
Arthur, I could go too... someday.
When it happens,
I want you to know one thing.

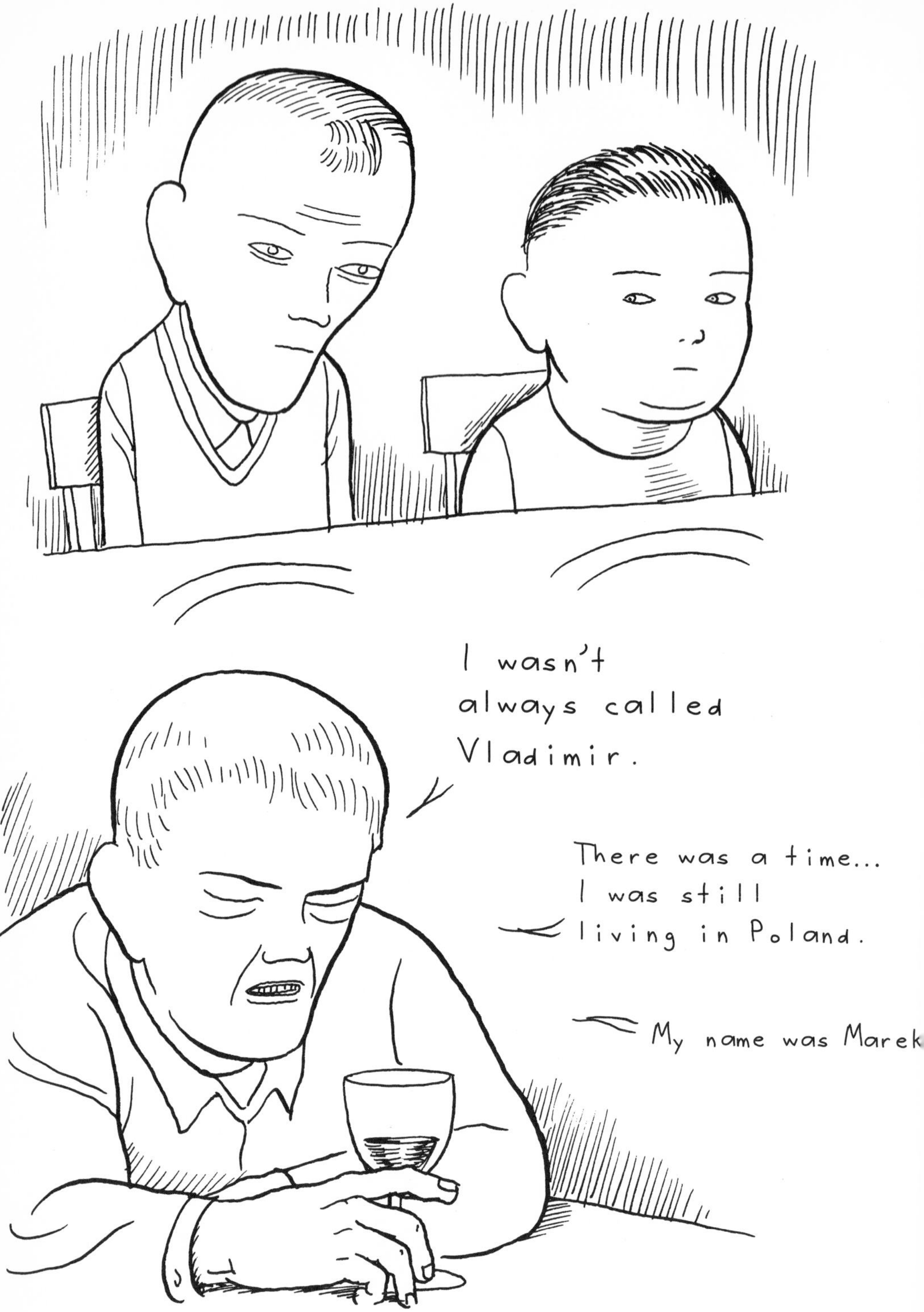
I wasn't always called Vladimir.
There was a time... I was still living in Poland.
My name was Marek

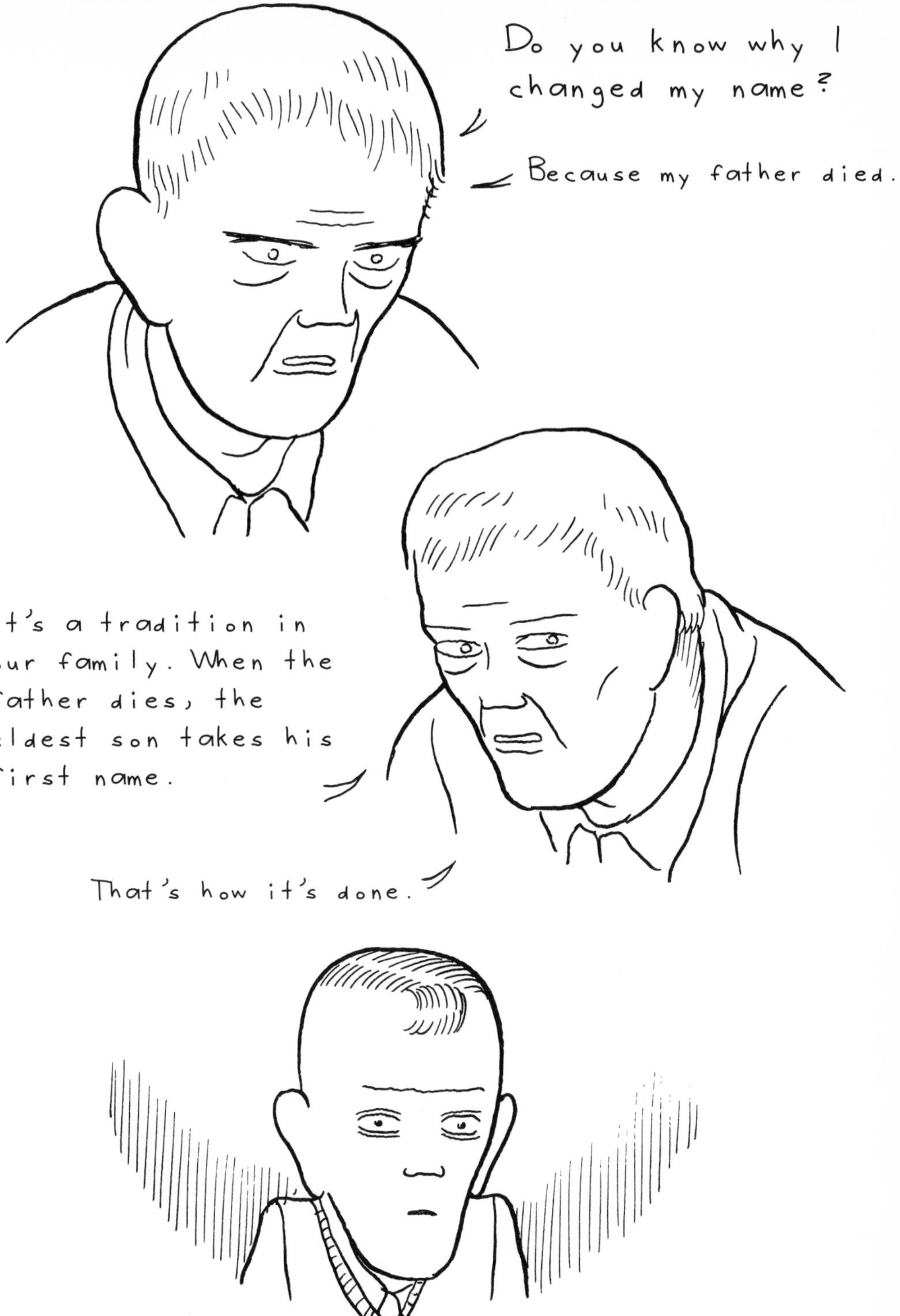
Do you know why I changed my name?
Because my father died.
It's a tradition in our family. When the father dies, the eldest son takes his first name.
That's how it's done.

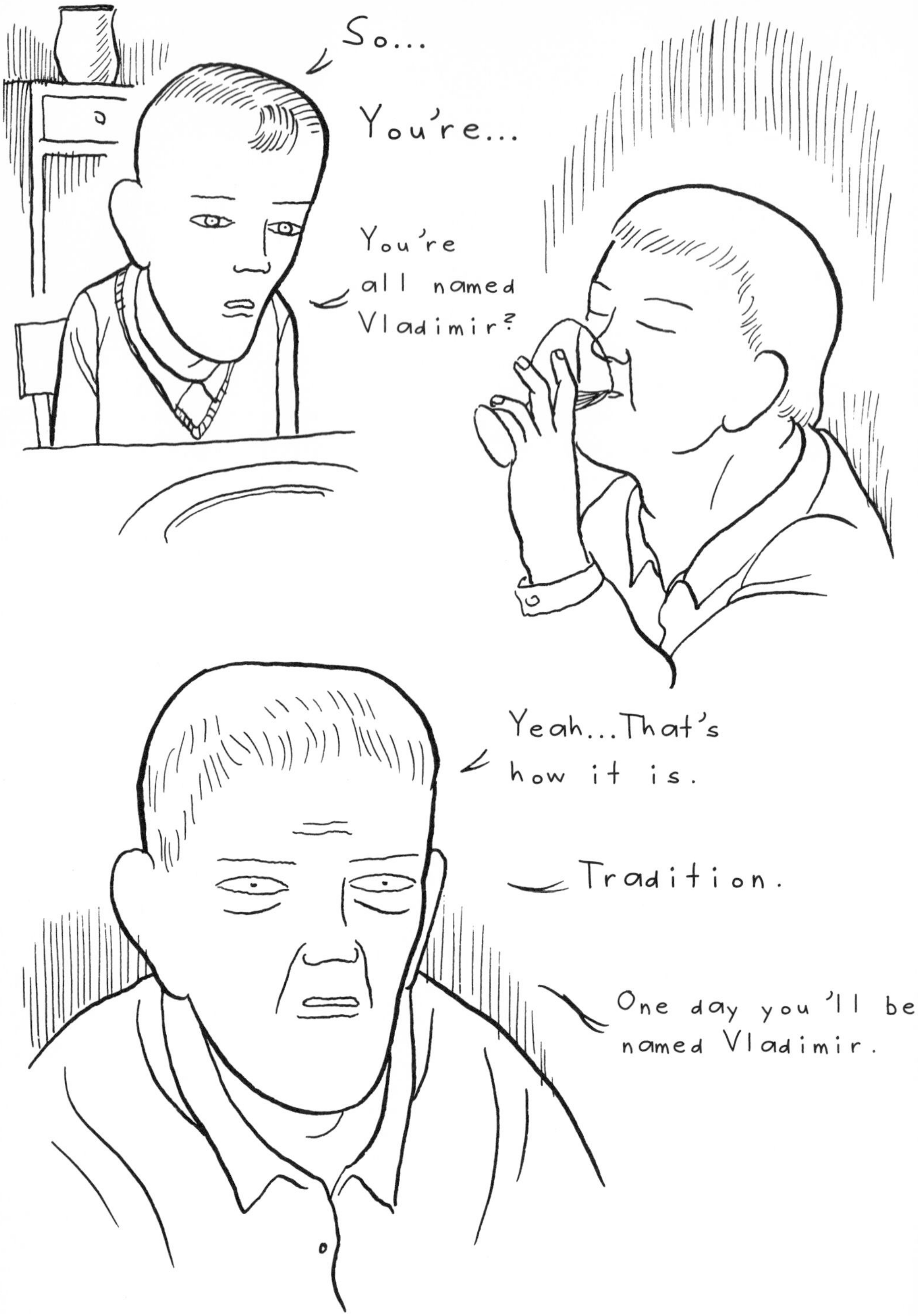
So...
You're...
You're all named Vladimir?
Yeah...That's how it is.
Tradition.
One day you'll be named Vladimir.

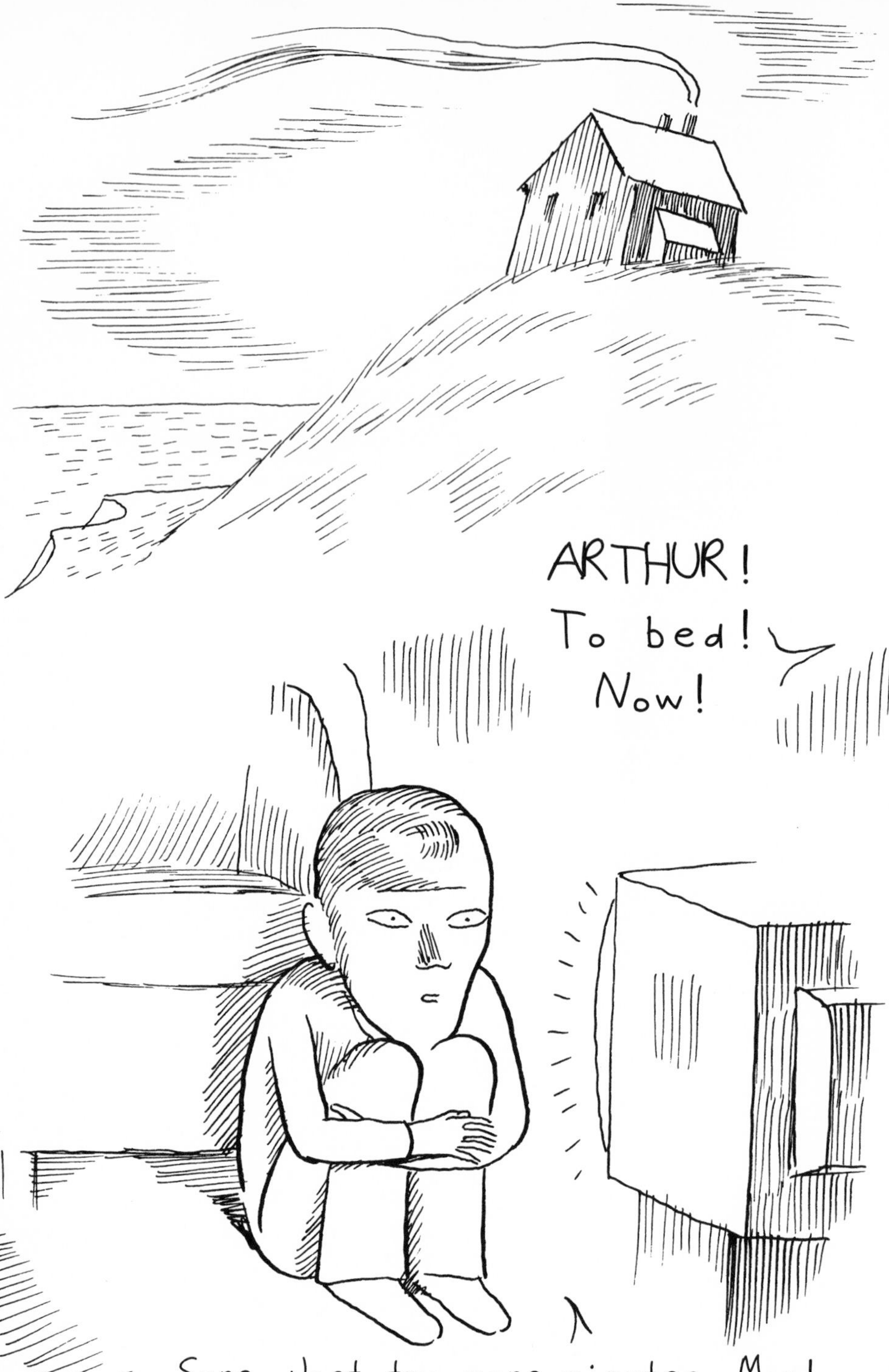
ARTHUR! To bed! Now!
Sure...Just two more minutes, Mom! X-Files is on.

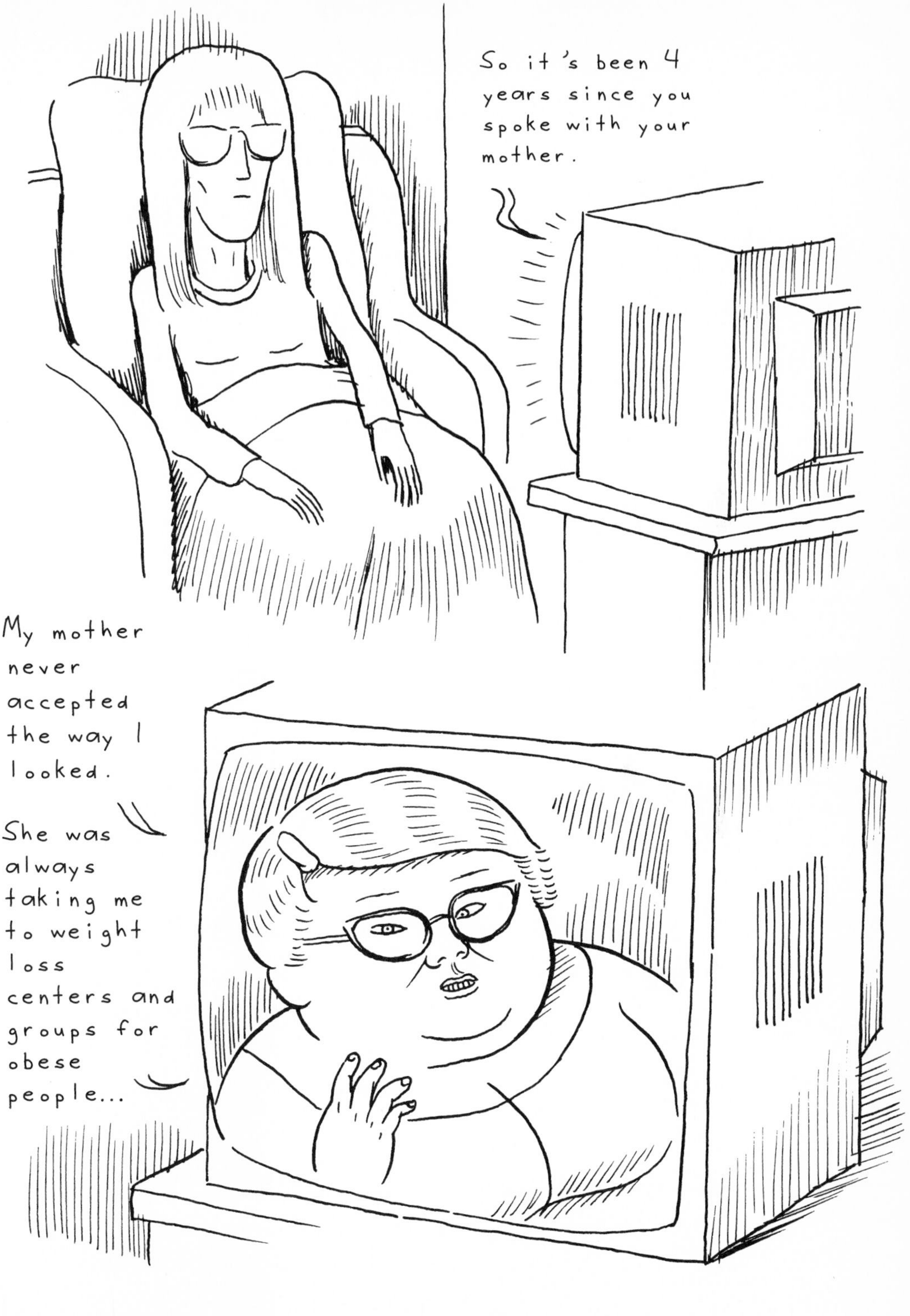

So it's been 4 years since you spoke with your mother.
My mother never accepted the way I looked.
She was always taking me to weight loss centers and groups for obese people...

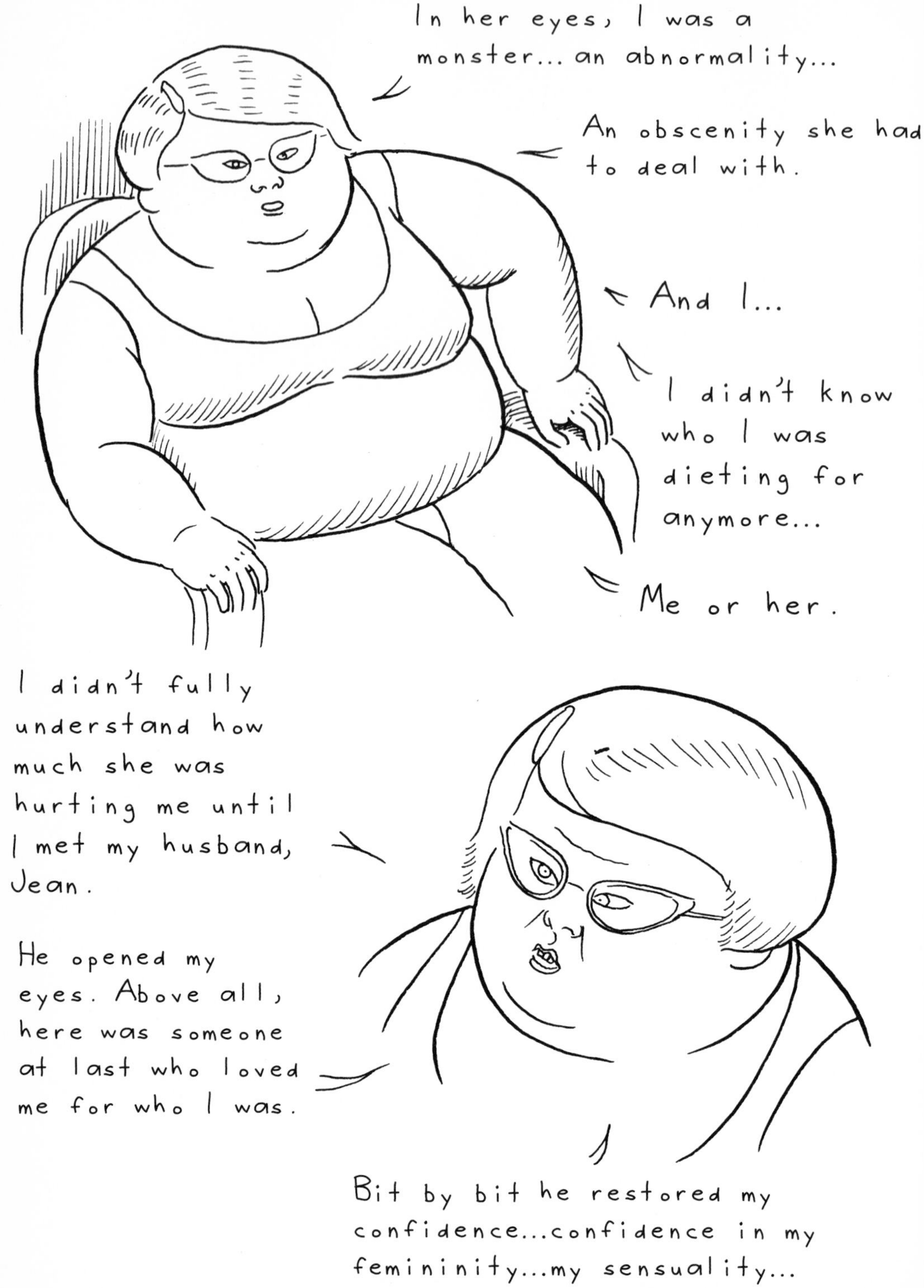
In her eyes, I was a monster... an abnormality...
An obscenity she had to deal with.
And I...
I didn't know who I was dieting for anymore...
Me or her.
I didn't fully understand how much she was hurting me until I met my husband, Jean.
He opened my eyes. Above all, here was someone at last who loved me for who I was.
Bit by bit he restored my confidence...confidence in my femininity...my sensuality...

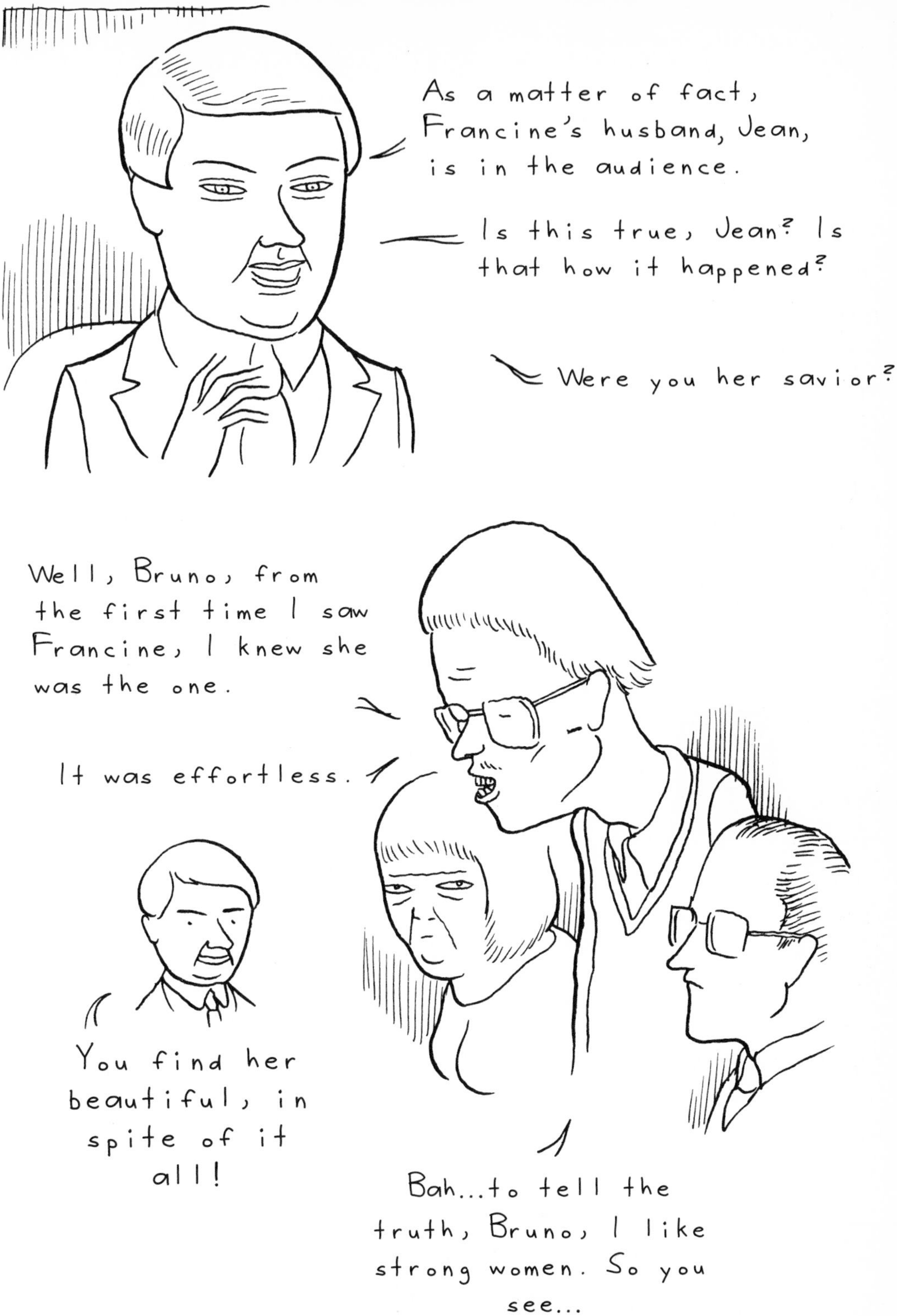
As a matter of fact, Francine's husband, Jean, is in the audience.
Is this true, Jean? Is that how it happened?
Were you her savior?
Well, Bruno, from the first time I saw Francine, I knew she was the one.
It was effortless.
You find her beautiful, in spite of it all!
Bah...to tell the truth, Bruno, I like strong women. So you see...

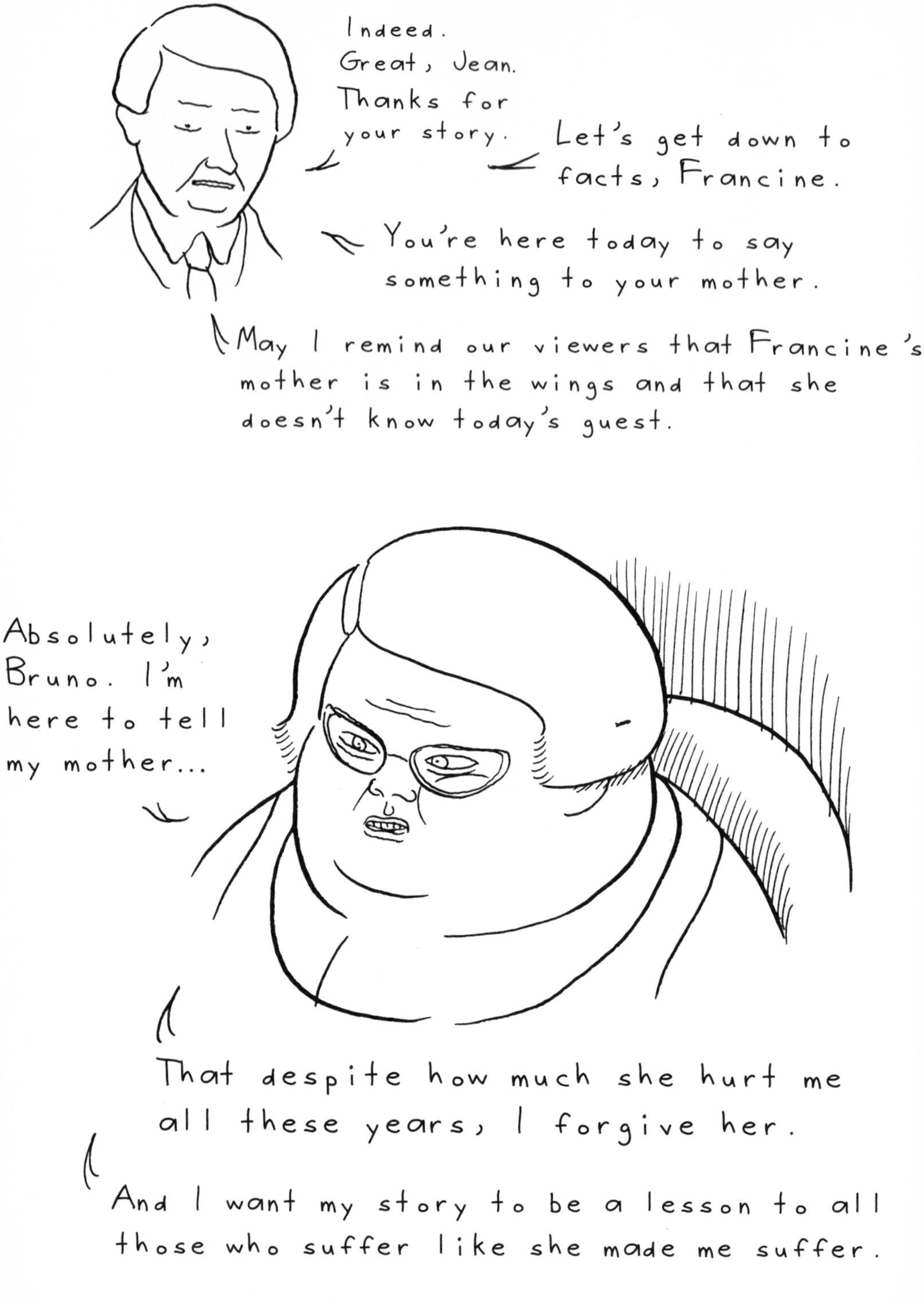
Indeed.
Great, Jean.
Thanks for your story.
Let's get down to facts, Francine.
You're here today to say something to your mother.
May I remind our viewers that Francine's mother is in the wings and that she doesn't know today's guest.
Absolutely, Bruno. I'm here to tell my mother...
That despite how much she hurt me all these years, I forgive her.
And I want my story to be a lesson to all those who suffer like she made me suffer.

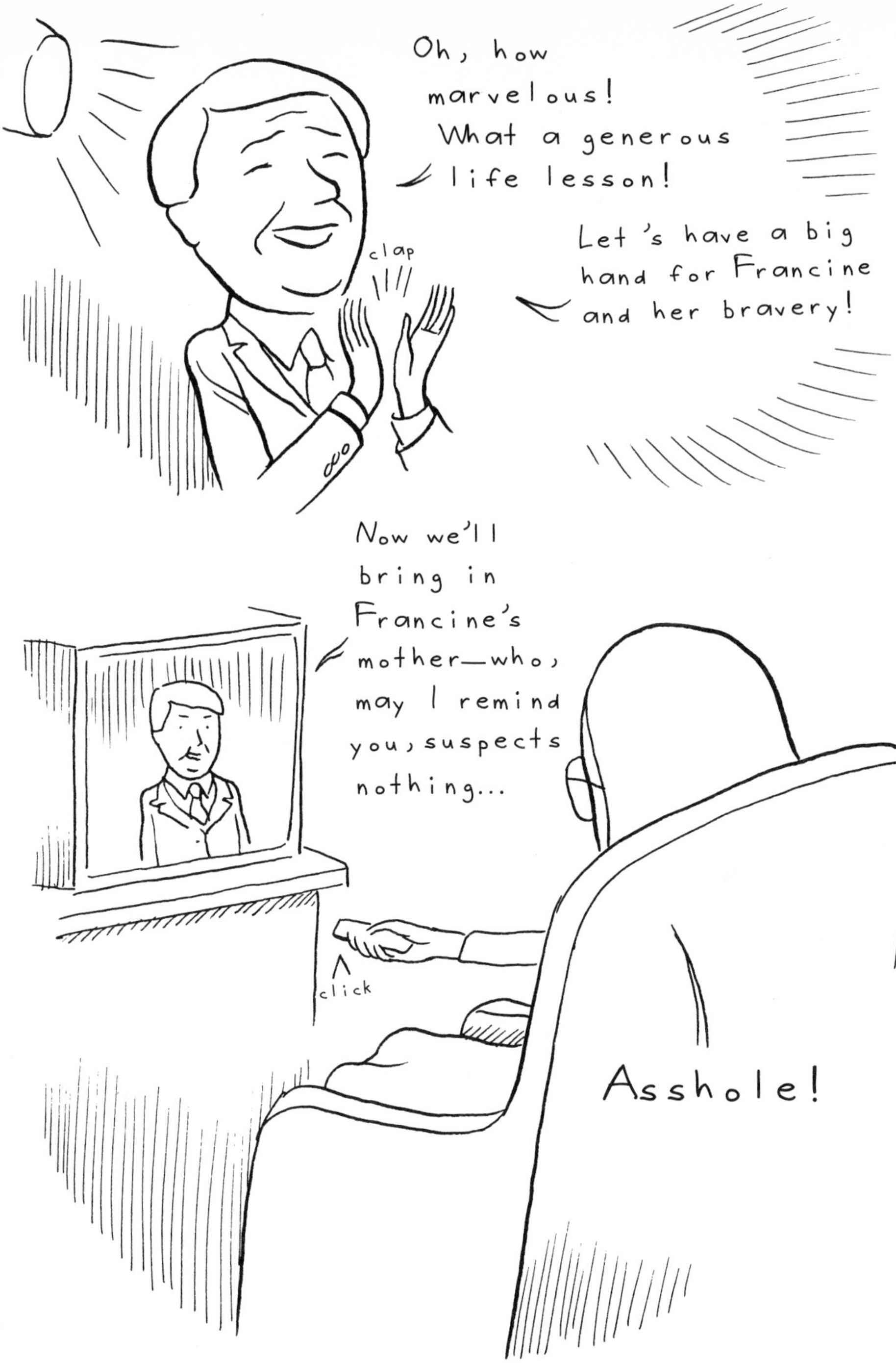
Oh, how marvelous! What a generous life lesson!
clap
Let's have a big hand for Francine and her bravery!
Now we'll bring in Francine's mother—who, may I remind you, suspects nothing...
click
Asshole!

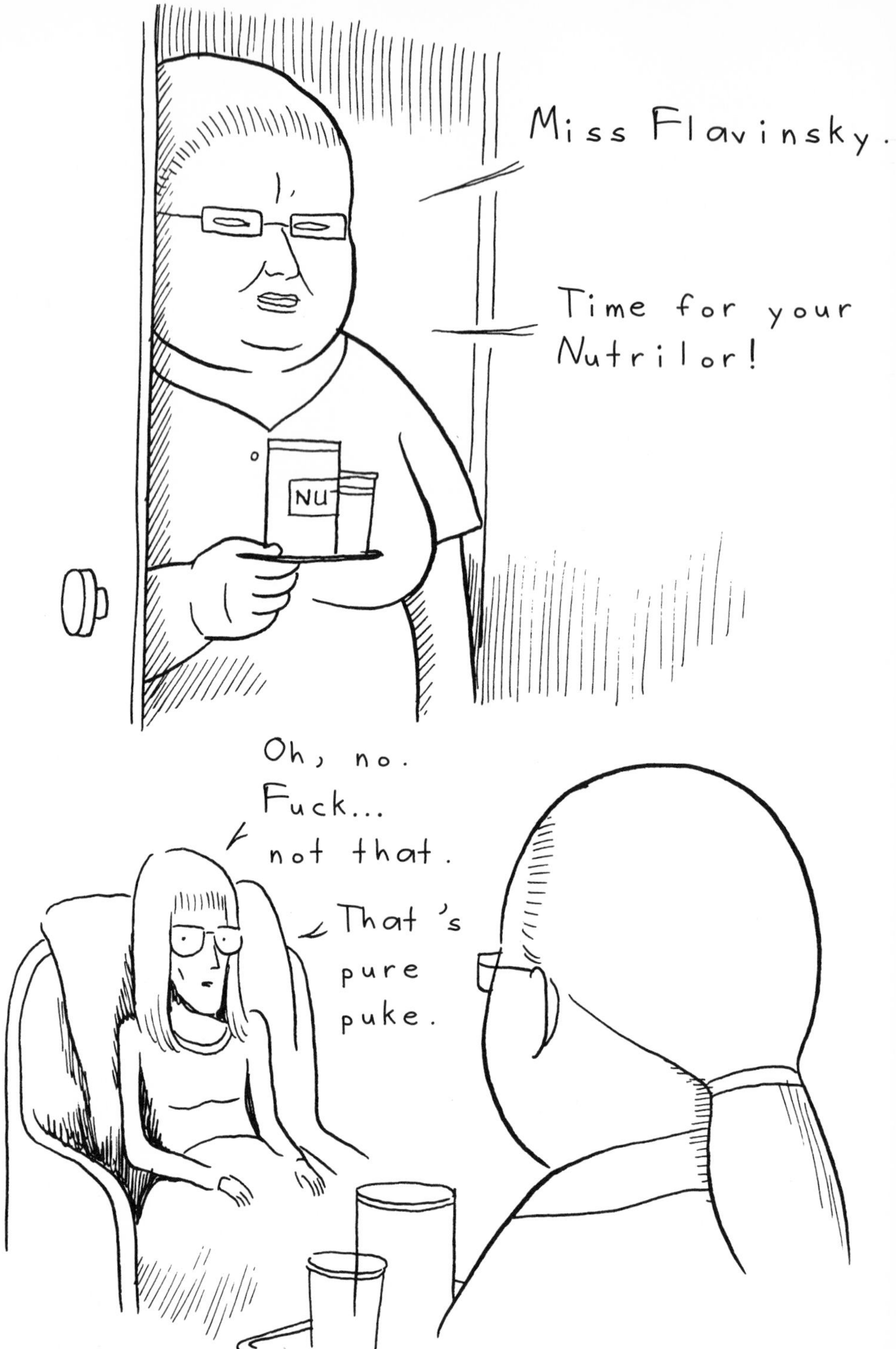
Miss Flavinsky.
Time for your Nutrilor!
NU
Oh, no. Fuck... not that.
That's pure puke.

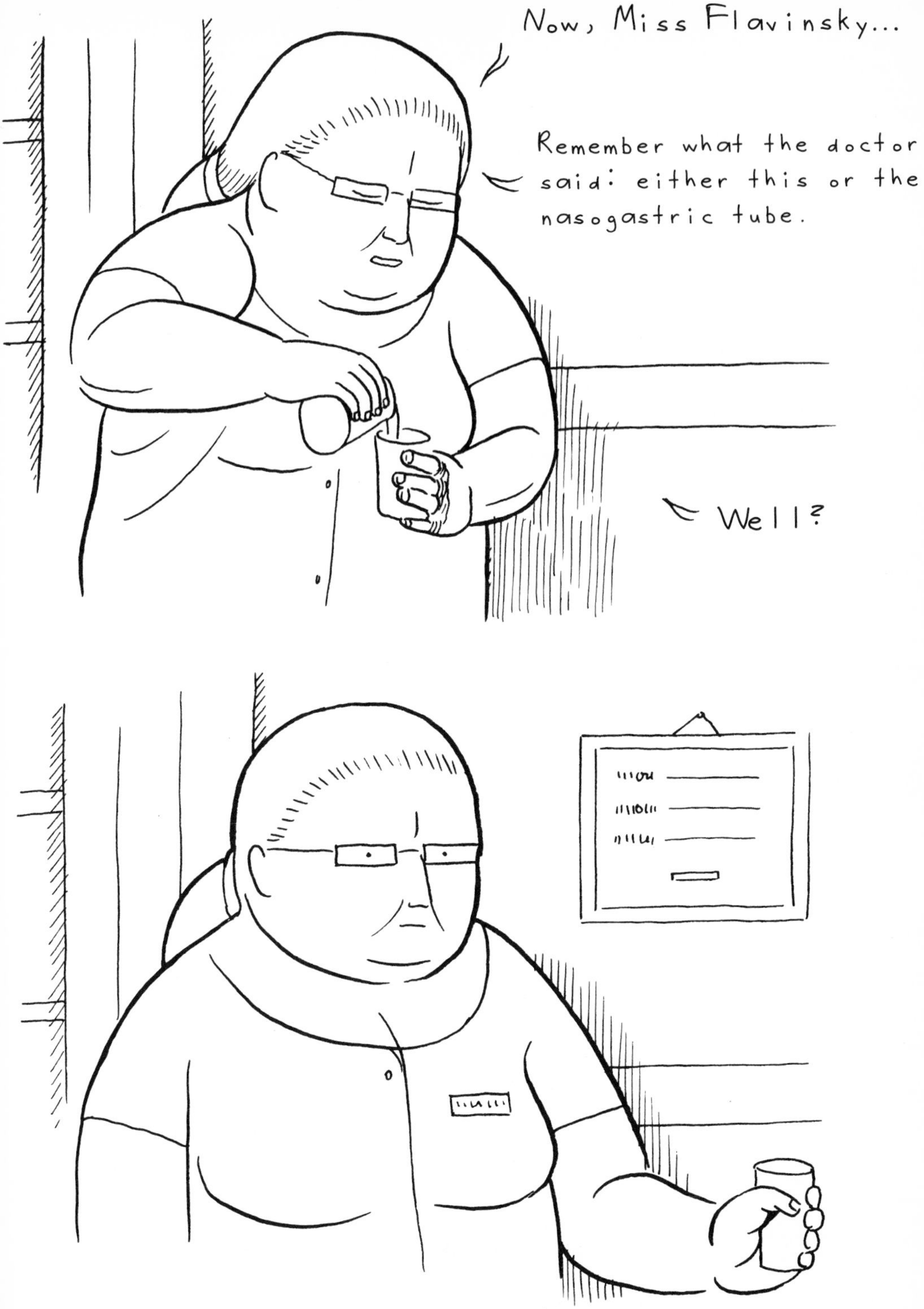
Now, Miss Flavinsky...
Remember what the doctor said: either this or the nasogastric tube.
Well?

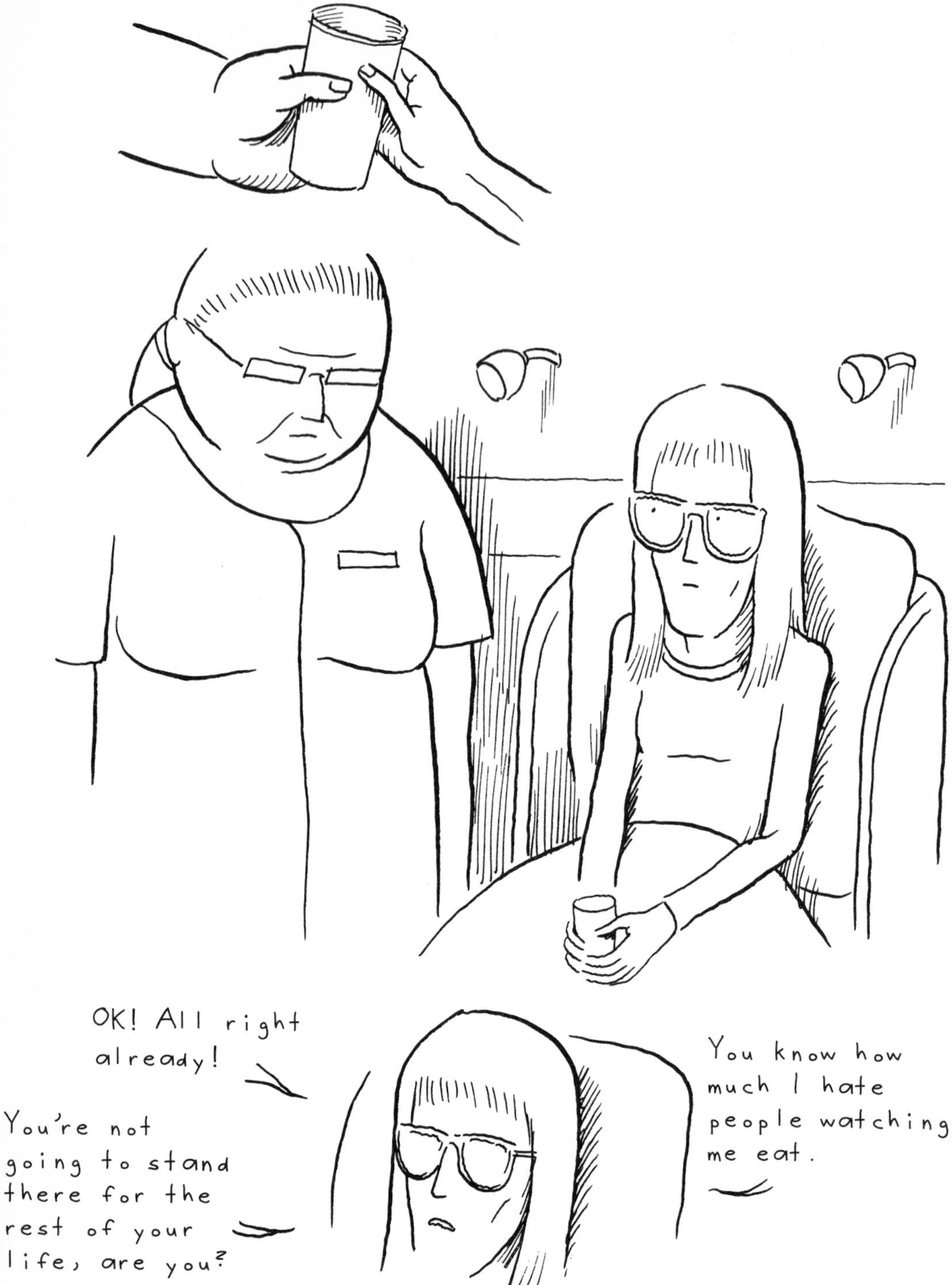
OK! All right already!
You're not going to stand there for the rest of your life, are you?
You know how much I hate people watching me eat.

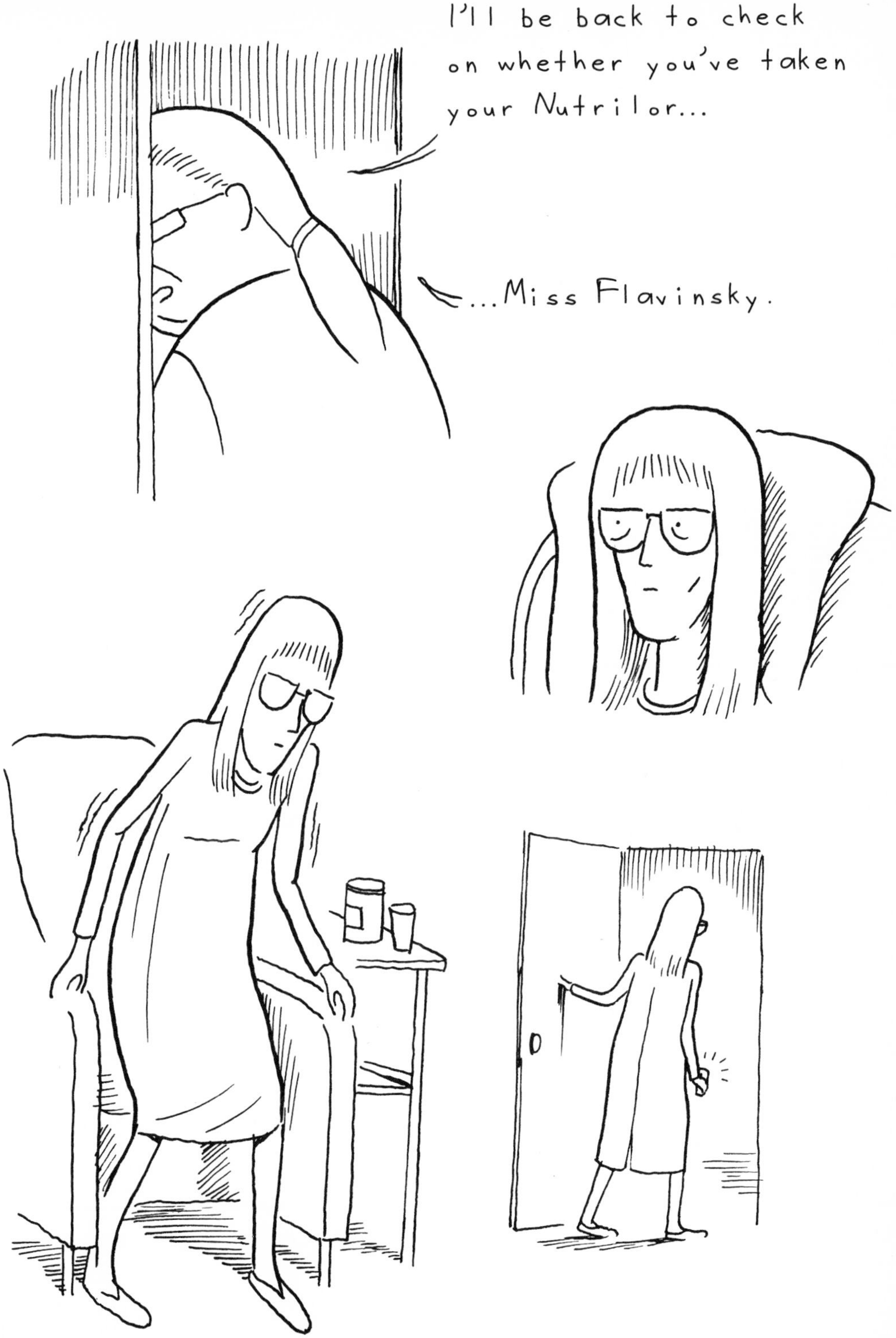
I'll be back to check on whether you've taken your Nutrilor...
...Miss Flavinsky.

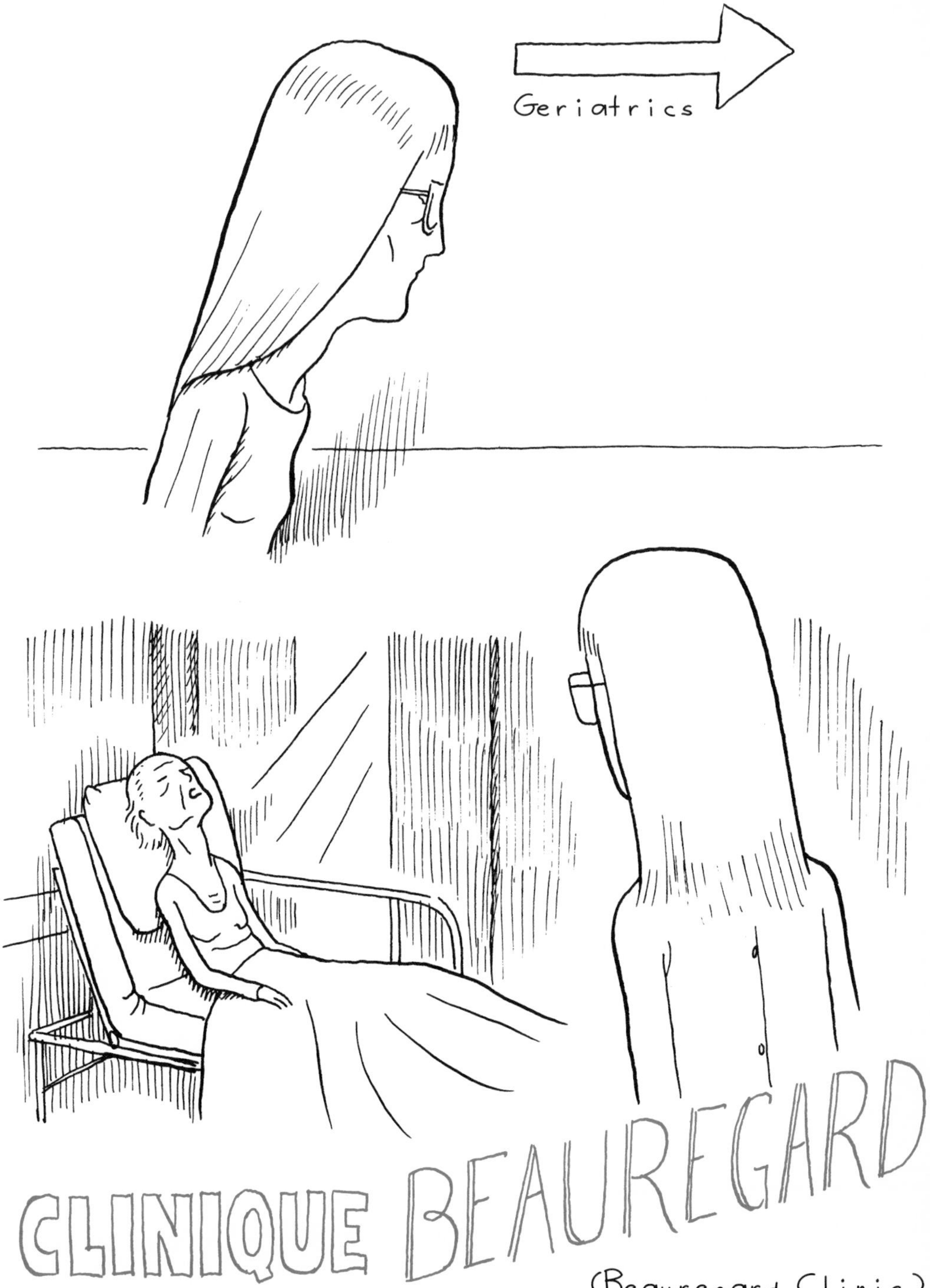
Geriatrics
CLINIQUE BEAUREGARD
(Beauregard Clinic)

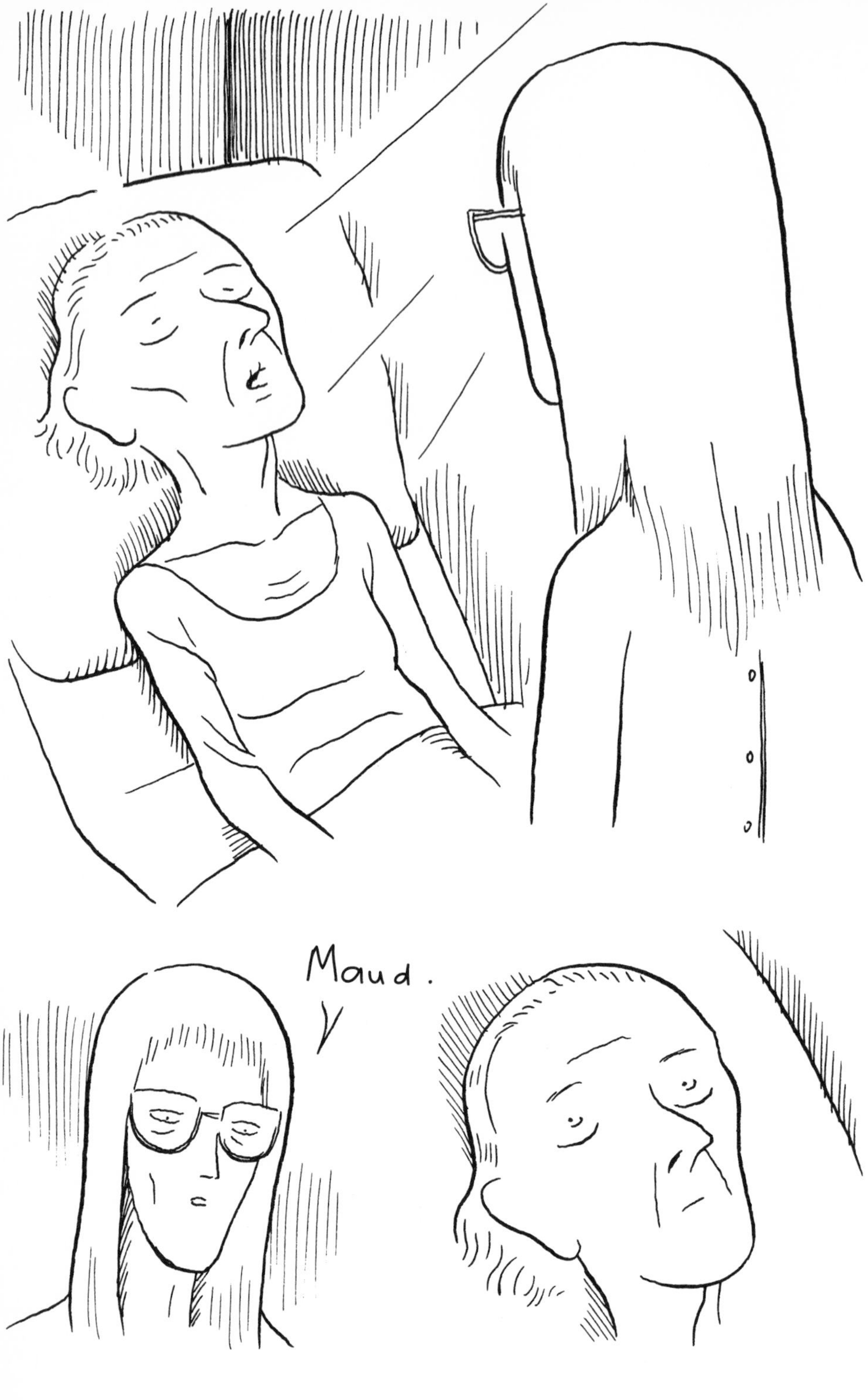
Maud.

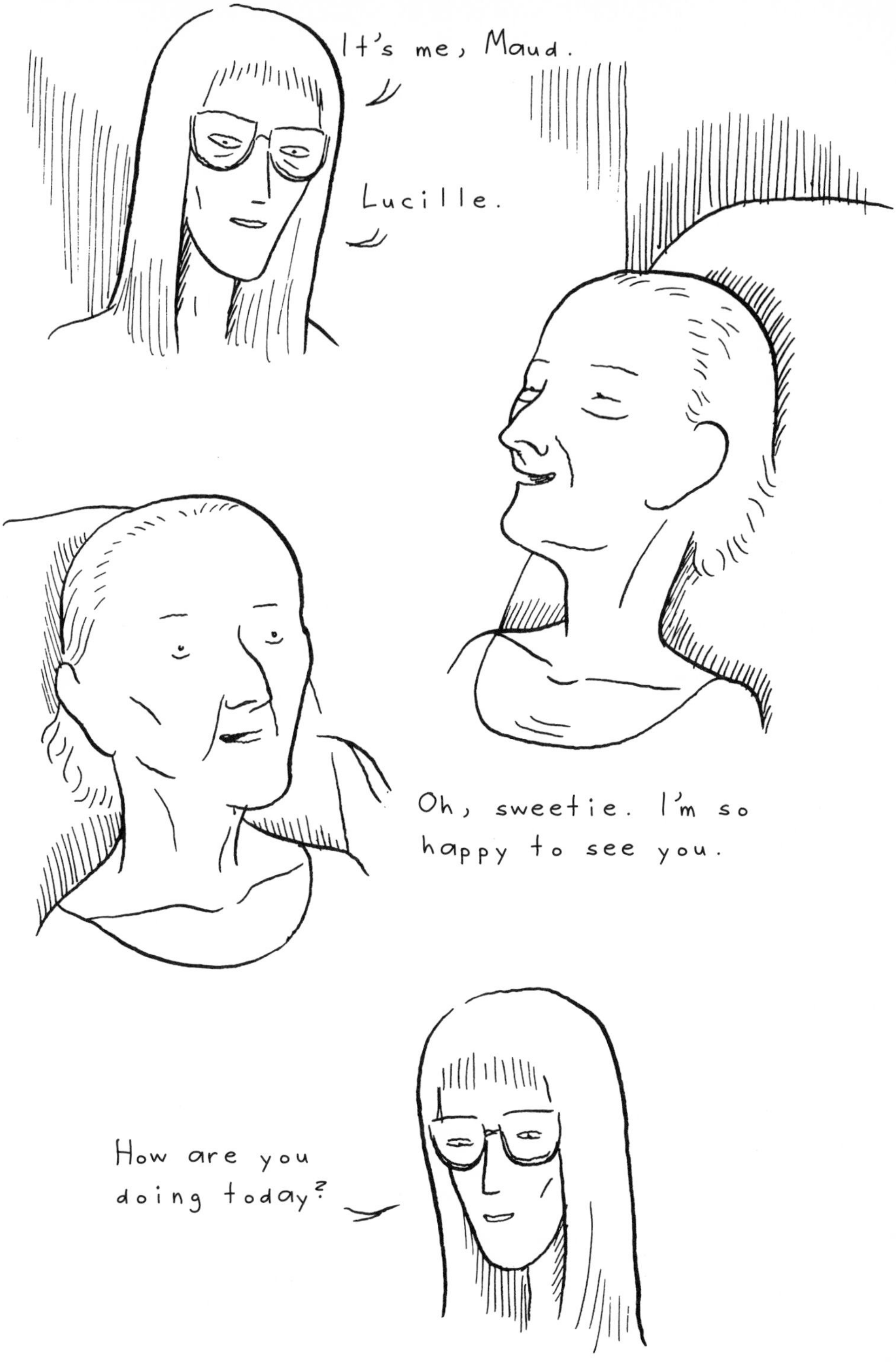
It's me, Maud.
Lucille.
Oh, sweetie. I'm so happy to see you.
How are you doing today?

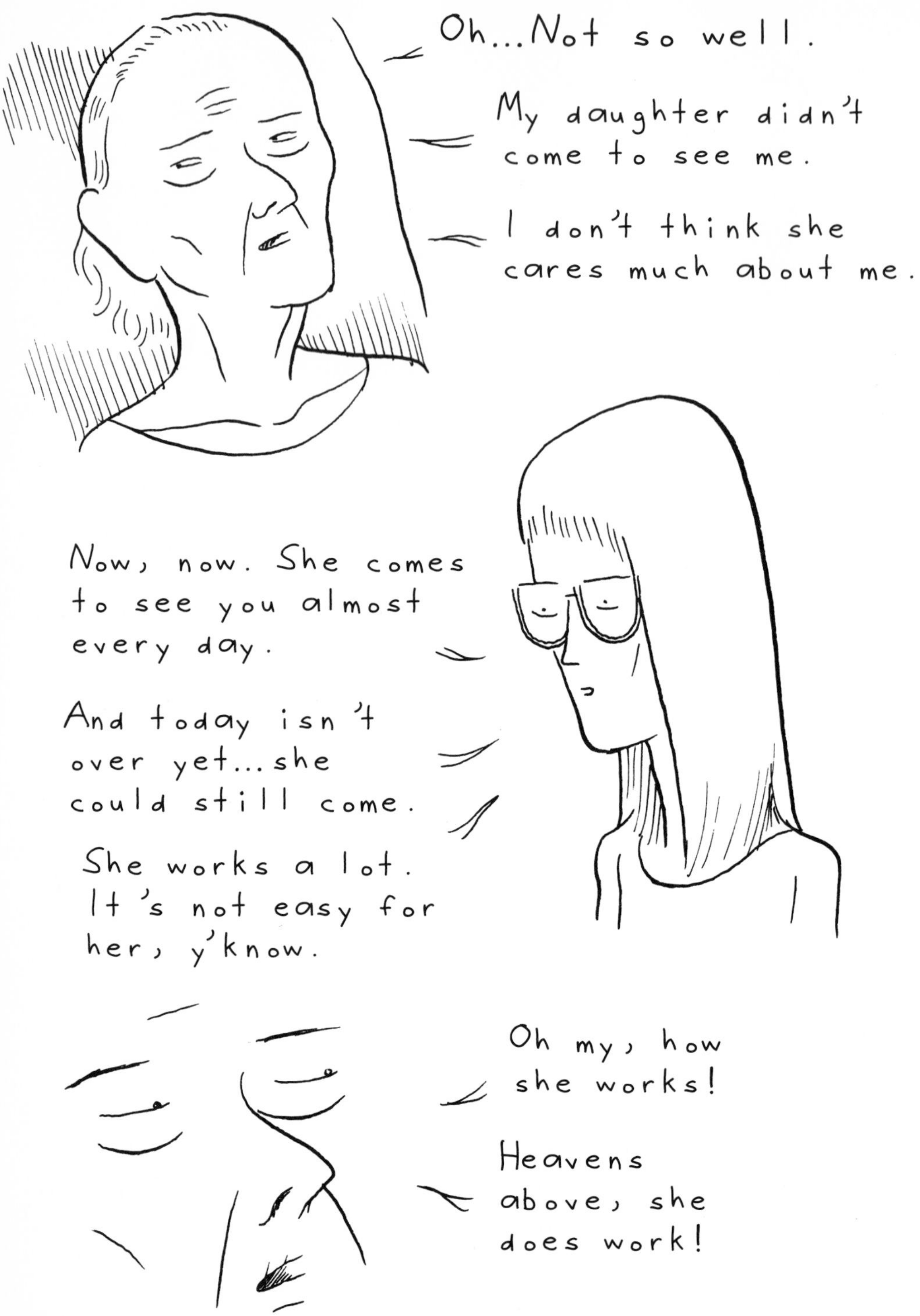
Oh...Not so well.
My daughter didn't come to see me.
I don't think she cares much about me.
Now, now. She comes to see you almost every day.
And today isn't over yet...she could still come.
She works a lot. It's not easy for her, y'know.
Oh my, how she works!
Heavens above, she does work!

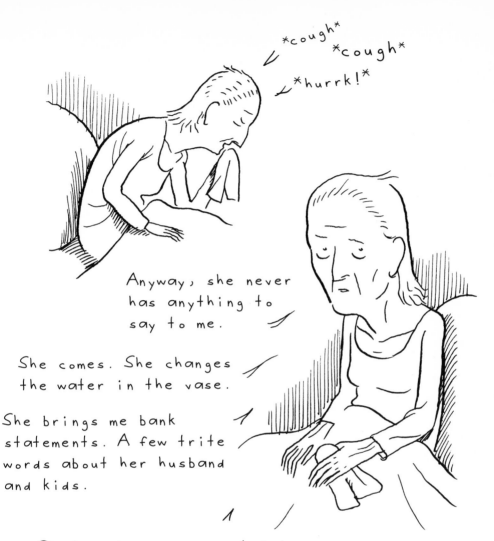

cough *cough* *hurrk!*

Anyway, she never has anything to say to me.

She comes. She changes the water in the vase.

She brings me bank statements. A few trite words about her husband and kids.

Don't get me wrong, I like my son-in-law a lot. But he's an artist. He doesn't have a cent. He's not going to support the family. But...

...not a single kind word from her... a smile...a gesture... how much would it cost her to smile a little?

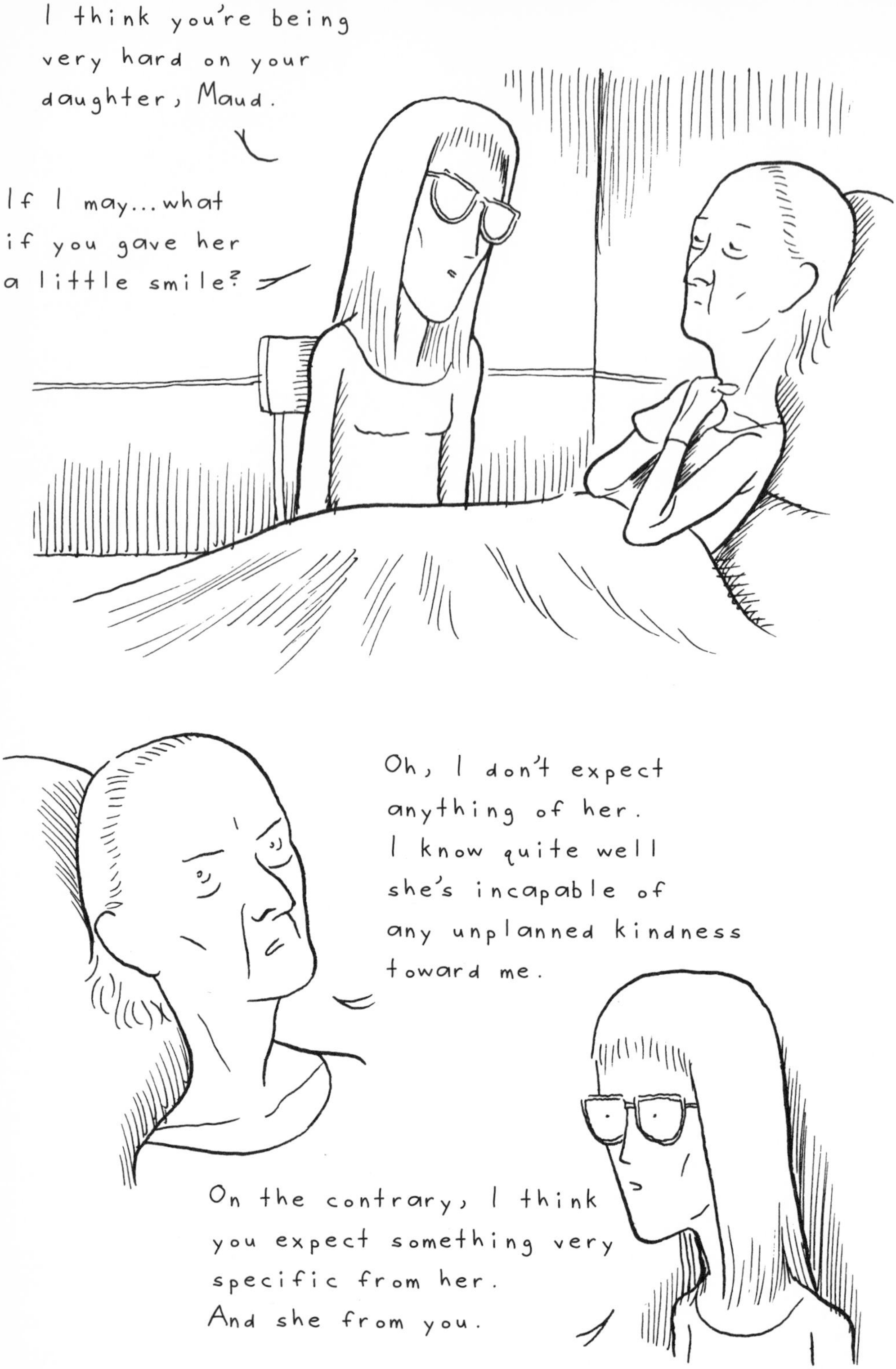
I think you're being very hard on your daughter, Maud.
If I may... what if you gave her a little smile?
Oh, I don't expect anything of her. I know quite well she's incapable of any unplanned kindness toward me.
On the contrary, I think you expect something very specific from her. And she from you.

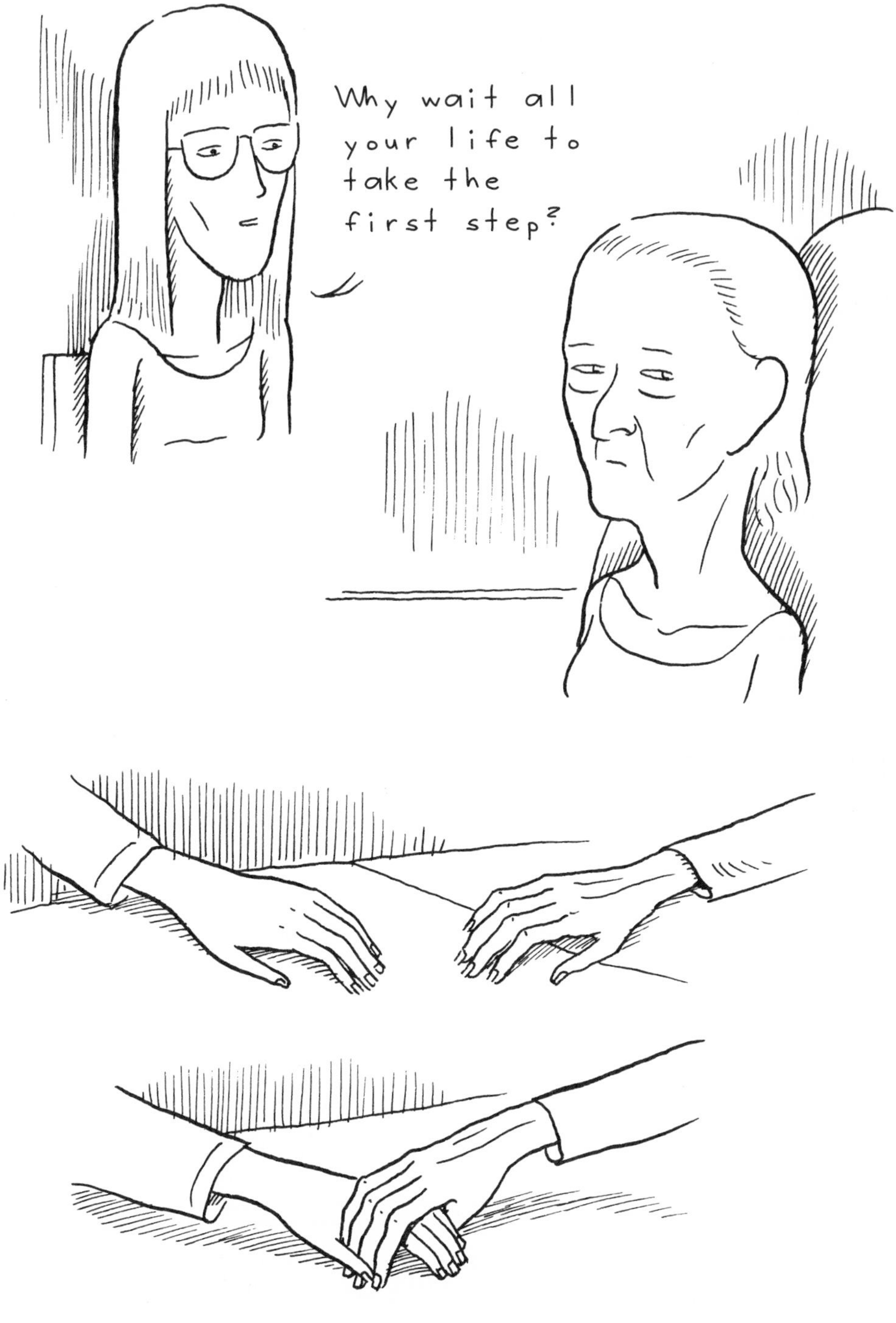
Why wait all your life to take the first step?

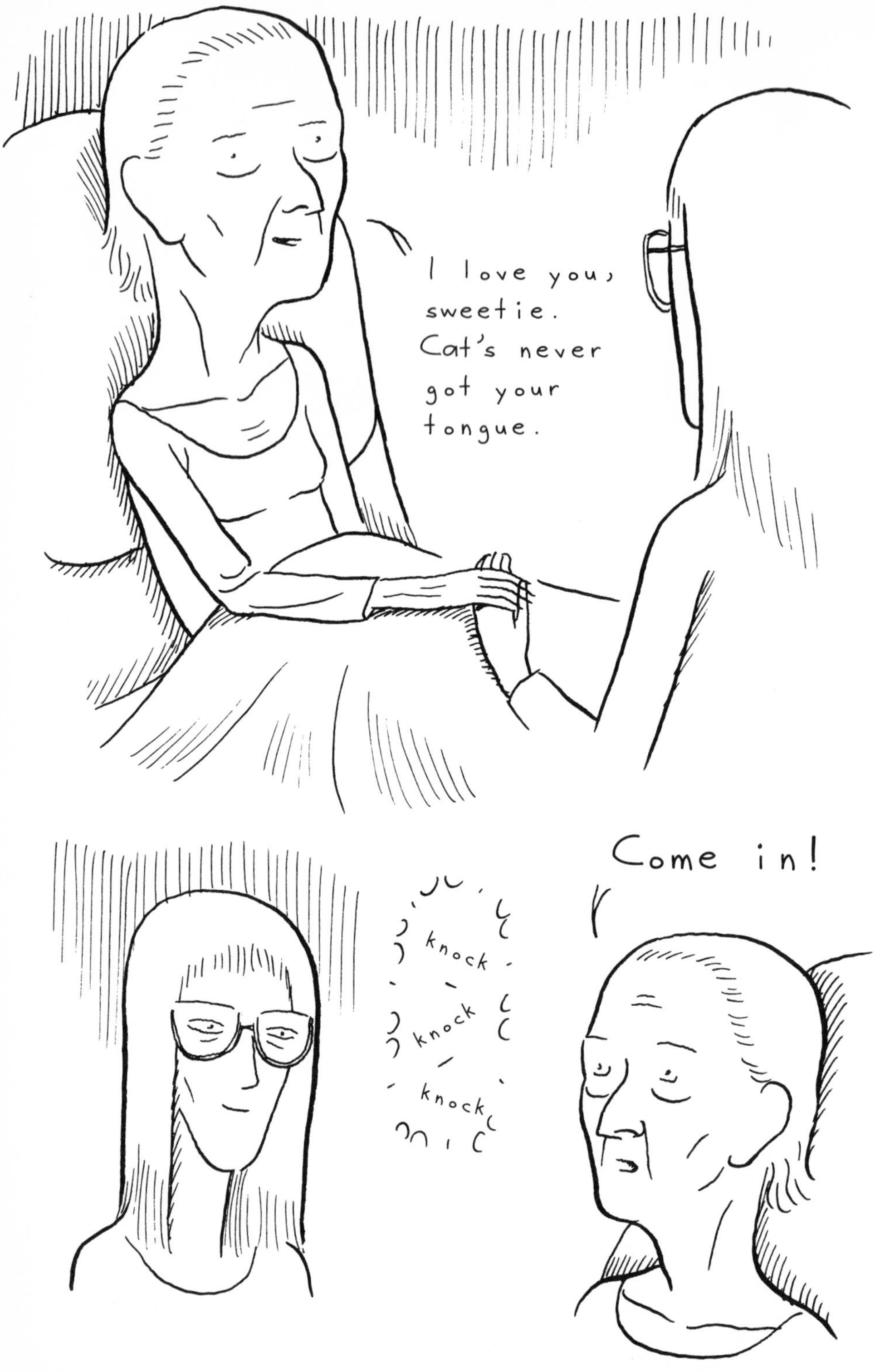
I love you, sweetie. Cat's never got your tongue.
knock knock knock
Come in!

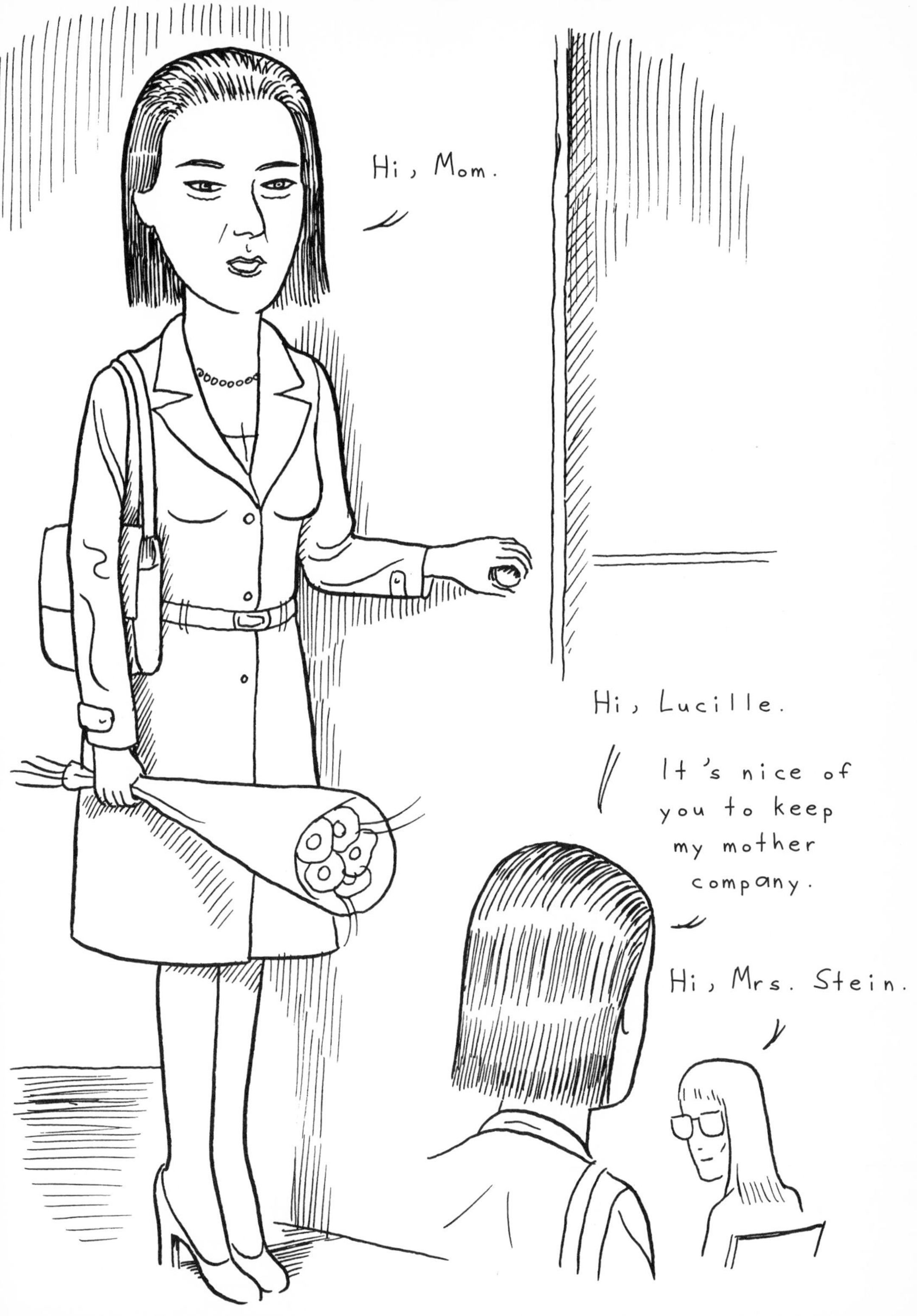

Hi, Mom.
Hi, Lucille.
It's nice of you to keep my mother company.
Hi, Mrs. Stein.

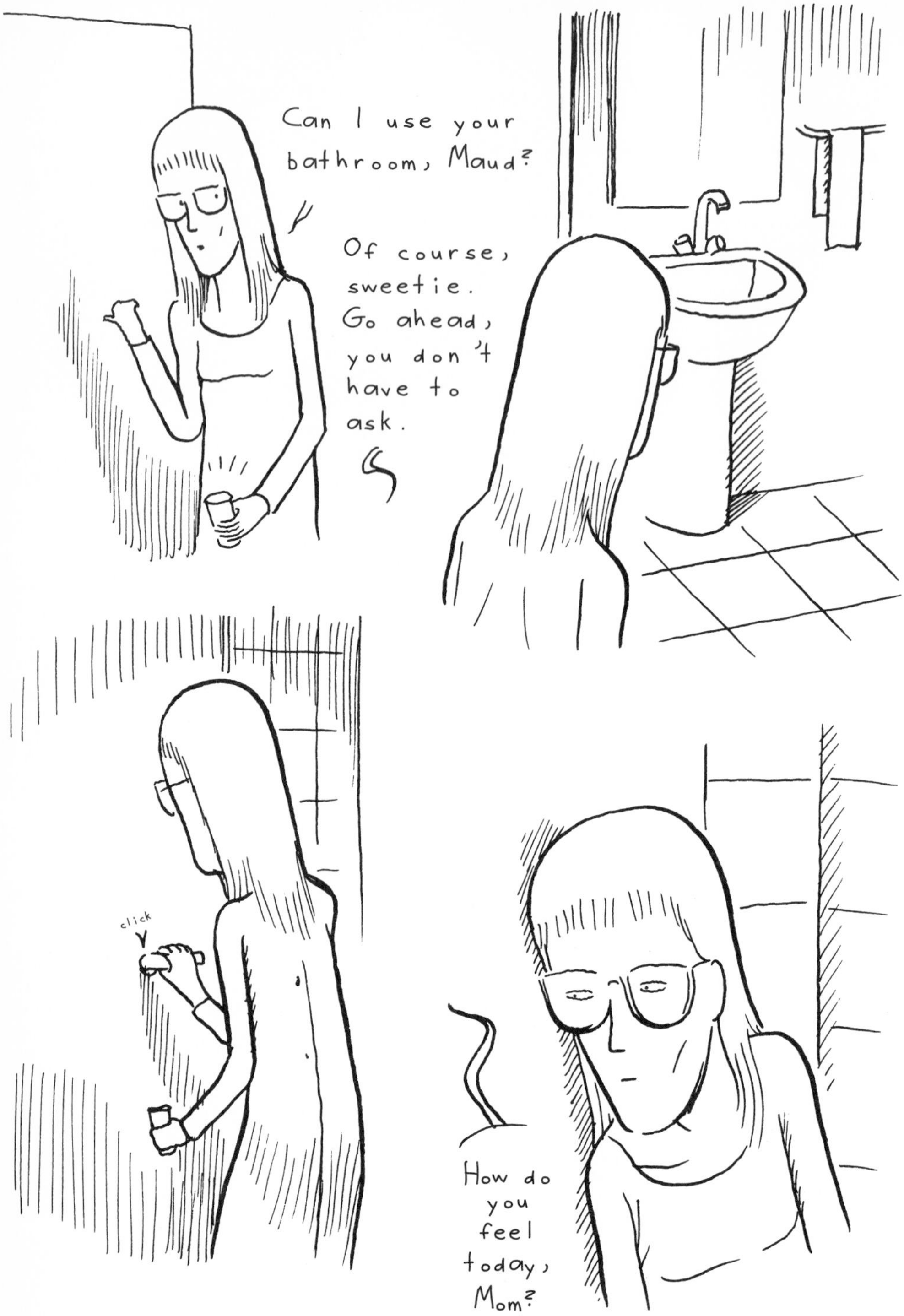

Can I use your bathroom, Maud?
Of course, sweetie. Go ahead, you don't have to ask.
click
How do you feel today, Mom?

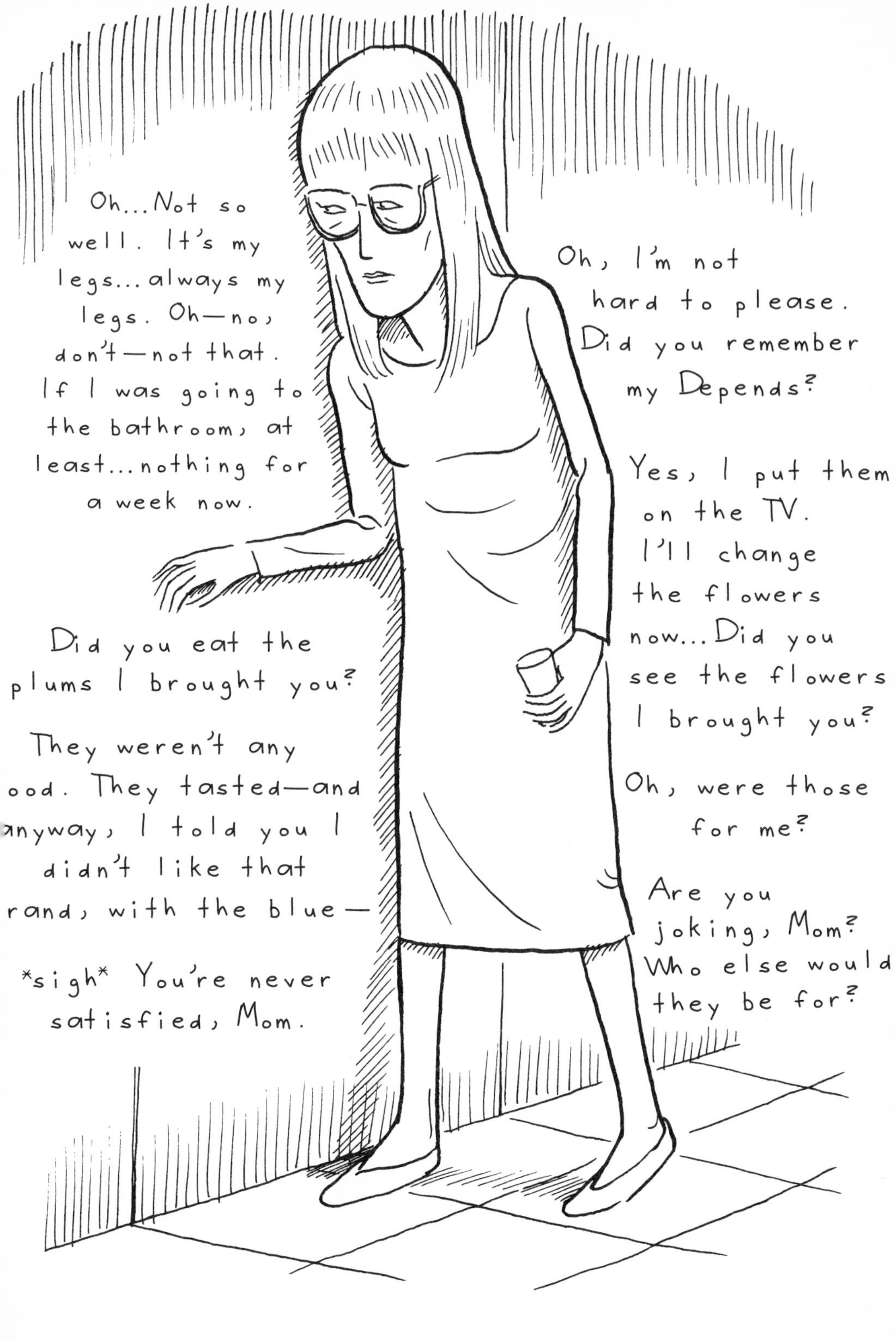

Oh... Not so well. It's my legs... always my legs. Oh—no, don't—not that. If I was going to the bathroom, at least... nothing for a week now.
Did you eat the plums I brought you?
They weren't any ood. They tasted—and anyway, I told you I didn't like that rand, with the blue—
sigh You're never satisfied, Mom.
Oh, I'm not hard to please. Did you remember my Depends?
Yes, I put them on the TV. I'll change the flowers now... Did you see the flowers I brought you?
Oh, were those for me?
Are you joking, Mom? Who else would they be for?

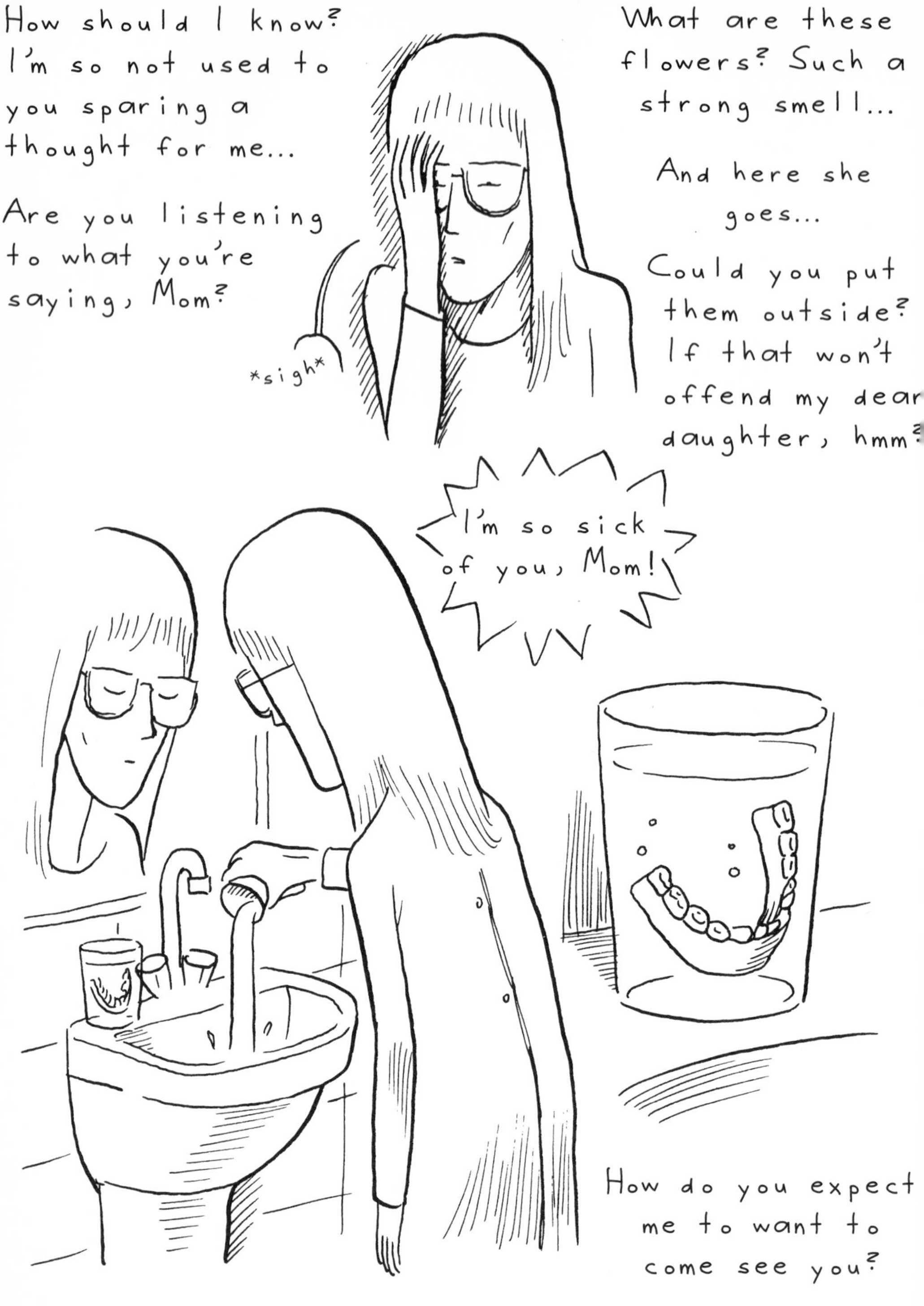
How should I know? I'm so not used to you sparing a thought for me...
Are you listening to what you're saying, Mom?
What are these flowers? Such a strong smell...
And here she goes...
Could you put them outside? If that won't offend my dear daughter, hmm?
sigh
I'm so sick of you, Mom!
How do you expect me to want to come see you?

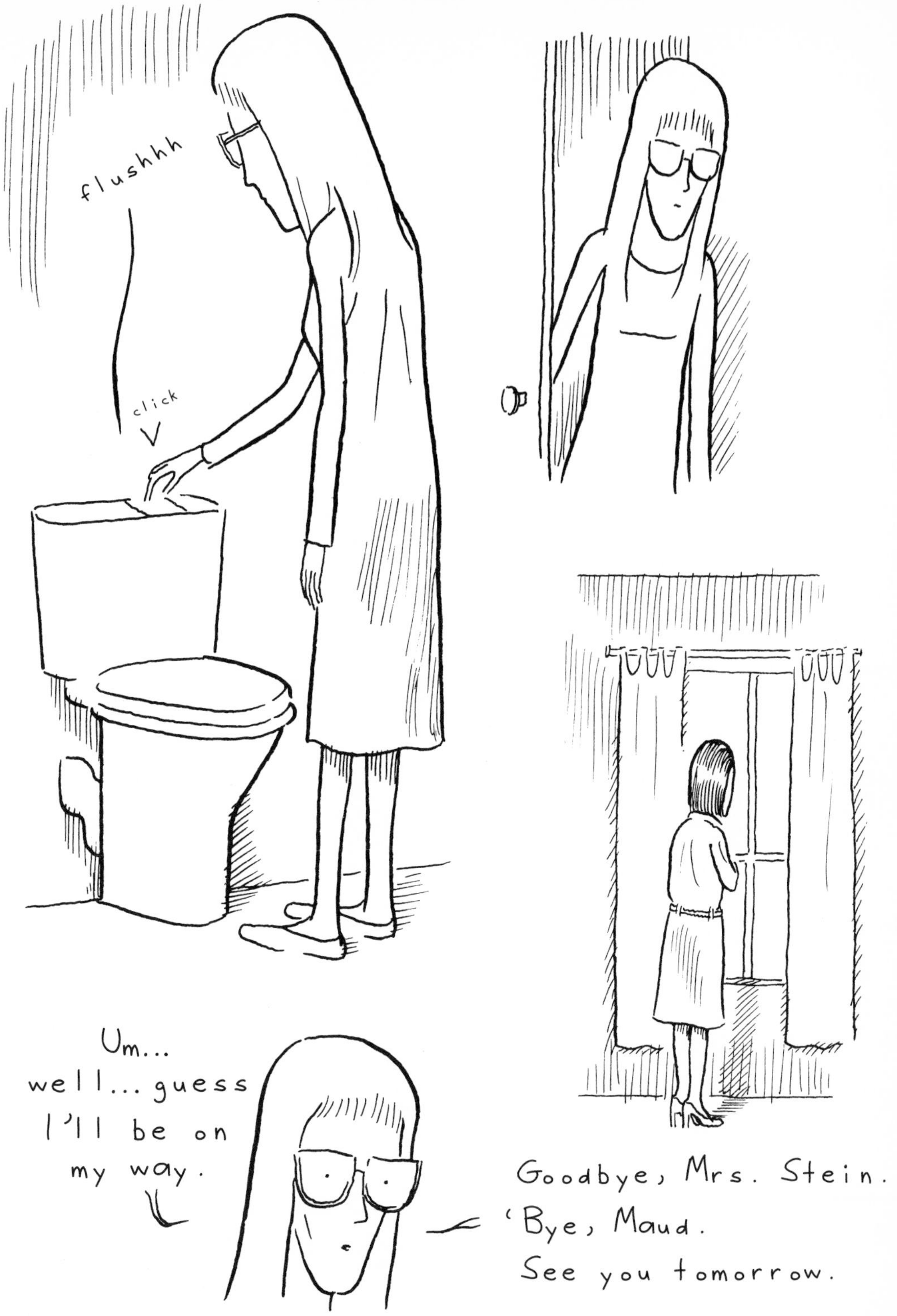
flushhh
click
Um... well... guess I'll be on my way.
Goodbye, Mrs. Stein.
'Bye, Maud. See you tomorrow.

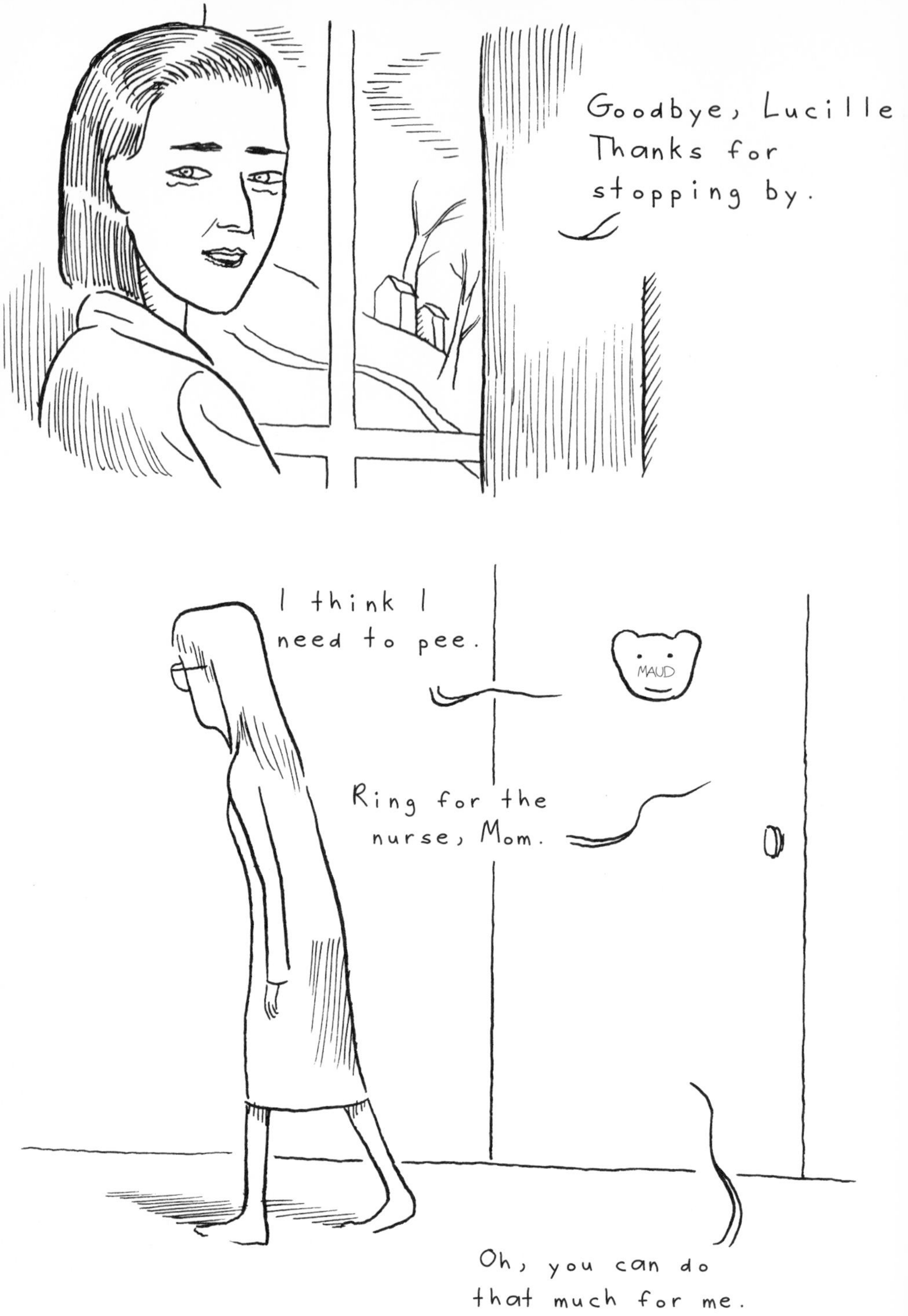
Goodbye, Lucille
Thanks for
stopping by.
I think I
need to pee.
MAUD
Ring for the
nurse, Mom.
Oh, you can do
that much for me.

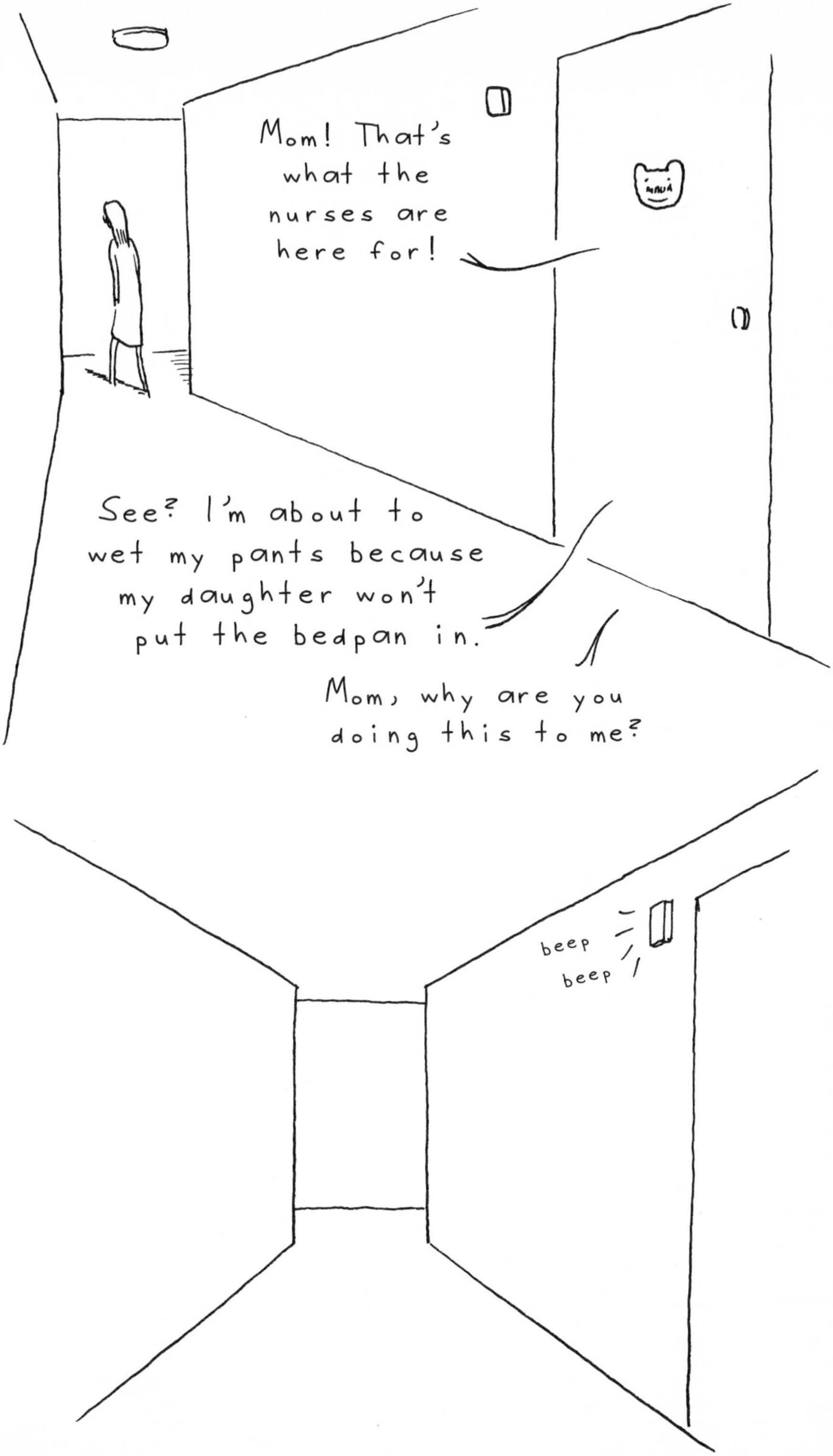

Mom! That's what the nurses are here for!
See? I'm about to wet my pants because my daughter won't put the bedpan in.
Mom, why are you doing this to me?
beep
beep

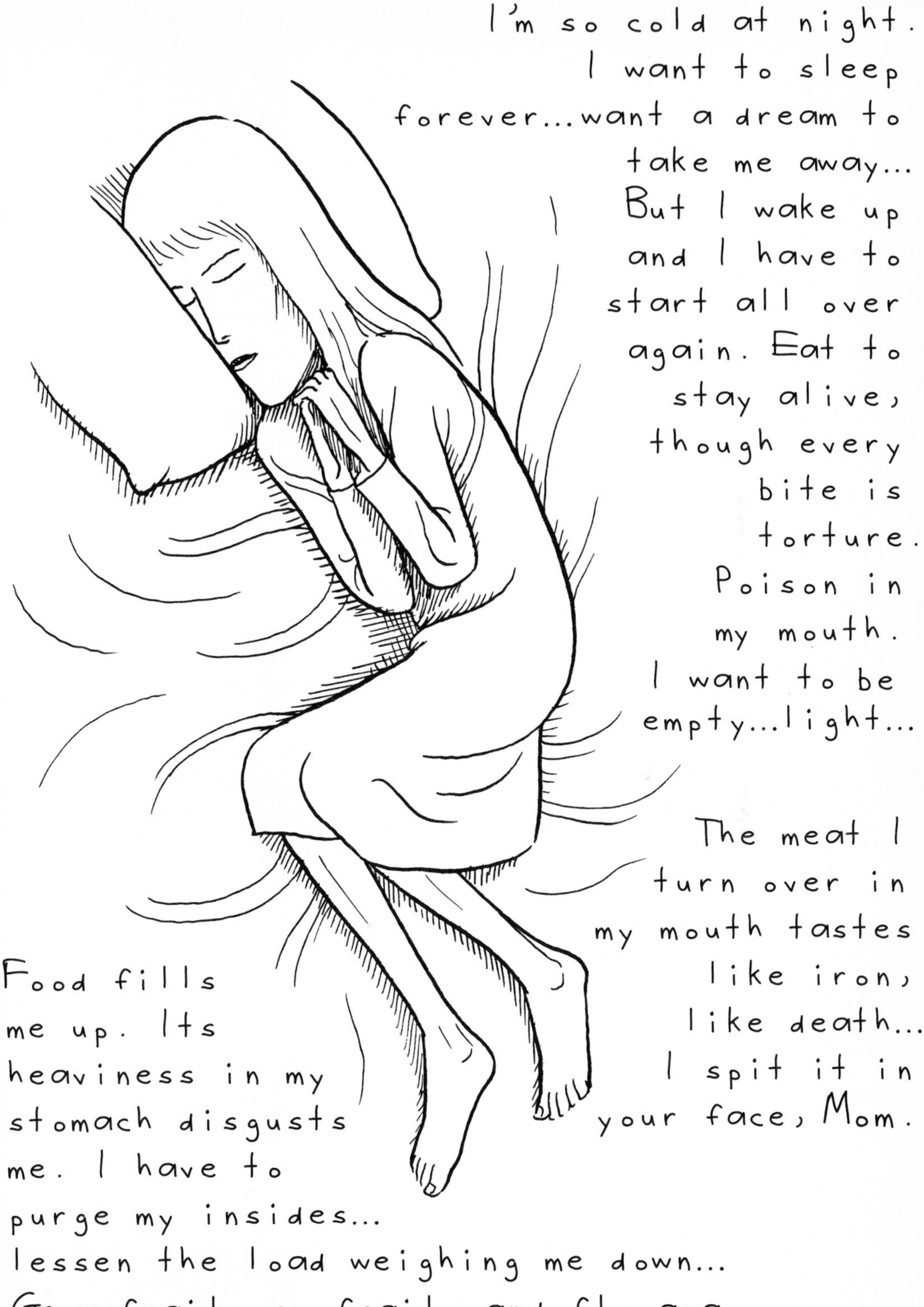
I'm so cold at night. I want to sleep forever...want a dream to take me away... But I wake up and I have to start all over again. Eat to stay alive, though every bite is torture. Poison in my mouth. I want to be empty...light...
The meat I turn over in my mouth tastes like iron, like death... I spit it in your face, Mom.
Food fills me up. Its heaviness in my stomach disgusts me. I have to purge my insides... lessen the load weighing me down... Grow frail, so frail, and fly away...

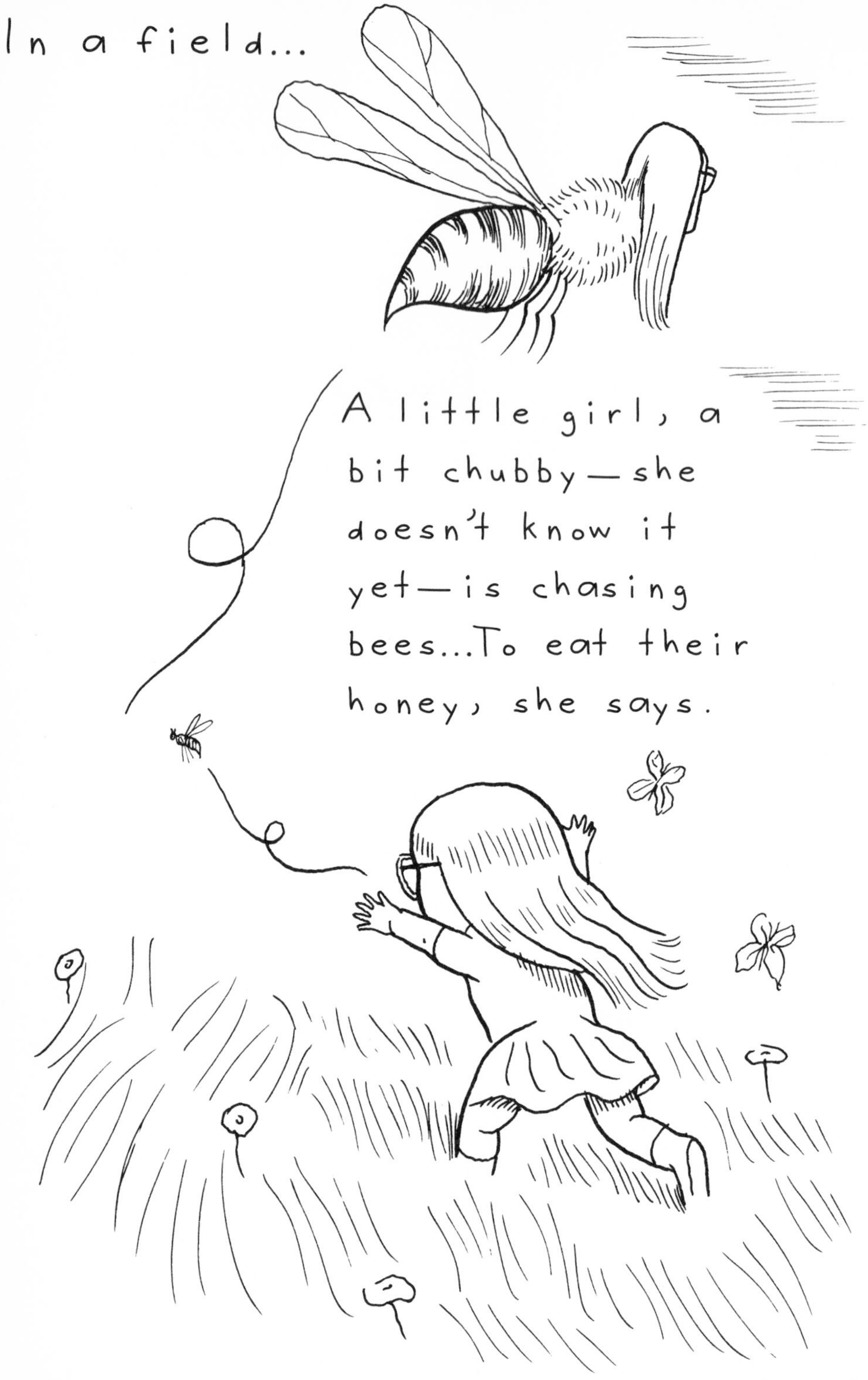
In a field...
A little girl, a bit chubby—she doesn't know it yet—is chasing bees...To eat their honey, she says.

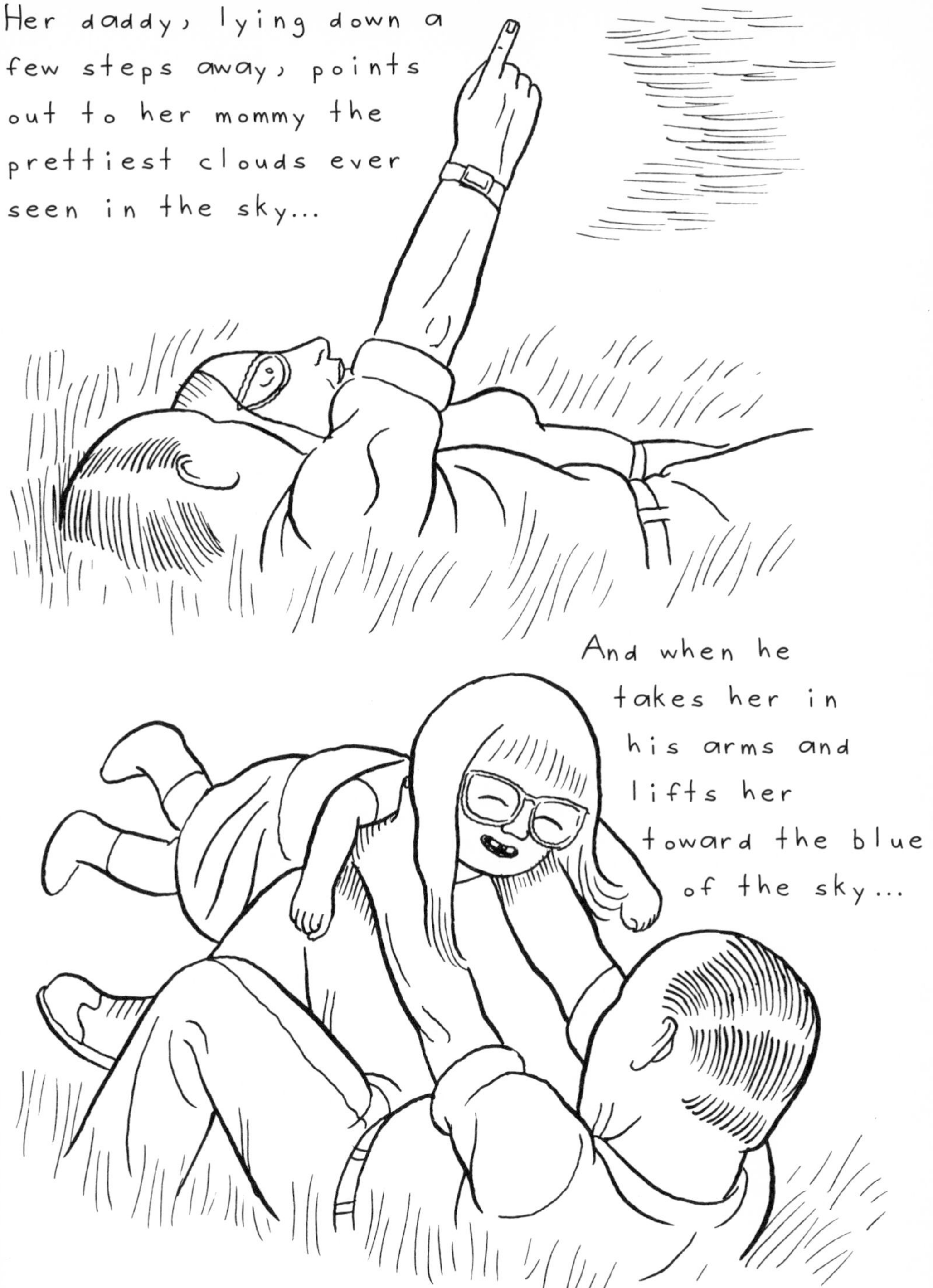
Her daddy, lying down a few steps away, points out to her mommy the prettiest clouds ever seen in the sky...
And when he takes her in his arms and lifts her toward the blue of the sky...
She feels so light...

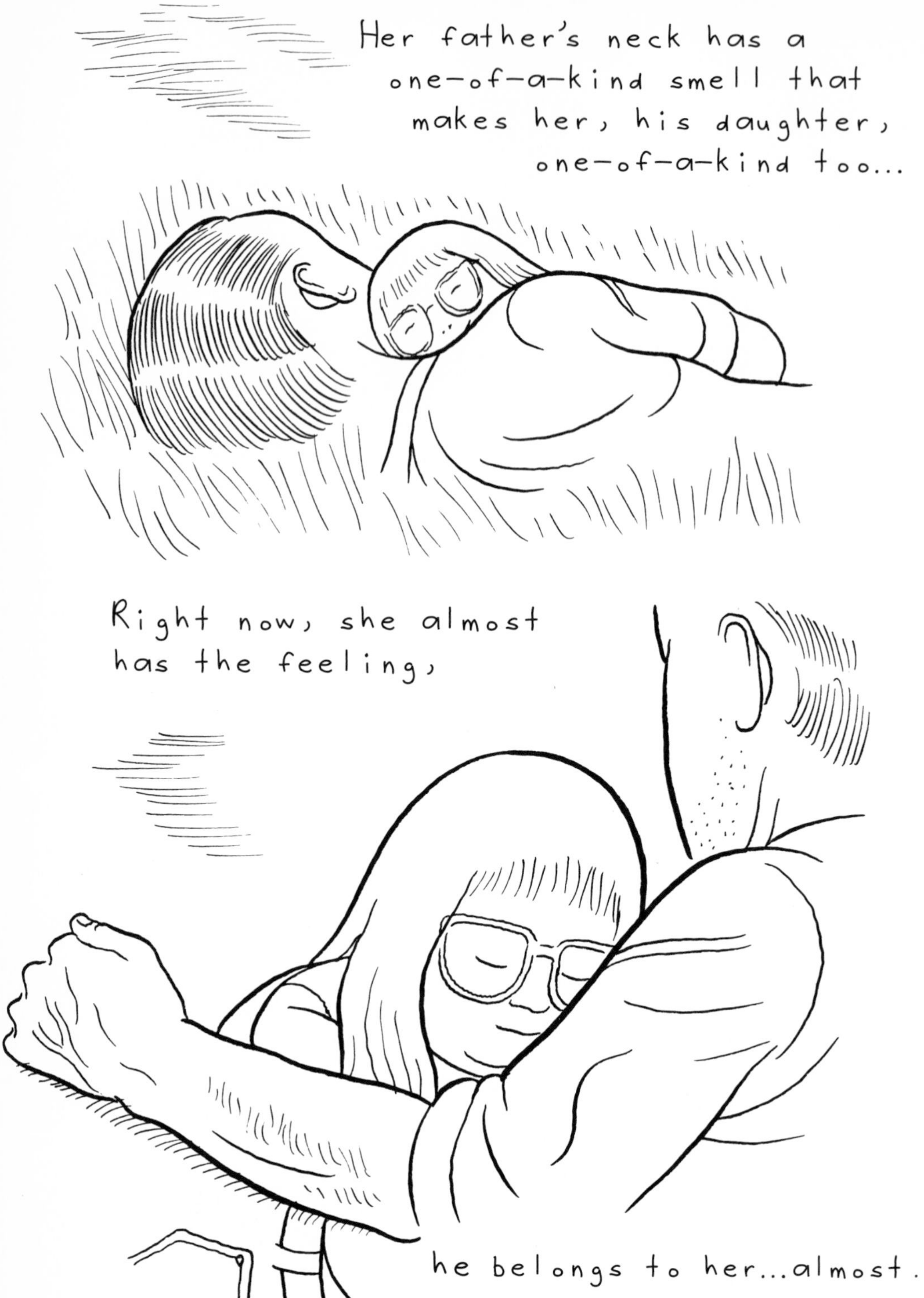
Her father's neck has a one-of-a-kind smell that makes her, his daughter, one-of-a-kind too...
Right now, she almost has the feeling,
he belongs to her...almost.

Not like that other time, a bit later...

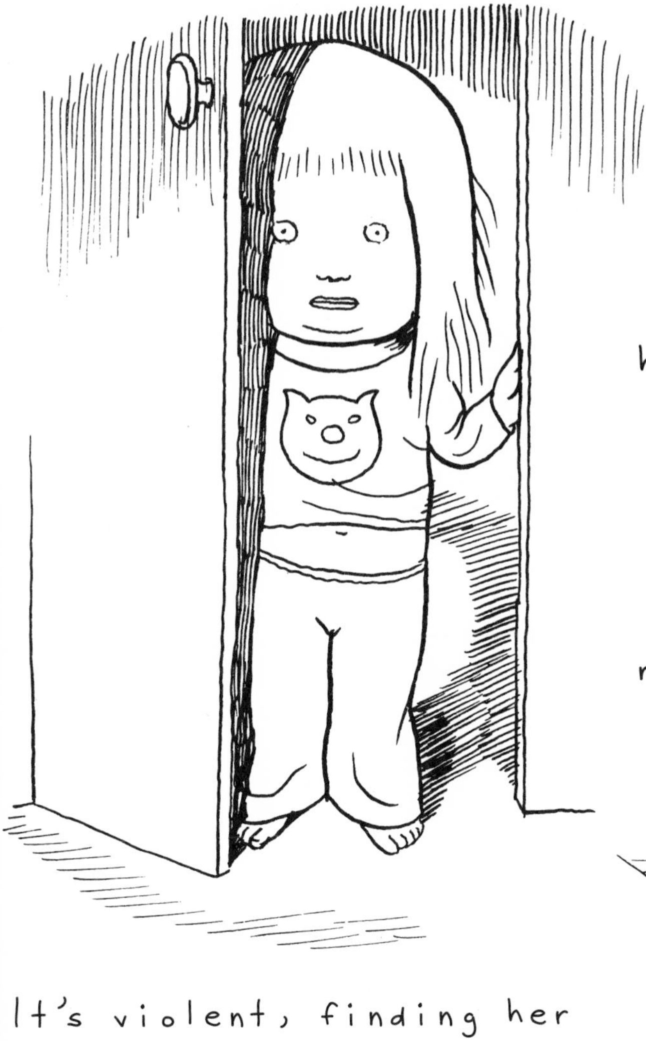

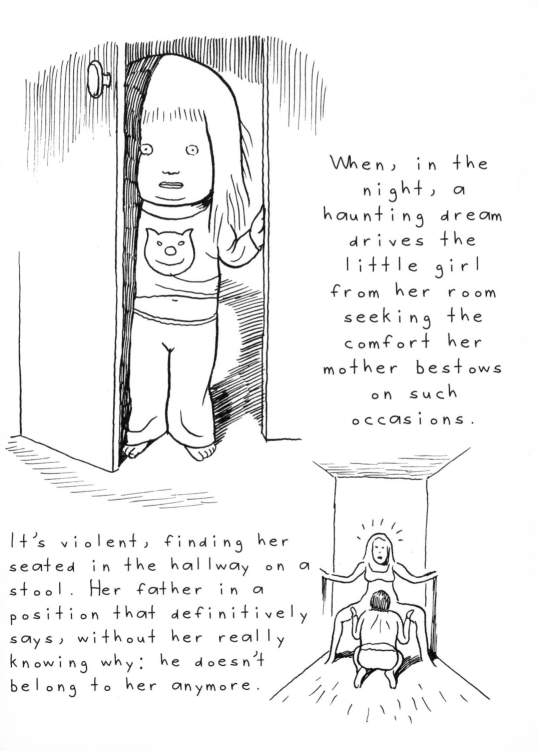

When, in the night, a haunting dream drives the little girl from her room seeking the comfort her mother bestows on such occasions.

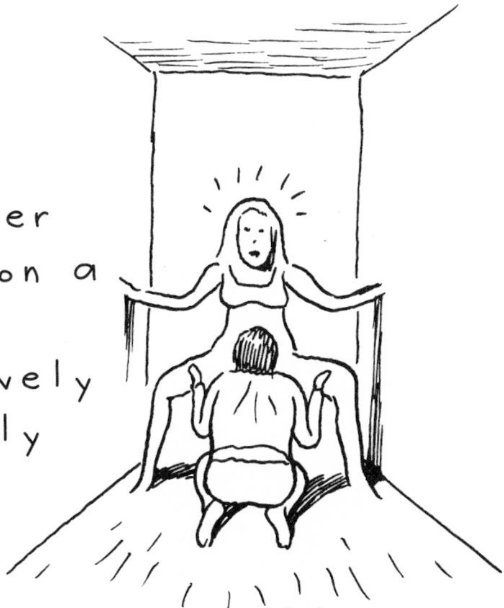

It's violent, finding her seated in the hallway on a stool. Her father in a position that definitively says, without her really knowing why: he doesn't belong to her anymore.

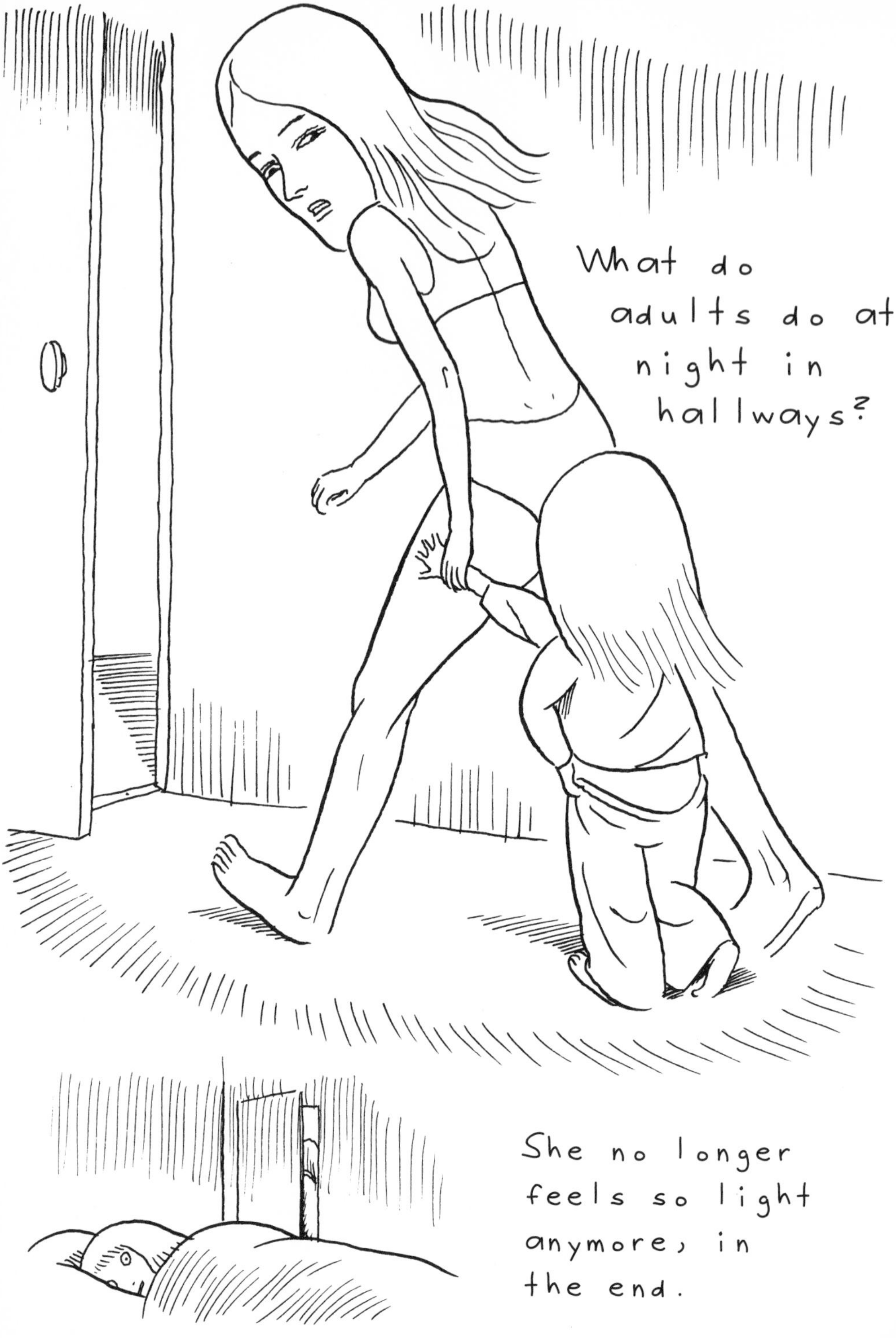
What do adults do at night in hallways?
She no longer feels so light anymore, in the end.

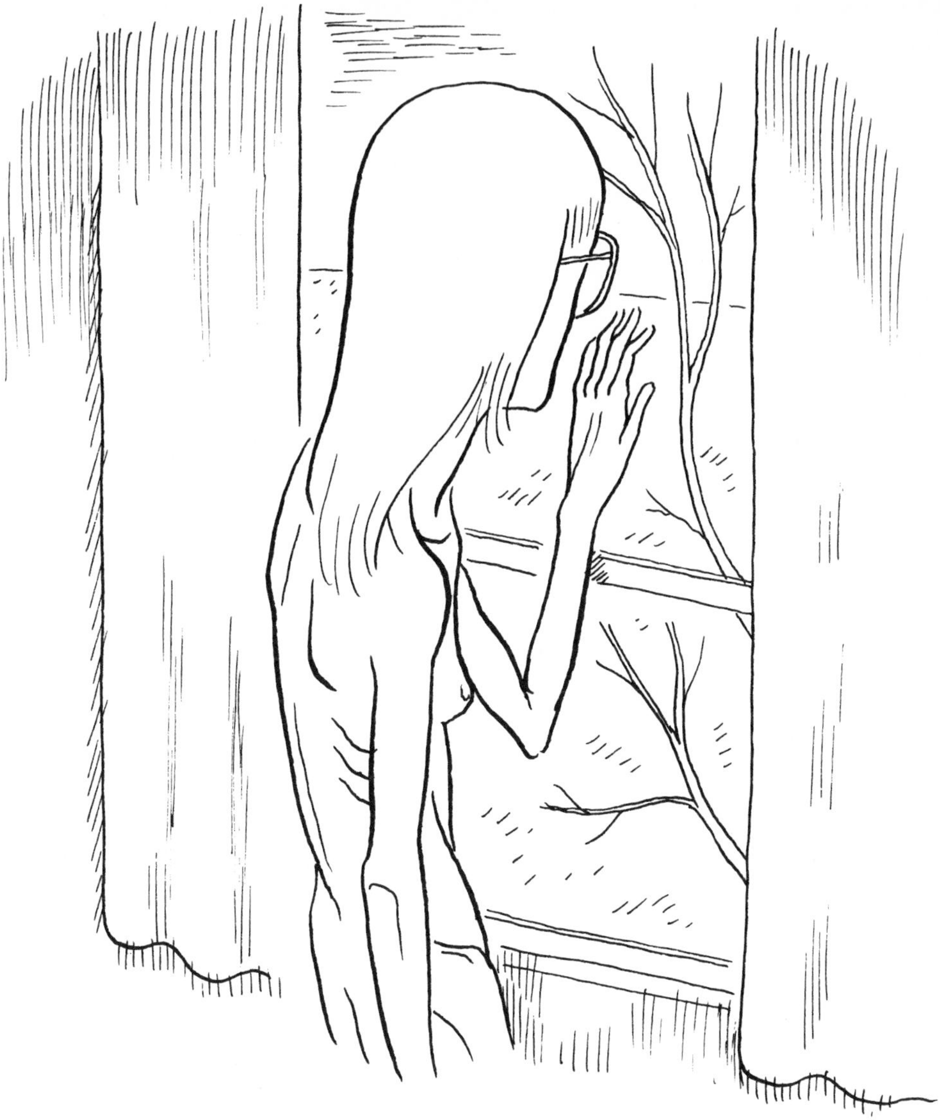

Odd... Ever since my weight dropped again and my "contract" with the doctors forbids visitors, I almost miss my mother.

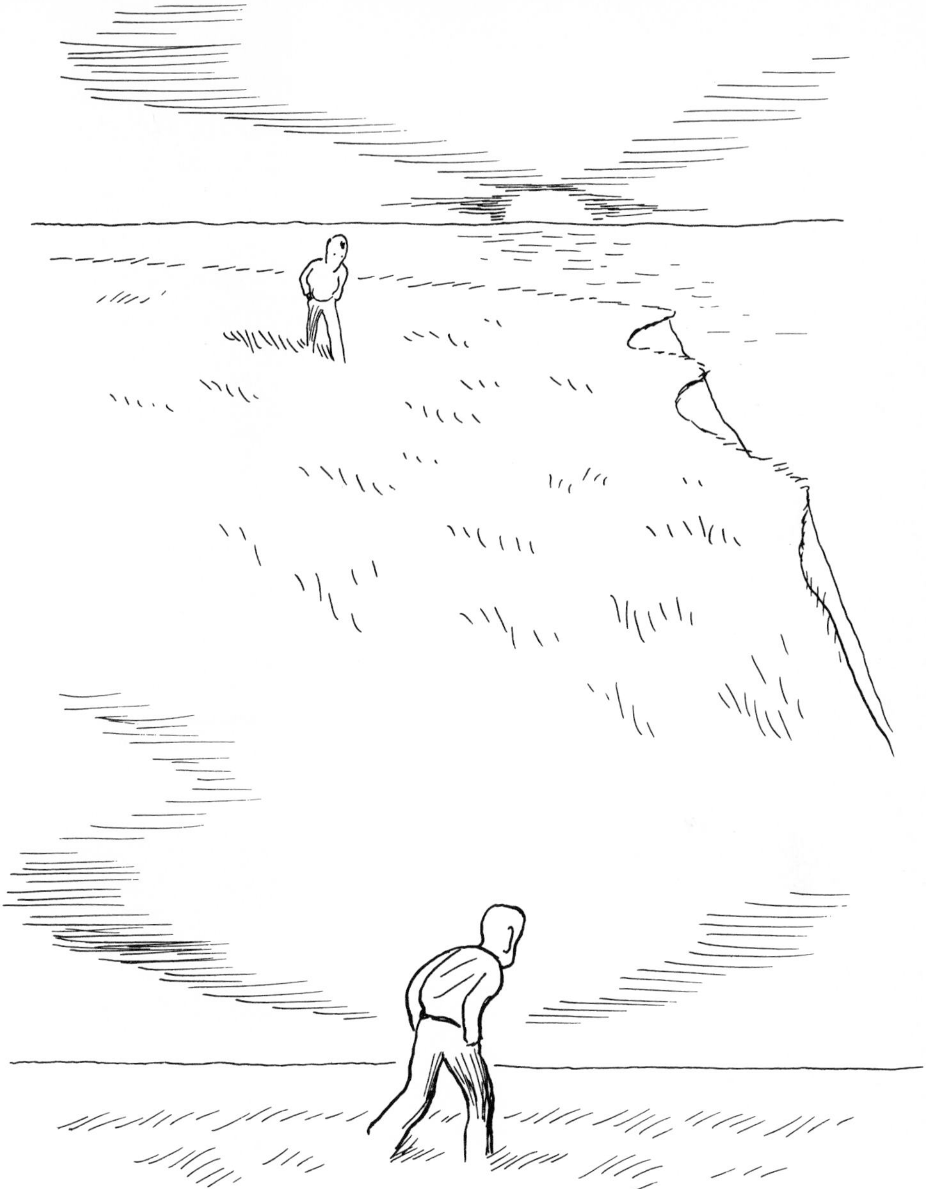

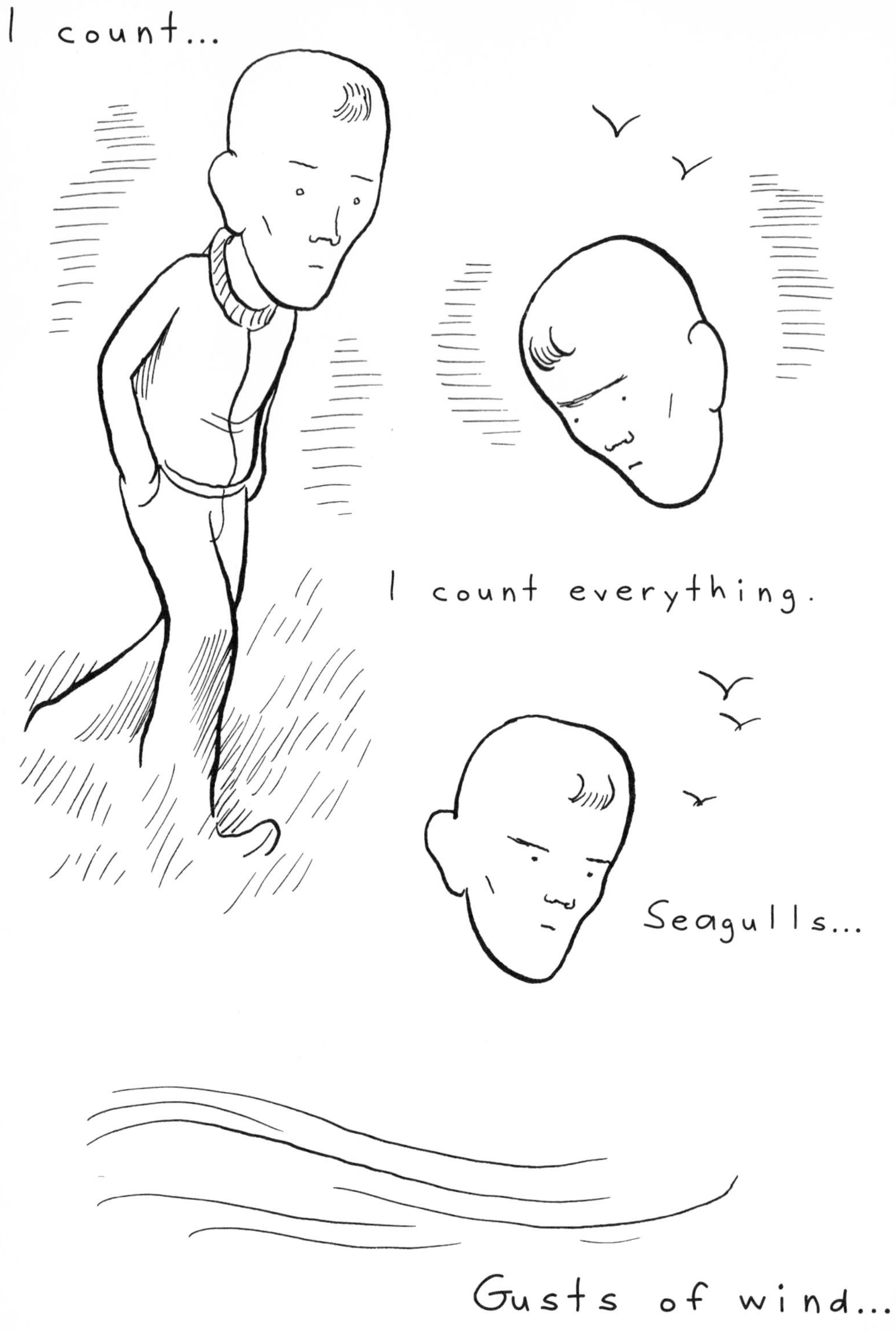
I count...
I count everything.
Seagulls...
Gusts of wind...

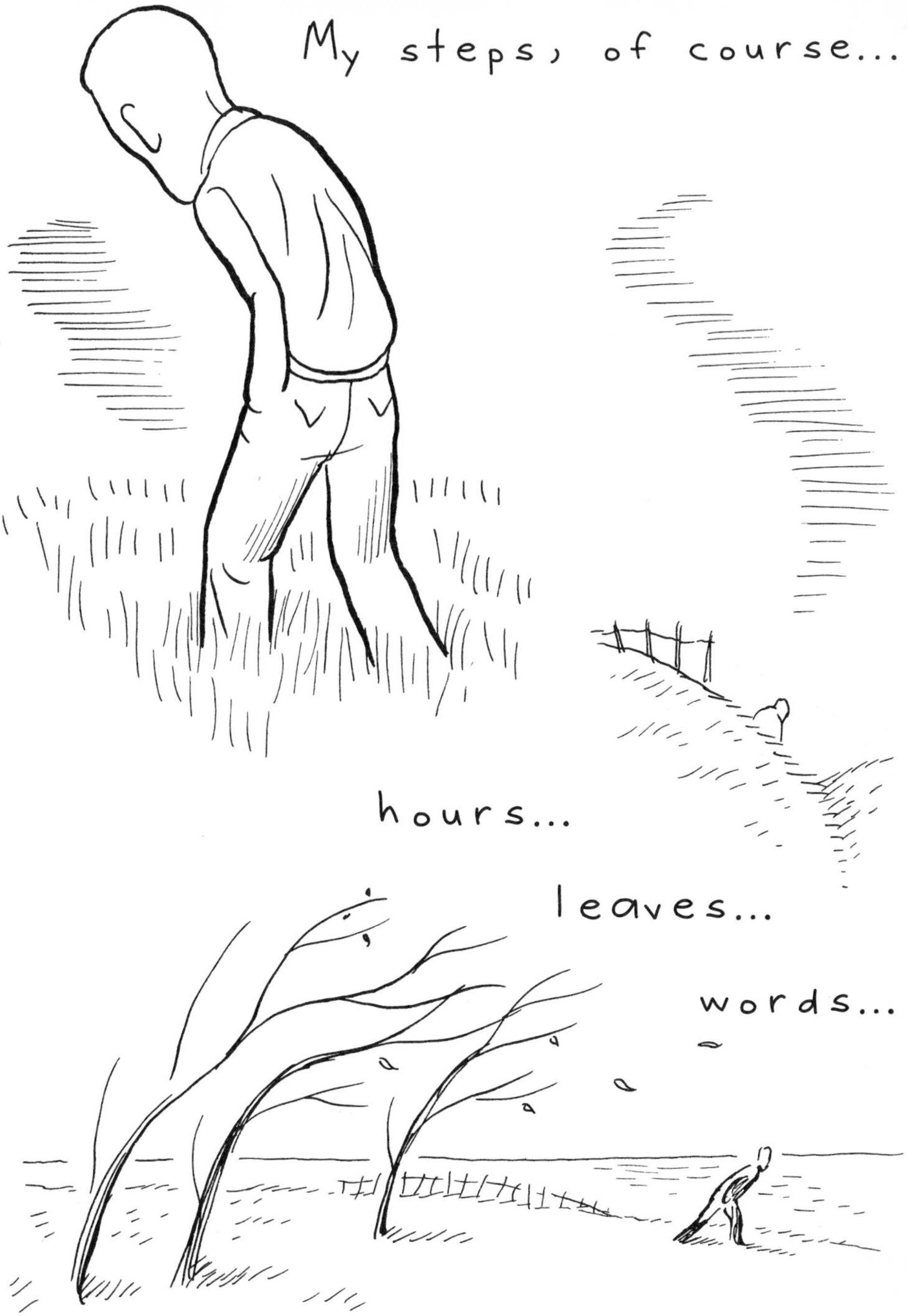

My steps, of course...
hours...
leaves...
words...
The words in these sentences.

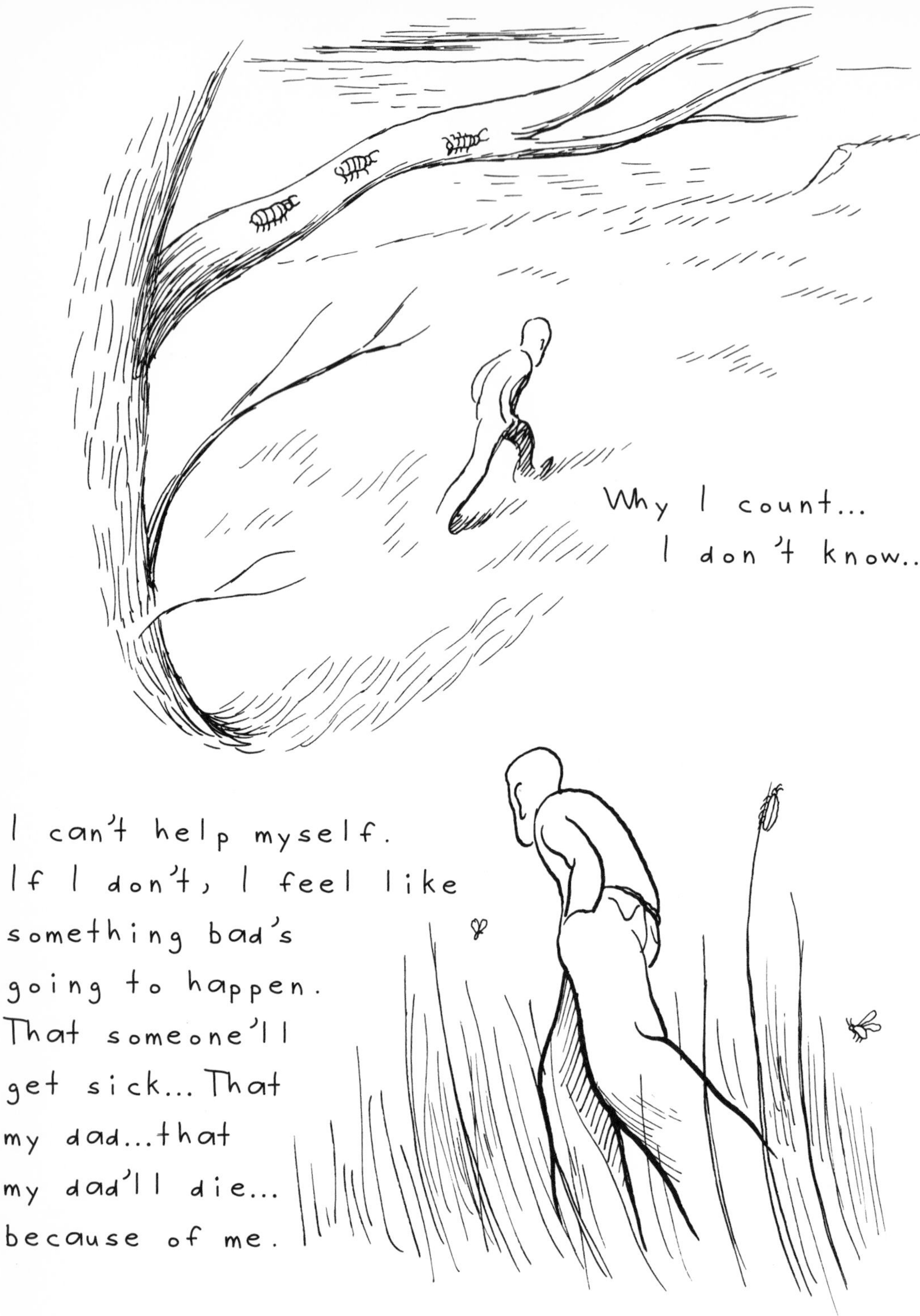
Why I count...
I don't know...
I can't help myself.
If I don't, I feel like
something bad's
going to happen.
That someone'll
get sick... That
my dad... that
my dad'll die...
because of me.

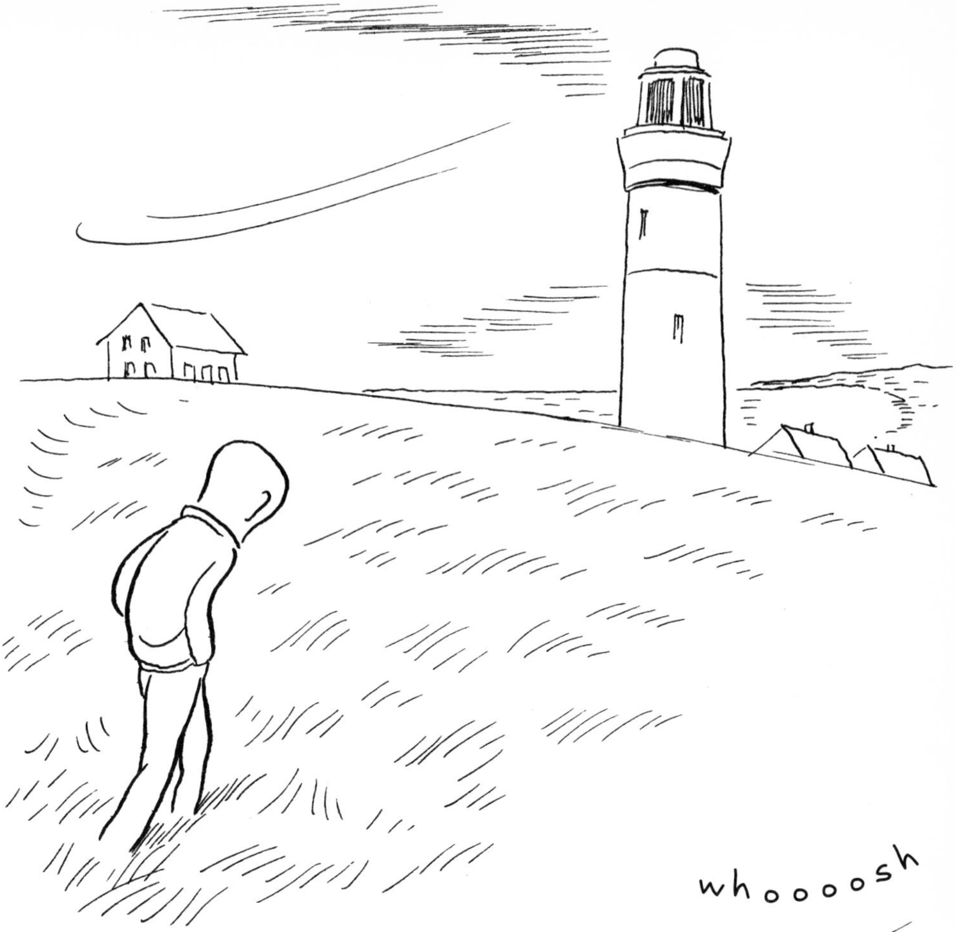

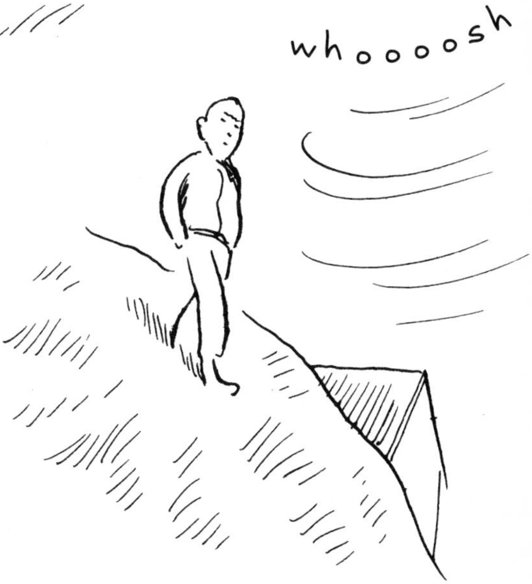
whoooosh

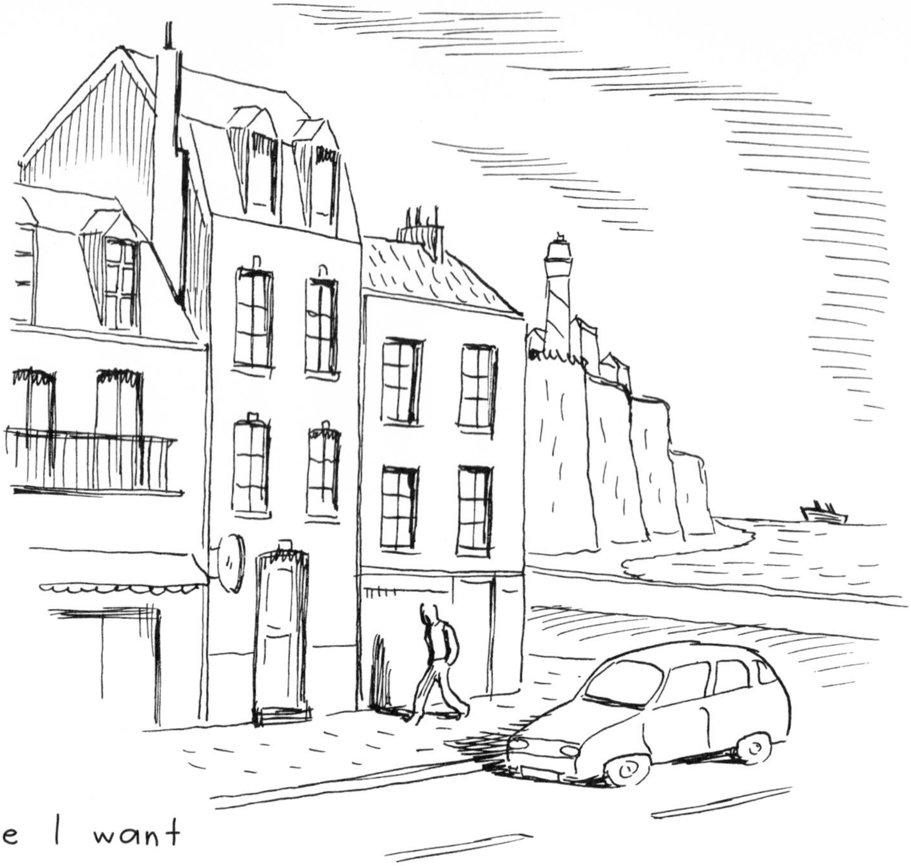

Maybe I want
him to die,
actually.

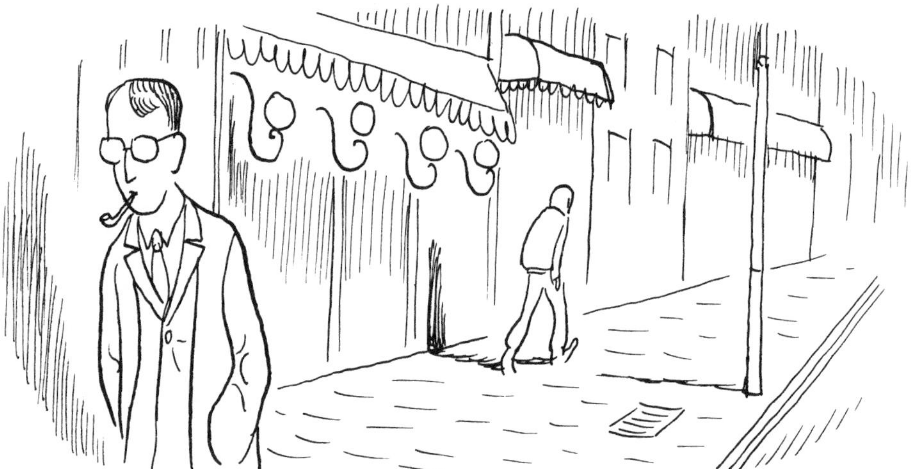

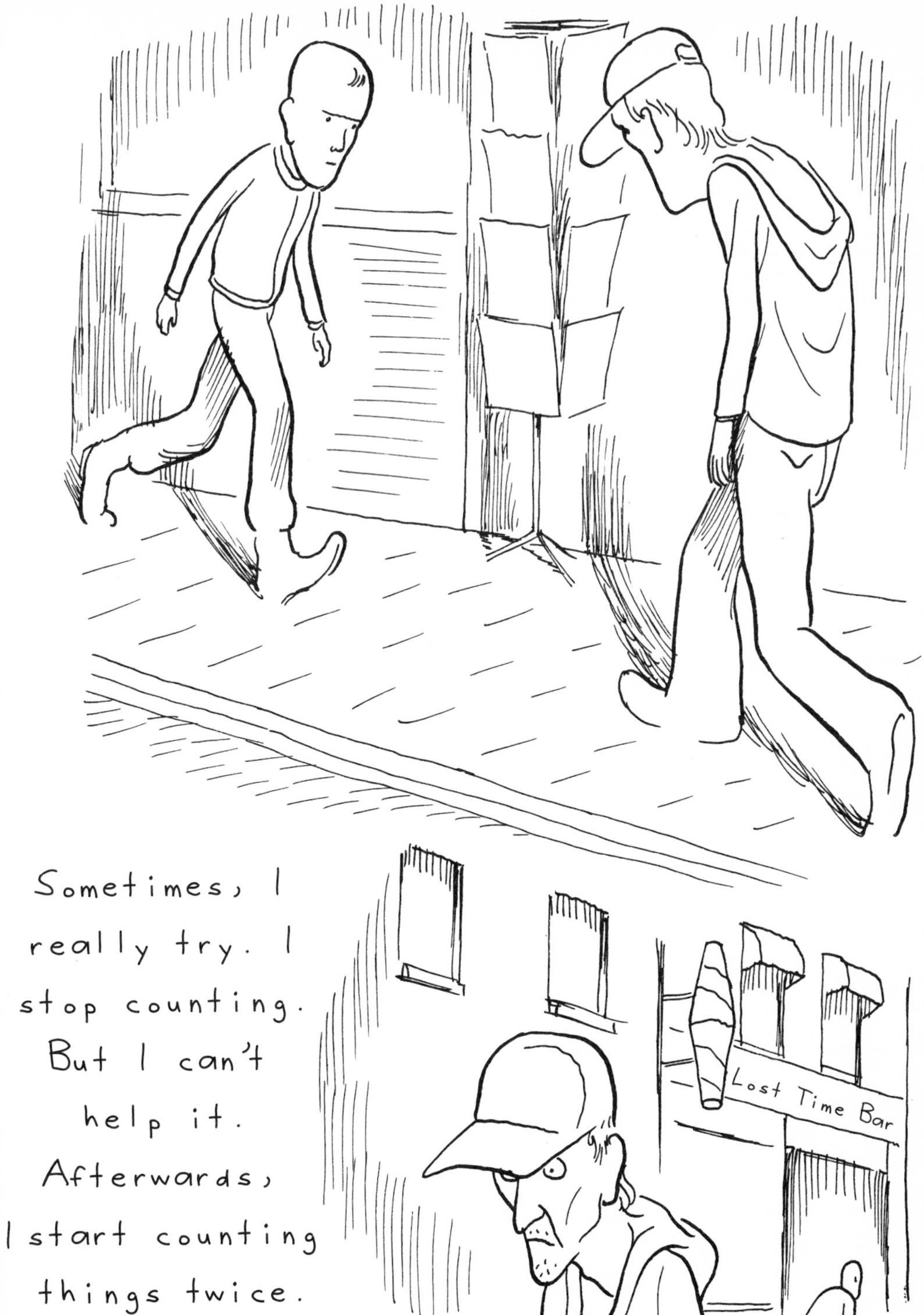
Sometimes, I really try. I stop counting. But I can't help it. Afterwards, I start counting things twice.
Lost Time Bar

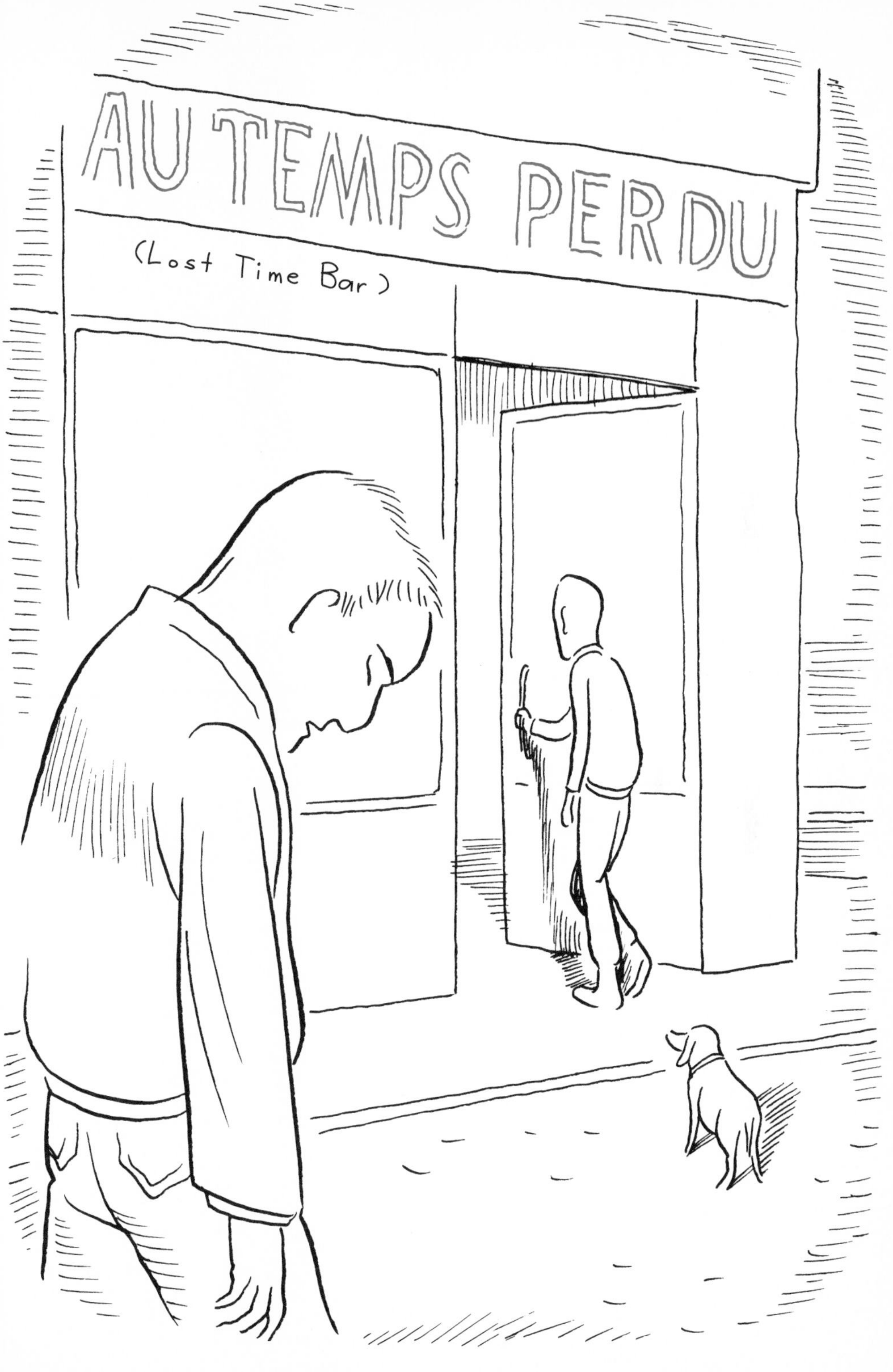
AU TEMPS PERDU
(Lost Time Bar)

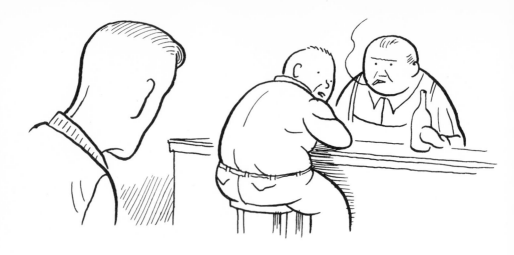

Uh...have you
seen my dad,
Mr. Jacky?

You! You're just
in time. Your
dad's in back,
and what with all
he's had, he's
starting to make
quite a scene.

You call yourselves sailors!
I say you're a buncha fairies who
run from a stiff breeze!

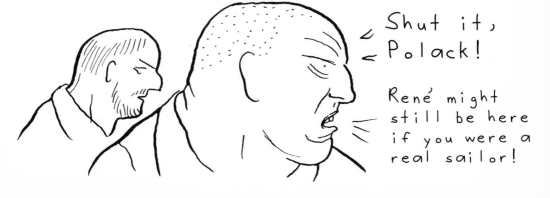

Shut it,
Polack!

René might
still be here
if you were a
real sailor!

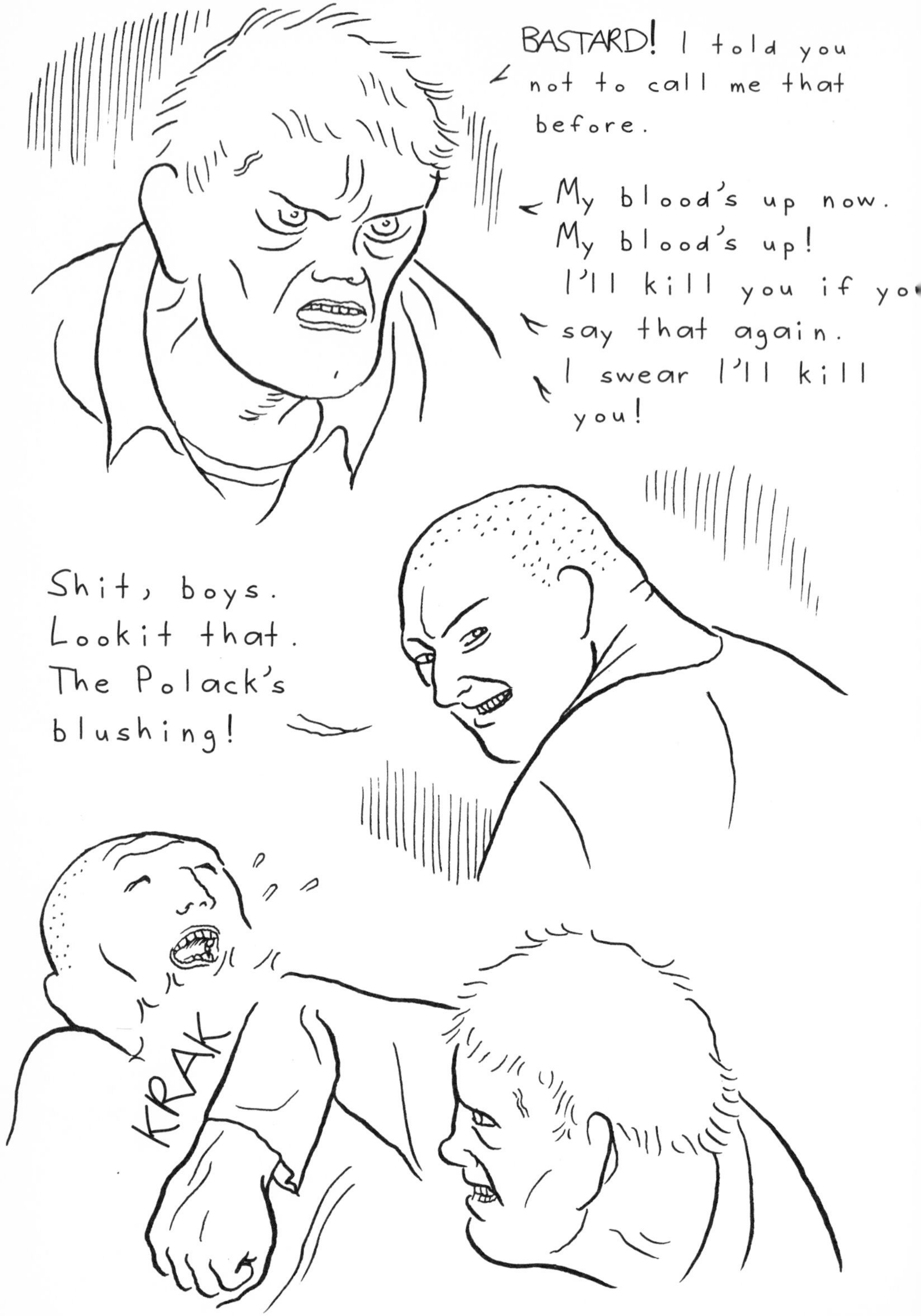
BASTARD! I told you not to call me that before.
My blood's up now. My blood's up! I'll kill you if you say that again. I swear I'll kill you!
Shit, boys. Lookit that. The Polack's blushing!
KRAK

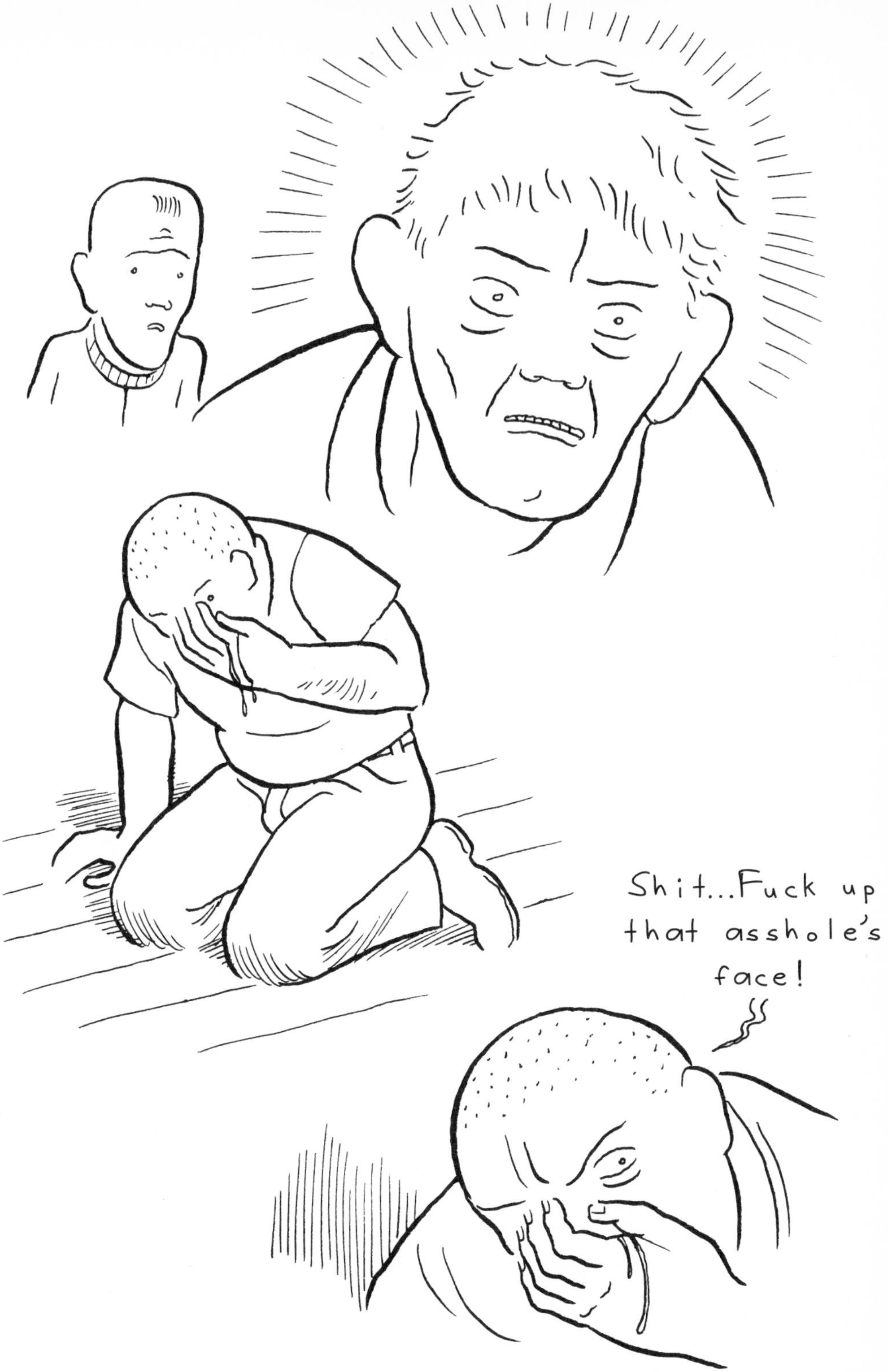
Shit...Fuck up that asshole's face!

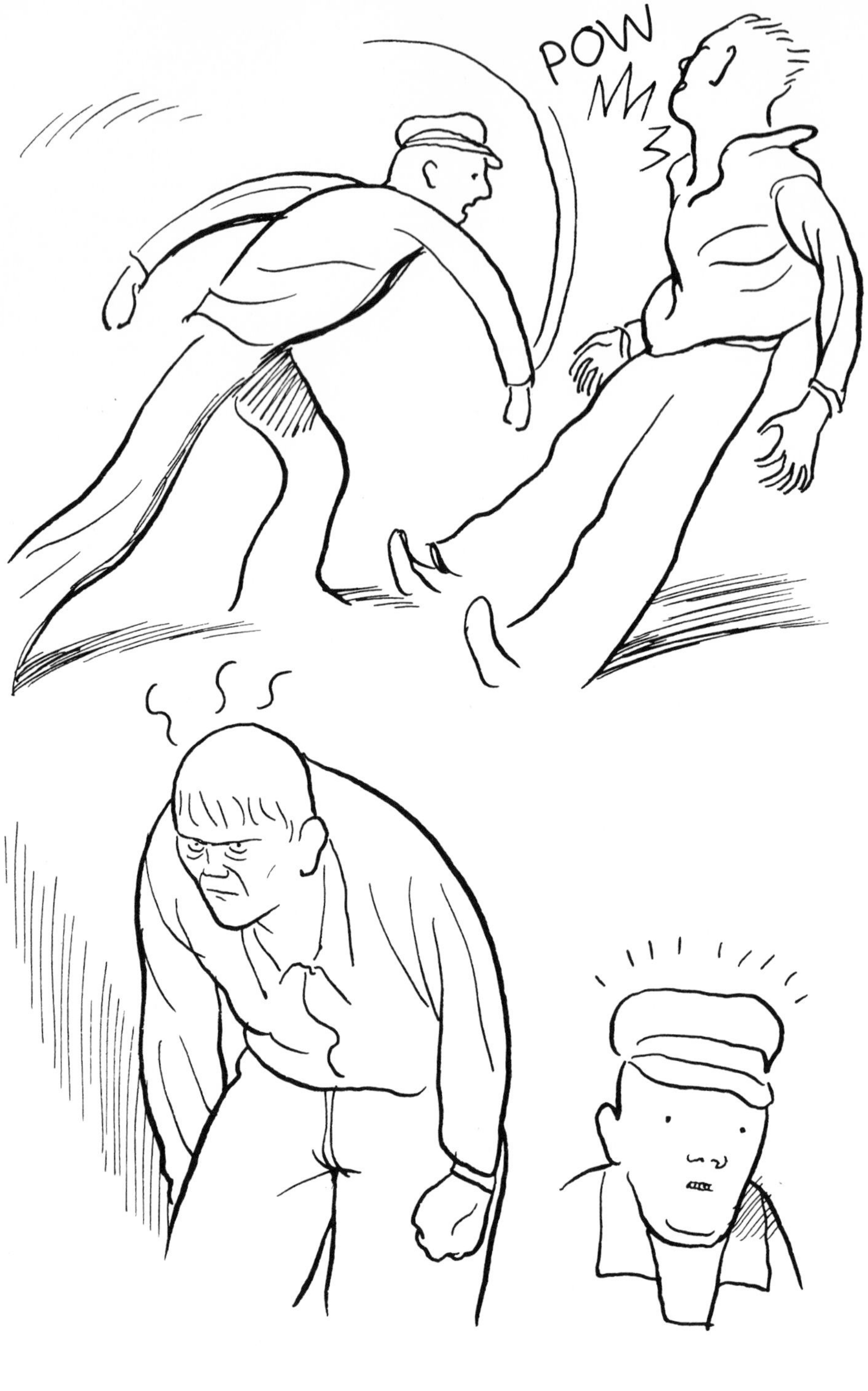
POW

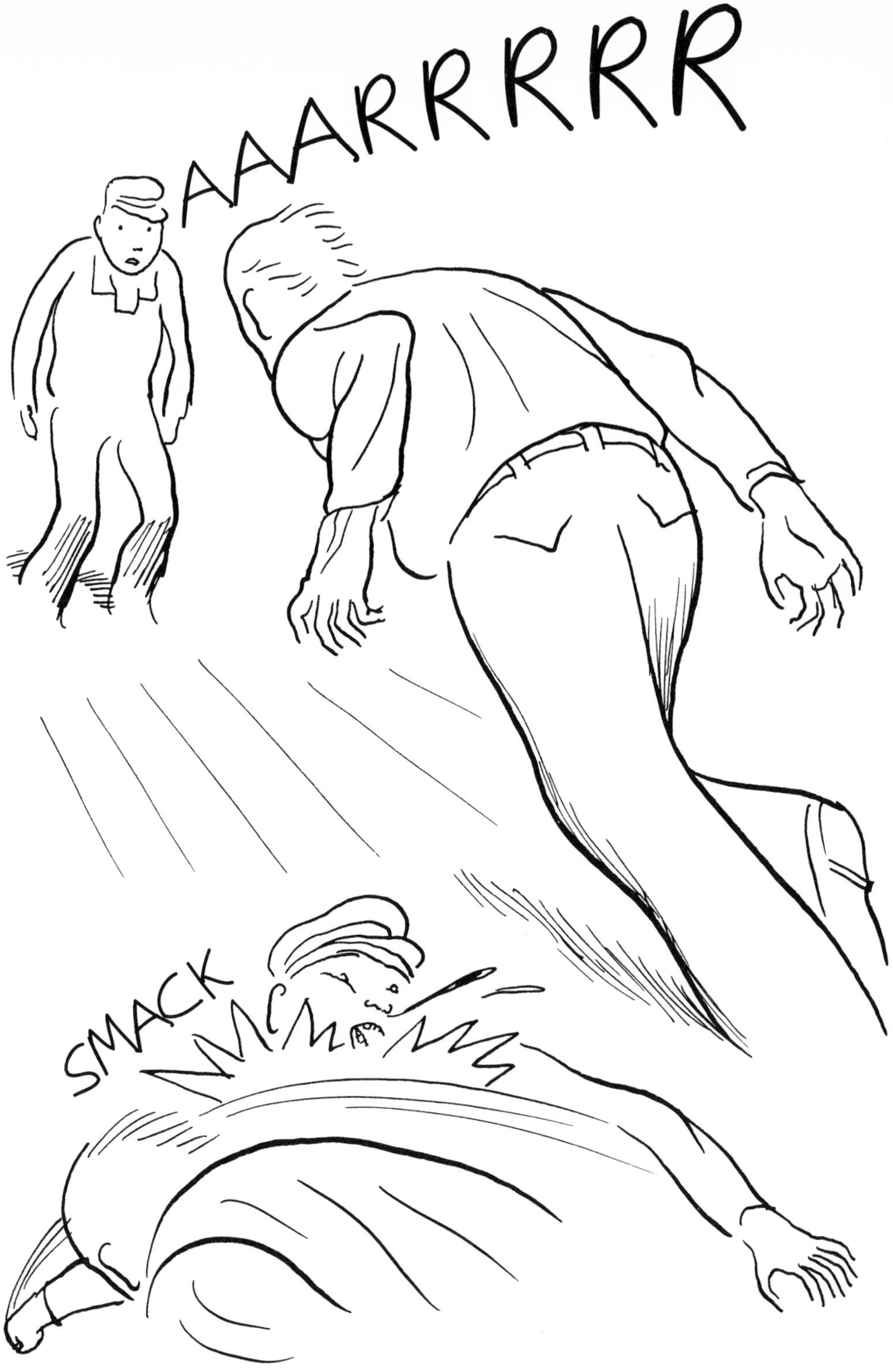
AAARRRRRR
SMACK

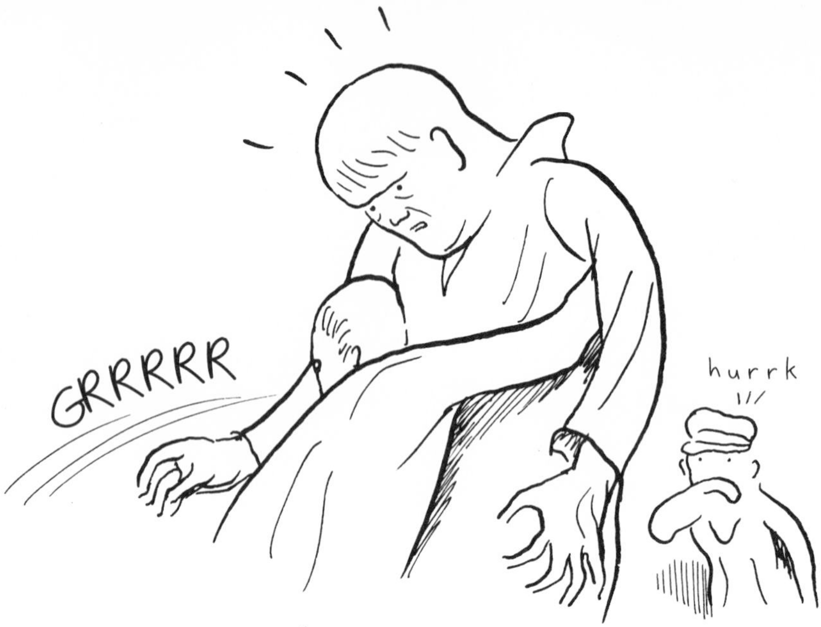
GRRRRR
hurrk

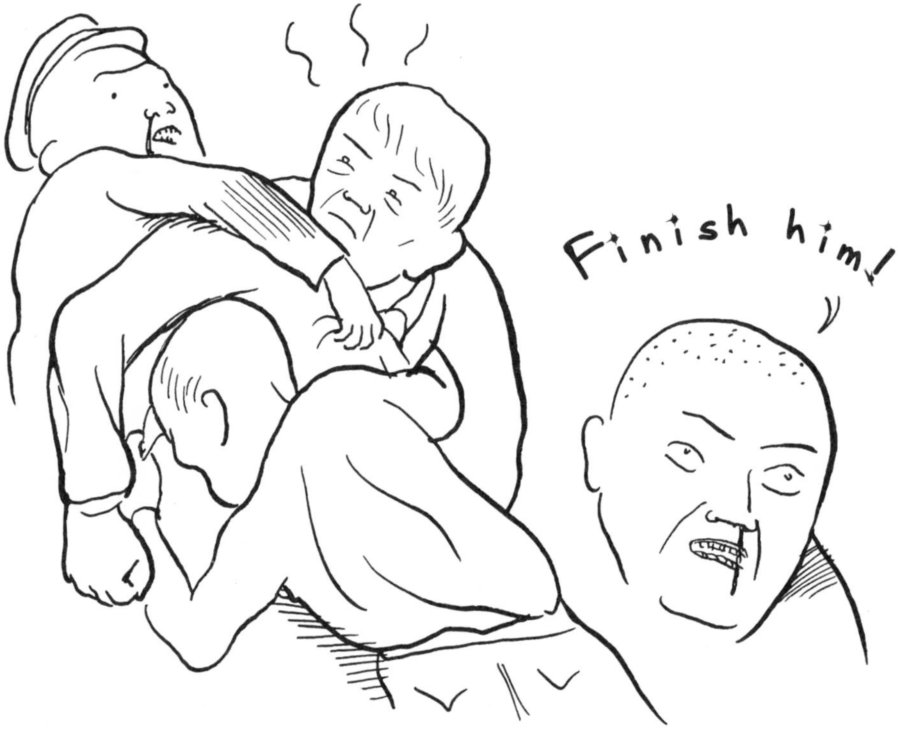
Finish him!

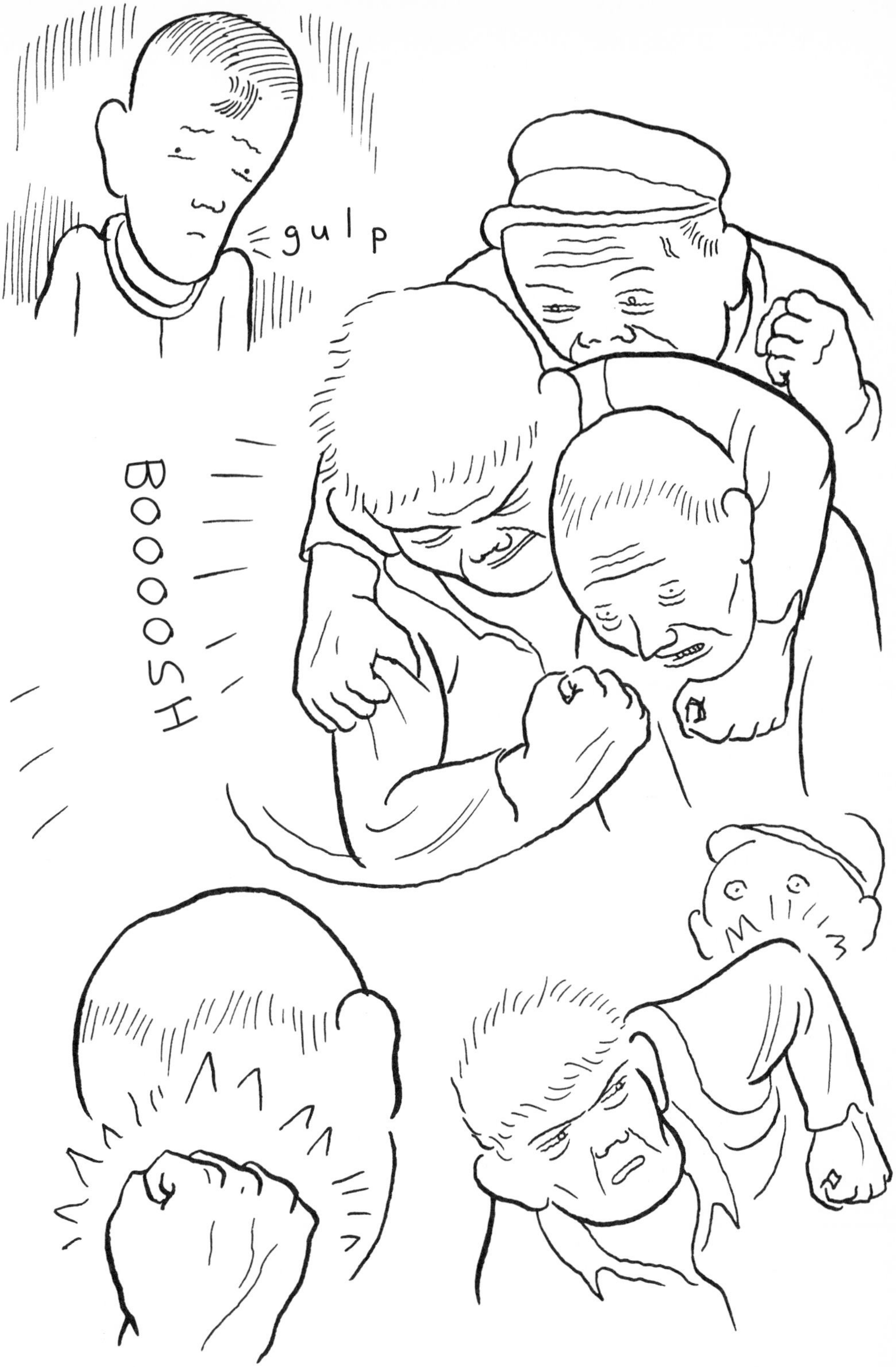
gulp
BOOOOSH

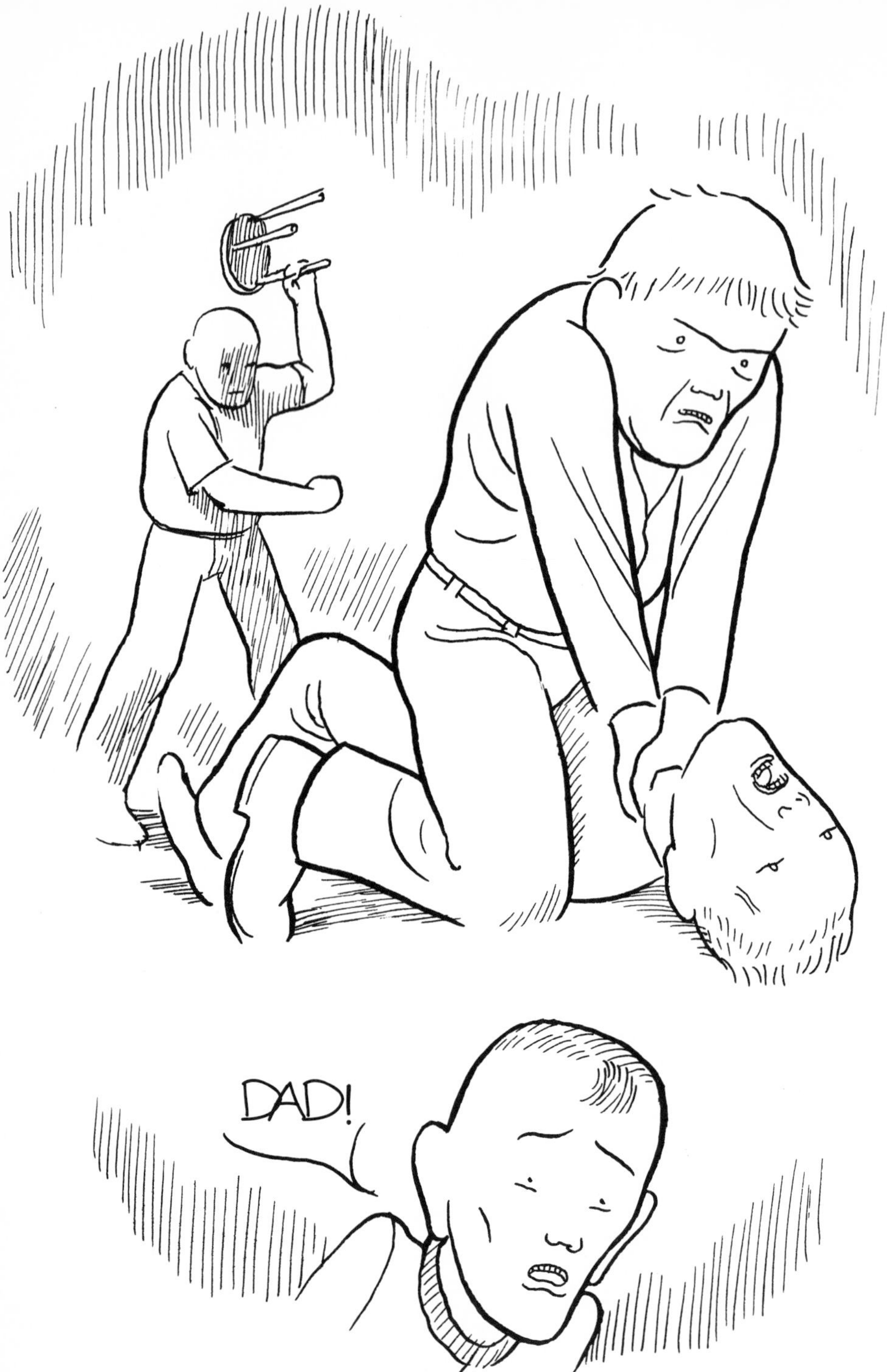
DAD!

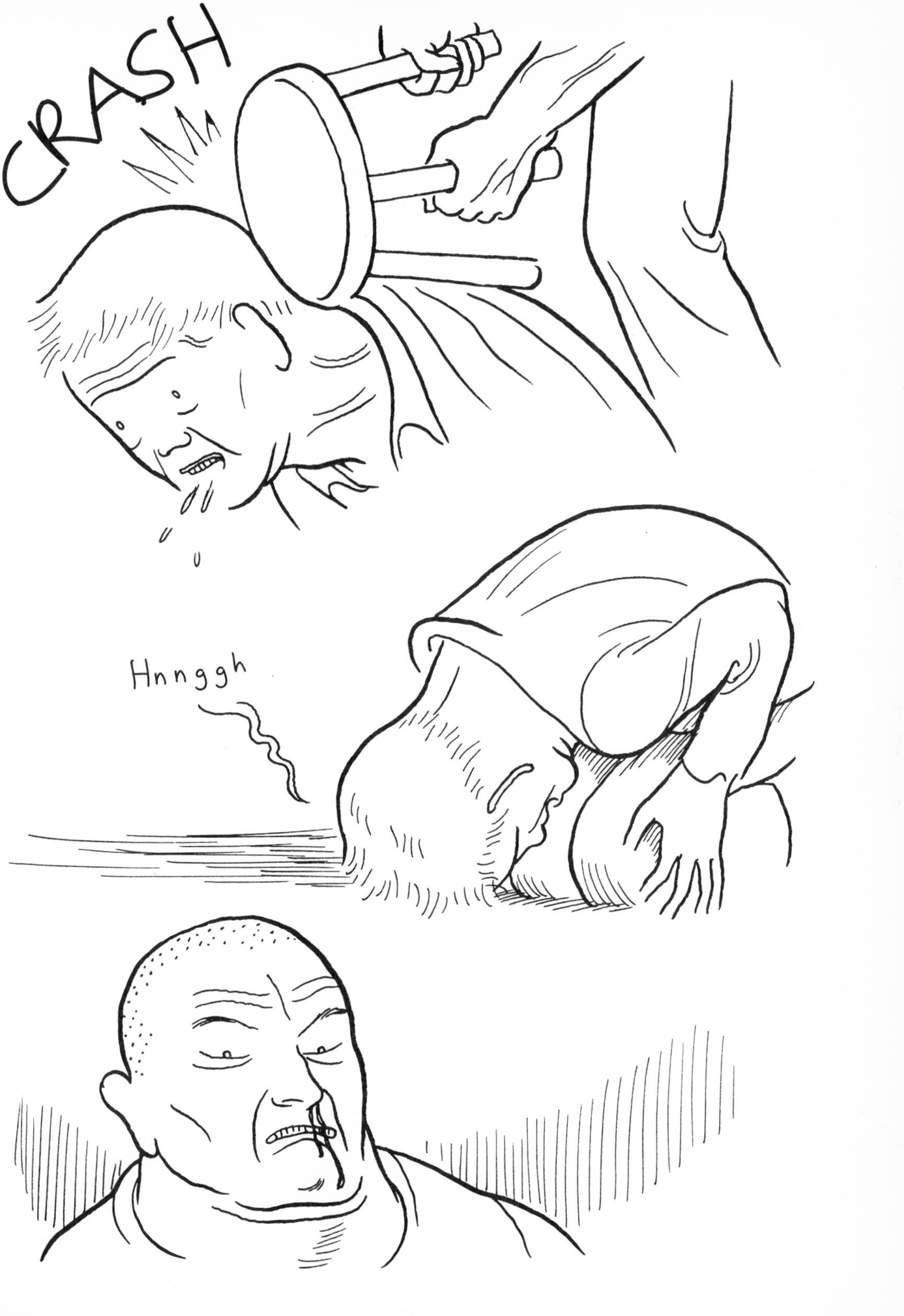
CRASH
Hnnggh

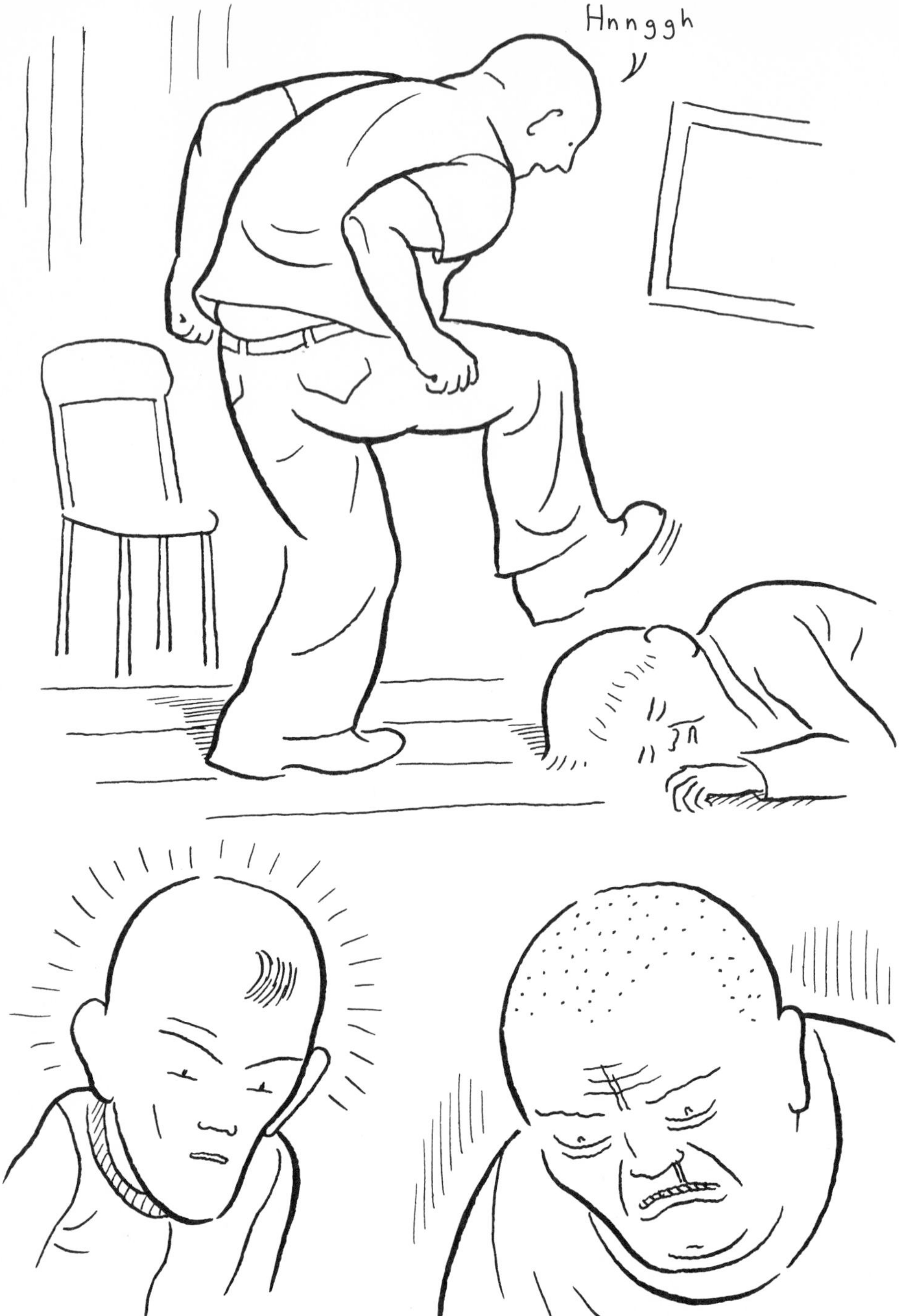
Hnnggh

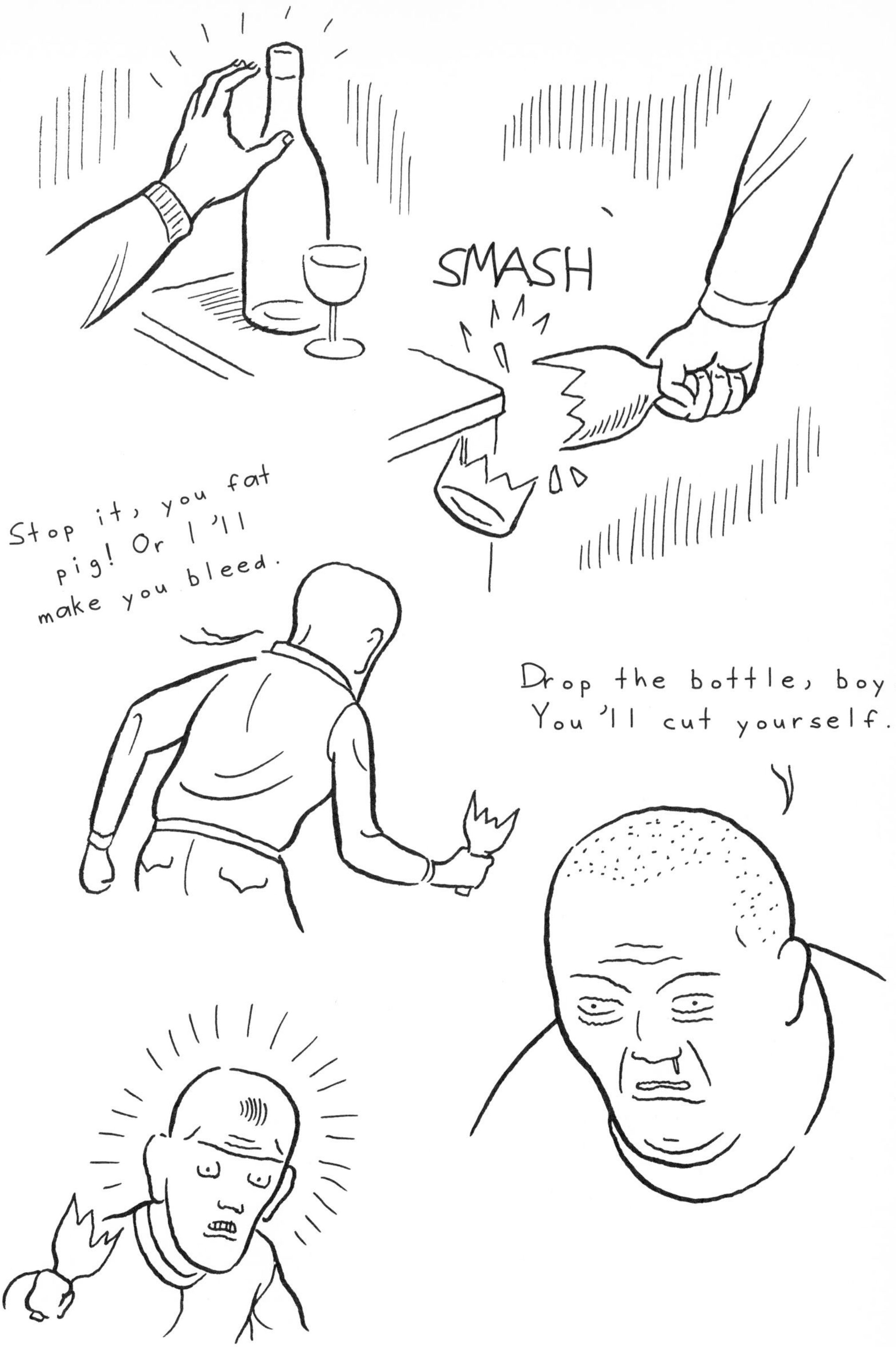
SMASH
Stop it, you fat pig! Or I'll make you bleed.
Drop the bottle, boy. You'll cut yourself.

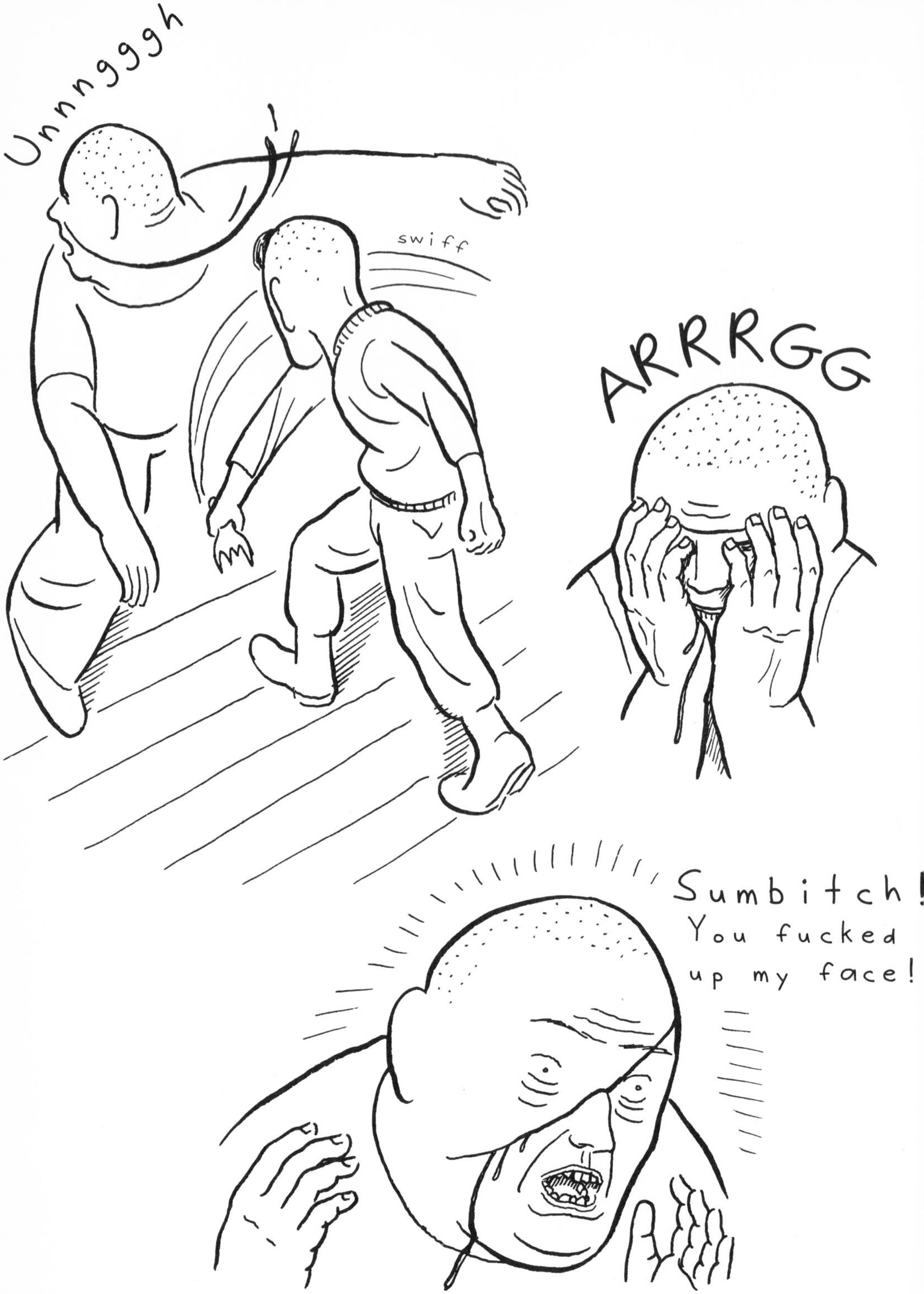
Unnngggh
swiff
ARRRGG
Sumbitch!
You fucked up my face!

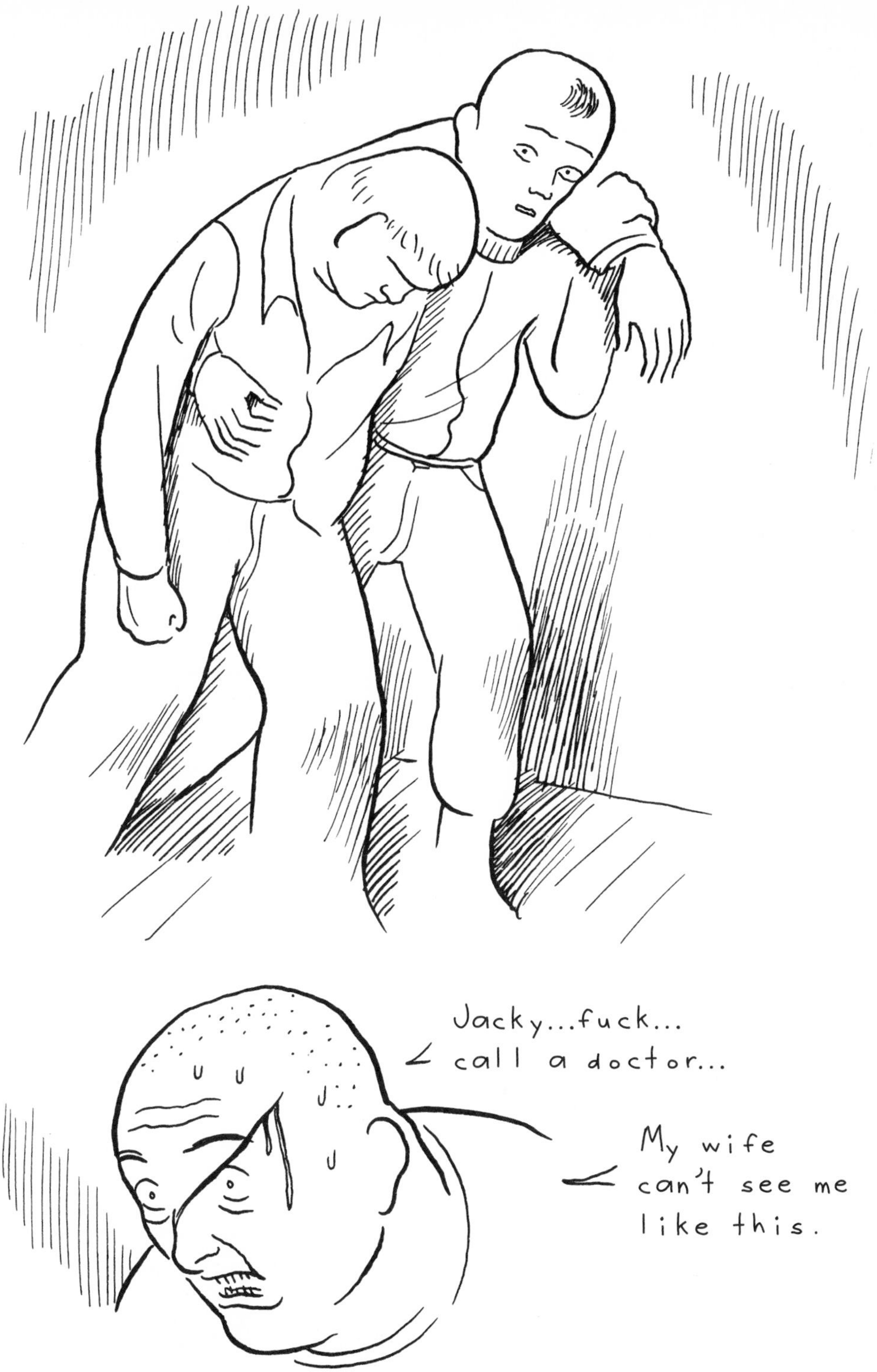
Jacky...fuck...
call a doctor...
My wife can't see me like this.

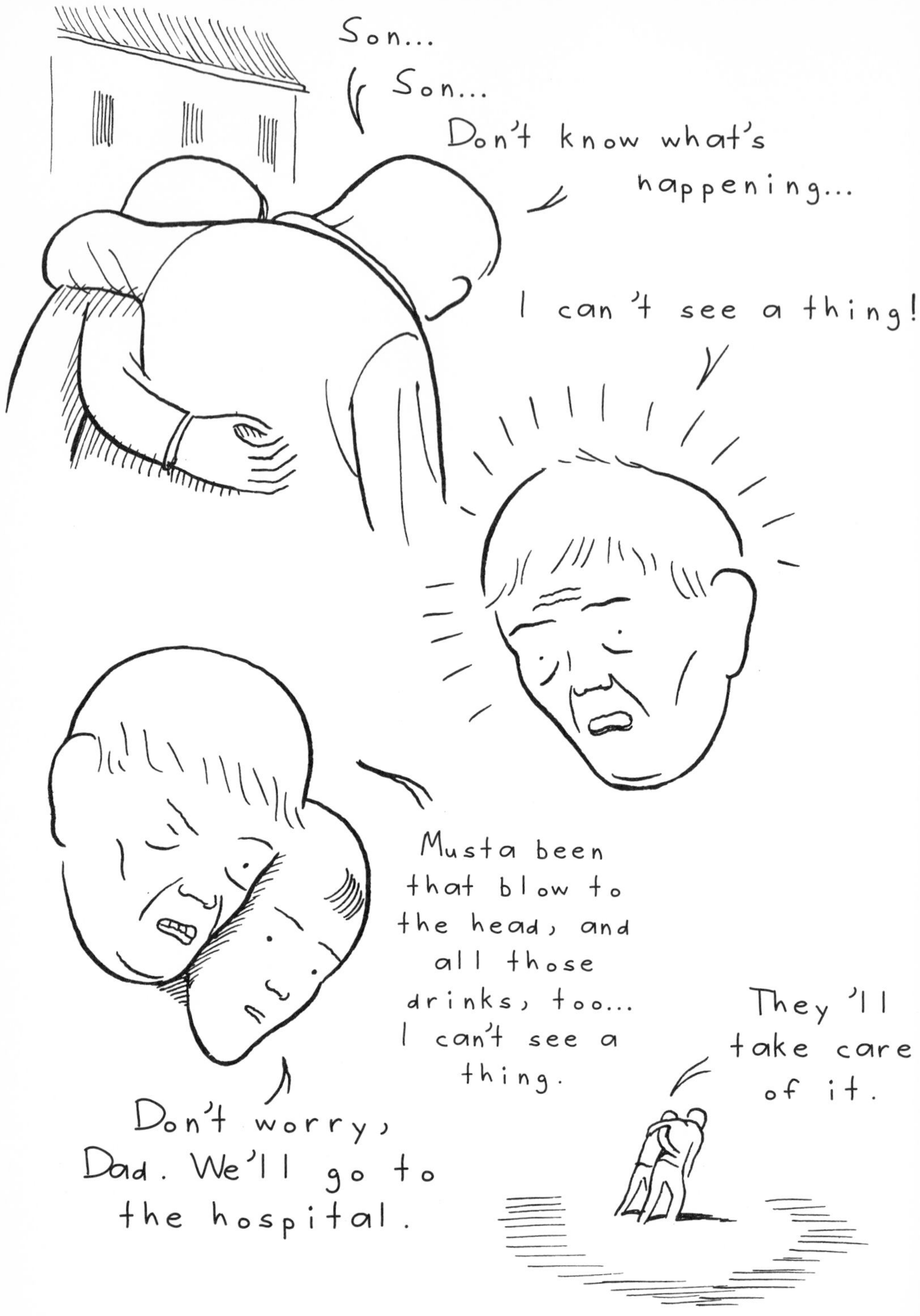
Son...
Son...
Don't know what's happening...
I can't see a thing!
Musta been that blow to the head, and all those drinks, too... I can't see a thing.
Don't worry, Dad. We'll go to the hospital.
They'll take care of it.

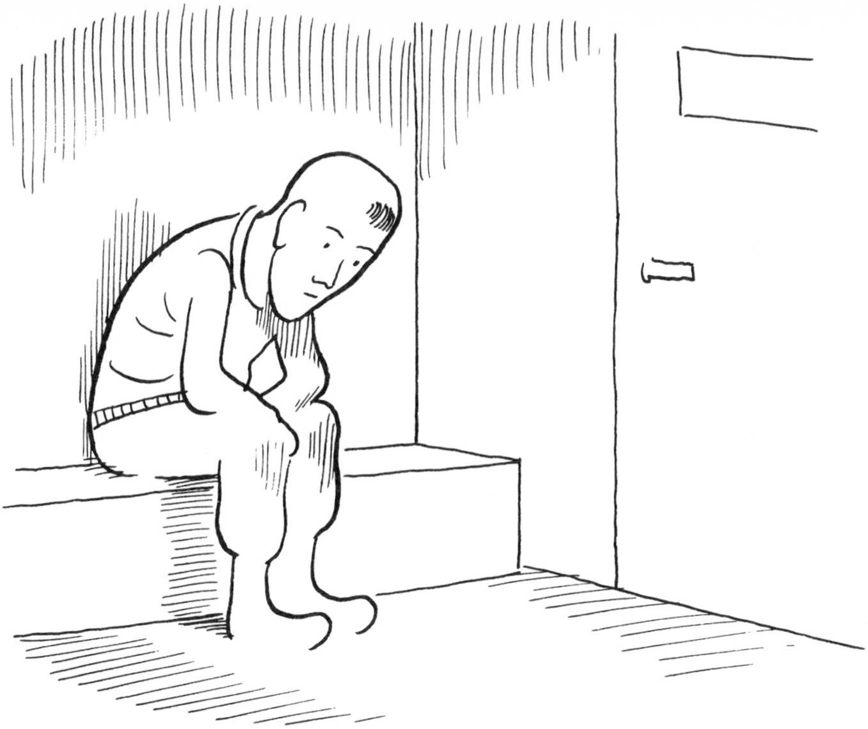

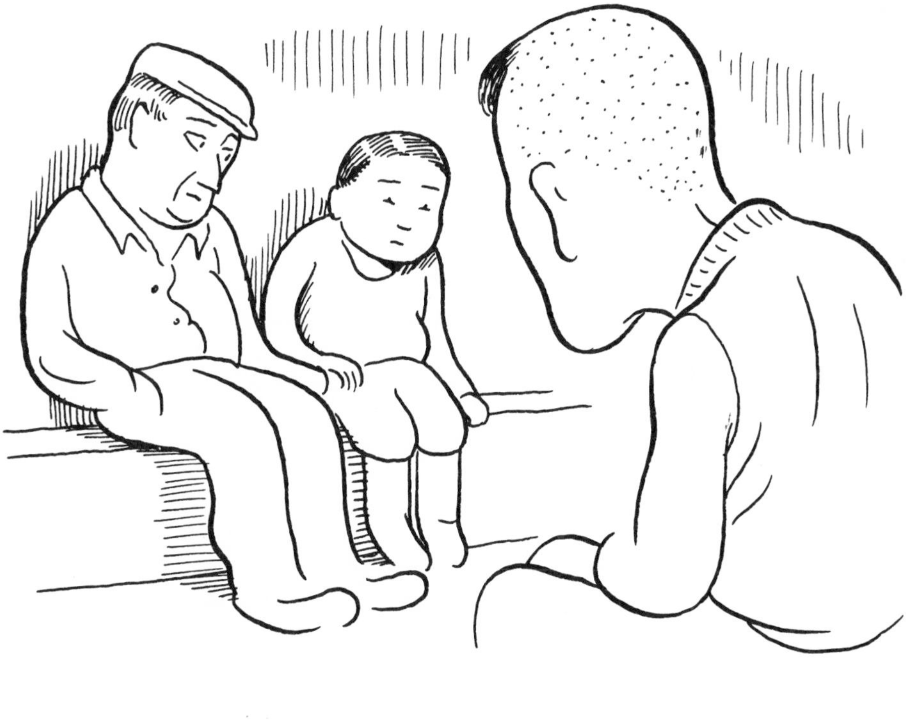

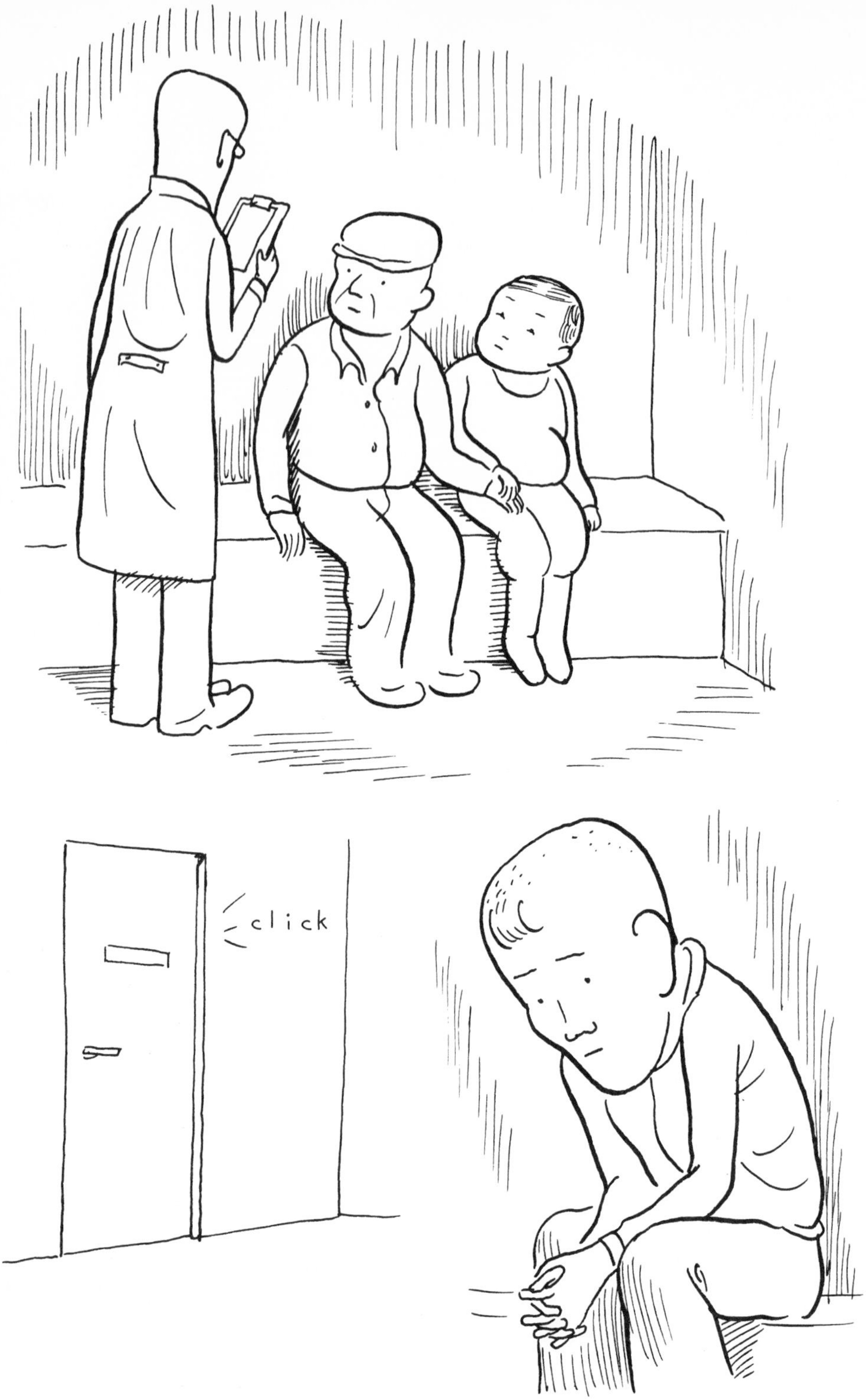
click

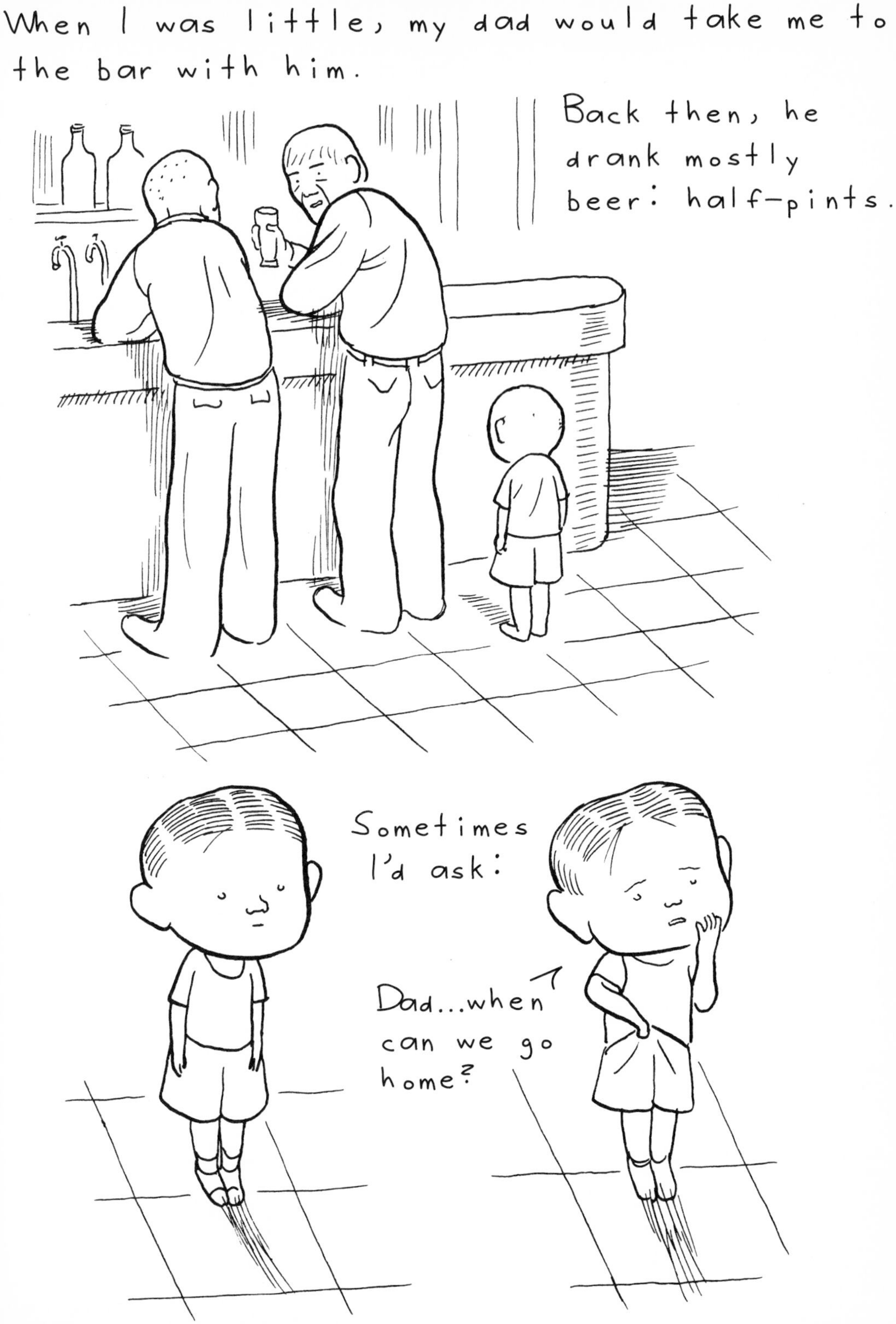
When I was little, my dad would take me to the bar with him.
Back then, he drank mostly beer: half-pints.
Sometimes I'd ask:
Dad...when can we go home?

He'd point to his glass with his big finger:

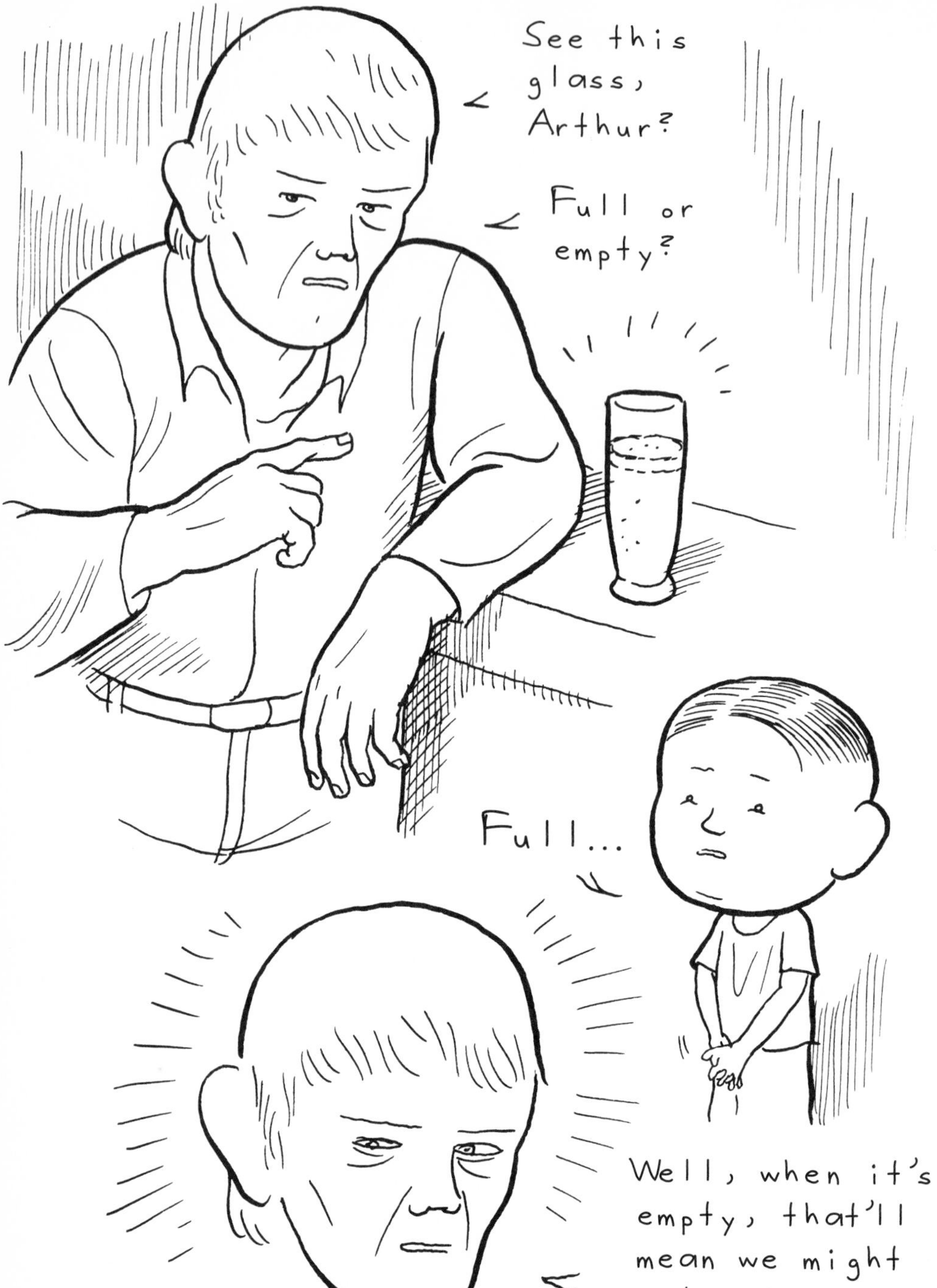
See this glass, Arthur?
Full or empty?
Full...
Well, when it's empty, that'll mean we might get going.

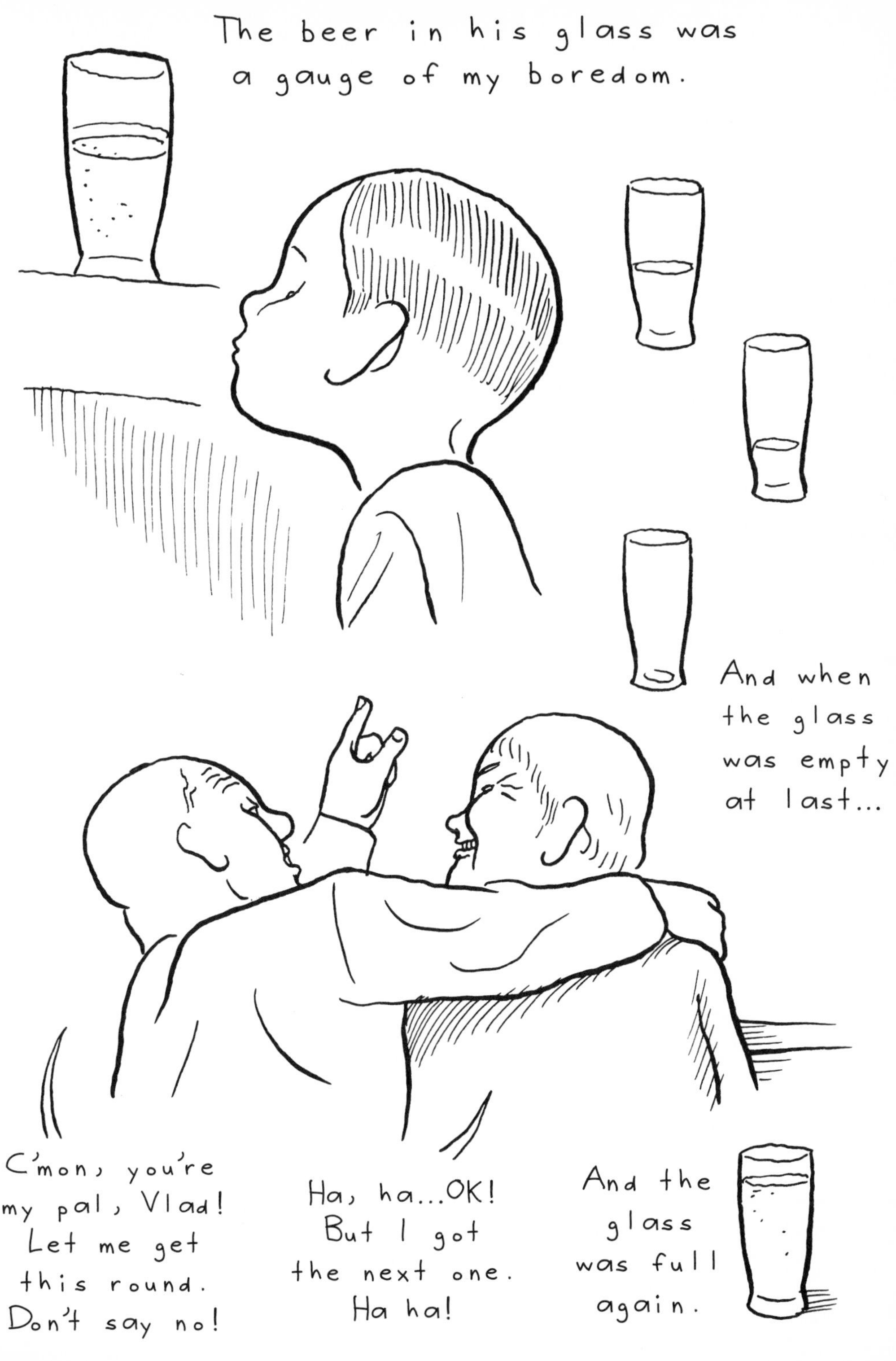
The beer in his glass was a gauge of my boredom.
And when the glass was empty at last...
C'mon, you're my pal, Vlad! Let me get this round. Don't say no!
Ha, ha...OK! But I got the next one. Ha ha!
And the glass was full again.

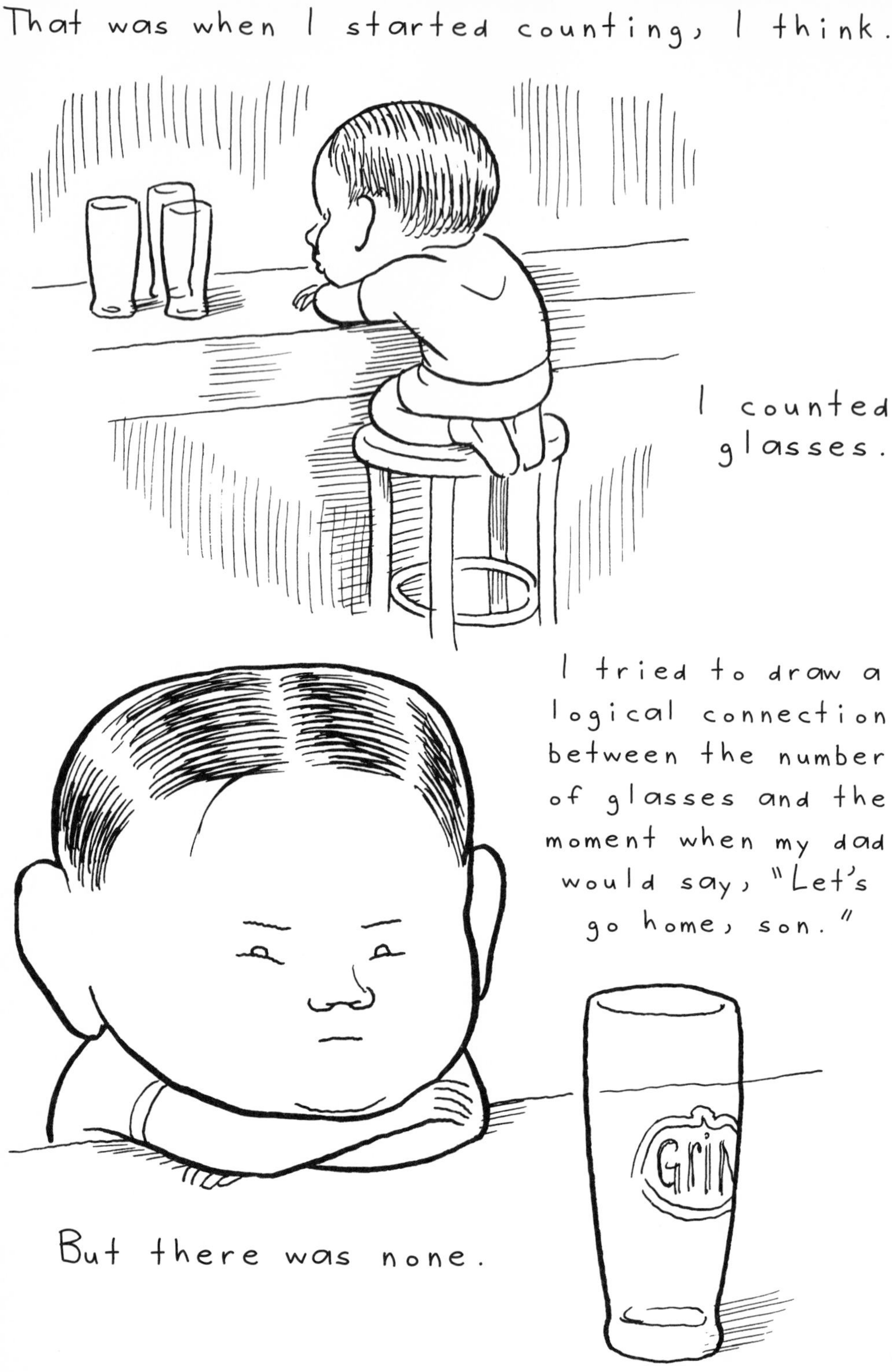
That was when I started counting, I think.
I counted glasses.
I tried to draw a logical connection between the number of glasses and the moment when my dad would say, "Let's go home, son."
But there was none.

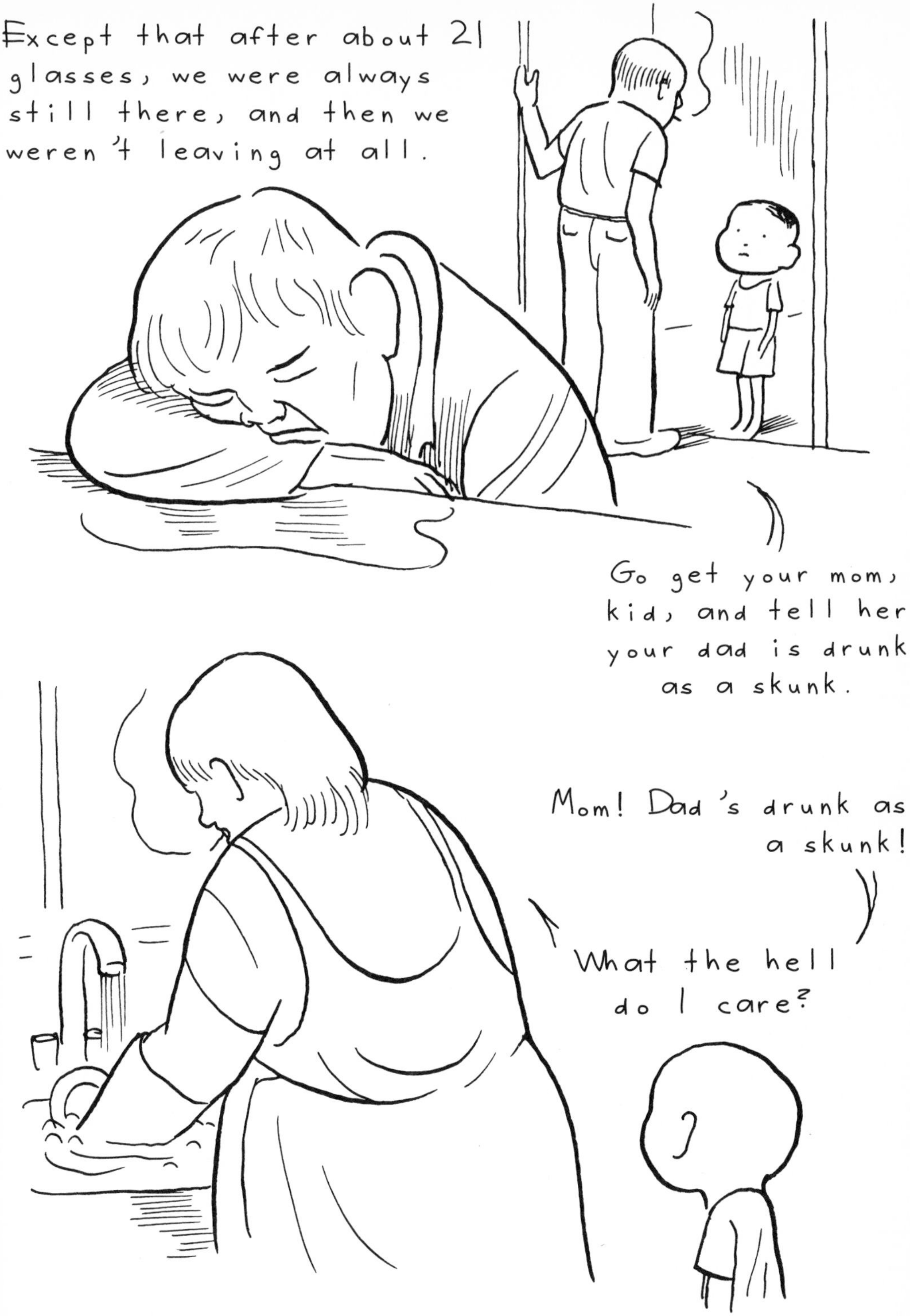
Except that after about 21 glasses, we were always still there, and then we weren't leaving at all.
Go get your mom, kid, and tell her your dad is drunk as a skunk.
Mom! Dad's drunk as a skunk!
What the hell do I care?

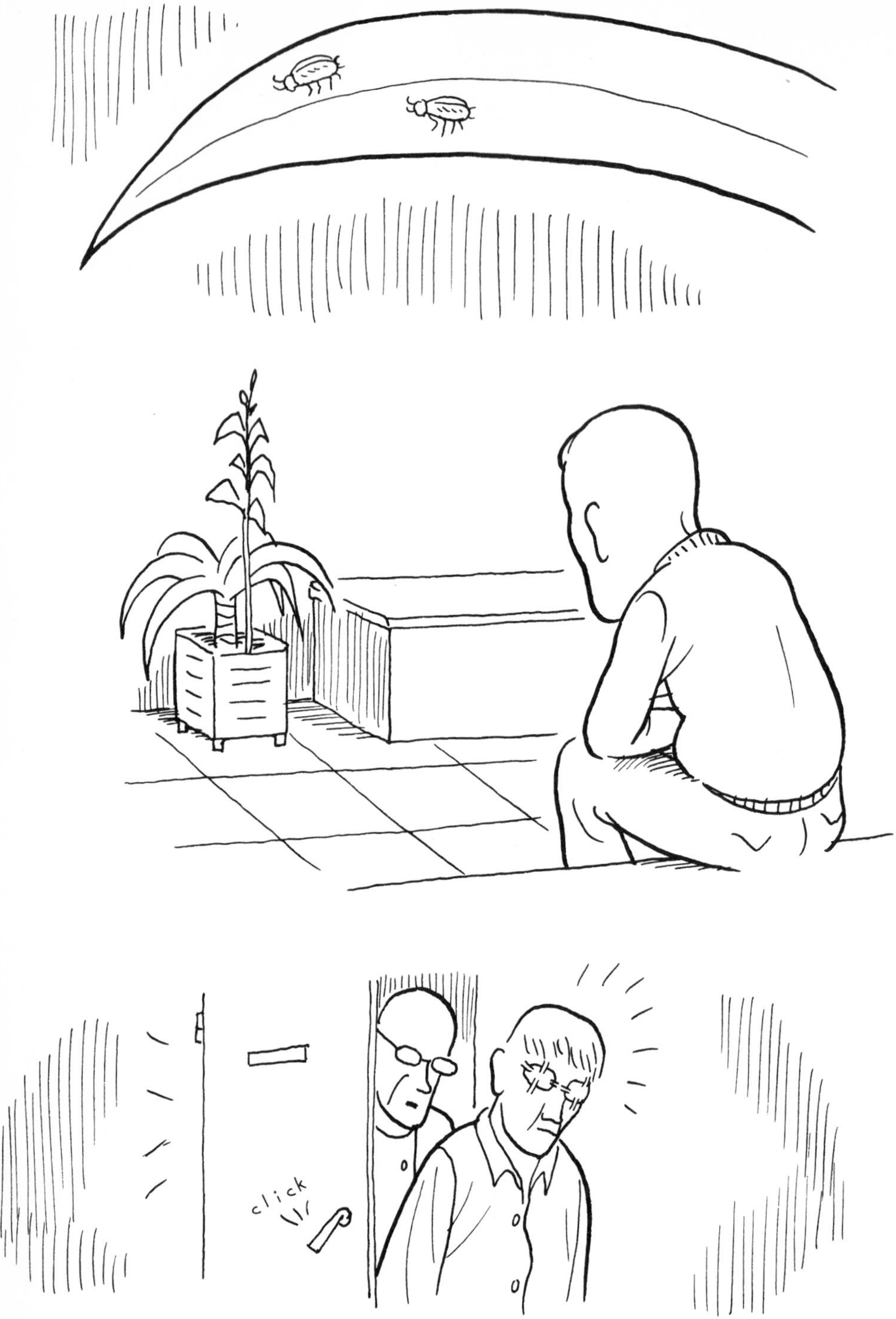
click

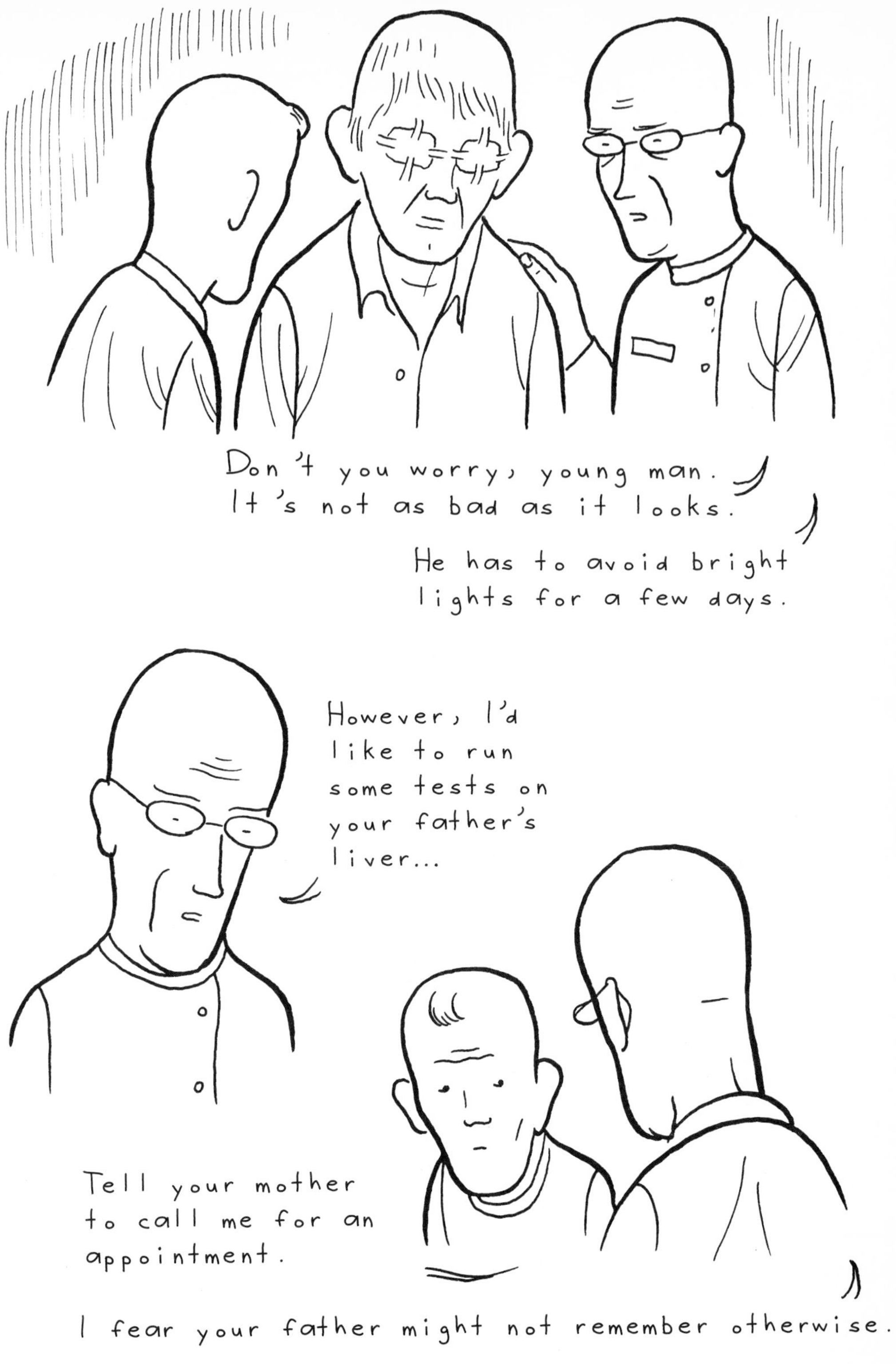
Don't you worry, young man. It's not as bad as it looks.
He has to avoid bright lights for a few days.
However, I'd like to run some tests on your father's liver...
Tell your mother to call me for an appointment.
I fear your father might not remember otherwise.

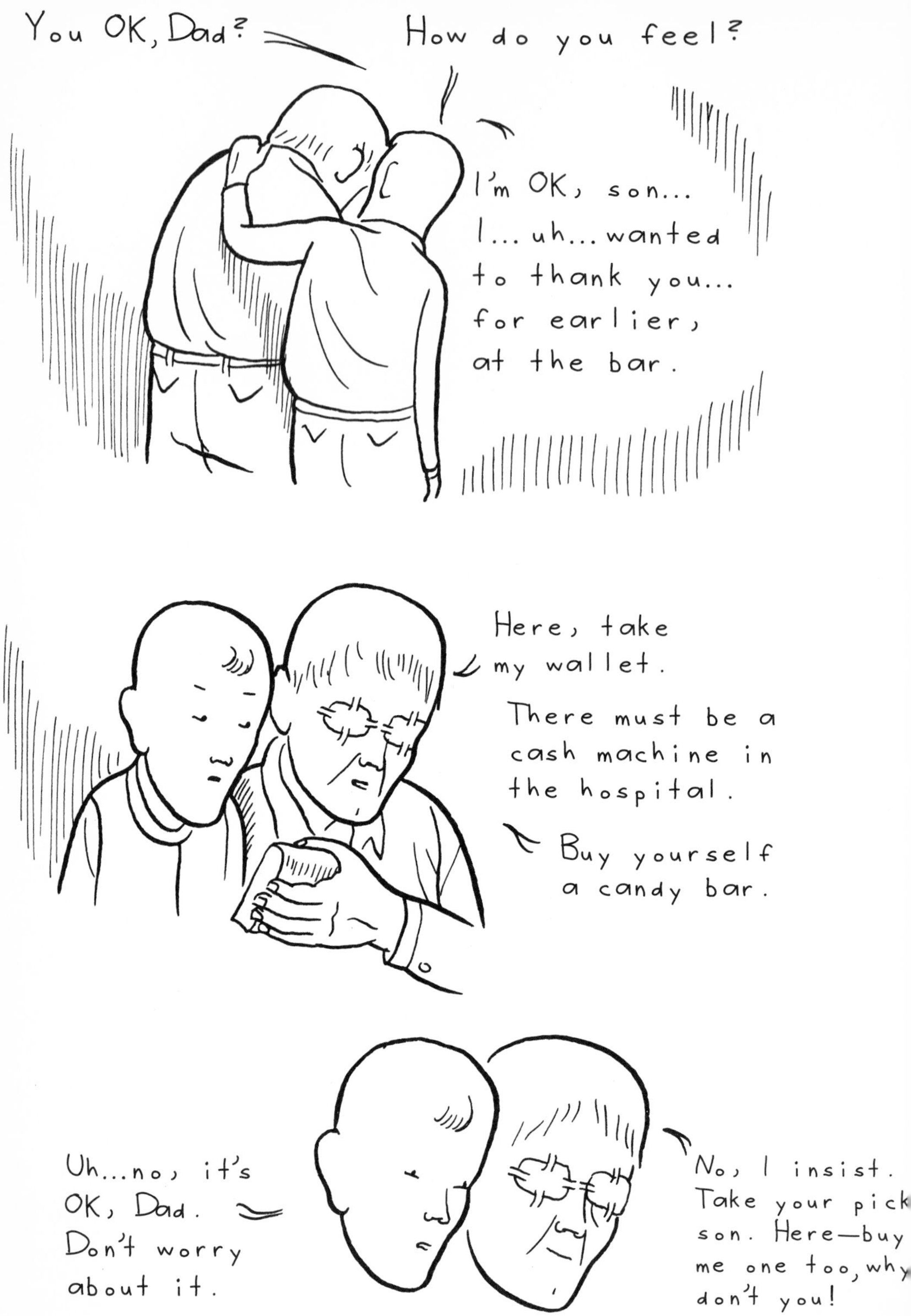

You OK, Dad?
How do you feel?
I'm OK, son... I... uh... wanted to thank you... for earlier, at the bar.
Here, take my wallet.
There must be a cash machine in the hospital.
Buy yourself a candy bar.
Uh...no, it's OK, Dad. Don't worry about it.
No, I insist. Take your pick son. Here—buy me one too, why don't you!

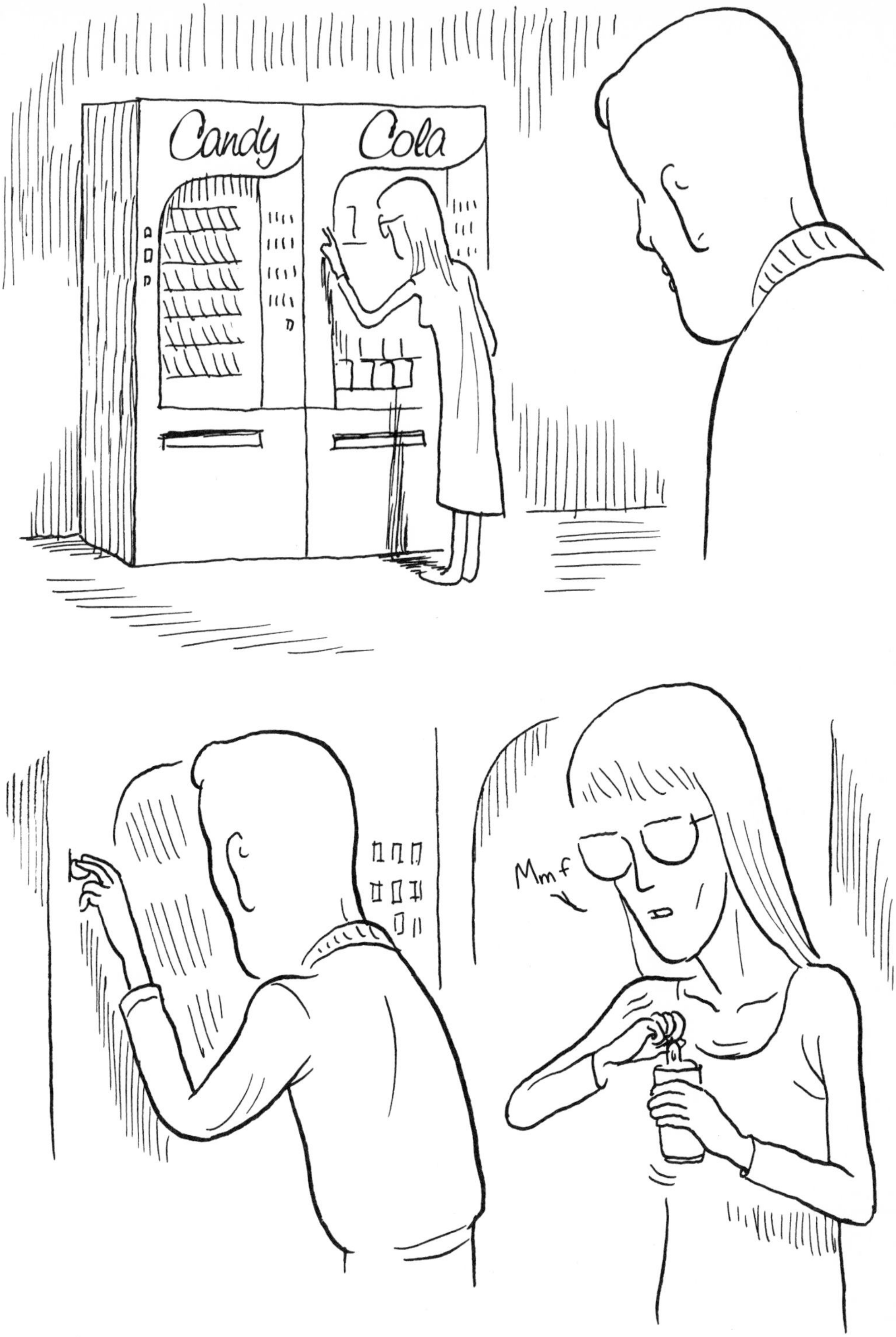
Candy
Cola
Mmf

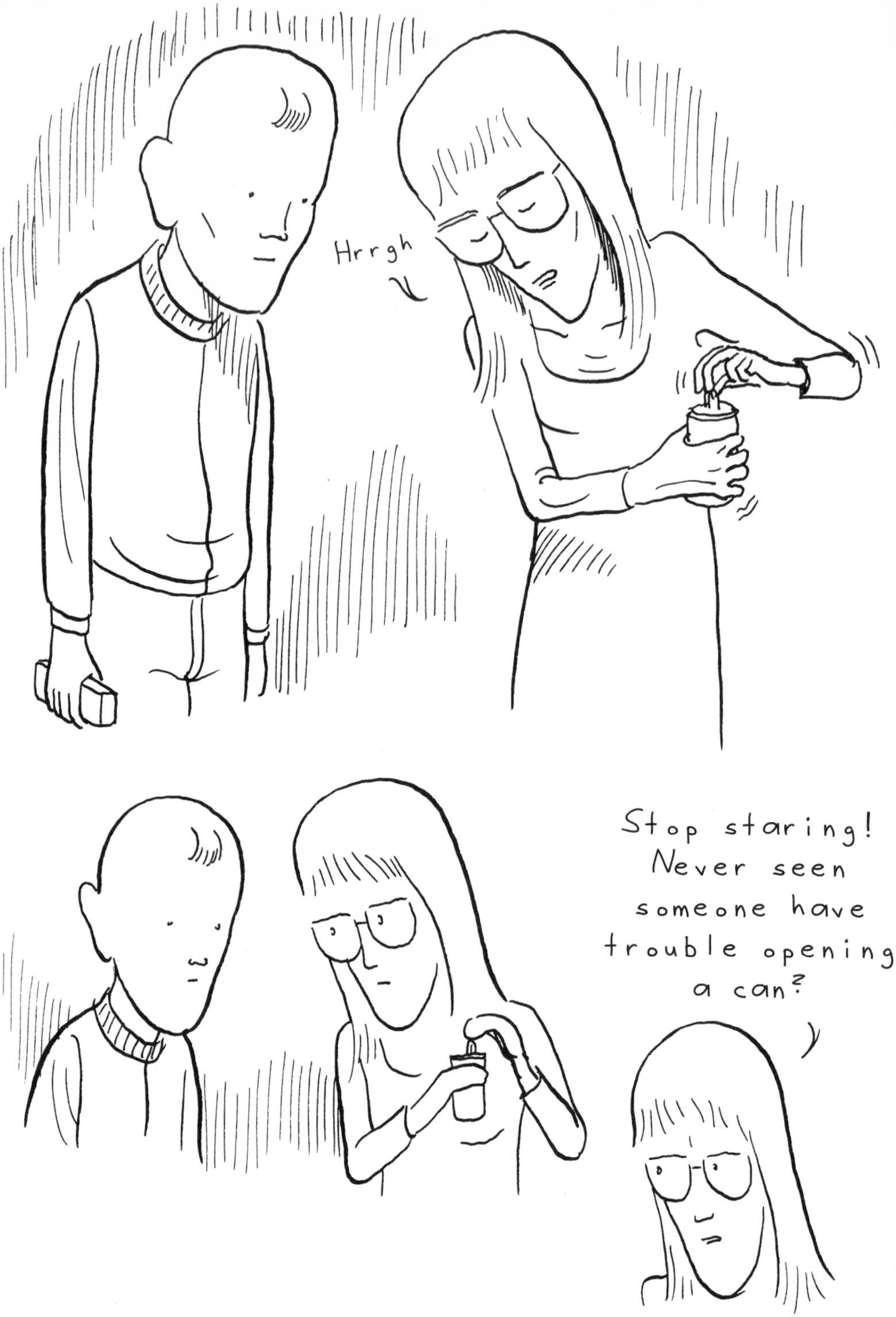
Hrrgh
Stop staring! Never seen someone have trouble opening a can?

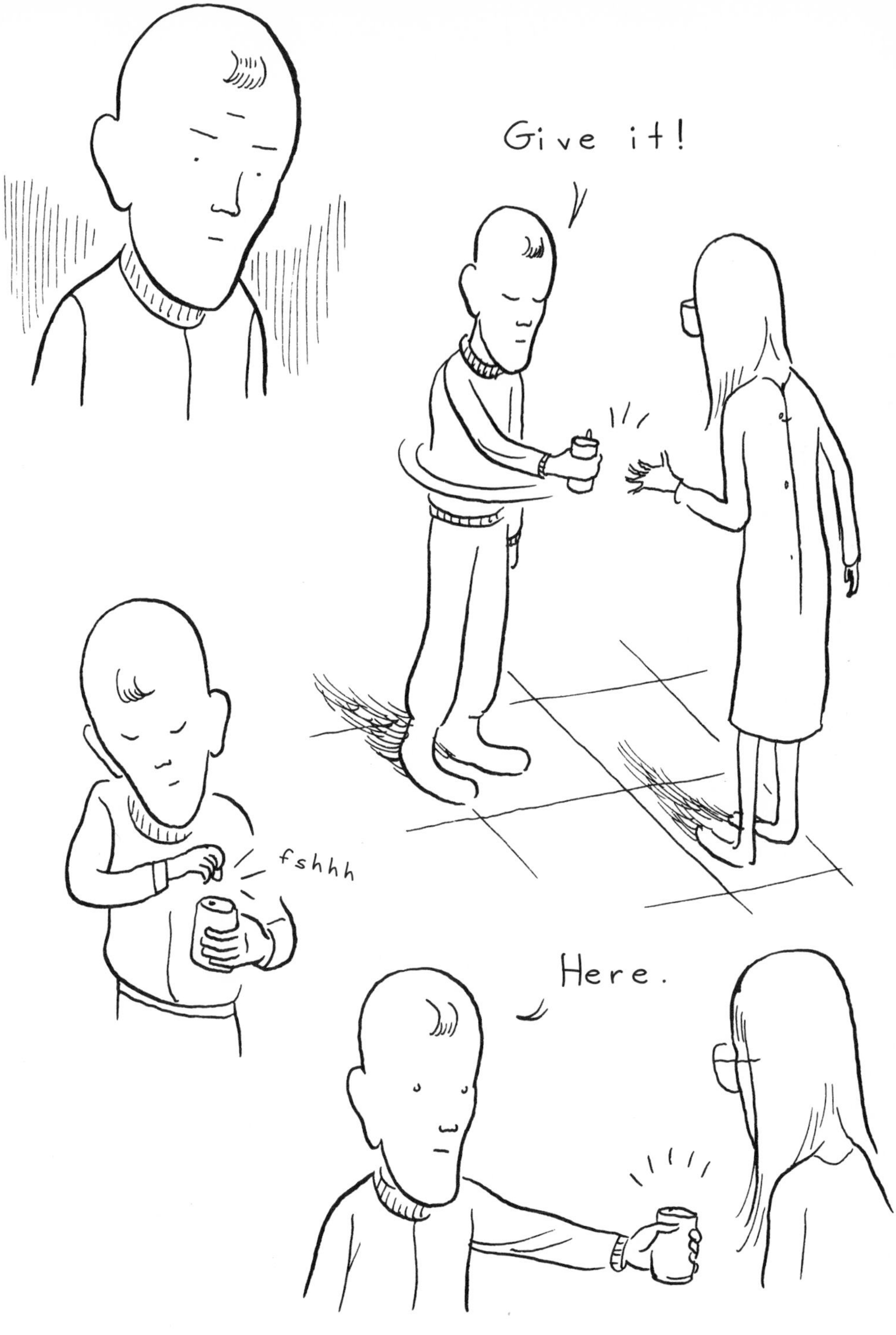
Give it!
fshhh
Here.

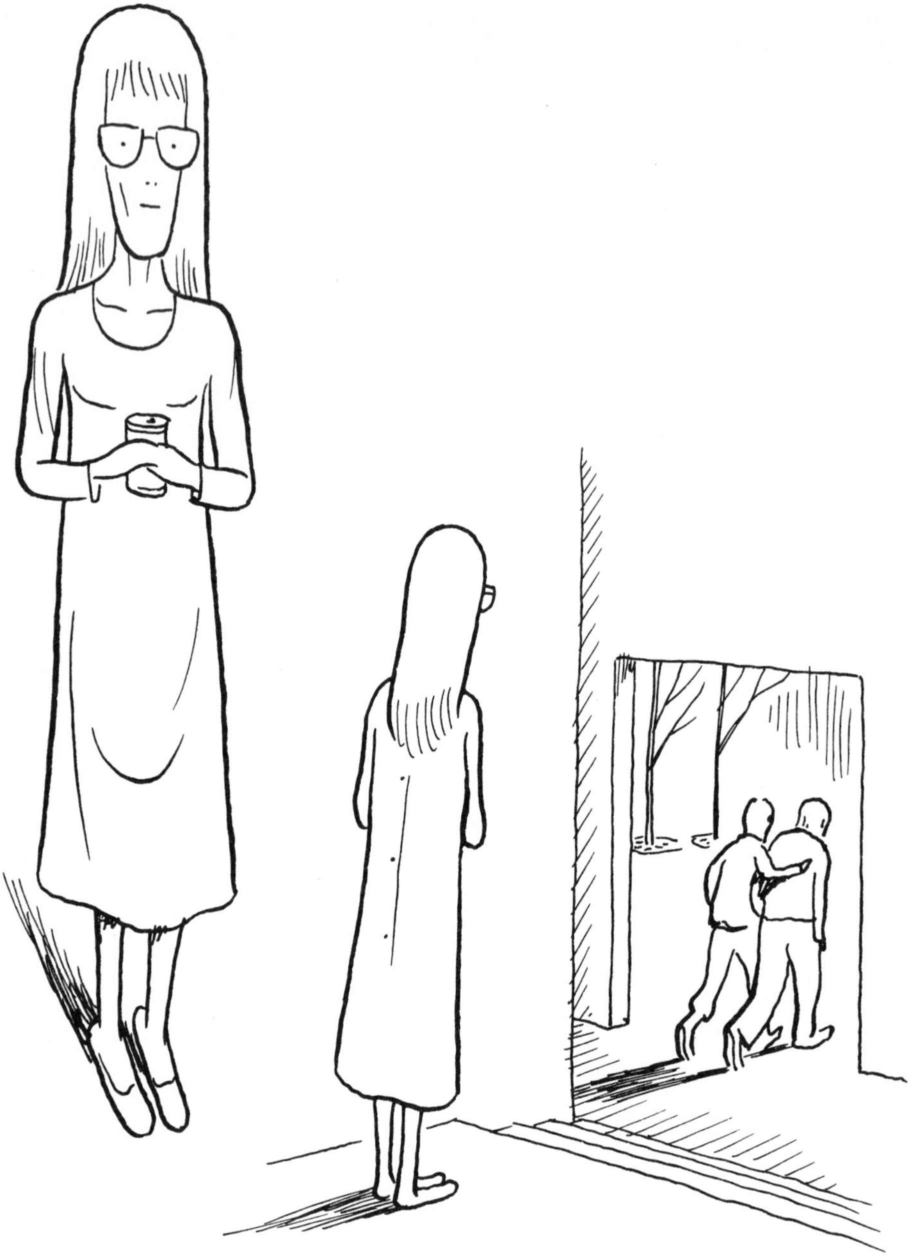

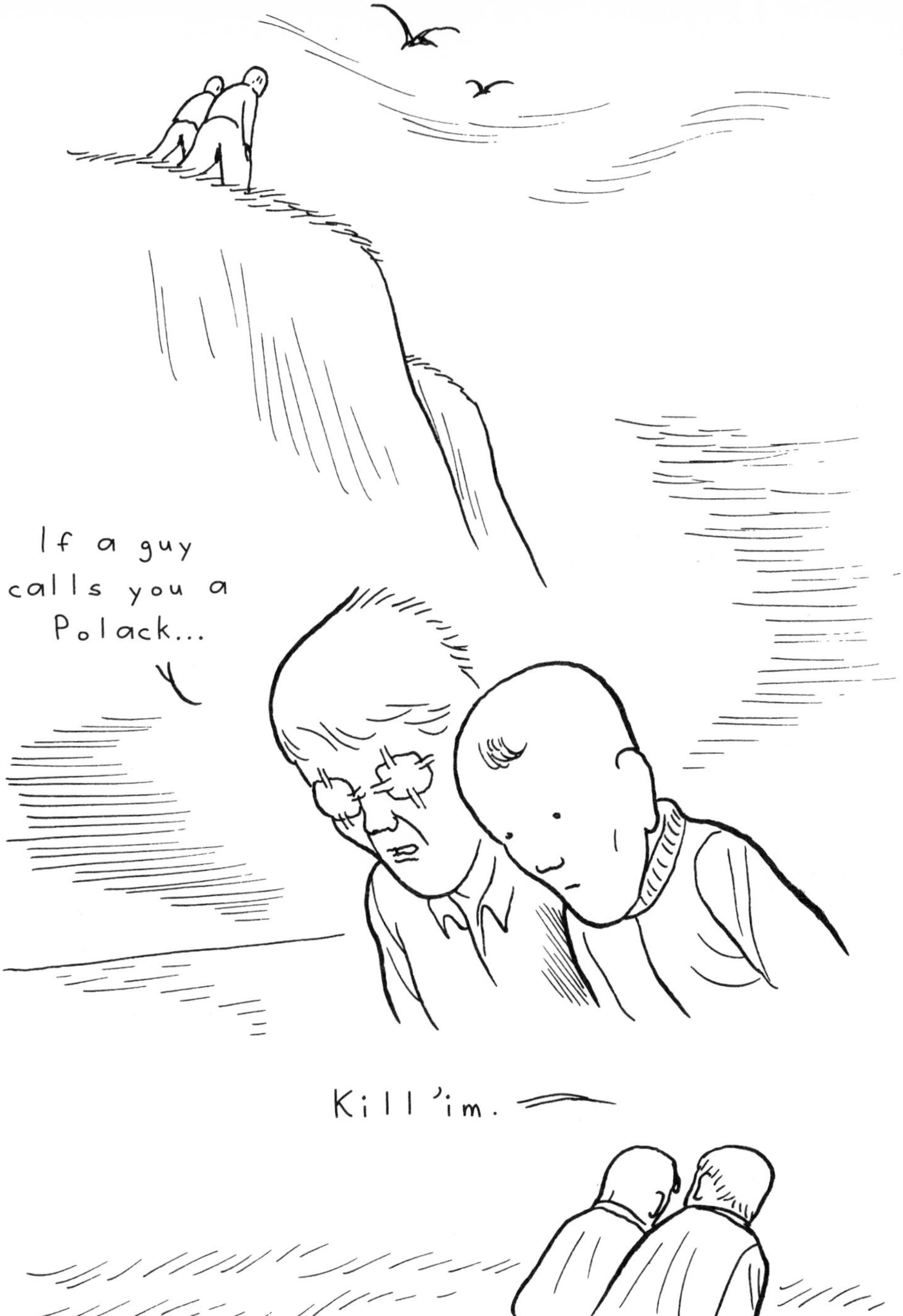
If a guy calls you a Polack...
Kill 'im.

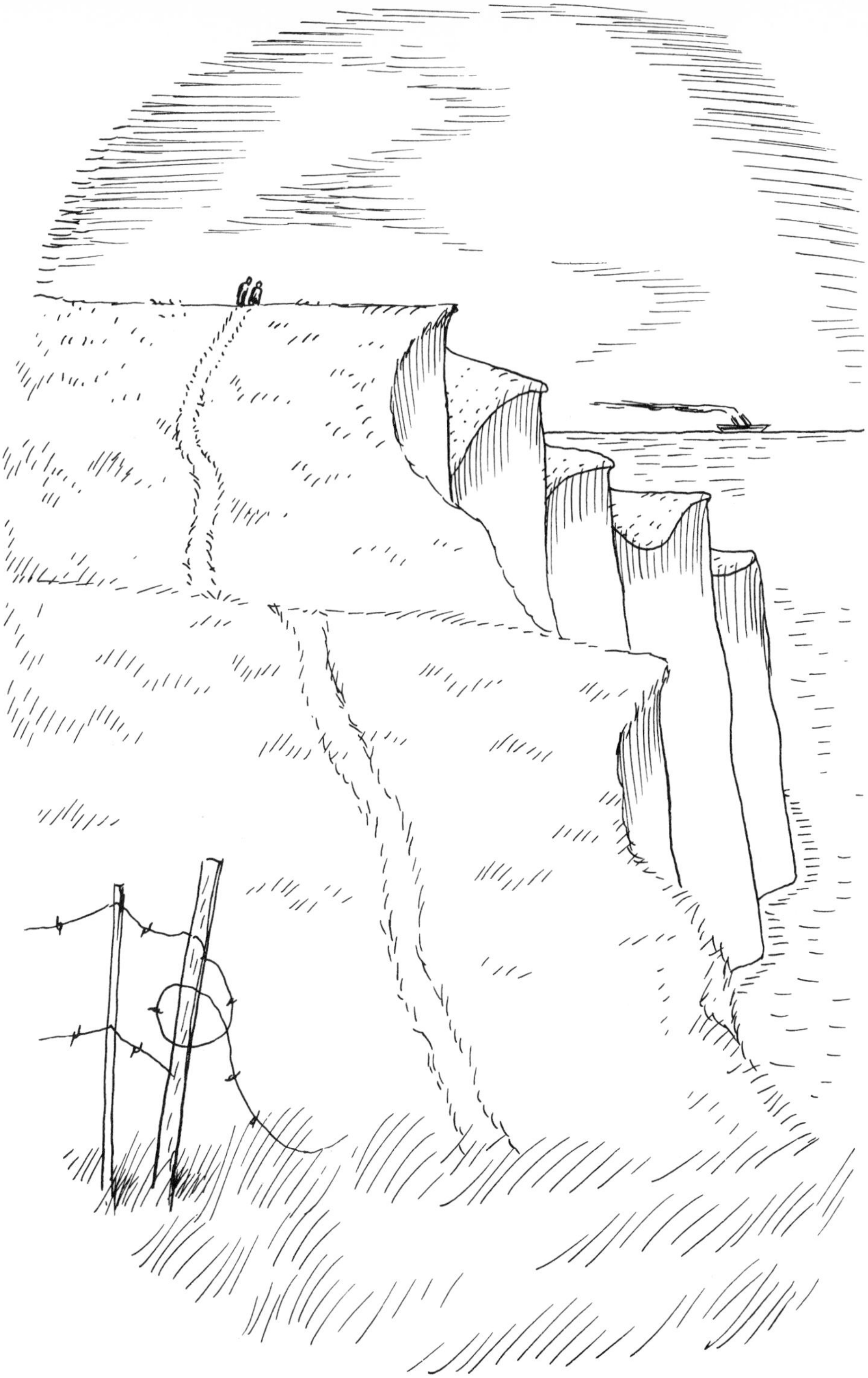

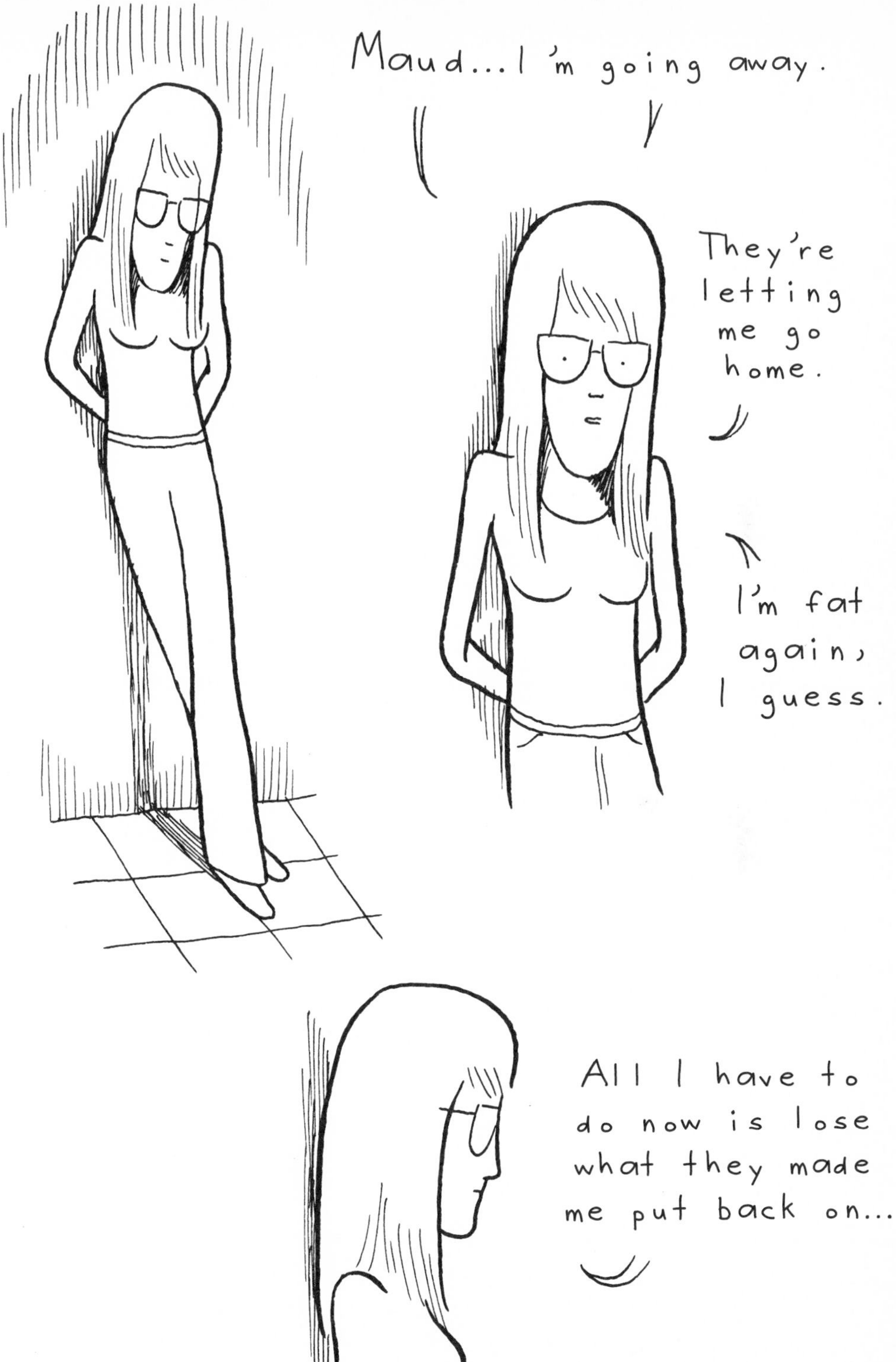
Maud... I'm going away.
They're letting me go home.
I'm fat again, I guess.
All I have to do now is lose what they made me put back on...

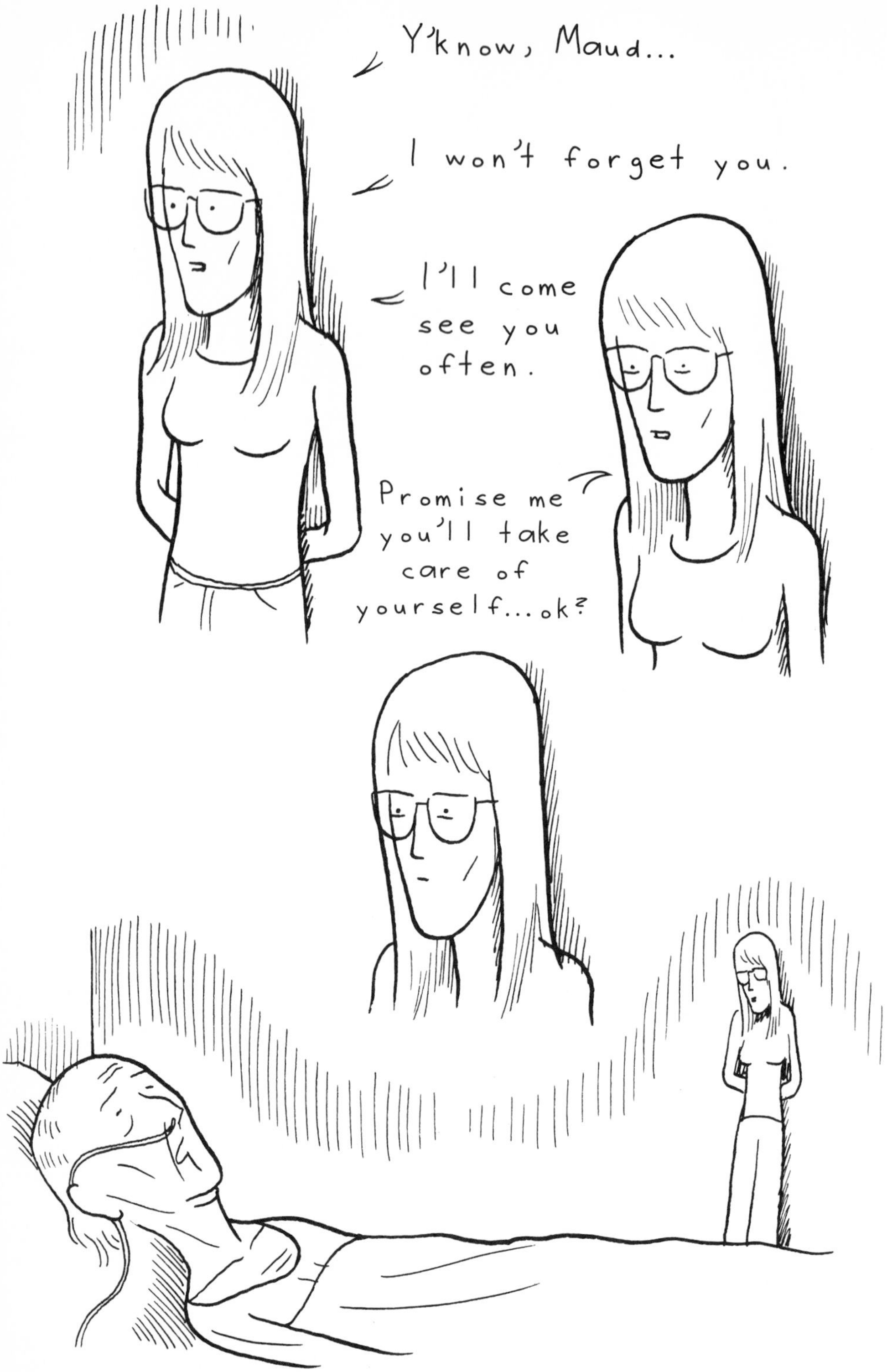
Y'know, Maud...
I won't forget you.
I'll come see you often.
Promise me you'll take care of yourself...ok?

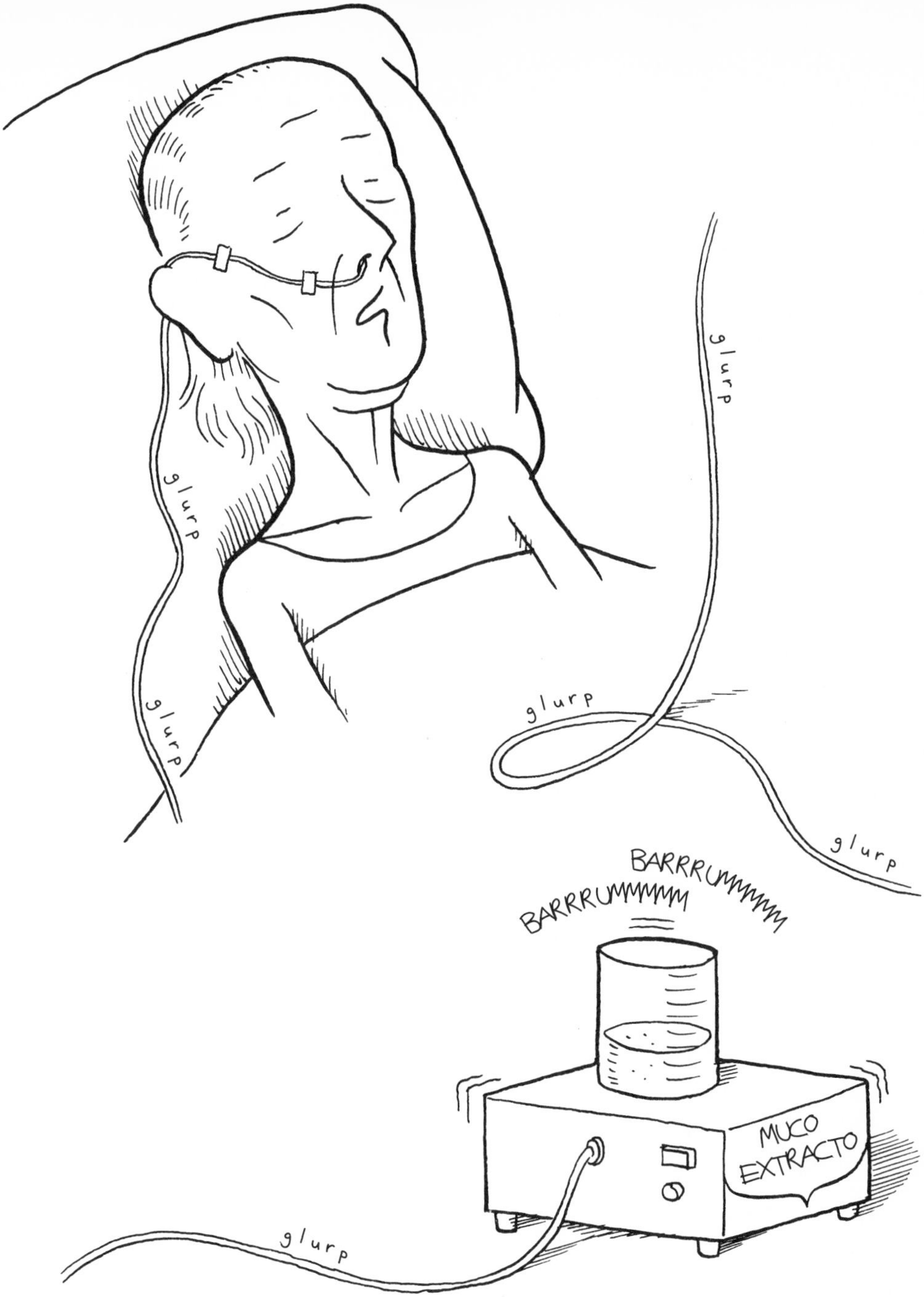
glurp
glurp
glurp
glurp
glurp
glurp
BARRRUMMMMM
BARRRUMMMMM
MUCO
EXTRACTO

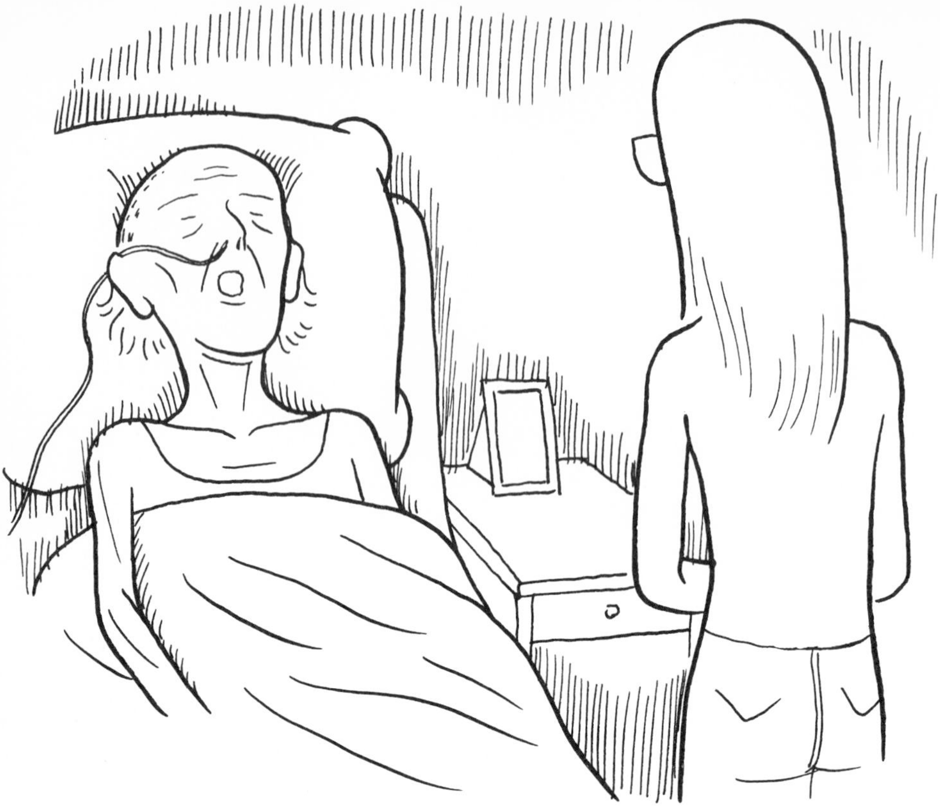
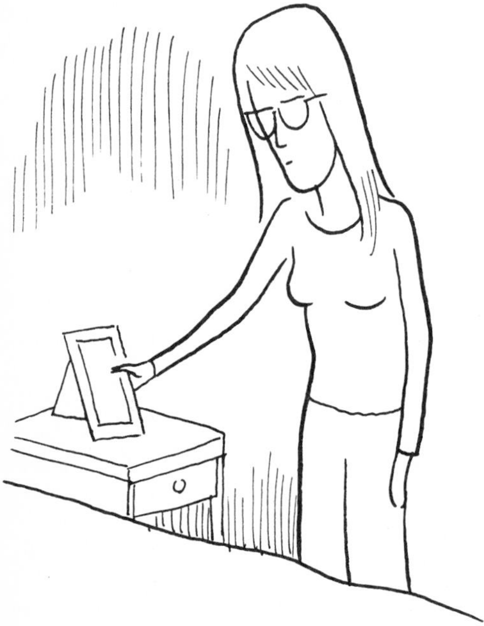
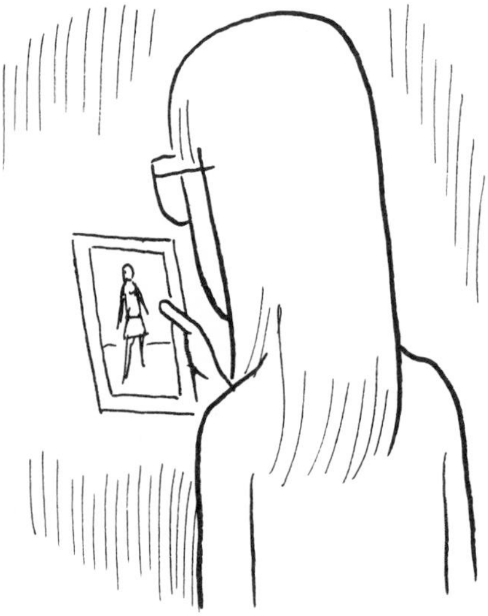

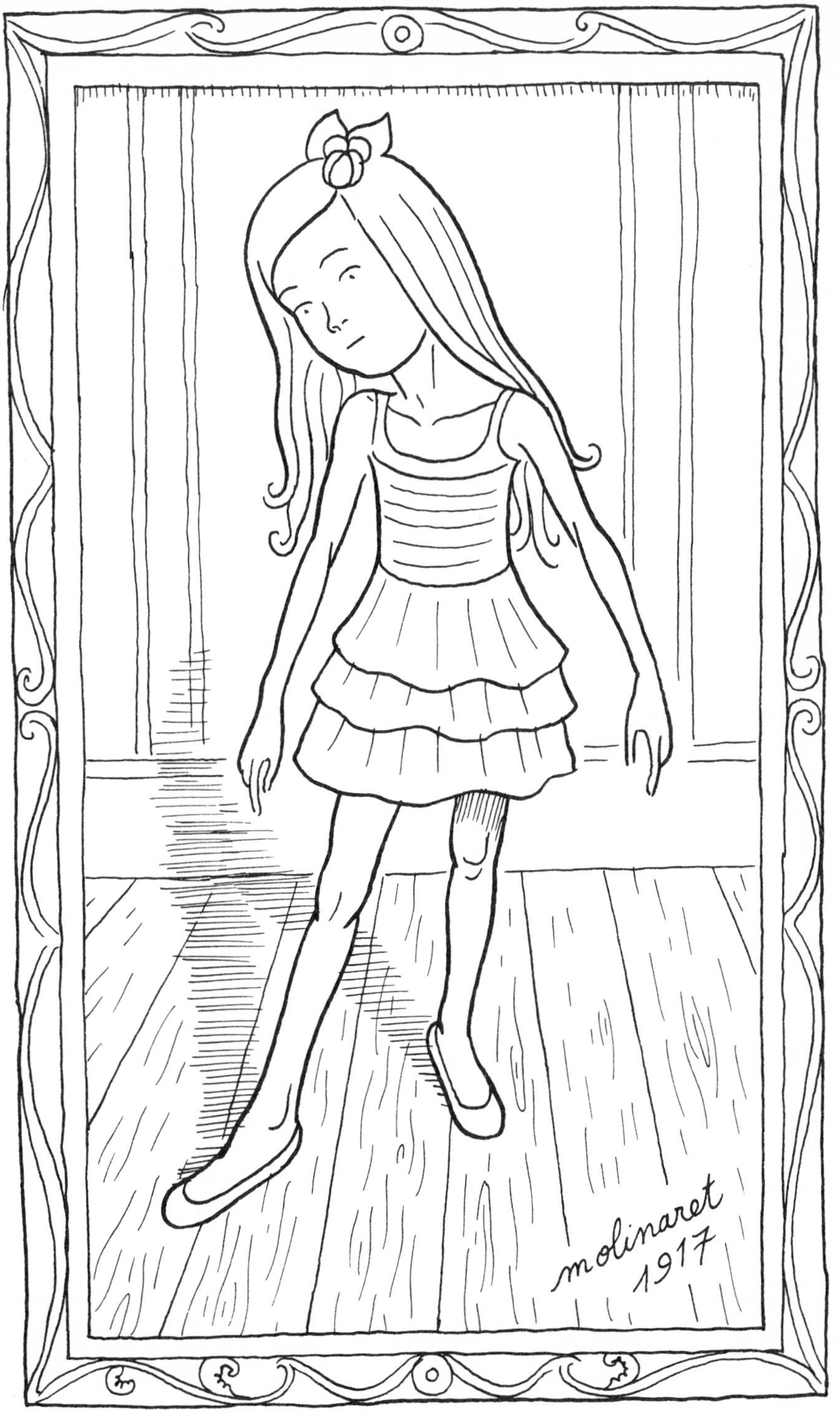
molinaret
1917

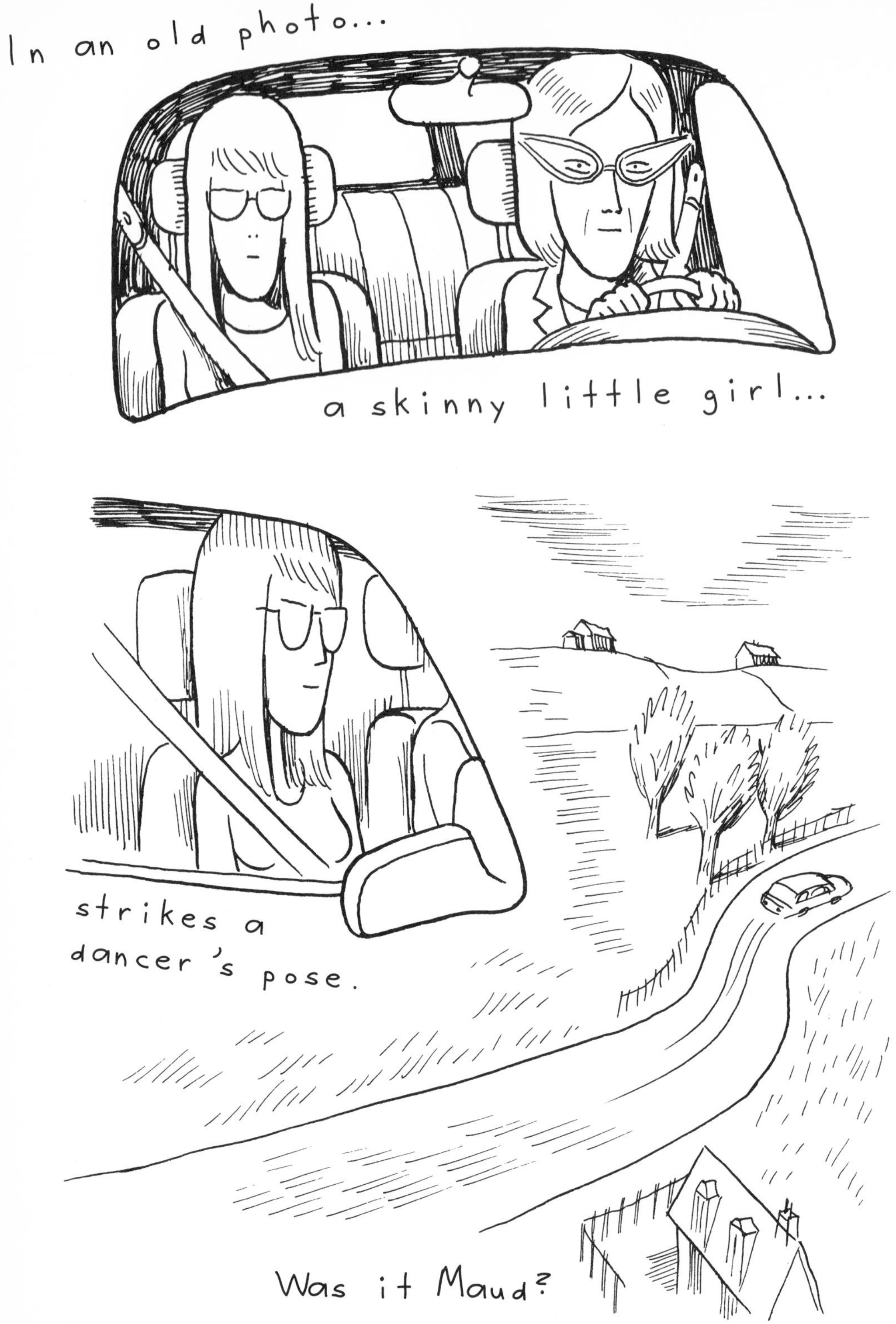
In an old photo...
a skinny little girl...
strikes a dancer's pose.
Was it Maud?

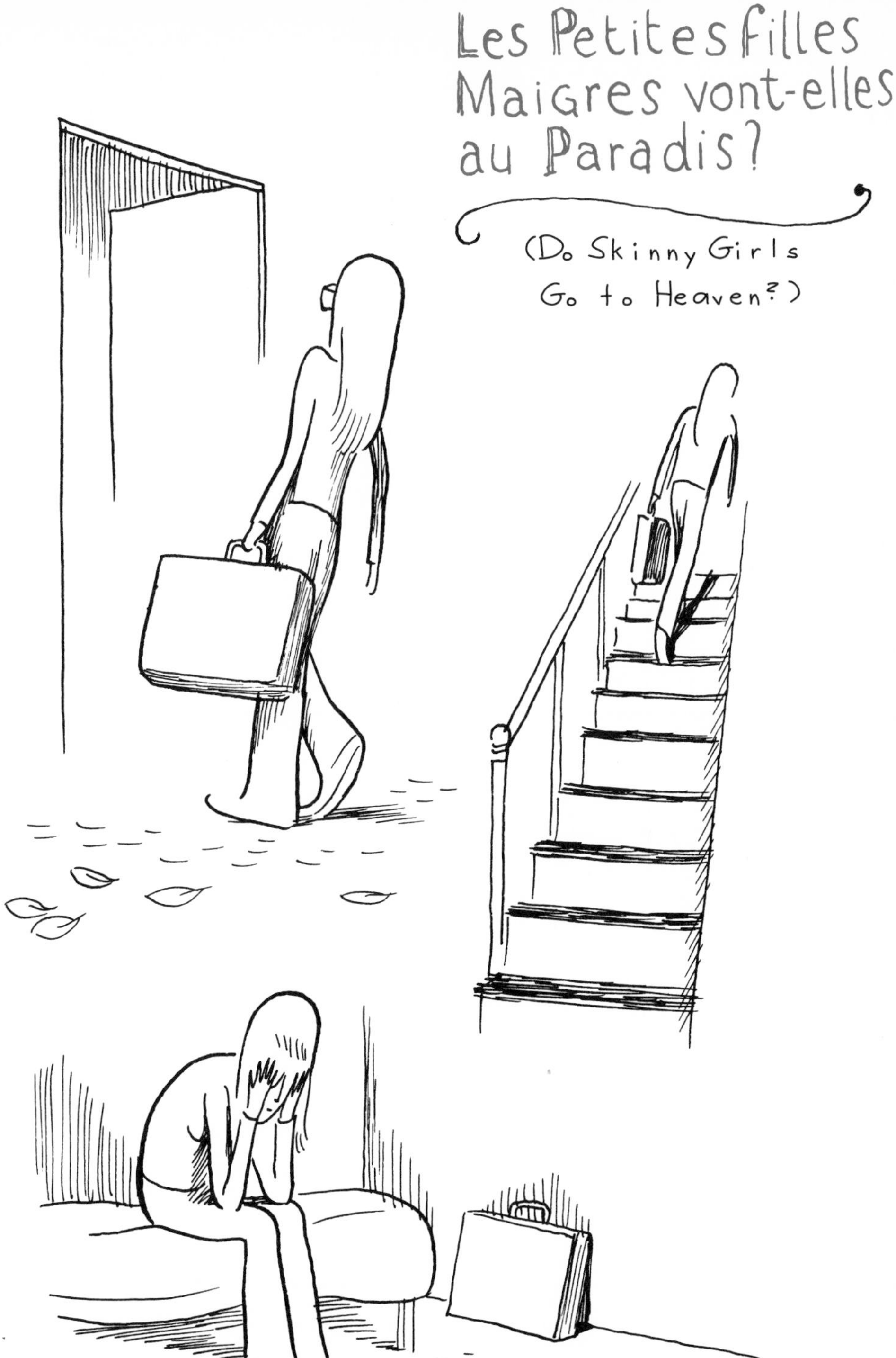
Les Petites filles Maigres vont-elles au Paradis?
(Do Skinny Girls Go to Heaven?)

Lucille?!
Set the table. Dinner'll be ready soon!
Hmm?

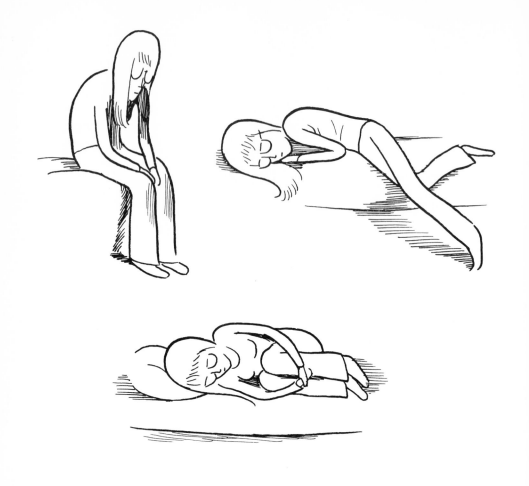

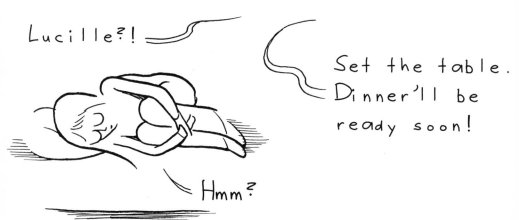

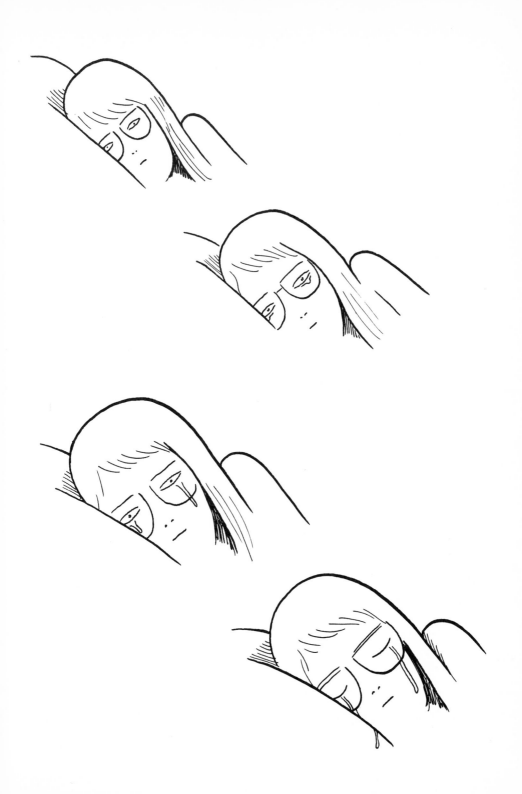

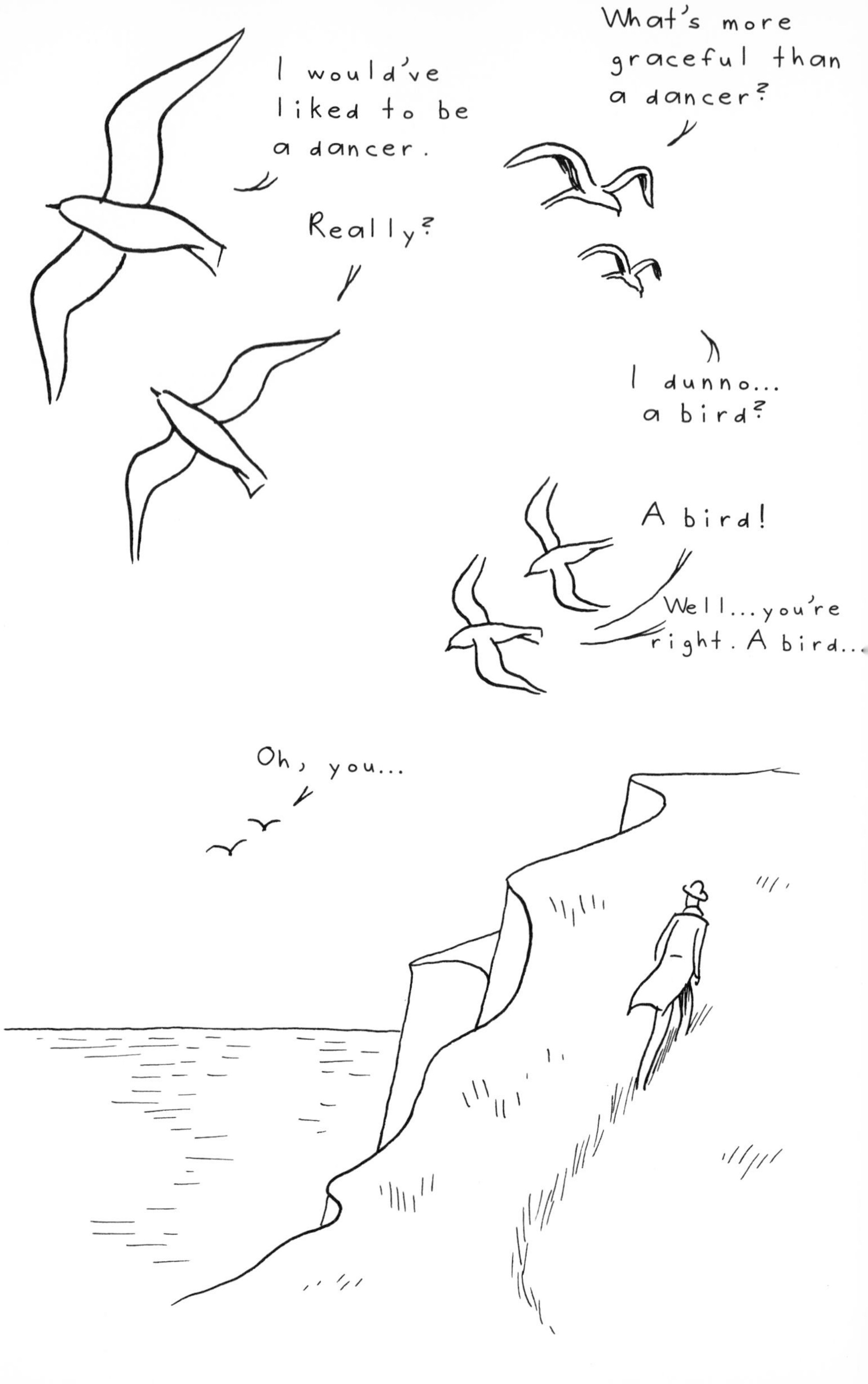
I would've liked to be a dancer.
Really?
What's more graceful than a dancer?
I dunno... a bird?
A bird!
Well... you're right. A bird...
Oh, you...

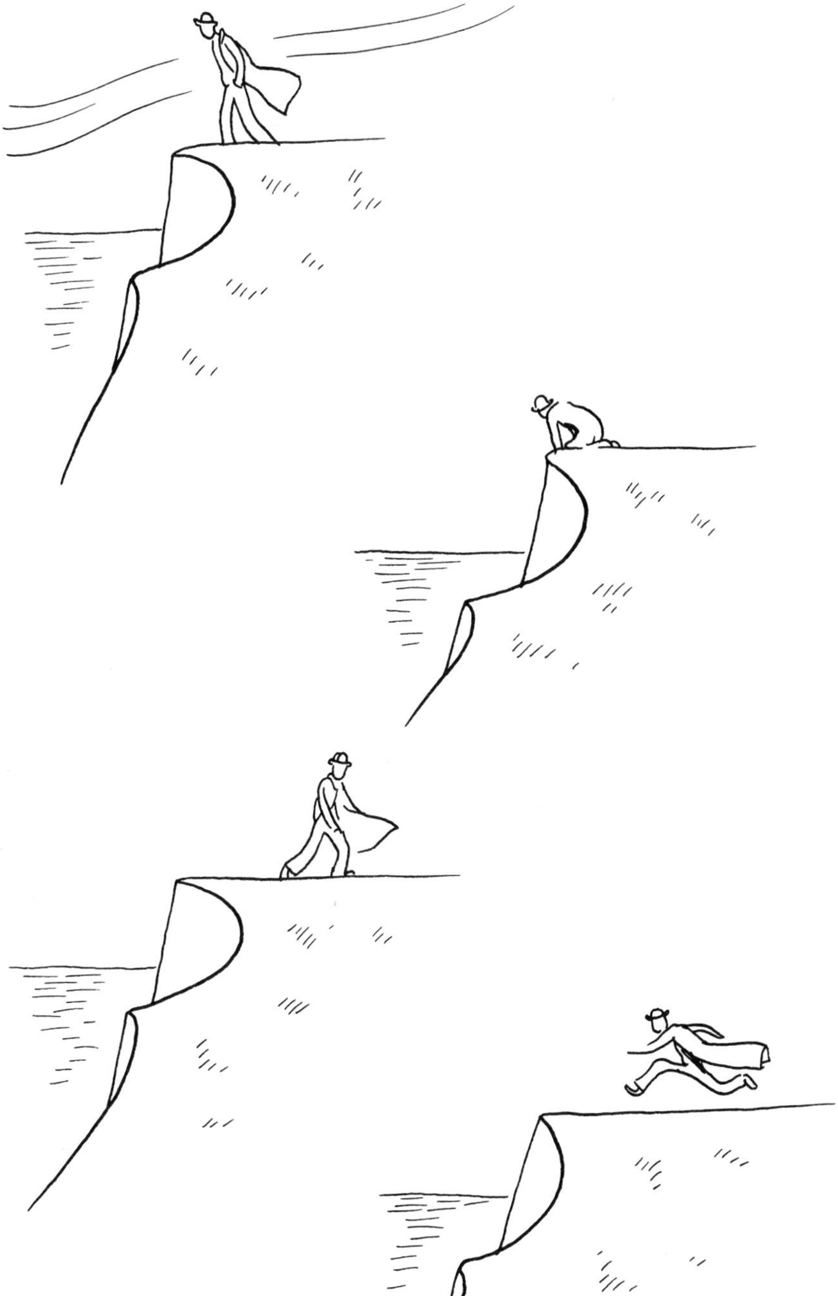

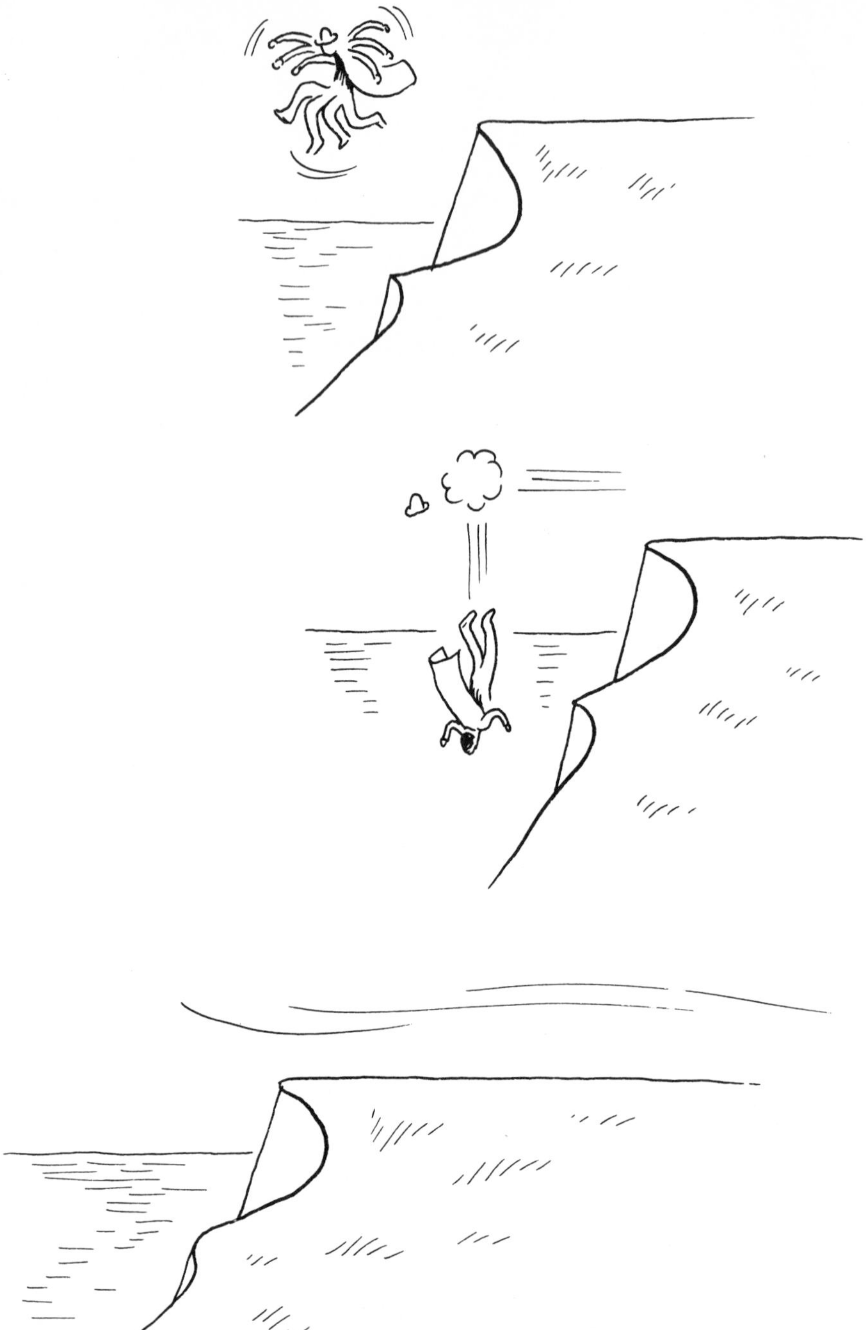

This is how the days go by: I'm lying down and I hurt. I can't stand contact between my limbs and my body. Bone against bone.

My mother thought we'd finally be able to share moments at meals.

Poor woman, she's so pissed off.

I definitely don't have breasts anymore. Two sad, empty bags. They disgust me.

They were rather pretty, I think. I never let a man touch them before... Now none will want to.

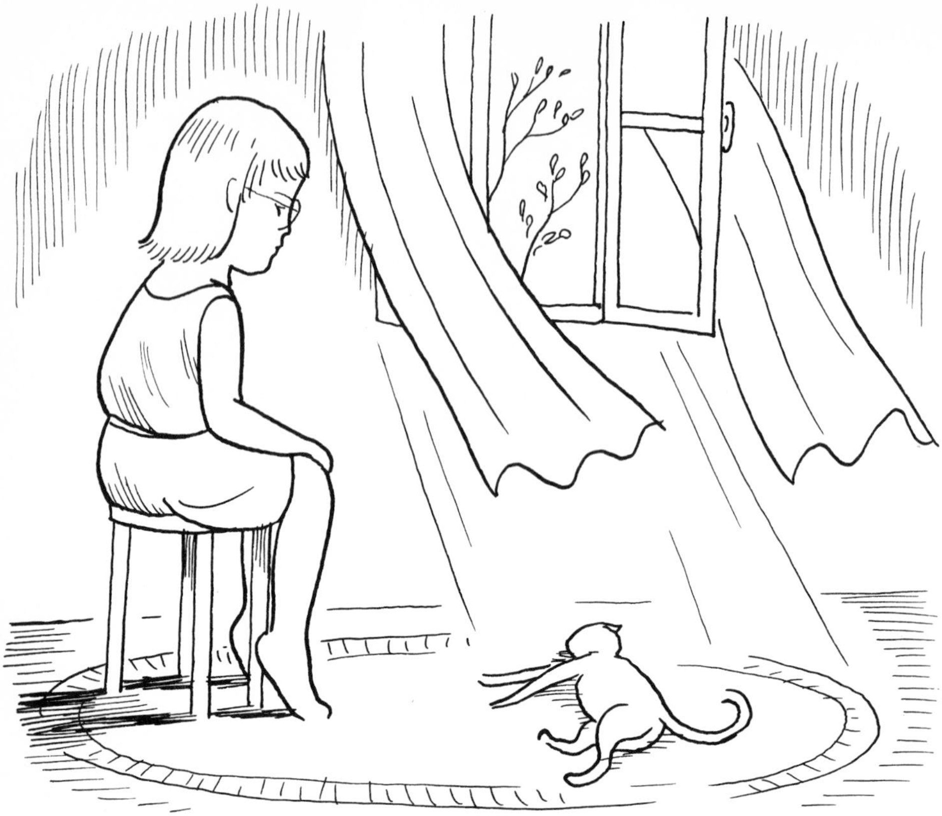

I remember the summer, as a chubby kid, when I realized my body type...We'd gone to the lake with a few friends.

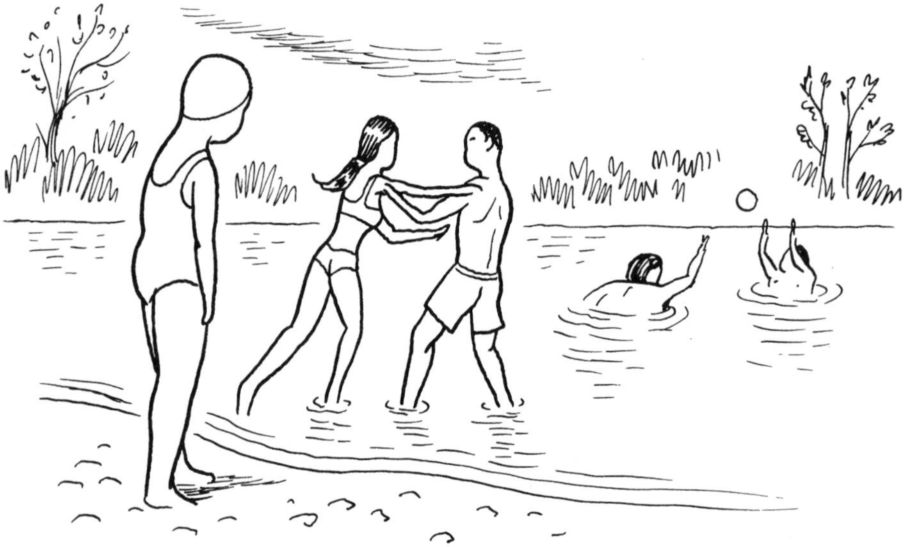

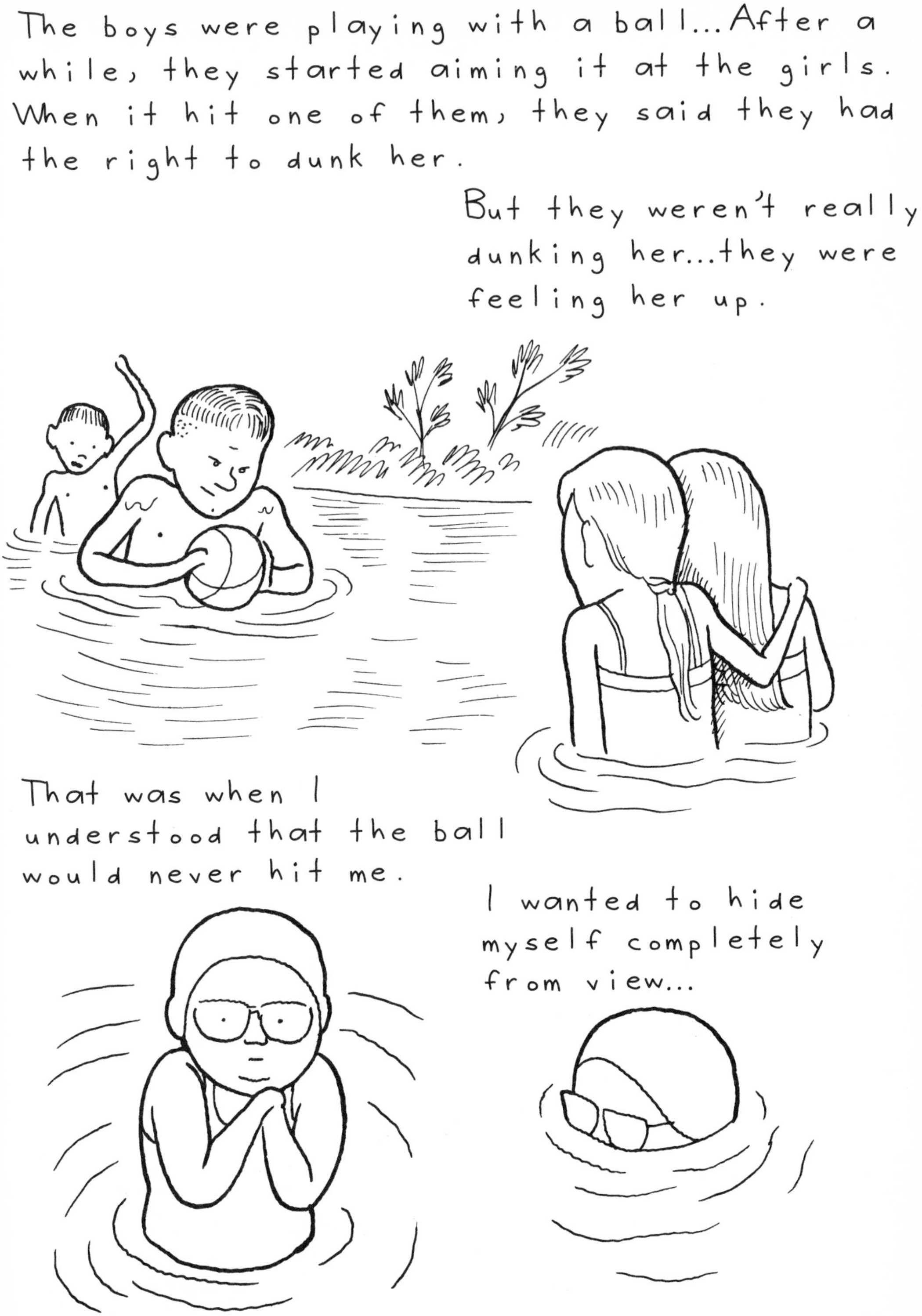
The boys were playing with a ball... After a while, they started aiming it at the girls. When it hit one of them, they said they had the right to dunk her.
But they weren't really dunking her... they were feeling her up.
That was when I understood that the ball would never hit me.
I wanted to hide myself completely from view...

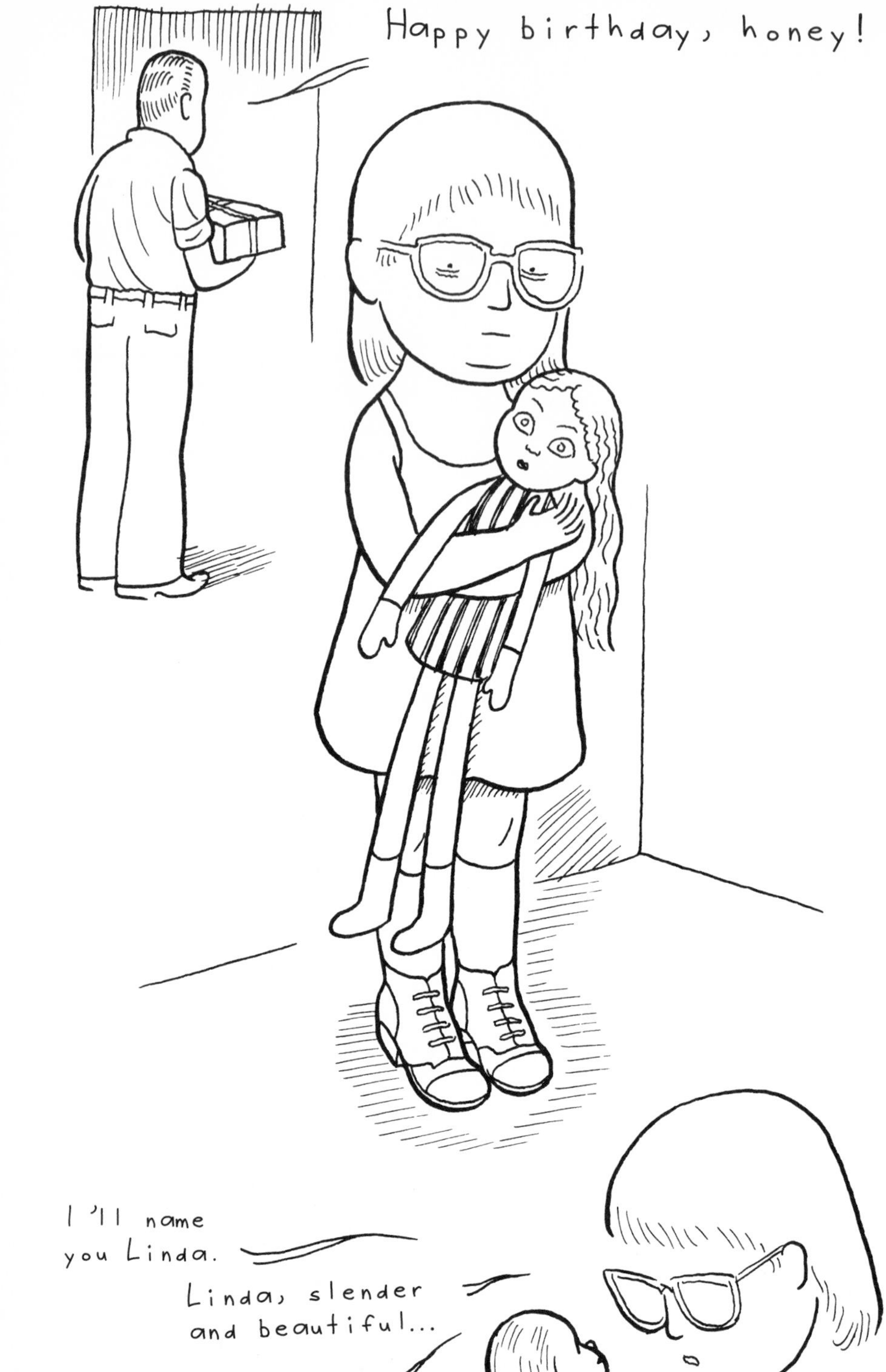
Happy birthday, honey!
I'll name you Linda.
Linda, slender and beautiful...
Slender as a thread.

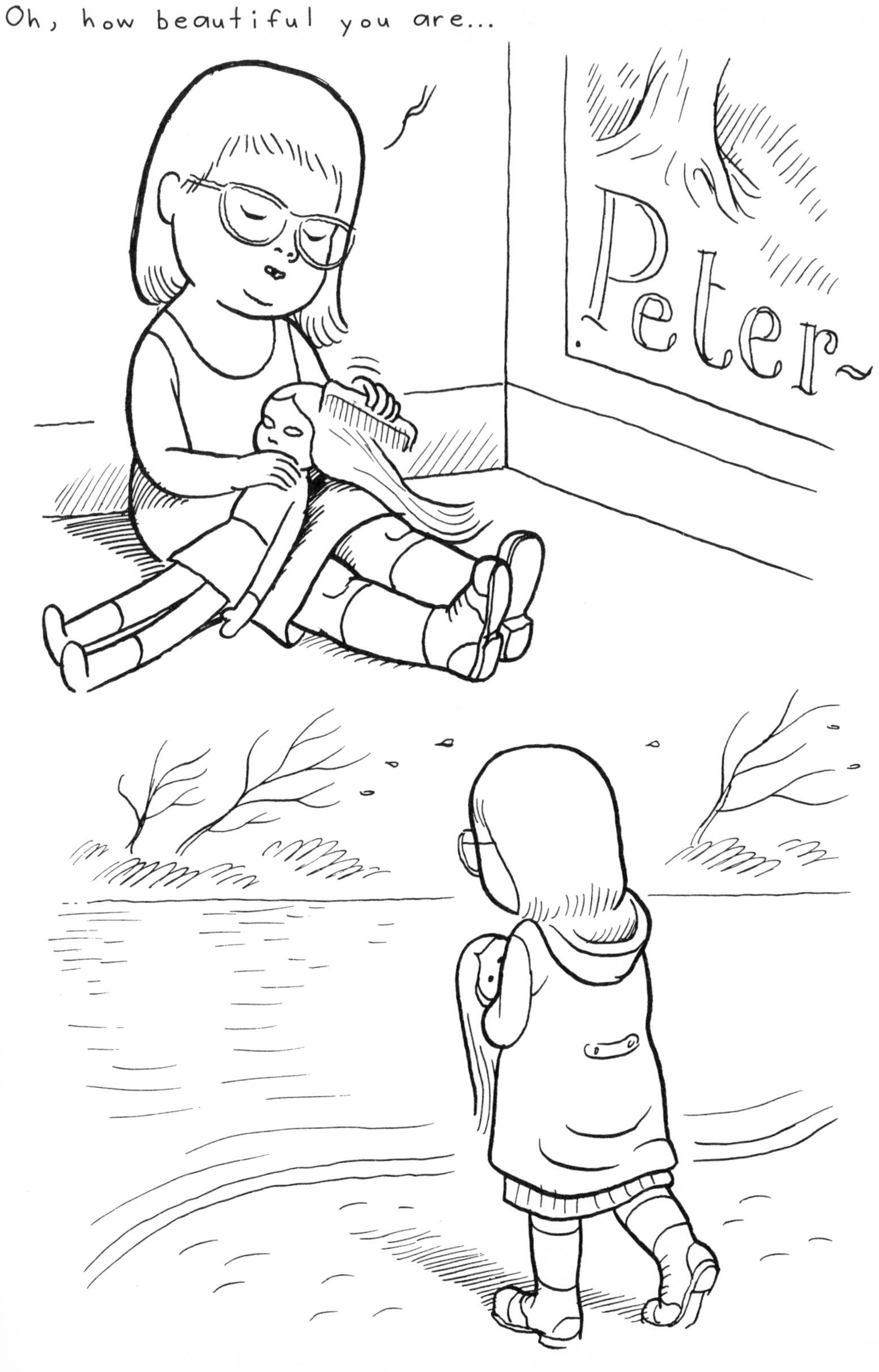
Oh, how beautiful you are...
Peter~

I took that doll with me everywhere...

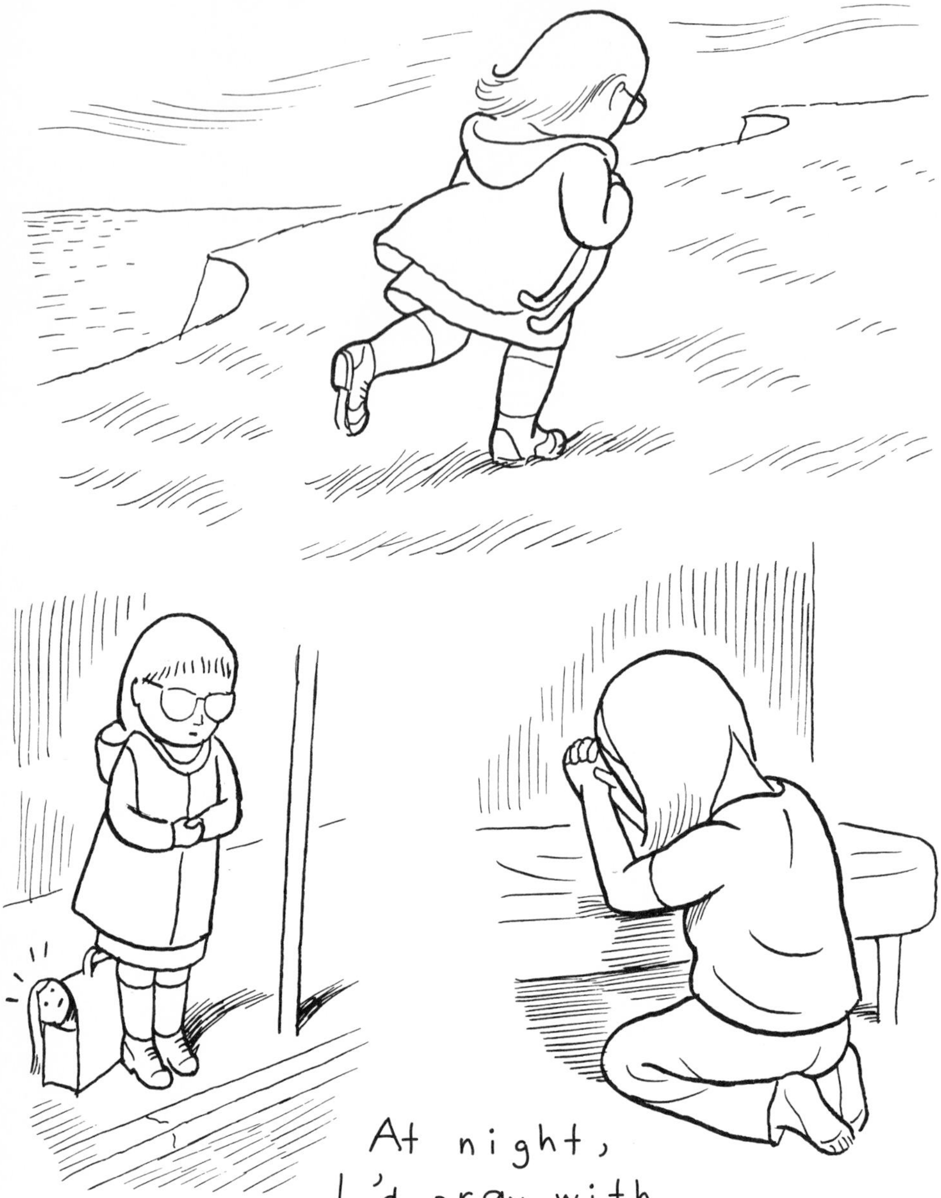

At night, I'd pray with her that one day I'd become beautiful, too.

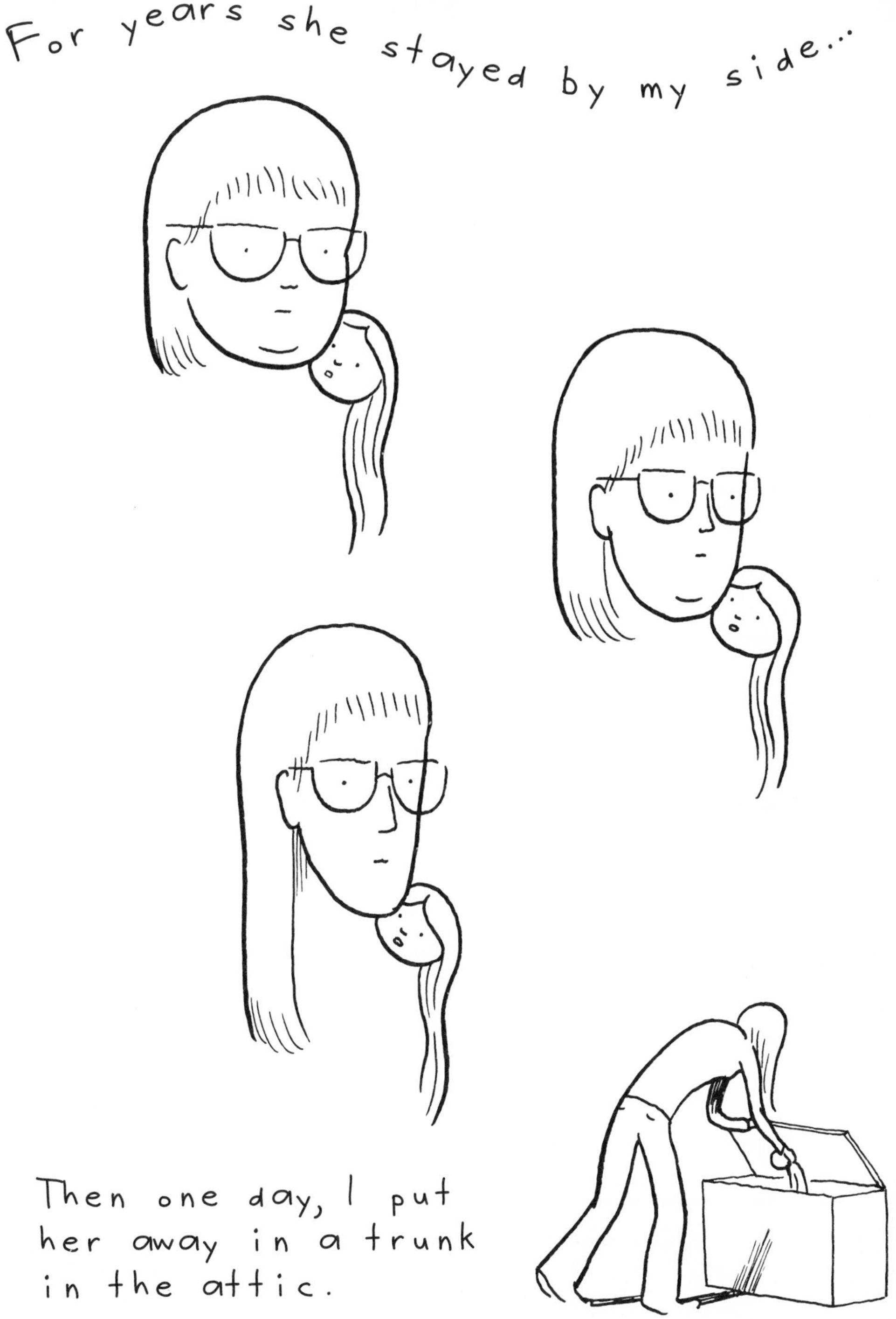
For years she stayed by my side...
Then one day, I put her away in a trunk in the attic.

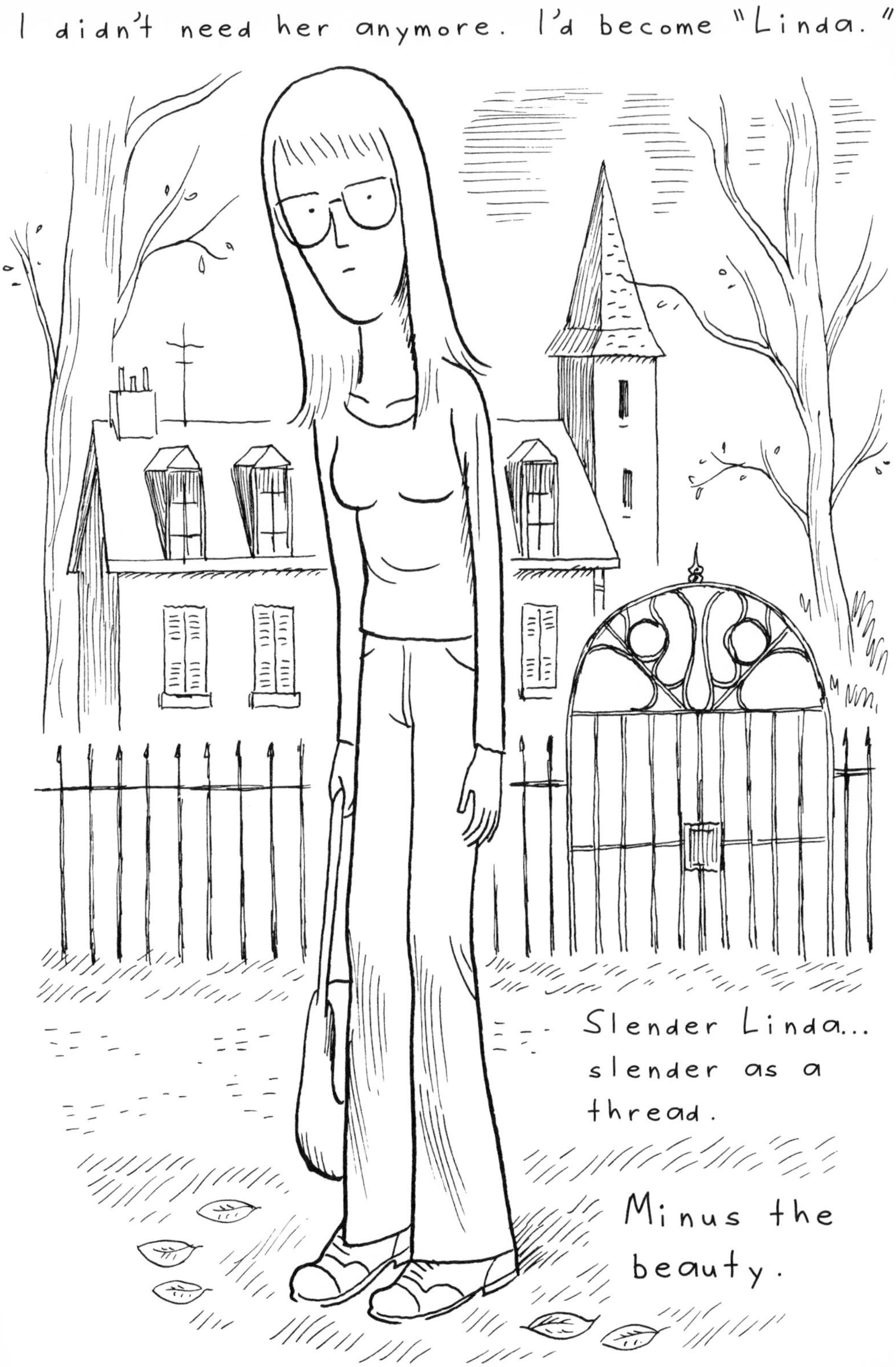
I didn't need her anymore. I'd become "Linda."
Slender Linda... slender as a thread.
Minus the beauty.

Wasn't I thin enough, that I had to get thinner?

I refuse all meals. My mother seems more worried than I am. I just don't get it, she says.

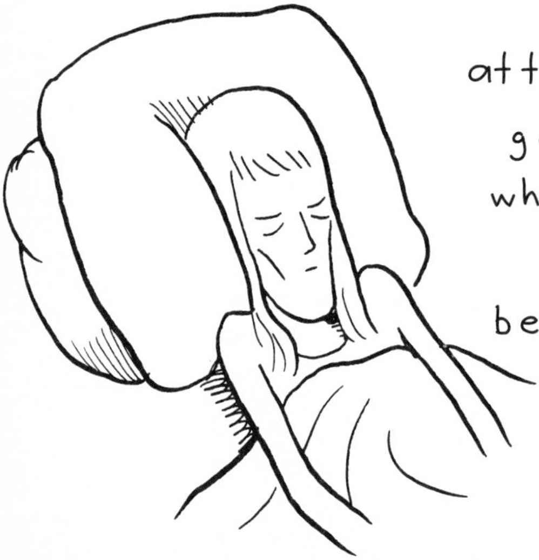

She says if it's attention I want, I've got it. But I think what I want is to be so thin my body becomes nonexistent... invisible.

Le fil

(The Thread)

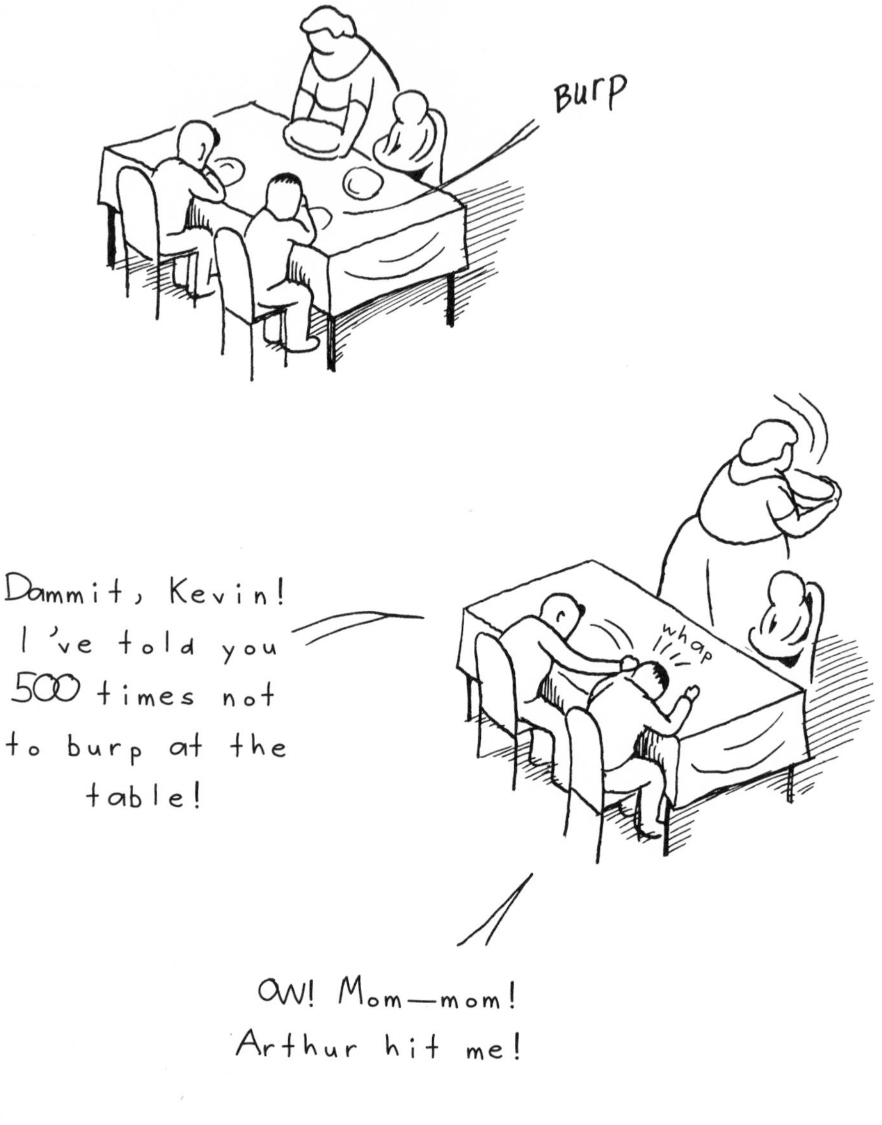

burp
Dammit, Kevin! I've told you 500 times not to burp at the table!
whap
OW! Mom—mom! Arthur hit me!

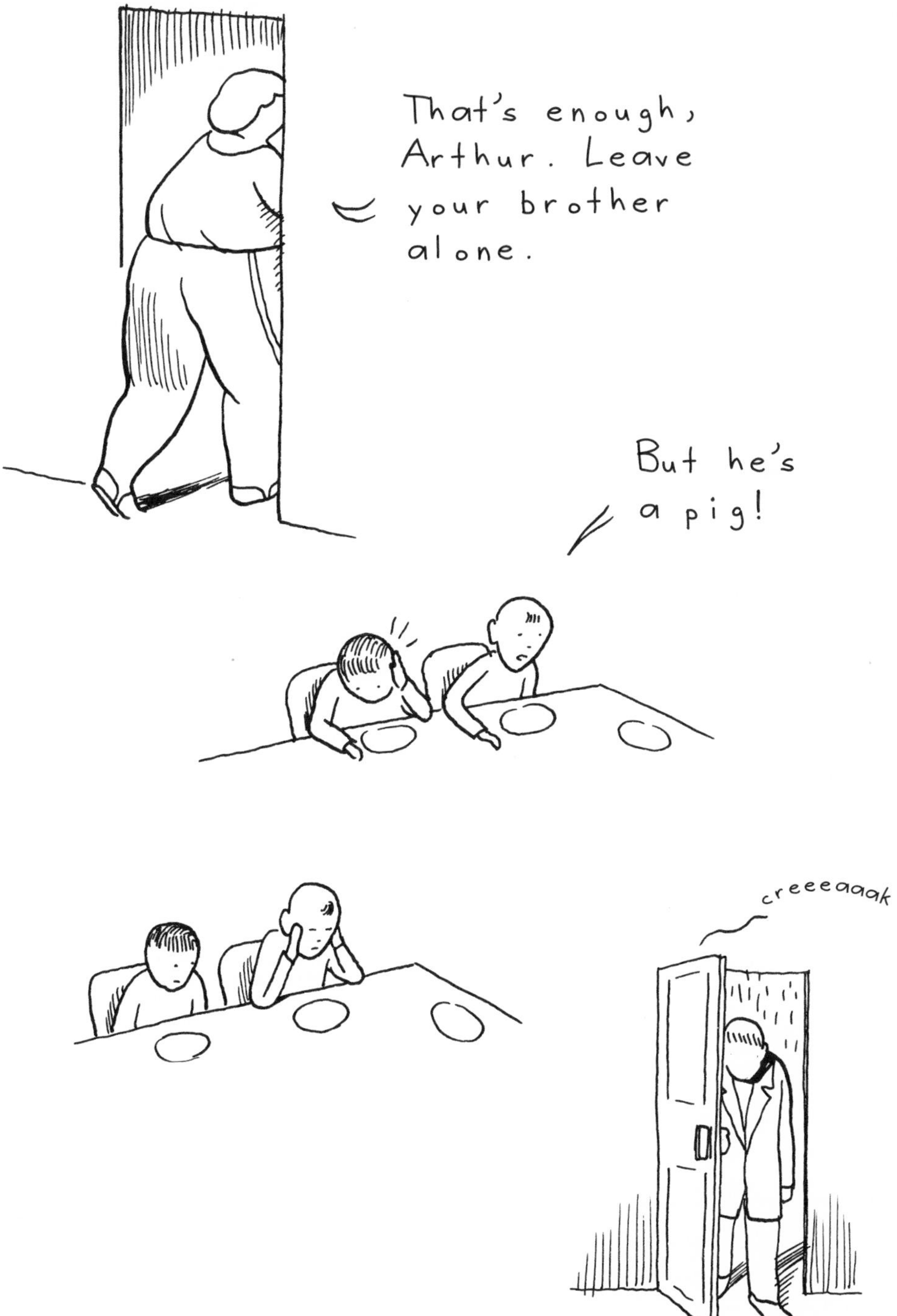
That's enough, Arthur. Leave your brother alone.
But he's a pig!
creeeaaak

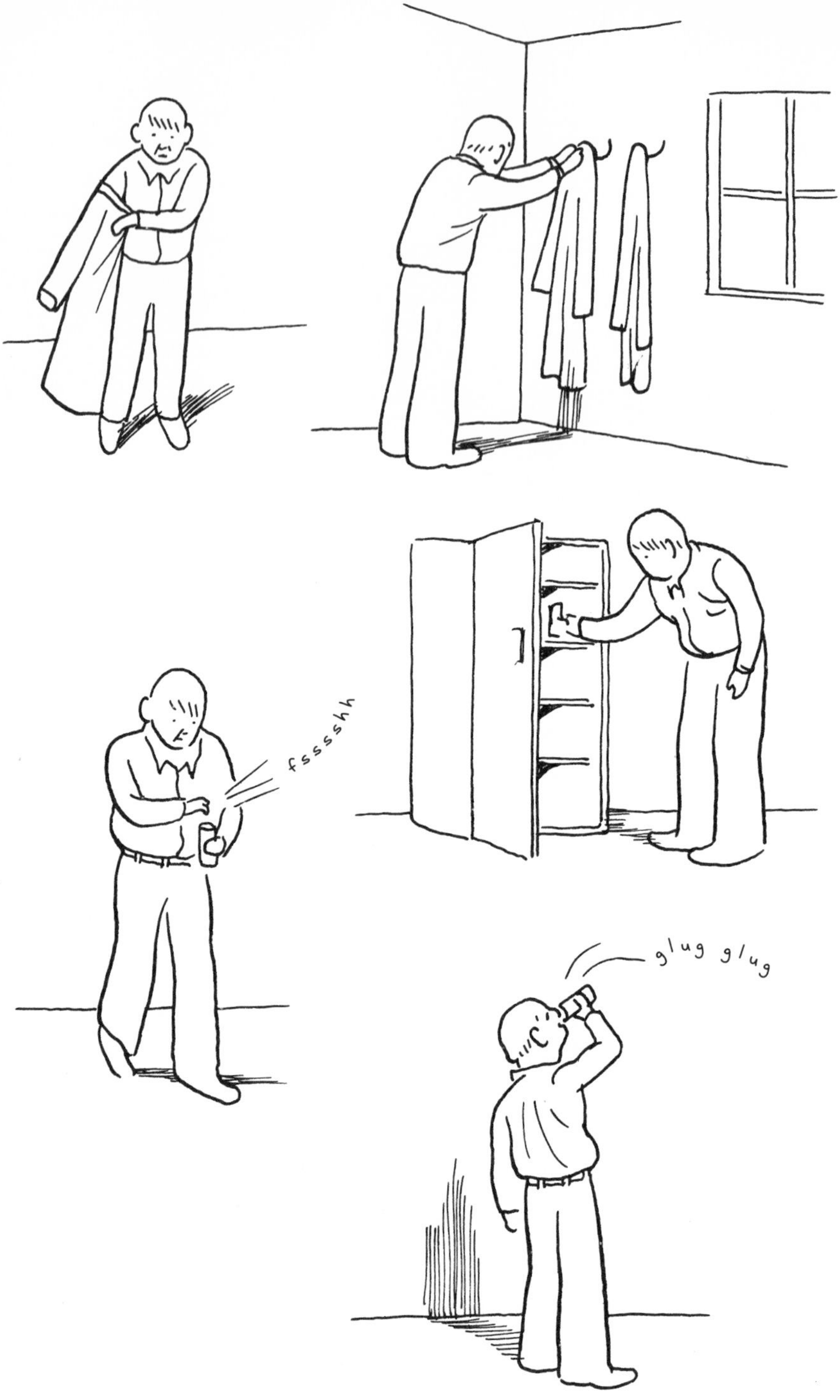
fssssshh
glug glug

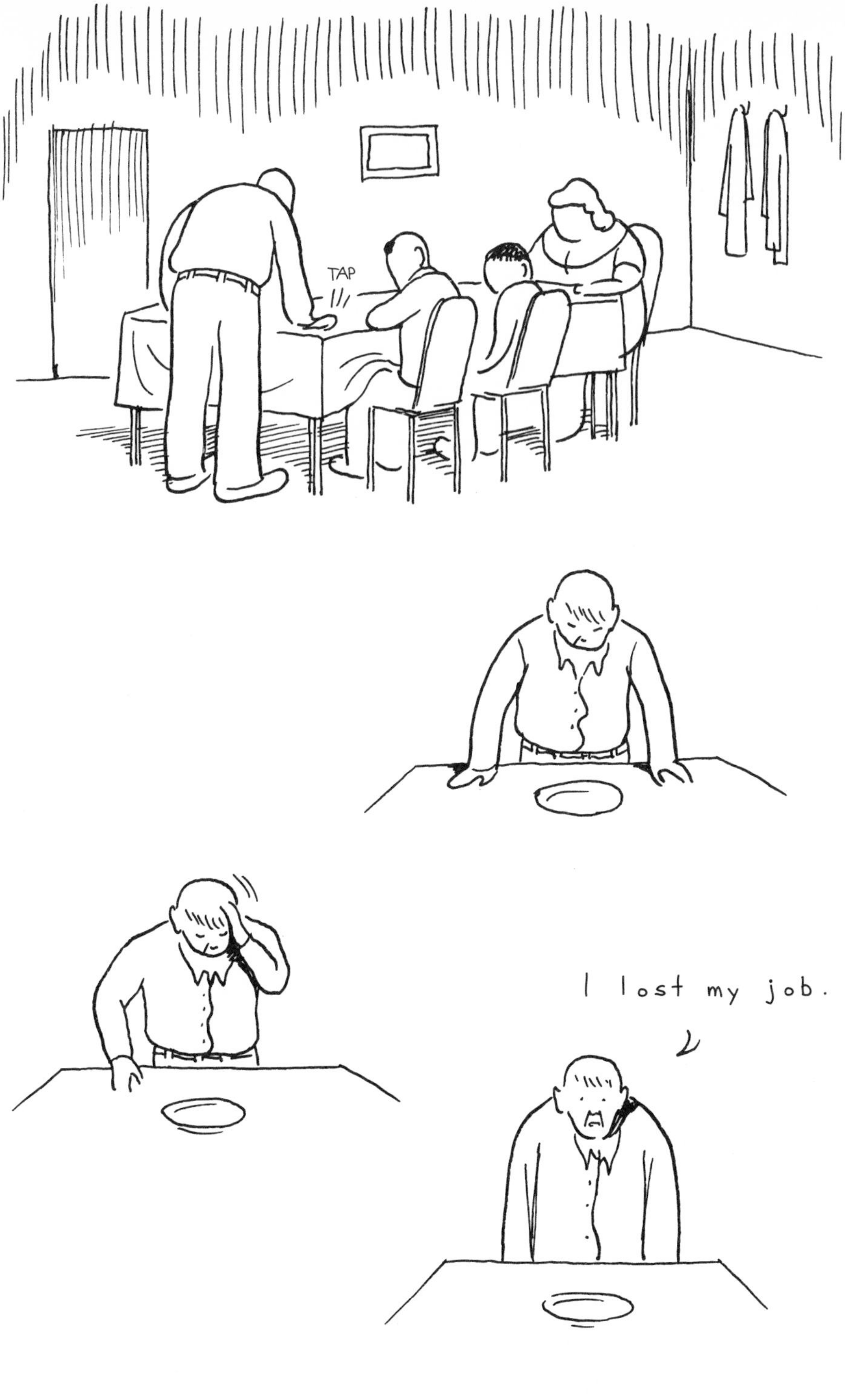
TAP
I lost my job.

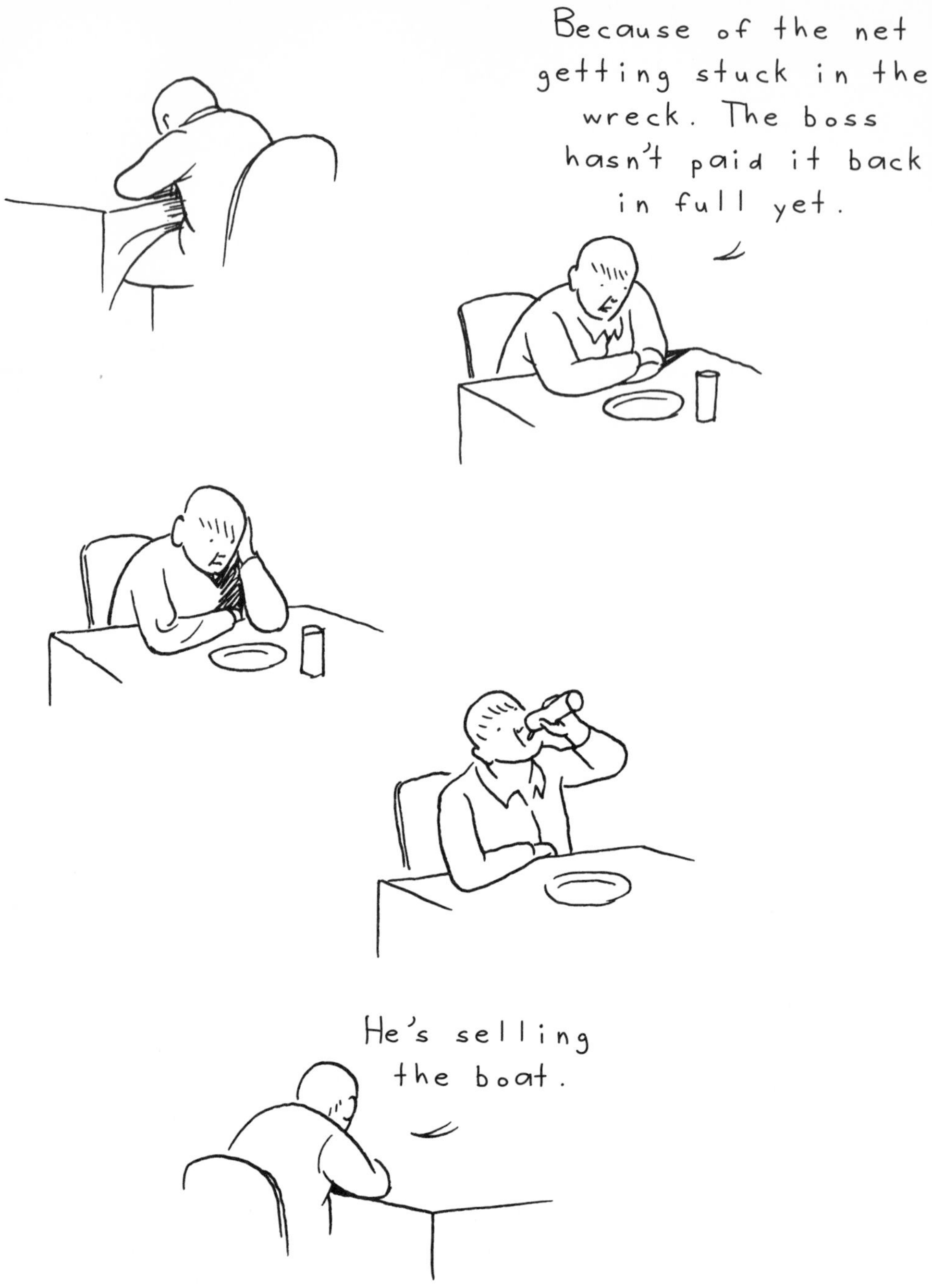
Because of the net getting stuck in the wreck. The boss hasn't paid it back in full yet.
He's selling the boat.

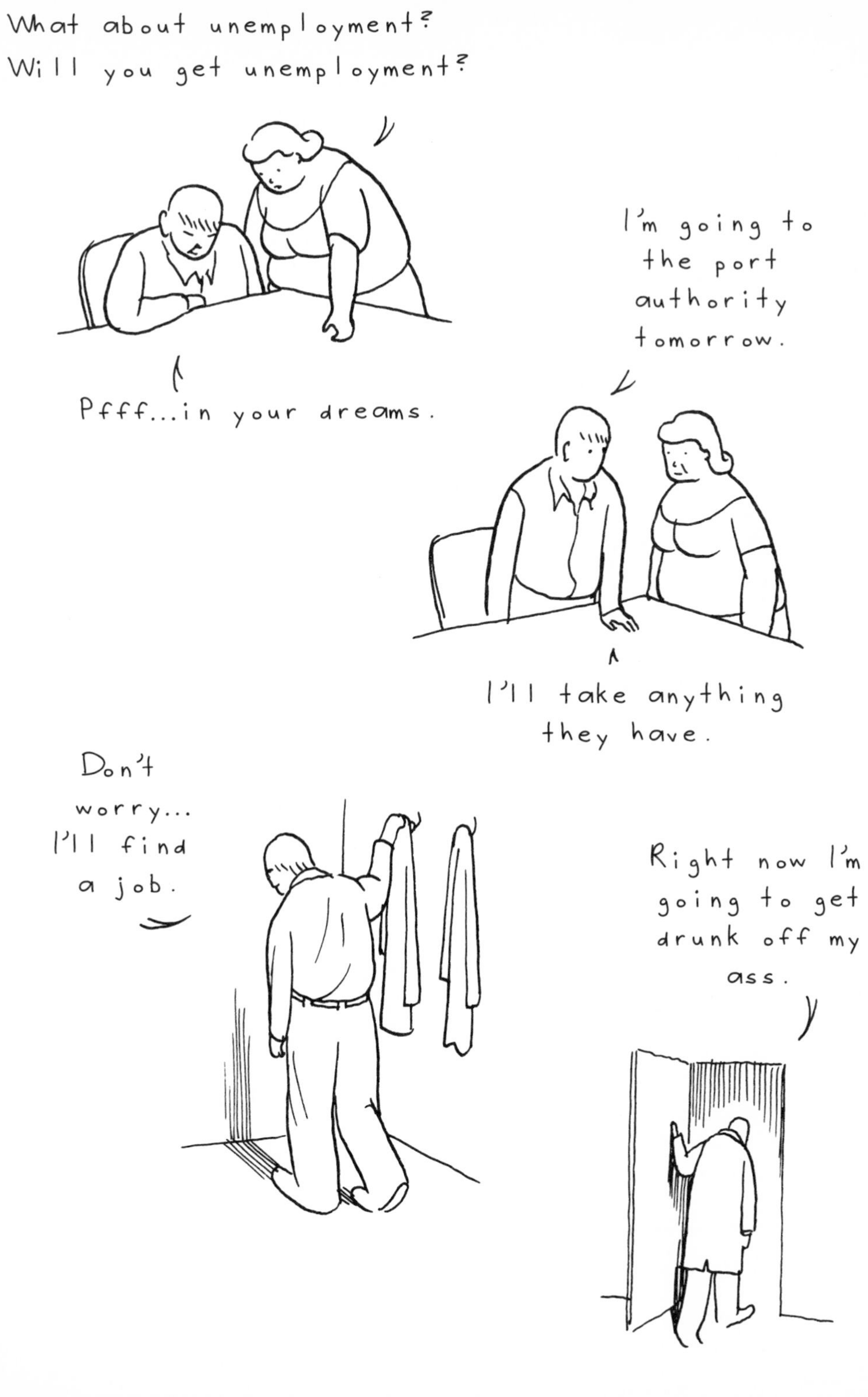
What about unemployment? Will you get unemployment?
Pfff...in your dreams.
I'm going to the port authority tomorrow.
I'll take anything they have.
Don't worry... I'll find a job.
Right now I'm going to get drunk off my ass.

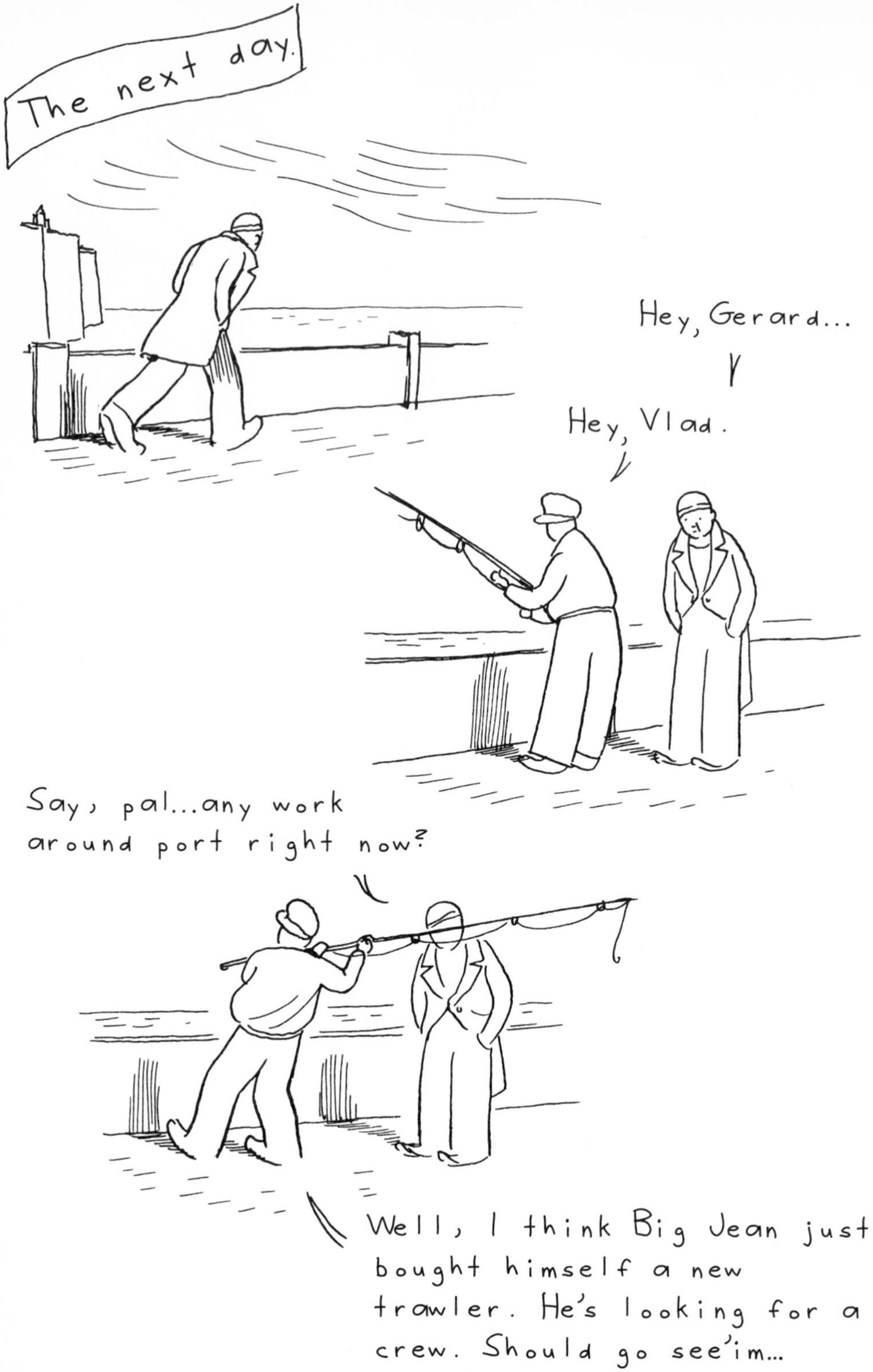
The next day.
Hey, Gerard...
Hey, Vlad.
Say, pal...any work around port right now?
Well, I think Big Jean just bought himself a new trawler. He's looking for a crew. Should go see'im...

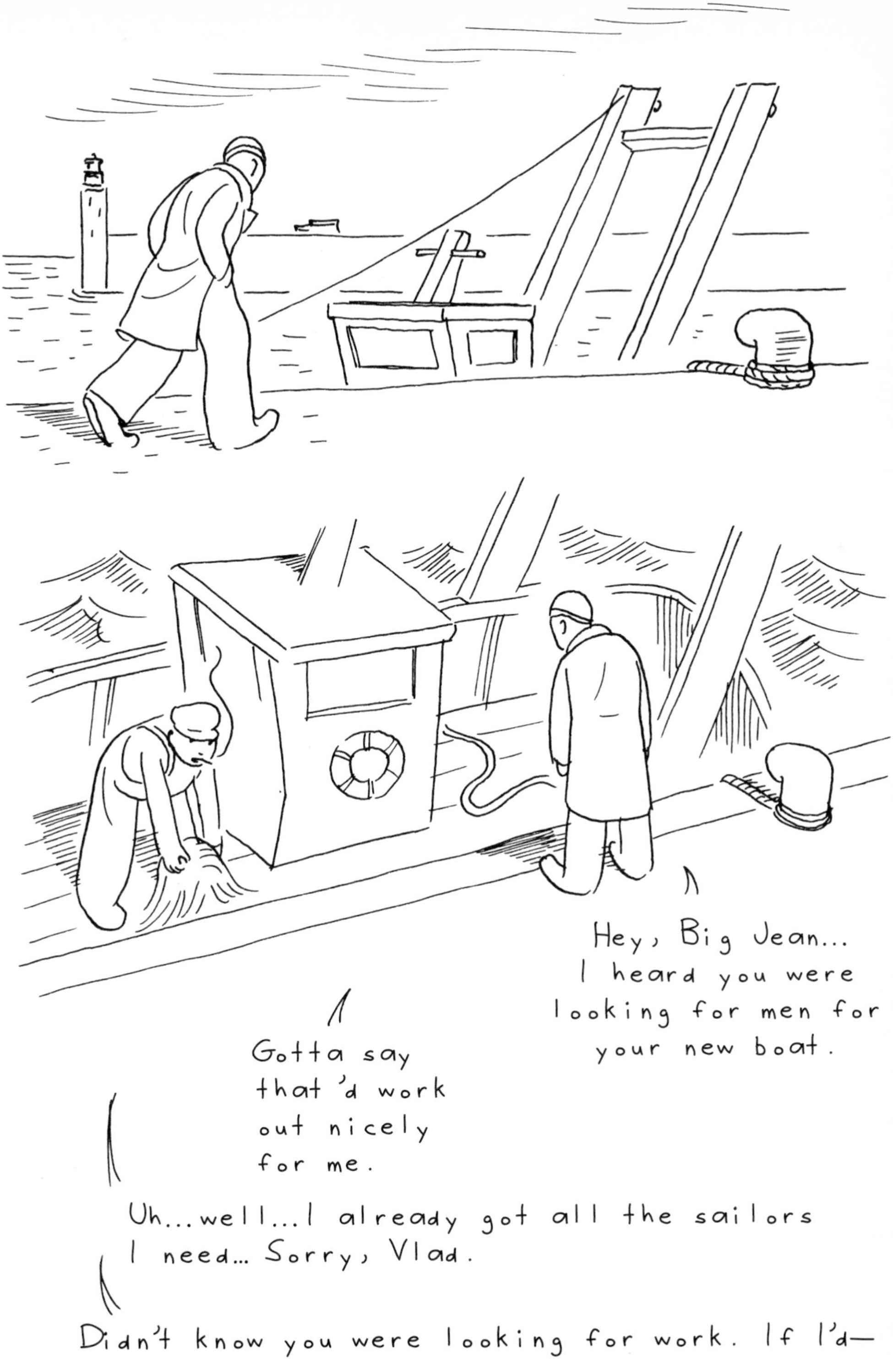
Hey, Big Jean... I heard you were looking for men for your new boat.
Gotta say that'd work out nicely for me.
Uh...well...I already got all the sailors I need... Sorry, Vlad.
Didn't know you were looking for work. If I'd—

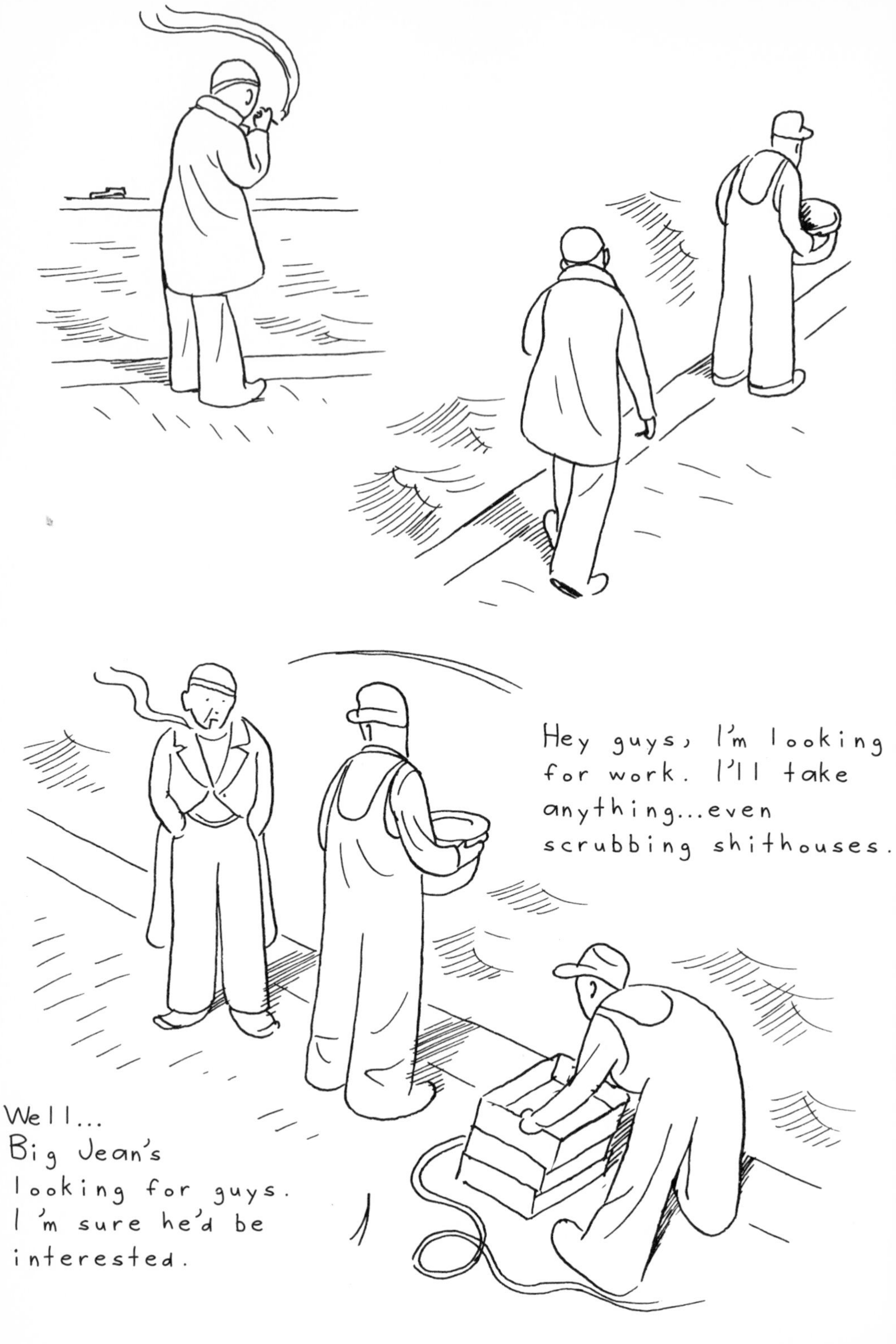
Hey guys, I'm looking for work. I'll take anything...even scrubbing shithouses.
Well... Big Jean's looking for guys. I'm sure he'd be interested.

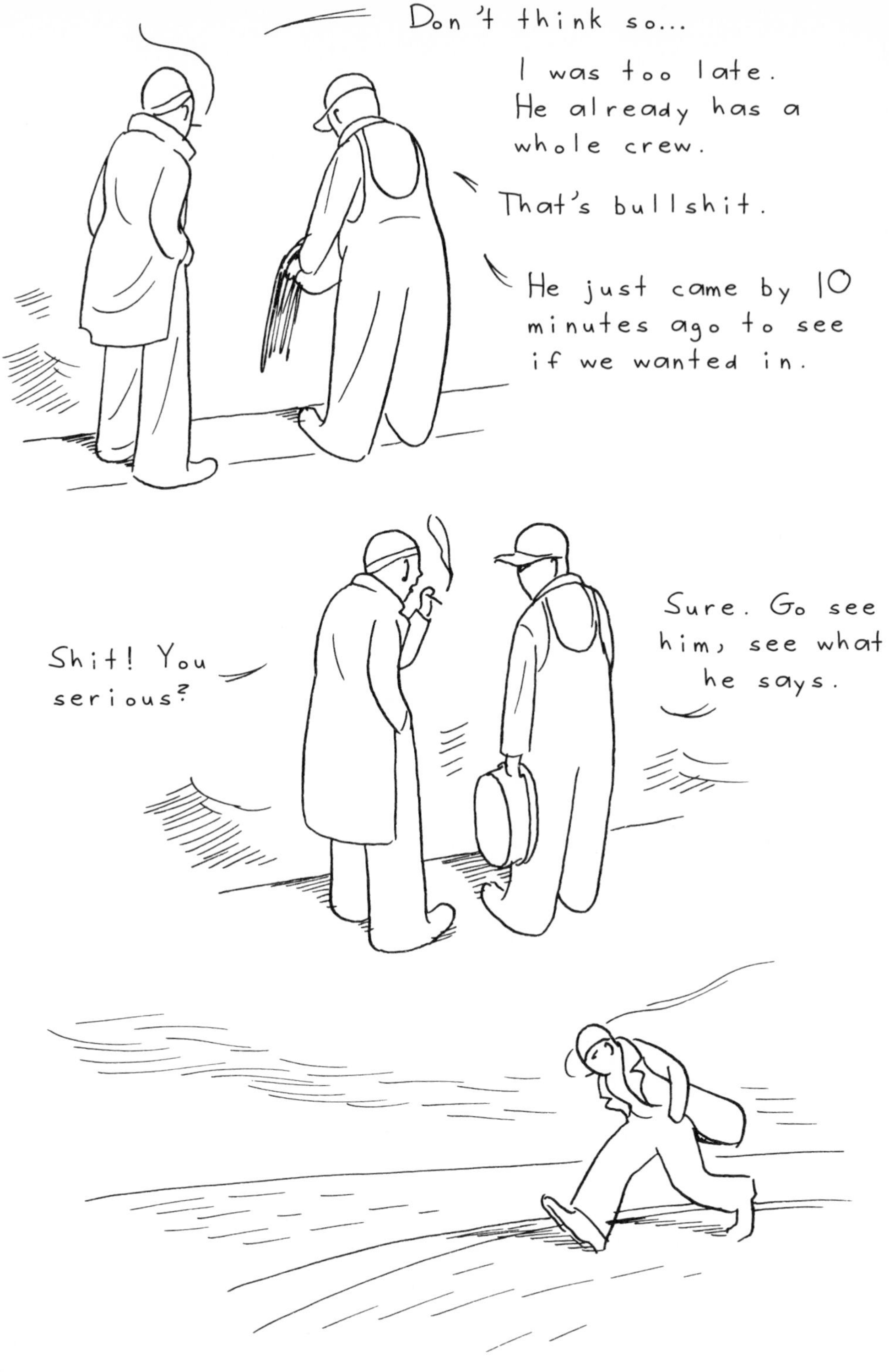
Don't think so...
I was too late. He already has a whole crew.
That's bullshit.
He just came by 10 minutes ago to see if we wanted in.
Shit! You serious?
Sure. Go see him, see what he says.

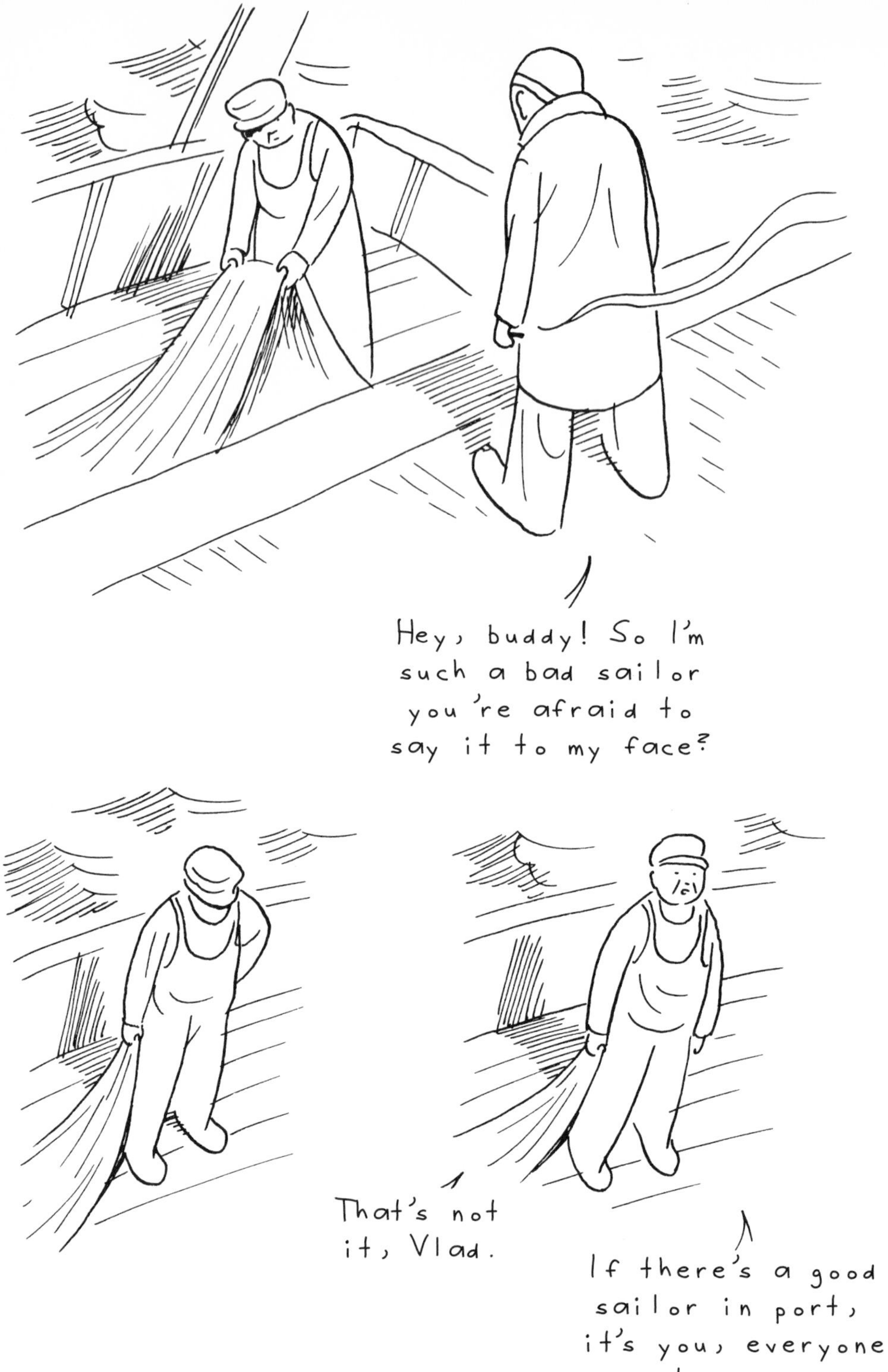
Hey, buddy! So I'm such a bad sailor you're afraid to say it to my face?
That's not it, Vlad.
If there's a good sailor in port, it's you, everyone knows...

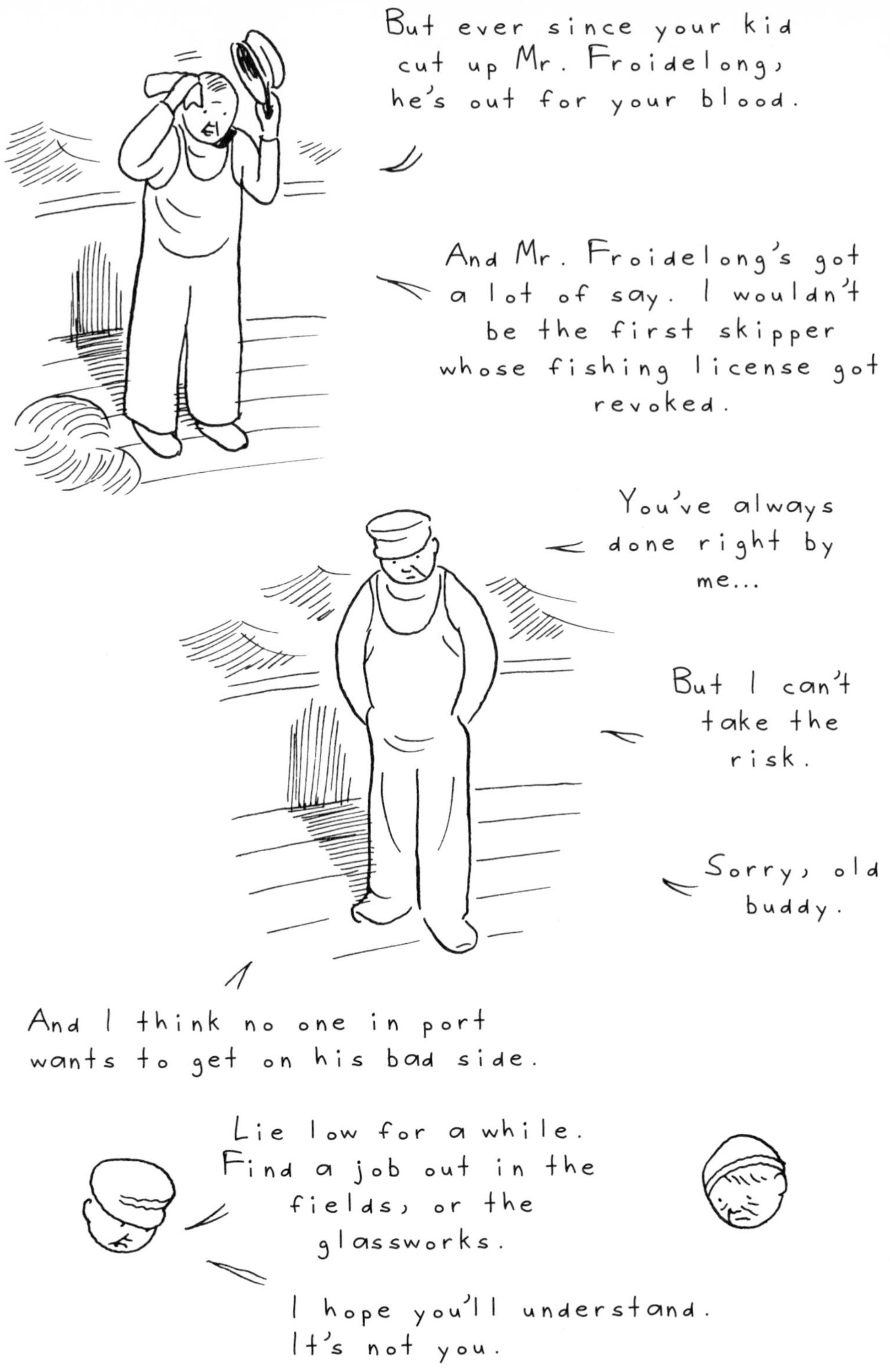
But ever since your kid cut up Mr. Froidelong, he's out for your blood.
And Mr. Froidelong's got a lot of say. I wouldn't be the first skipper whose fishing license got revoked.
You've always done right by me...
But I can't take the risk.
Sorry, old buddy.
And I think no one in port wants to get on his bad side.
Lie low for a while. Find a job out in the fields, or the glassworks.
I hope you'll understand. It's not you.

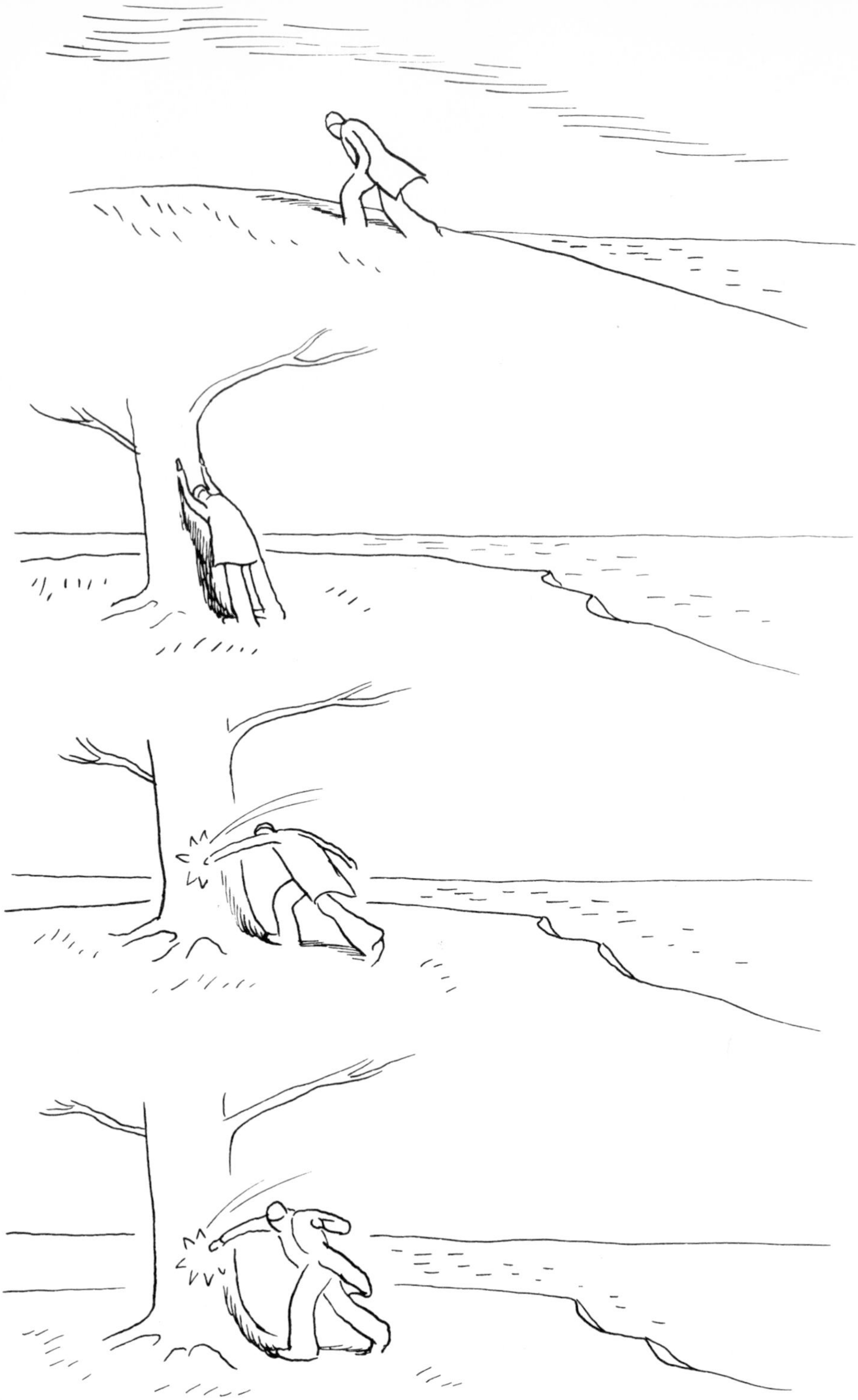

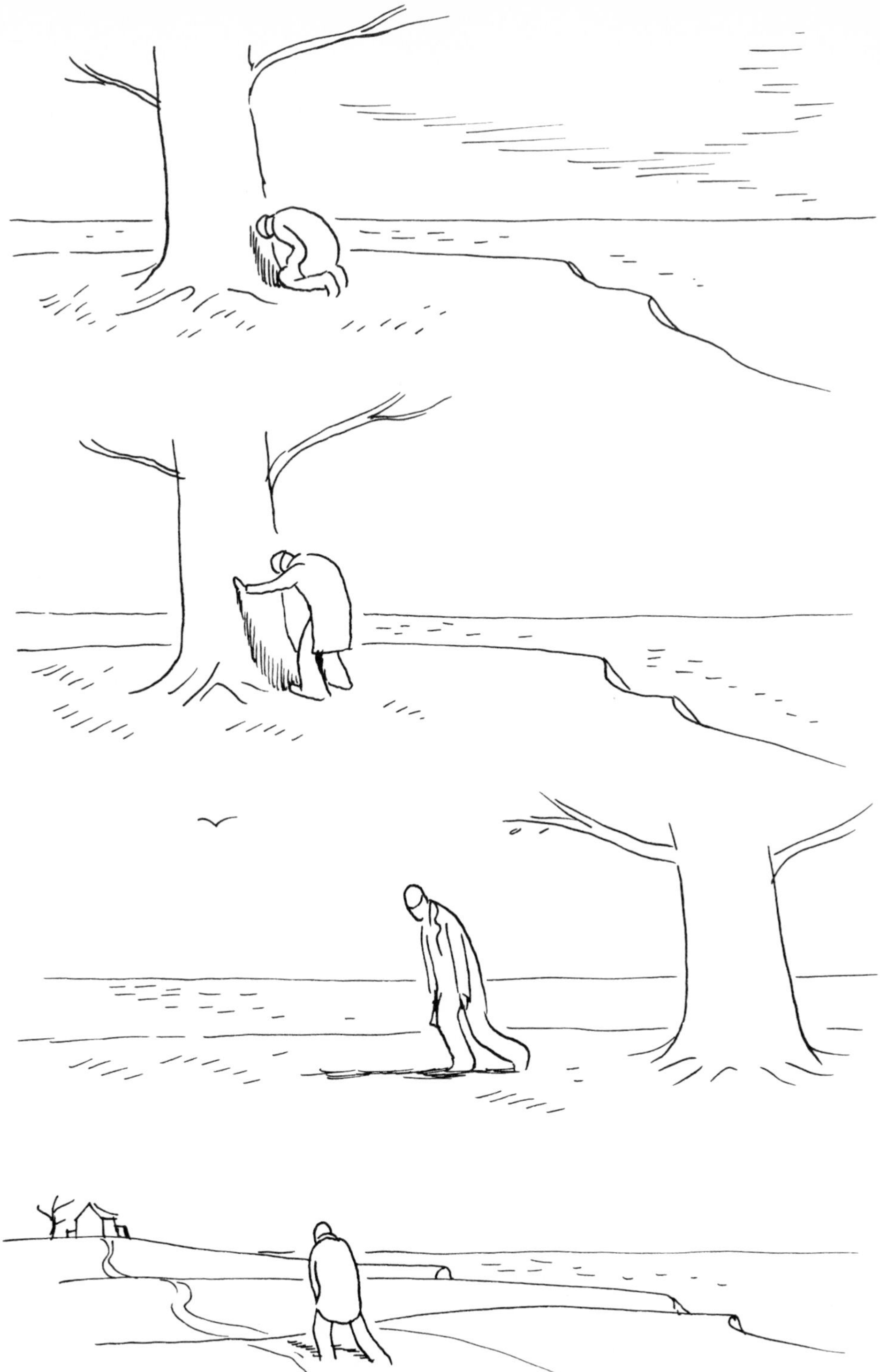

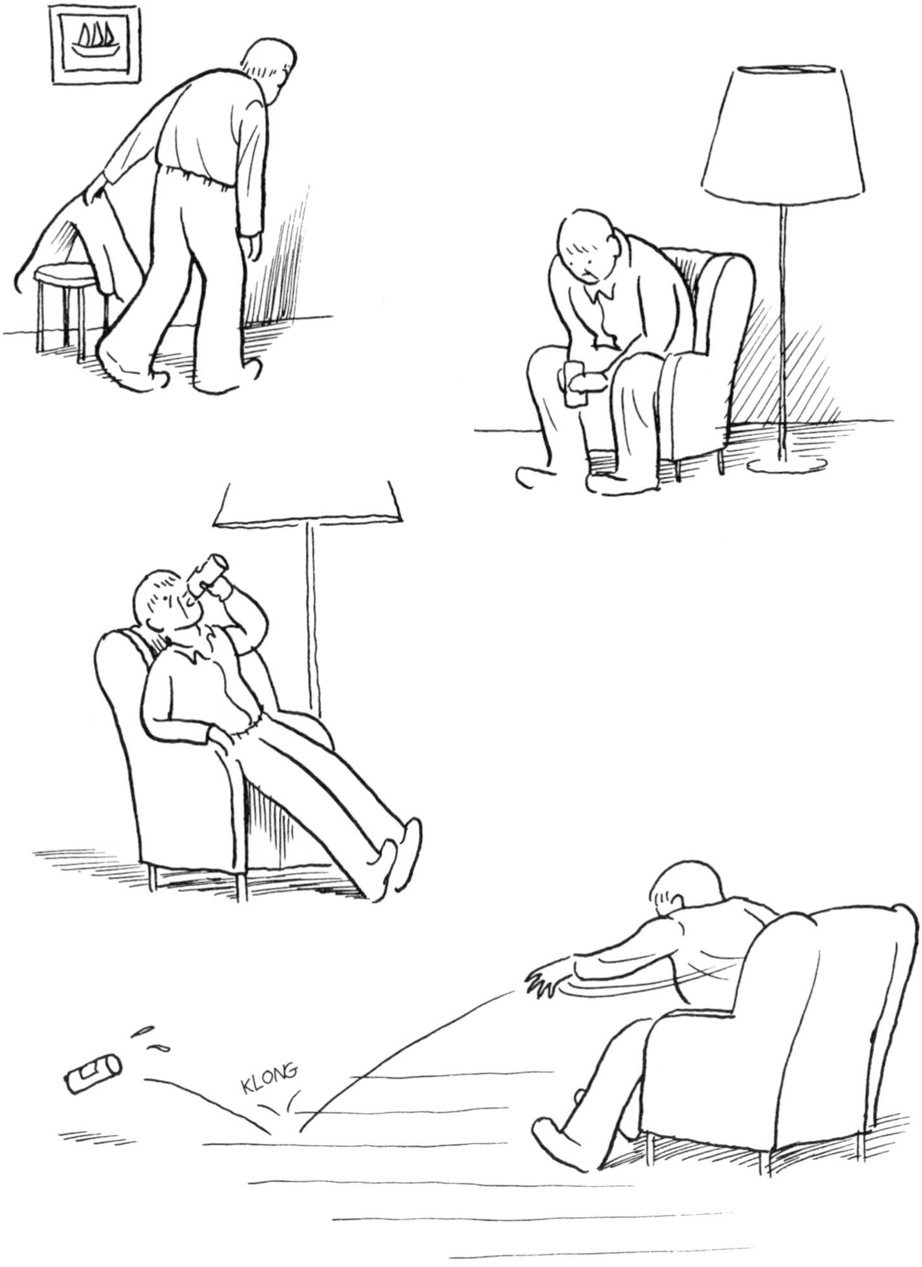
KLONG

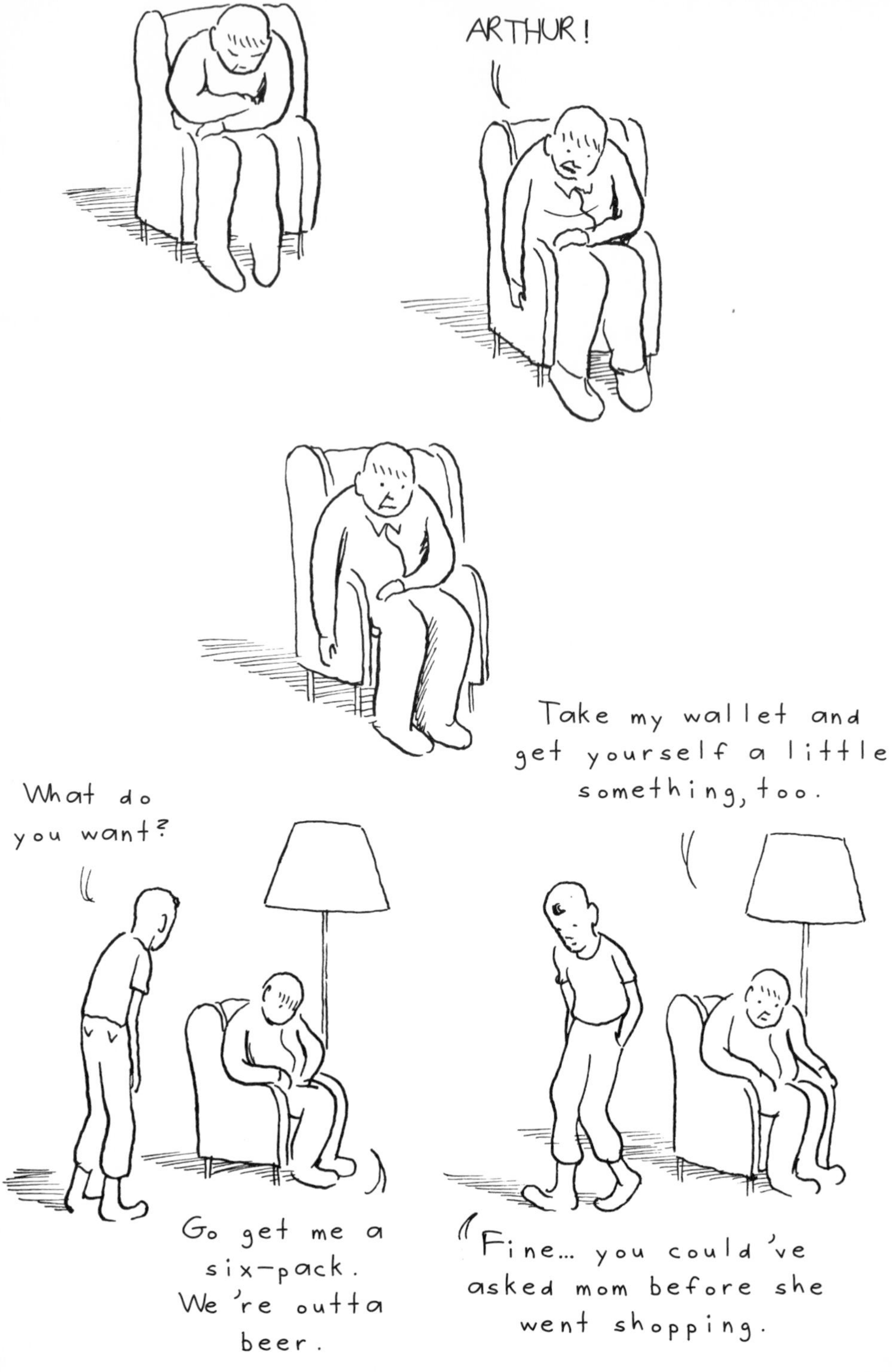
ARTHUR!
What do you want?
Go get me a six-pack. We're outta beer.
Take my wallet and get yourself a little something, too.
Fine... you could've asked mom before she went shopping.

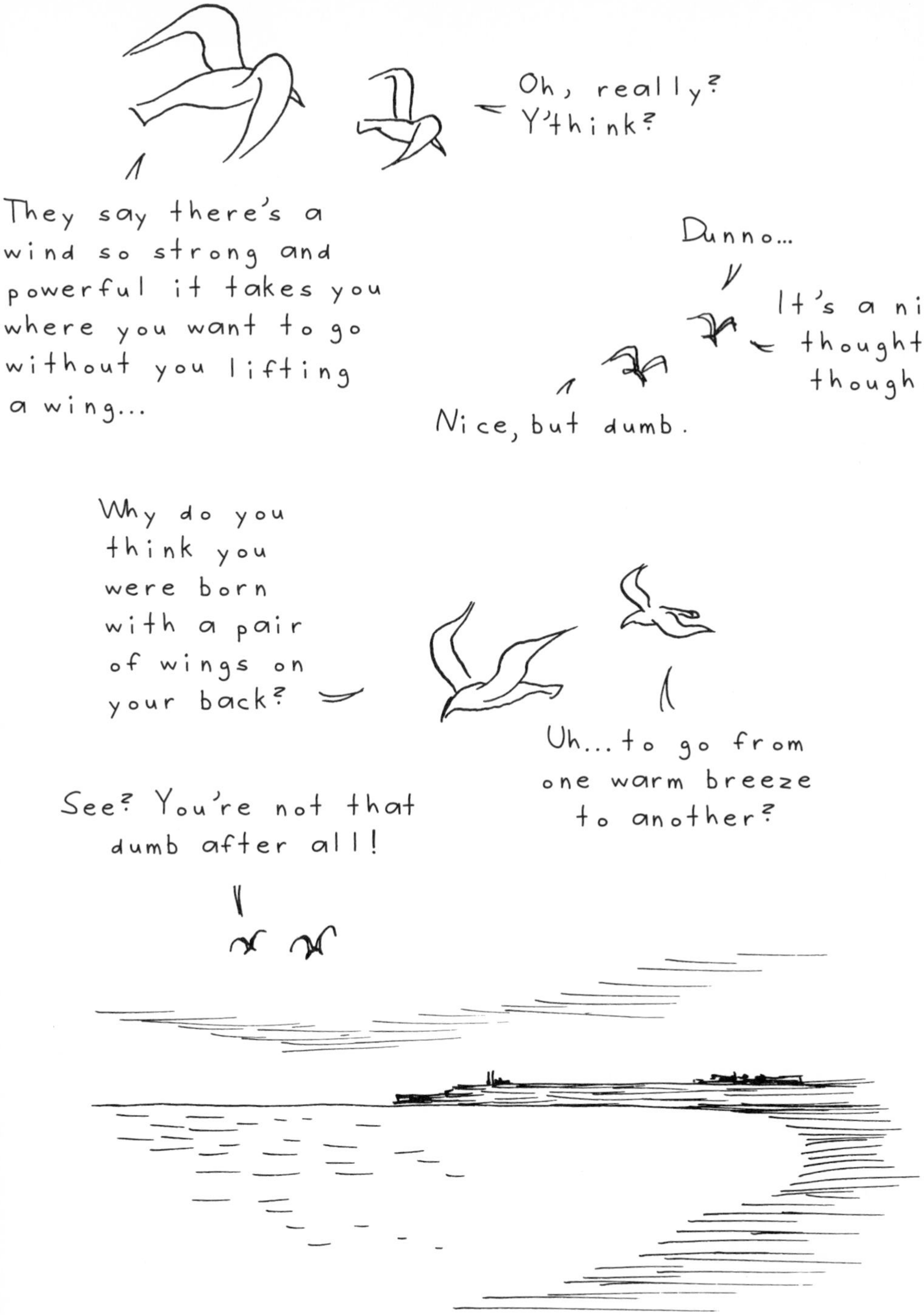
Oh, really? Y'think?
They say there's a wind so strong and powerful it takes you where you want to go without you lifting a wing...
Dunno...
It's a nice thought, though.
Nice, but dumb.
Why do you think you were born with a pair of wings on your back?
Uh... to go from one warm breeze to another?
See? You're not that dumb after all!

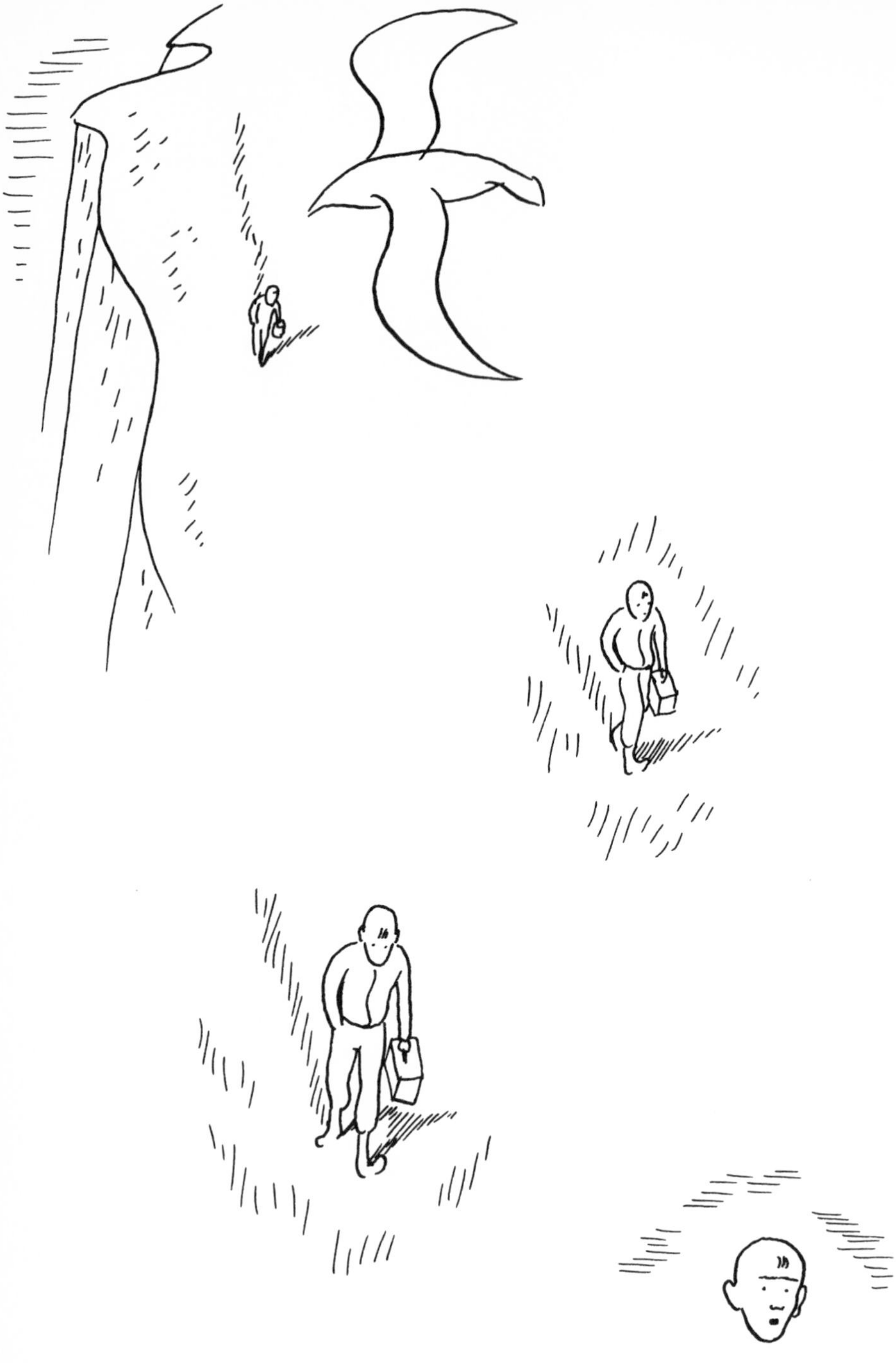

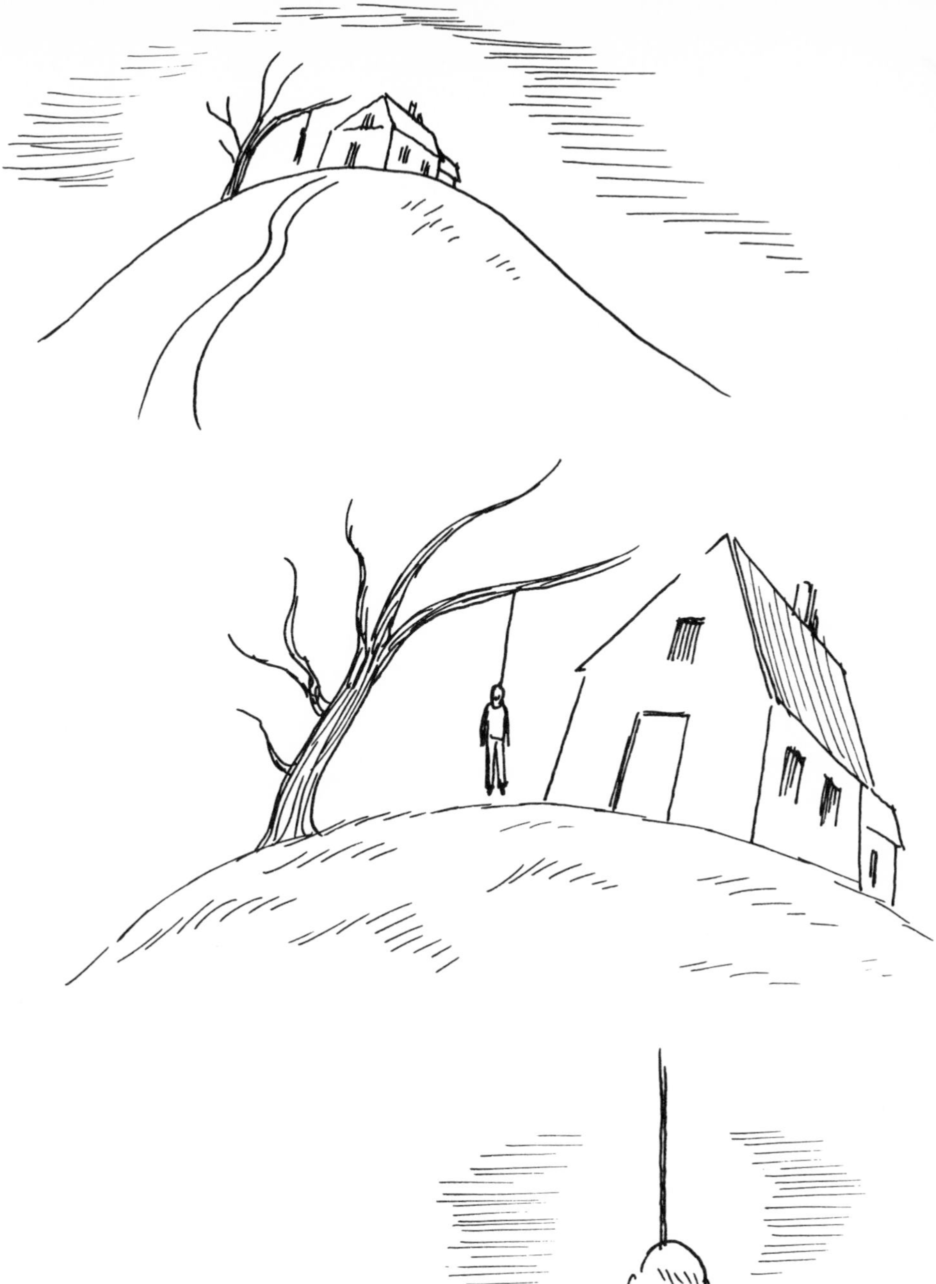

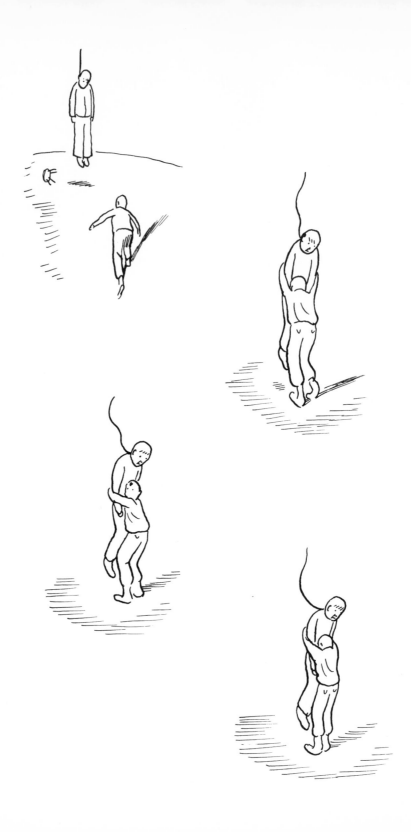

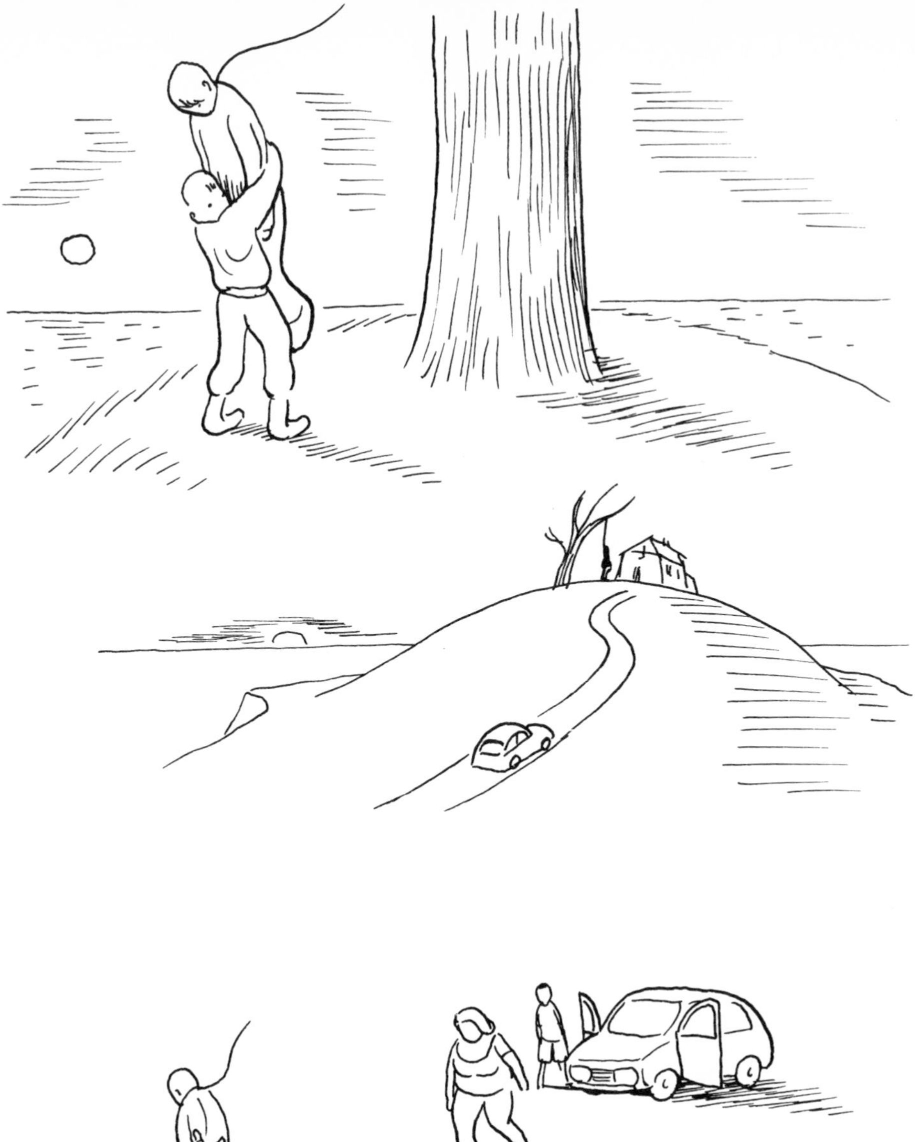

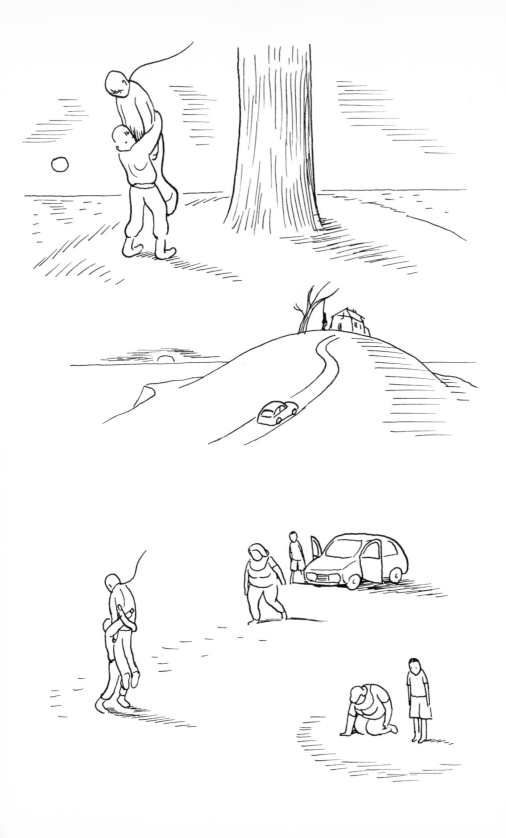

Let him go, Arthur...
He's dead already.

Le fils

(The Son)

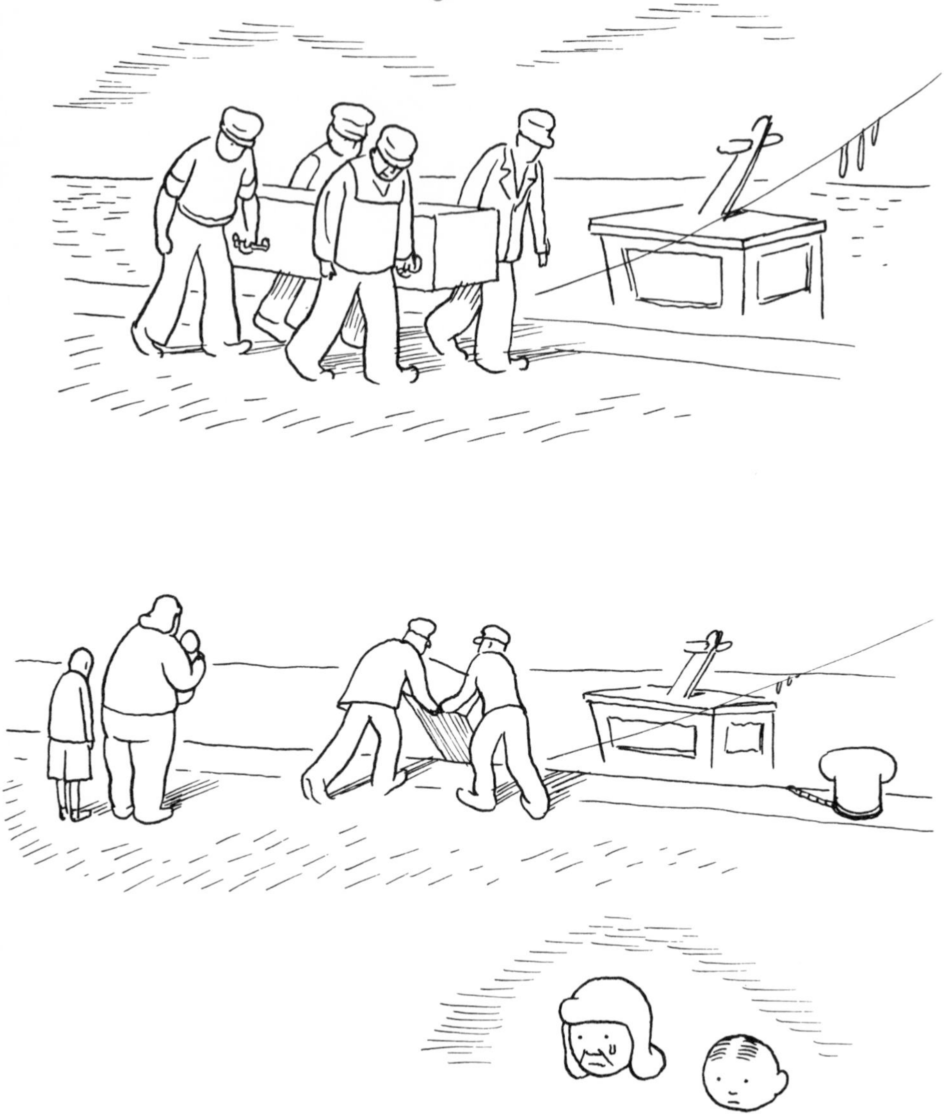

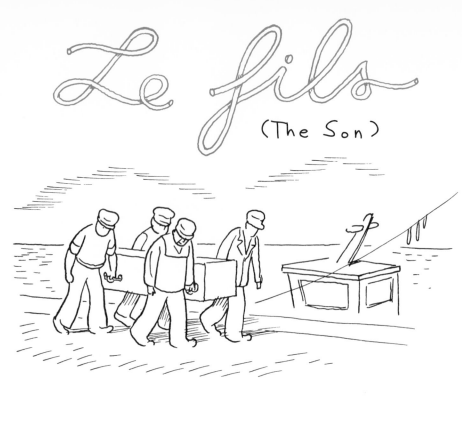

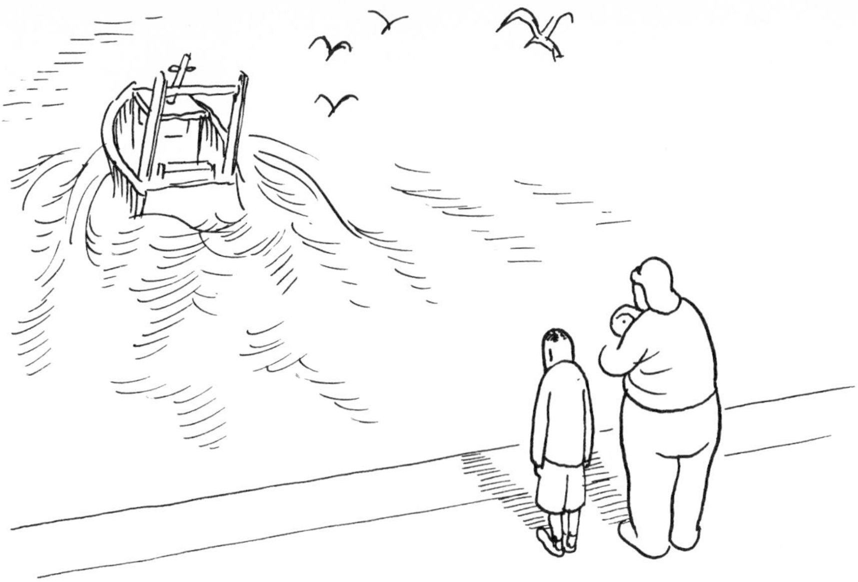

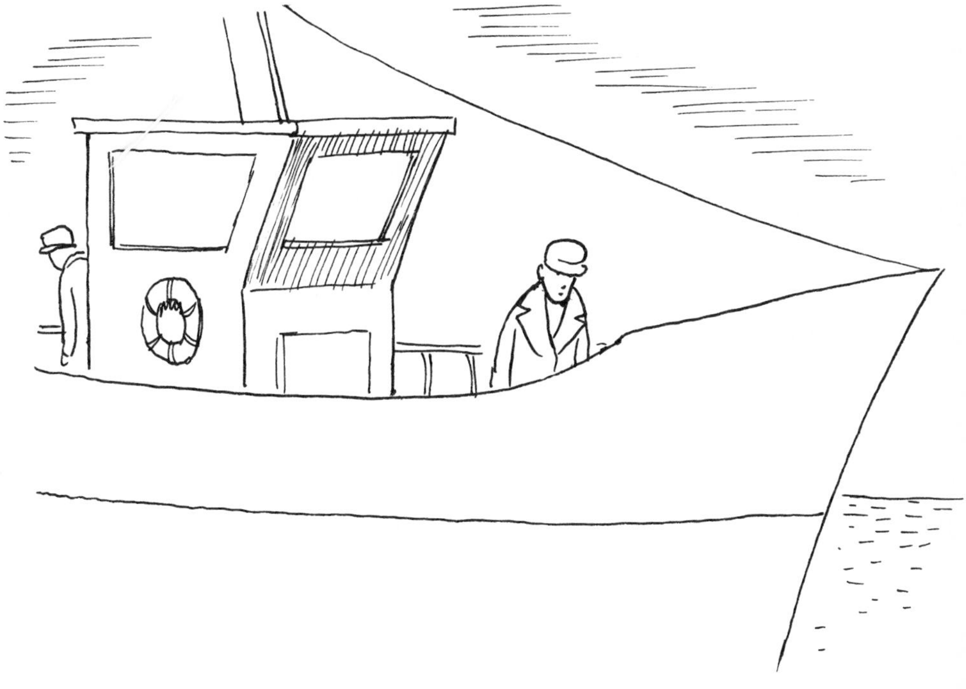

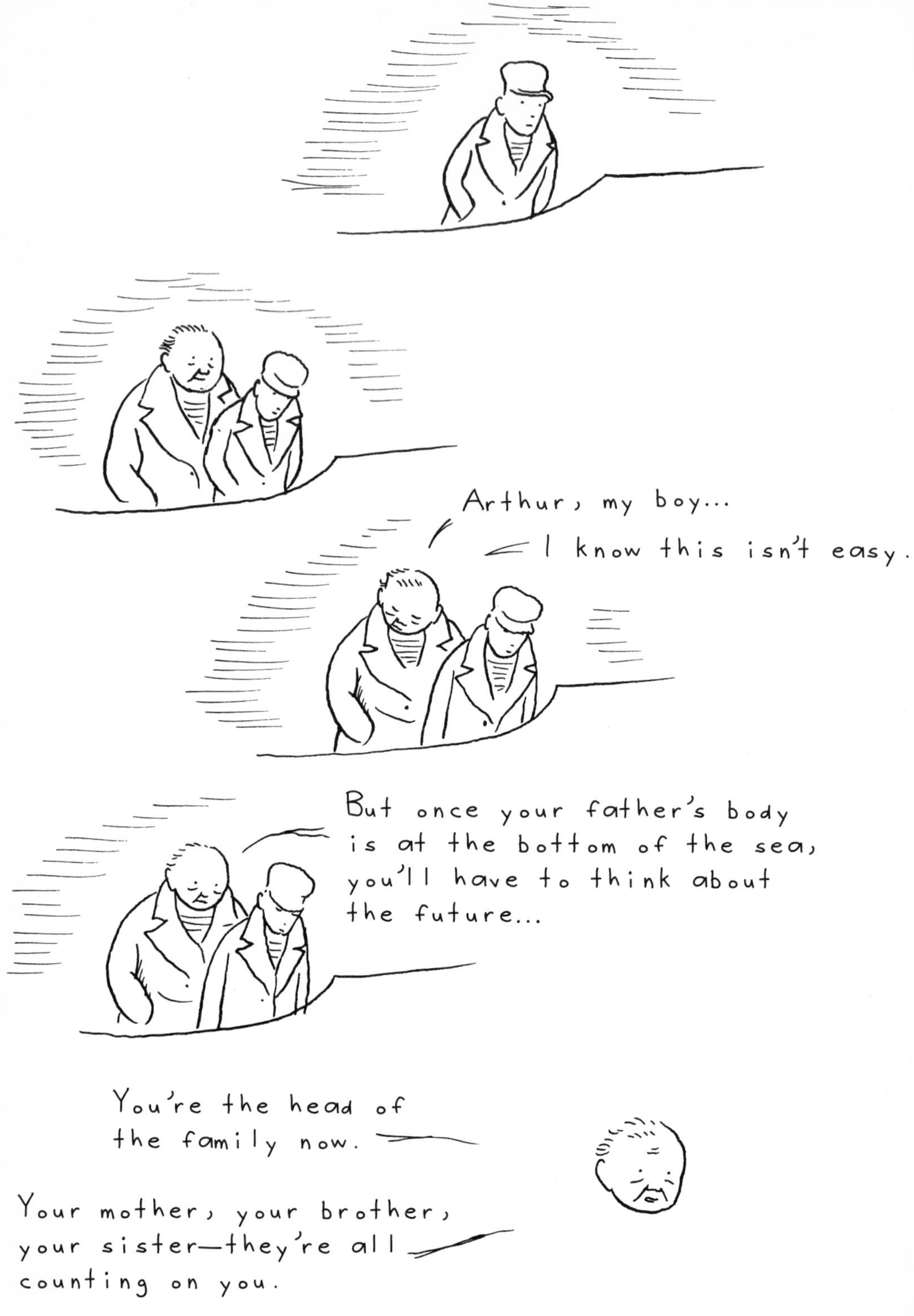
Arthur, my boy...
I know this isn't easy.
But once your father's body is at the bottom of the sea, you'll have to think about the future...
You're the head of the family now.
Your mother, your brother, your sister—they're all counting on you.

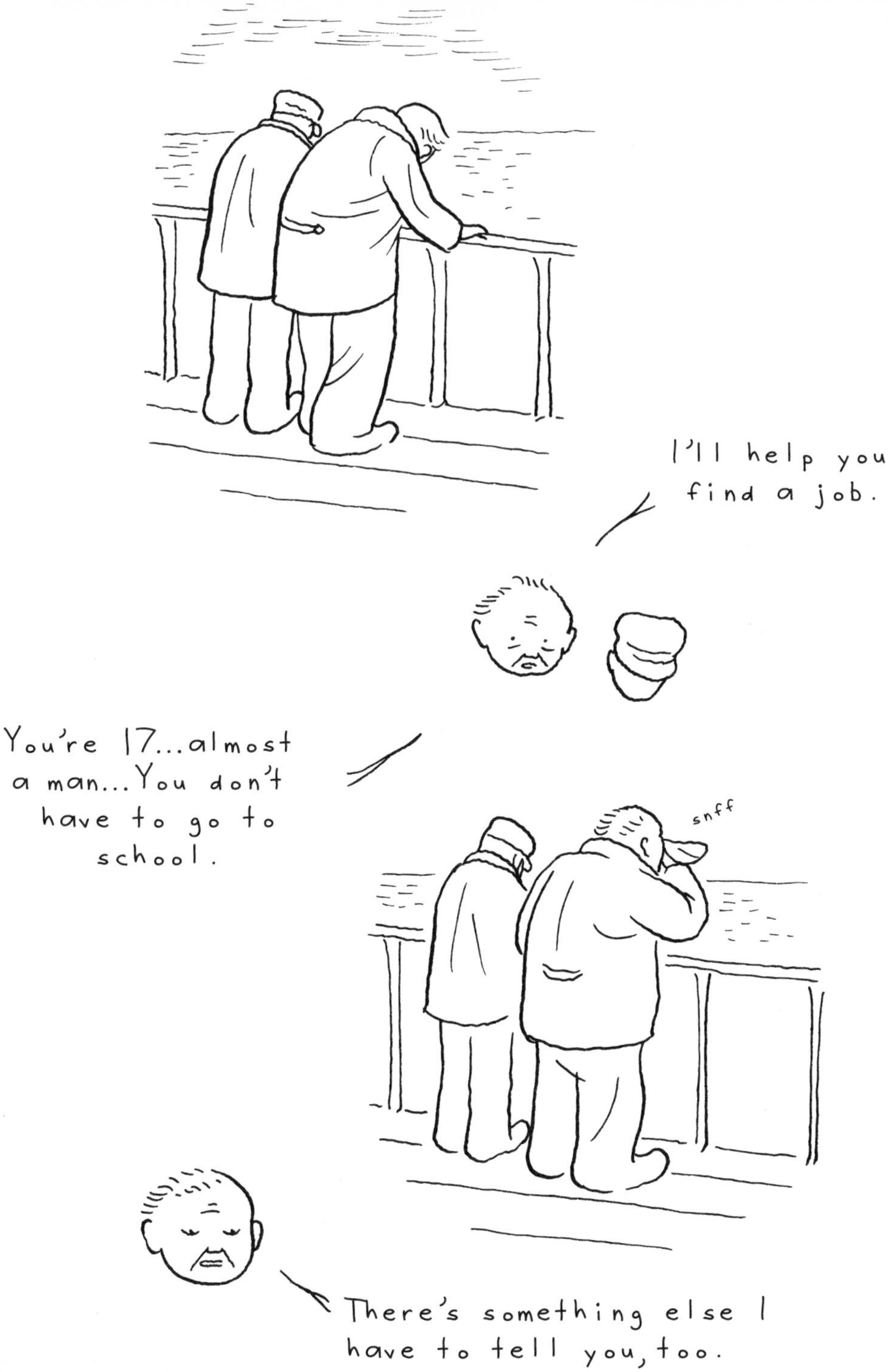
I'll help you find a job.
You're 17...almost a man...You don't have to go to school.
snff
There's something else I have to tell you, too.

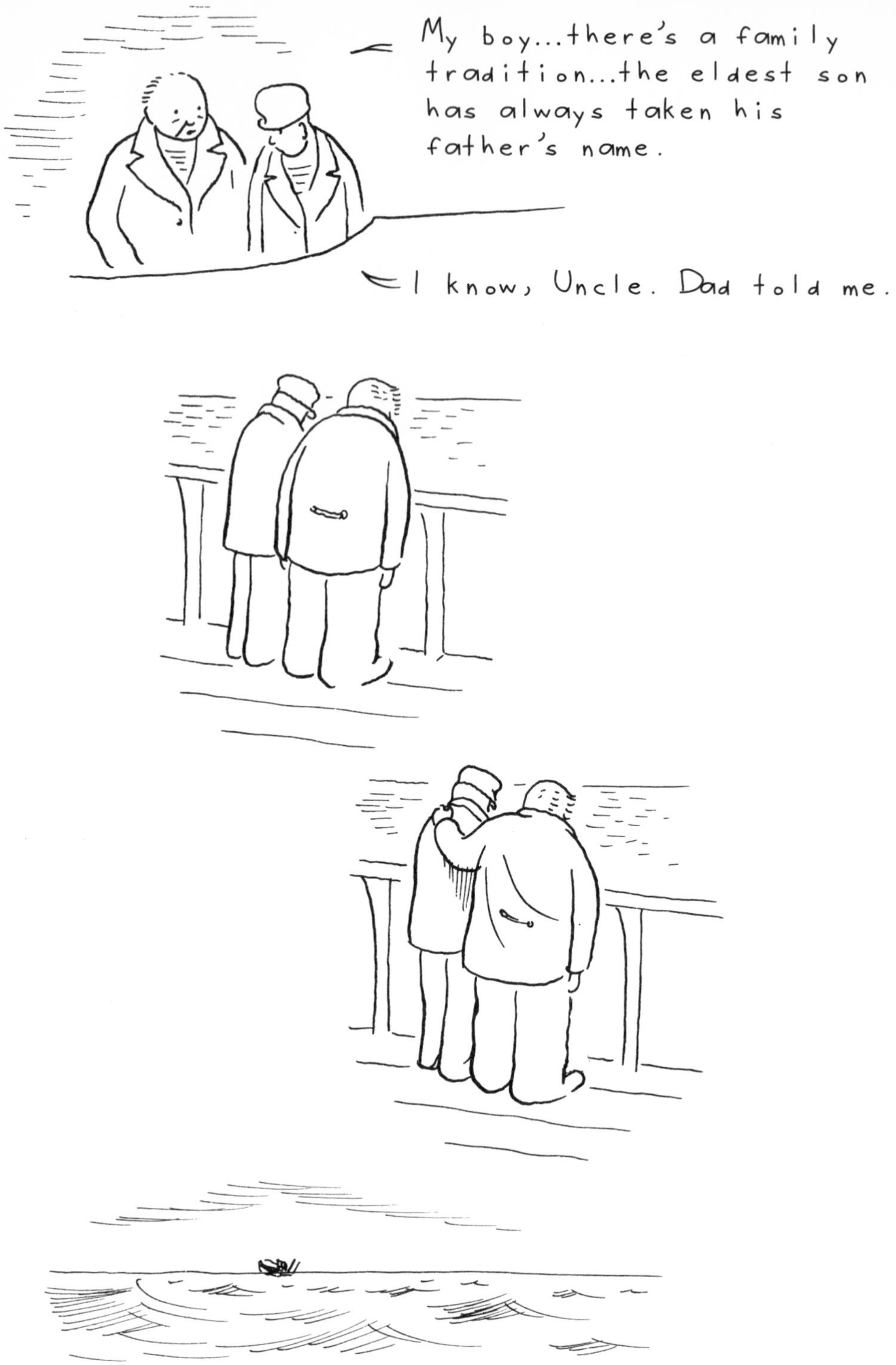
My boy...there's a family tradition...the eldest son has always taken his father's name.
I know, Uncle. Dad told me.

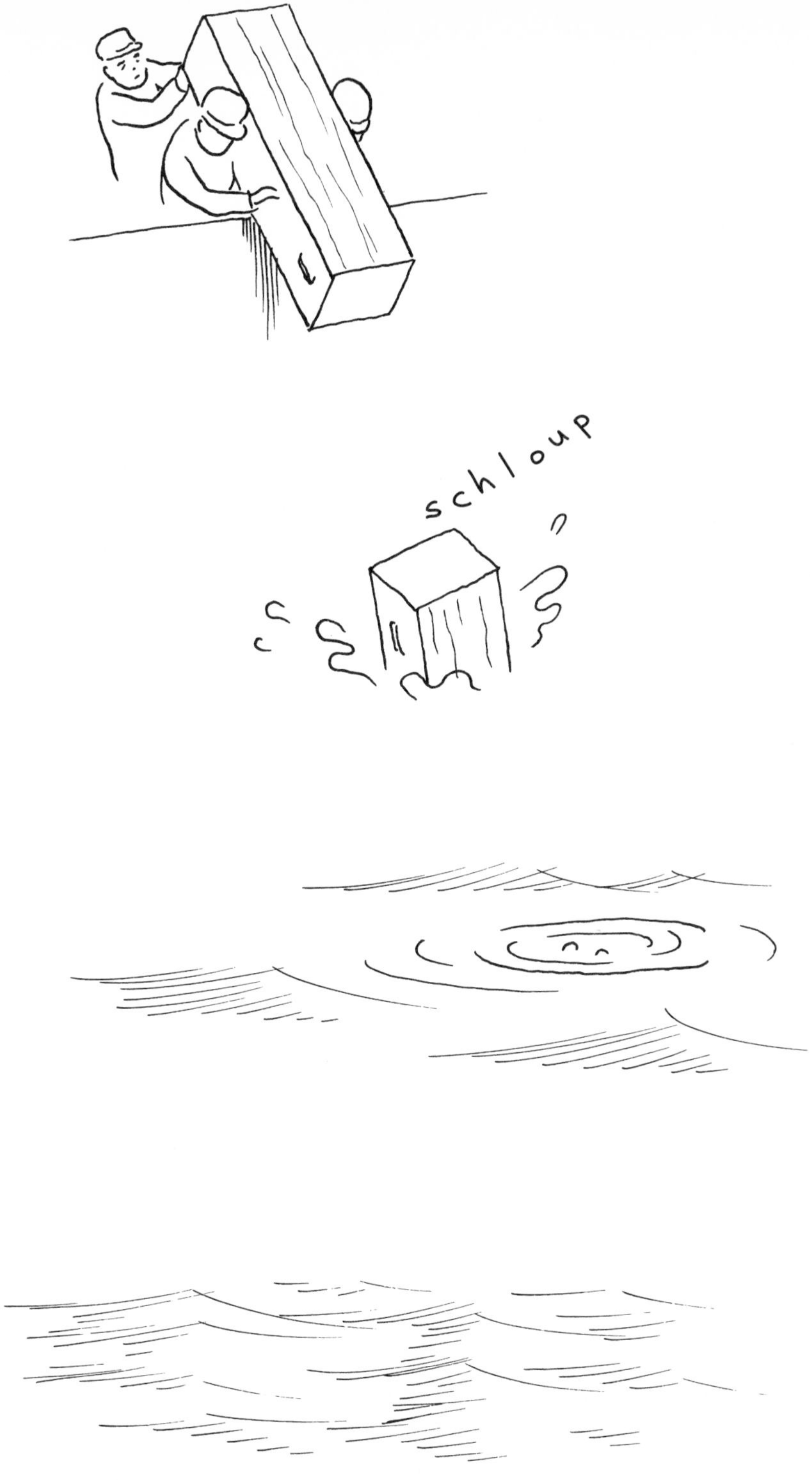
schloup

Où Êtes Vous Mon Amour?

(Where Are You, My Love?)

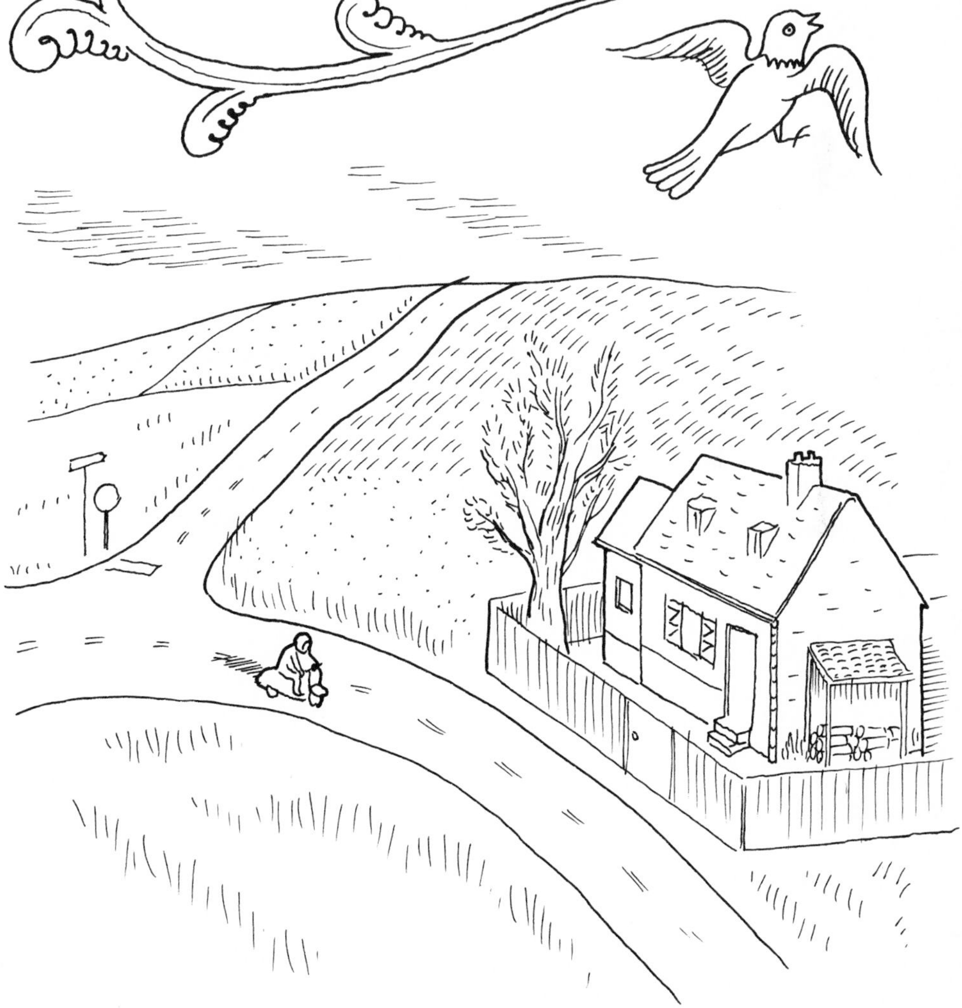

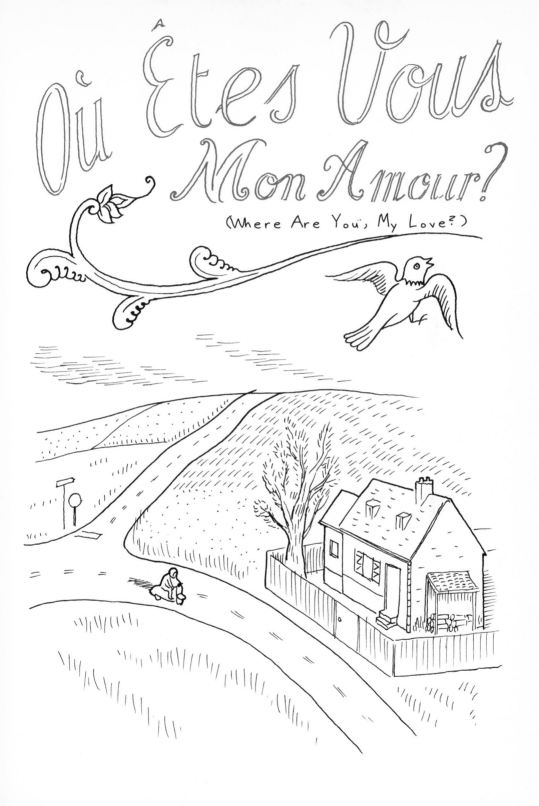

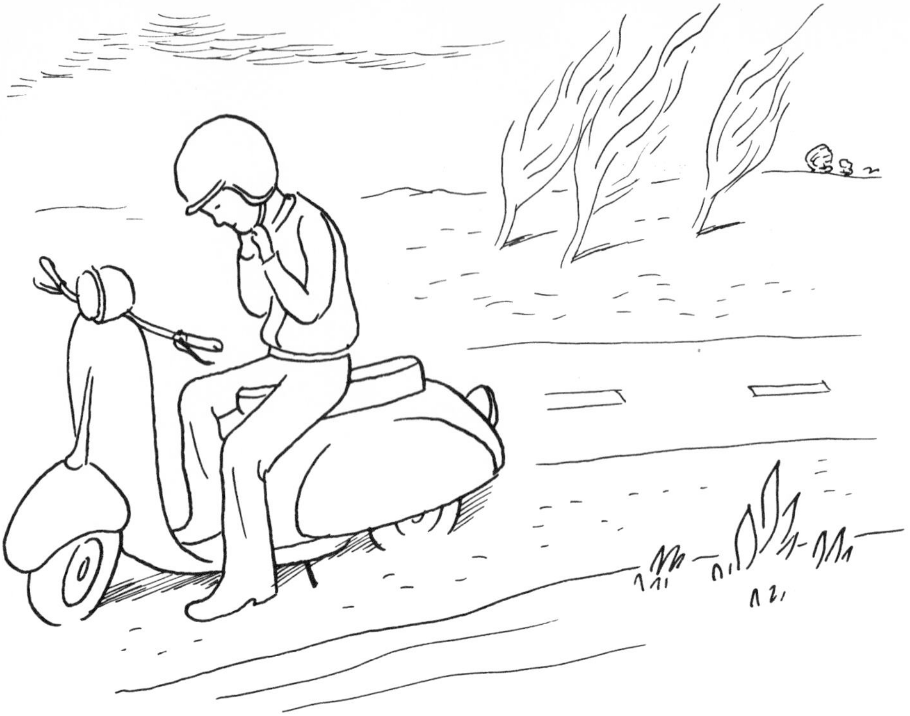

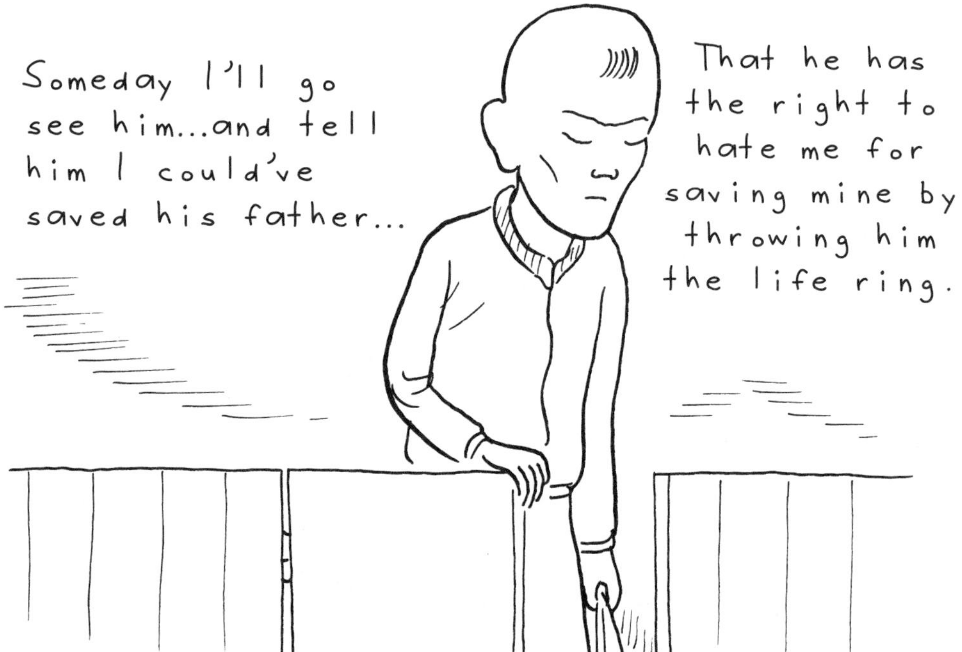
Someday I'll go see him...and tell him I could've saved his father...
That he has the right to hate me for saving mine by throwing him the life ring.

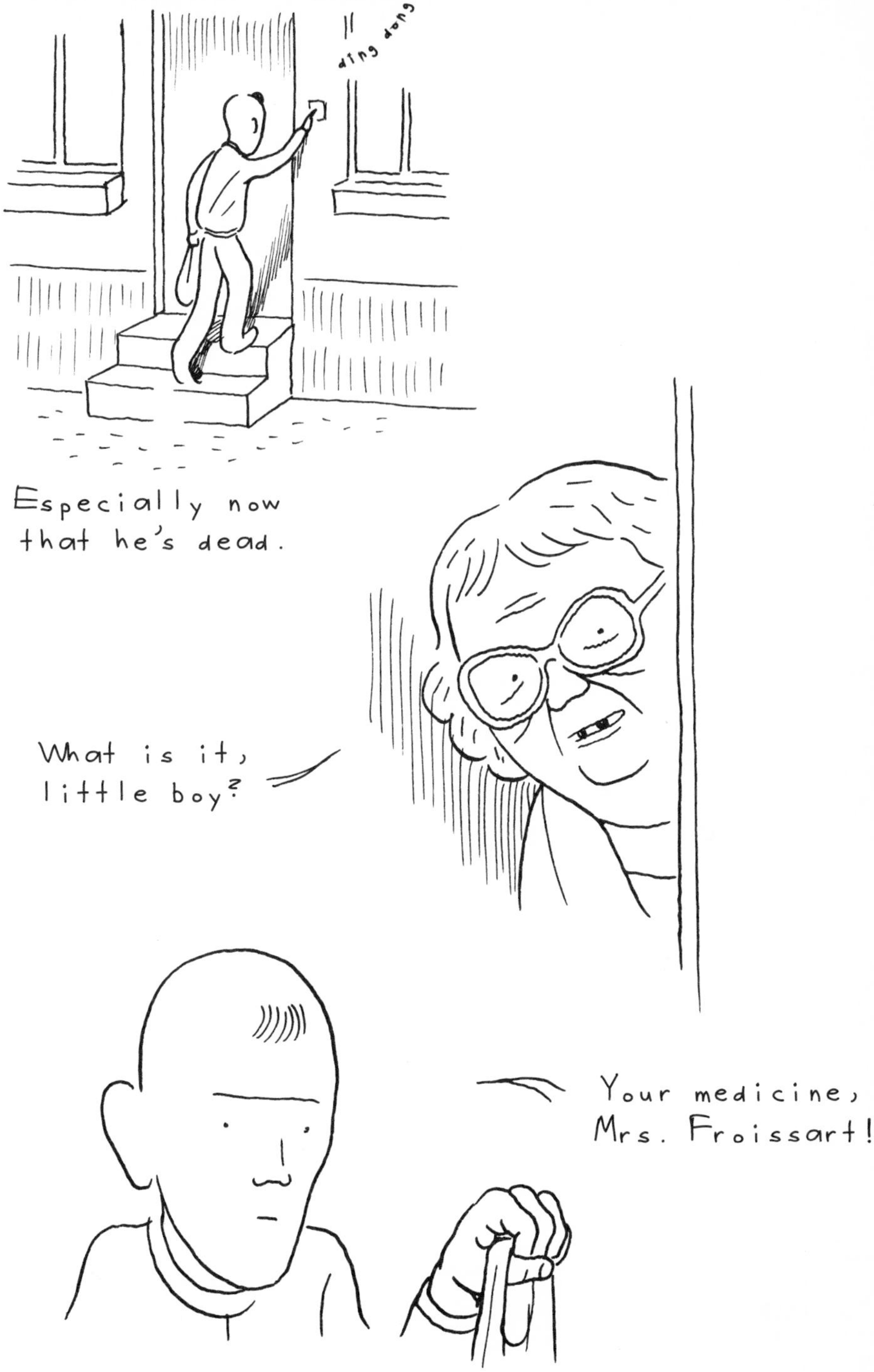
ding dong
Especially now that he's dead.
What is it, little boy?
Your medicine, Mrs. Froissart!

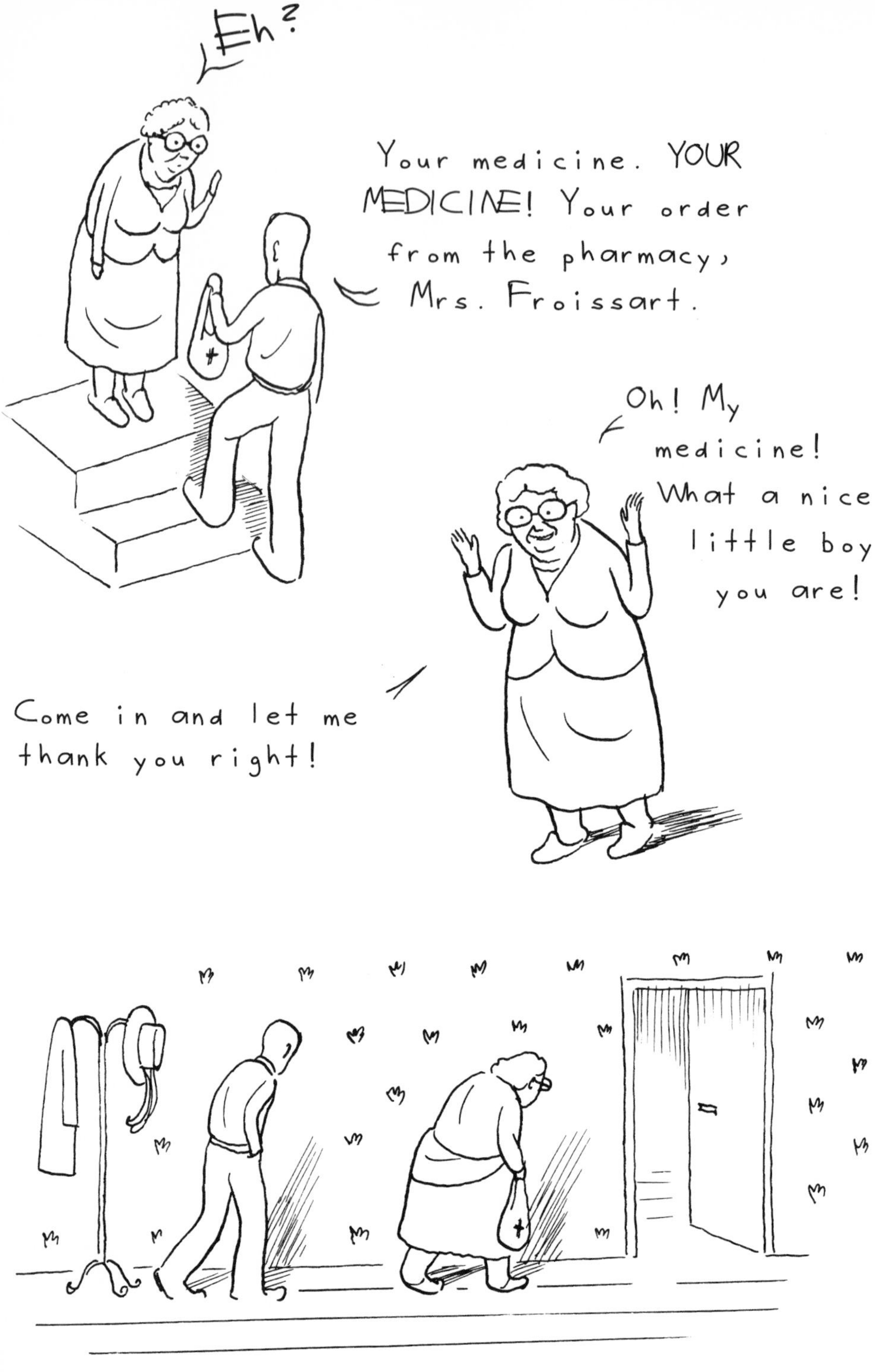
Eh?
Your medicine. YOUR MEDICINE! Your order from the pharmacy, Mrs. Froissart.
Oh! My medicine! What a nice little boy you are!
Come in and let me thank you right!

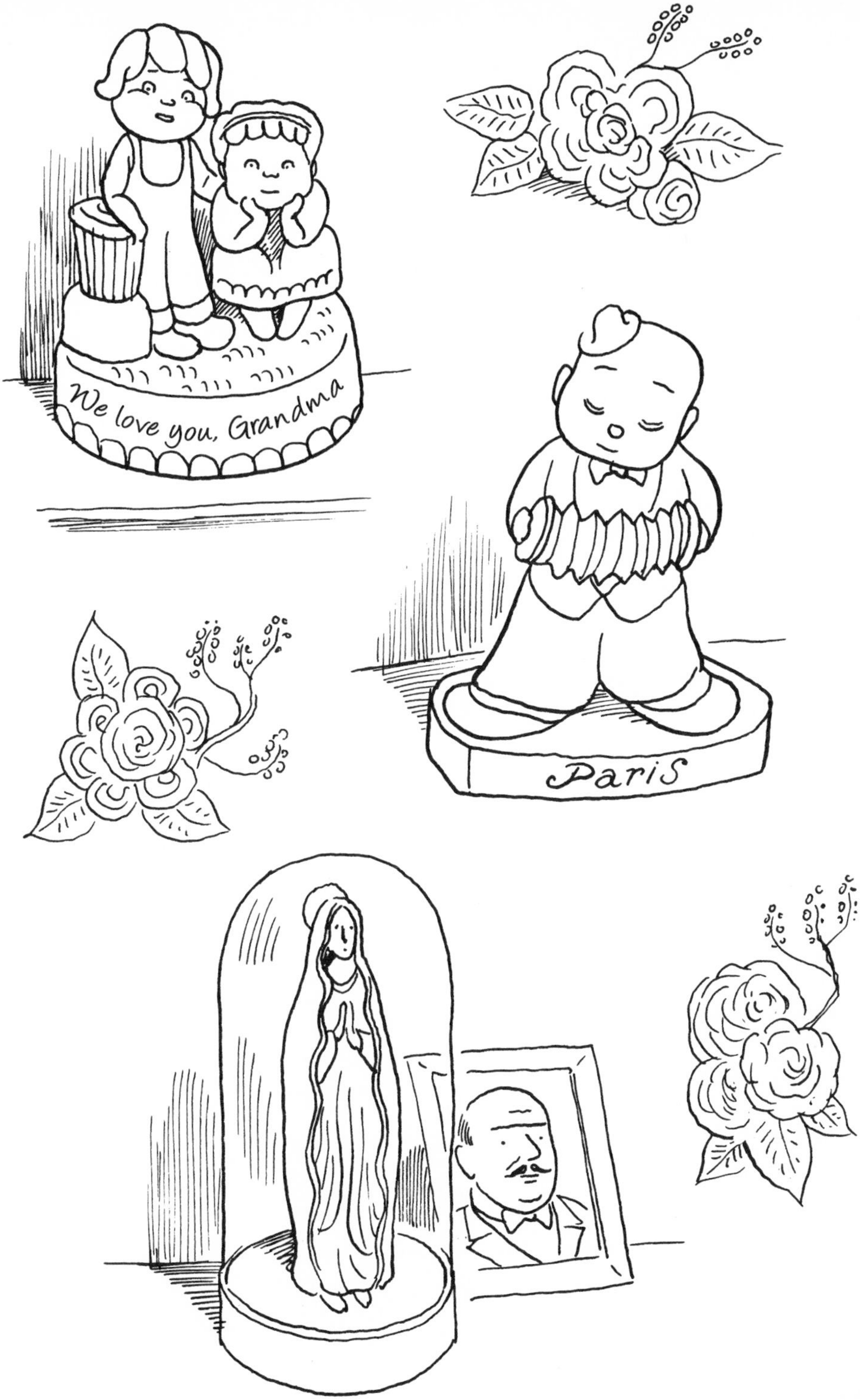
We love you, Grandma
Paris

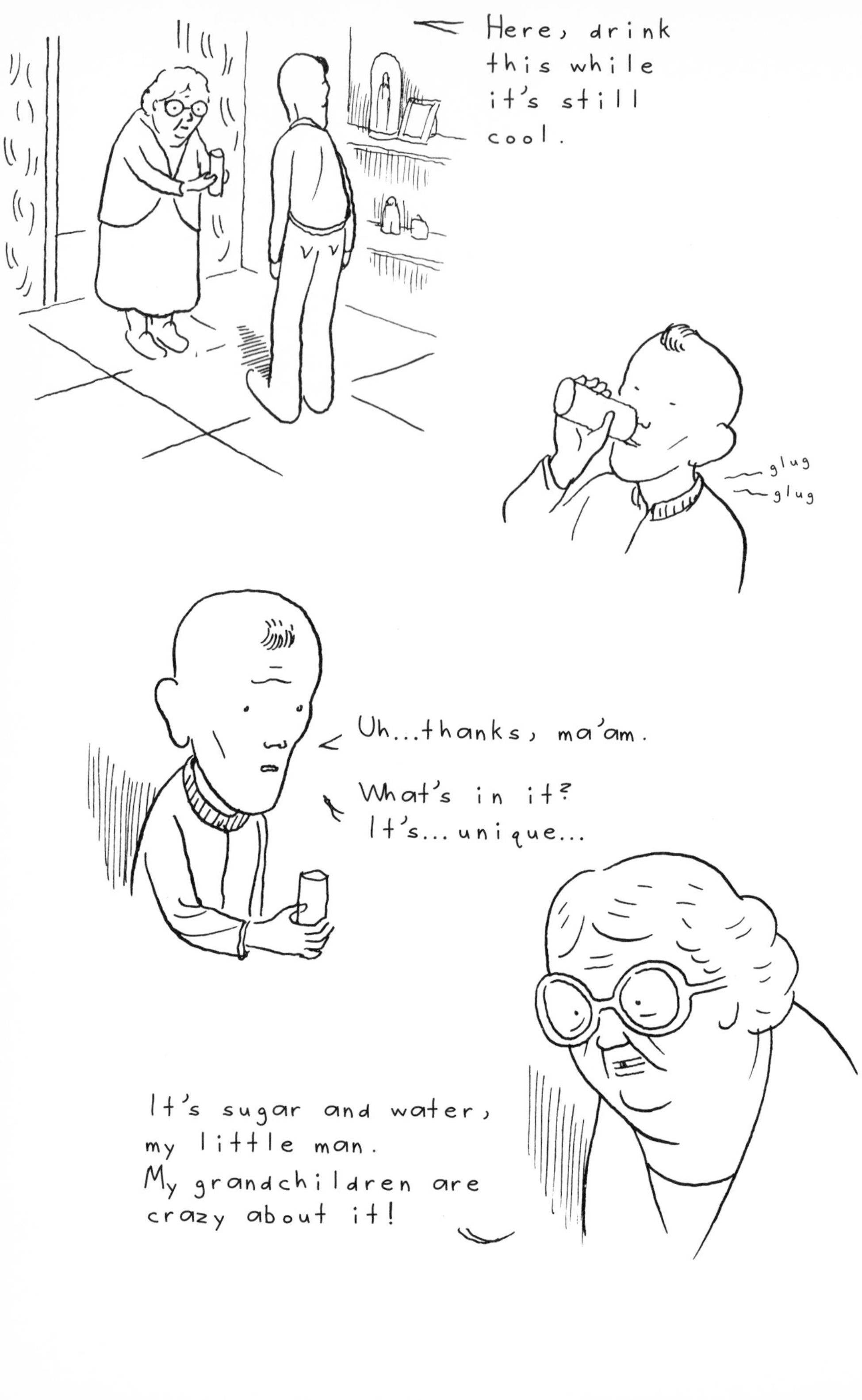
Here, drink this while it's still cool.
glug glug
Uh...thanks, ma'am.
What's in it? It's... unique...
It's sugar and water, my little man. My grandchildren are crazy about it!

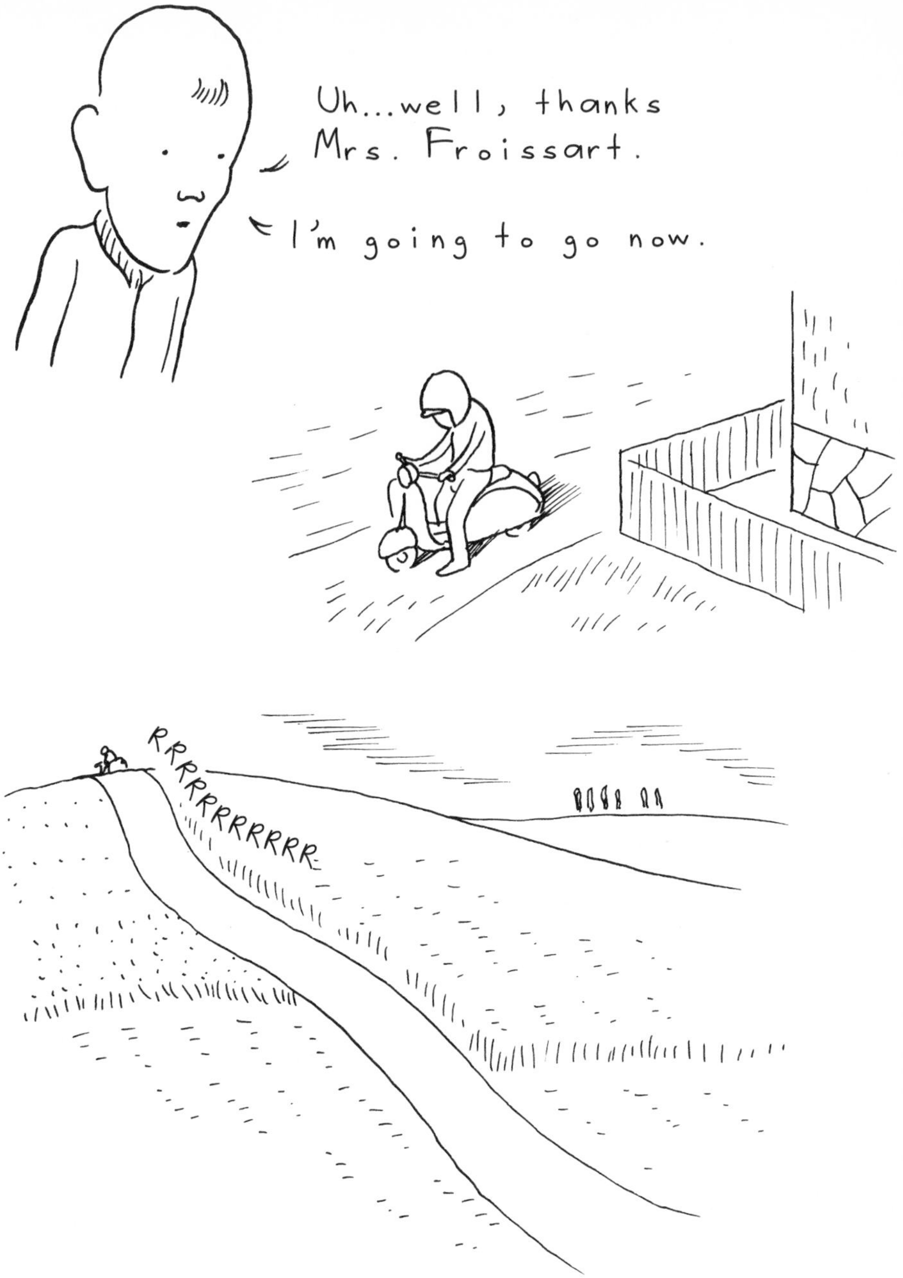
Uh...well, thanks Mrs. Froissart.
I'm going to go now.
RRRRRRRRRRR

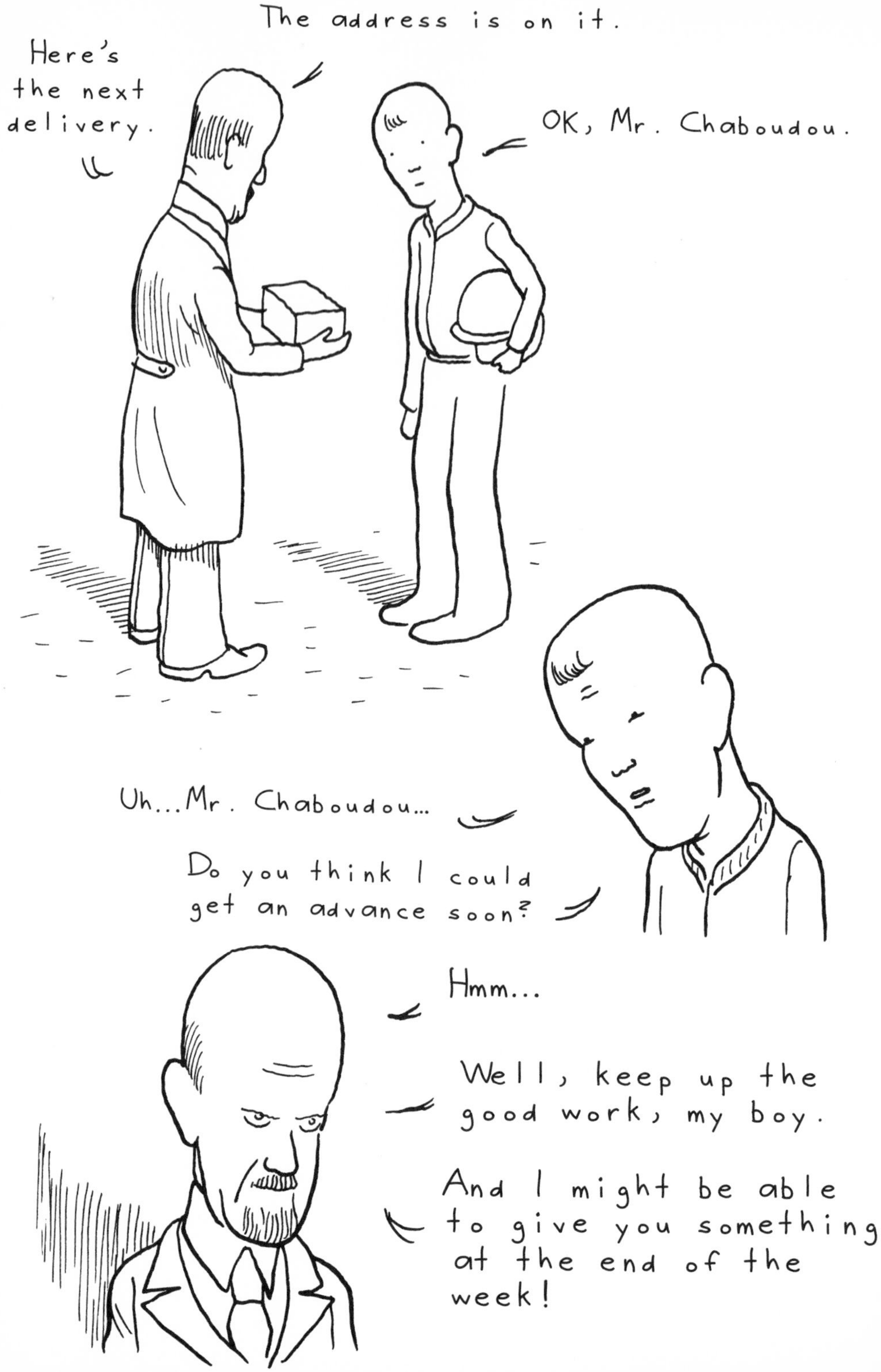
Here's the next delivery.
The address is on it.
OK, Mr. Chaboudou.
Uh... Mr. Chaboudou...
Do you think I could get an advance soon?
Hmm...
Well, keep up the good work, my boy.
And I might be able to give you something at the end of the week!

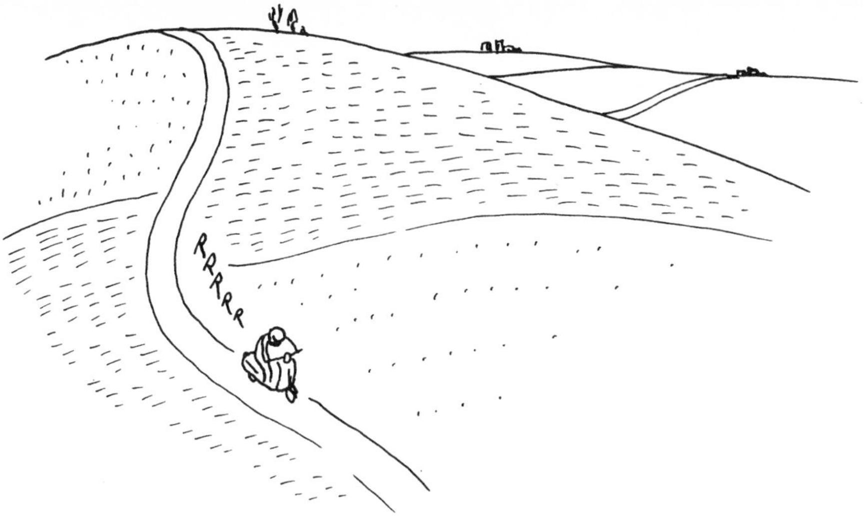
RRRRR

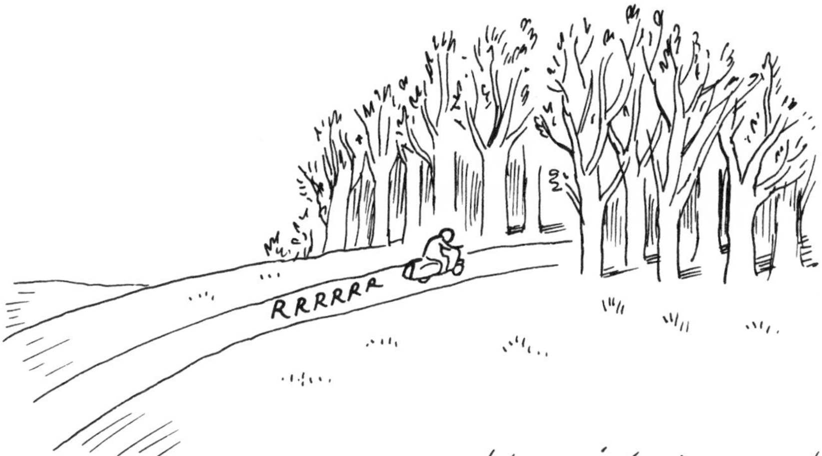
RRRRRR

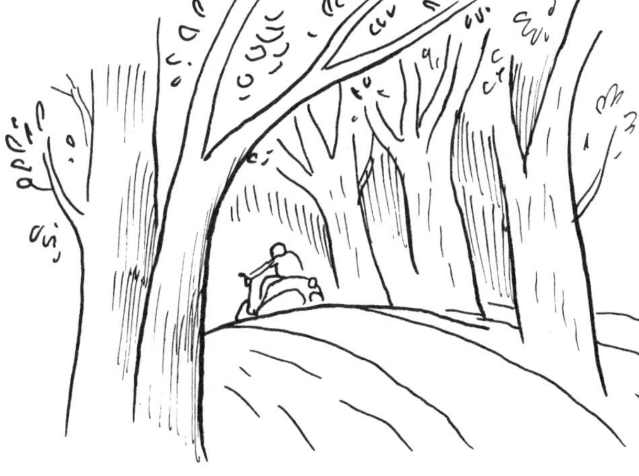

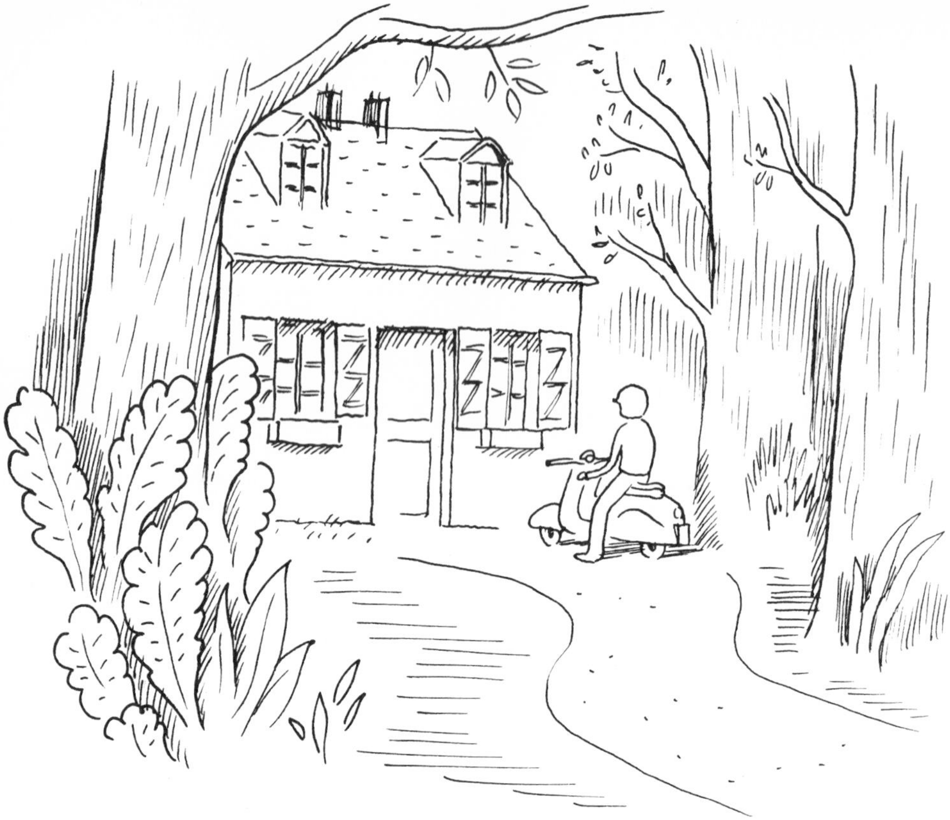

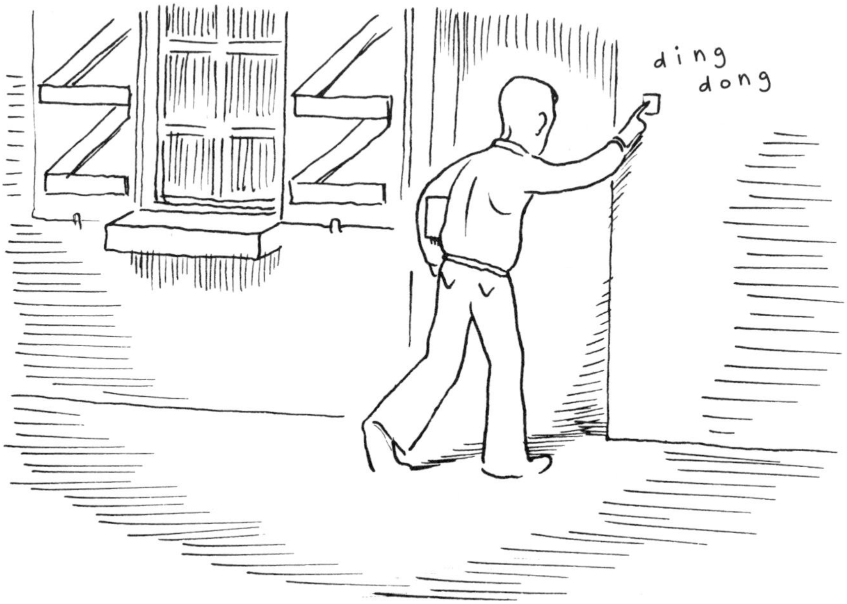
ding dong

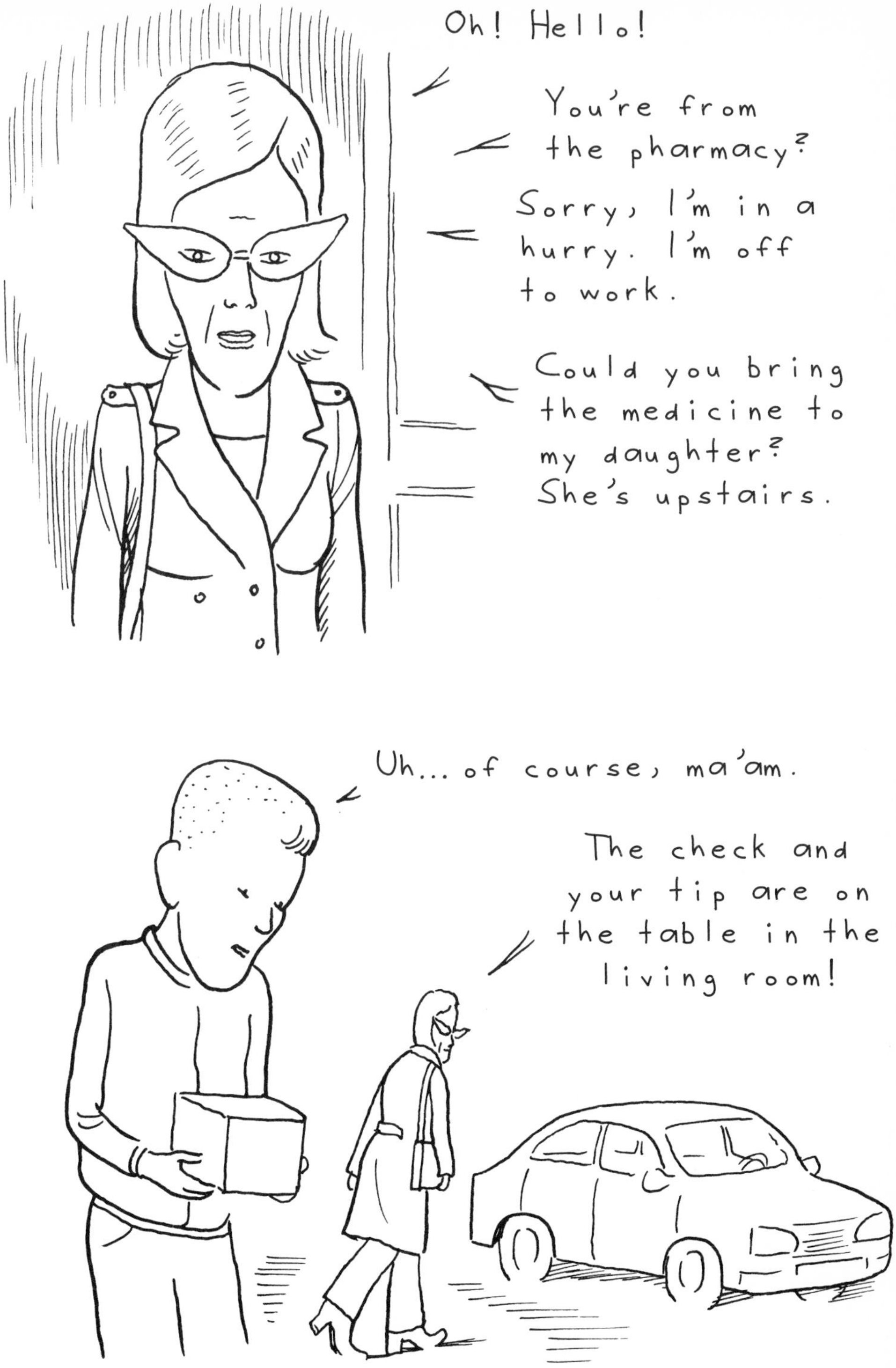
Oh! Hello!
You're from the pharmacy?
Sorry, I'm in a hurry. I'm off to work.
Could you bring the medicine to my daughter? She's upstairs.
Uh... of course, ma'am.
The check and your tip are on the table in the living room!

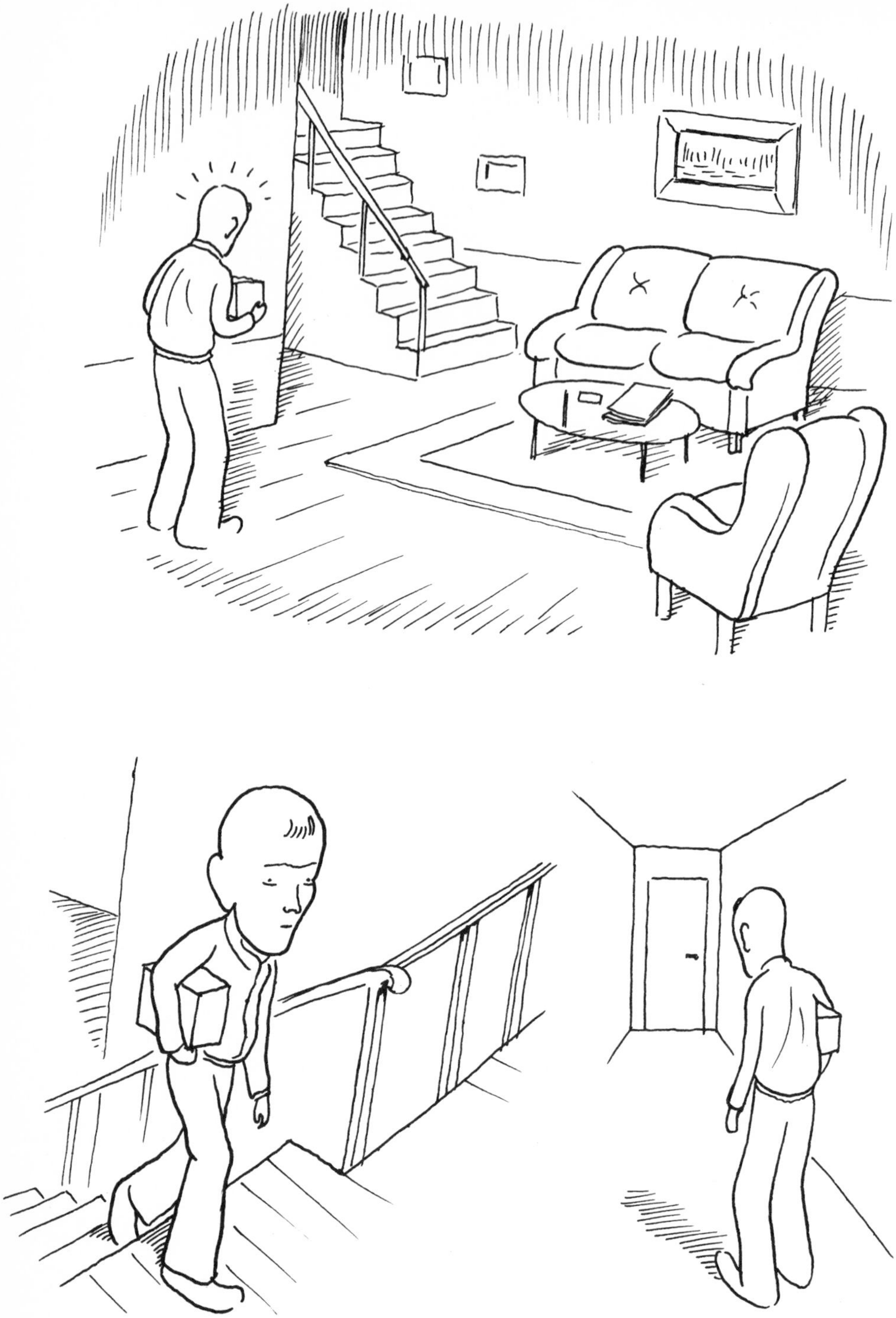

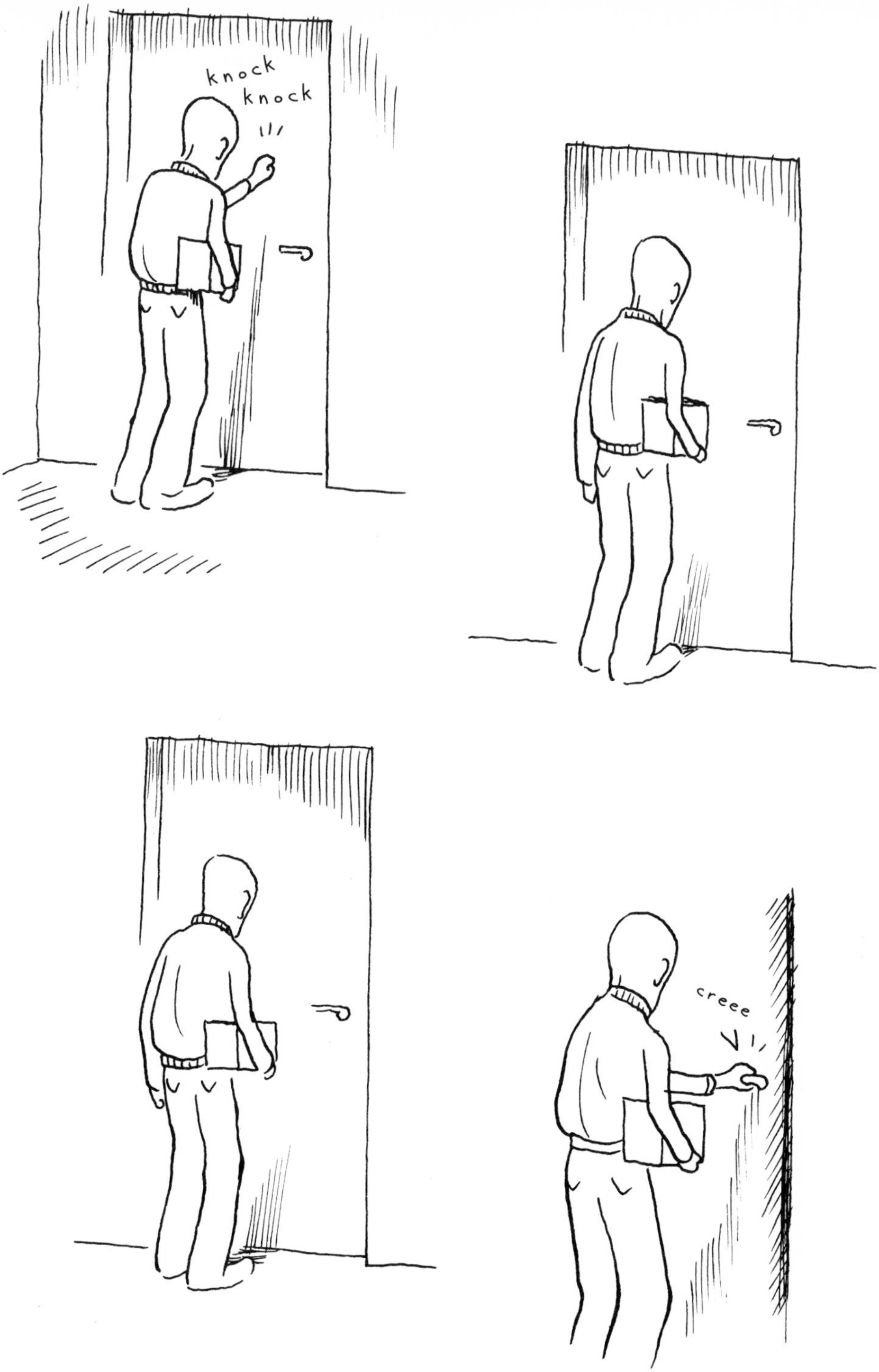
knock
knock
creee

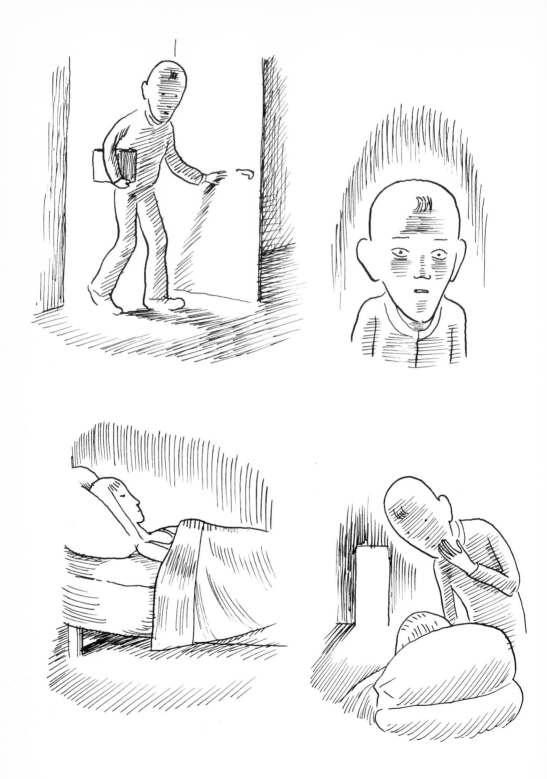

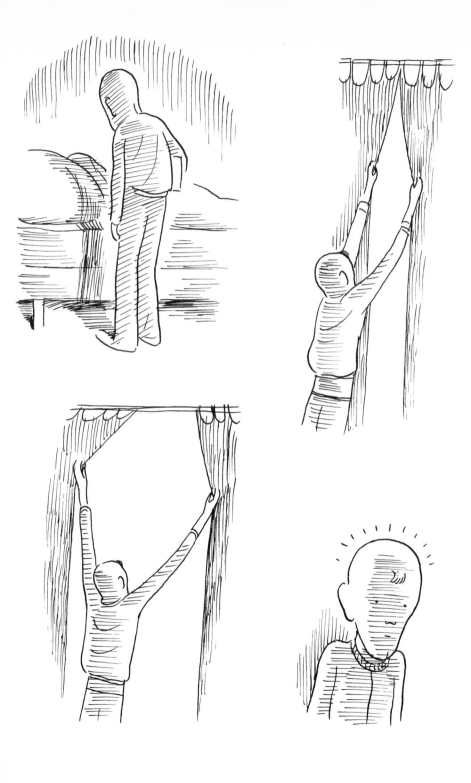

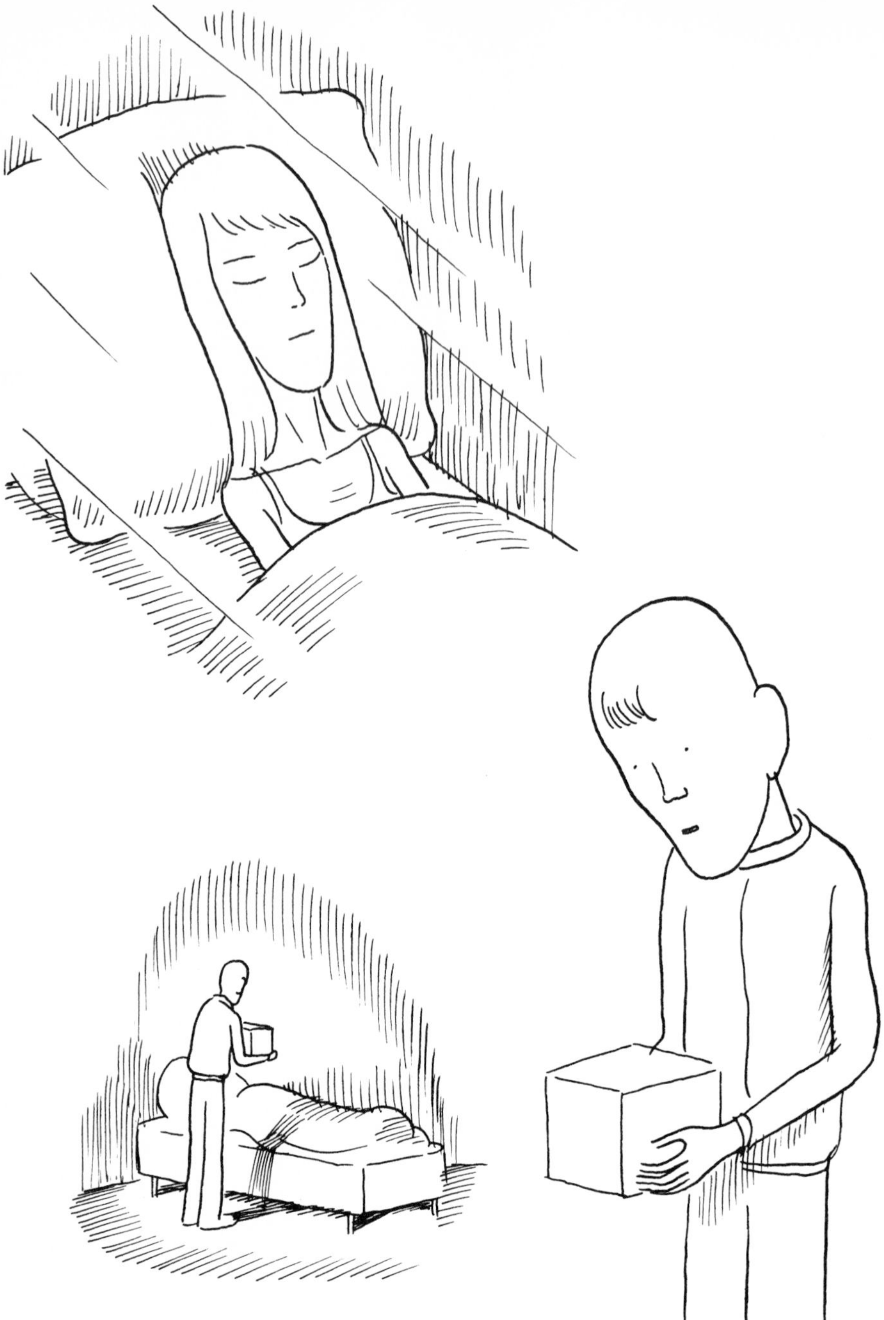

Can you be
more fragile?

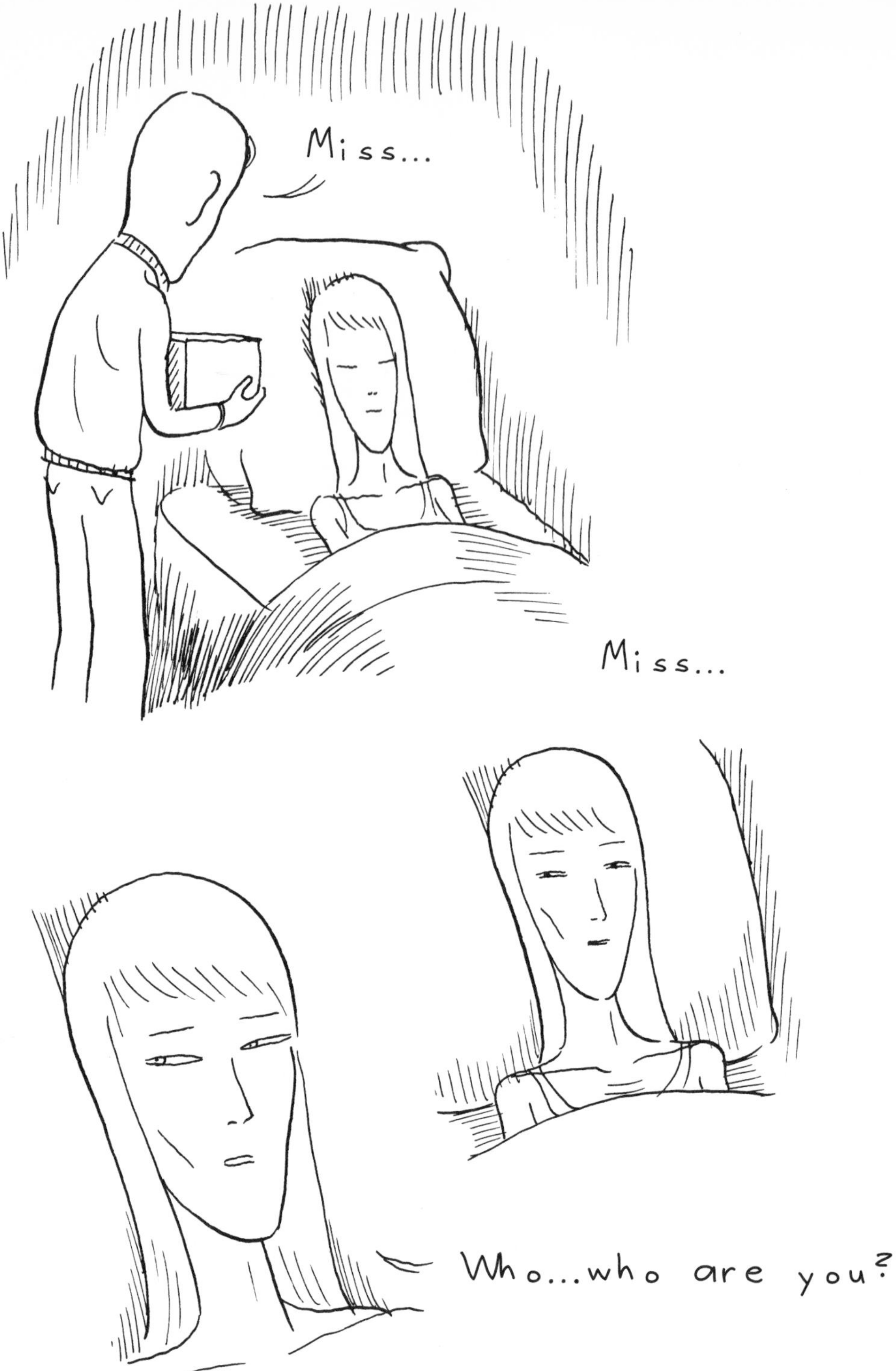
Miss...
Miss...
Who...who are you?

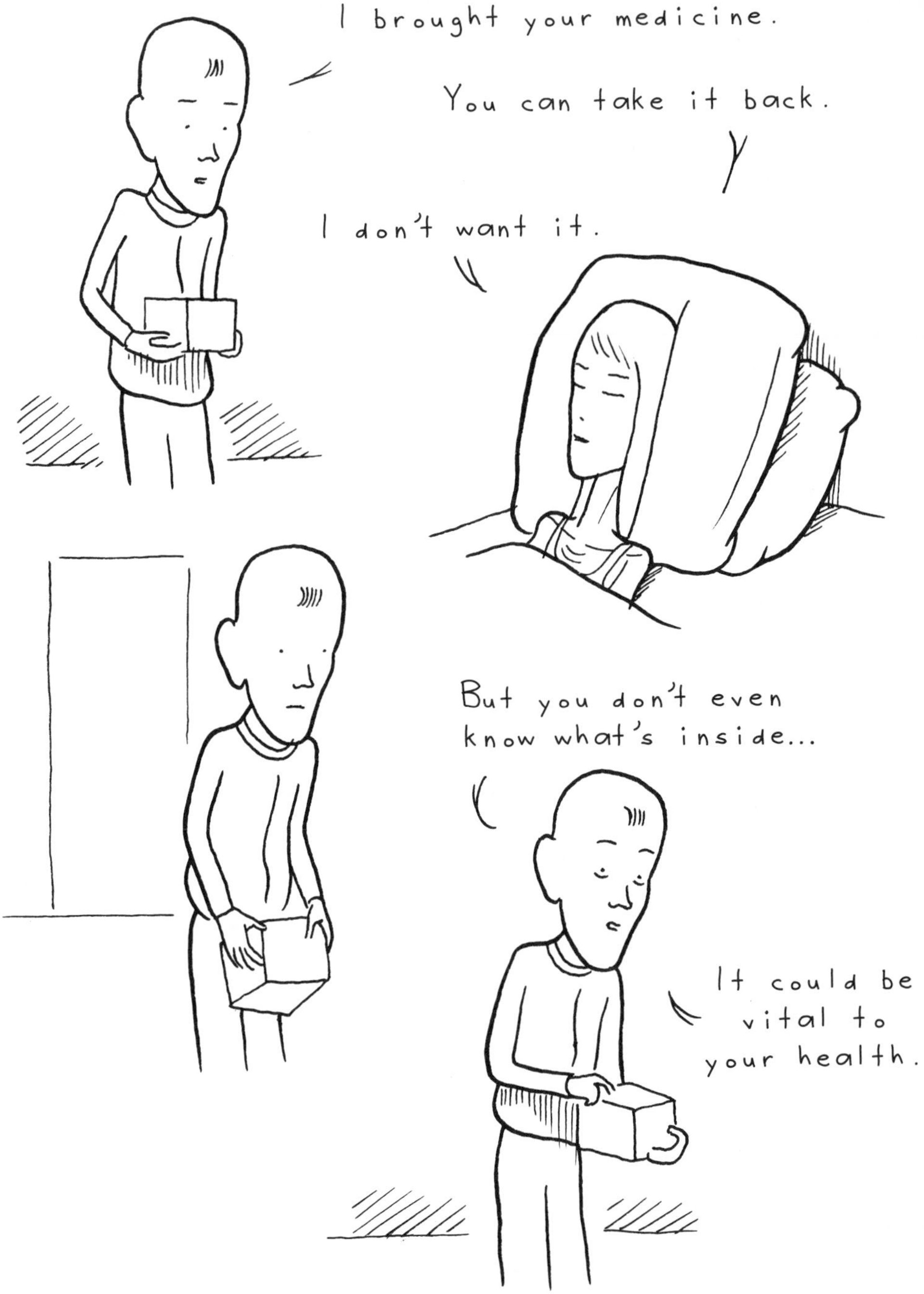
I brought your medicine.
You can take it back.
I don't want it.
But you don't even know what's inside...
It could be vital to your health.

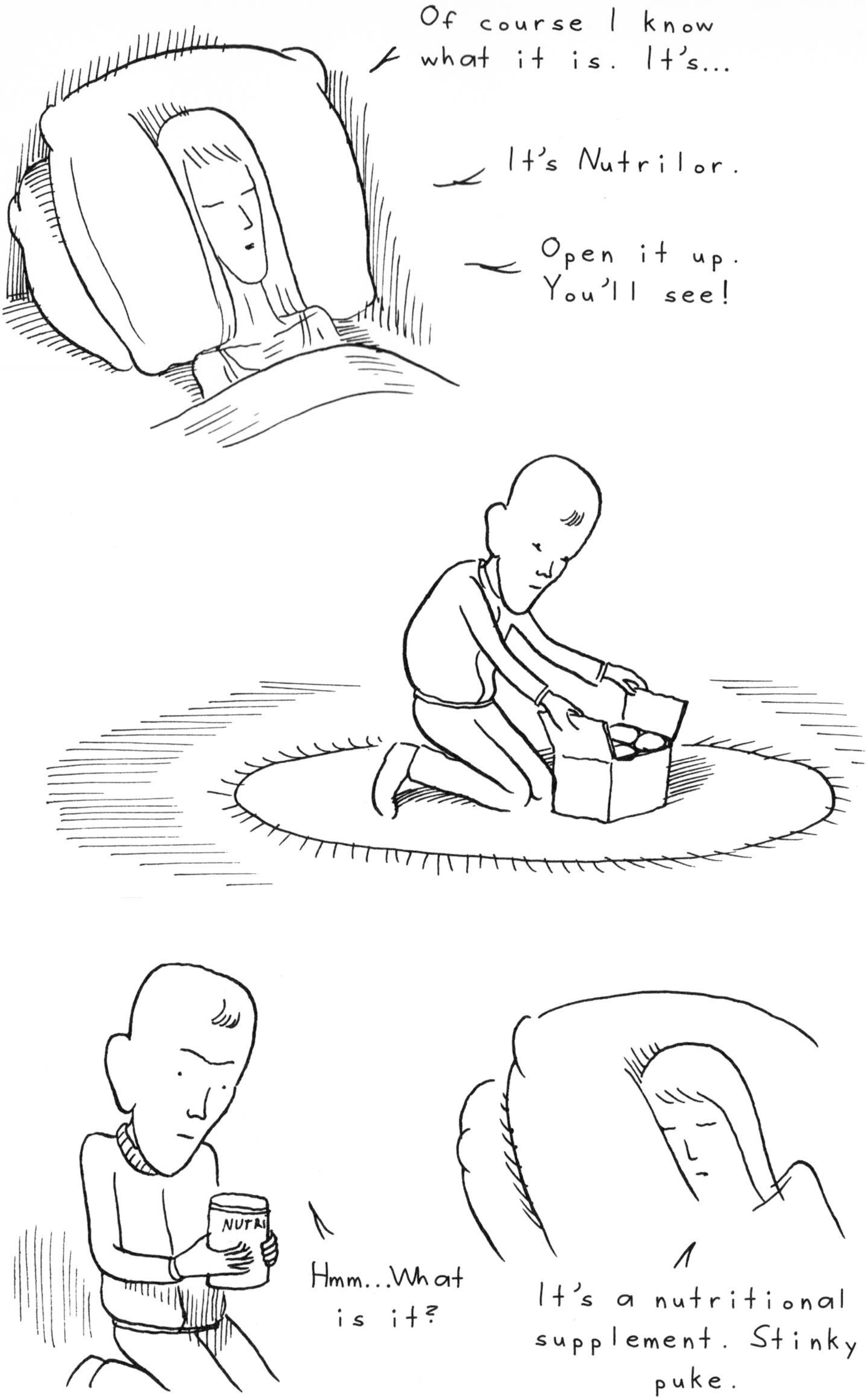
Of course I know what it is. It's...
It's Nutrilor.
Open it up. You'll see!
NUTRI
Hmm...What is it?
It's a nutritional supplement. Stinky puke.

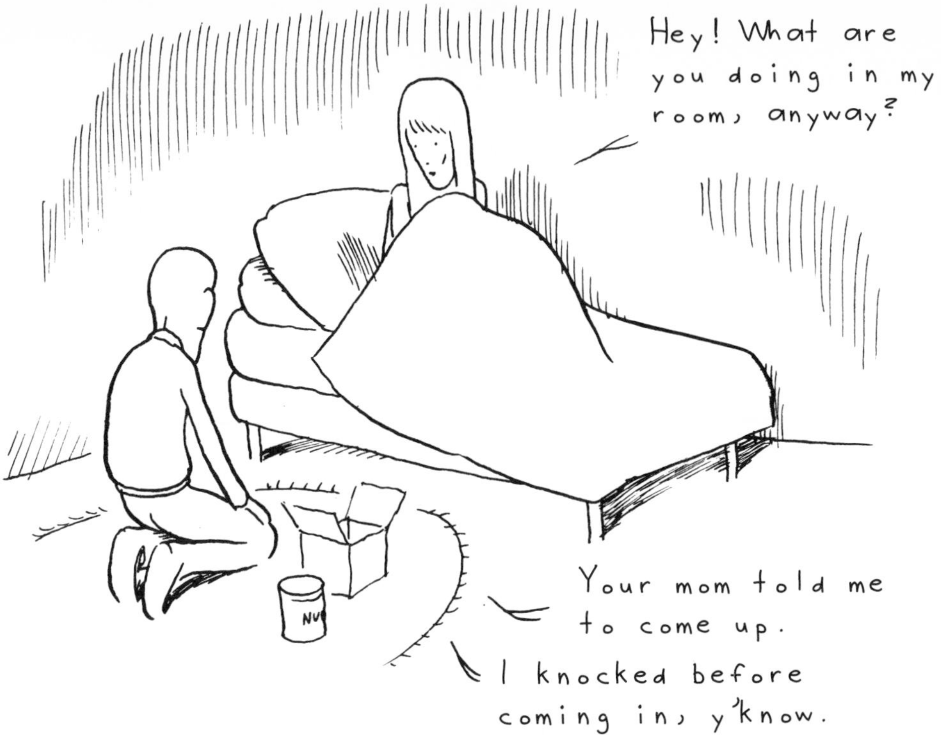
Hey! What are you doing in my room, anyway?
Your mom told me to come up.
I knocked before coming in, y'know.

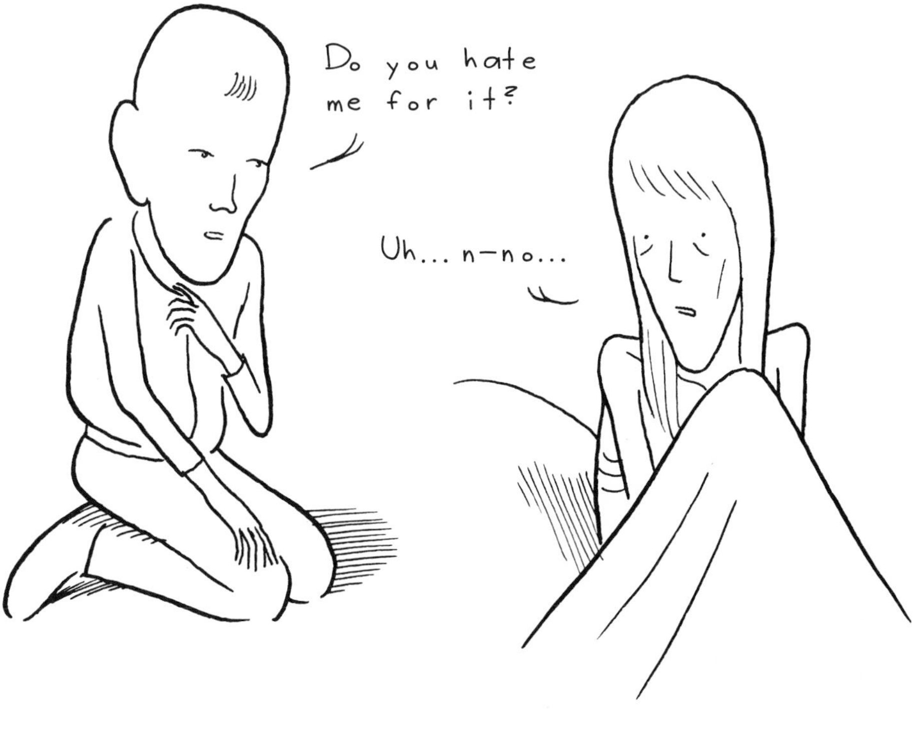
Do you hate me for it?
Uh... n-no...

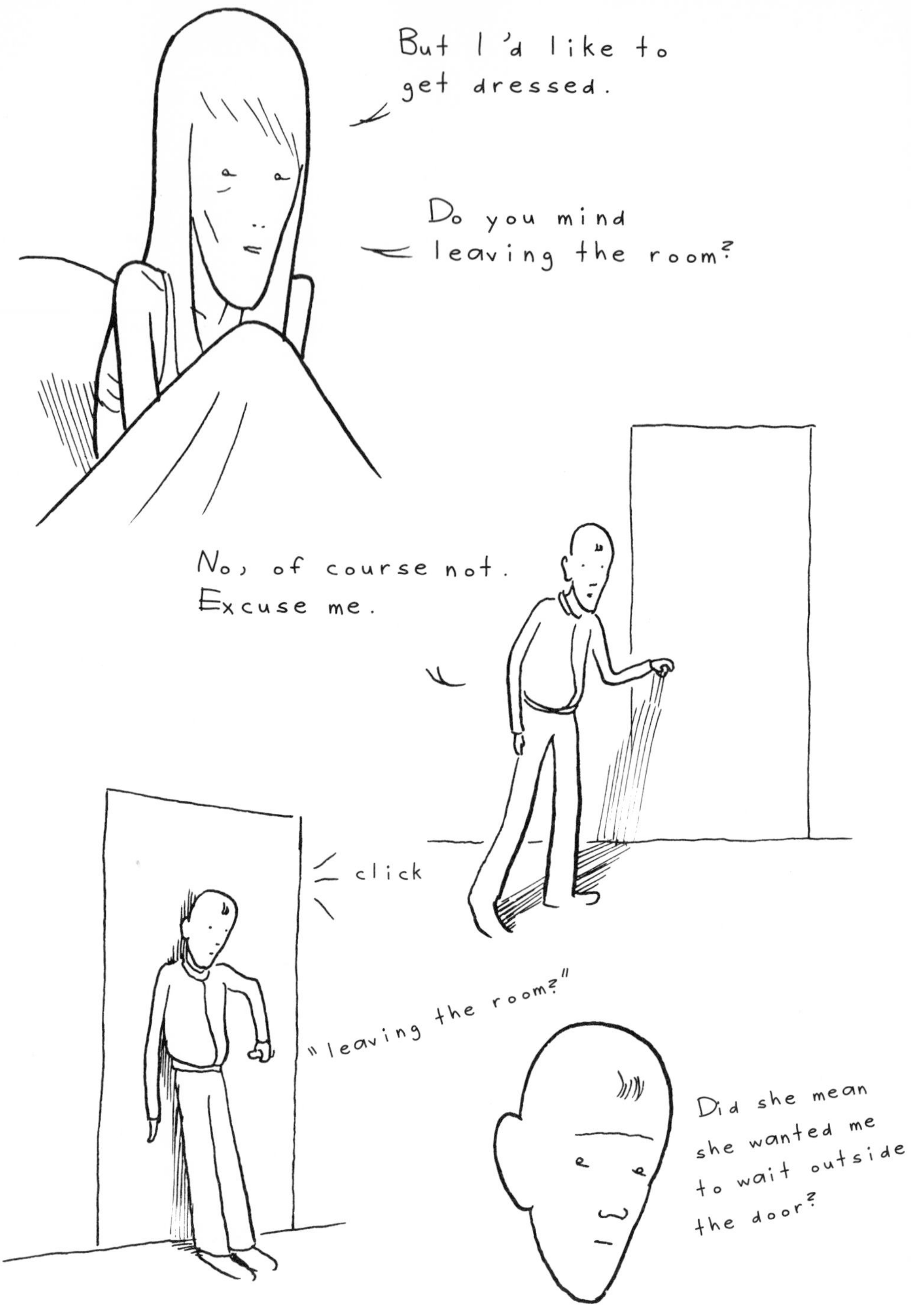

But I'd like to get dressed.
Do you mind leaving the room?
No, of course not. Excuse me.
click
"leaving the room?"
Did she mean she wanted me to wait outside the door?

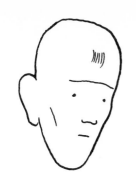

We hardly know each other... why would she want me to wait?

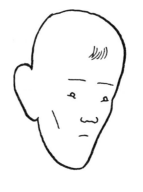

But now I've stepped out without saying goodbye, so it'd be rude to leave.

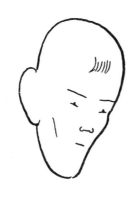

The best thing to do would be to say goodbye through the door...

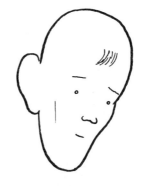

And if she really wants me to stay, she'll say so.

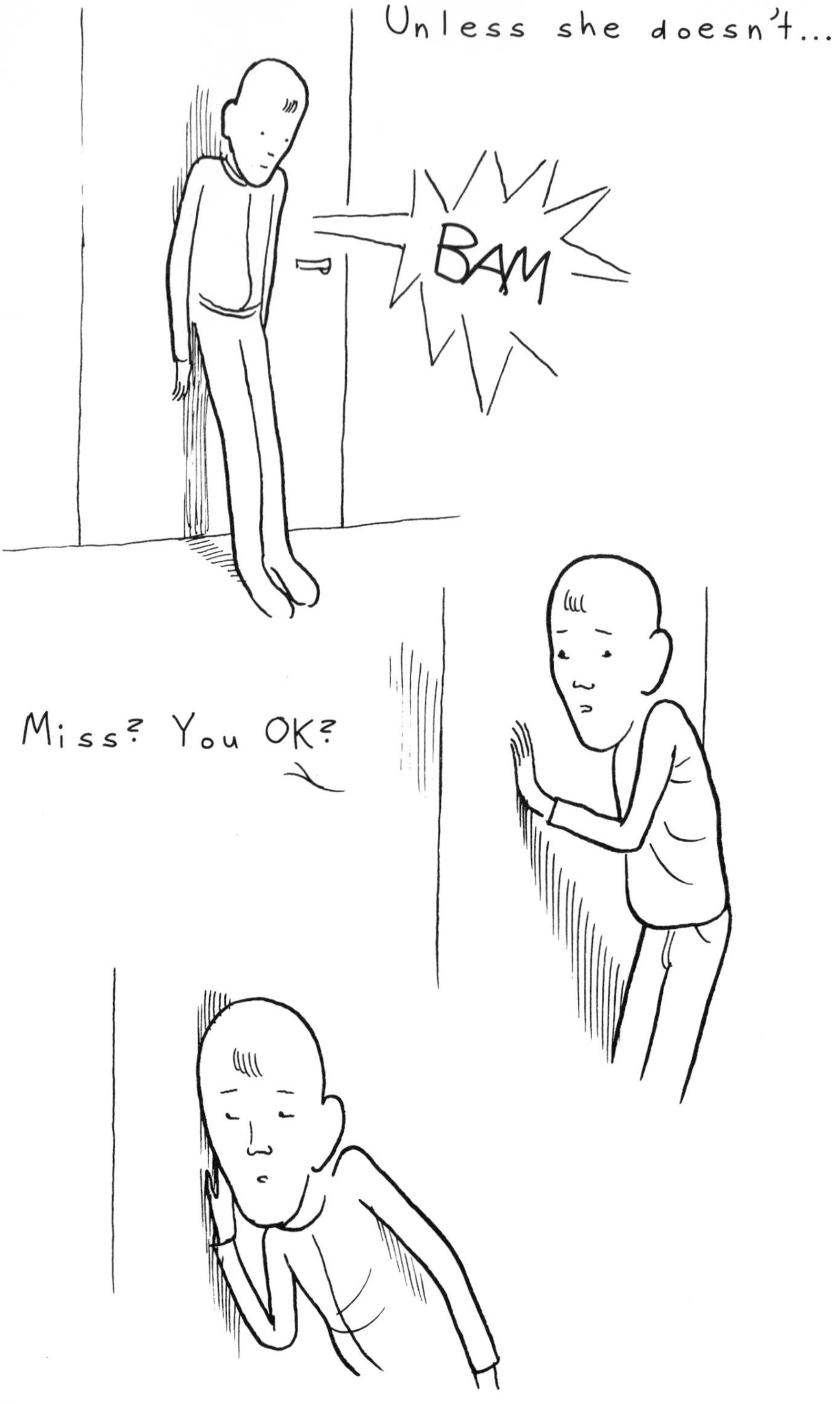
Unless she doesn't...
BAM
Miss? You OK?

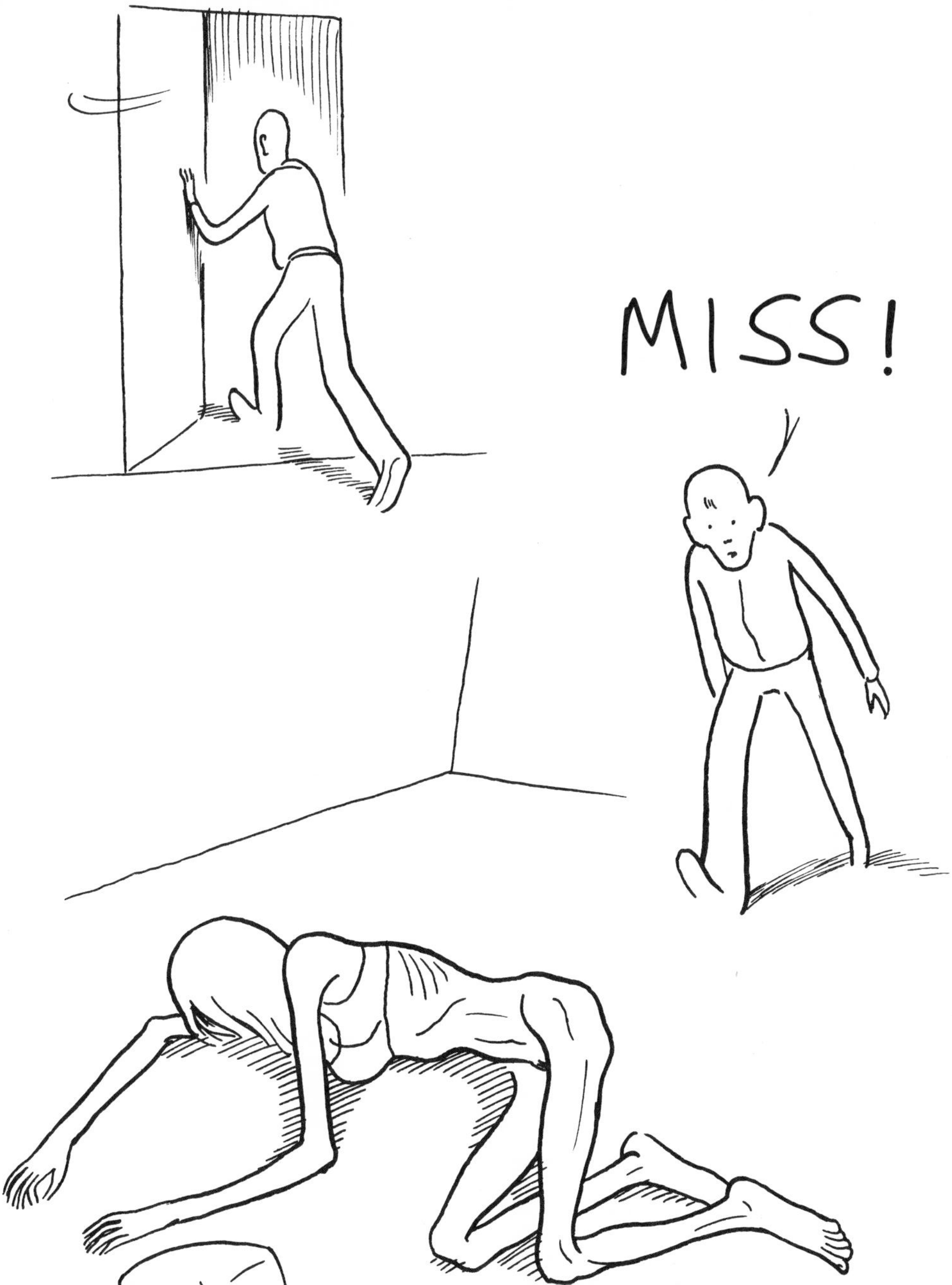
MISS!

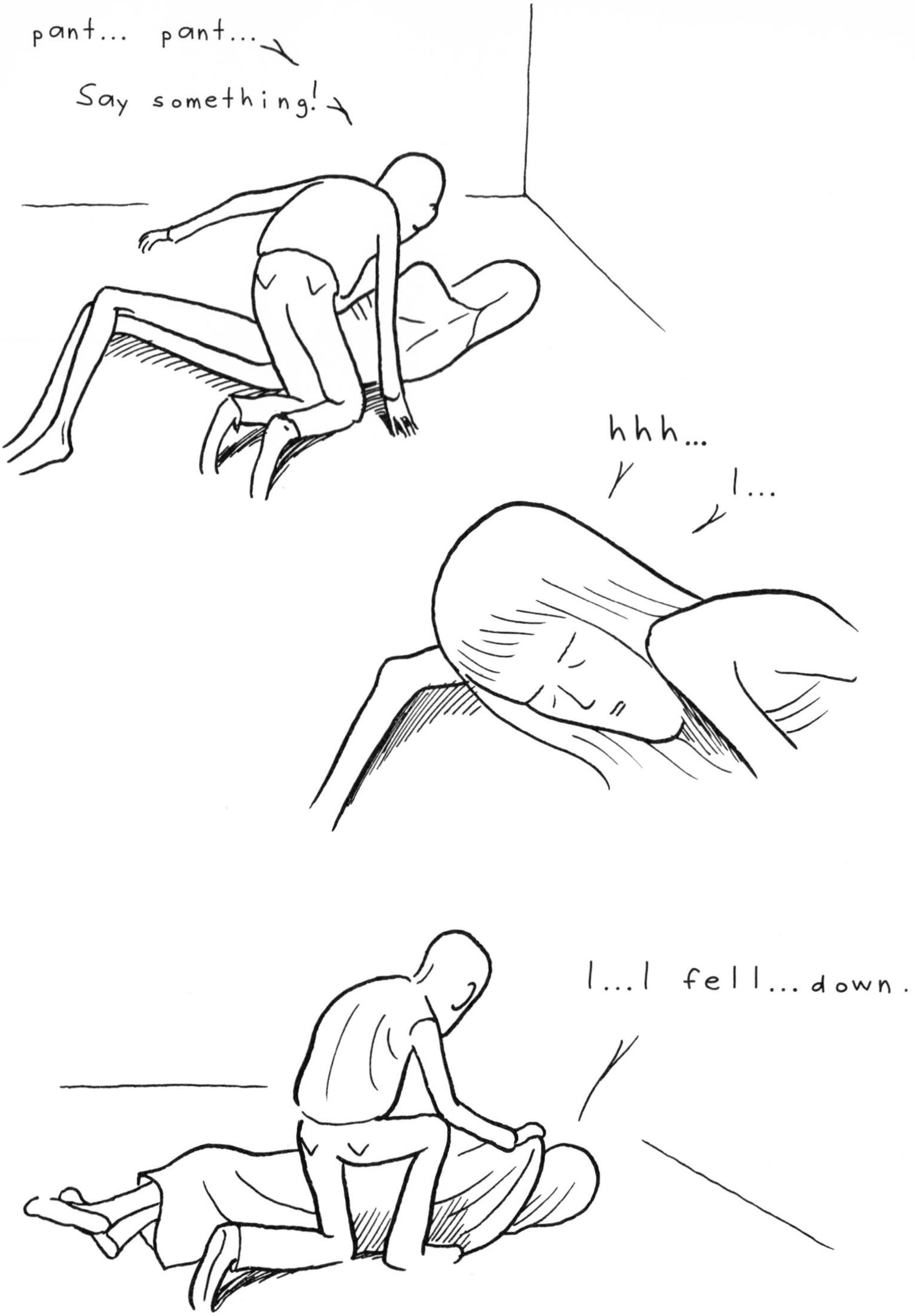
pant... pant...
Say something!
hhh...
I...
I...I fell...down.

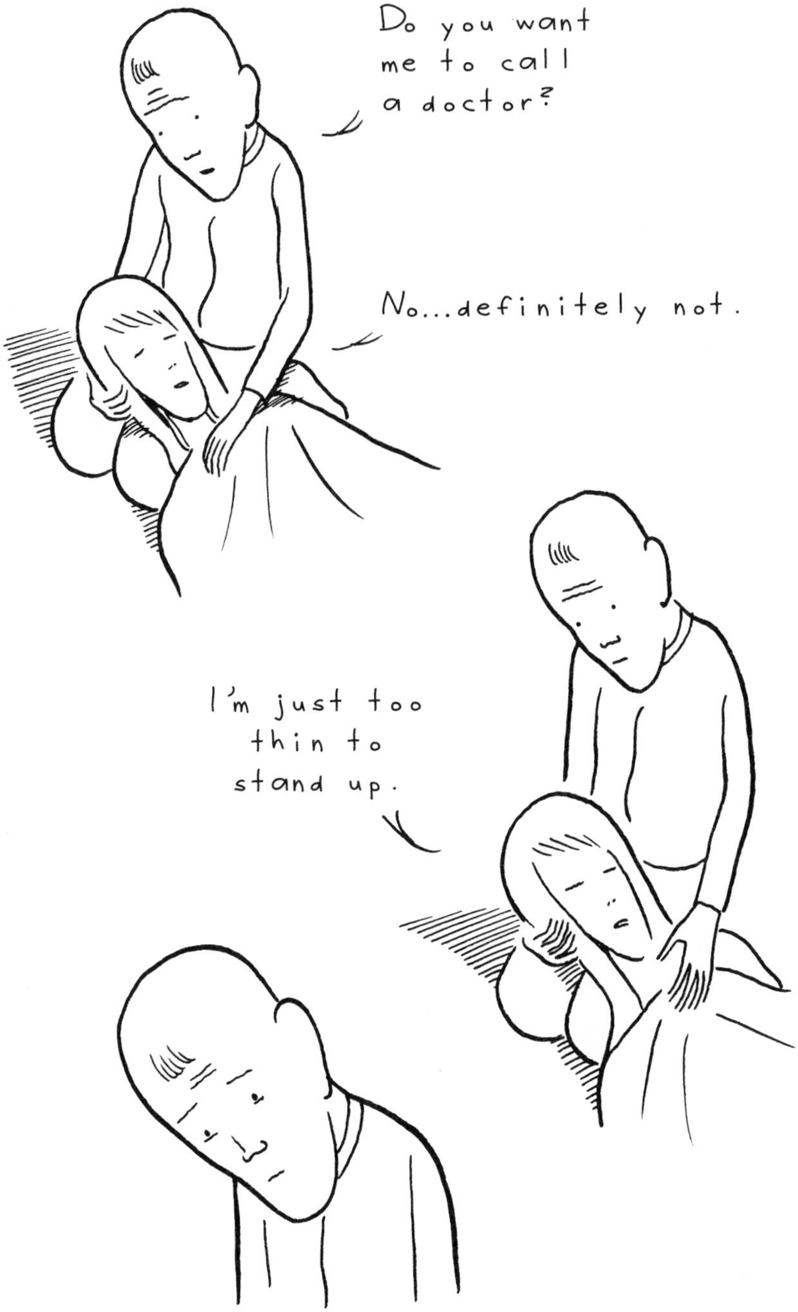
Do you want me to call a doctor?
No...definitely not.
I'm just too thin to stand up.

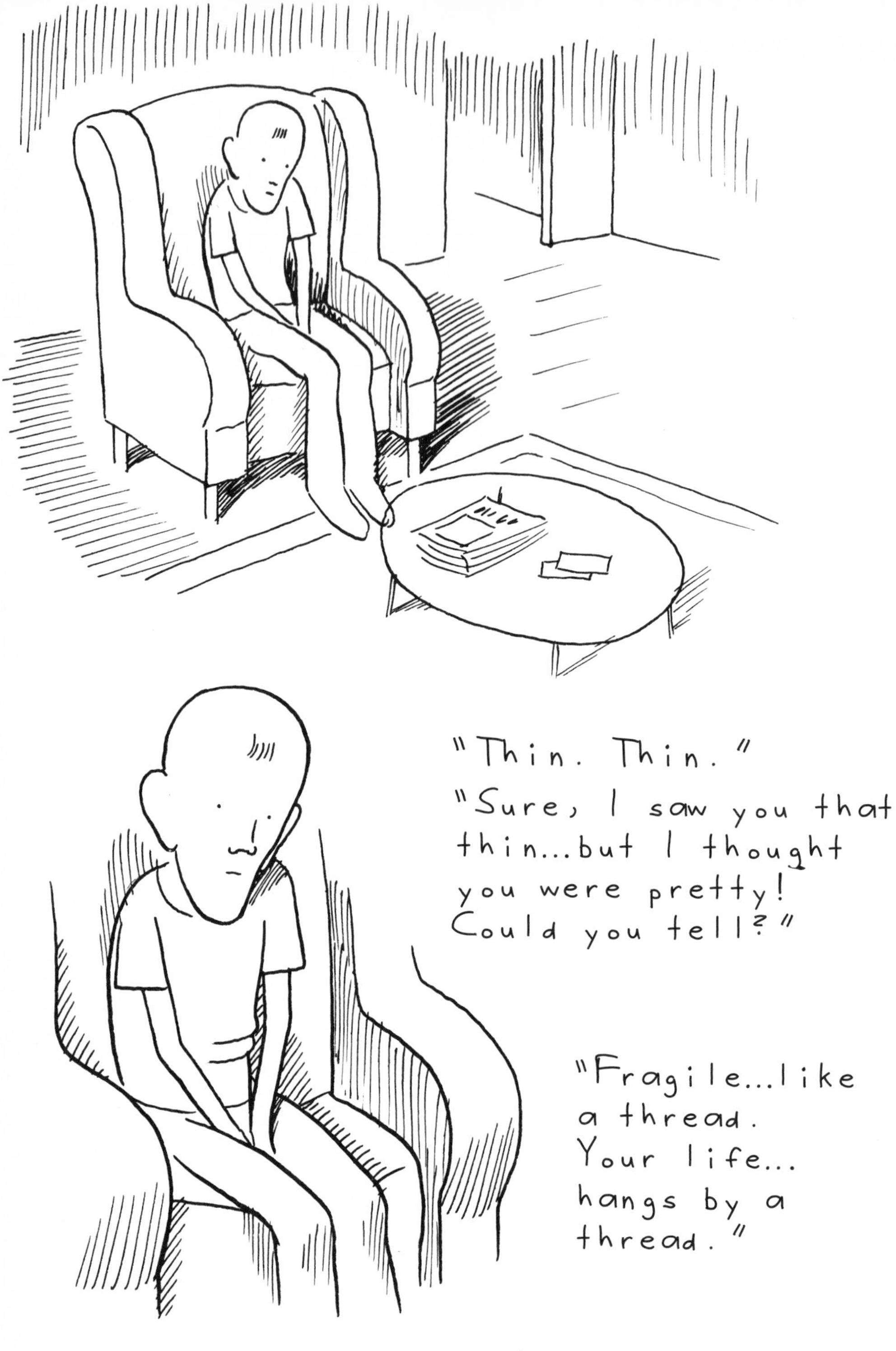
"Thin. Thin."
"Sure, I saw you that thin...but I thought you were pretty! Could you tell?"
"Fragile...like a thread. Your life... hangs by a thread."

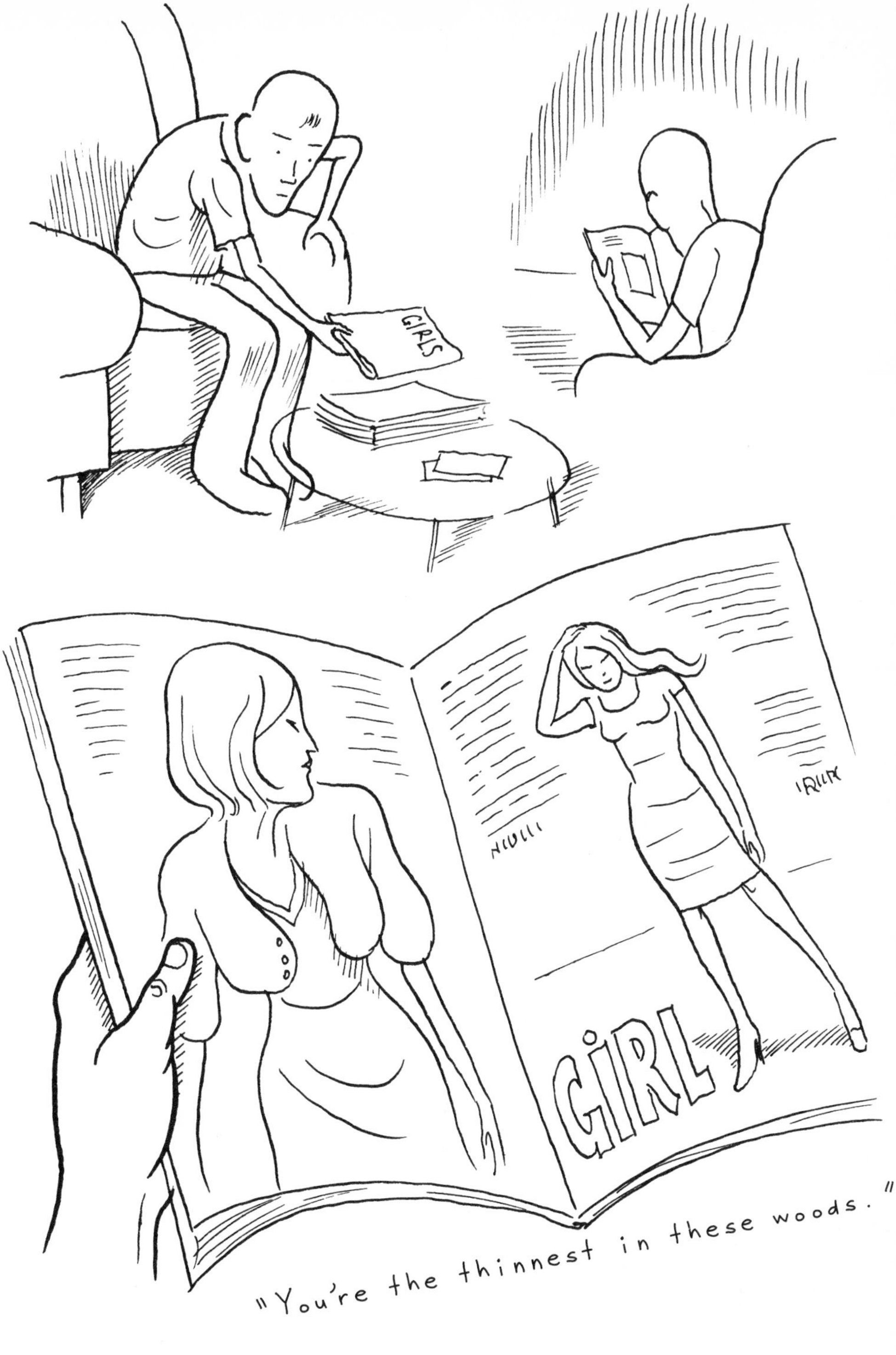
GIRLS
GIRL

"You're the thinnest in these woods."

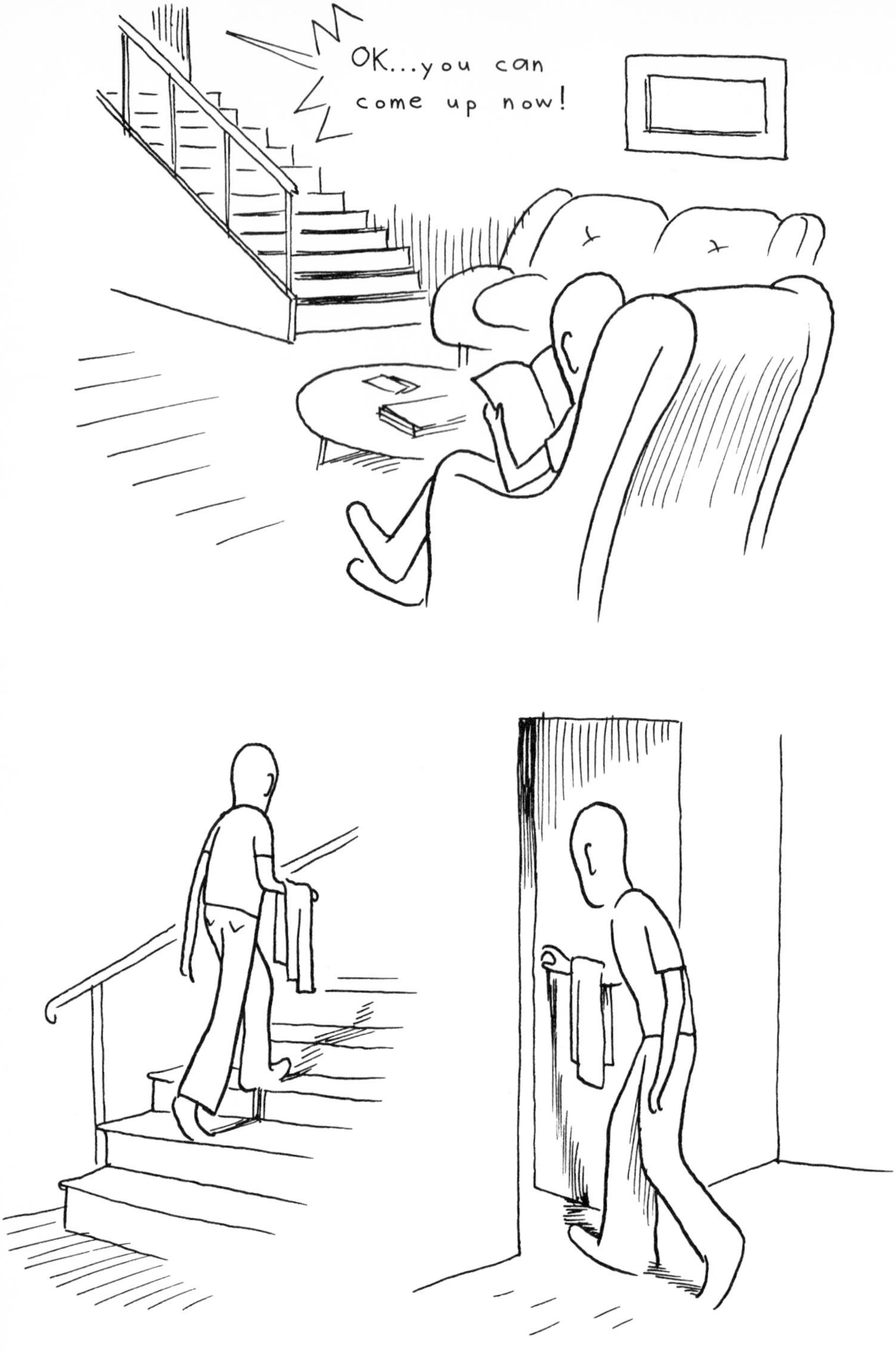
OK...you can come up now!

"In these woods..."

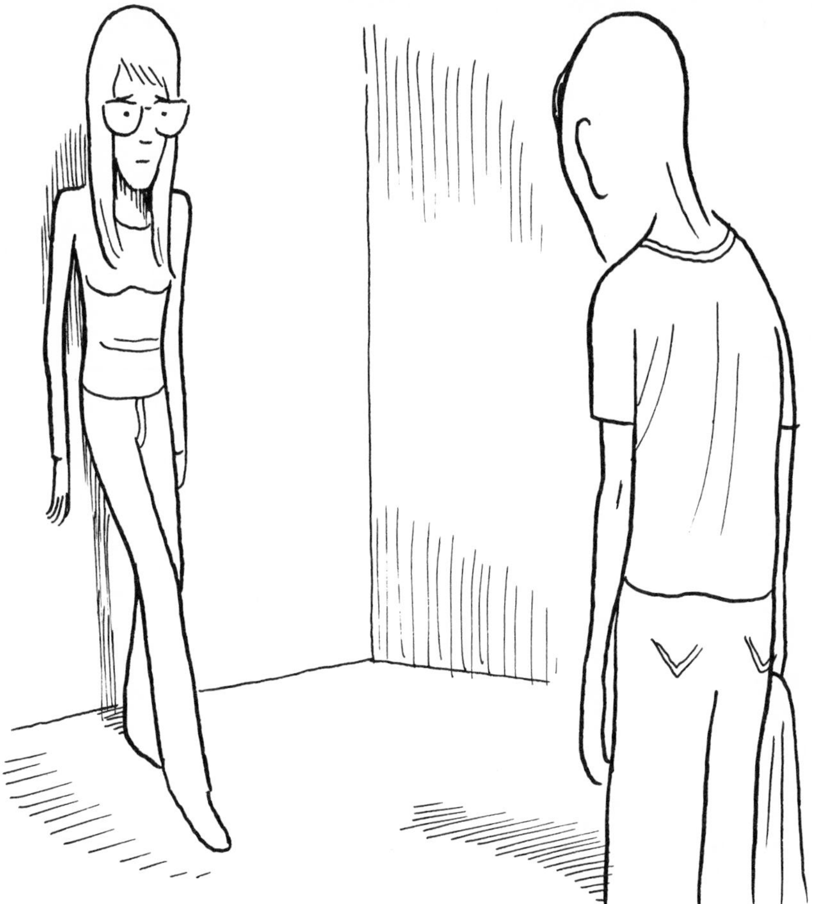

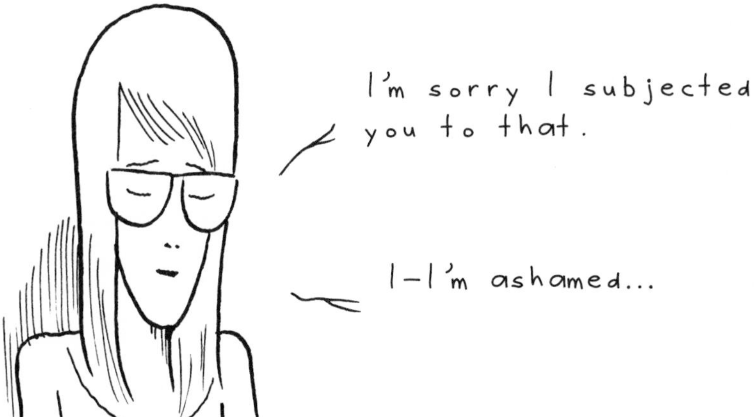
I'm sorry I subjected you to that.
I-I'm ashamed...

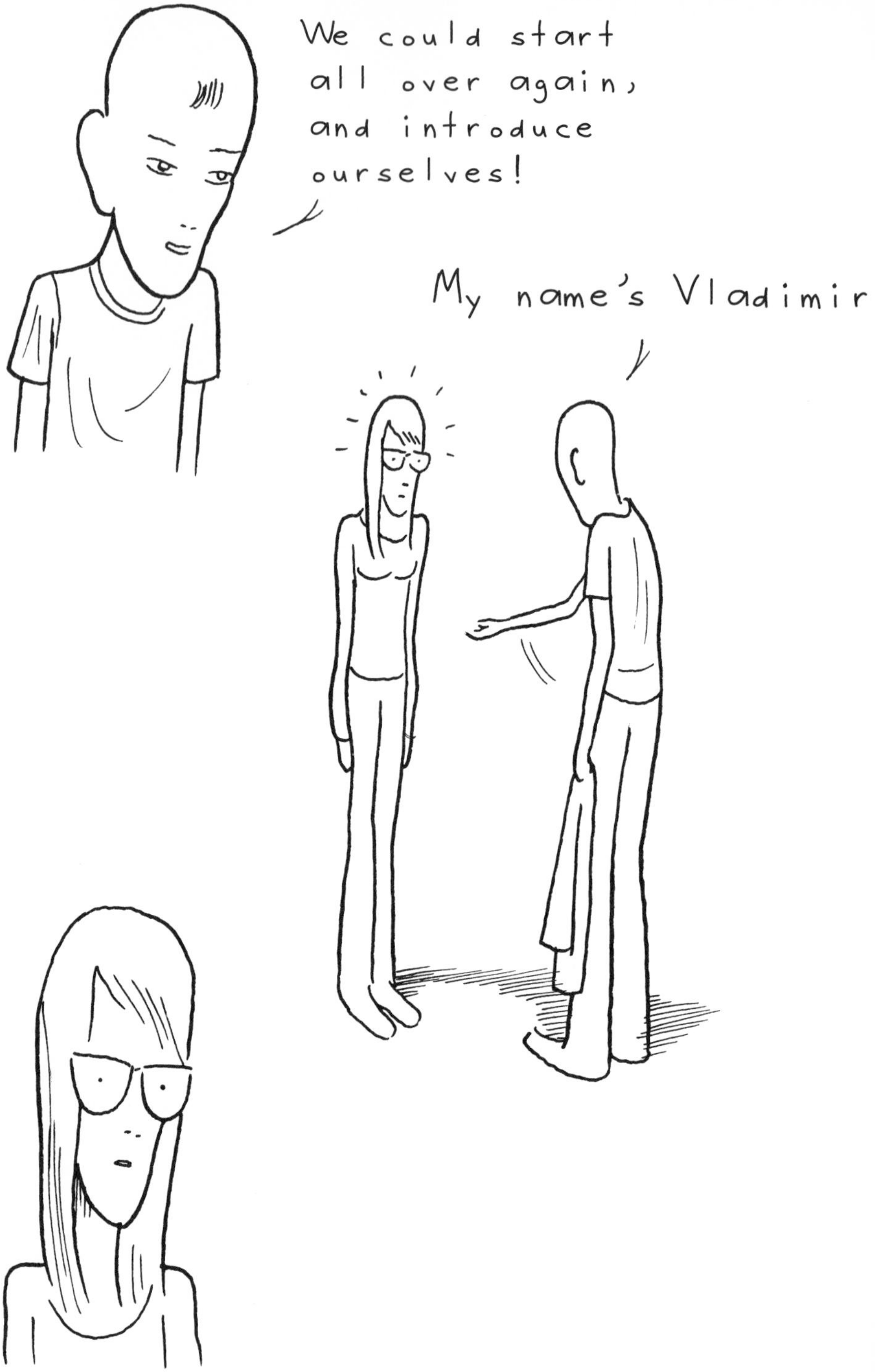
We could start all over again, and introduce ourselves!
My name's Vladimir.

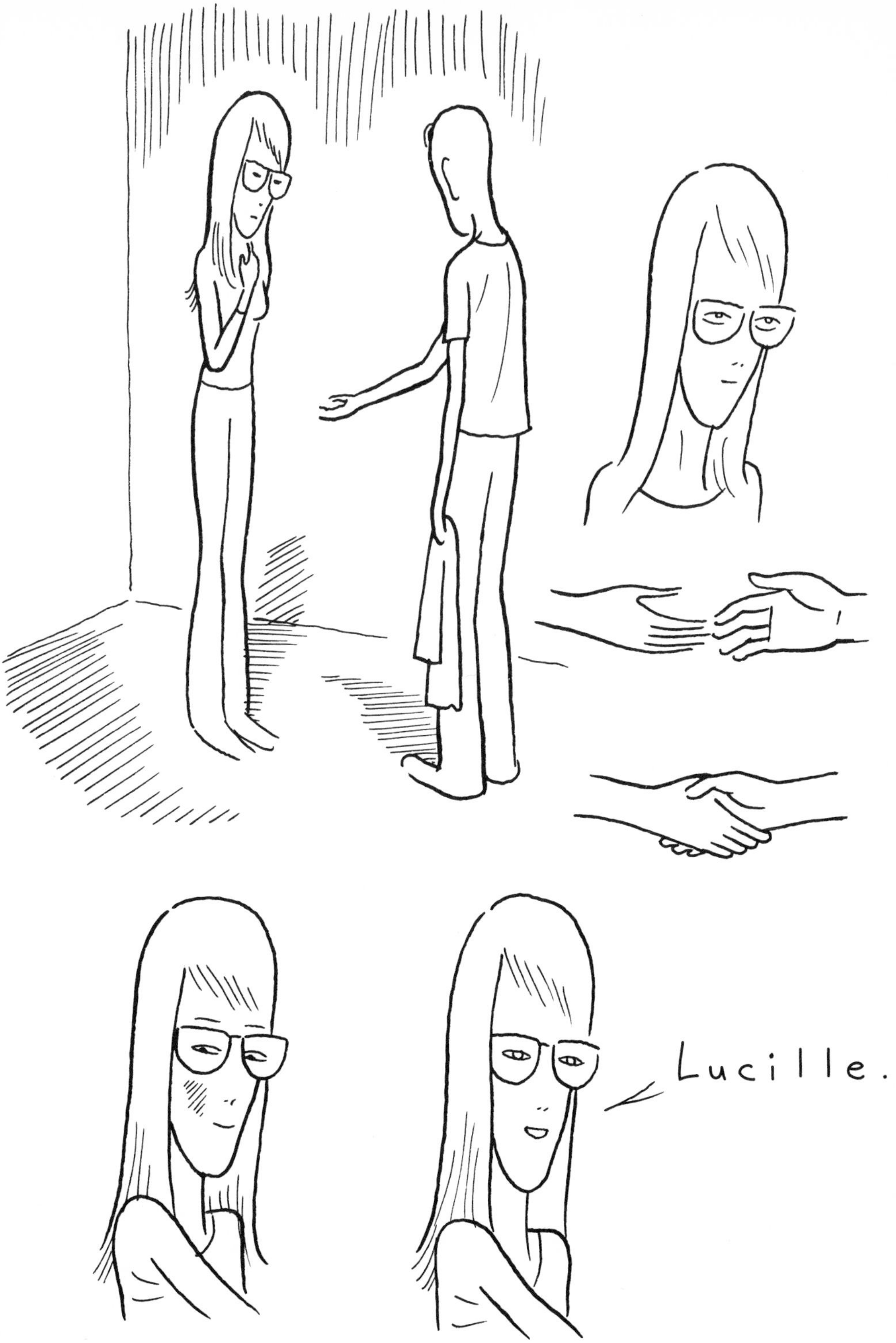
Lucille.

"Do you remember?"

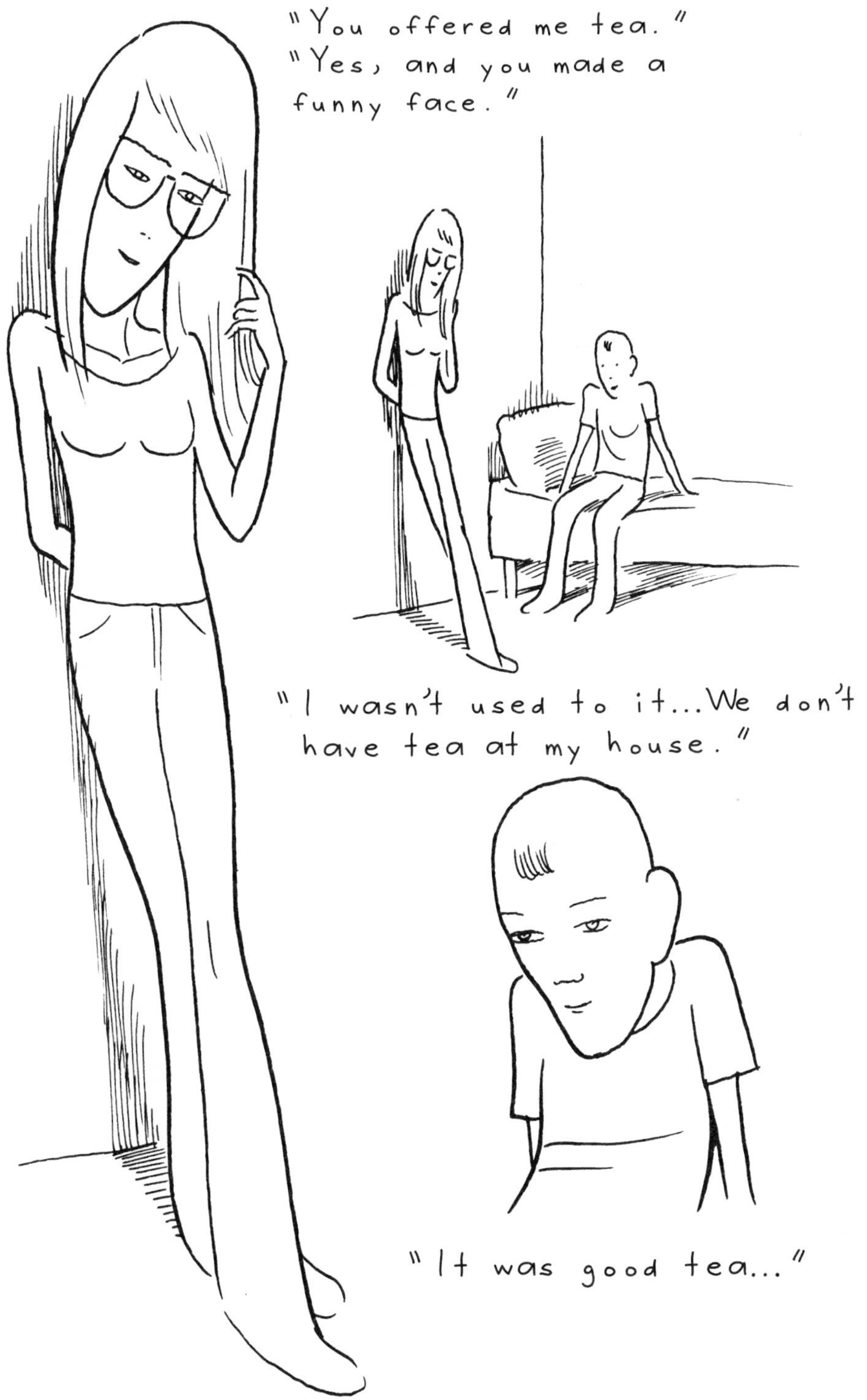
"You offered me tea."
"Yes, and you made a funny face."
"I wasn't used to it...We don't have tea at my house."
"It was good tea..."

"We didn't want to move. But it was weird, being there...together..."

"You talked about your mother. And a bit about your illness."

"It was easy to talk to you. You were still a stranger, and at the same time you'd seen all of me already."

"You talked about your father. You were very touching. I felt stupid...I had both my parents."

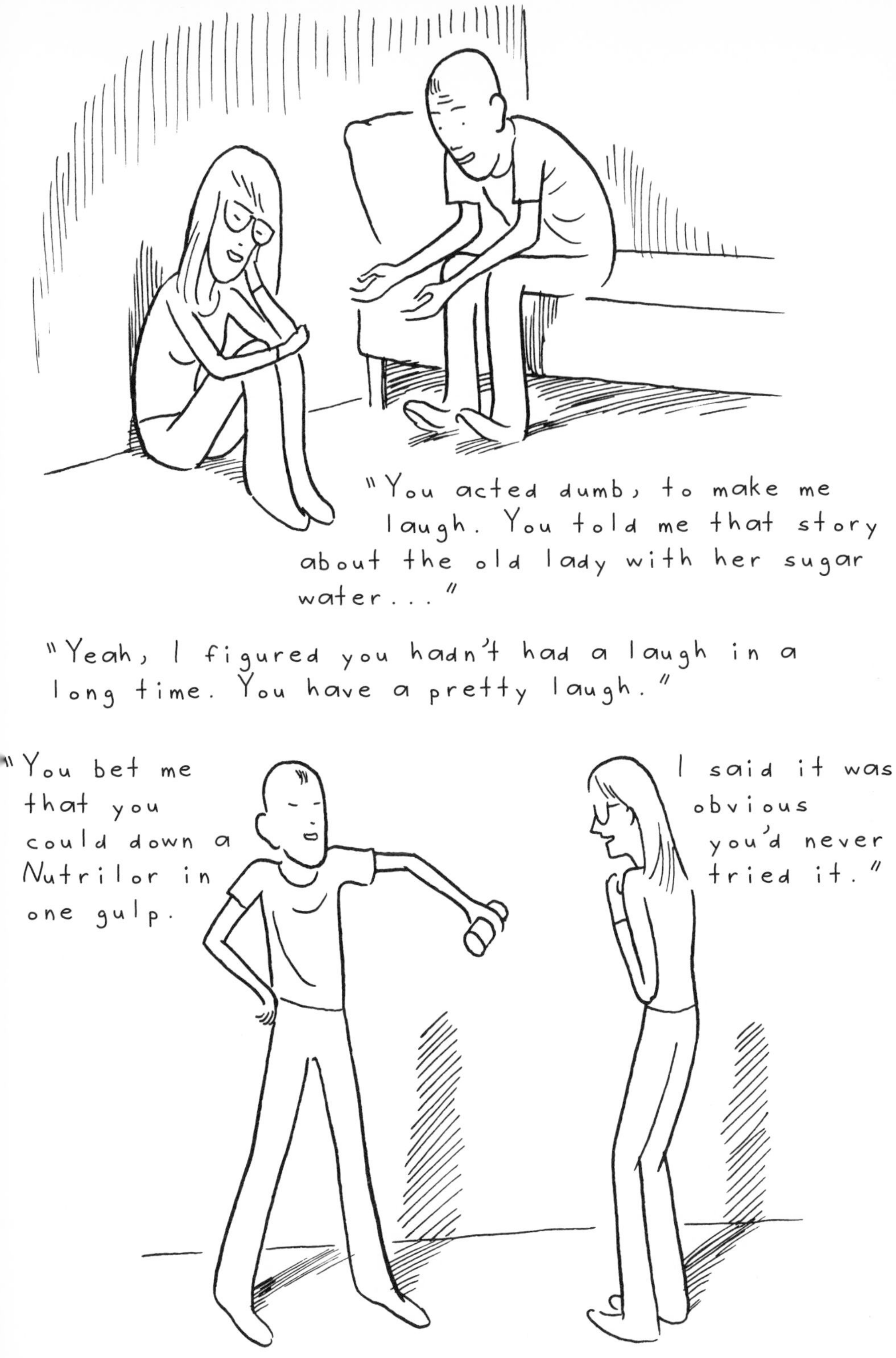
"You acted dumb, to make me laugh. You told me that story about the old lady with her sugar water..."
"Yeah, I figured you hadn't had a laugh in a long time. You have a pretty laugh."
"You bet me that you could down a Nutrilor in one gulp.
I said it was obvious you'd never tried it."

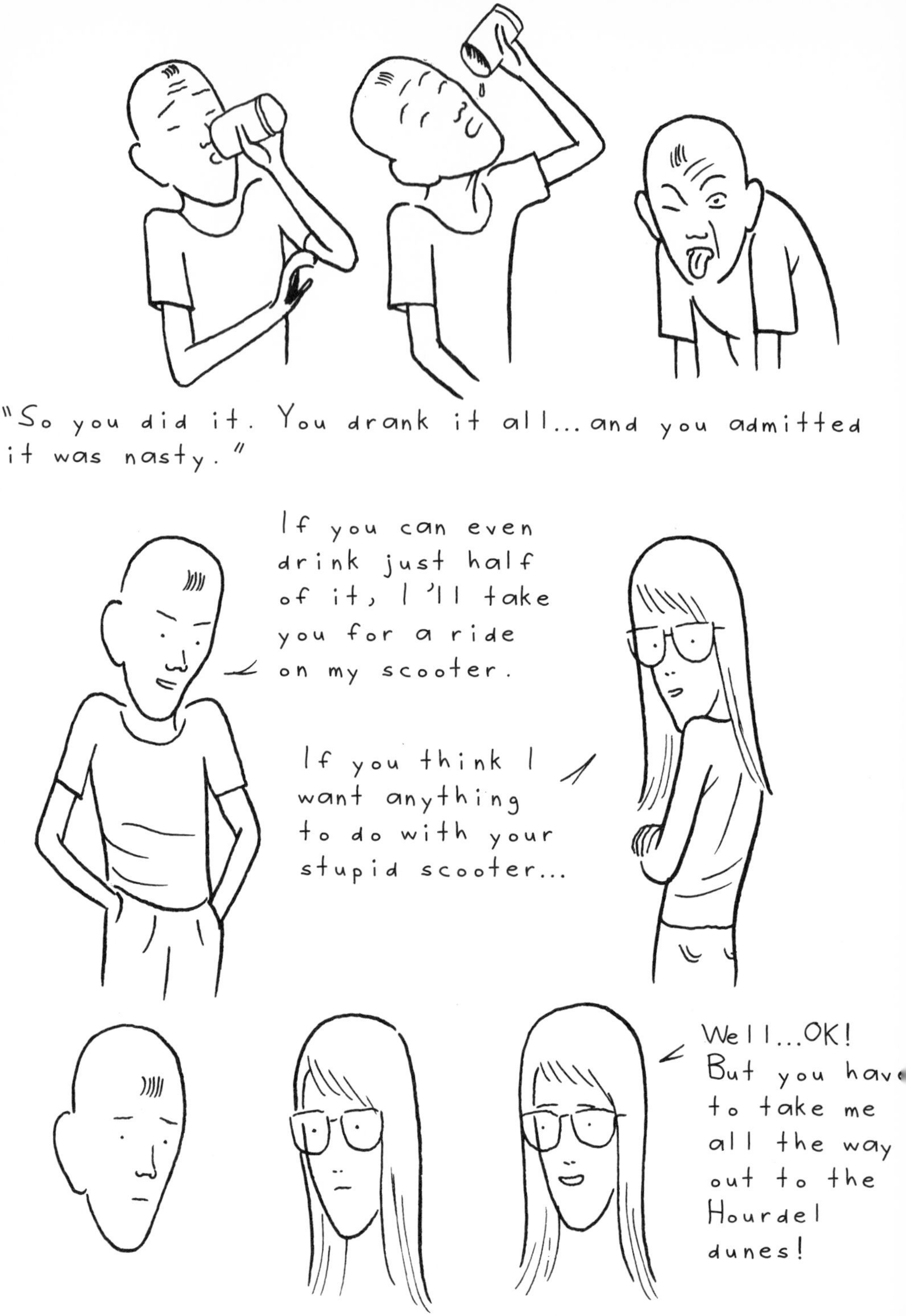
"So you did it. You drank it all... and you admitted it was nasty."
If you can even drink just half of it, I'll take you for a ride on my scooter.
If you think I want anything to do with your stupid scooter...
Well...OK! But you hav to take me all the way out to the Hourdel dunes!

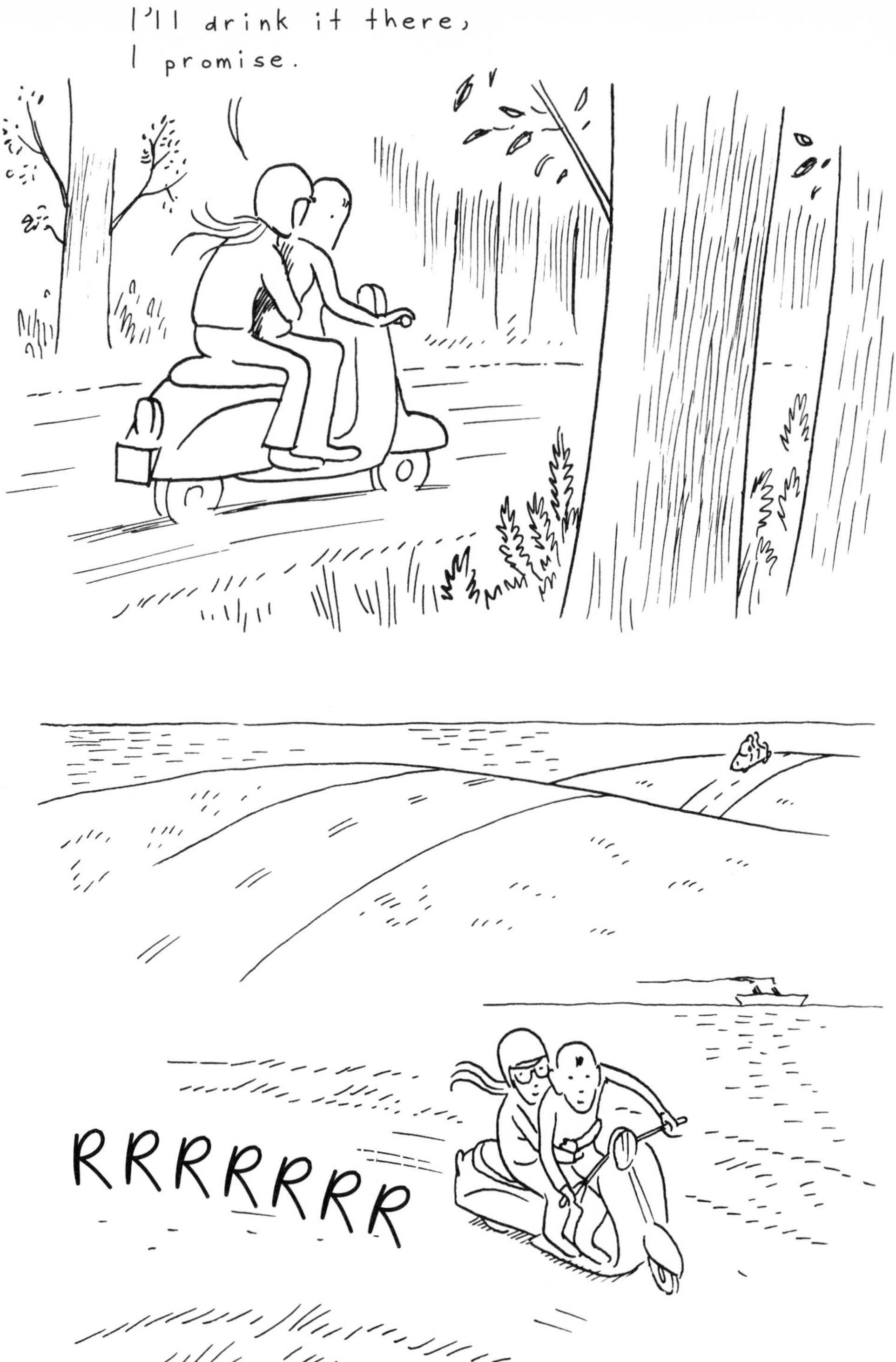
I'll drink it there, I promise.
RRRRRRRR

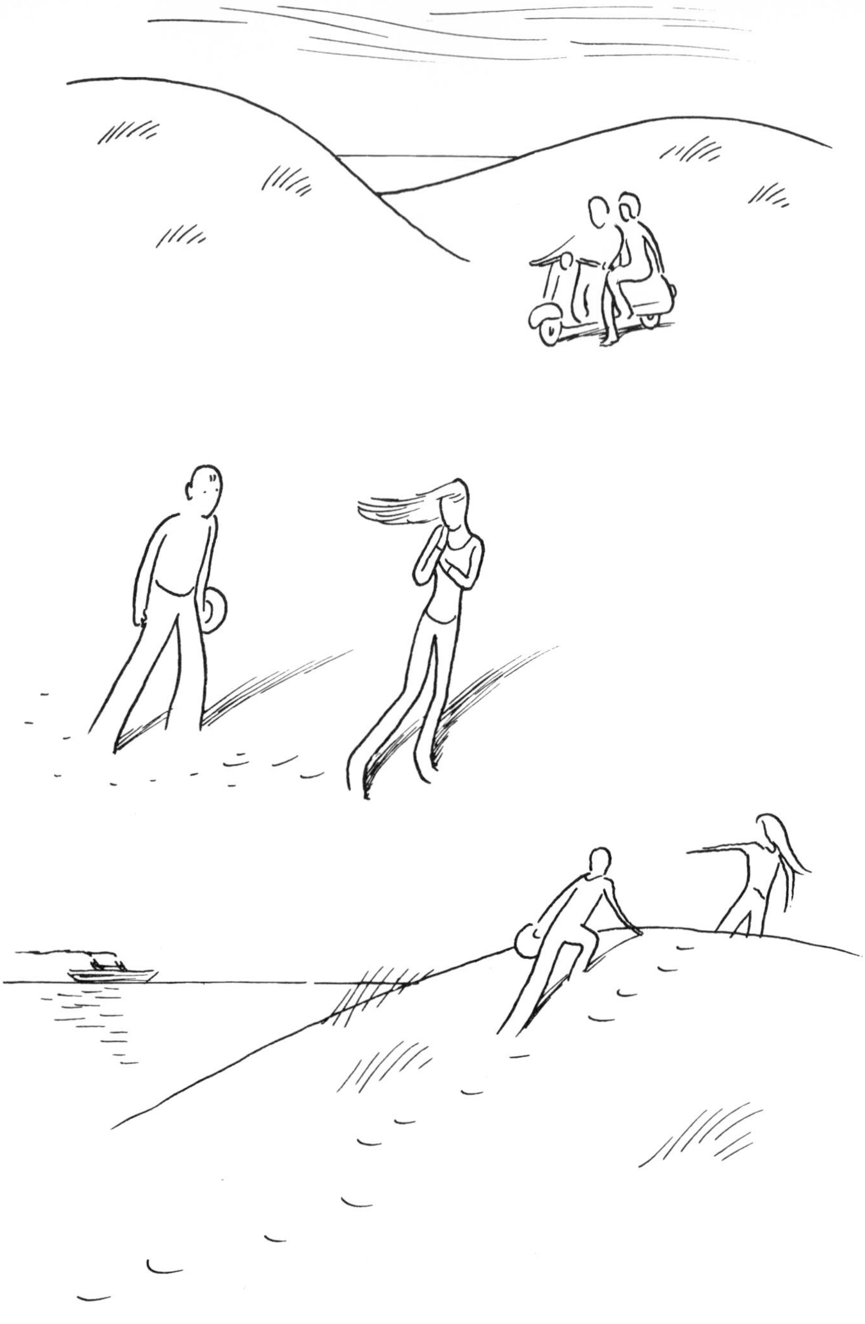

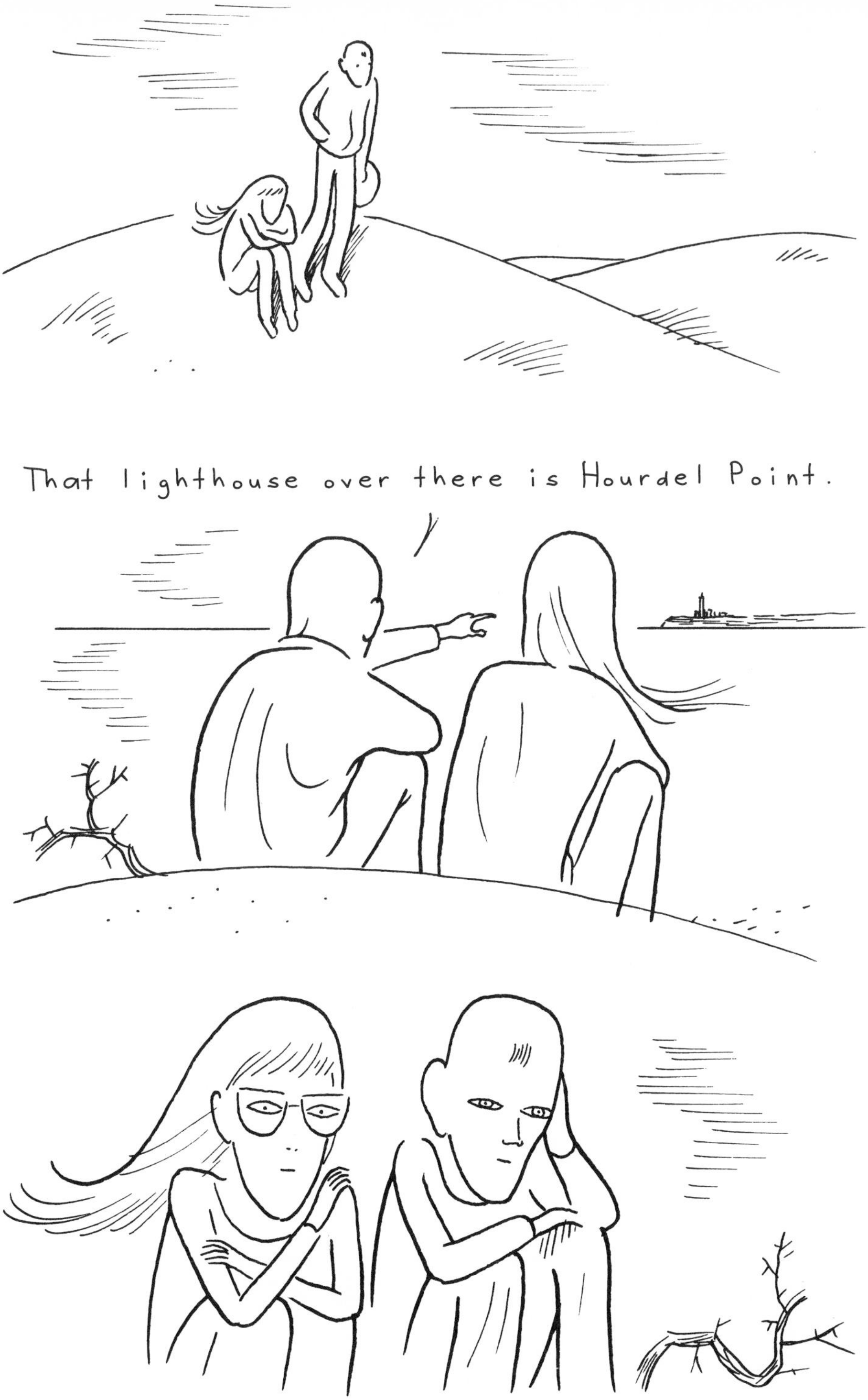
That lighthouse over there is Hourdel Point.

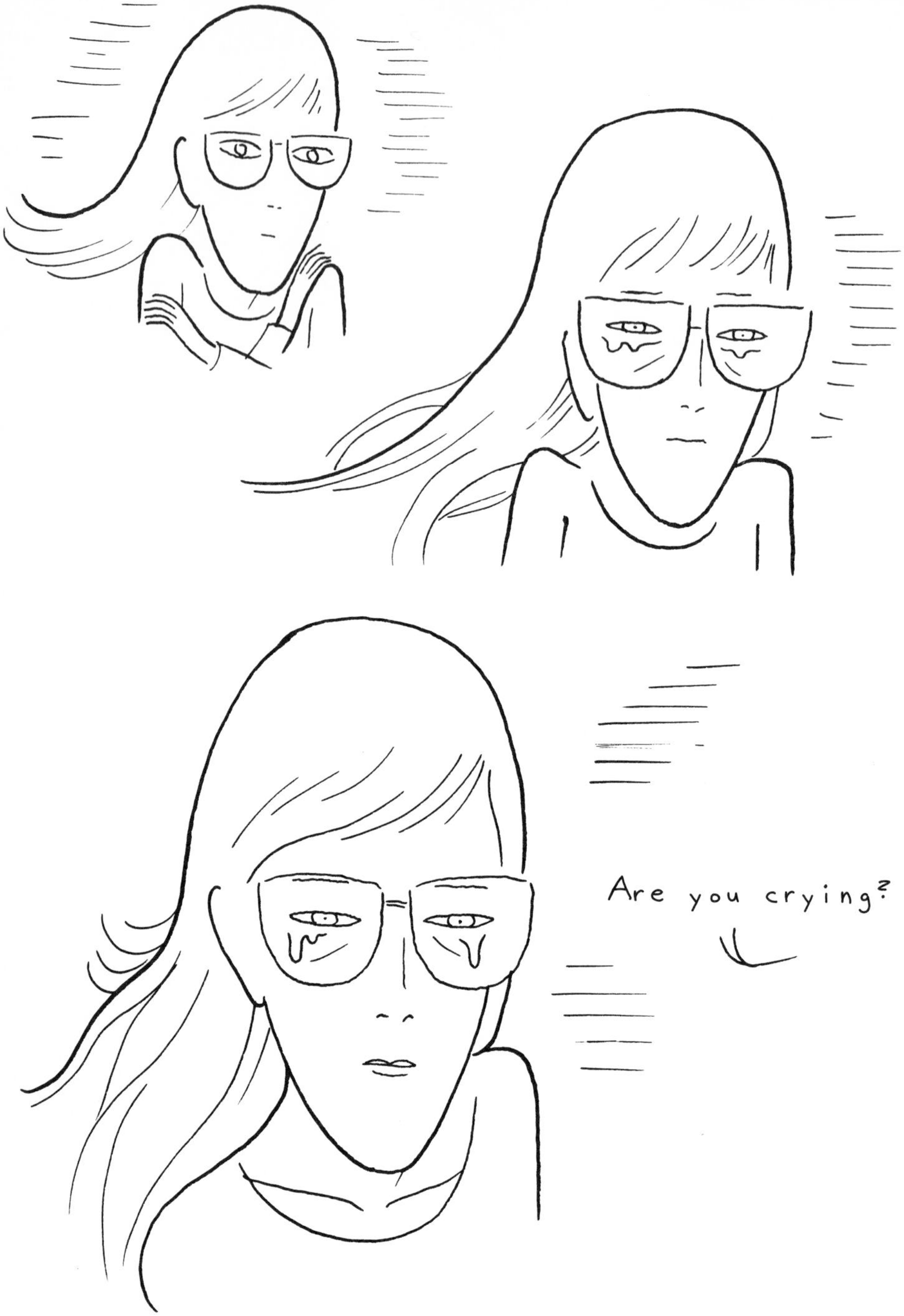
Are you crying?

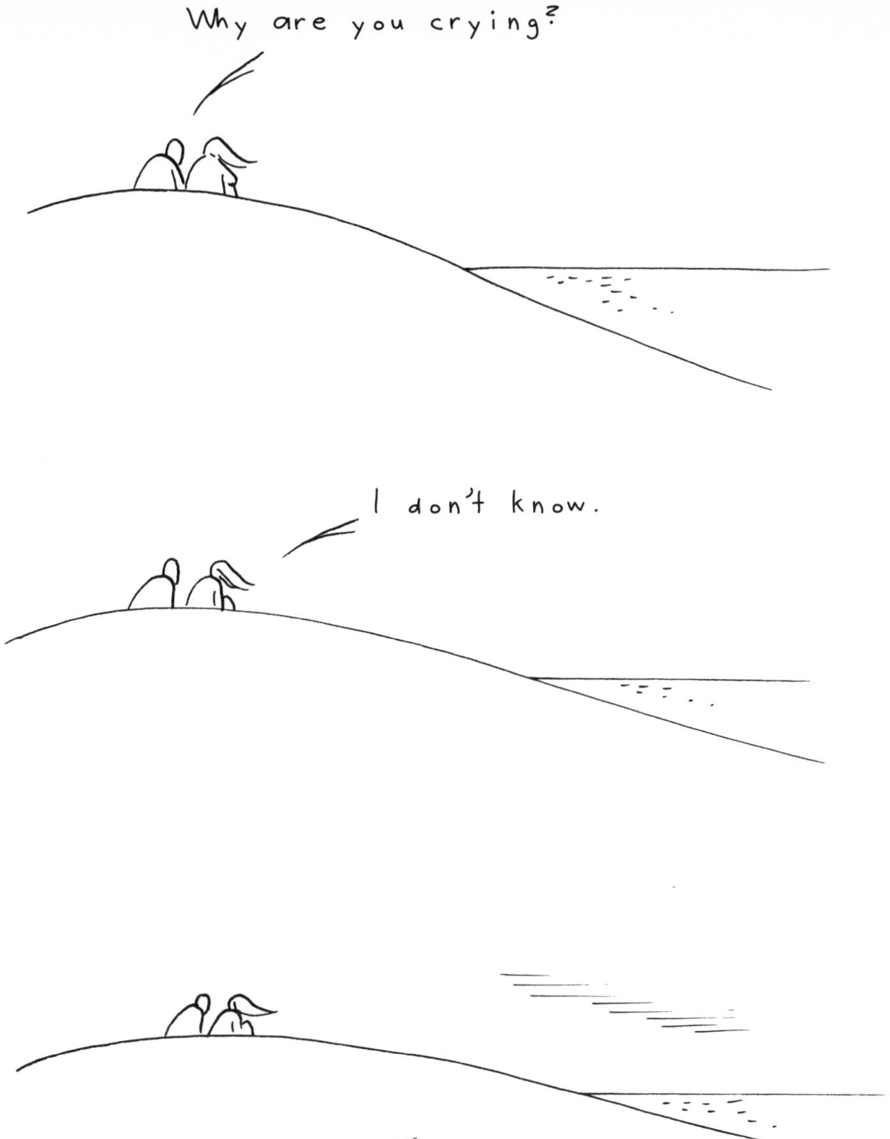
Why are you crying?
I don't know.

"I said you didn't have to drink the Nutrilor...that it was just a game.

But you wanted to anyway. You explained you didn't like eating in front of people. So you went into an old blockhouse that smelled like piss and shit and drank the Nutrilor."

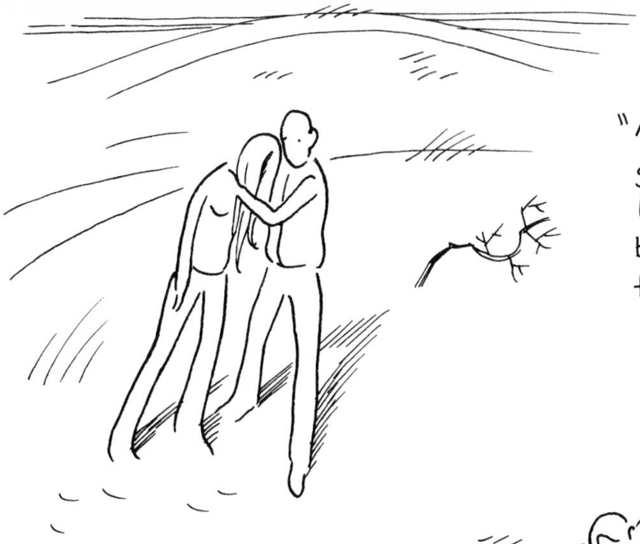

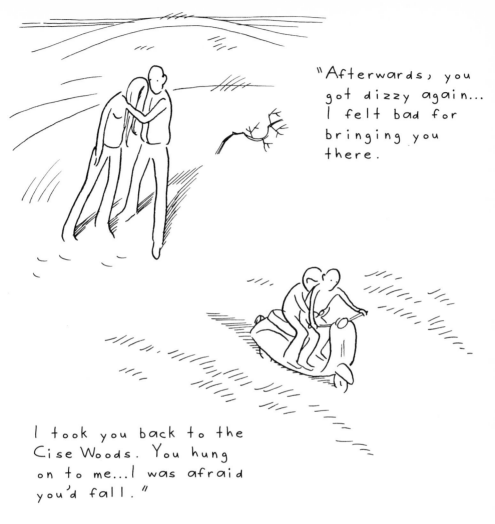

"Afterwards, you got dizzy again... I felt bad for bringing you there.

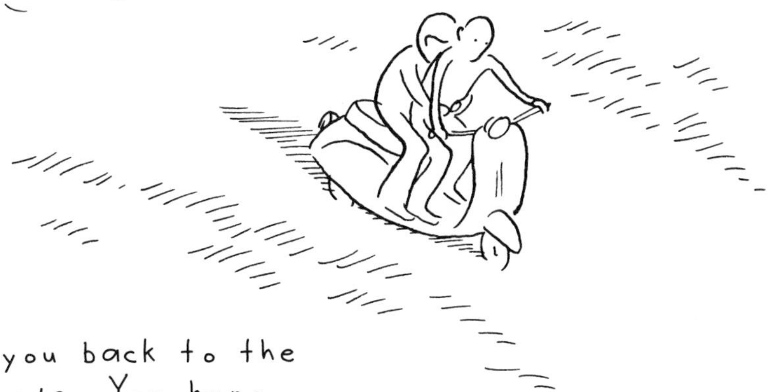

I took you back to the Cise Woods. You hung on to me...I was afraid you'd fall."

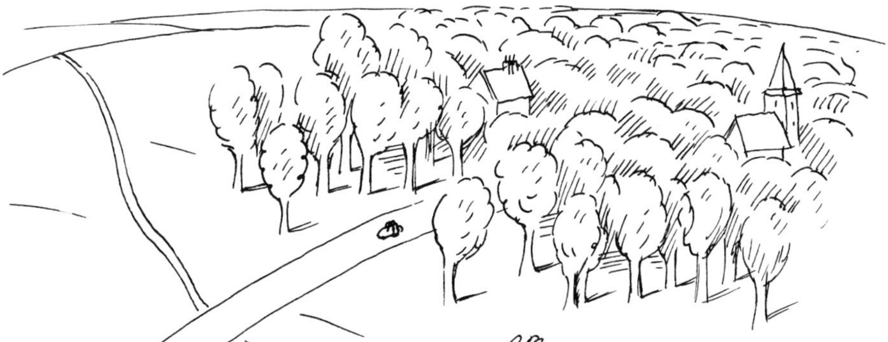

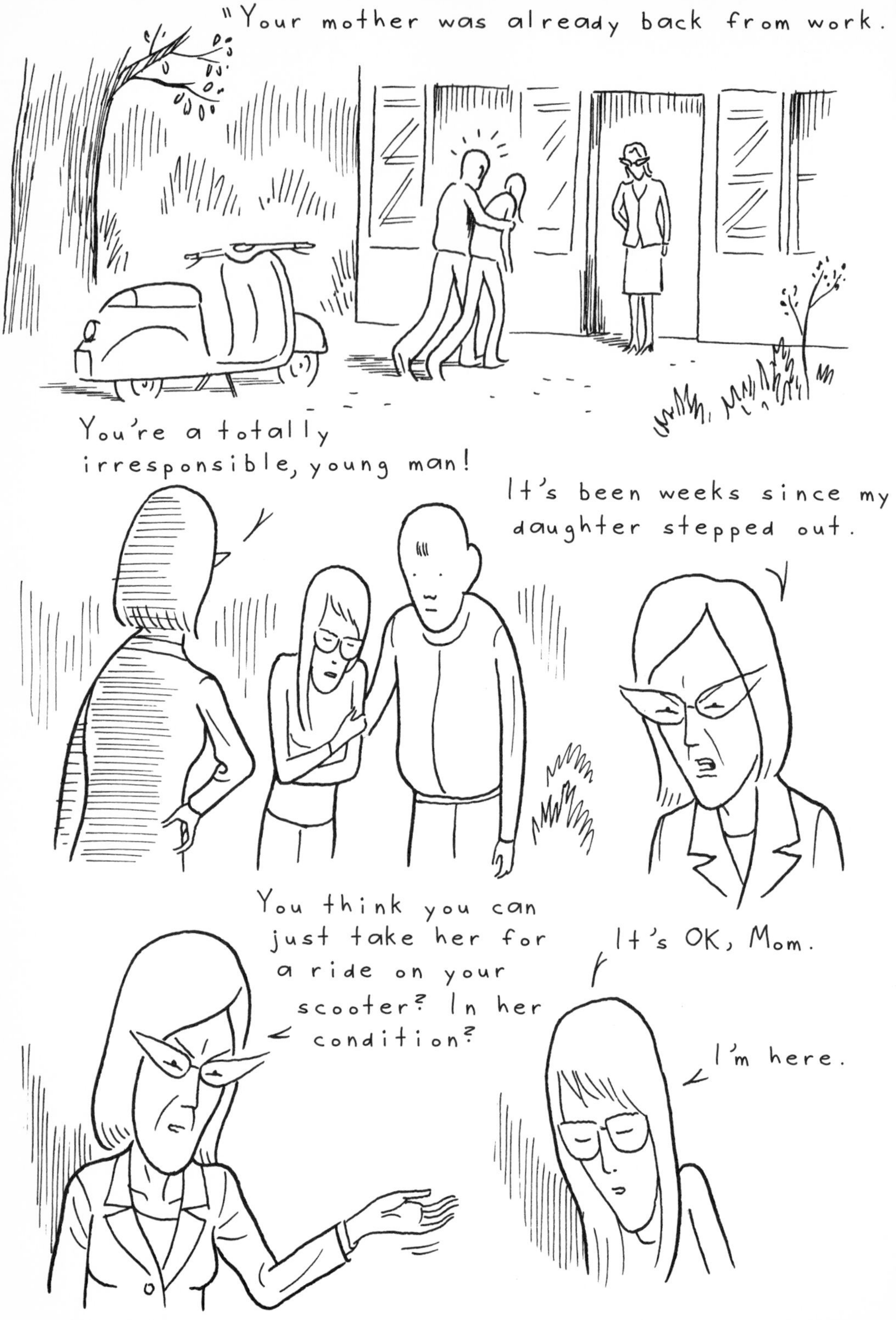
"Your mother was already back from work.
You're a totally irresponsible, young man!
It's been weeks since my daughter stepped out.
You think you can just take her for a ride on your scooter? In her condition?
It's OK, Mom.
I'm here.

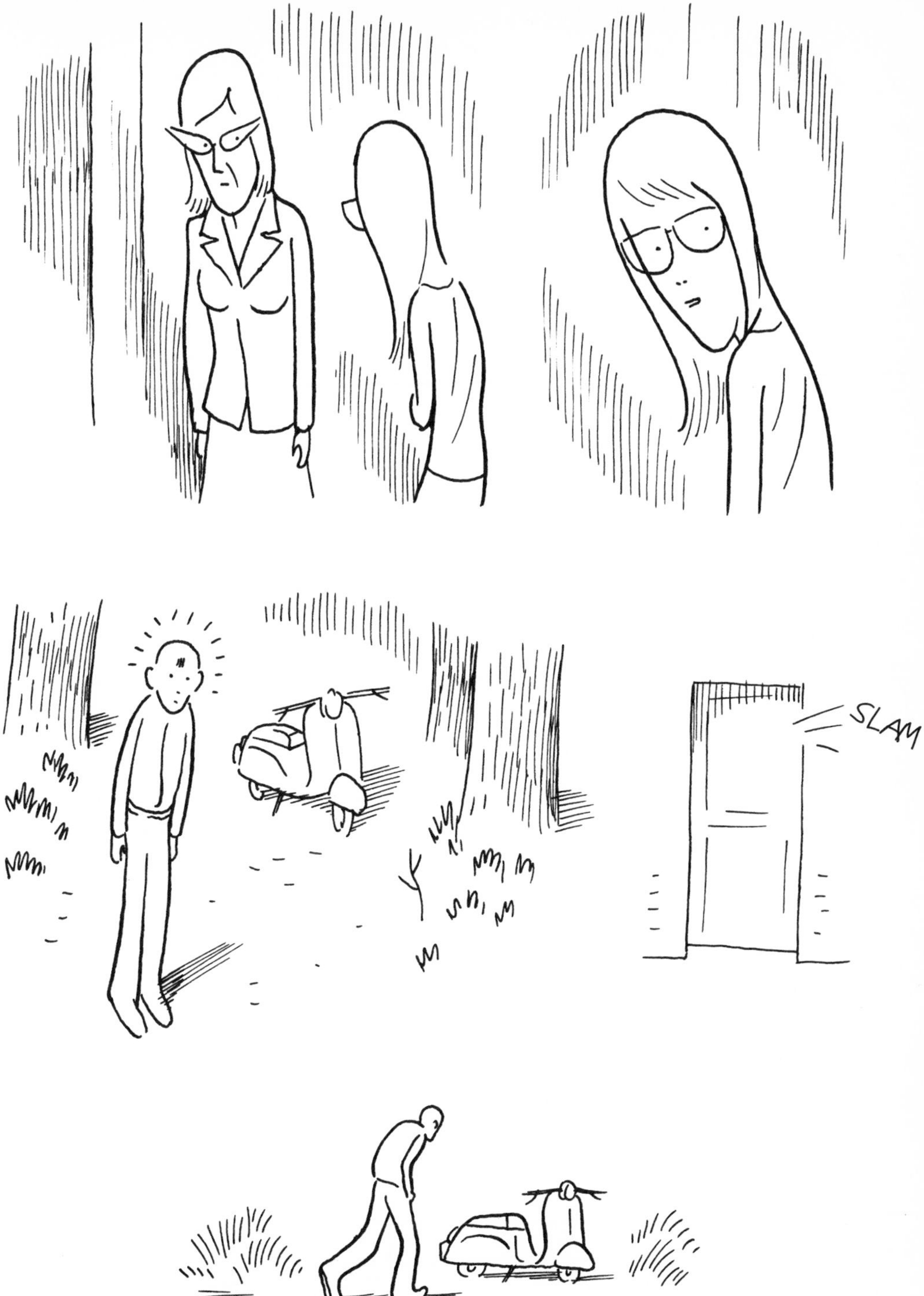
SLAM

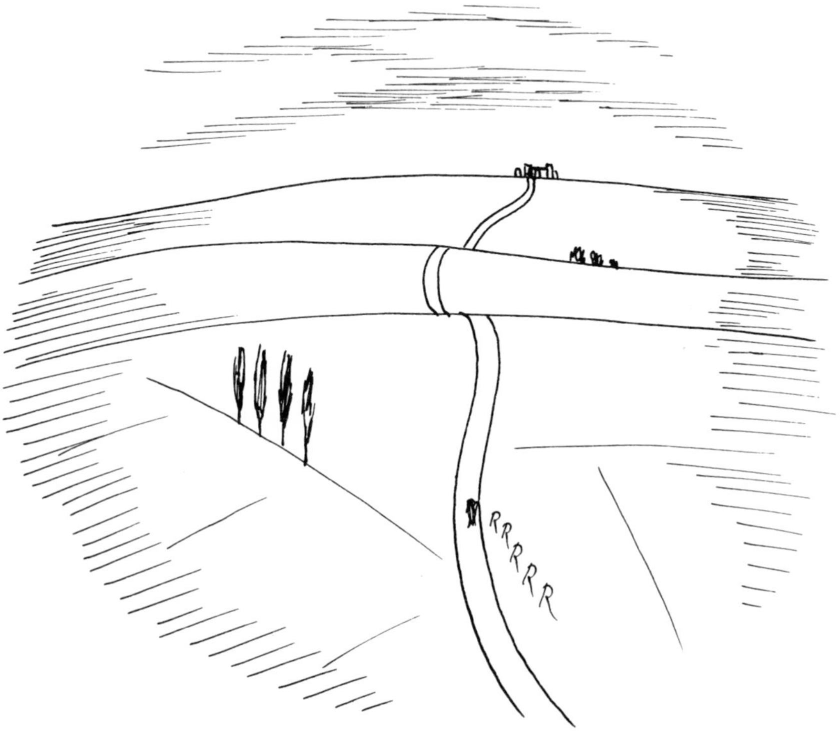
RRRRR

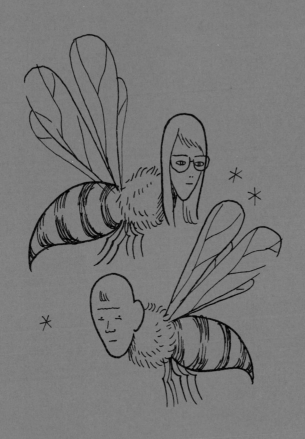

LA LIGNE
(The Line)

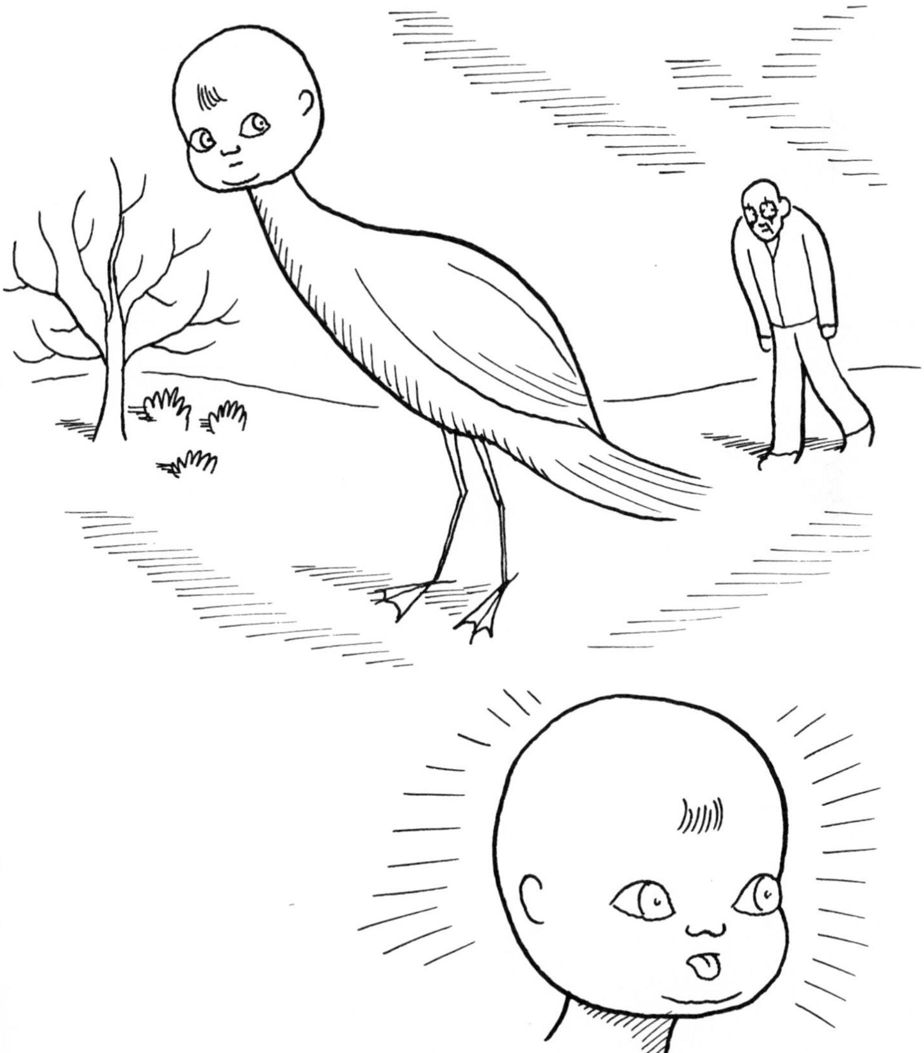

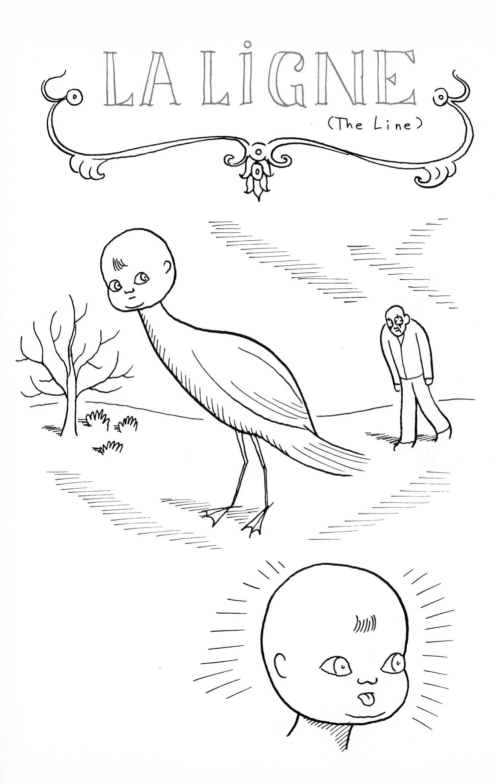

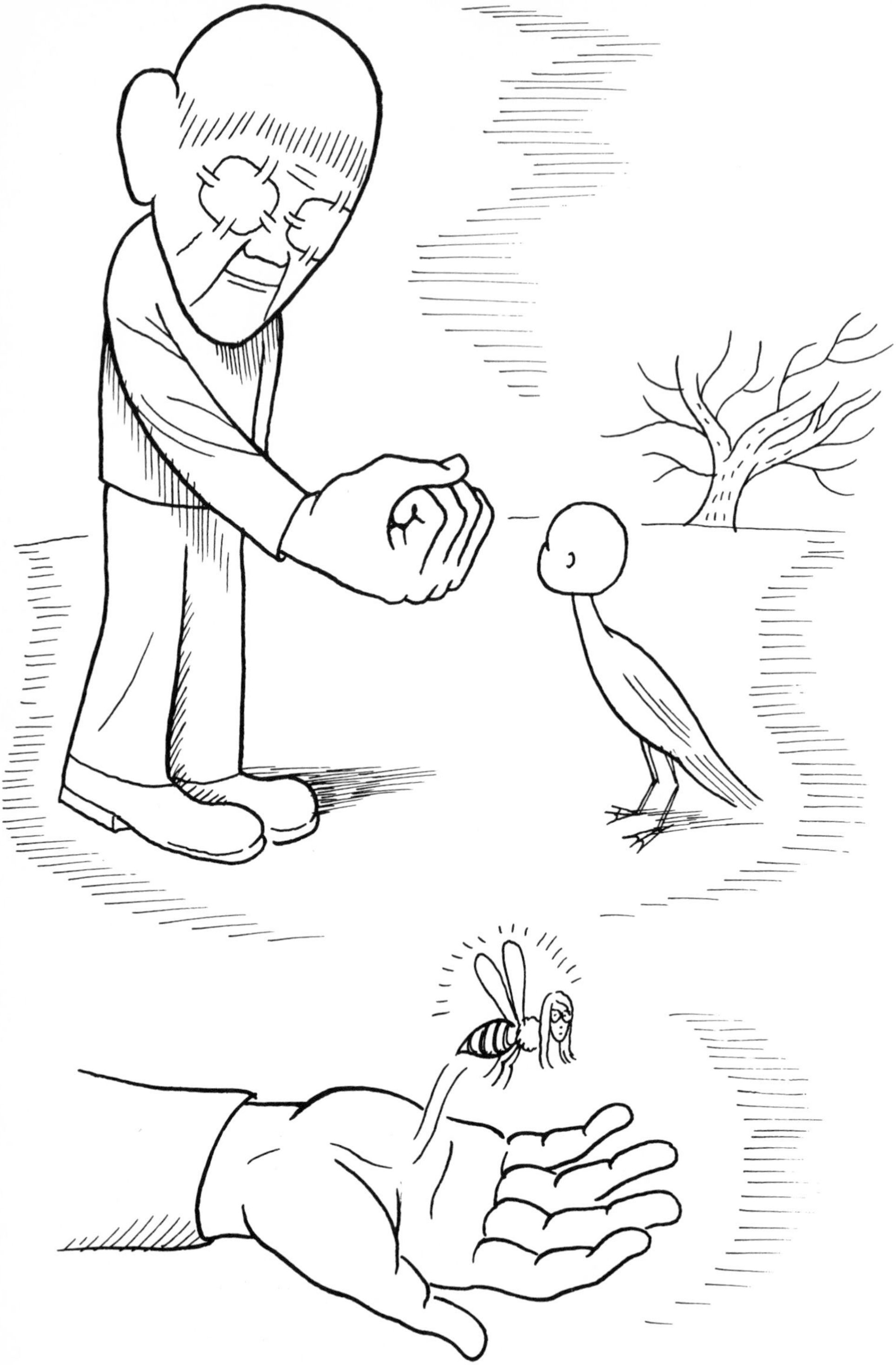

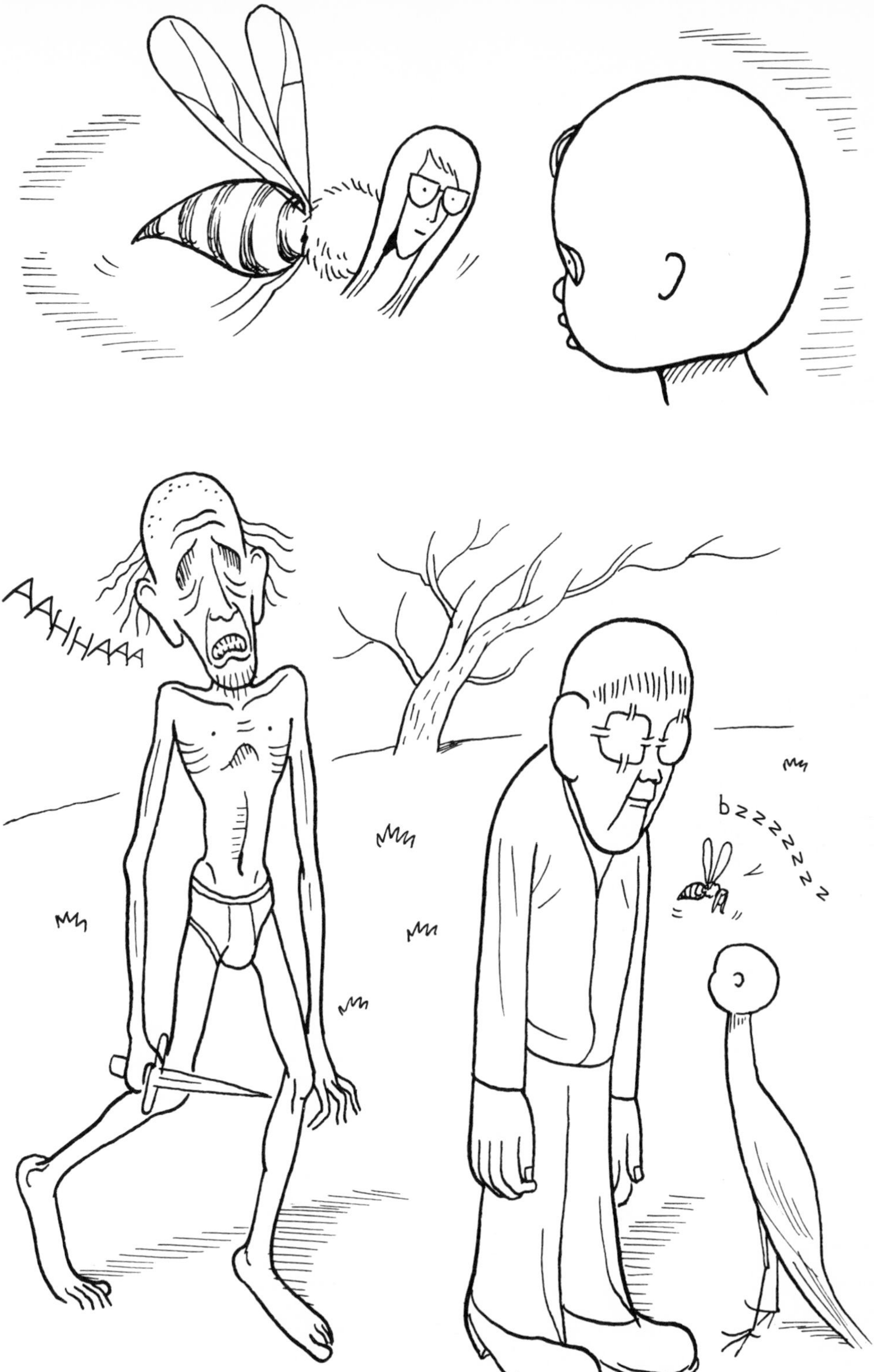
AAHHAAA
bzzzzzzzz

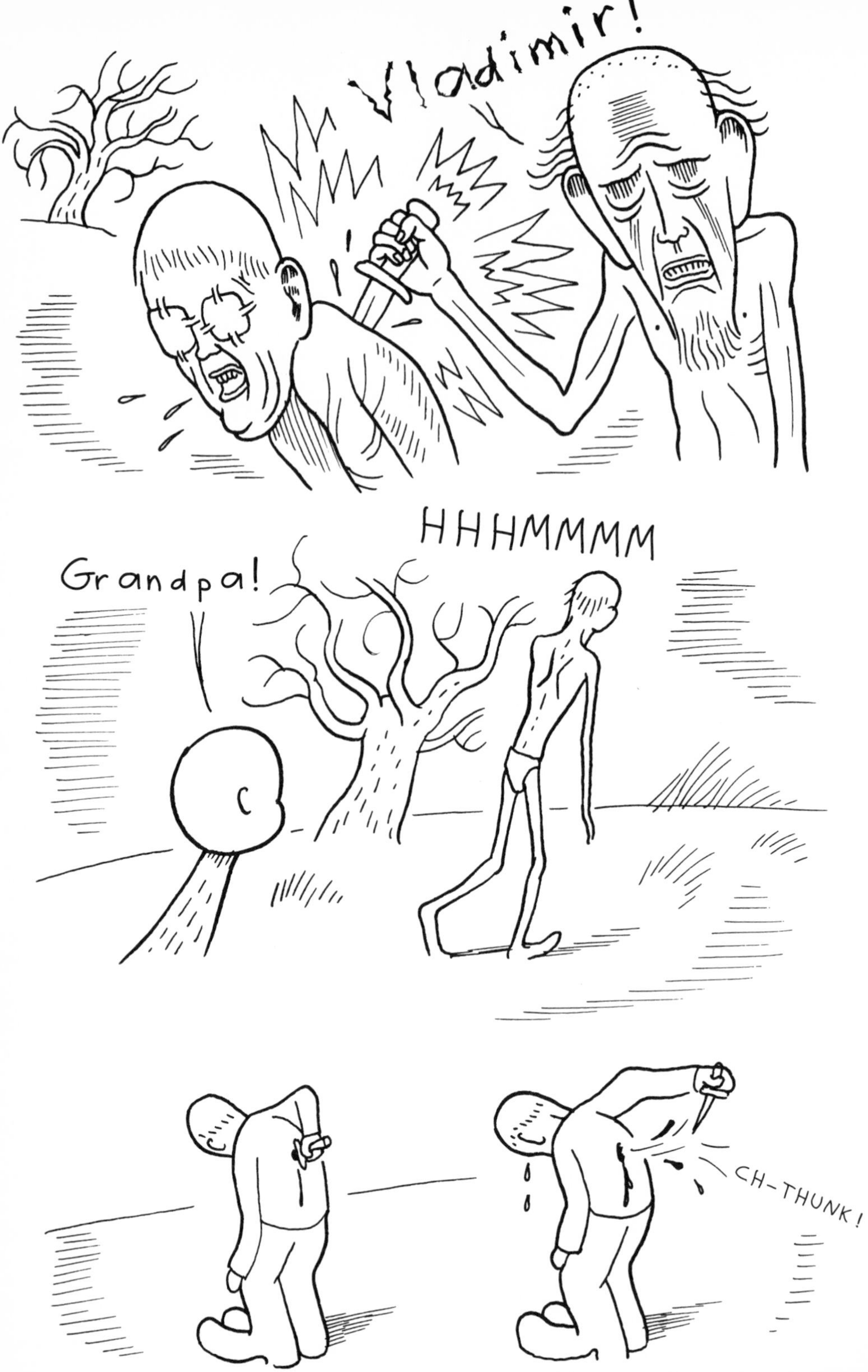
Vladimir!
Grandpa!
HHHMMMM
CH-THUNK!

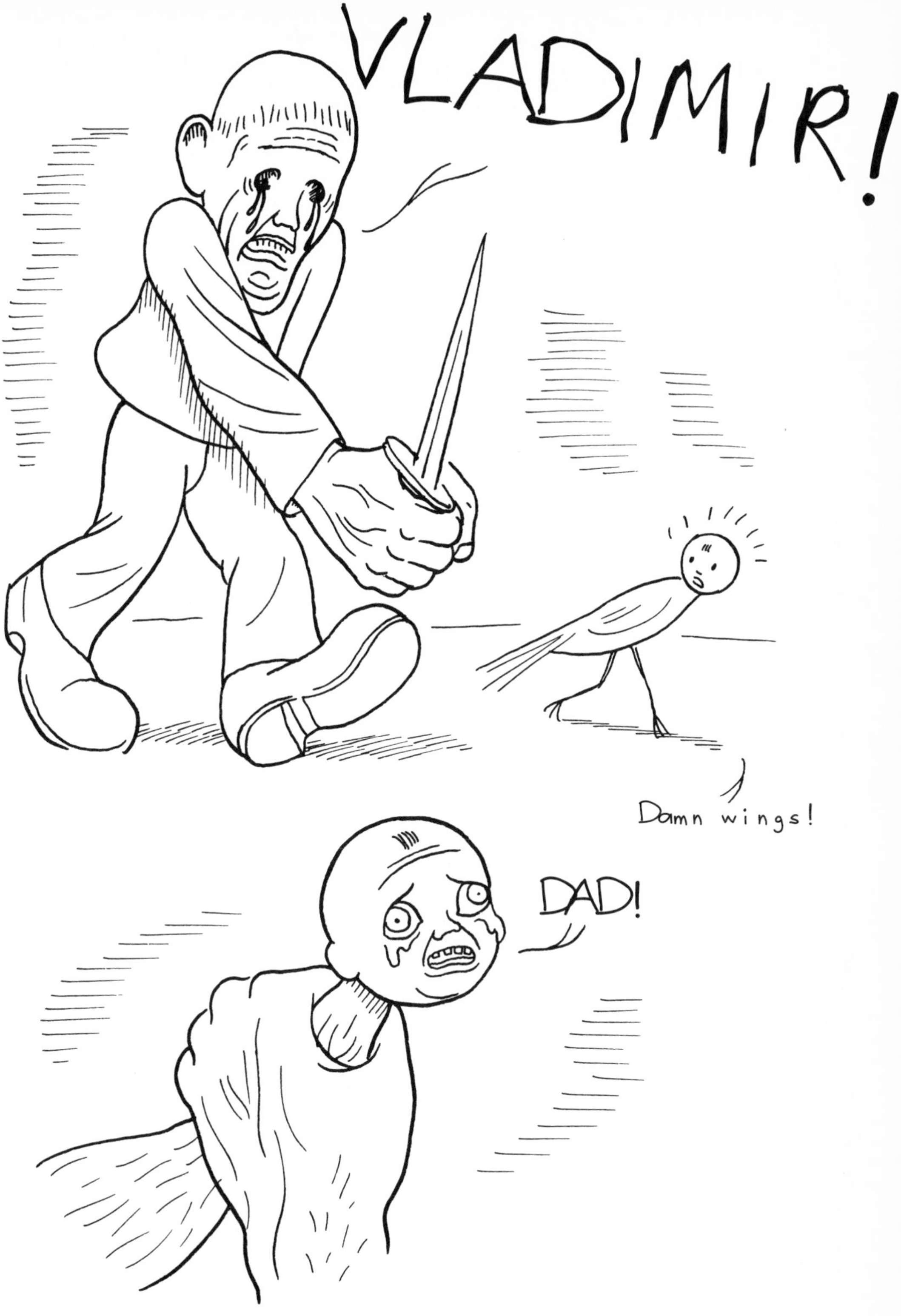
VLADIMIR!
Damn wings!
DAD!

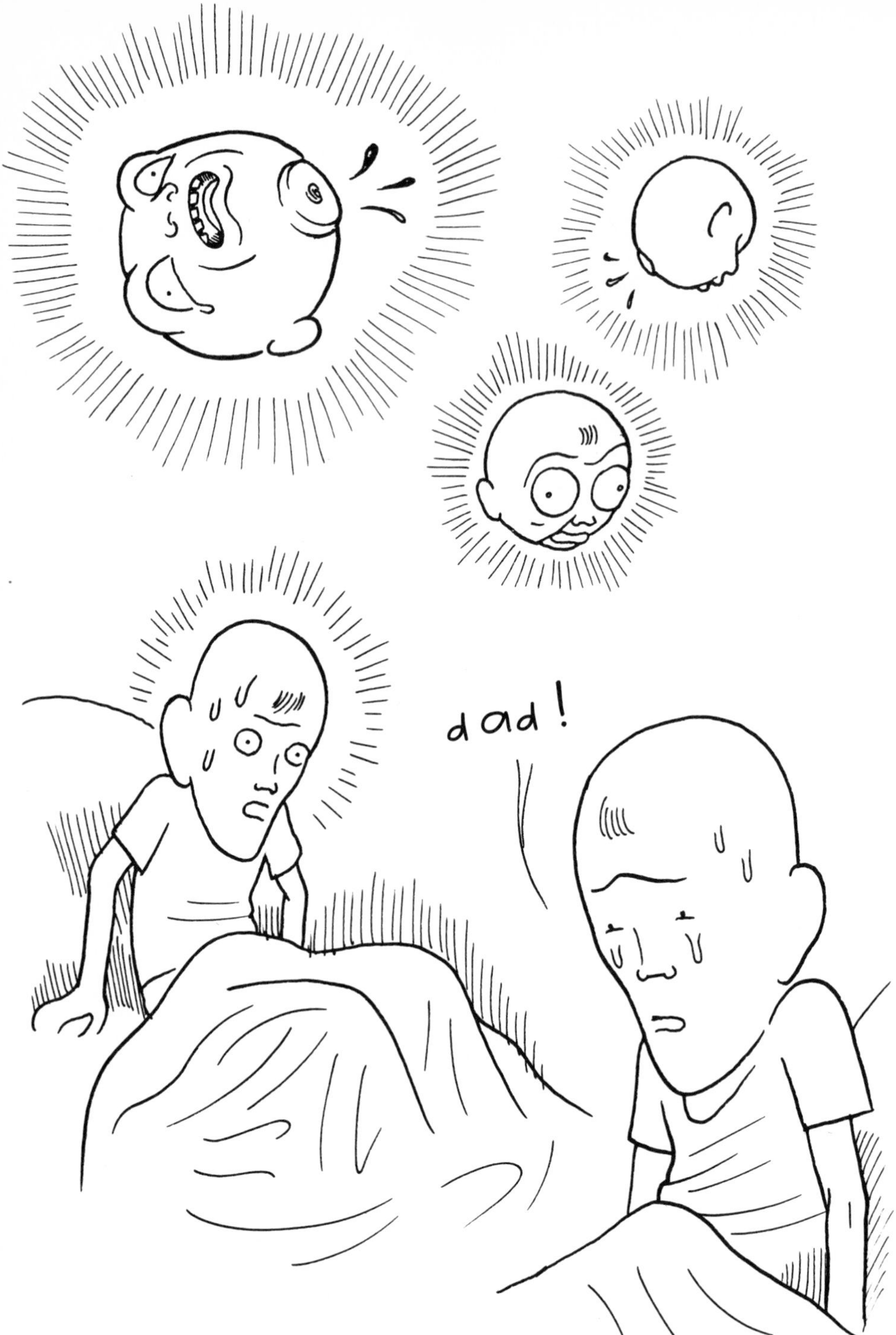
dad!

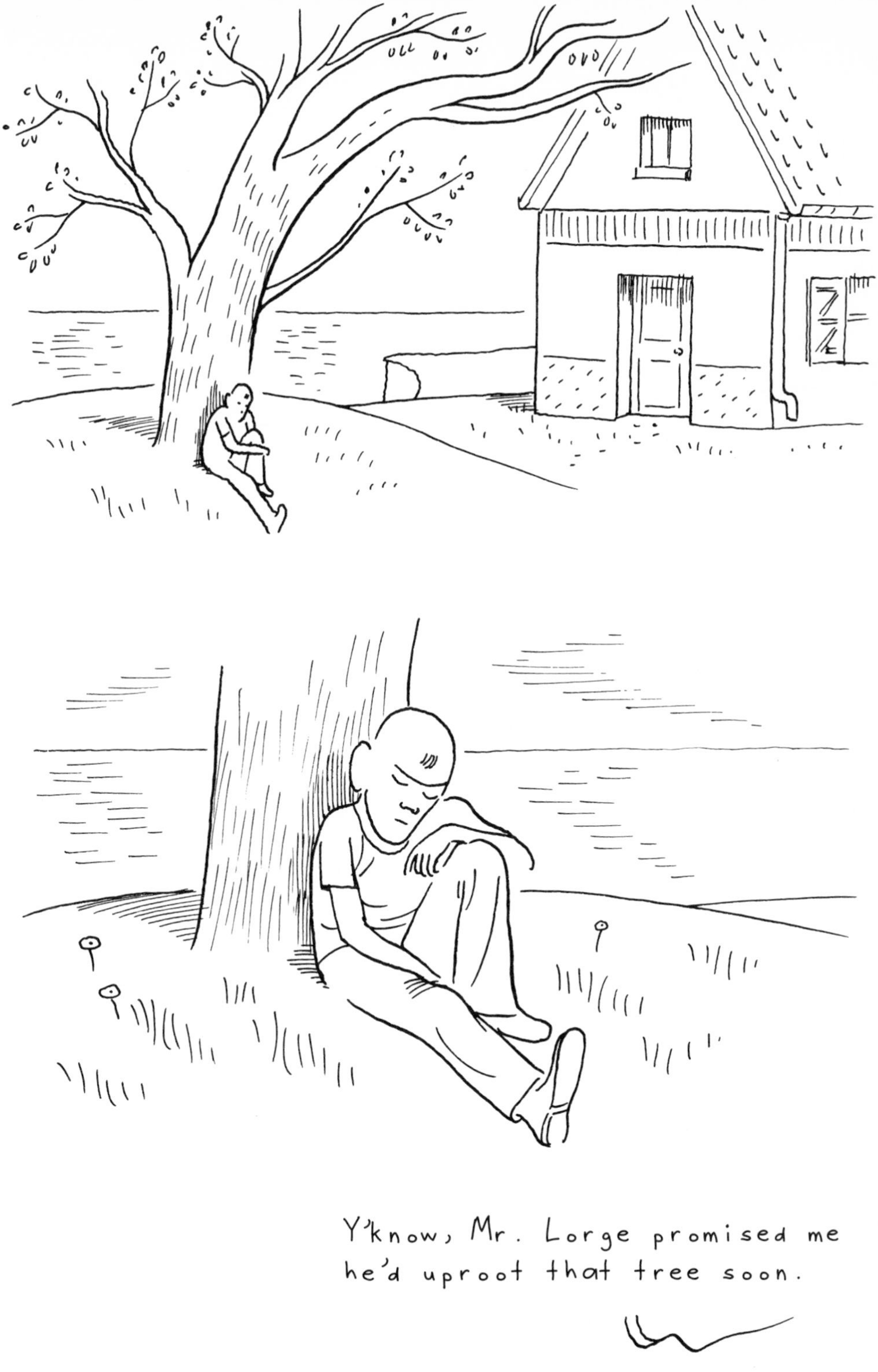
Y'know, Mr. Lorge promised me he'd uproot that tree soon.

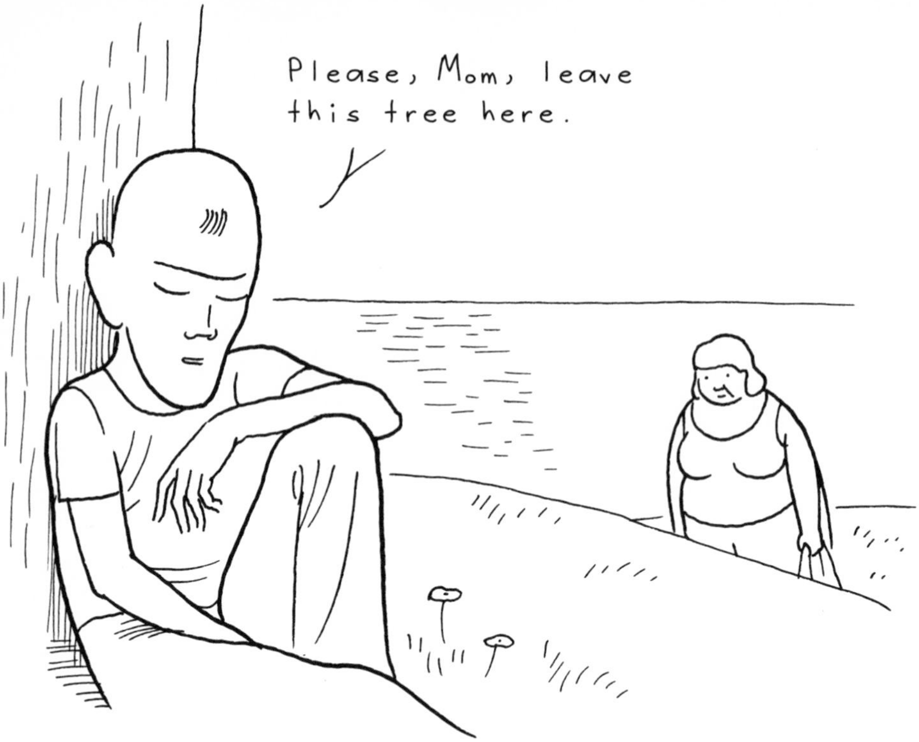
Please, Mom, leave
this tree here.

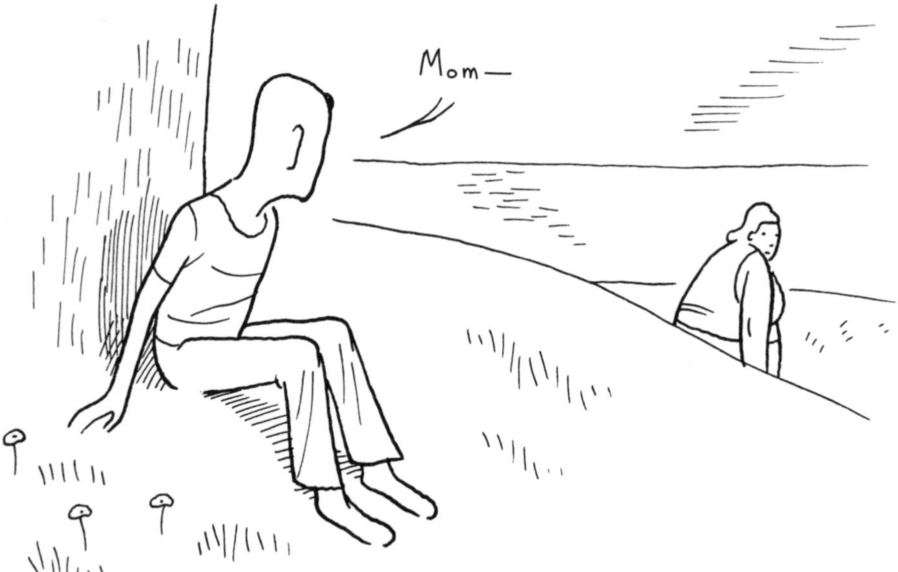
Mom—

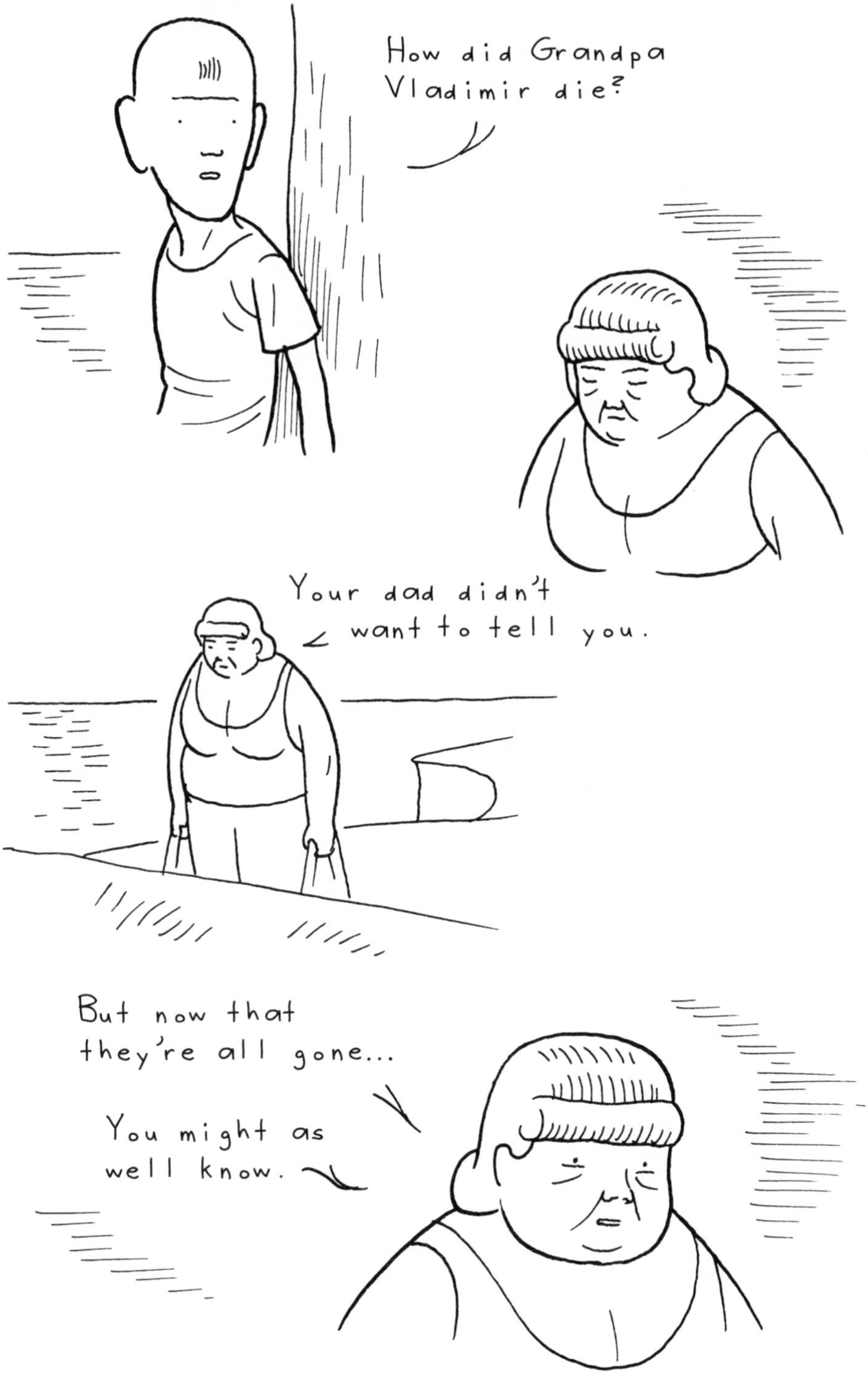
How did Grandpa Vladimir die?
Your dad didn't want to tell you.
But now that they're all gone...
You might as well know.

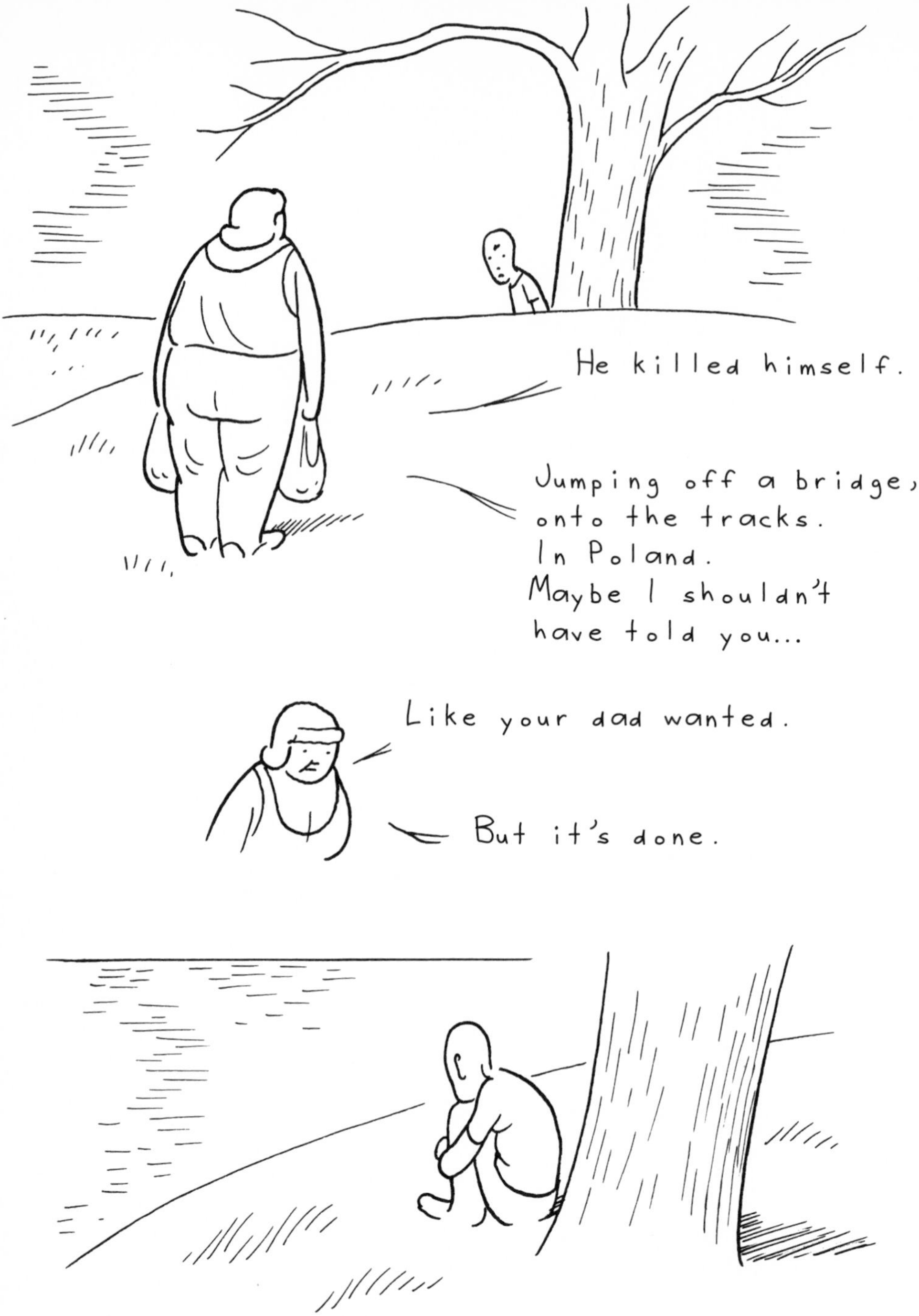
He killed himself.
Jumping off a bridge, onto the tracks. In Poland. Maybe I shouldn't have told you...
Like your dad wanted.
But it's done.

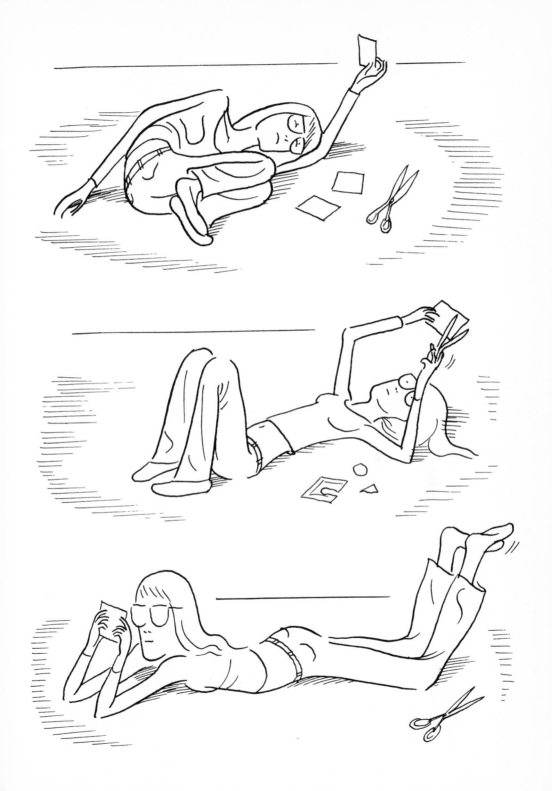

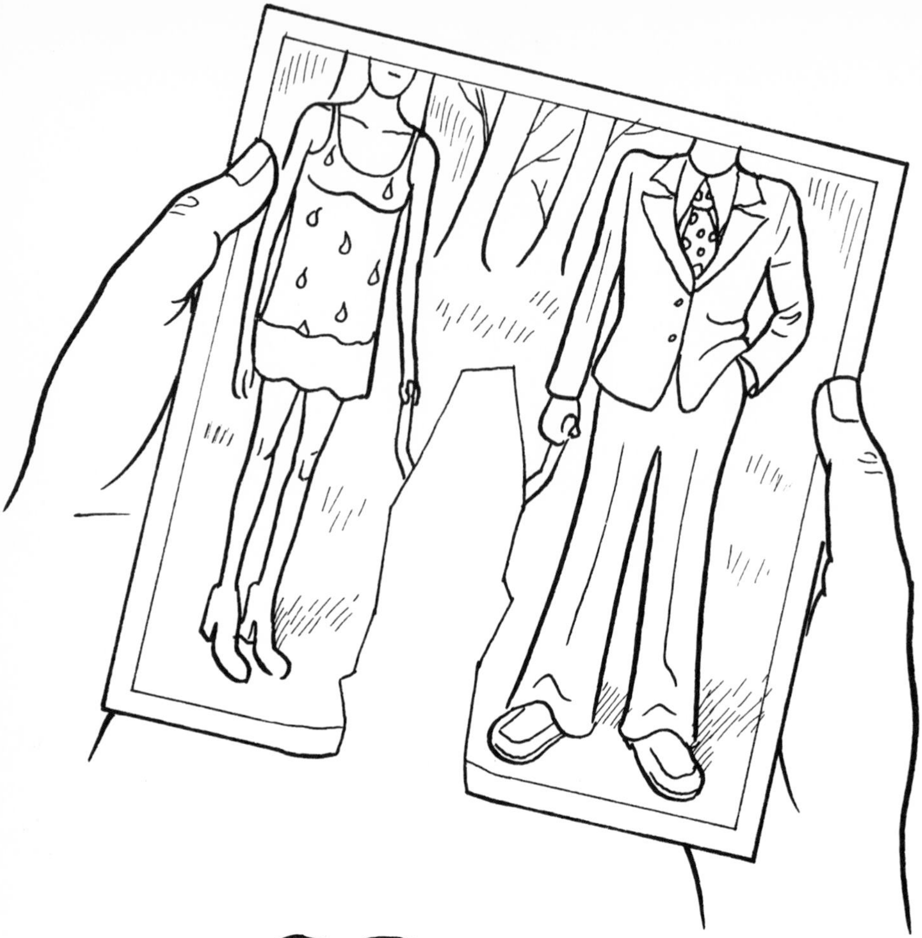

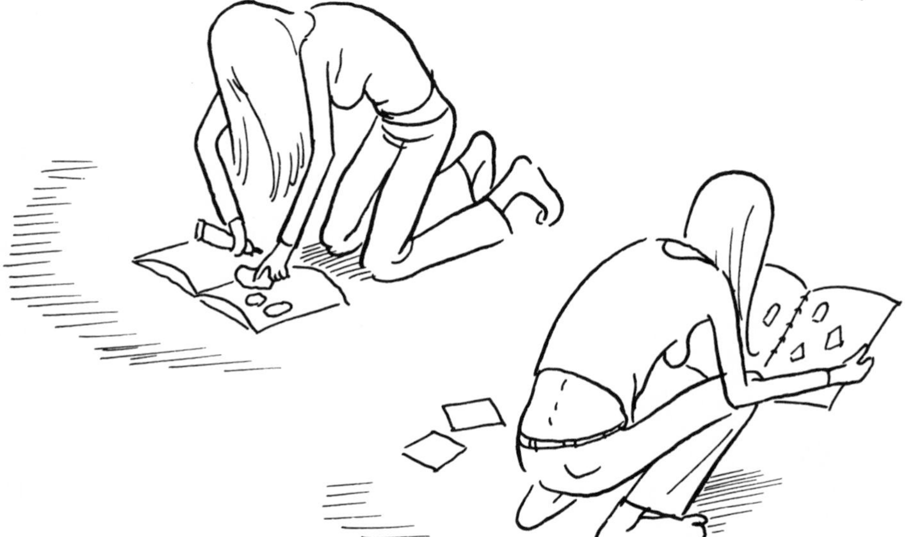

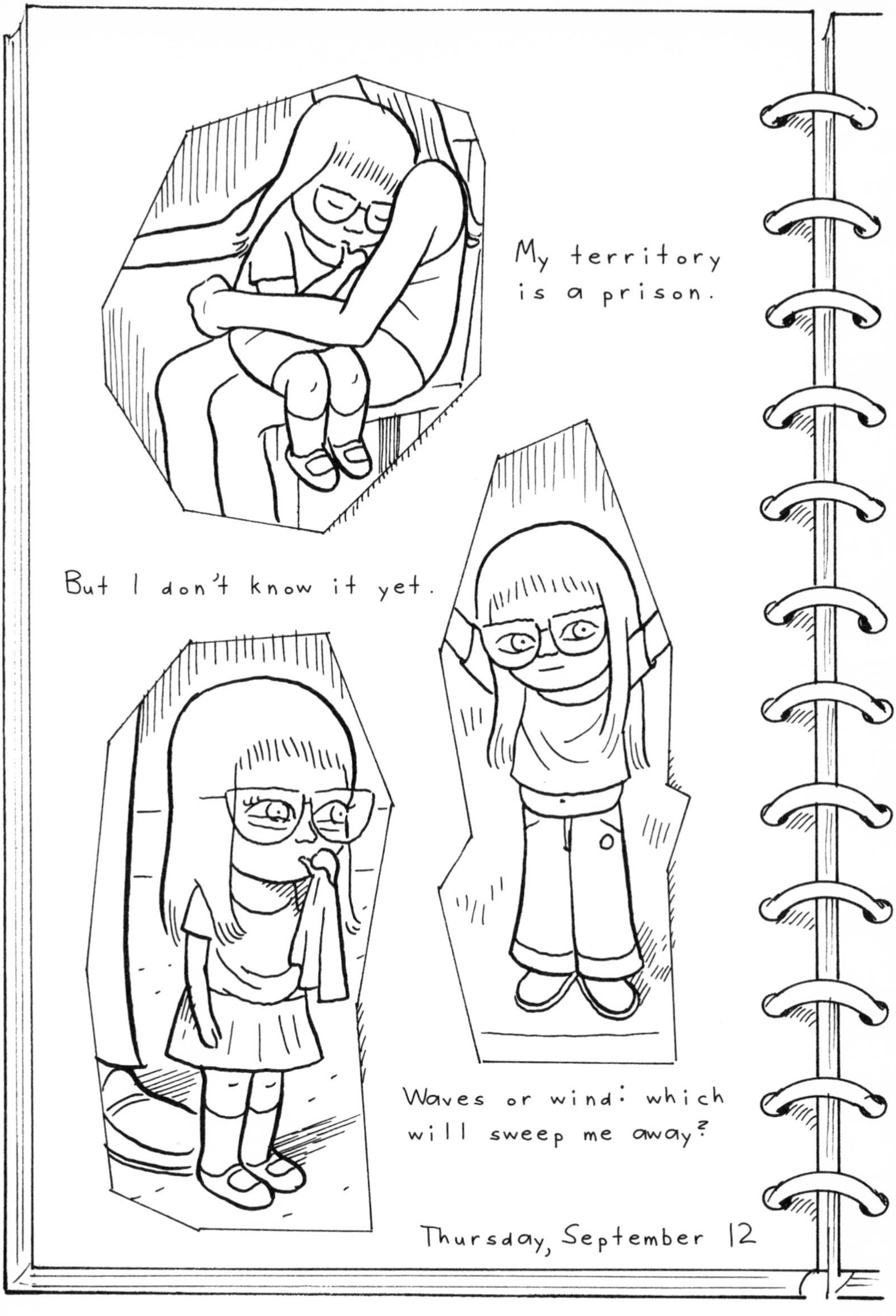
My territory is a prison.
But I don't know it yet.
Waves or wind: which will sweep me away?
Thursday, September 12

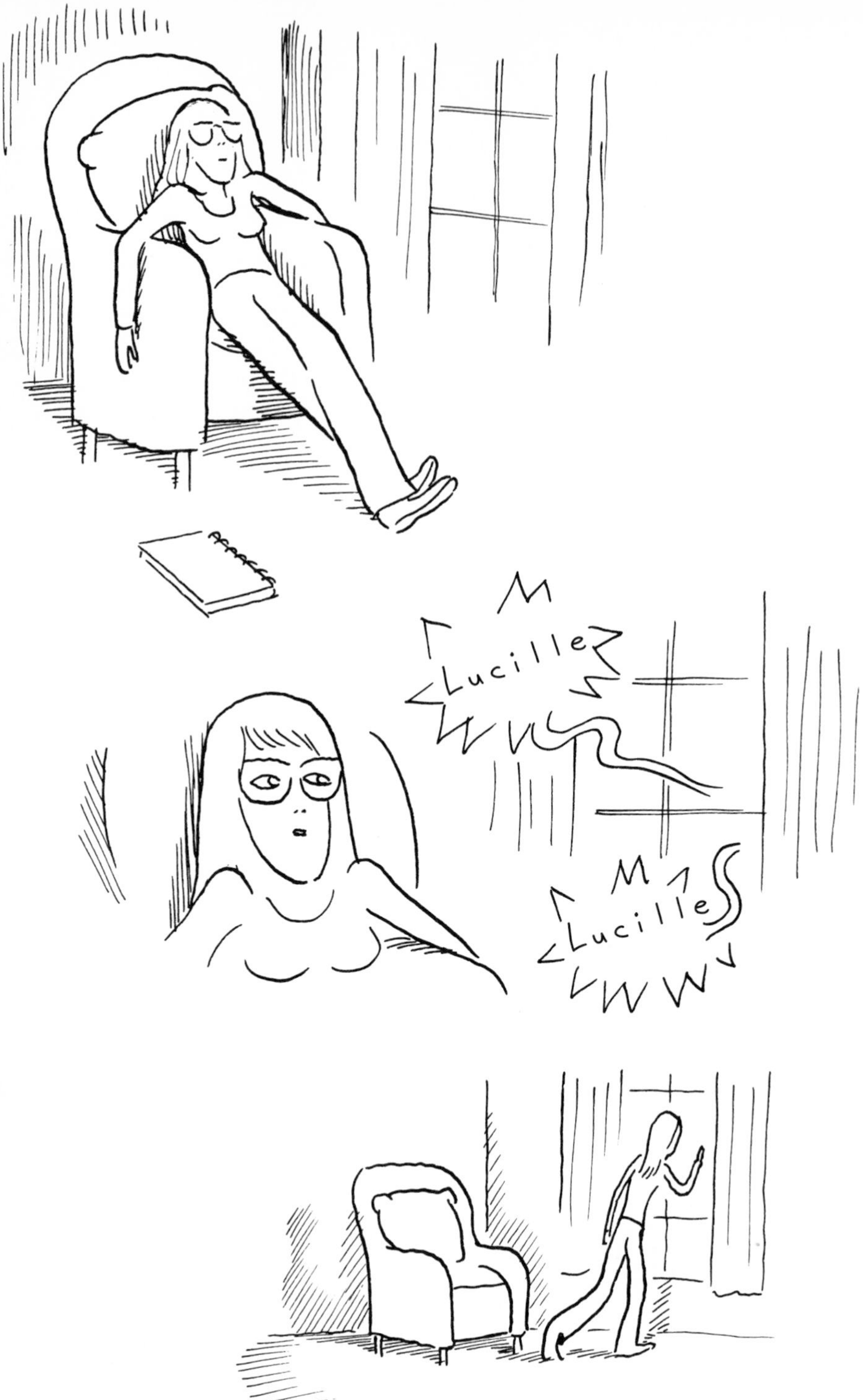
Lucille
Lucille

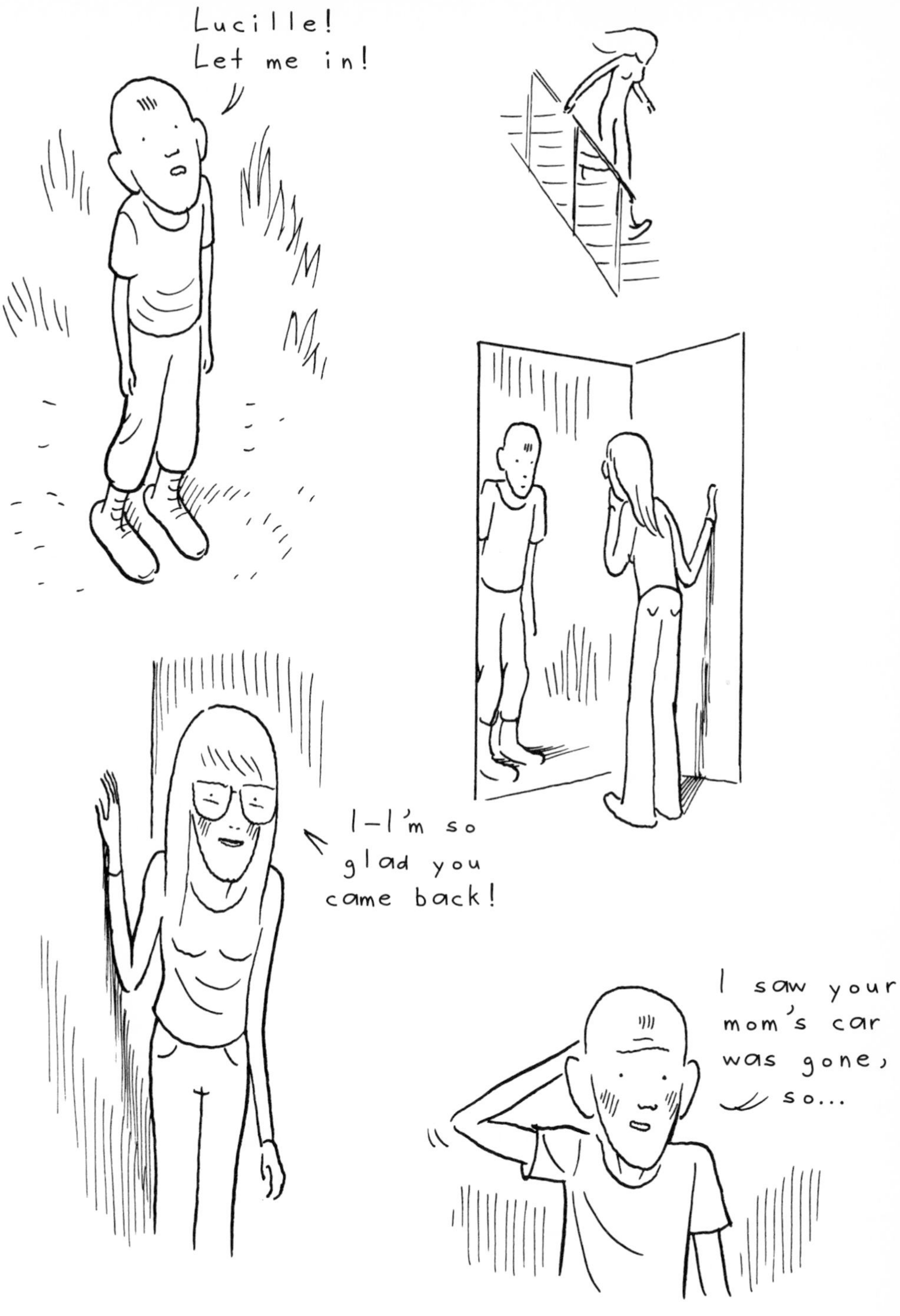
Lucille!
Let me in!
I-I'm so glad you came back!
I saw your mom's car was gone, so...

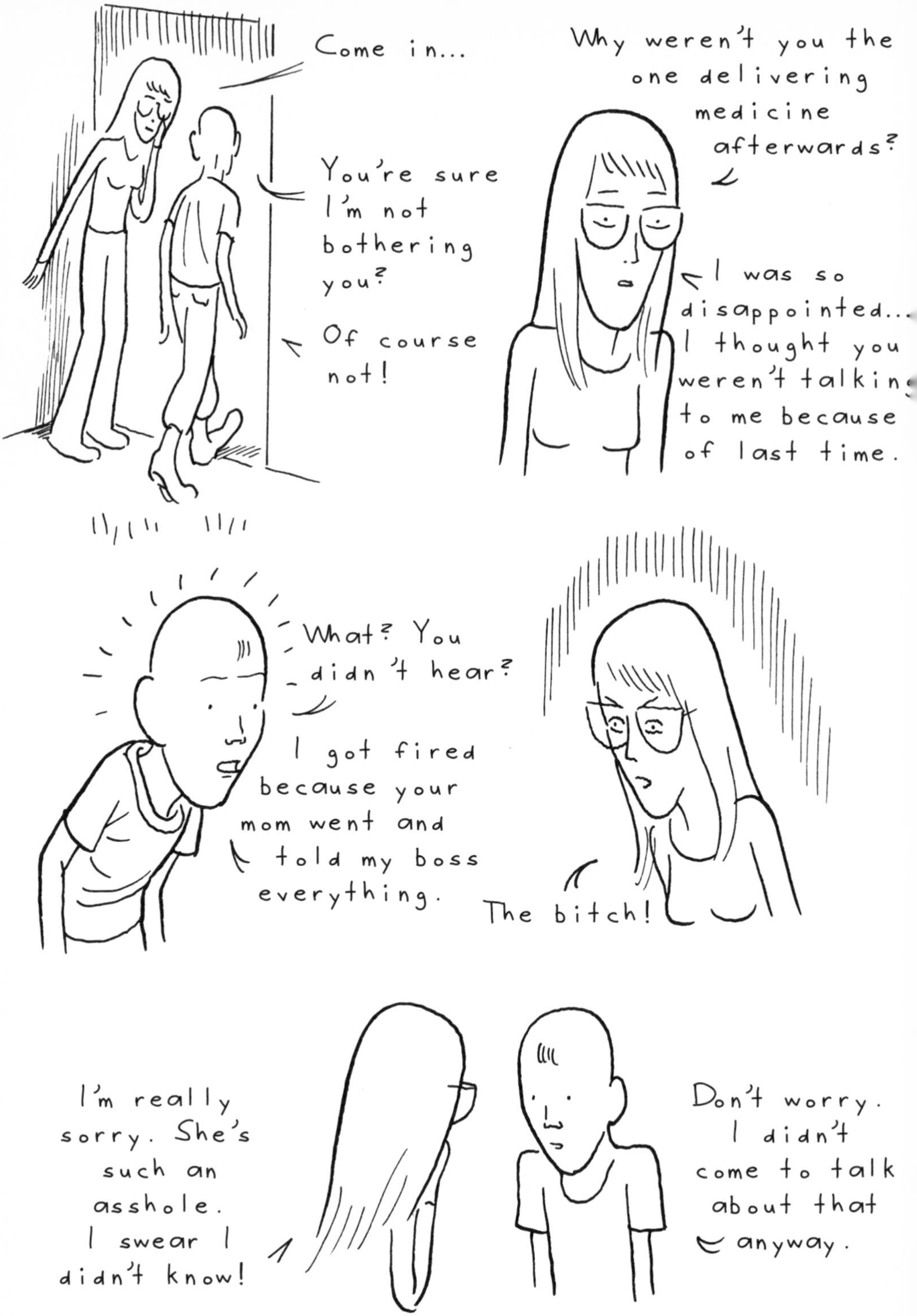
Come in...
You're sure I'm not bothering you?
Of course not!
Why weren't you the one delivering medicine afterwards?
I was so disappointed... I thought you weren't talking to me because of last time.
What? You didn't hear?
I got fired because your mom went and told my boss everything.
The bitch!
I'm really sorry. She's such an asshole. I swear I didn't know!
Don't worry. I didn't come to talk about that anyway.

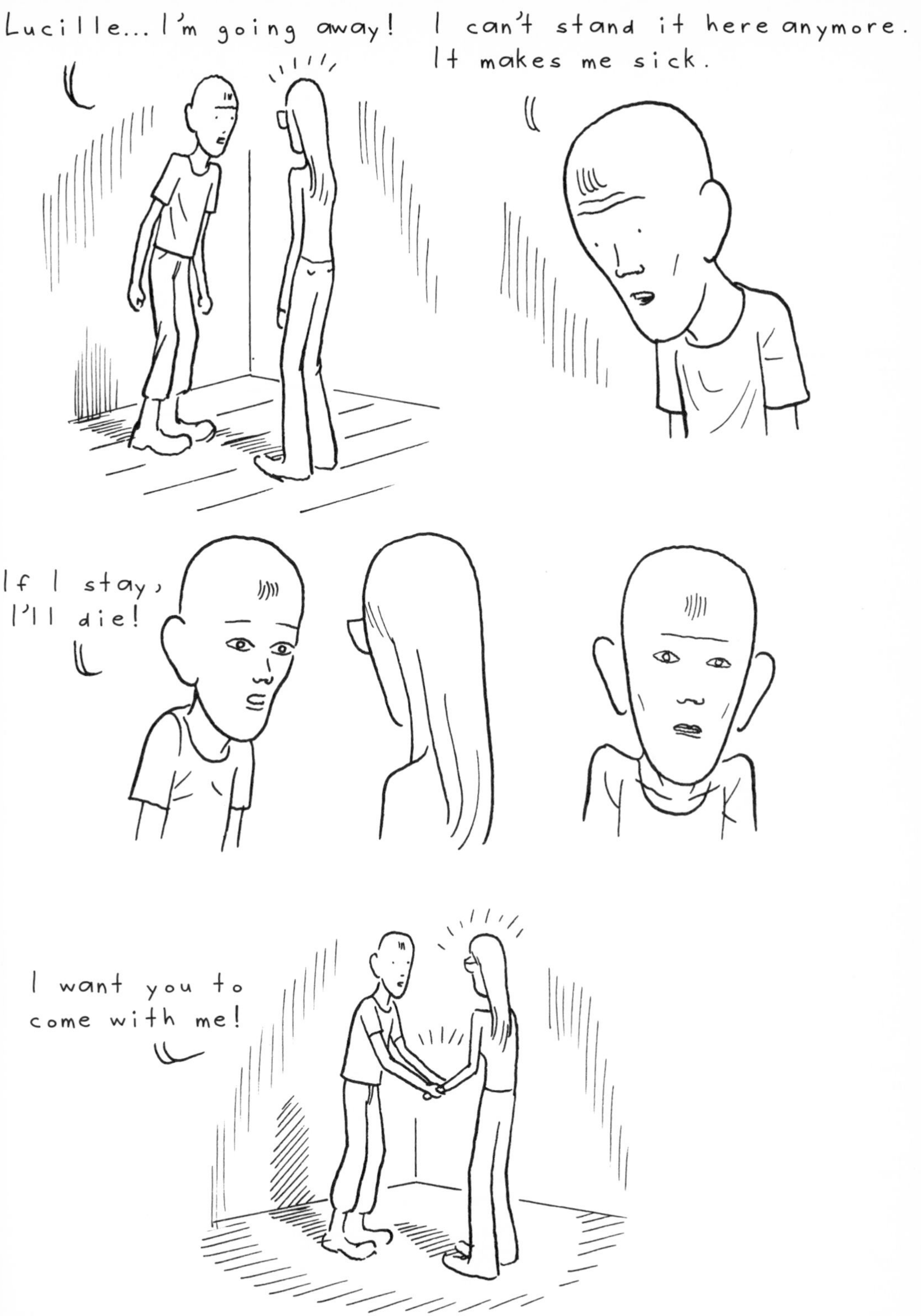
Lucille... I'm going away!
I can't stand it here anymore. It makes me sick.
If I stay, I'll die!
I want you to come with me!

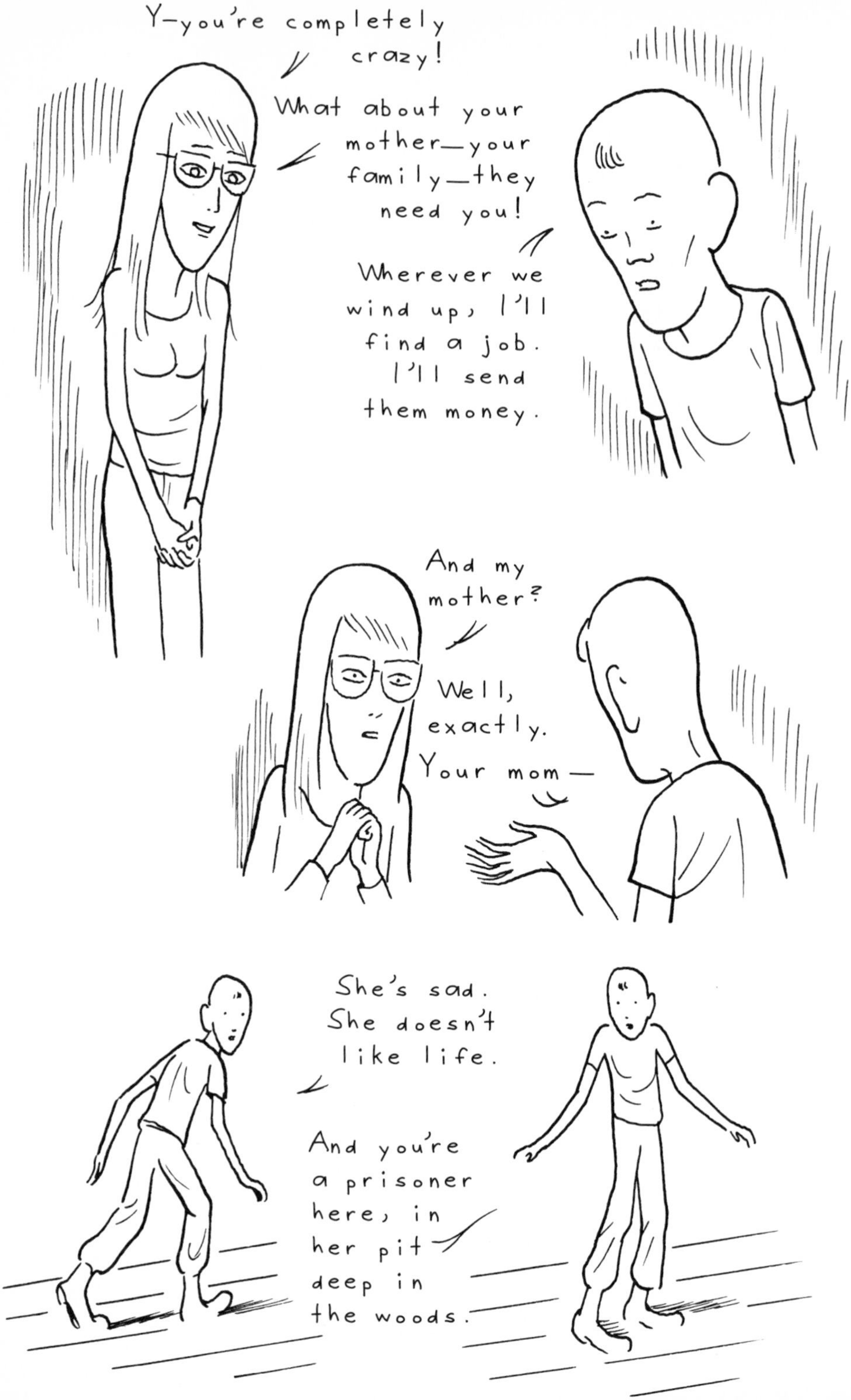
Y—you're completely crazy!
What about your mother—your family—they need you!
Wherever we wind up, I'll find a job. I'll send them money.
And my mother?
Well, exactly. Your mom—
She's sad. She doesn't like life.
And you're a prisoner here, in her pit deep in the woods.

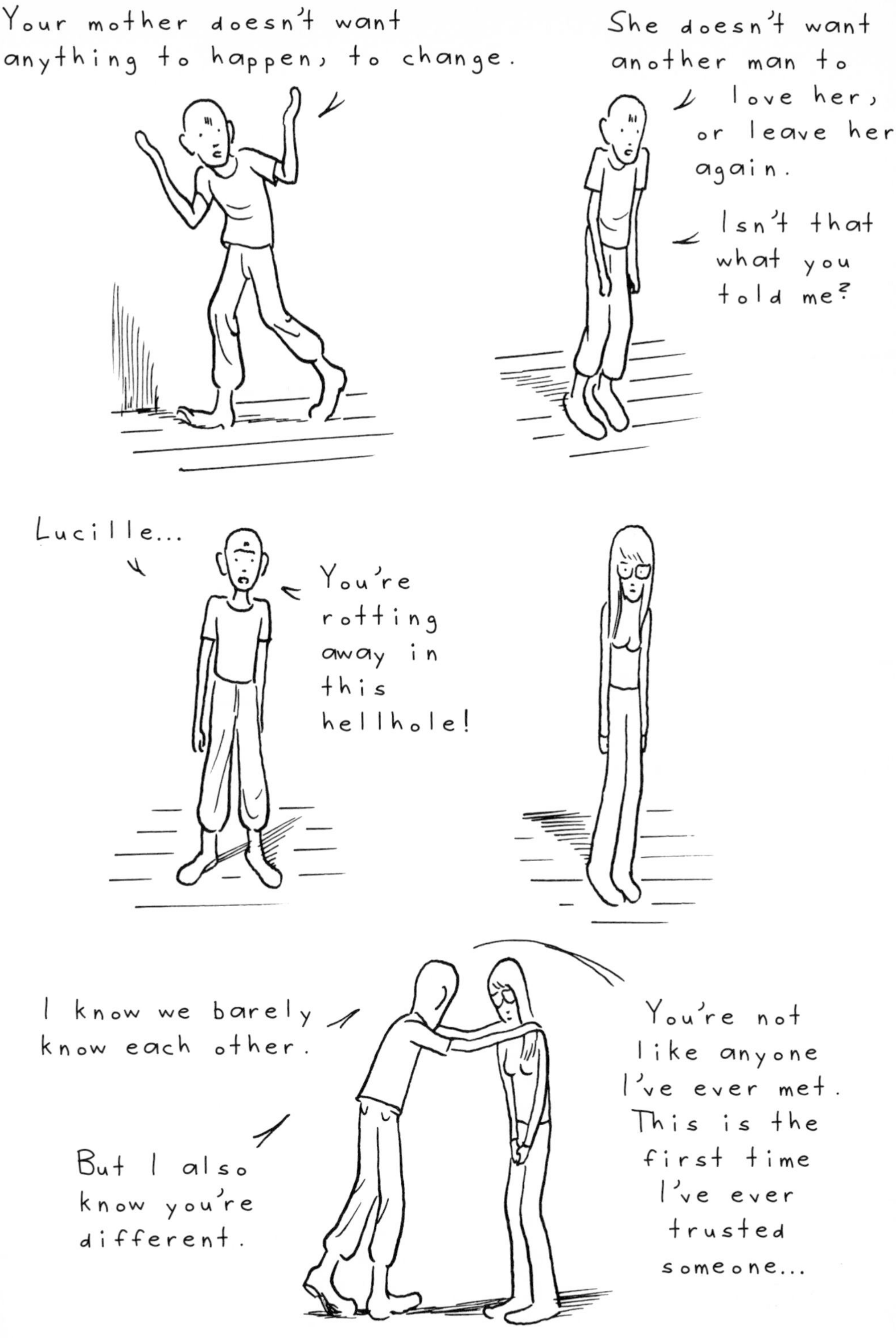
Your mother doesn't want anything to happen, to change.
She doesn't want another man to love her, or leave her again.
Isn't that what you told me?
Lucille...
You're rotting away in this hellhole!
I know we barely know each other.
But I also know you're different.
You're not like anyone I've ever met. This is the first time I've ever trusted someone...

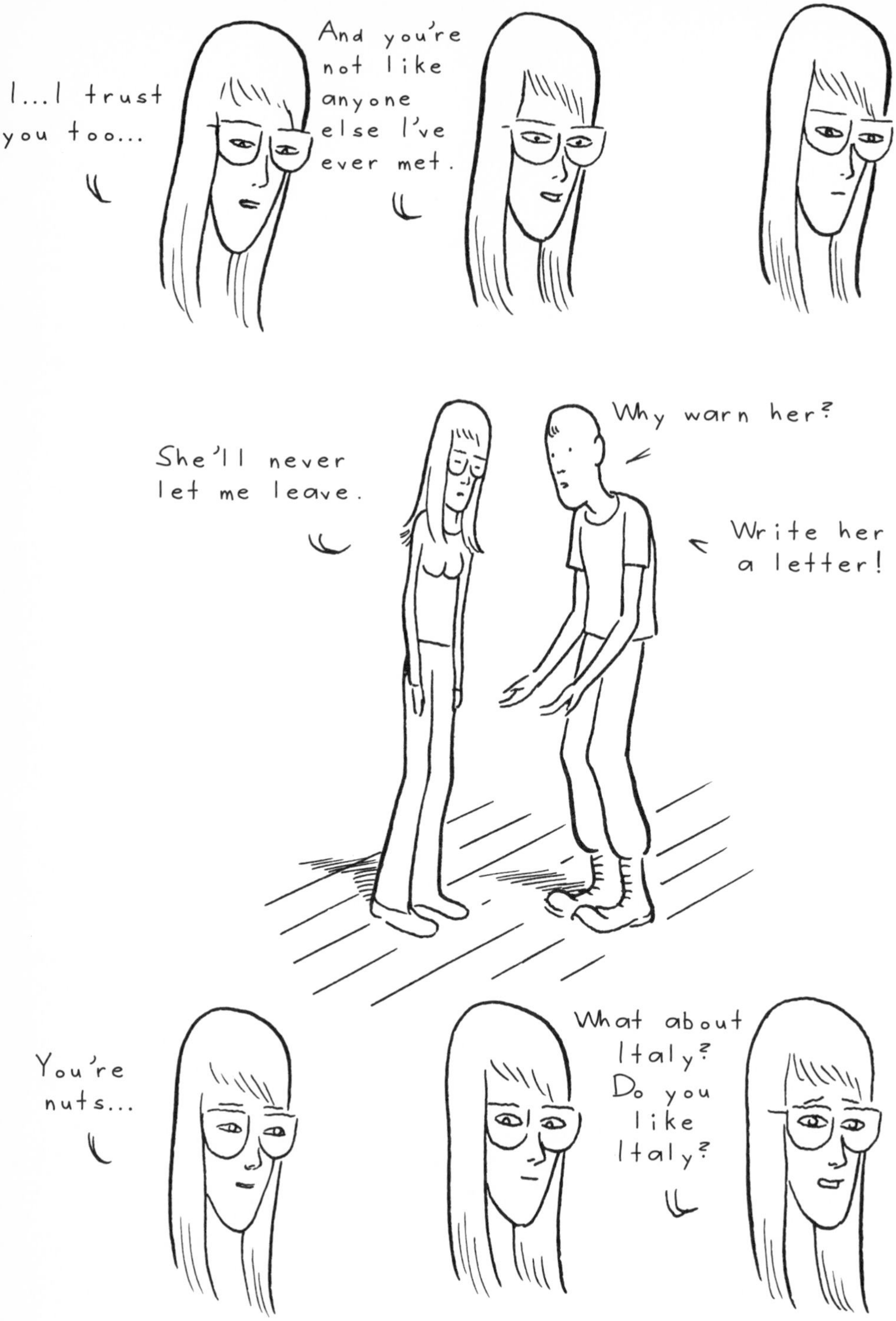
I...I trust you too...
And you're not like anyone else I've ever met.
She'll never let me leave.
Why warn her?
Write her a letter!
You're nuts...
What about Italy? Do you like Italy?

"That's how we left. I grabbed my things, and you had yours on your scooter already."

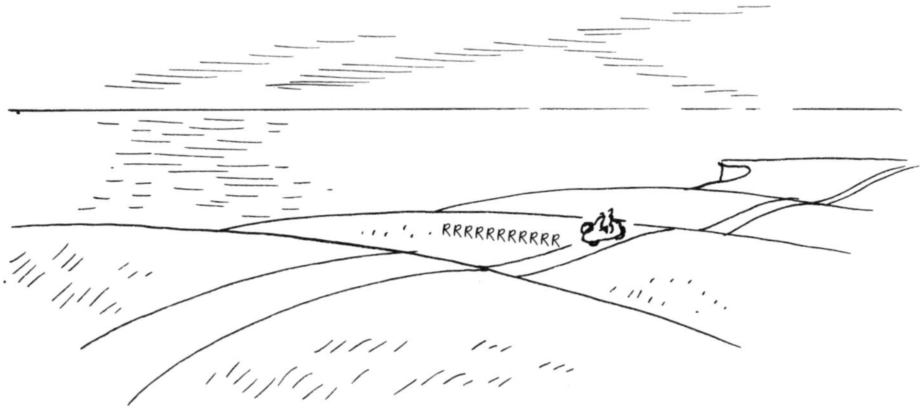
RRRRRRRRRRRR

"We stopped at a bank, I withdrew all I could from the account my father had opened for me before leaving for Tokyo."

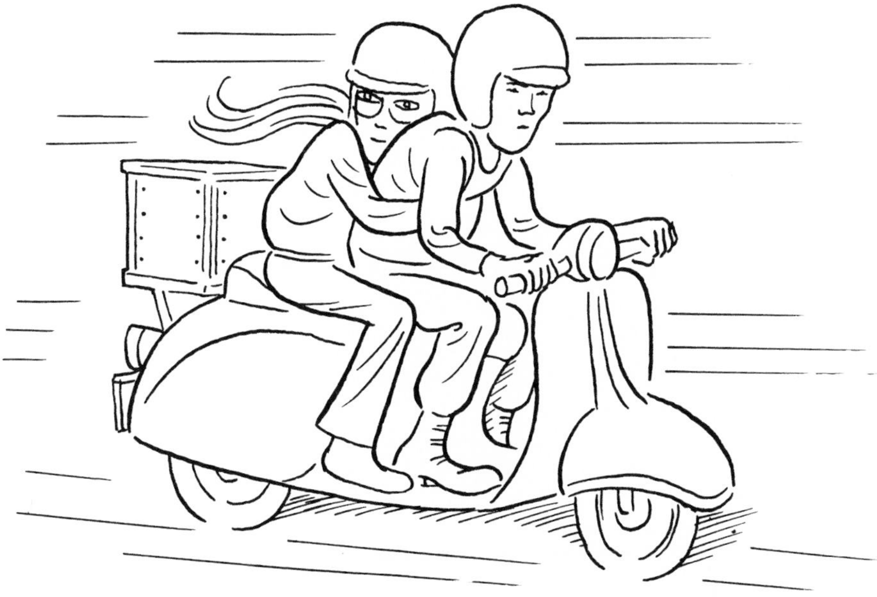

"We took the train. We saw the cliffs of Tréort dwindle away."

"We wondered what color the water would be in Italy. Here it was like the chalk it lapped at every day of the year, summer and winter..."

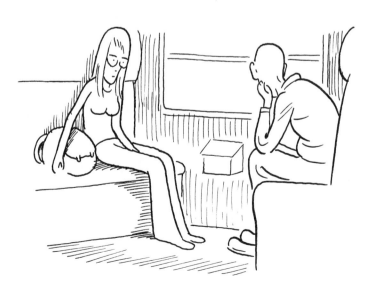

"I was scared..."

"But you were there."

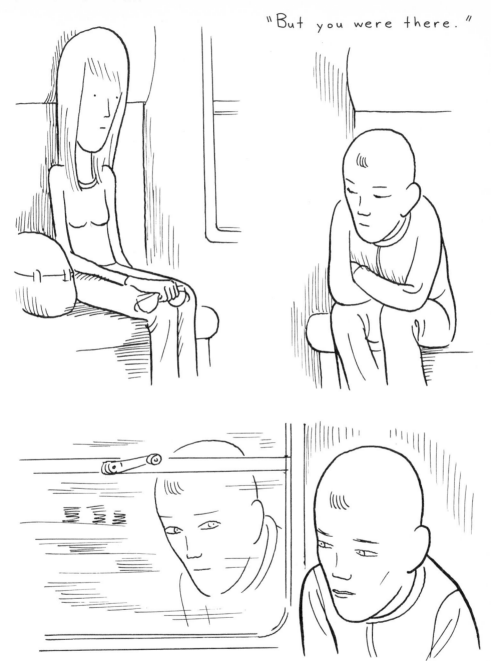

"You were scared, too..."
"But it was different now. You weren't alone anymore either."

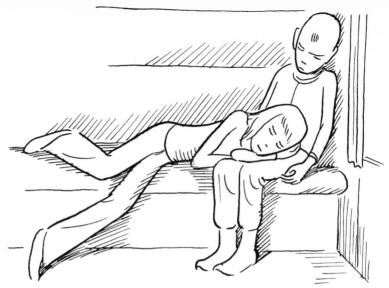

Gare du Nord. Final stop.
All passengers must leave the train.

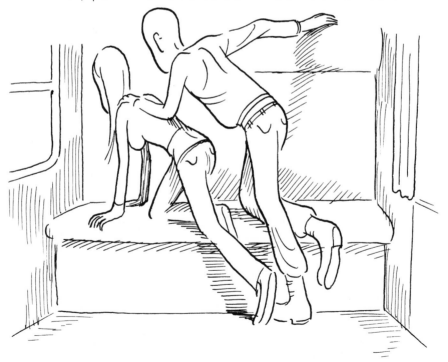

"And then Paris was upon us... before we
even knew it."

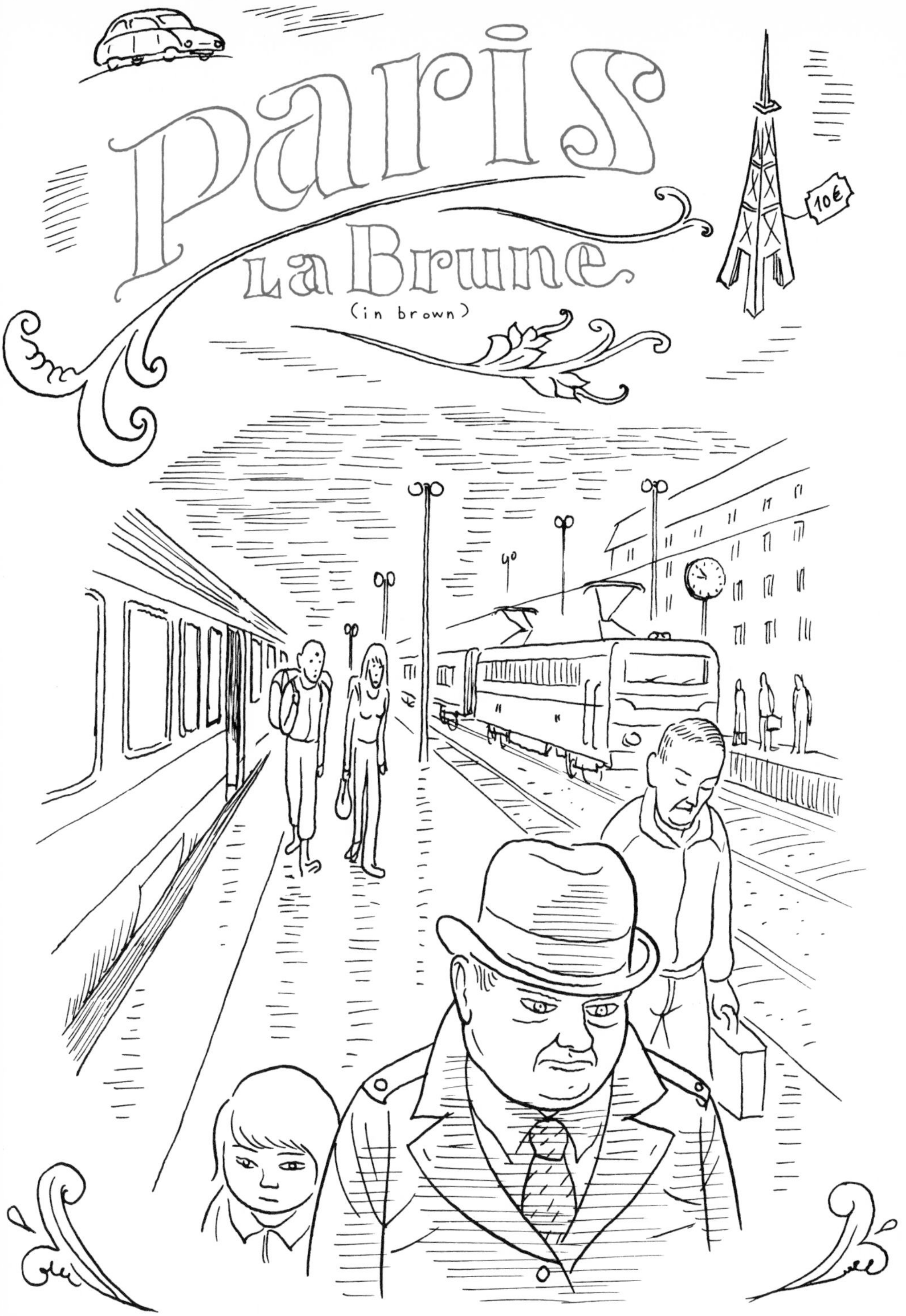
Paris
La Brune
(in brown)
10€

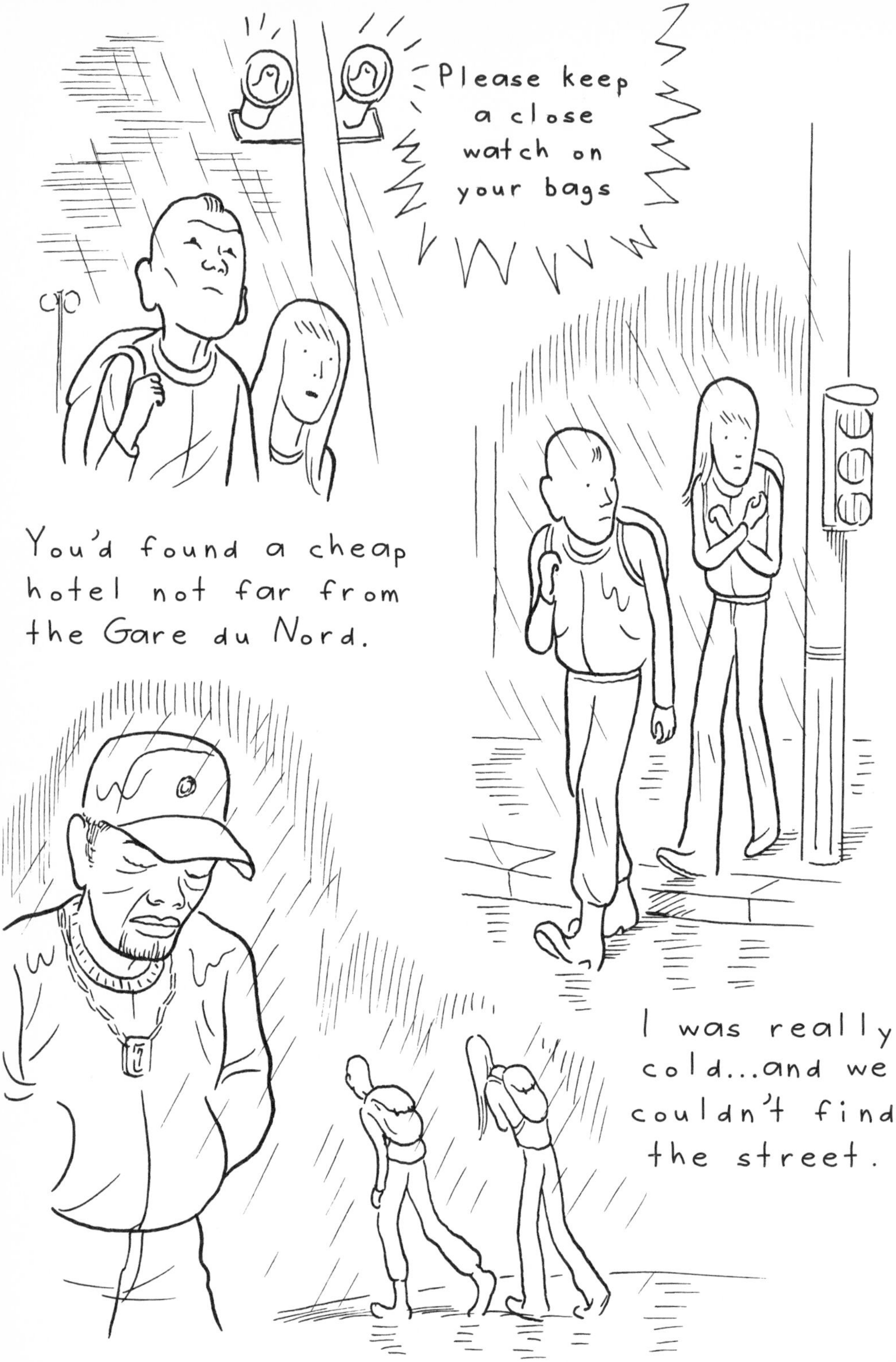
Please keep a close watch on your bags
You'd found a cheap hotel not far from the Gare du Nord.
I was really cold...and we couldn't find the street.

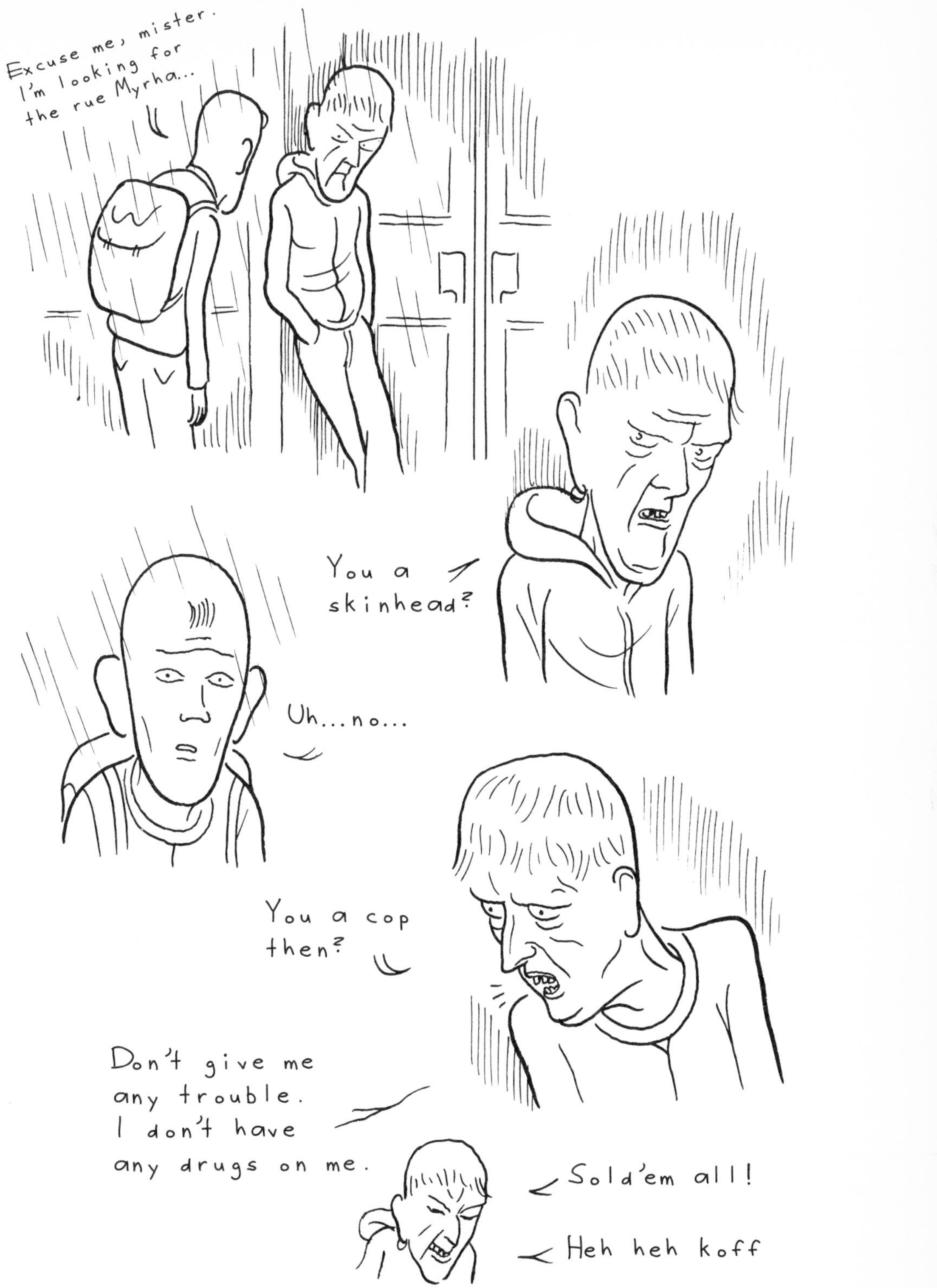
Excuse me, mister. I'm looking for the rue Myrha...
You a skinhead?
Uh... no...
You a cop then?
Don't give me any trouble. I don't have any drugs on me.
Sold'em all!
Heh heh koff

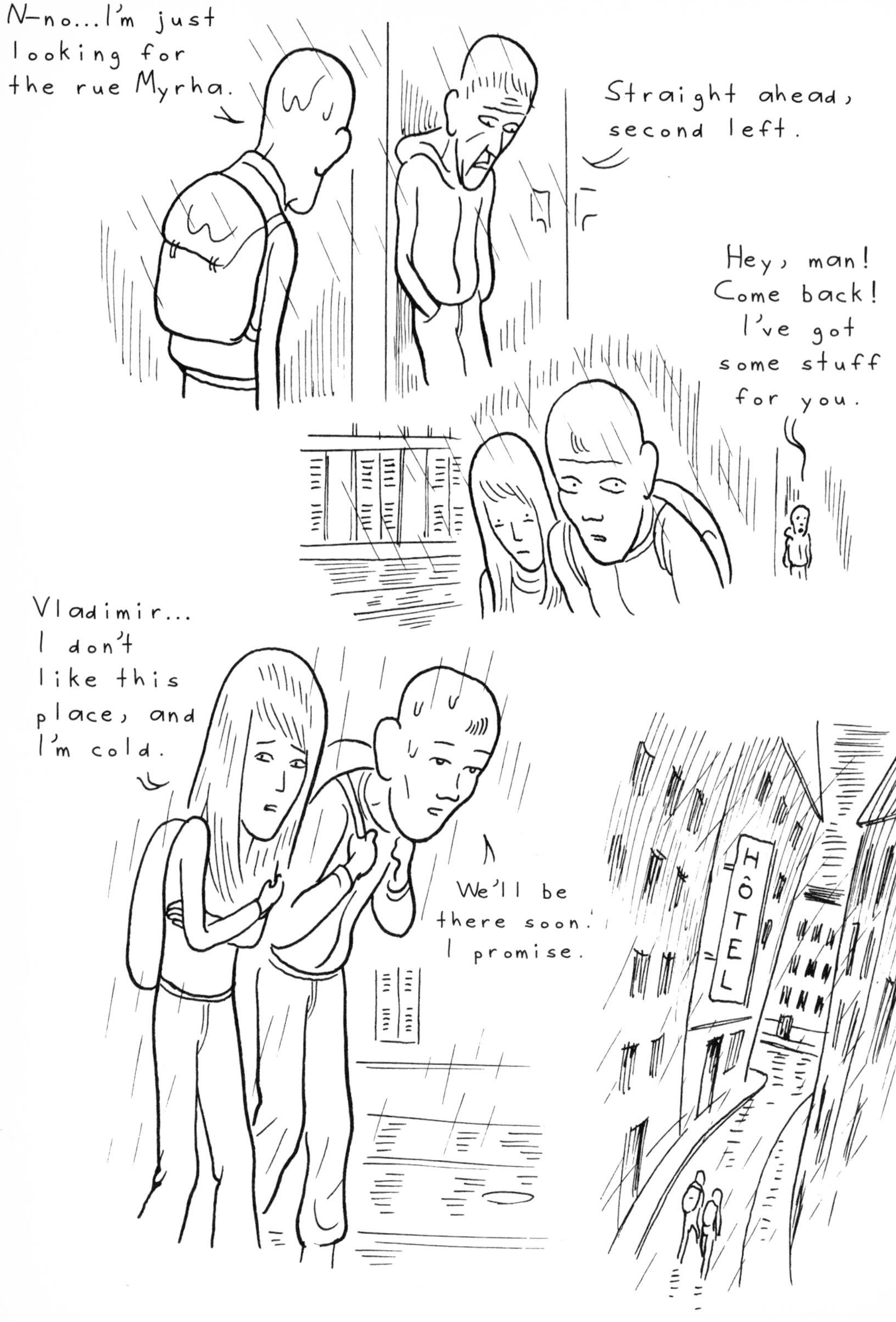
N—no...I'm just looking for the rue Myrha.
Straight ahead, second left.
Hey, man! Come back! I've got some stuff for you.
Vladimir... I don't like this place, and I'm cold.
We'll be there soon. I promise.
HÔTEL

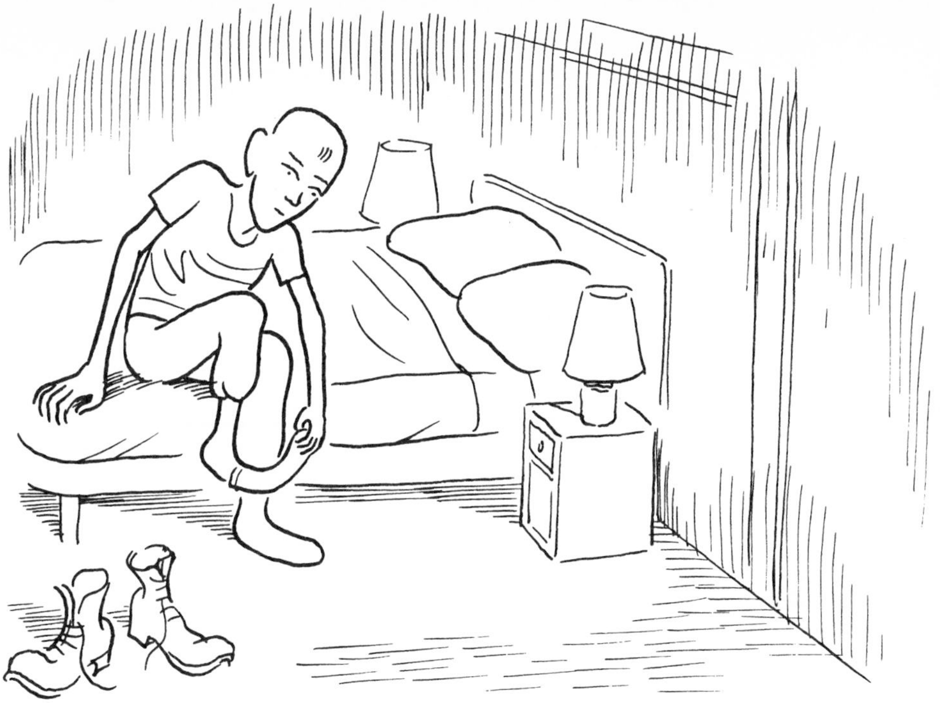
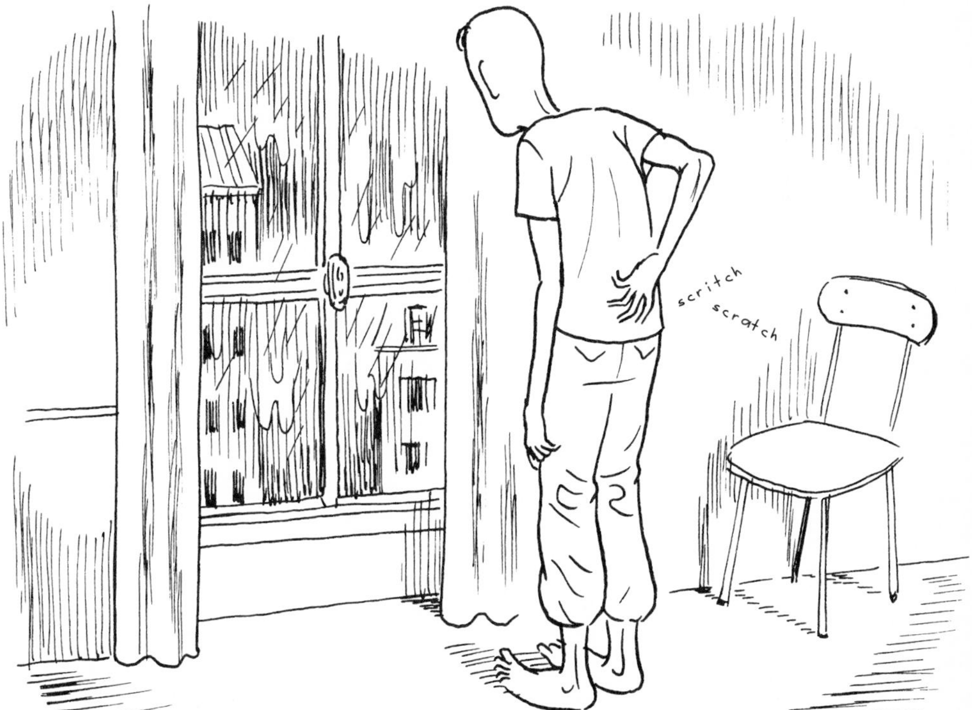
scritch
scratch

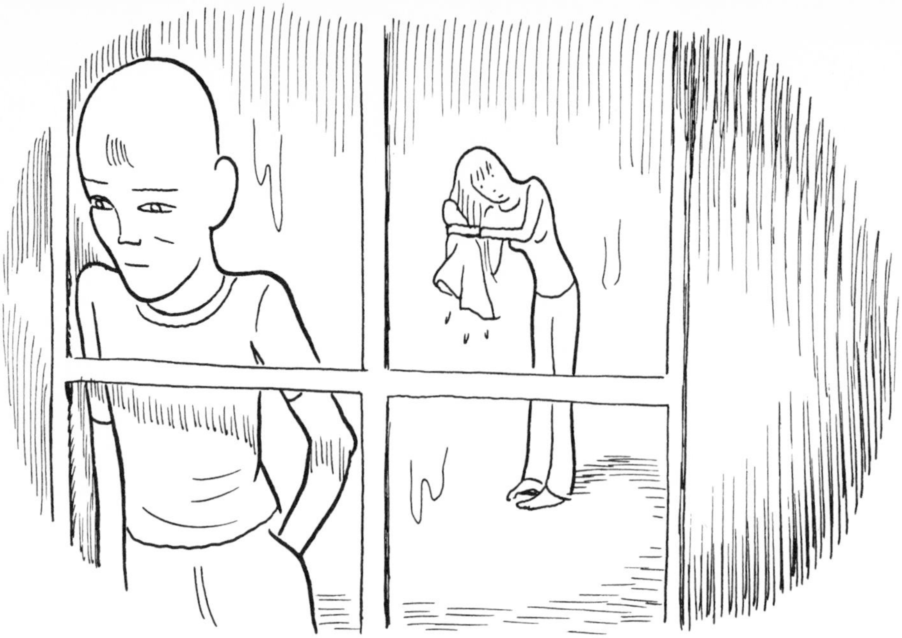

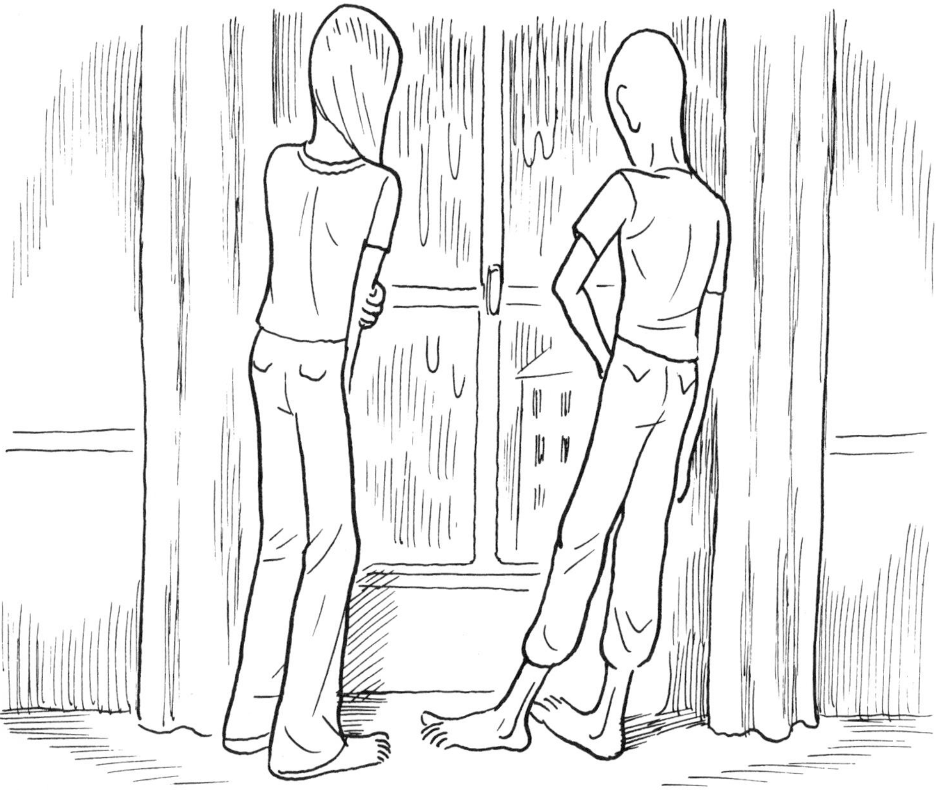

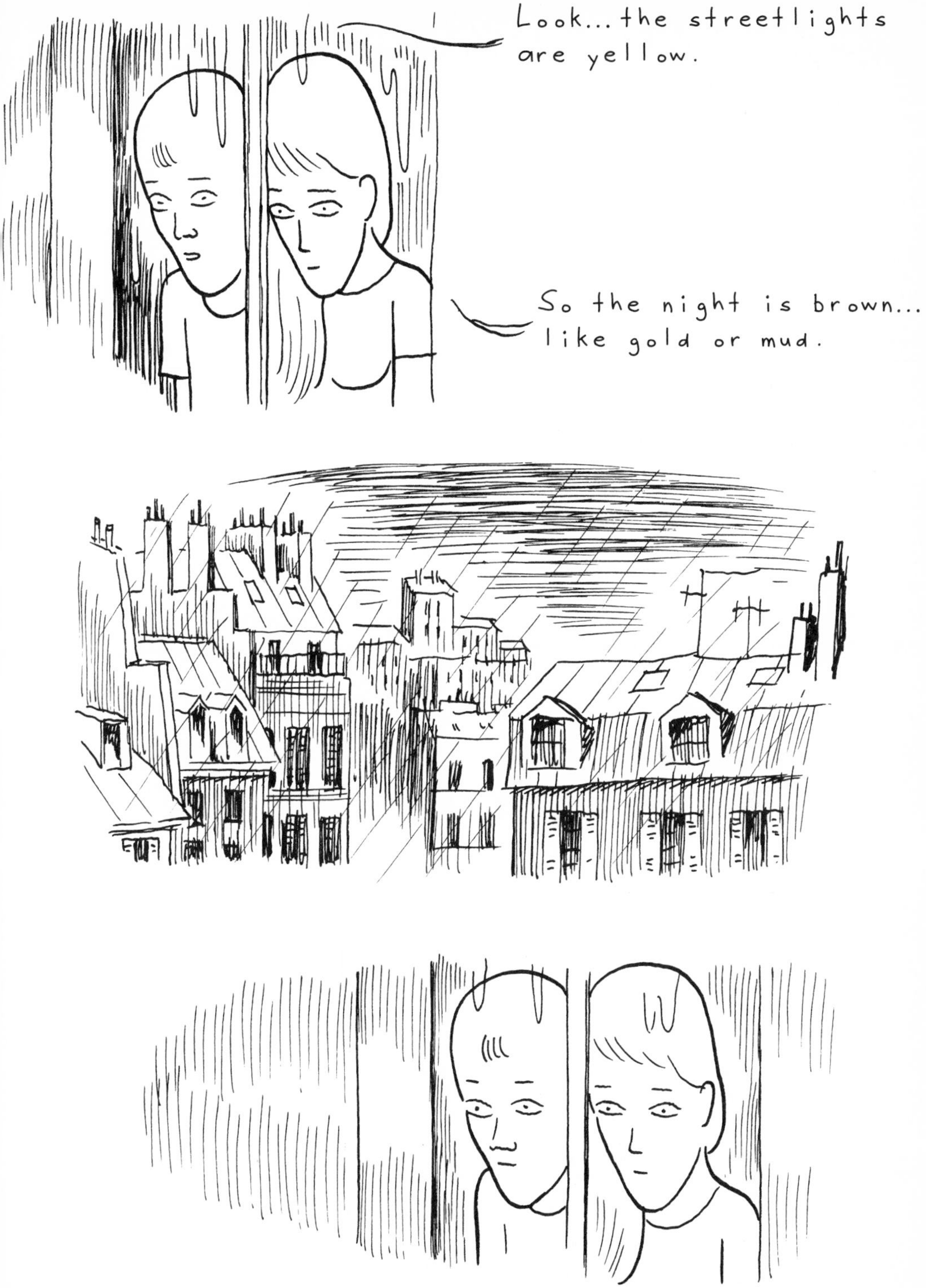
Look... the streetlights are yellow.
So the night is brown... like gold or mud.

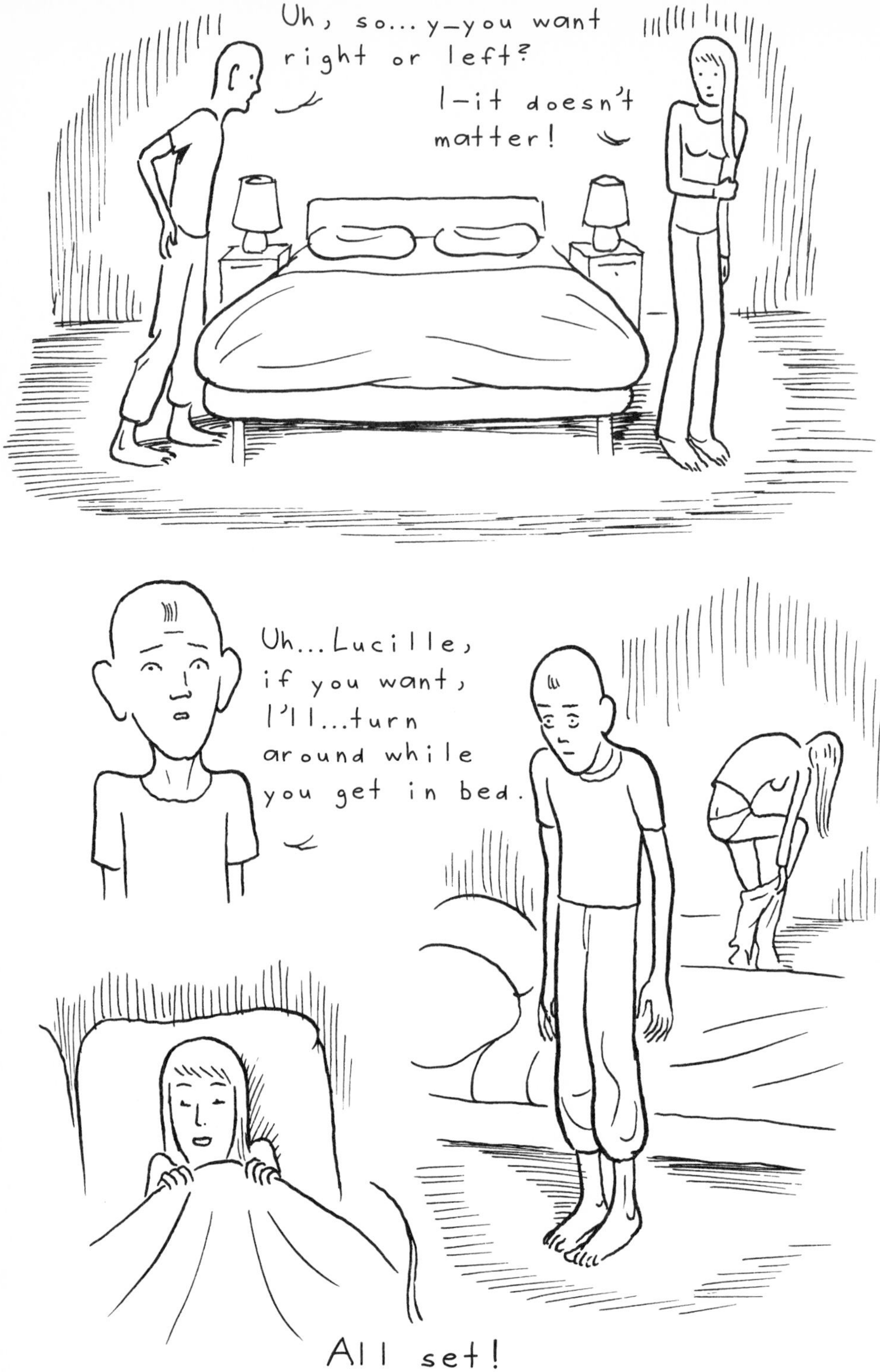
Uh, so... y—you want right or left?
I—it doesn't matter!
Uh... Lucille, if you want, I'll... turn around while you get in bed.
All set!

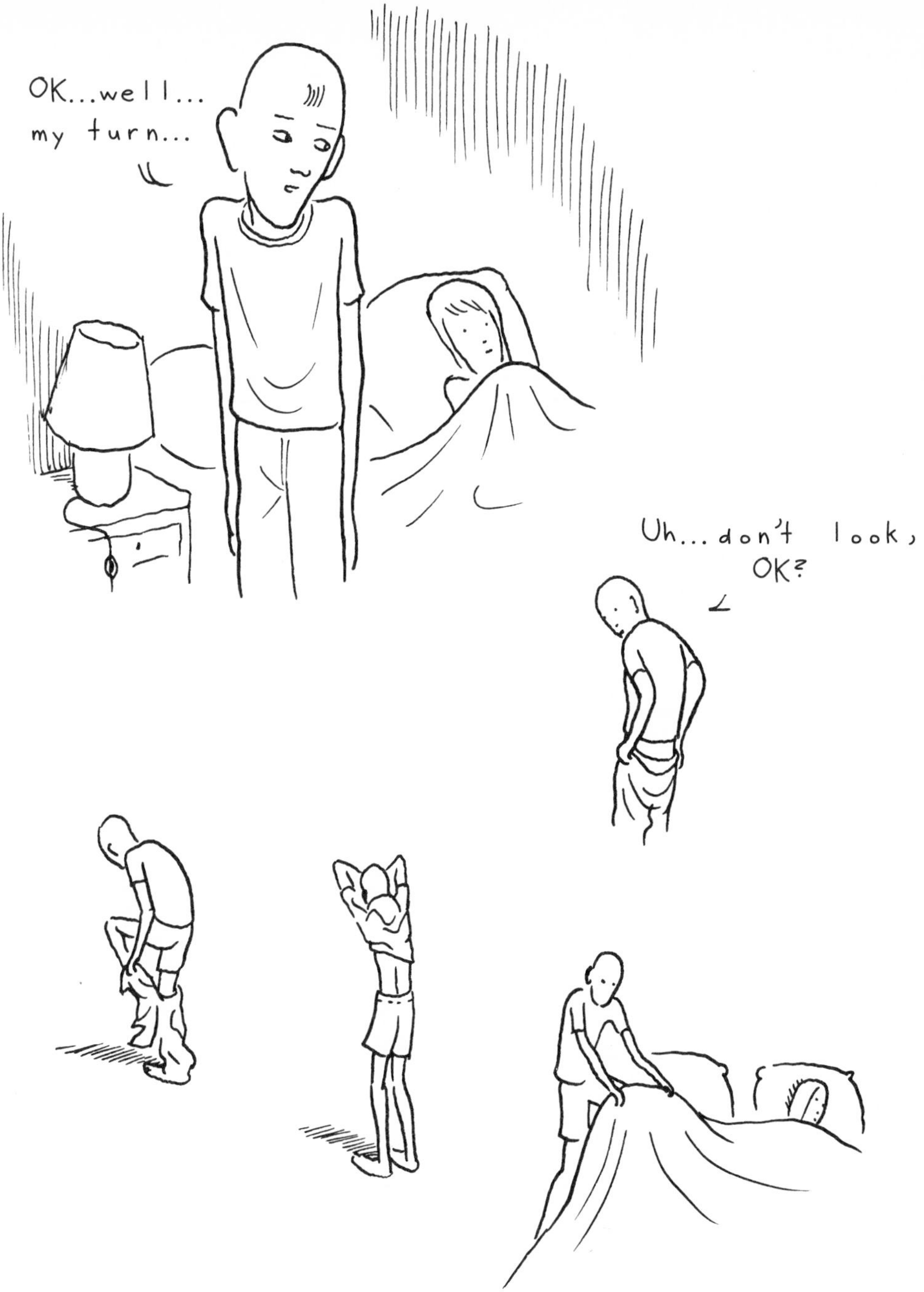
OK...well... my turn...
Uh...don't look, OK?

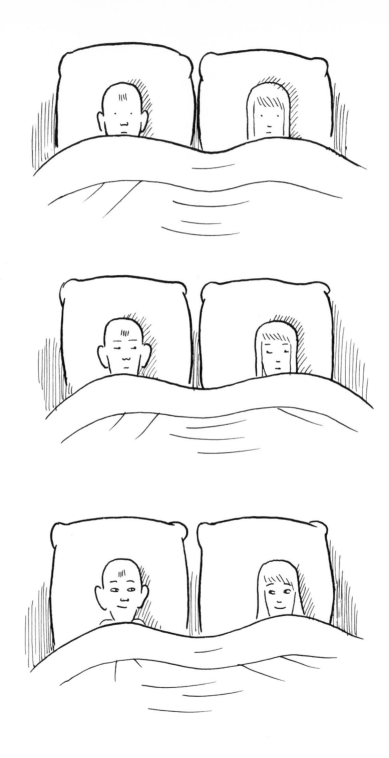

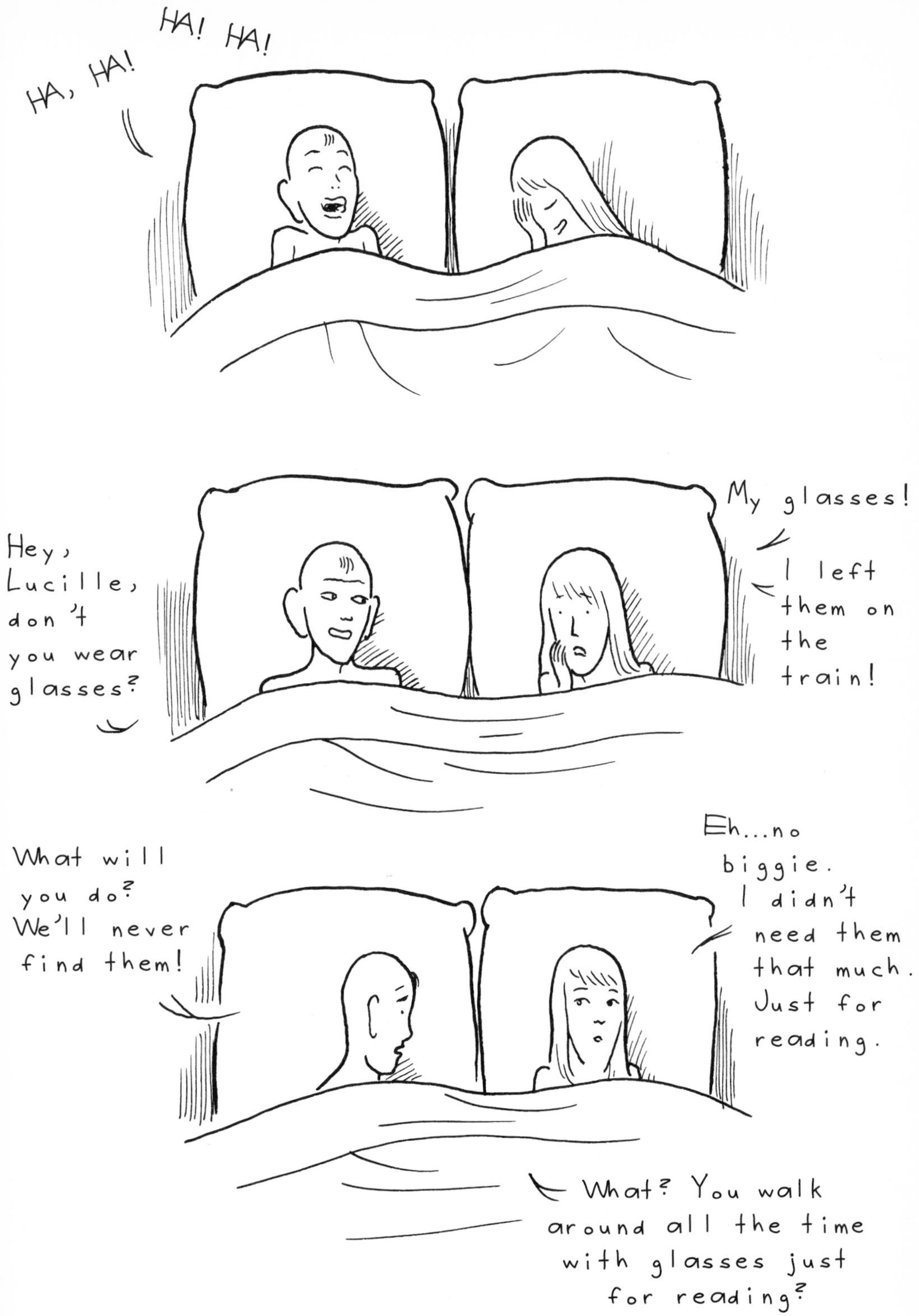
HA, HA!
HA! HA!
Hey, Lucille, don't you wear glasses?
My glasses!
I left them on the train!
What will you do? We'll never find them!
Eh...no biggie. I didn't need them that much. Just for reading.
What? You walk around all the time with glasses just for reading?

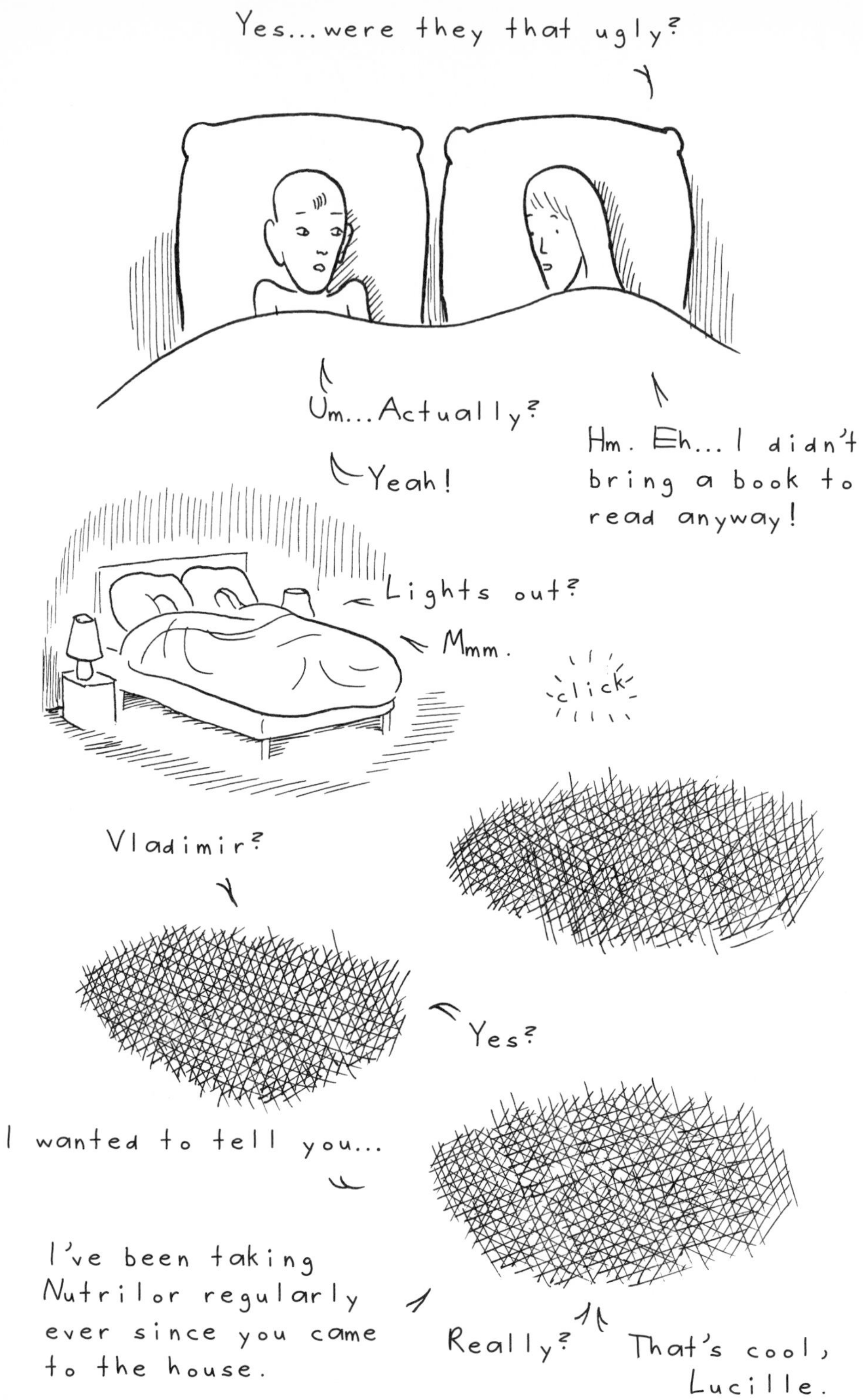
Yes... were they that ugly?
Um... Actually?
Hm. Eh... I didn't bring a book to read anyway!
Yeah!
Lights out?
Mmm.
click
Vladimir?
Yes?
I wanted to tell you...
I've been taking Nutrilor regularly ever since you came to the house.
Really?
That's cool, Lucille.

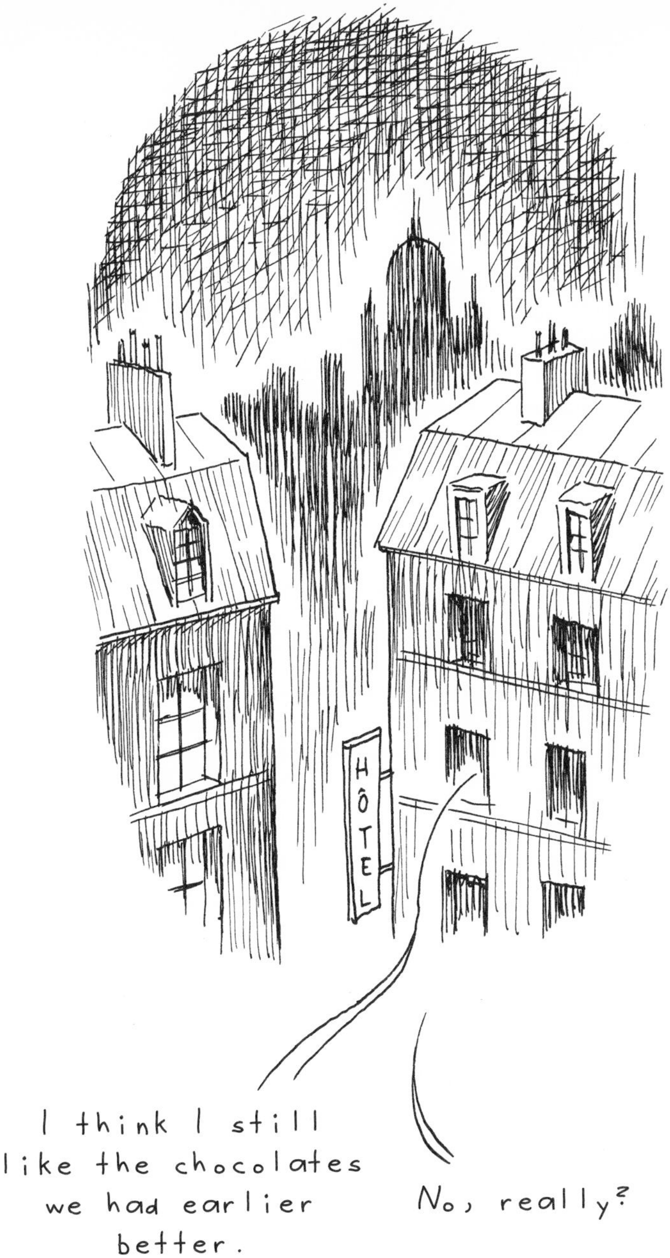
HÔTEL
I think I still like the chocolates we had earlier better.
No, really?

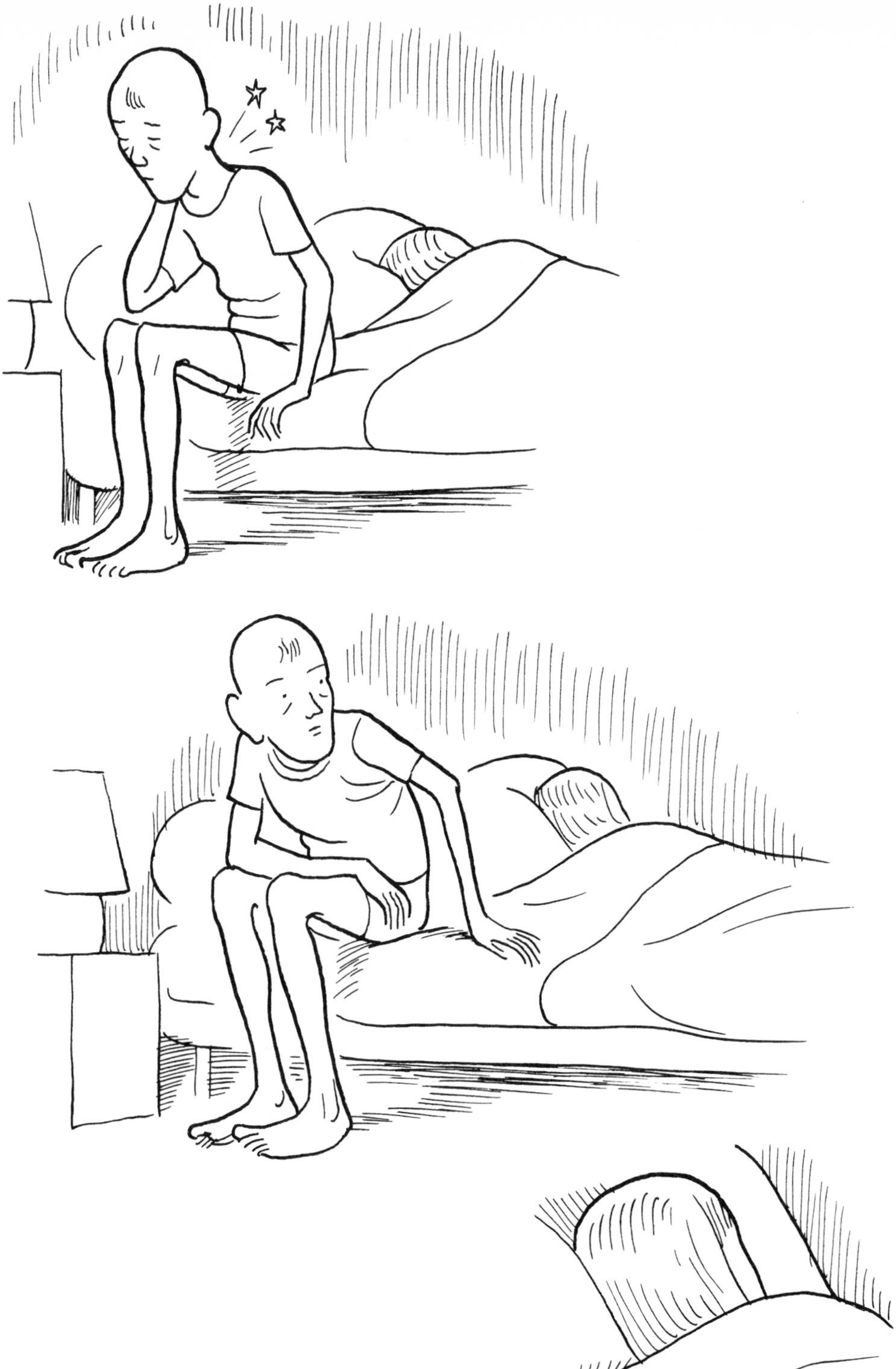

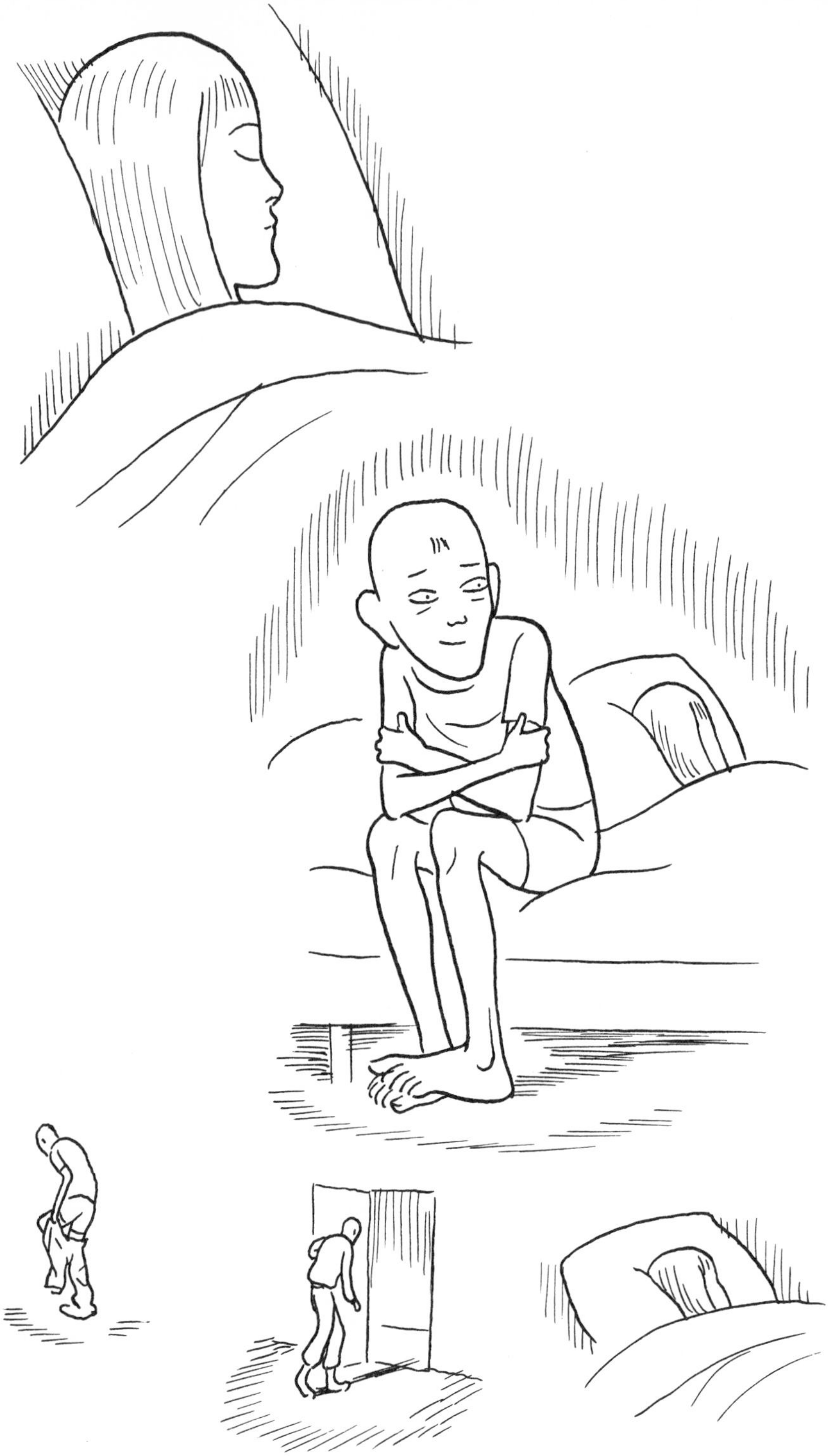

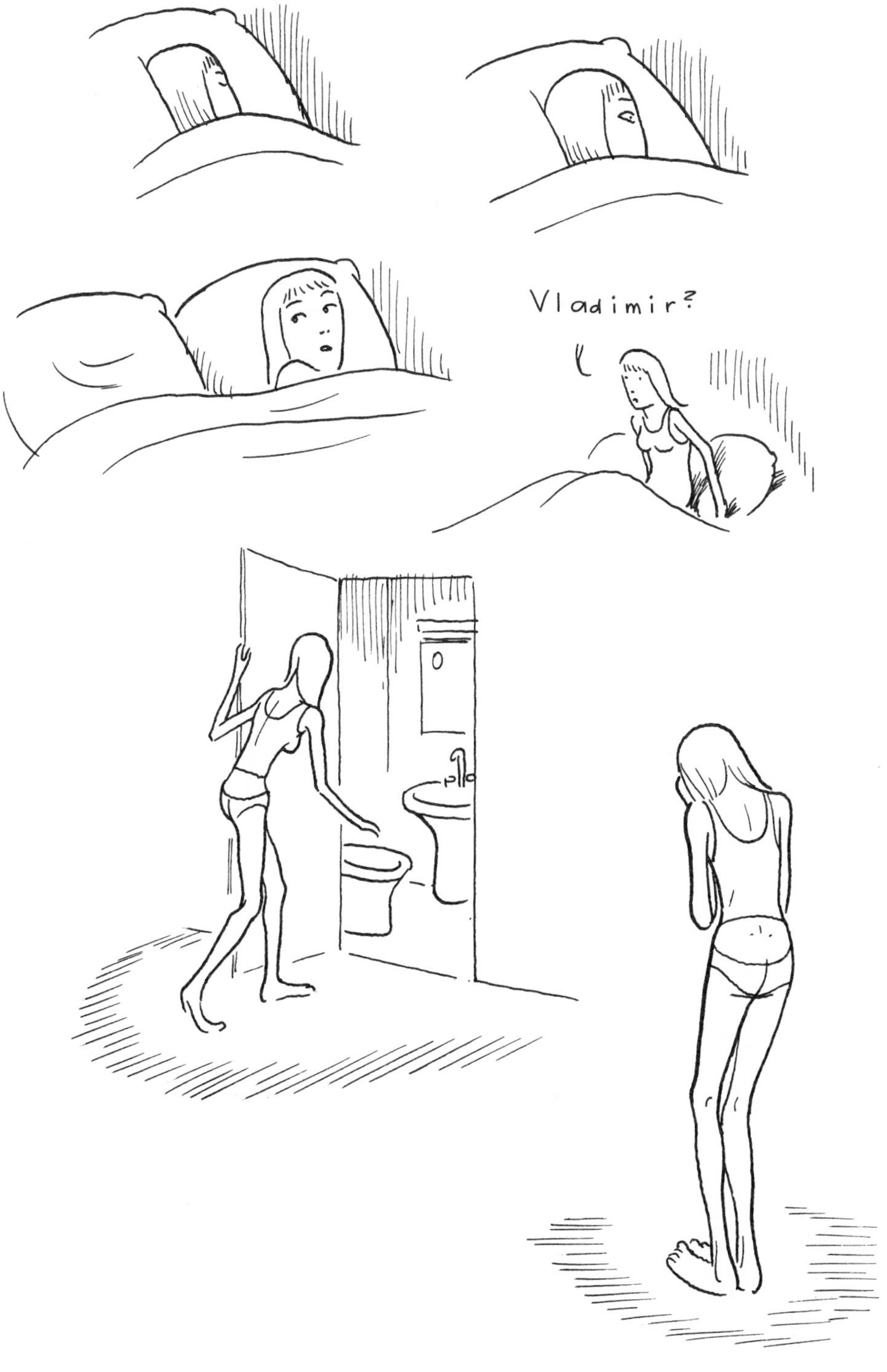
Vladimir?

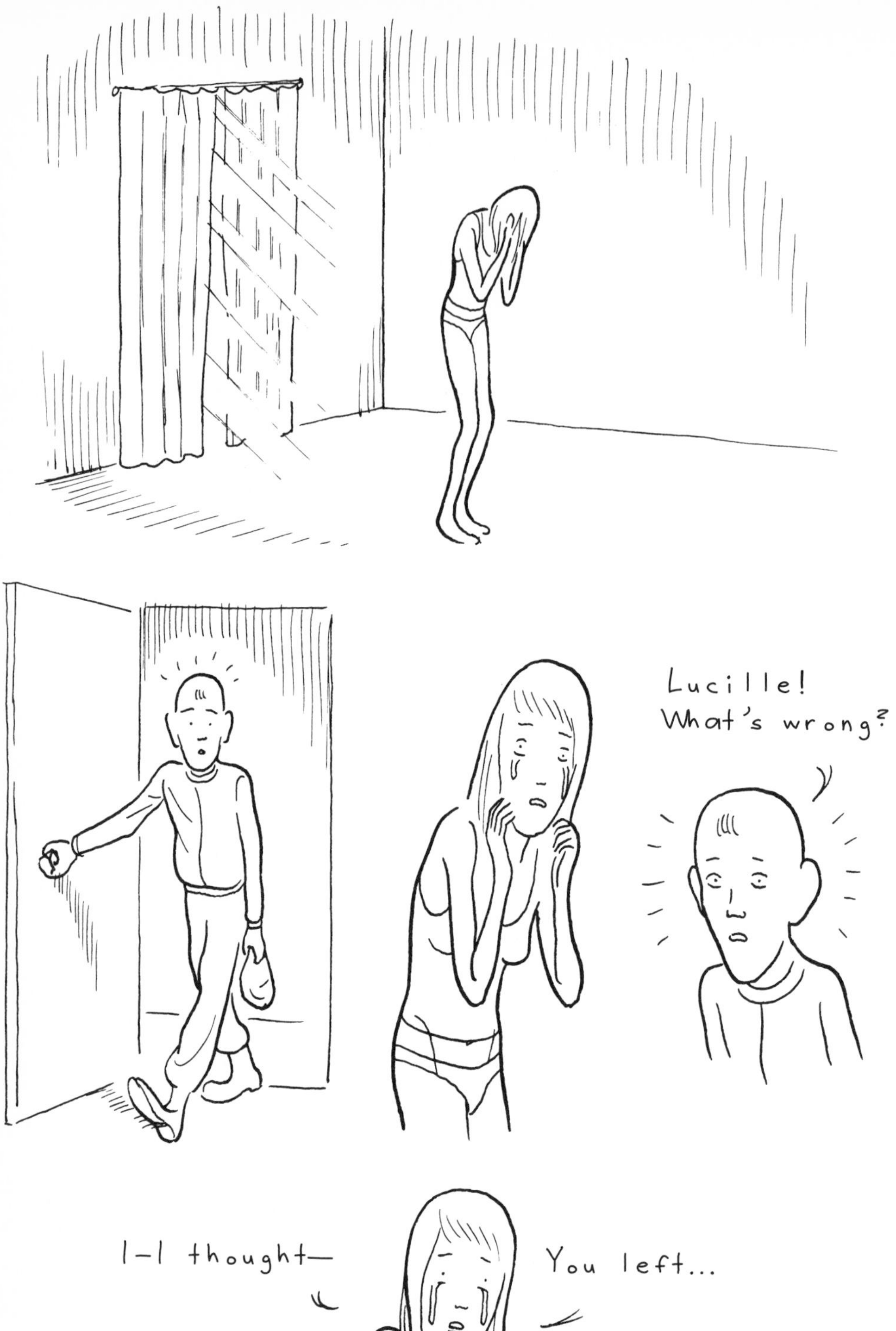
Lucille!
What's wrong?
I-I thought—
You left...

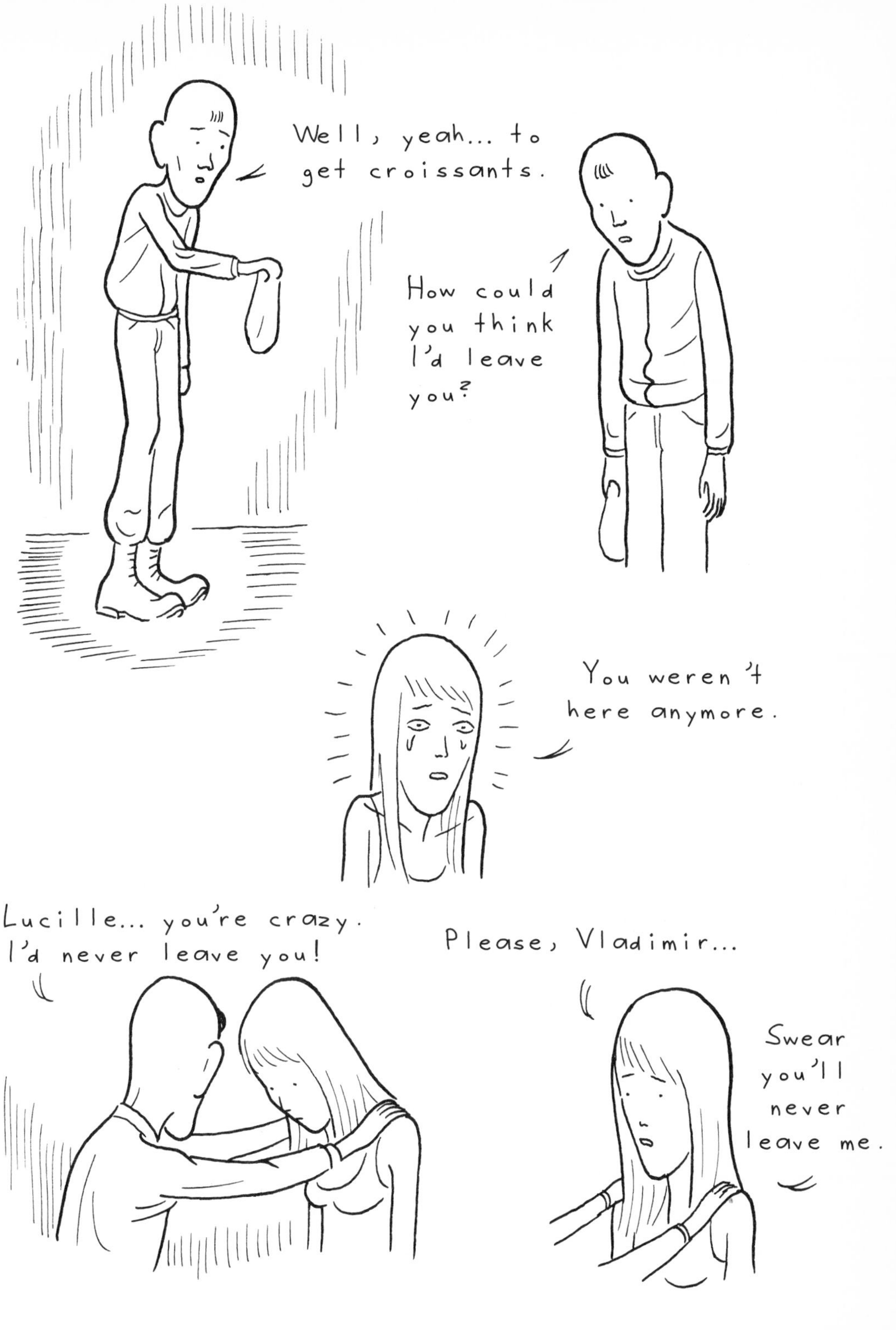
Well, yeah... to get croissants.
How could you think I'd leave you?
You weren't here anymore.
Lucille... you're crazy. I'd never leave you!
Please, Vladimir...
Swear you'll never leave me.

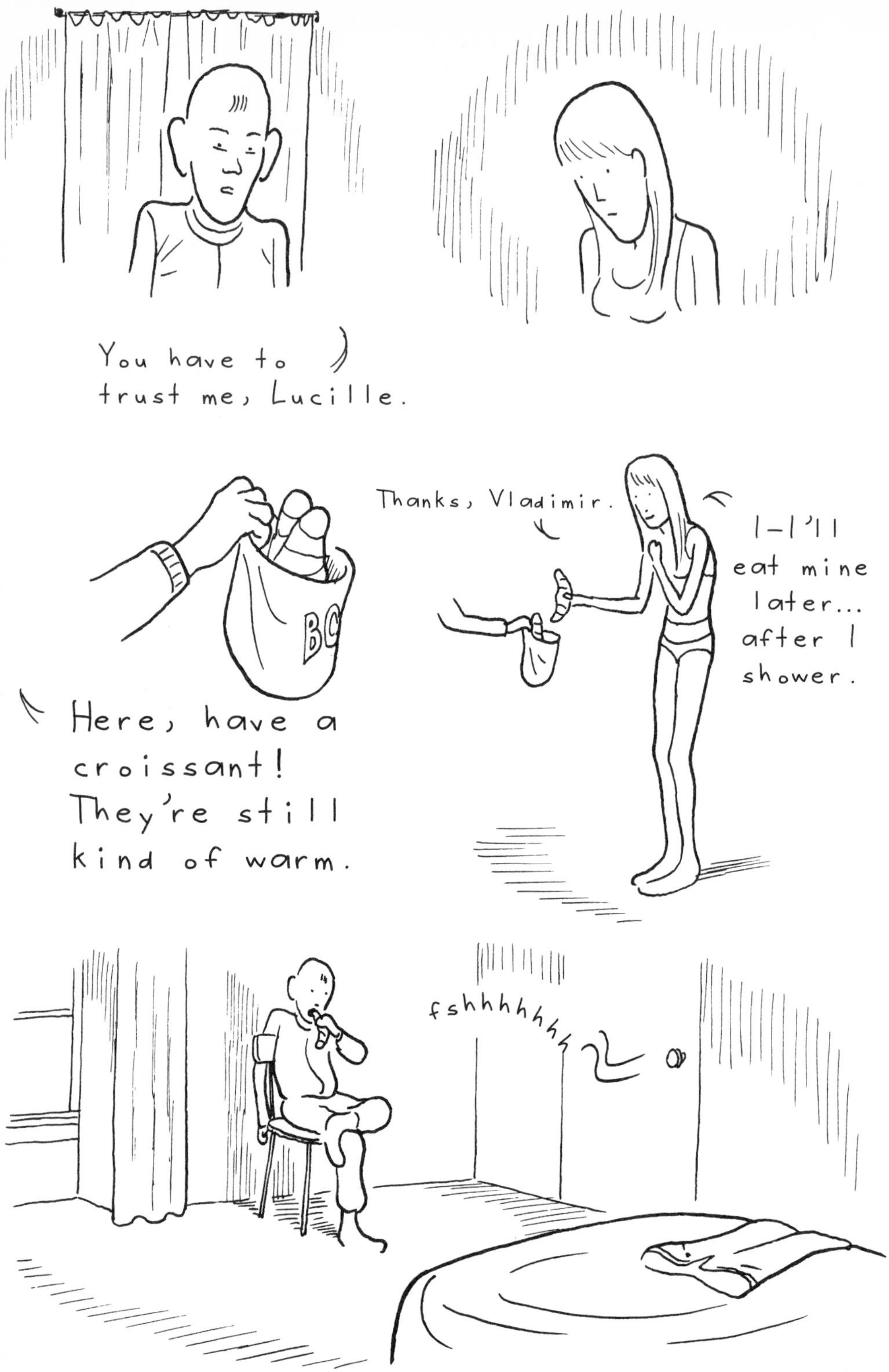
You have to trust me, Lucille.
Here, have a croissant! They're still kind of warm.
Thanks, Vladimir.
I-I'll eat mine later... after I shower.
fshhhhhhh

Our train for Italy was leaving that night.

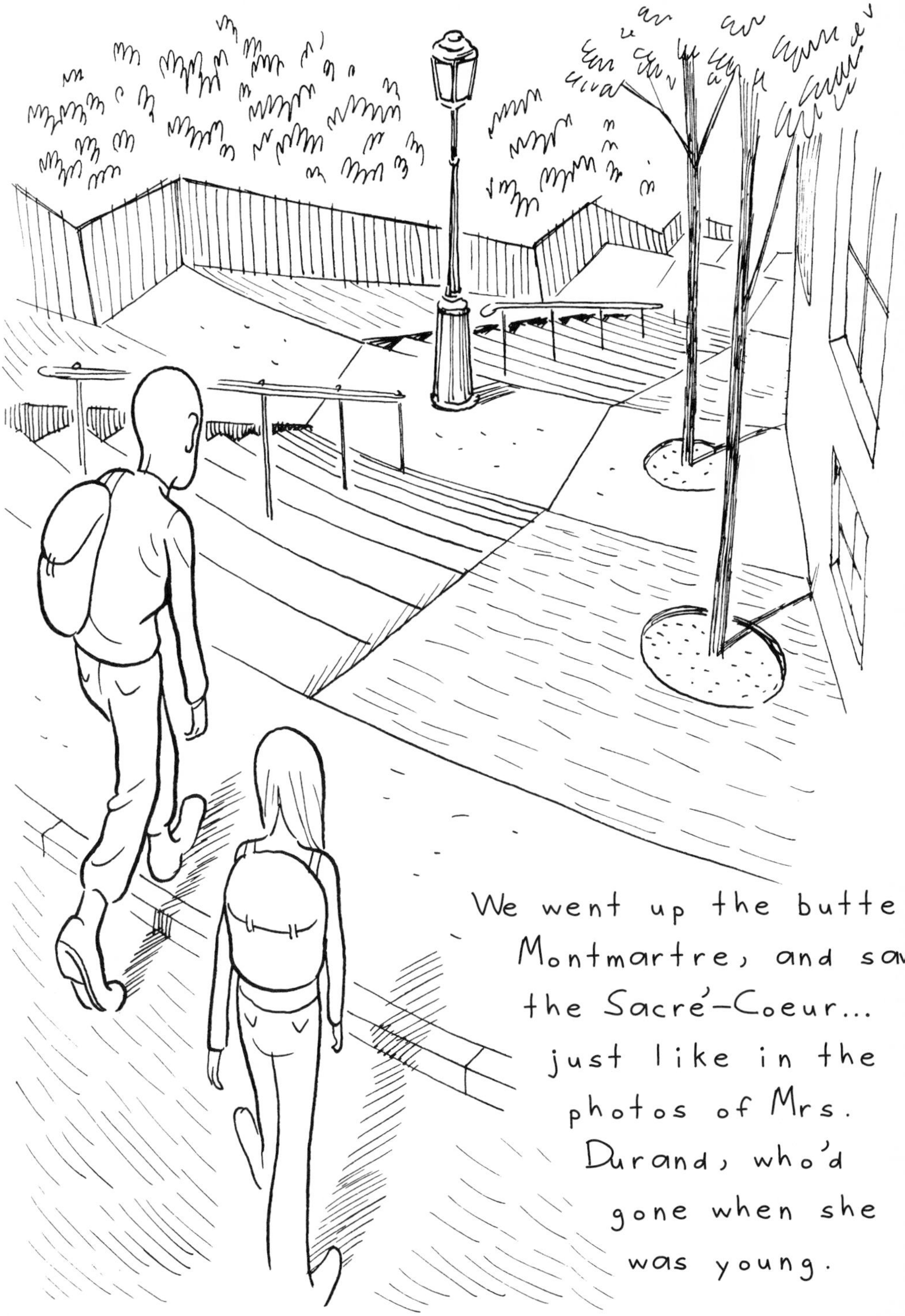
We went up the butte Montmartre, and saw the Sacré-Coeur... just like in the photos of Mrs. Durand, who'd gone when she was young.

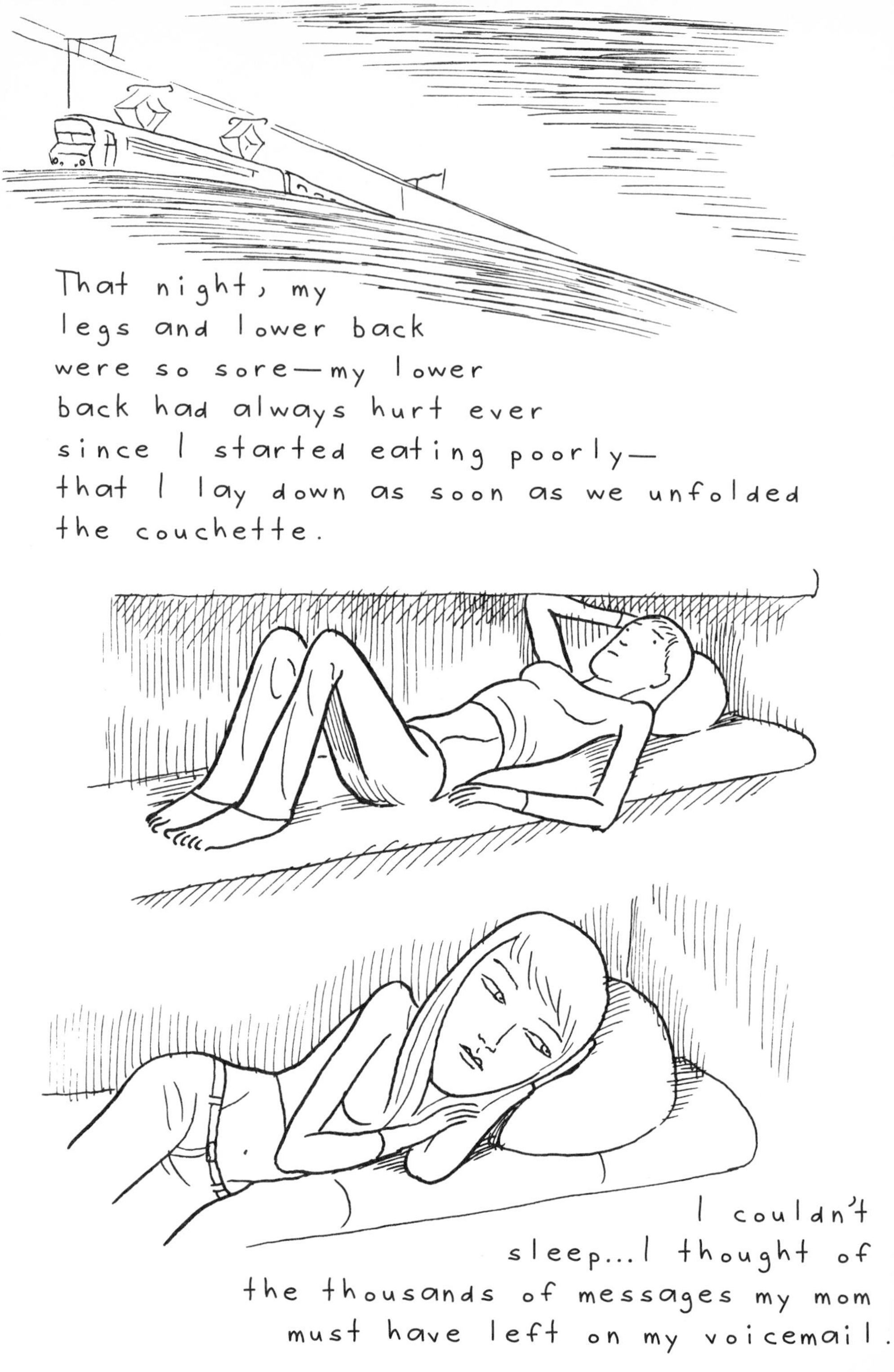
That night, my legs and lower back were so sore—my lower back had always hurt ever since I started eating poorly—that I lay down as soon as we unfolded the couchette.
I couldn't sleep... I thought of the thousands of messages my mom must have left on my voicemail.

"Vladimir?

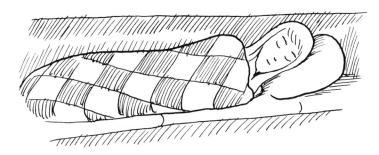

Do you remember...

...the first time we met?"

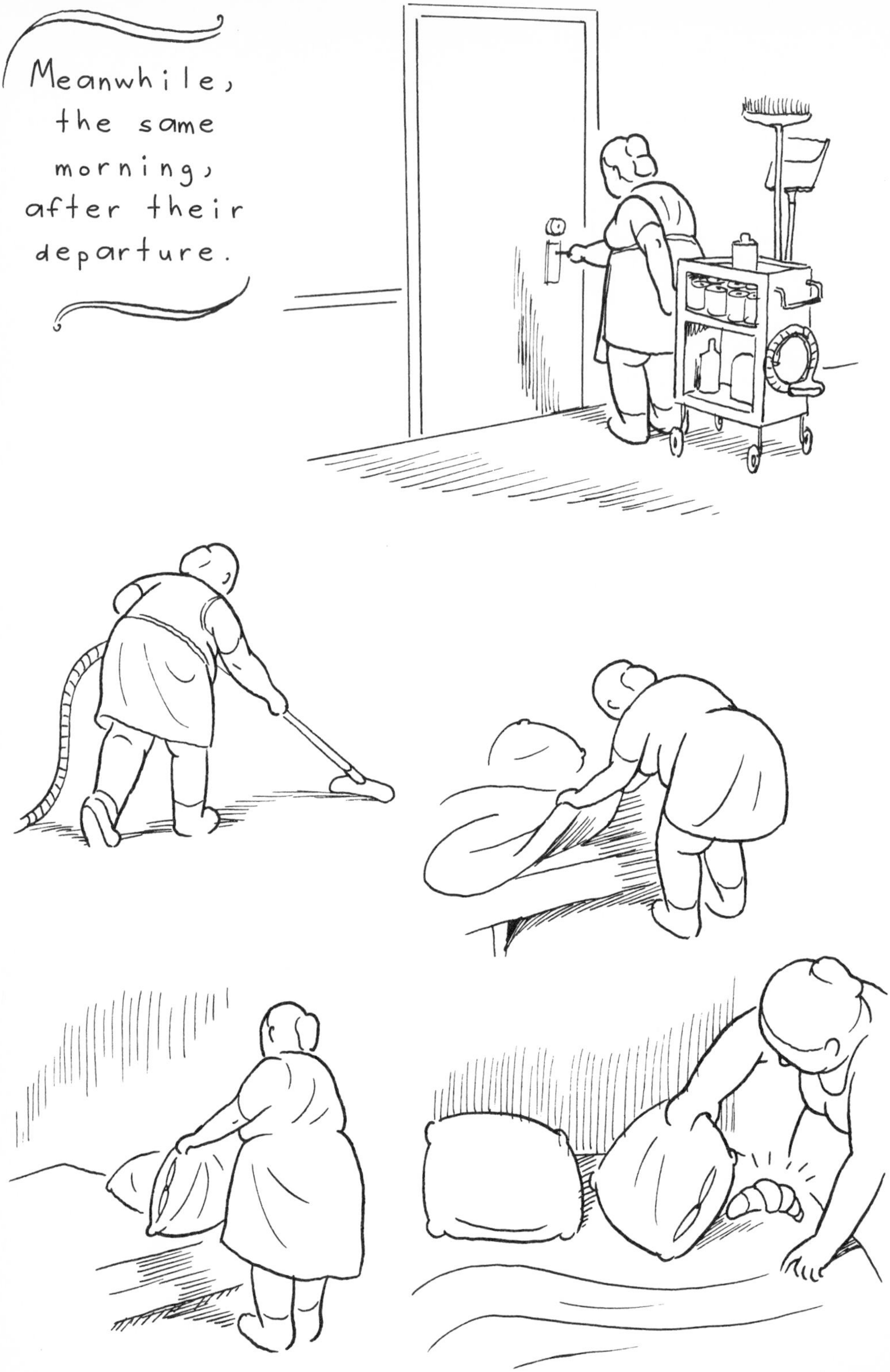
Meanwhile, the same morning, after their departure.

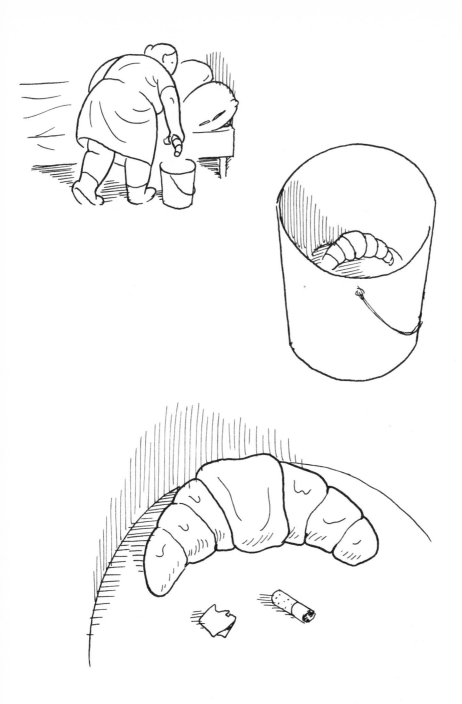

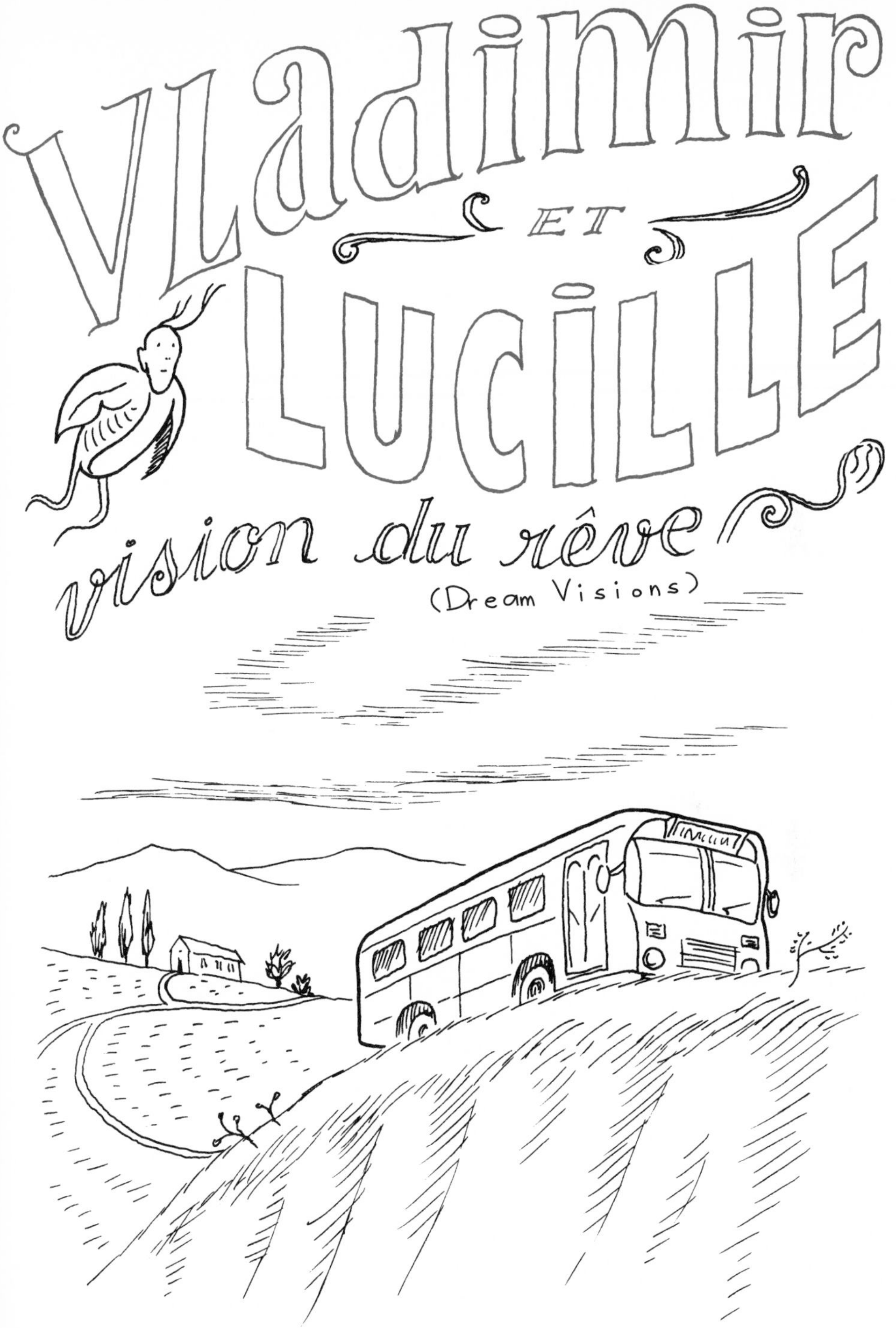
Vladimir
et
Lucille
vision du rêve
(Dream Visions)

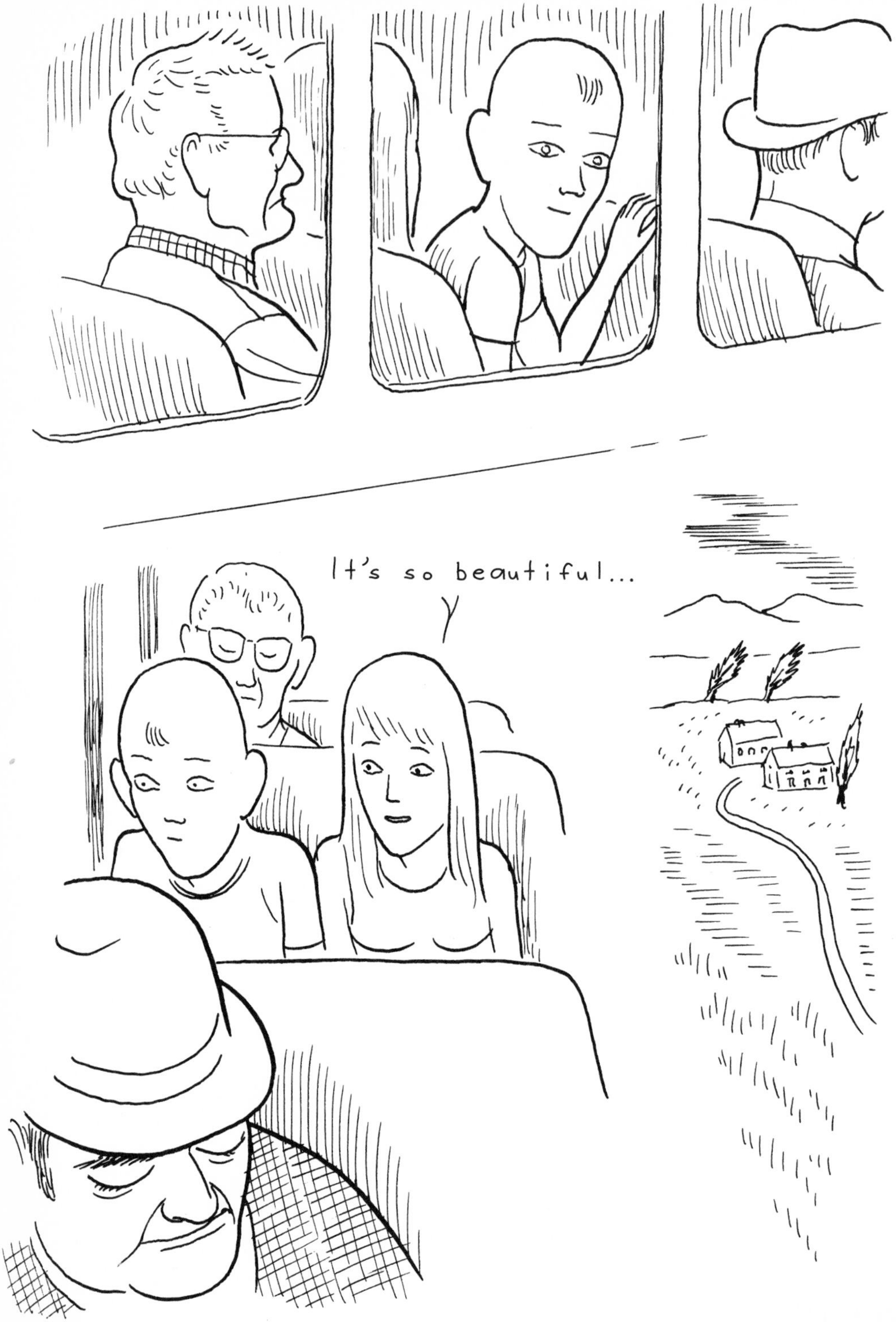
It's so beautiful...

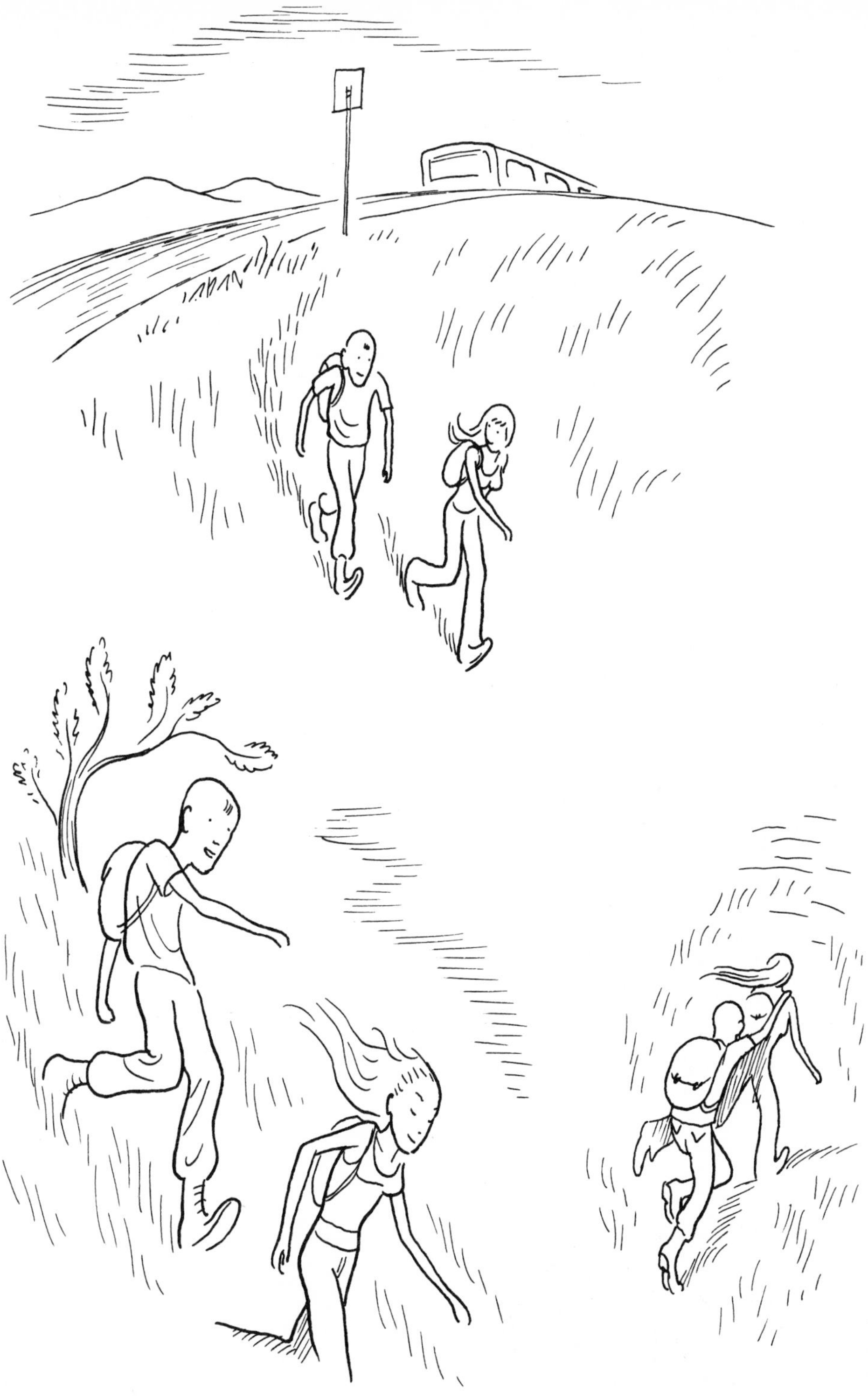

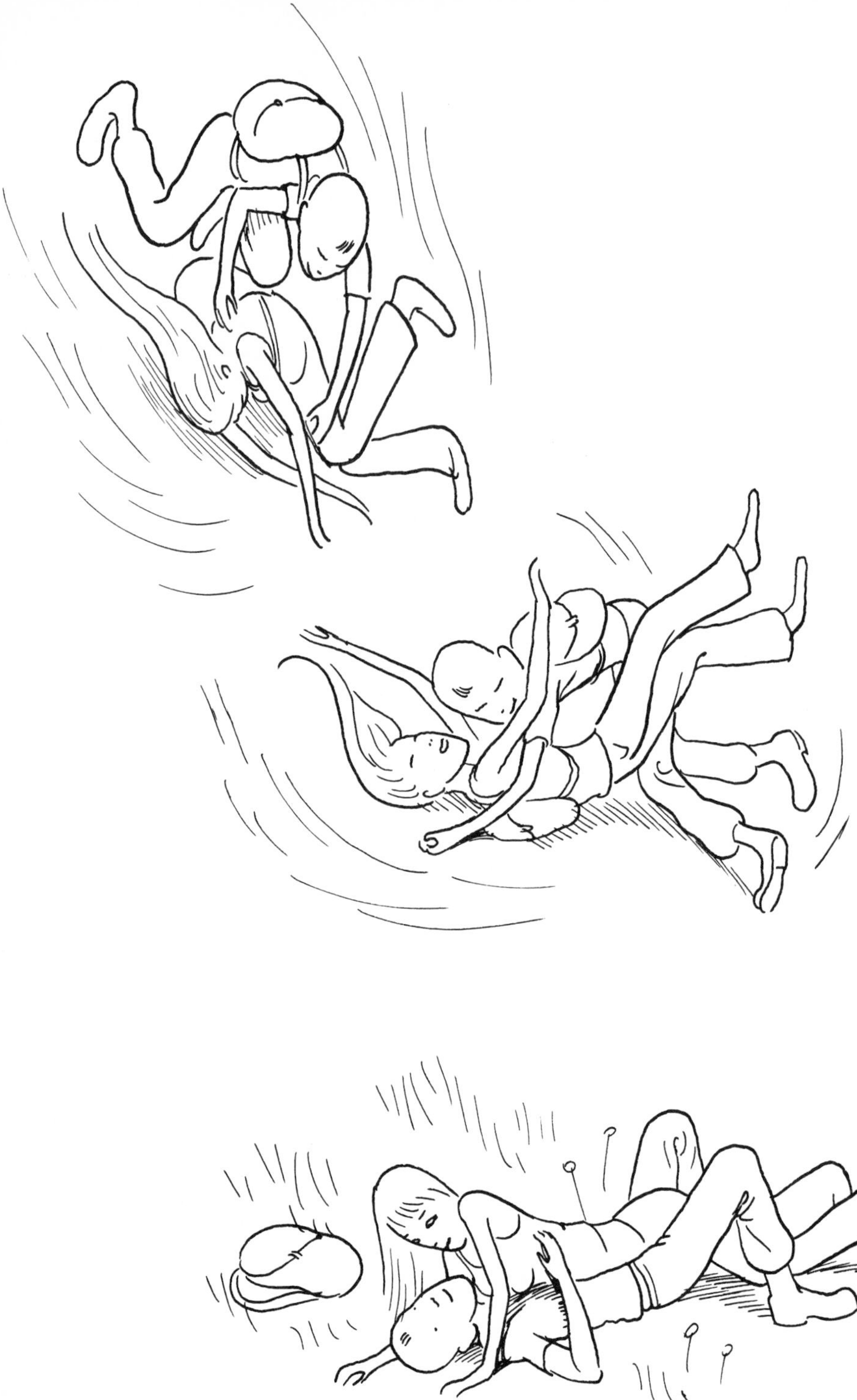

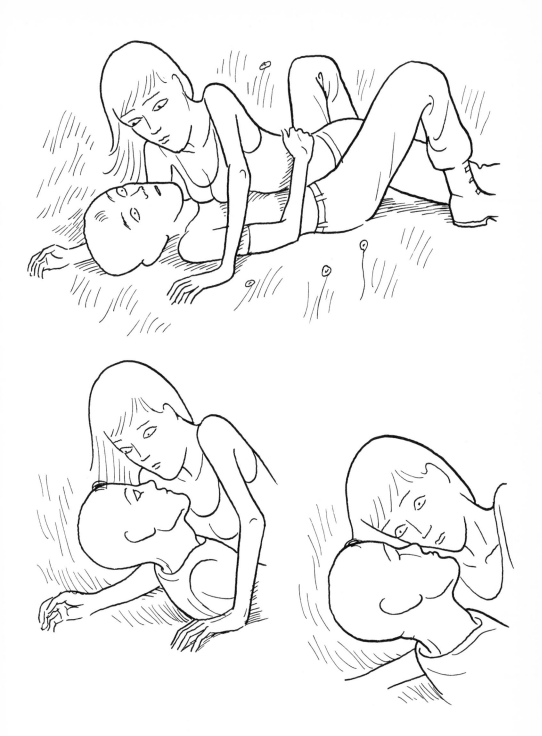

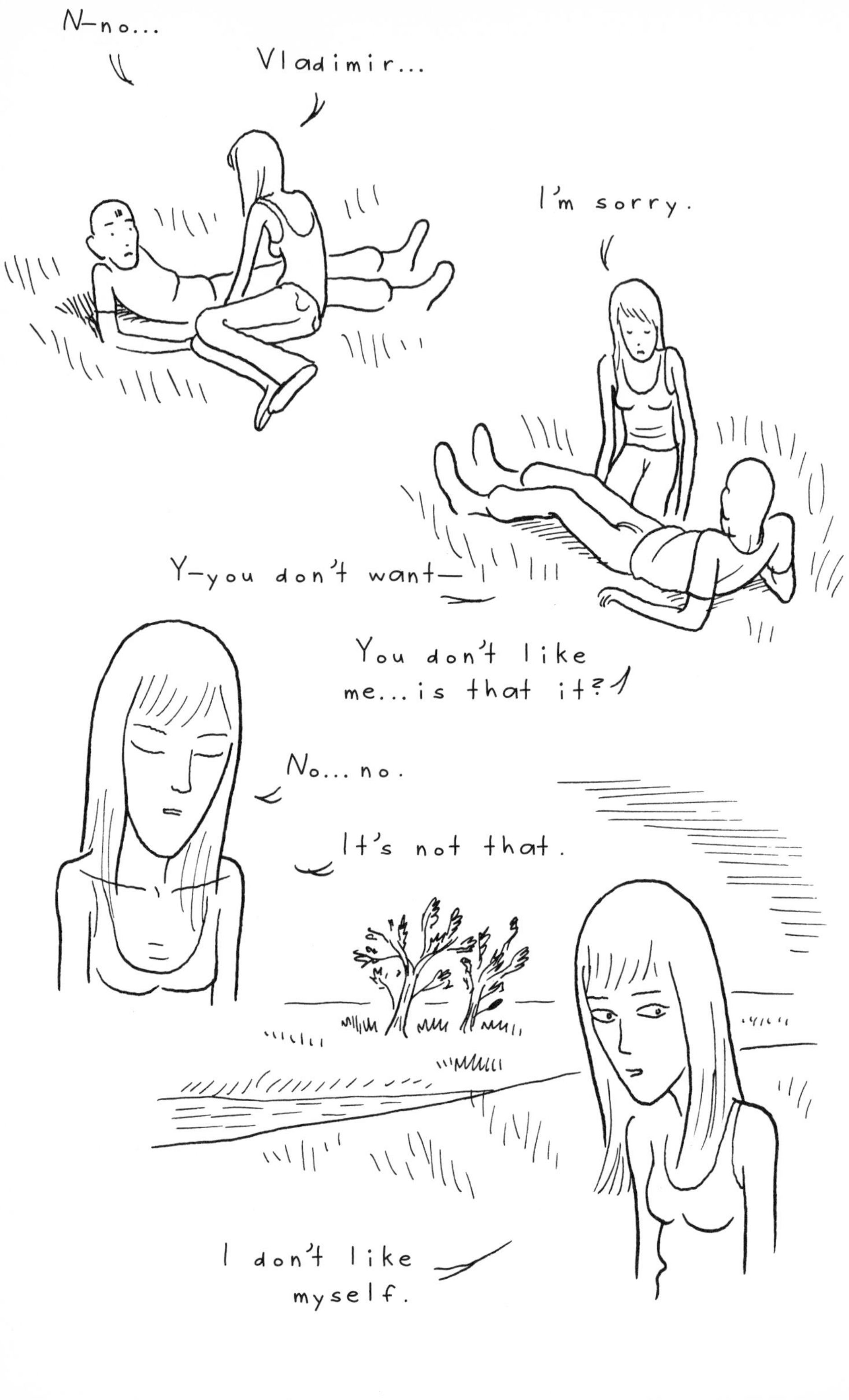
N—no...
Vladimir...
I'm sorry.
Y—you don't want—
You don't like me... is that it?
No... no.
It's not that.
I don't like myself.

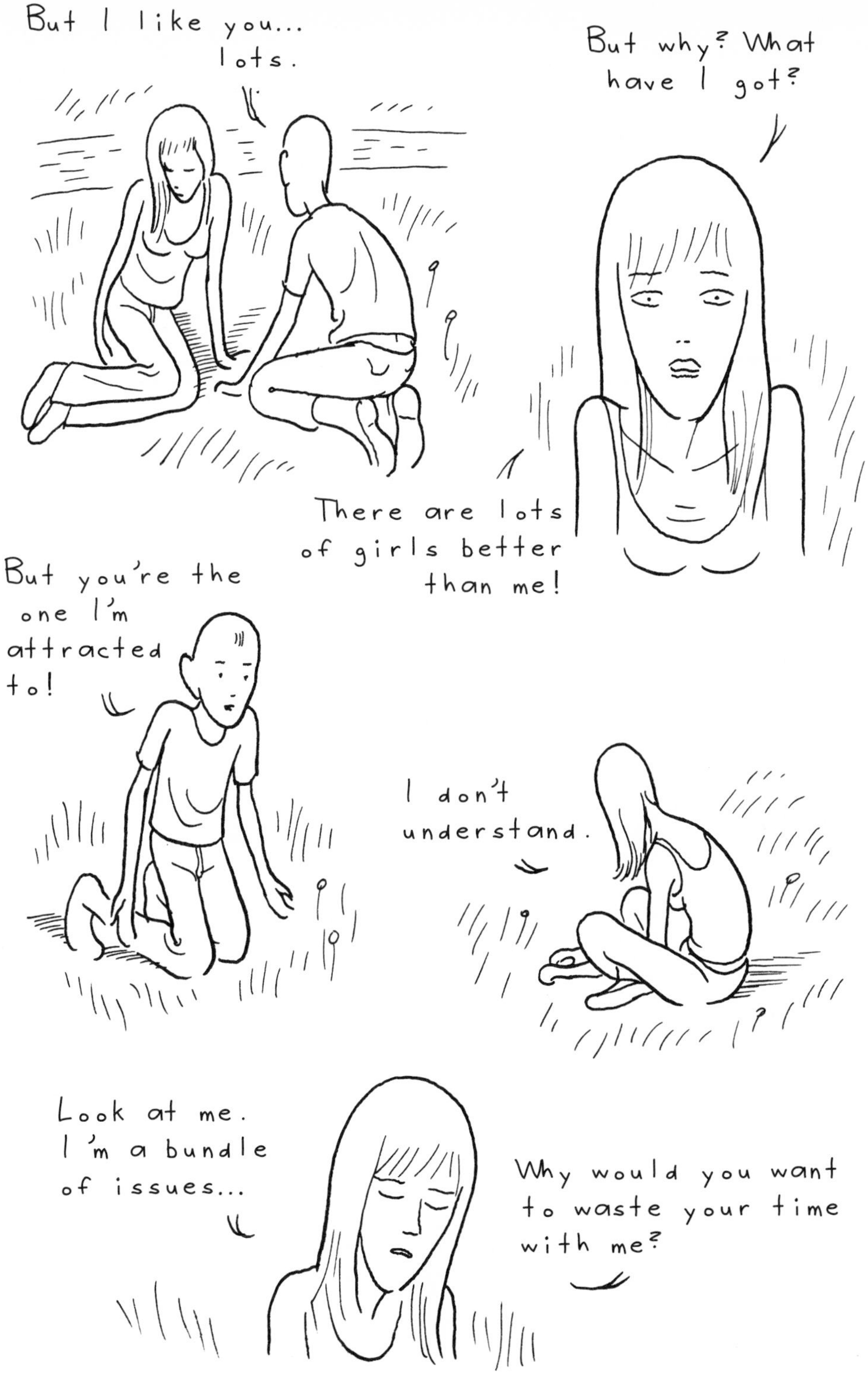

But I like you... lots.
But why? What have I got?
There are lots of girls better than me!
But you're the one I'm attracted to!
I don't understand.
Look at me. I'm a bundle of issues...
Why would you want to waste your time with me?

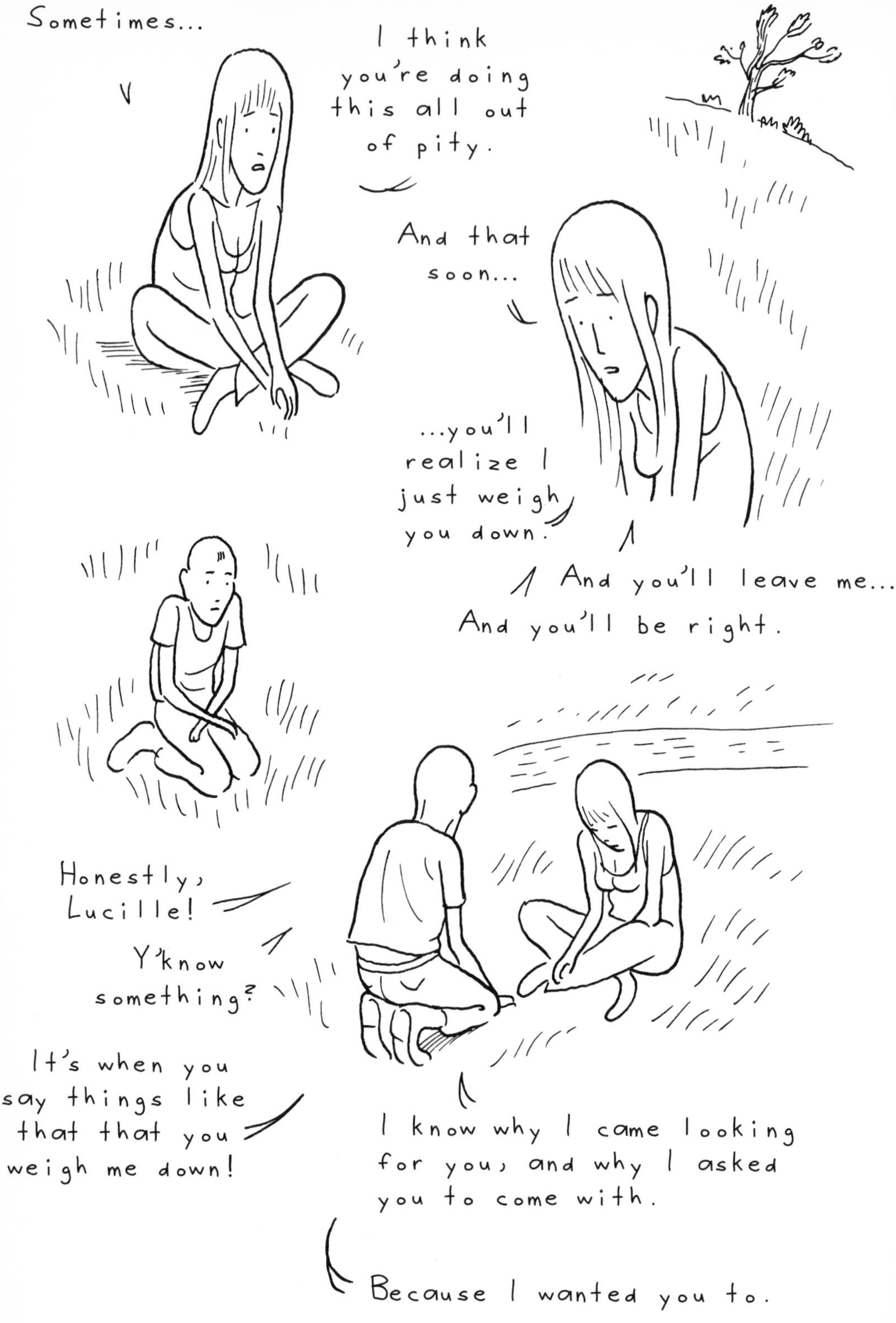
Sometimes...
I think you're doing this all out of pity.
And that soon...
...you'll realize I just weigh you down.
And you'll leave me...
And you'll be right.
Honestly, Lucille!
Y'know something?
It's when you say things like that that you weigh me down!
I know why I came looking for you, and why I asked you to come with.
Because I wanted you to.

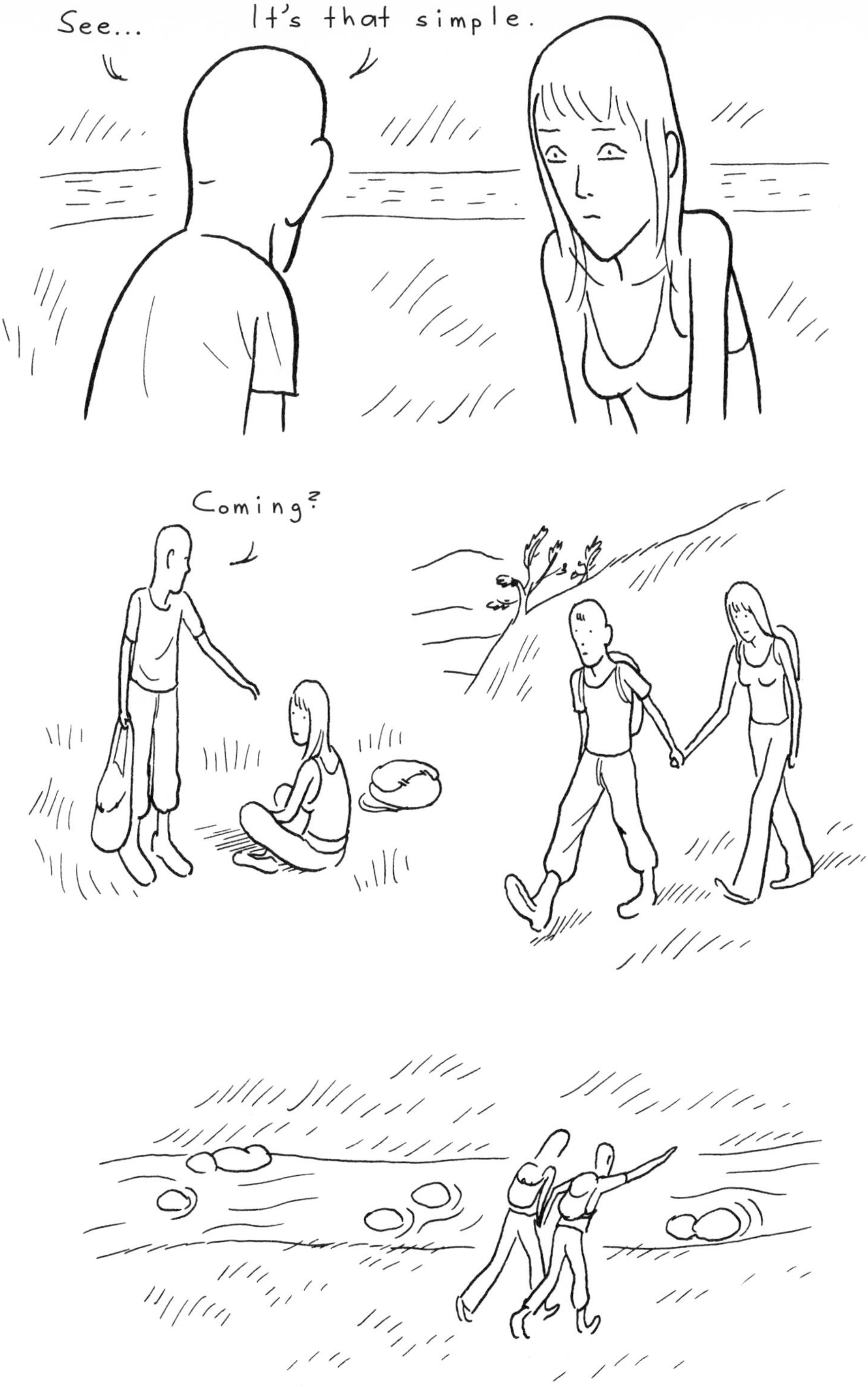

See...
It's that simple.
Coming?

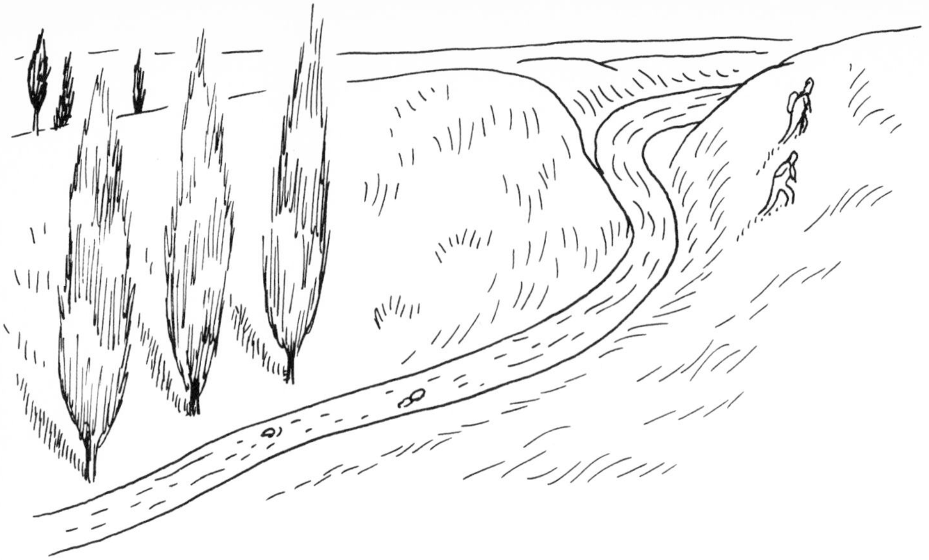

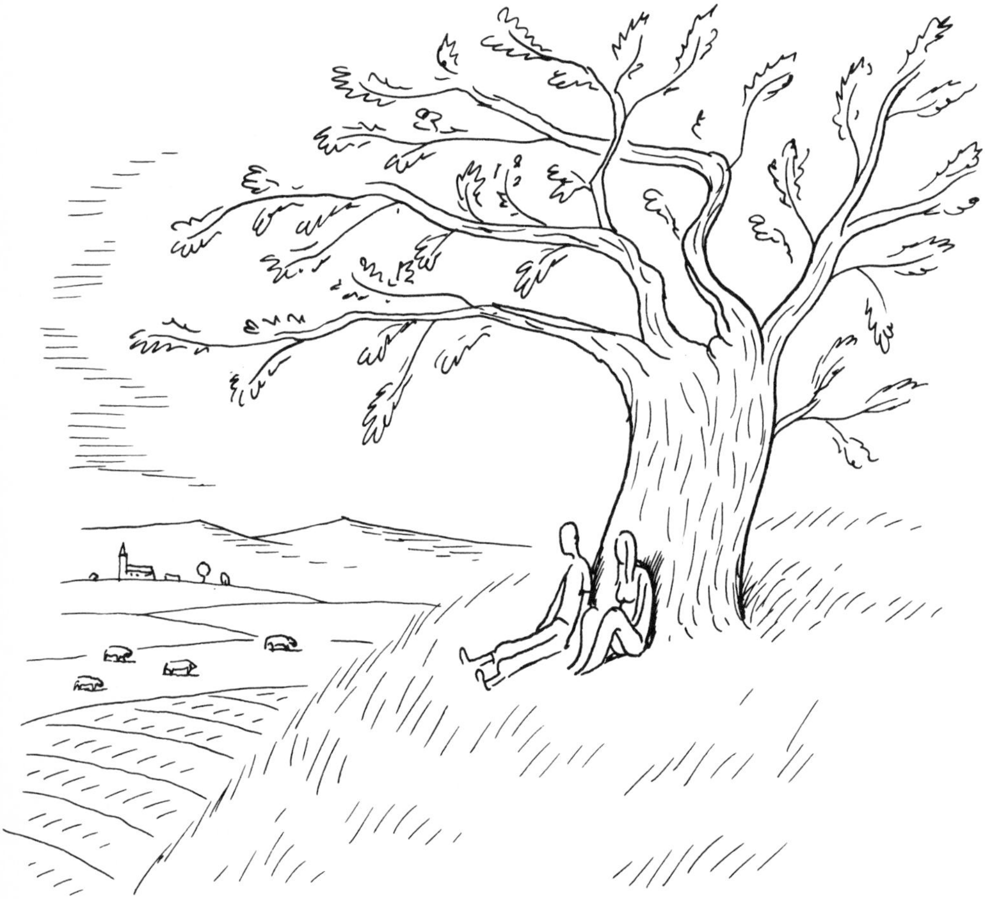

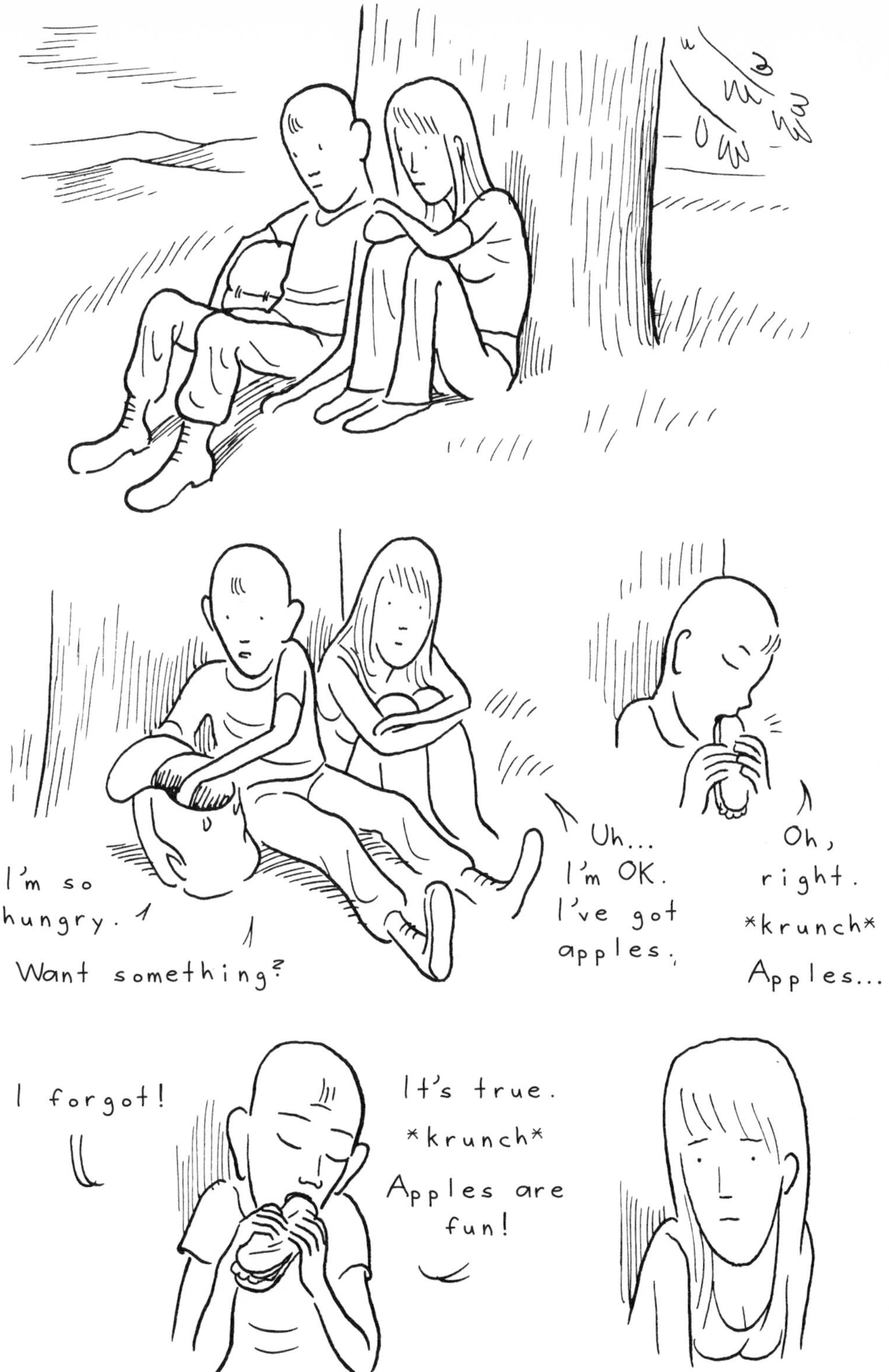
I'm so hungry.
Want something?
Uh... I'm OK. I've got apples.
Oh, right. *krunch* Apples...
I forgot!
It's true. *krunch* Apples are fun!

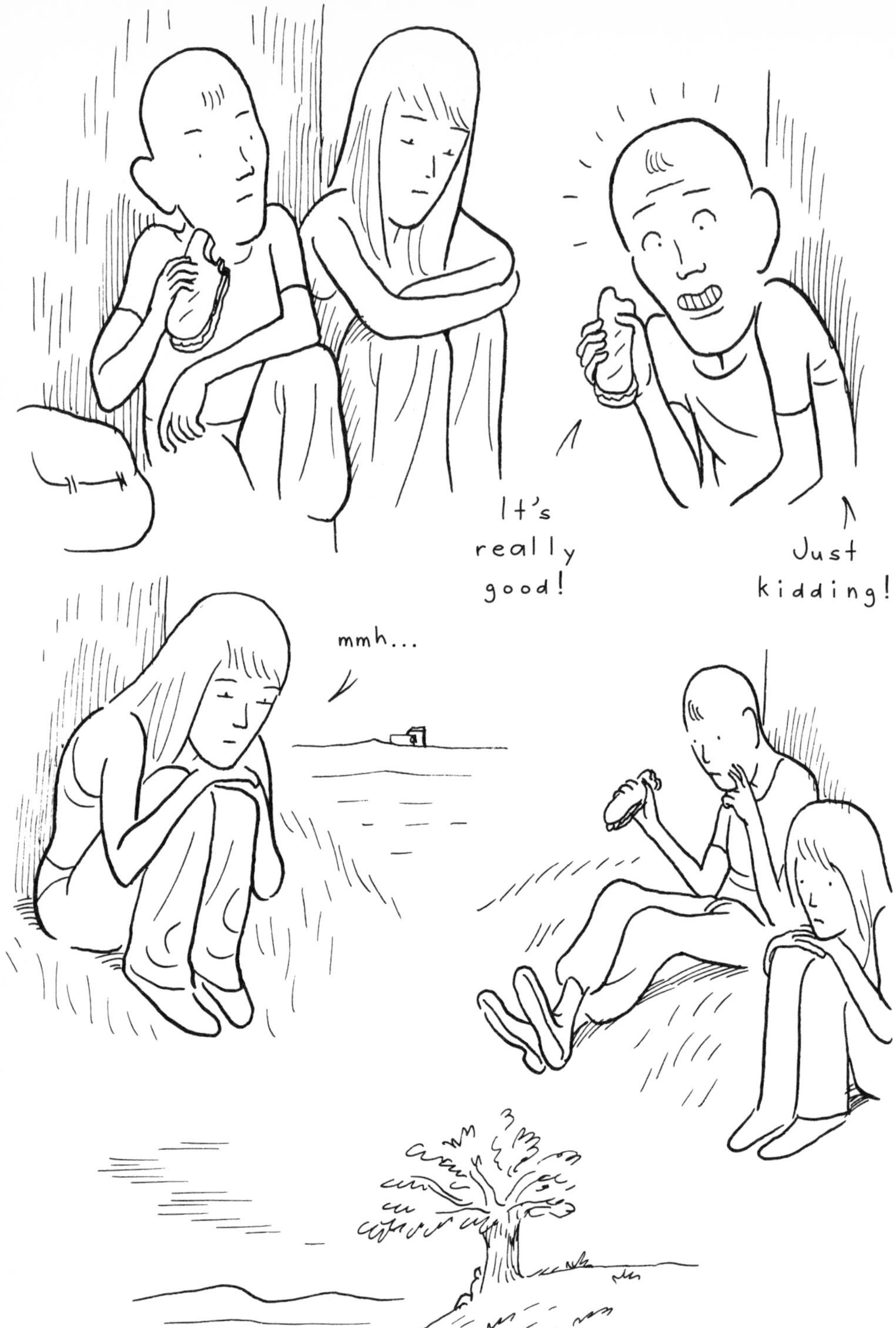
It's really good!
Just kidding!
mmh...

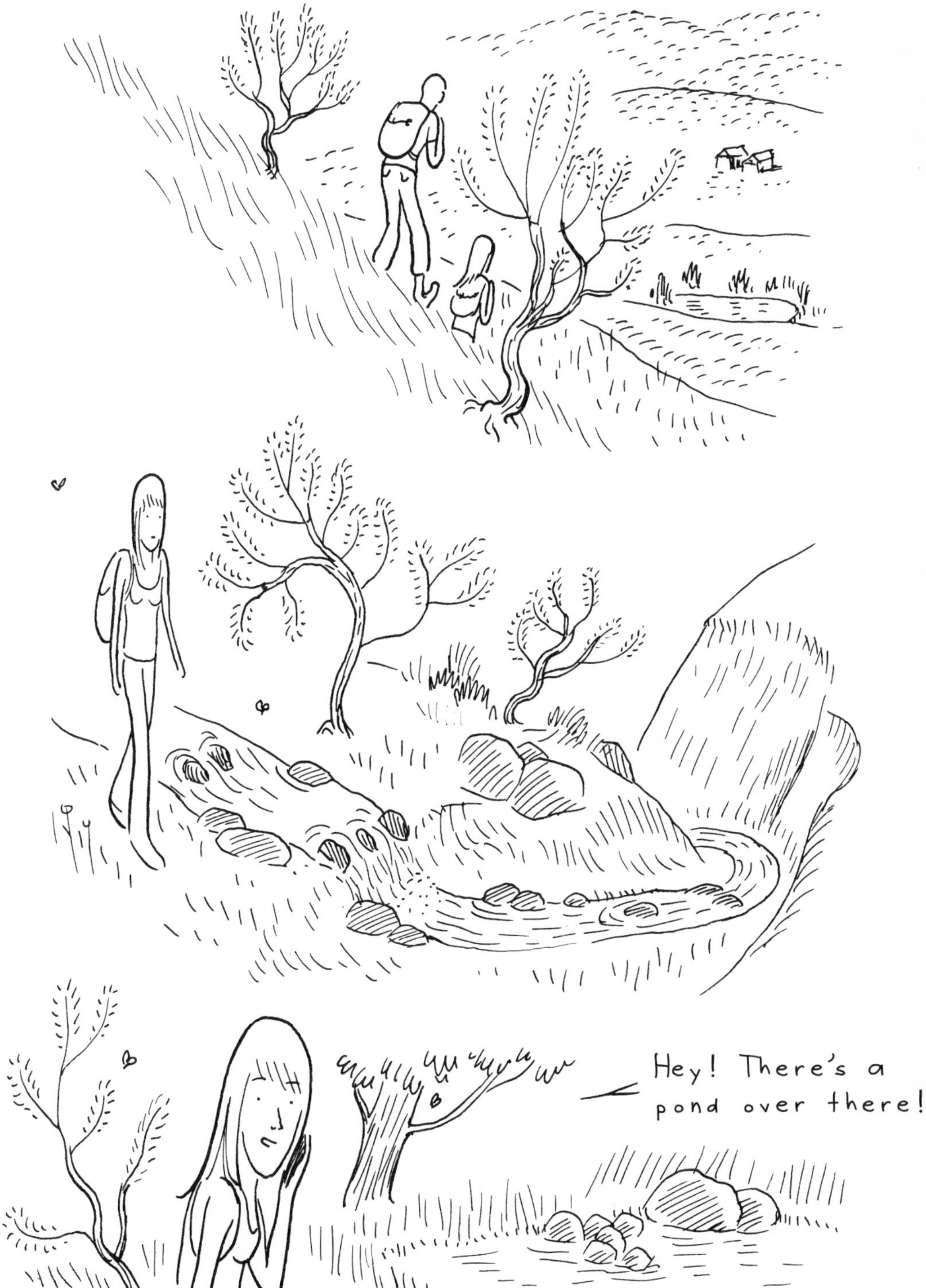
Hey! There's a pond over there!

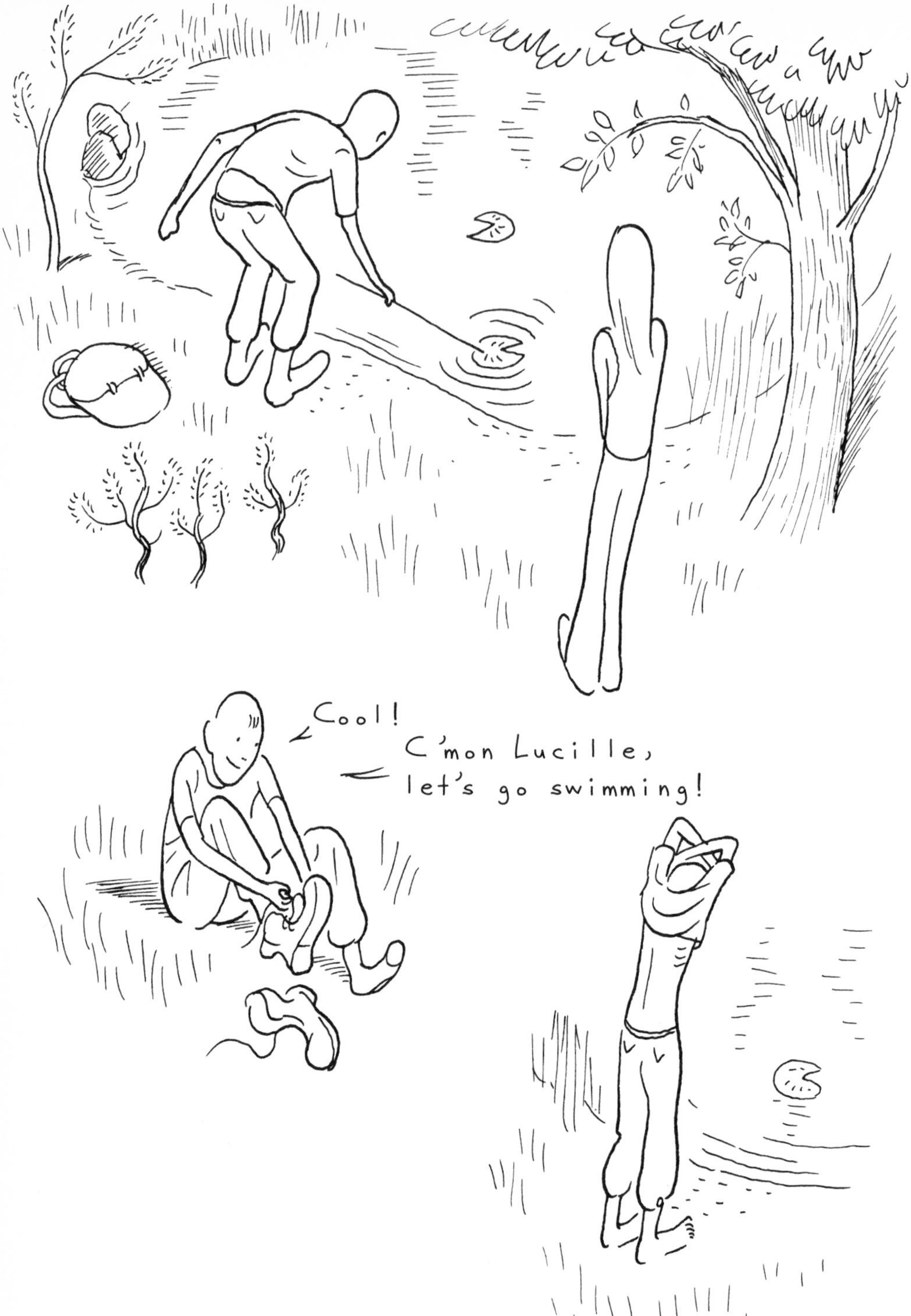
Cool!
C'mon Lucille, let's go swimming!

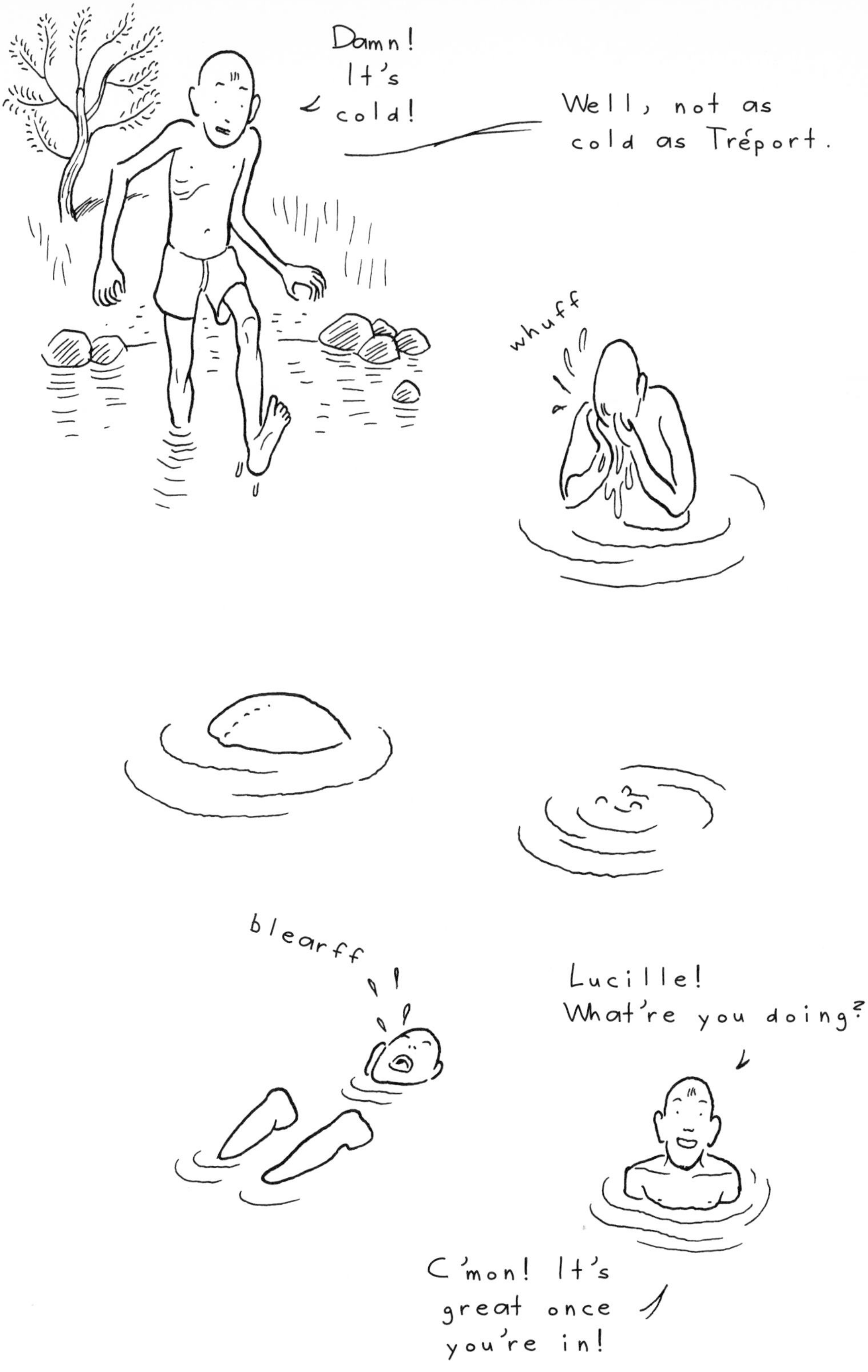
Damn! It's cold!
Well, not as cold as Tréport.
whuff
blearff
Lucille! What're you doing?
C'mon! It's great once you're in!

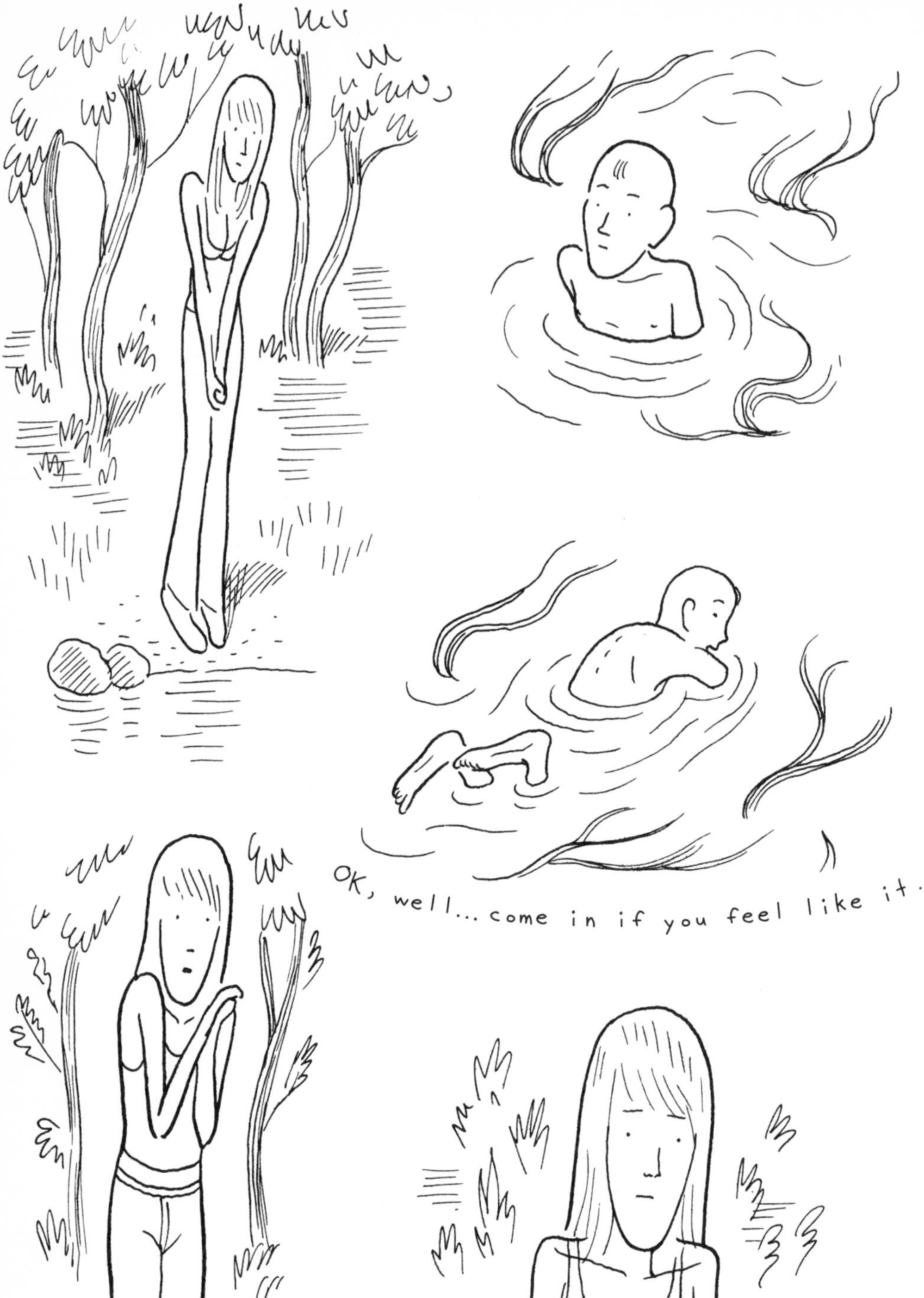
OK, well... come in if you feel like it.

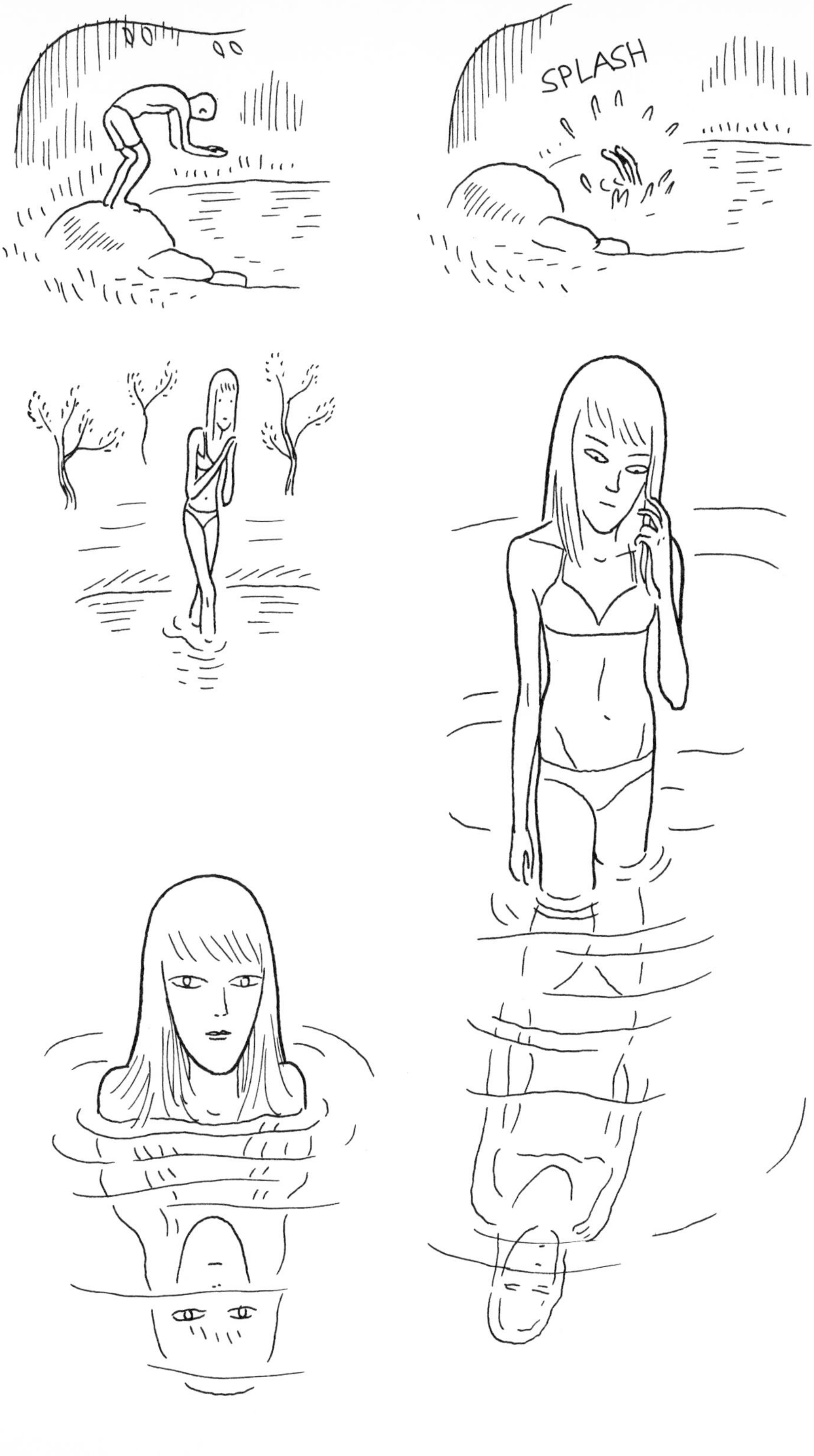
SPLASH

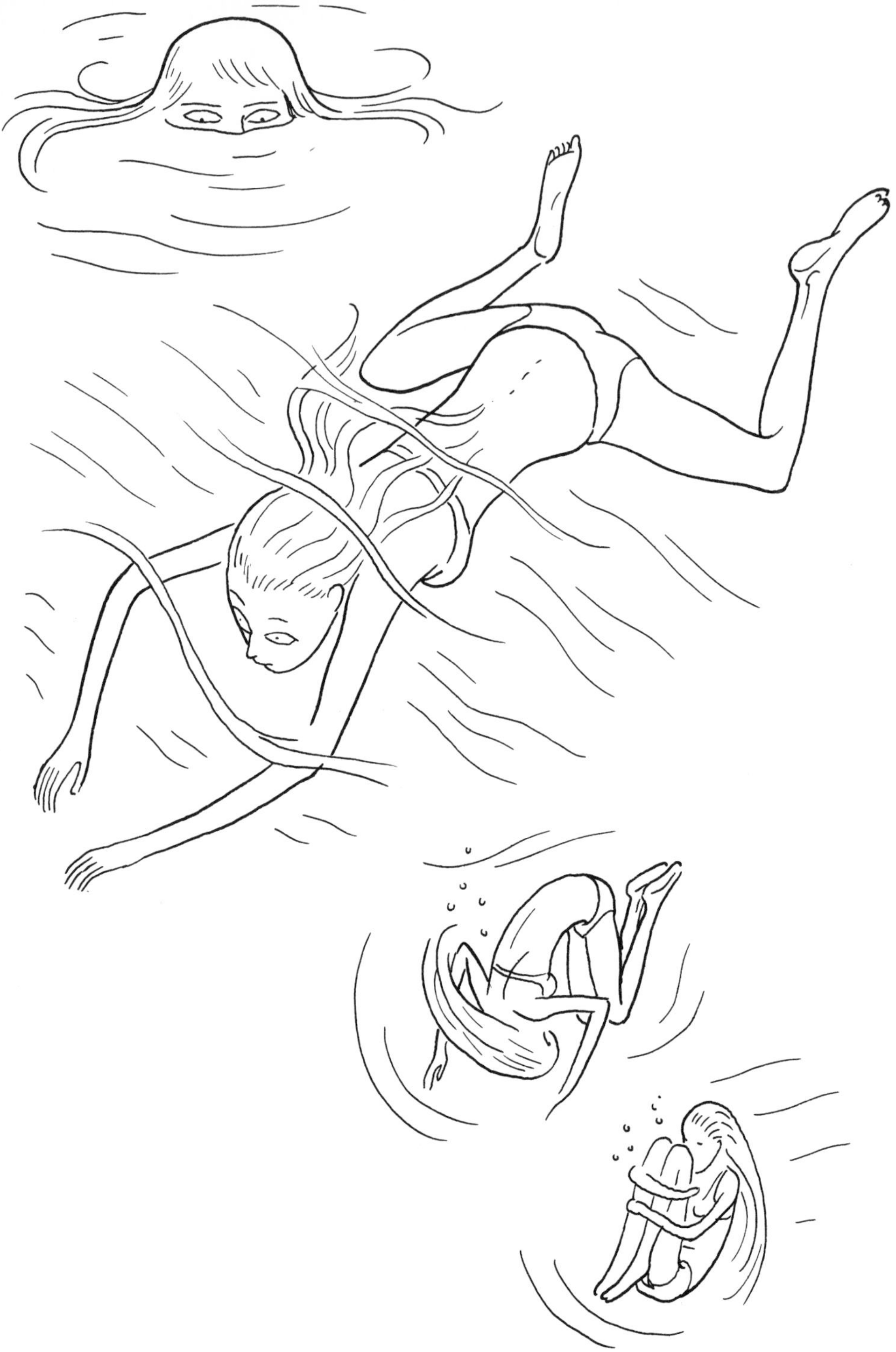

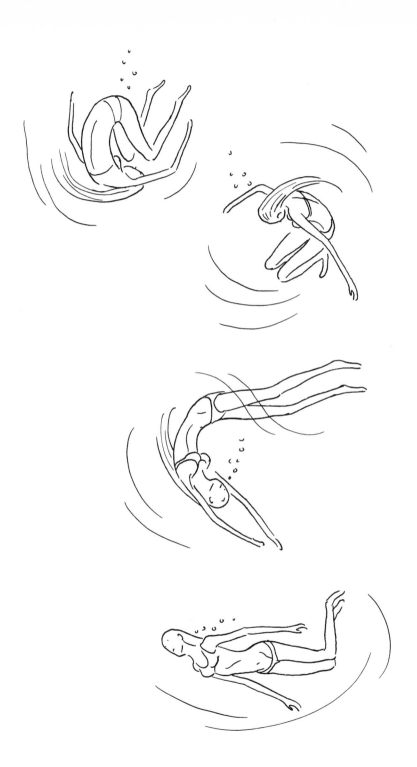

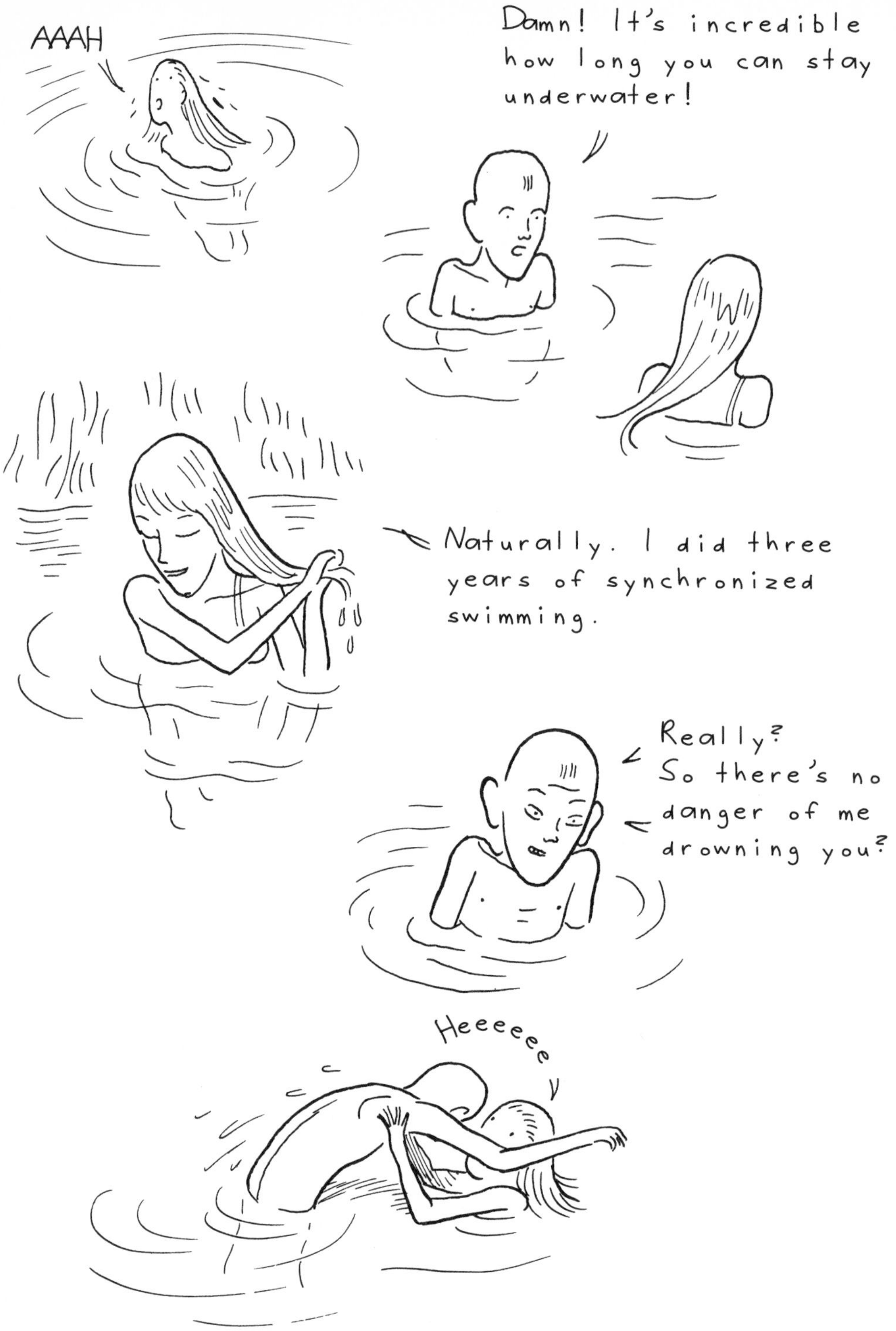

AAAH
Damn! It's incredible how long you can stay underwater!
Naturally. I did three years of synchronized swimming.
Really? So there's no danger of me drowning you?
Heeeeeee

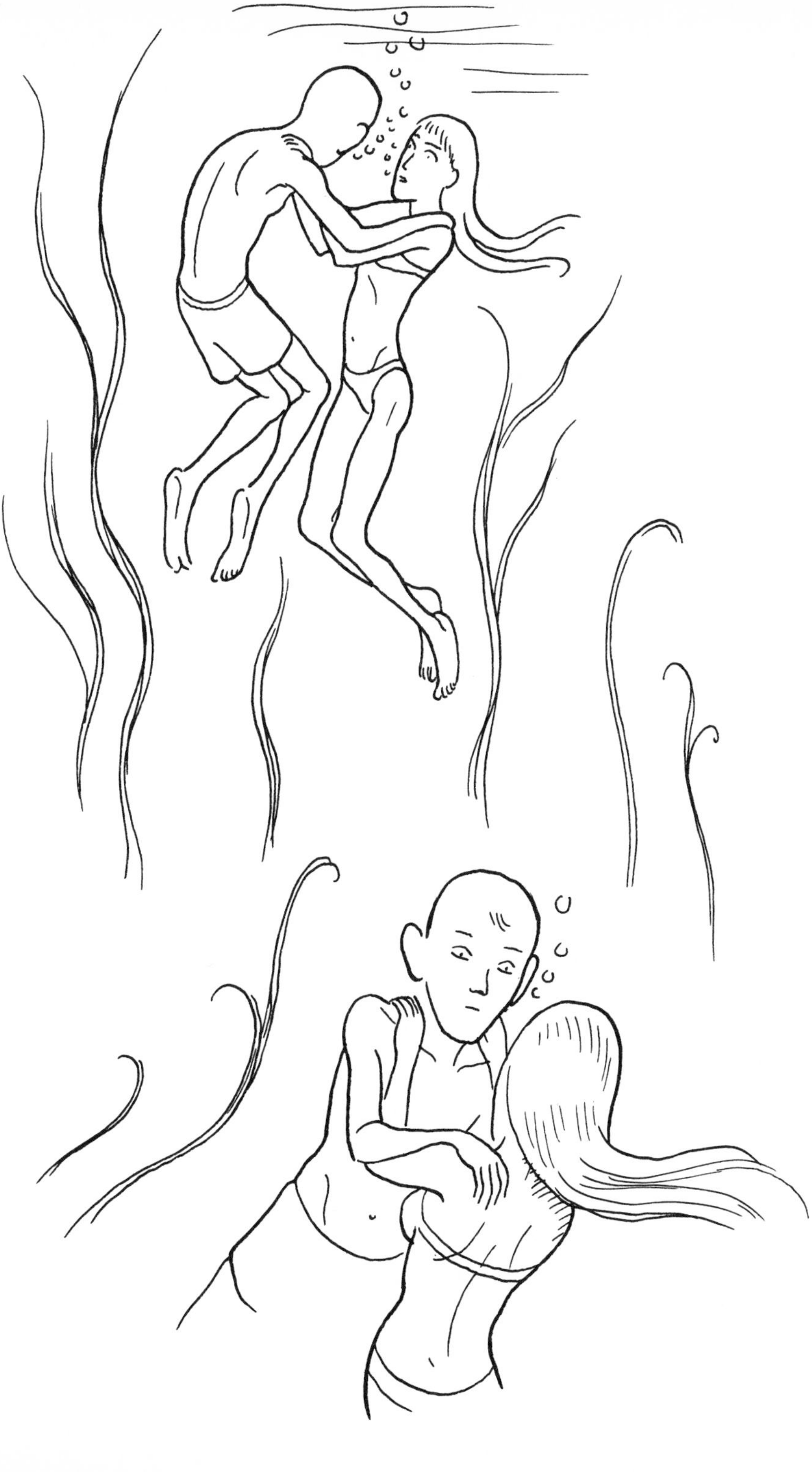

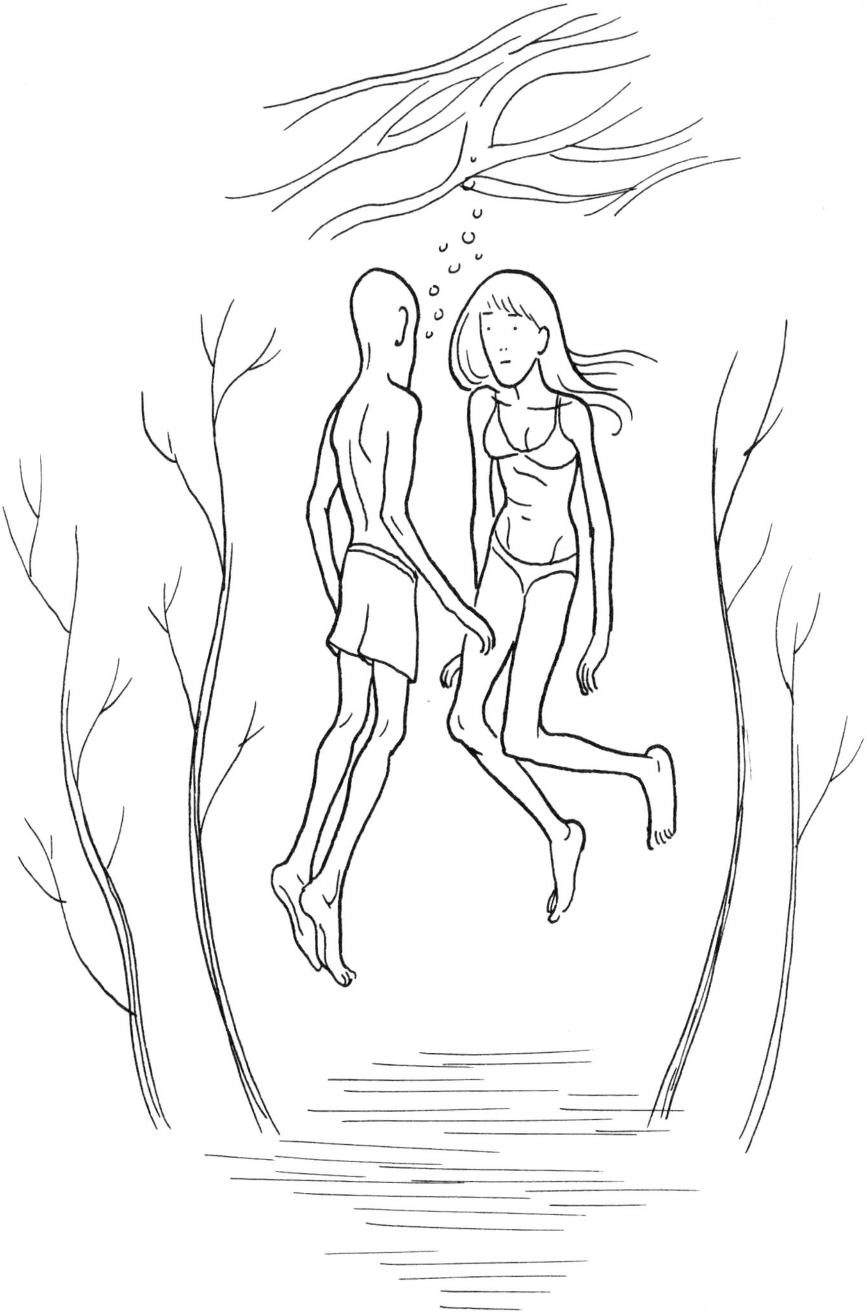

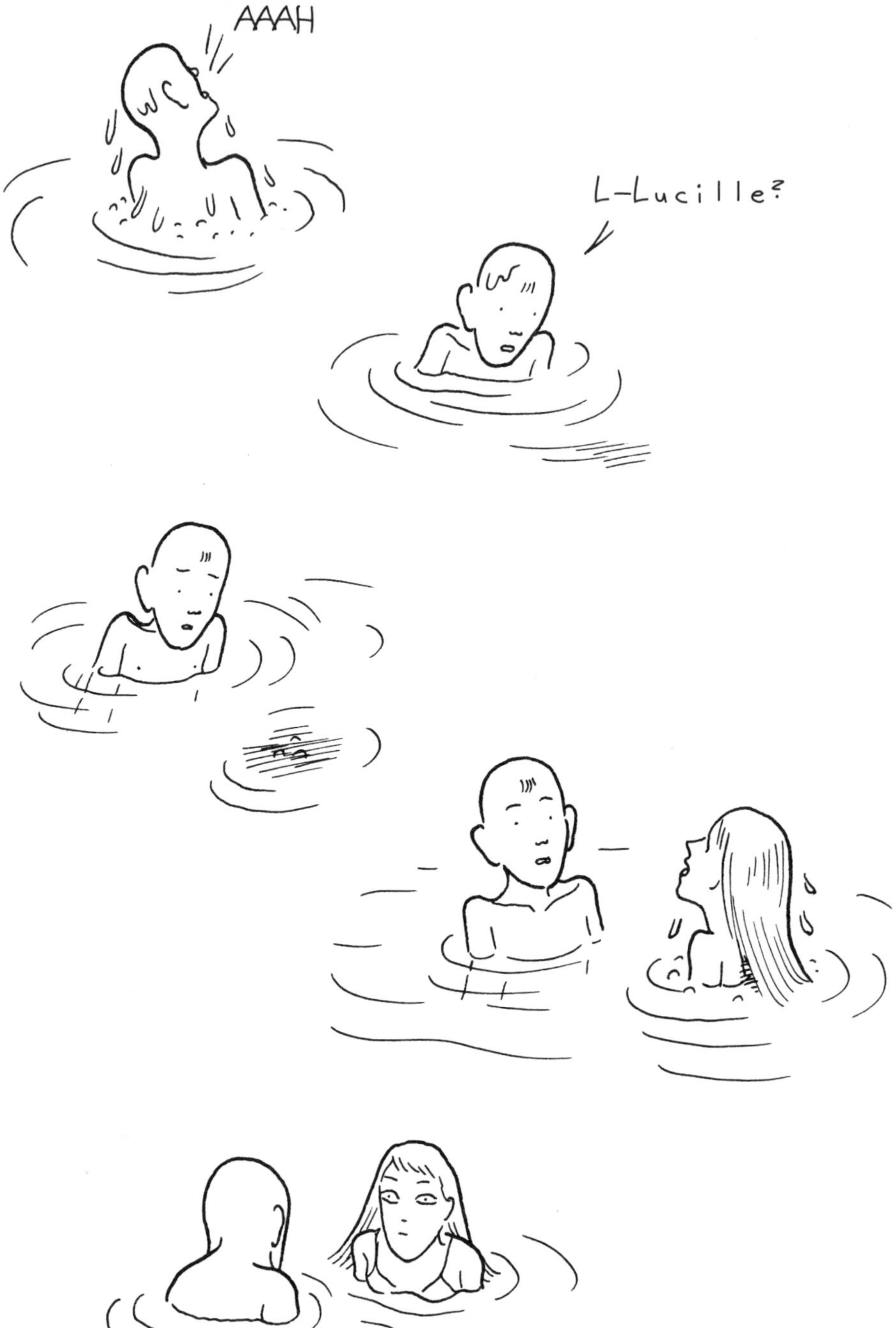
AAAH
L-Lucille?

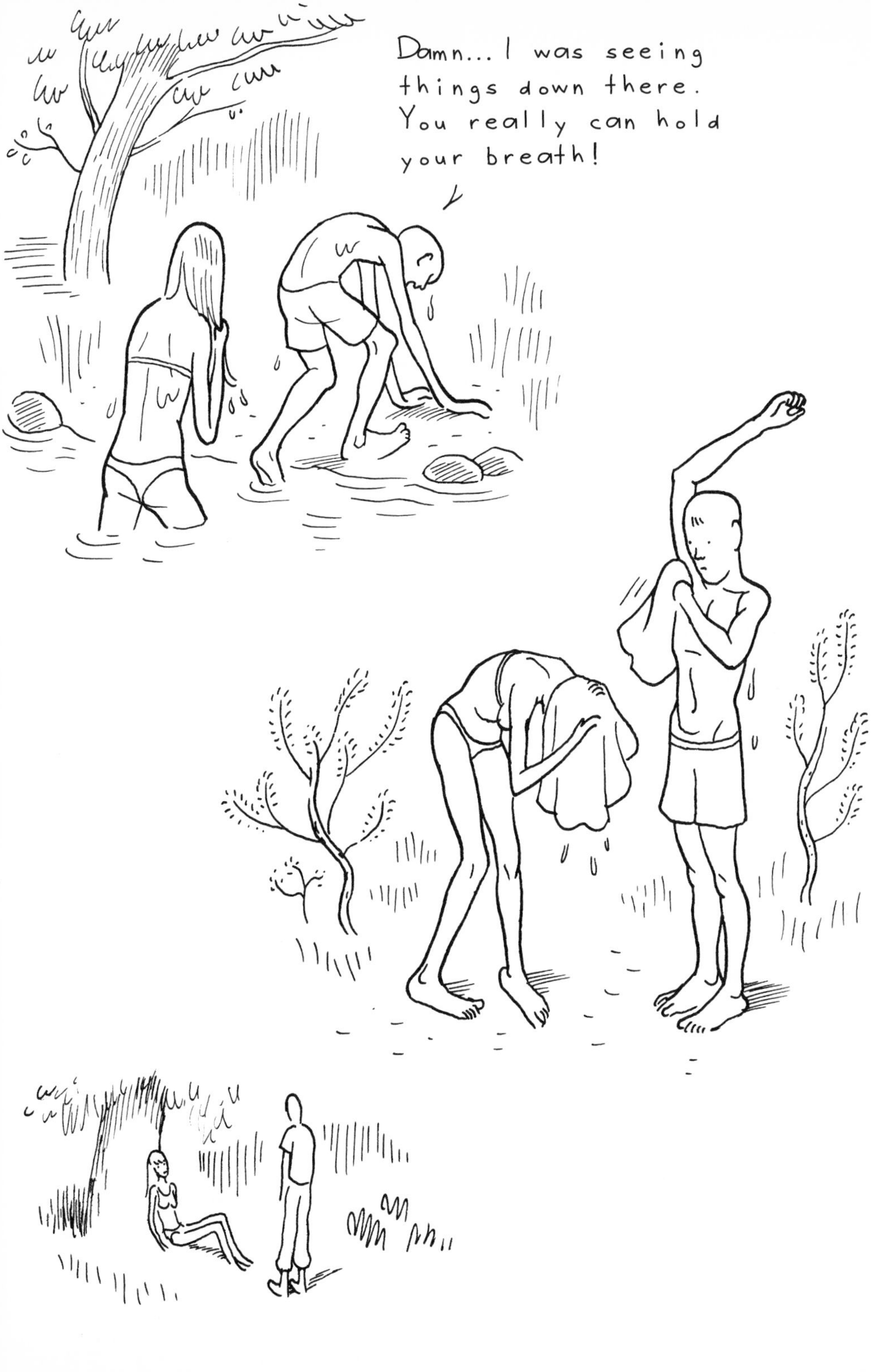
Damn... I was seeing things down there. You really can hold your breath!

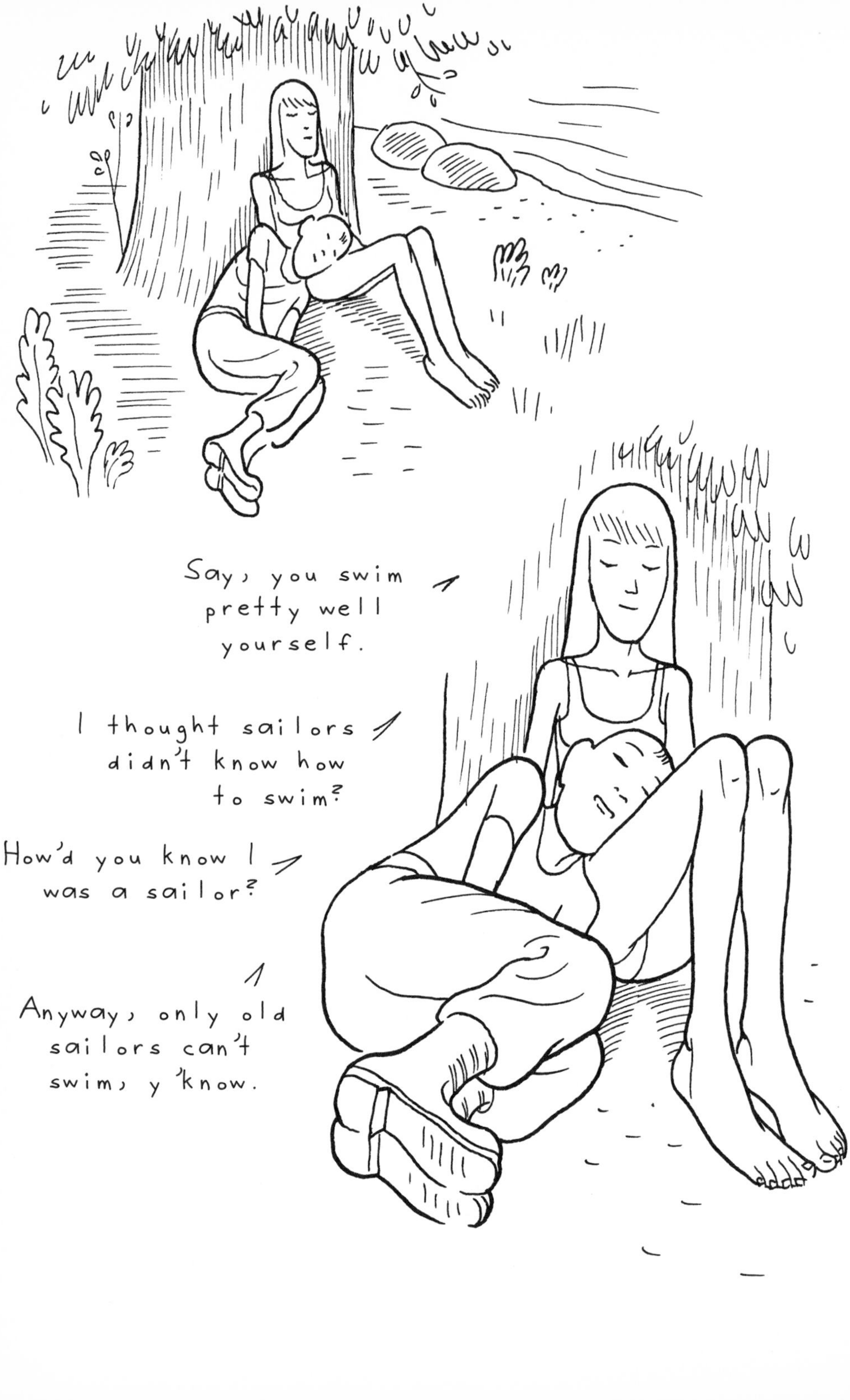
Say, you swim pretty well yourself.
I thought sailors didn't know how to swim?
How'd you know I was a sailor?
Anyway, only old sailors can't swim, y'know.

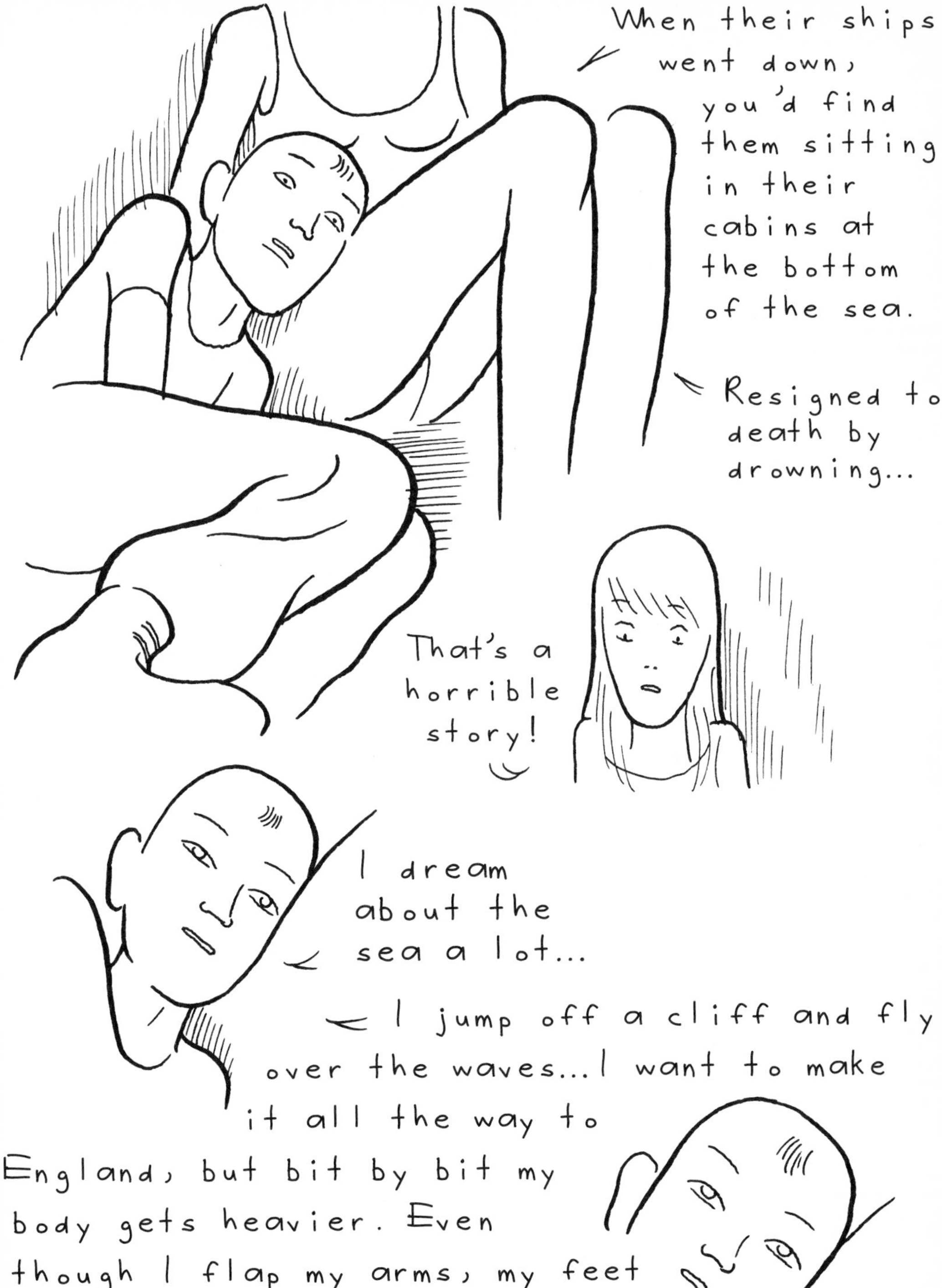

When their ships went down, you'd find them sitting in their cabins at the bottom of the sea.
Resigned to death by drowning...
That's a horrible story!
I dream about the sea a lot...
I jump off a cliff and fly over the waves... I want to make it all the way to England, but bit by bit my body gets heavier. Even though I flap my arms, my feet start dragging in the water.

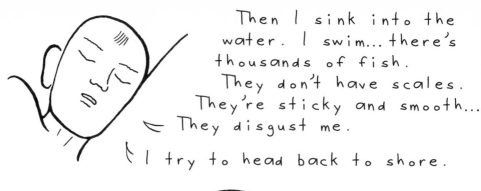

Then I sink into the water. I swim...there's thousands of fish.
They don't have scales. They're sticky and smooth... They disgust me.
I try to head back to shore.

A few weeks ago I read that a famous dancer went to the cliff between Ault and Tréport.

And threw himself off...

What a weird last dance, right?

Hmm...

Y'know... I don't really... Dancing isn't my thing.

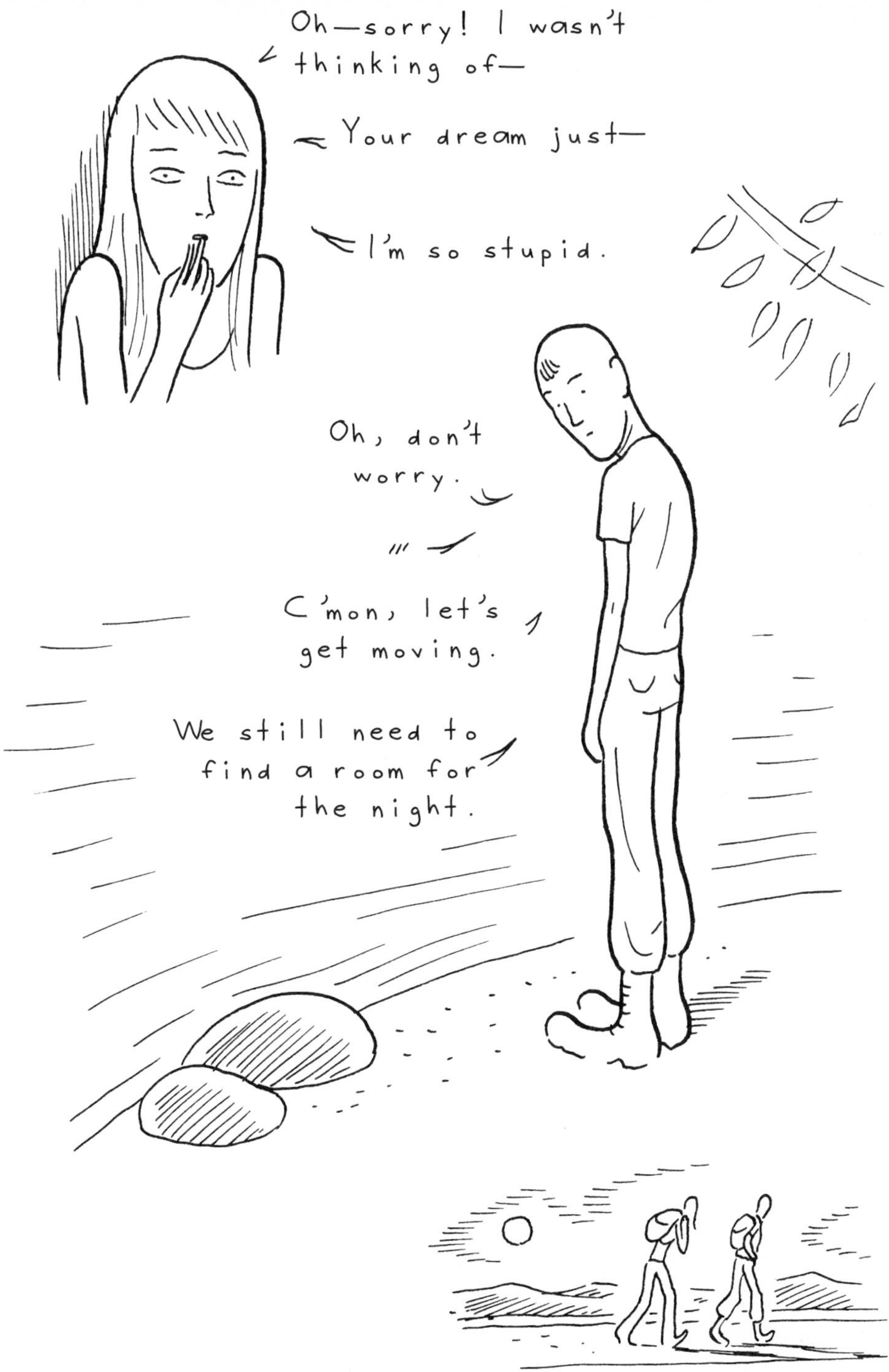
Oh—sorry! I wasn't thinking of—
Your dream just—
I'm so stupid.
Oh, don't worry.
///
C'mon, let's get moving.
We still need to find a room for the night.

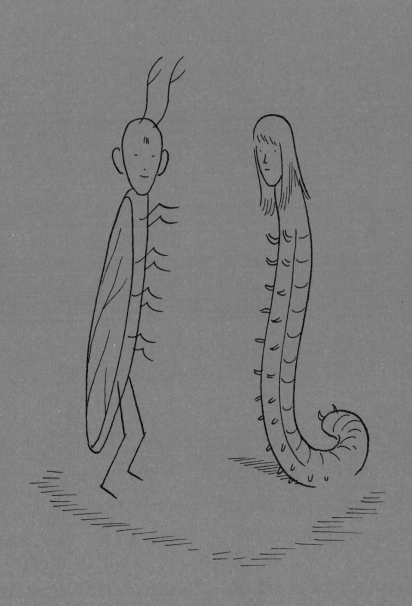

La Nuit Les Chemins Disparaîssent

(At Night the Roads Disappear)

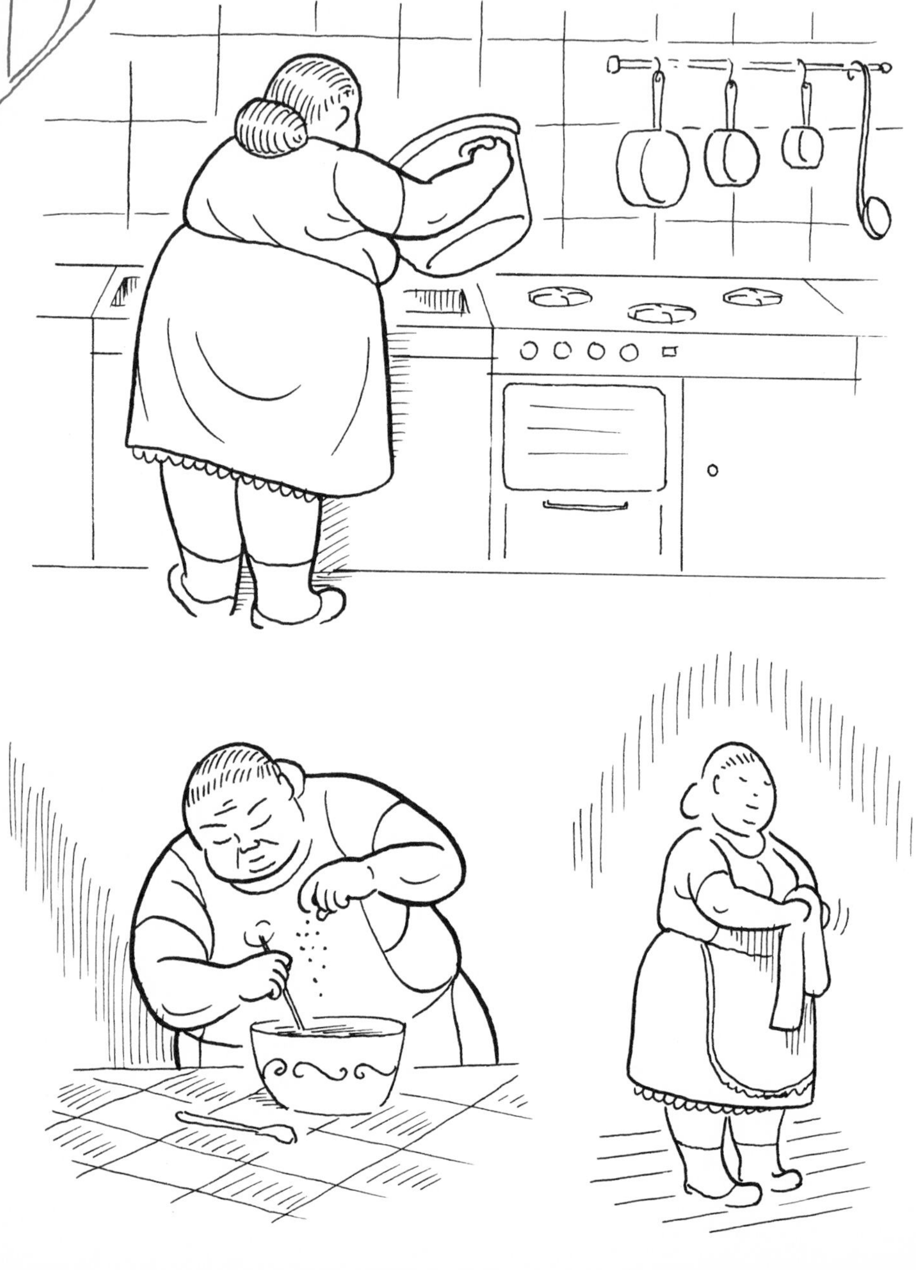

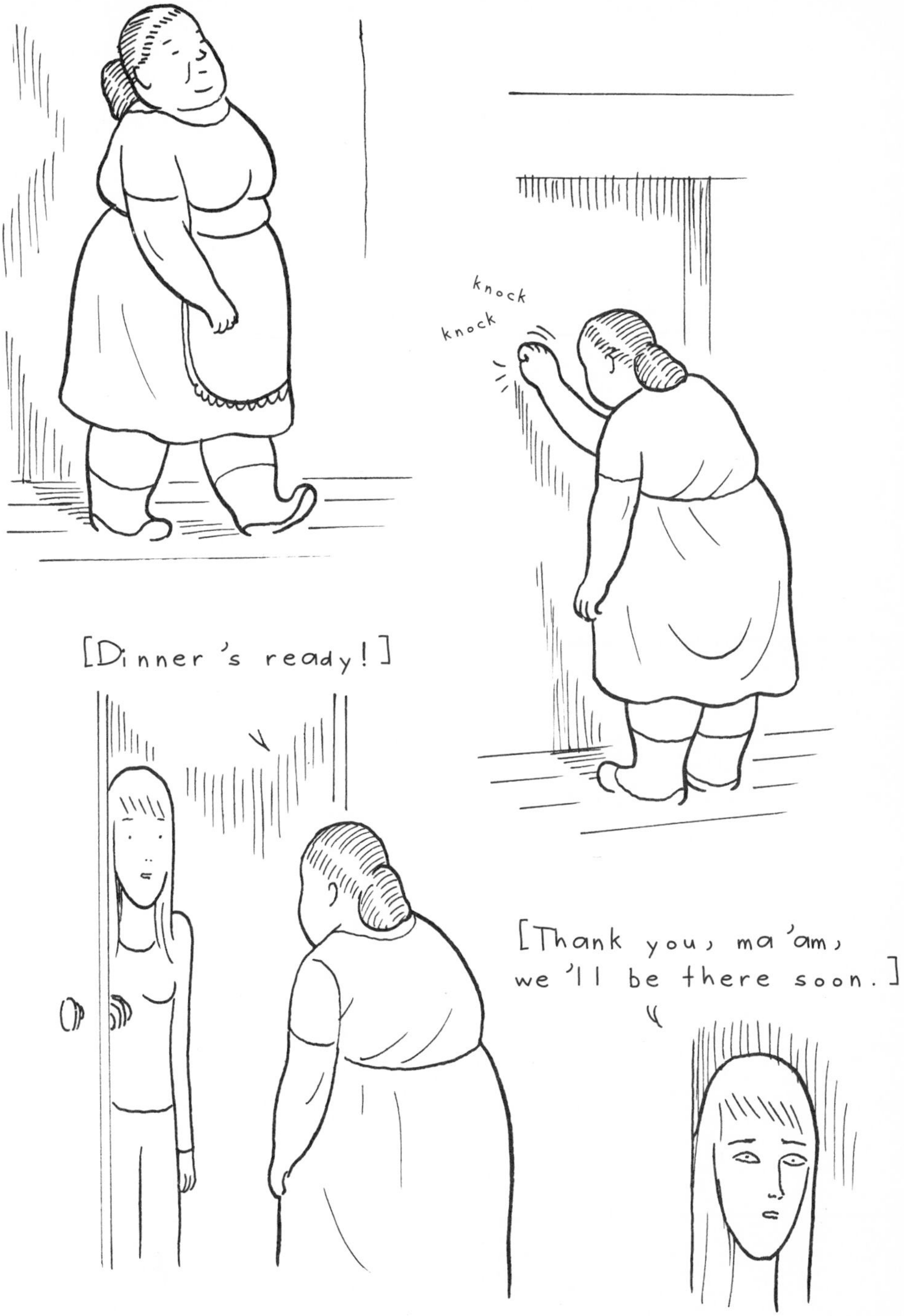
knock
knock
[Dinner's ready!]
[Thank you, ma'am, we'll be there soon.]

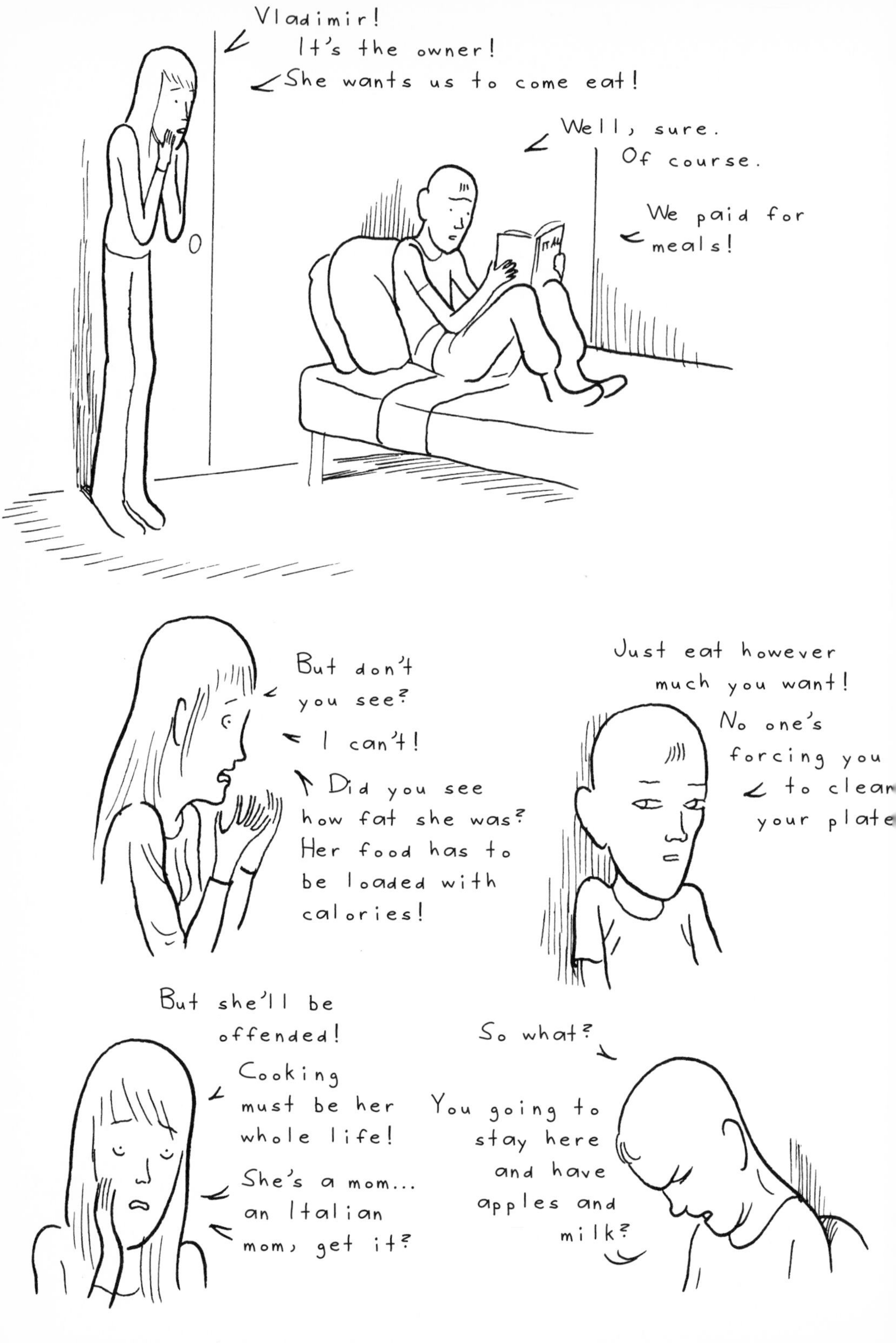
Vladimir! It's the owner! She wants us to come eat!
Well, sure. Of course.
We paid for meals!
But don't you see?
I can't!
Did you see how fat she was? Her food has to be loaded with calories!
Just eat however much you want!
No one's forcing you to clean your plate
But she'll be offended!
Cooking must be her whole life!
She's a mom... an Italian mom, get it?
So what?
You going to stay here and have apples and milk?

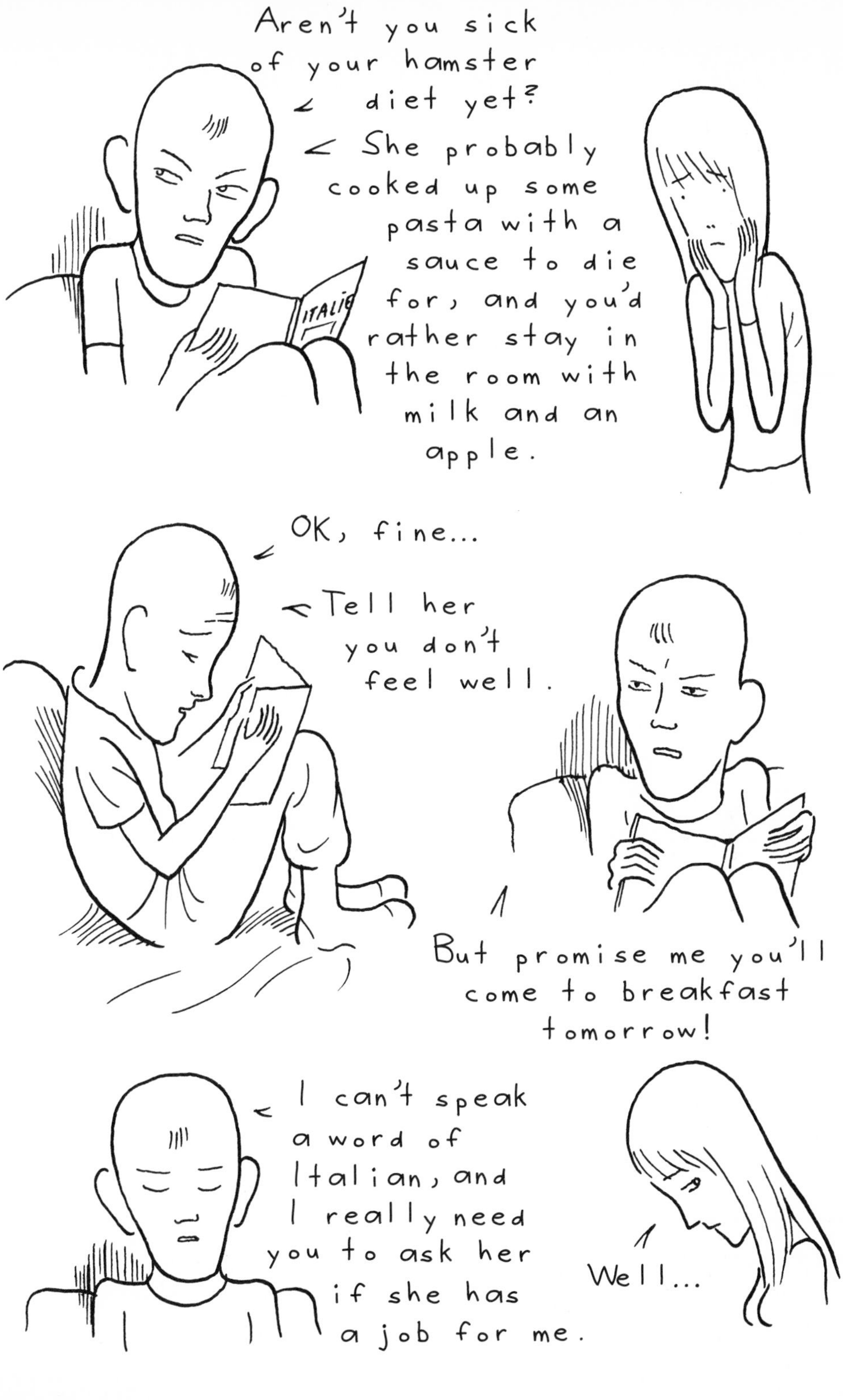
Aren't you sick of your hamster diet yet?
She probably cooked up some pasta with a sauce to die for, and you'd rather stay in the room with milk and an apple.
OK, fine...
Tell her you don't feel well.
But promise me you'll come to breakfast tomorrow!
I can't speak a word of Italian, and I really need you to ask her if she has a job for me.
Well...

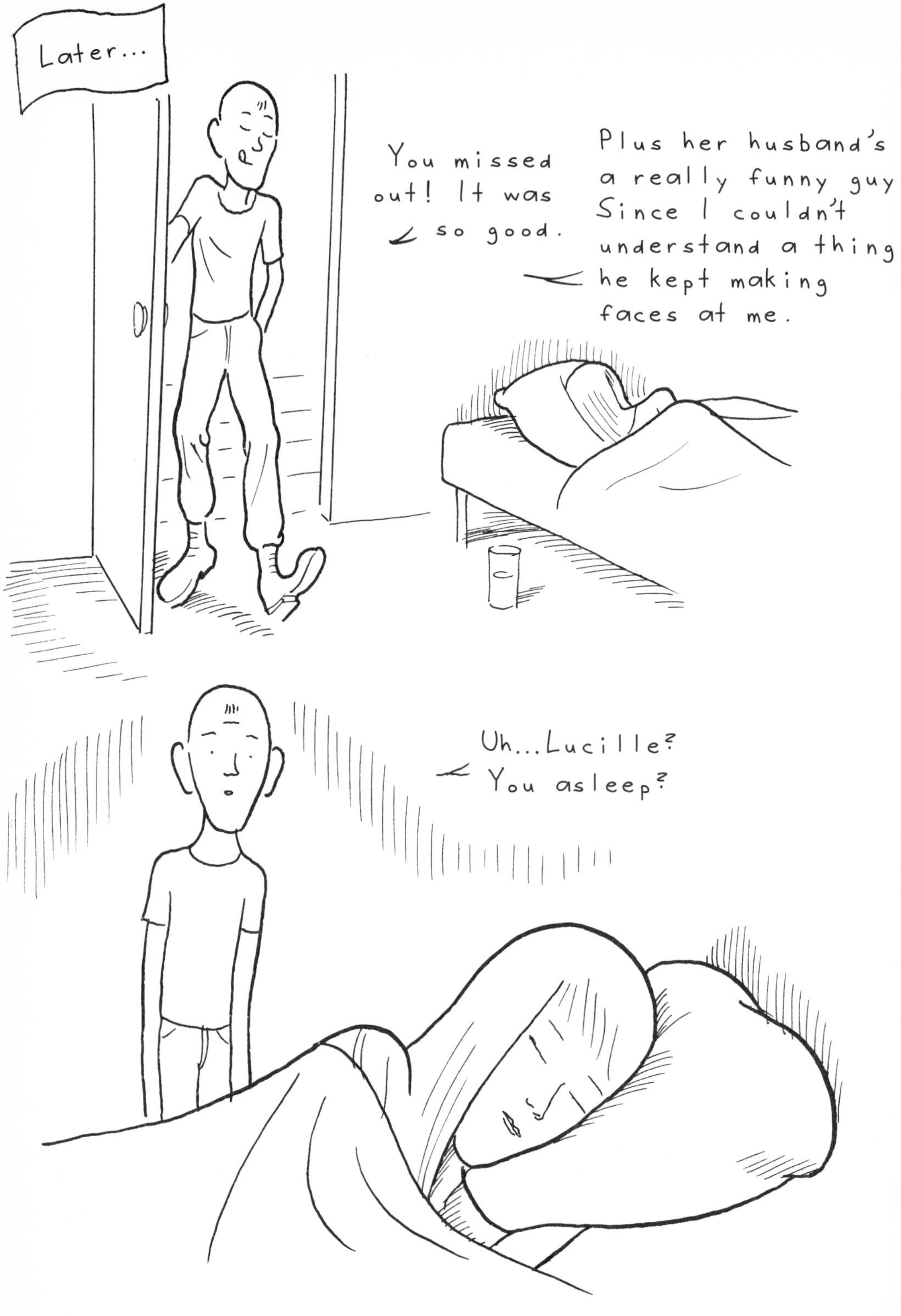
Later...
You missed out! It was so good.
Plus her husband's a really funny guy Since I couldn't understand a thing he kept making faces at me.
Uh...Lucille? You asleep?

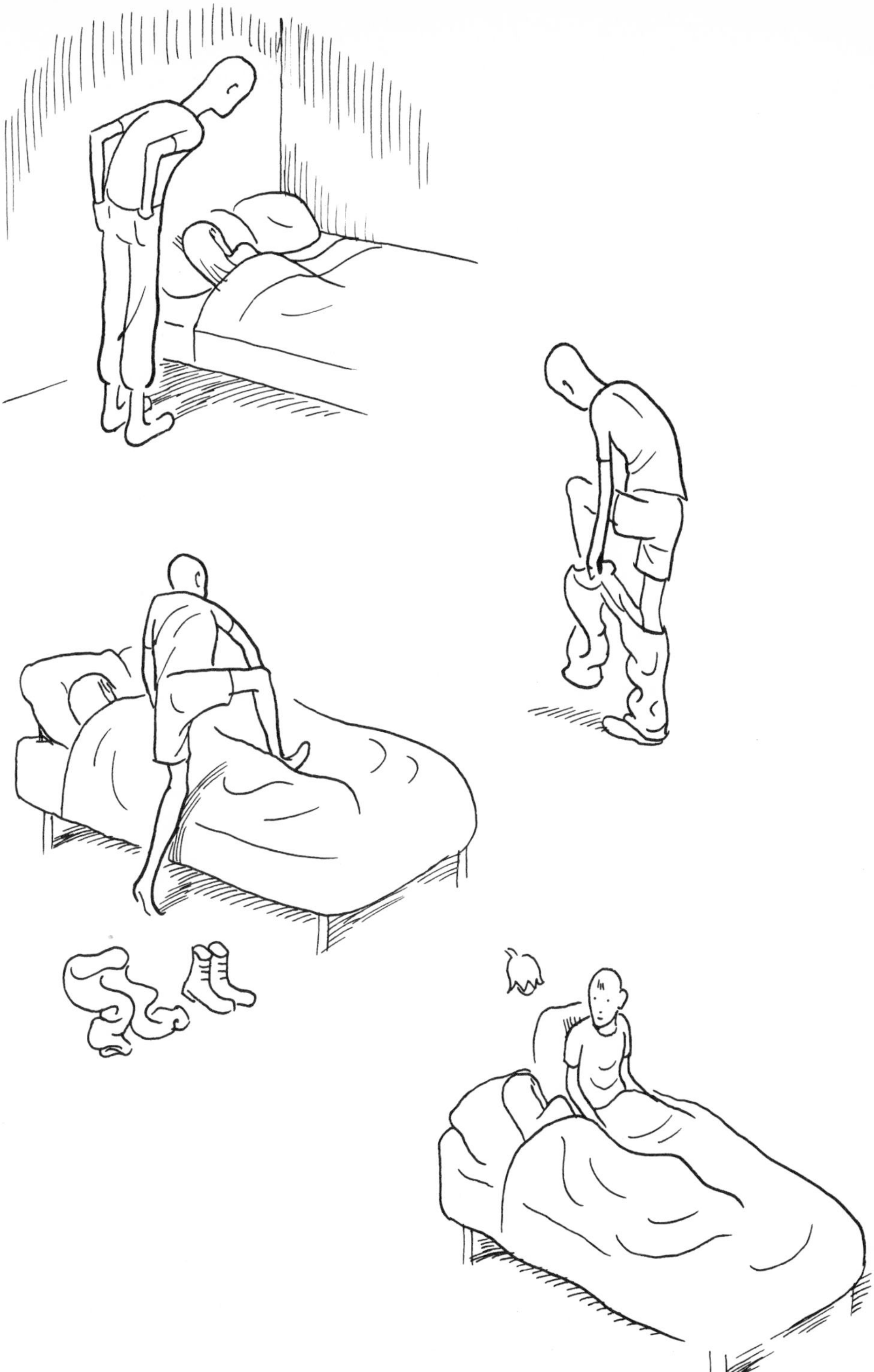

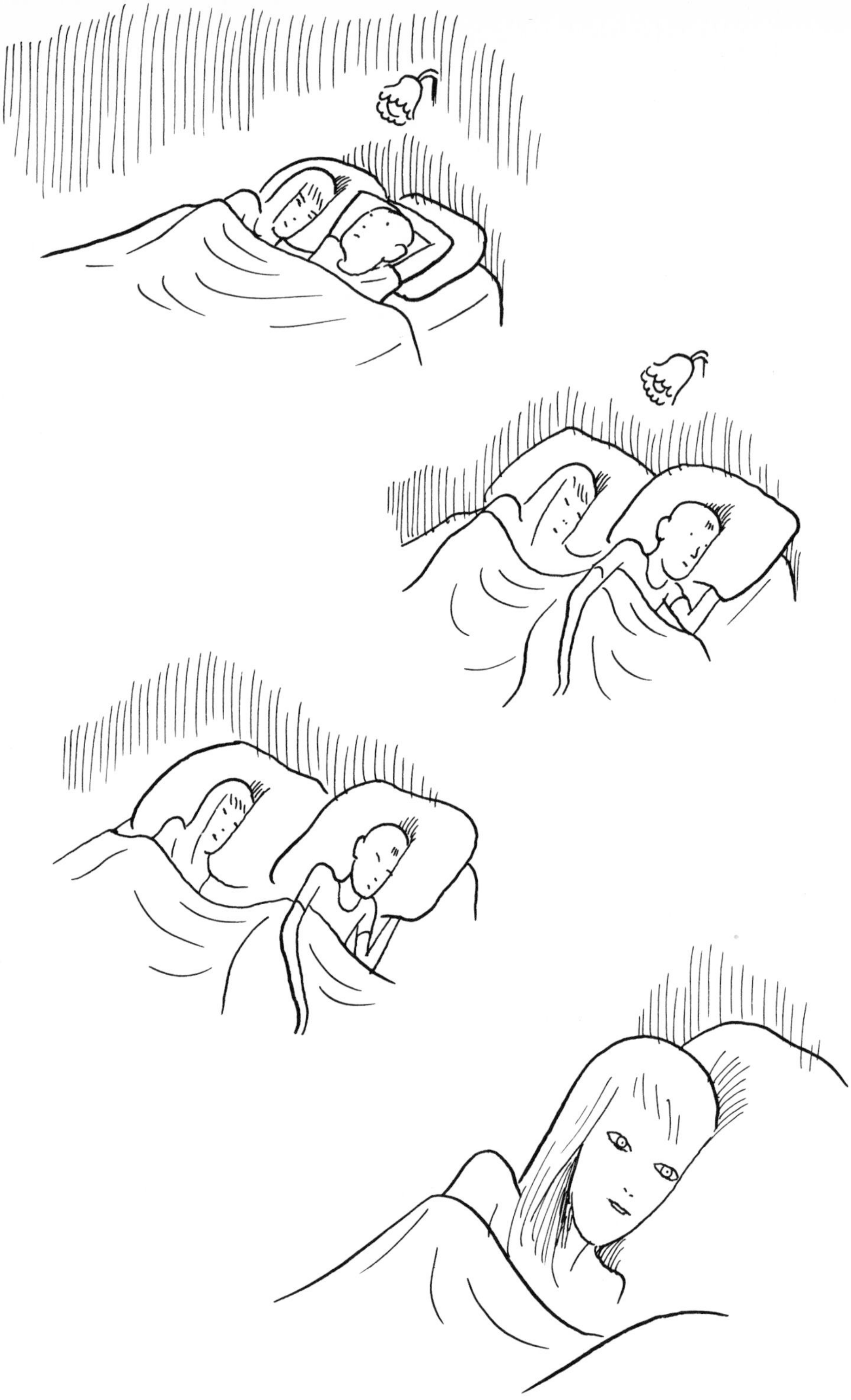

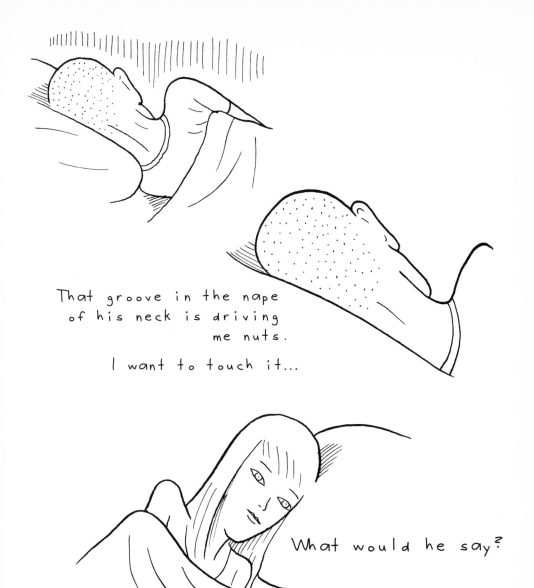

That groove in the nape
of his neck is driving
me nuts.

I want to touch it...

What would he say?

I want to, but I'm afraid.
Maybe if I study it long enough,
in great detail, it'll be like I did.

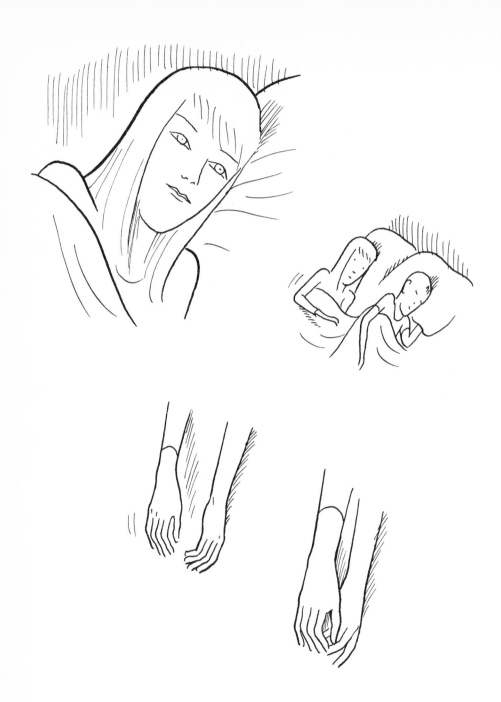

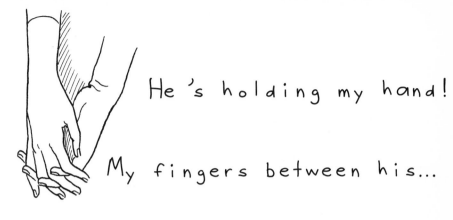

He's holding my hand!

My fingers between his...

What's he thinking of right now?

Is he thinking the same thing?

My heart's about to leap out of my chest.

I feel numb all over, I can't feel my body anymore... My feet are all electrified.

I'm doing it!

I'm touching a man!

He's turning over!
He must be turning over to kiss me!

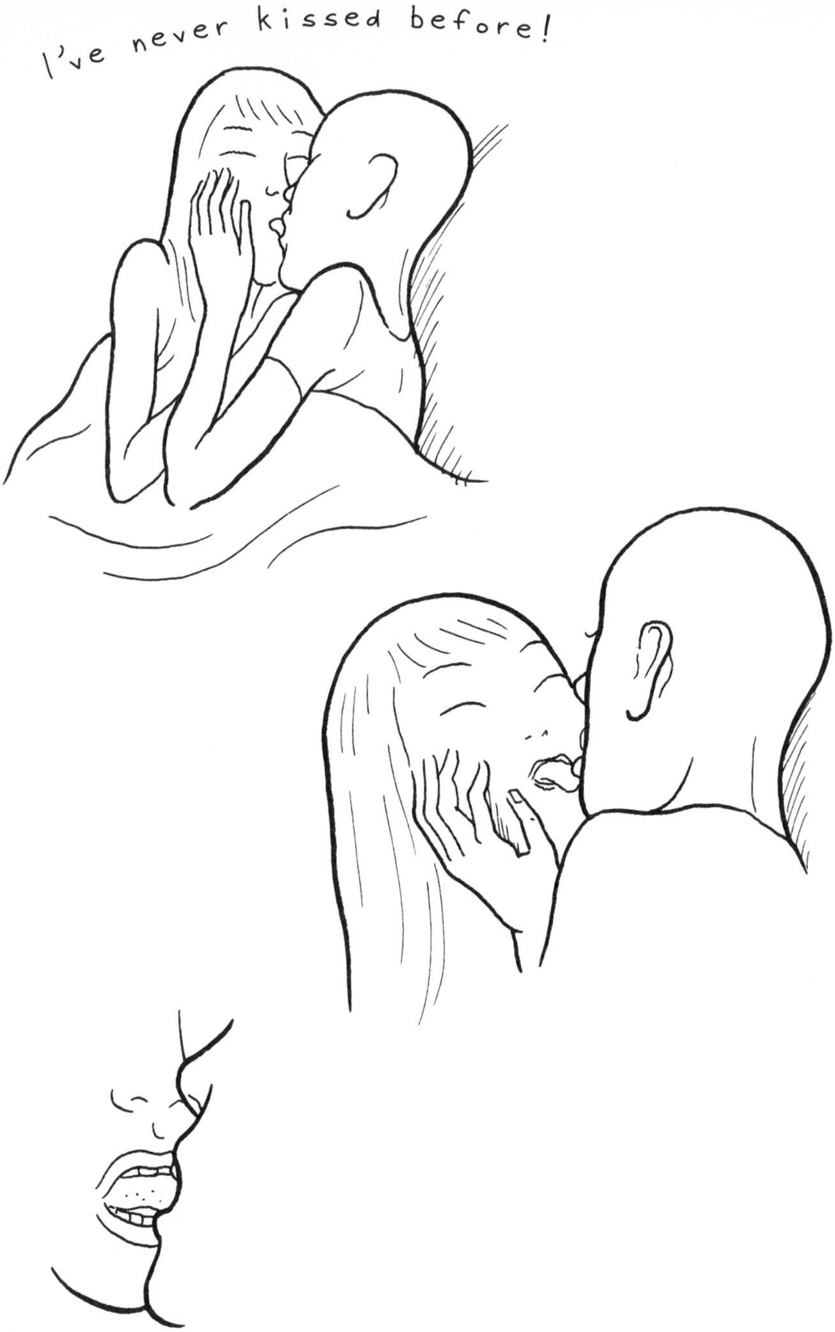
I've never kissed before!

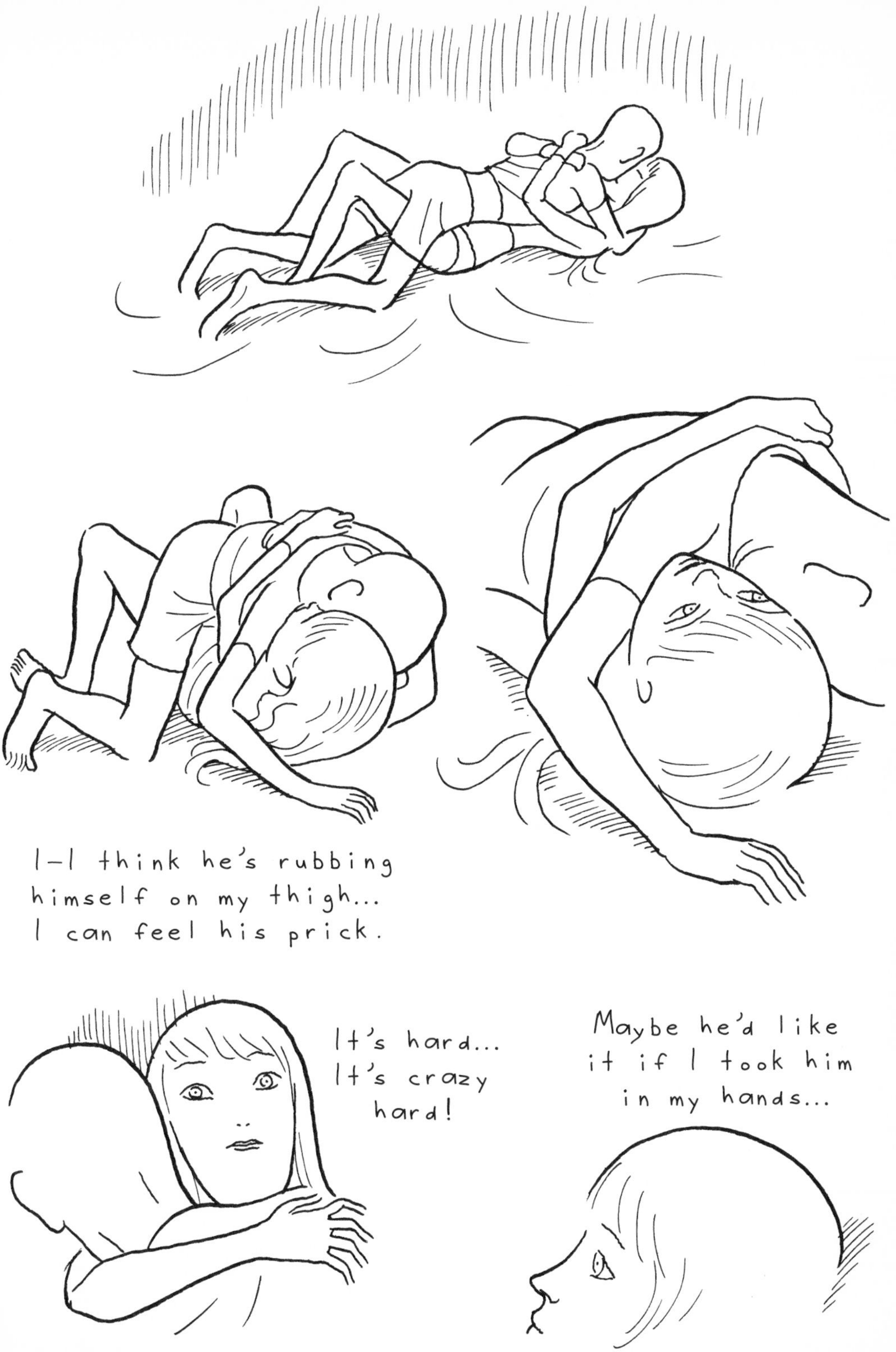
I-I think he's rubbing himself on my thigh... I can feel his prick.
It's hard... It's crazy hard!
Maybe he'd like it if I took him in my hands...

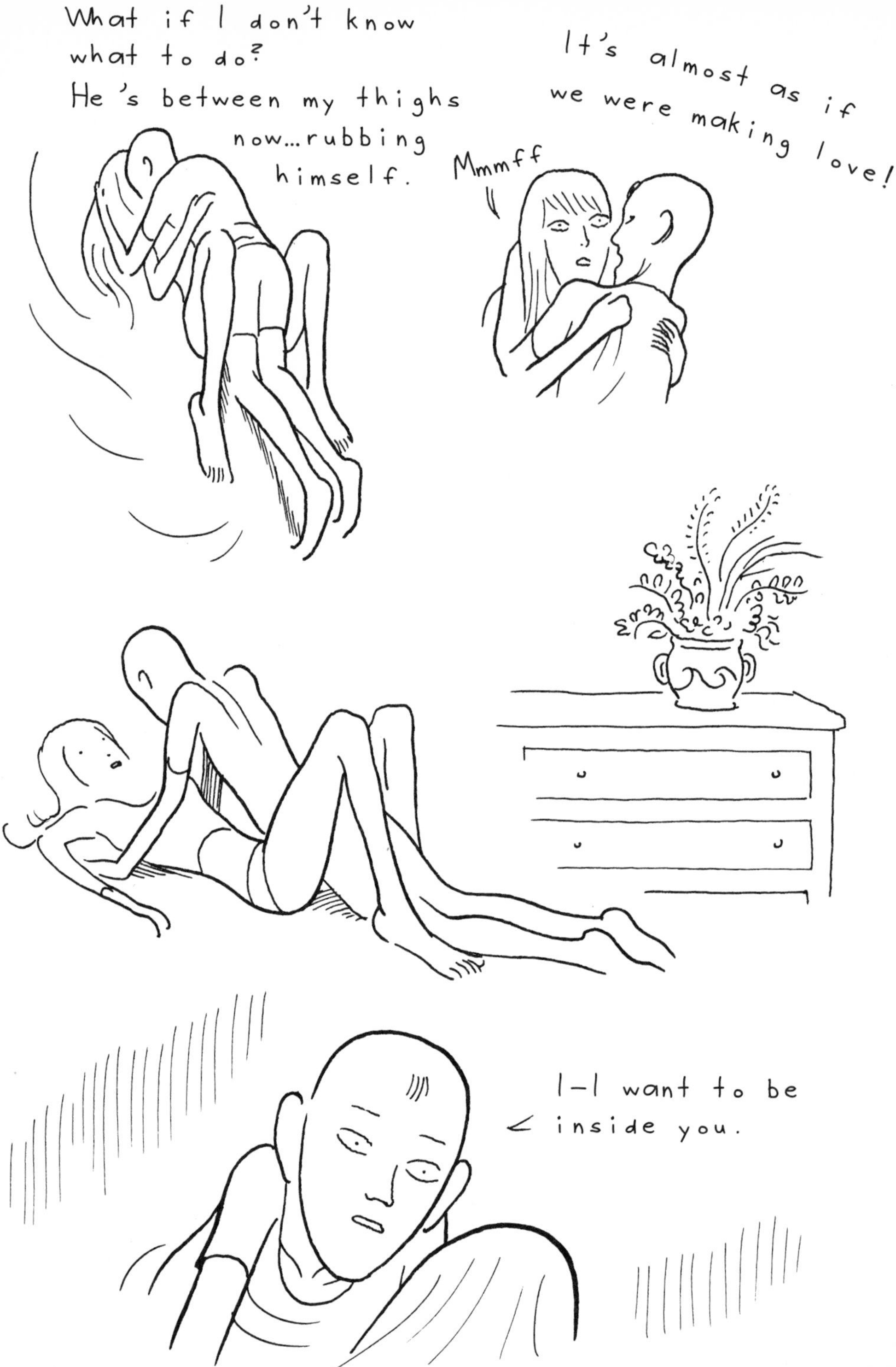
What if I don't know what to do?
He's between my thighs now...rubbing himself.
Mmmff
It's almost as if we were making love!
I-I want to be inside you.

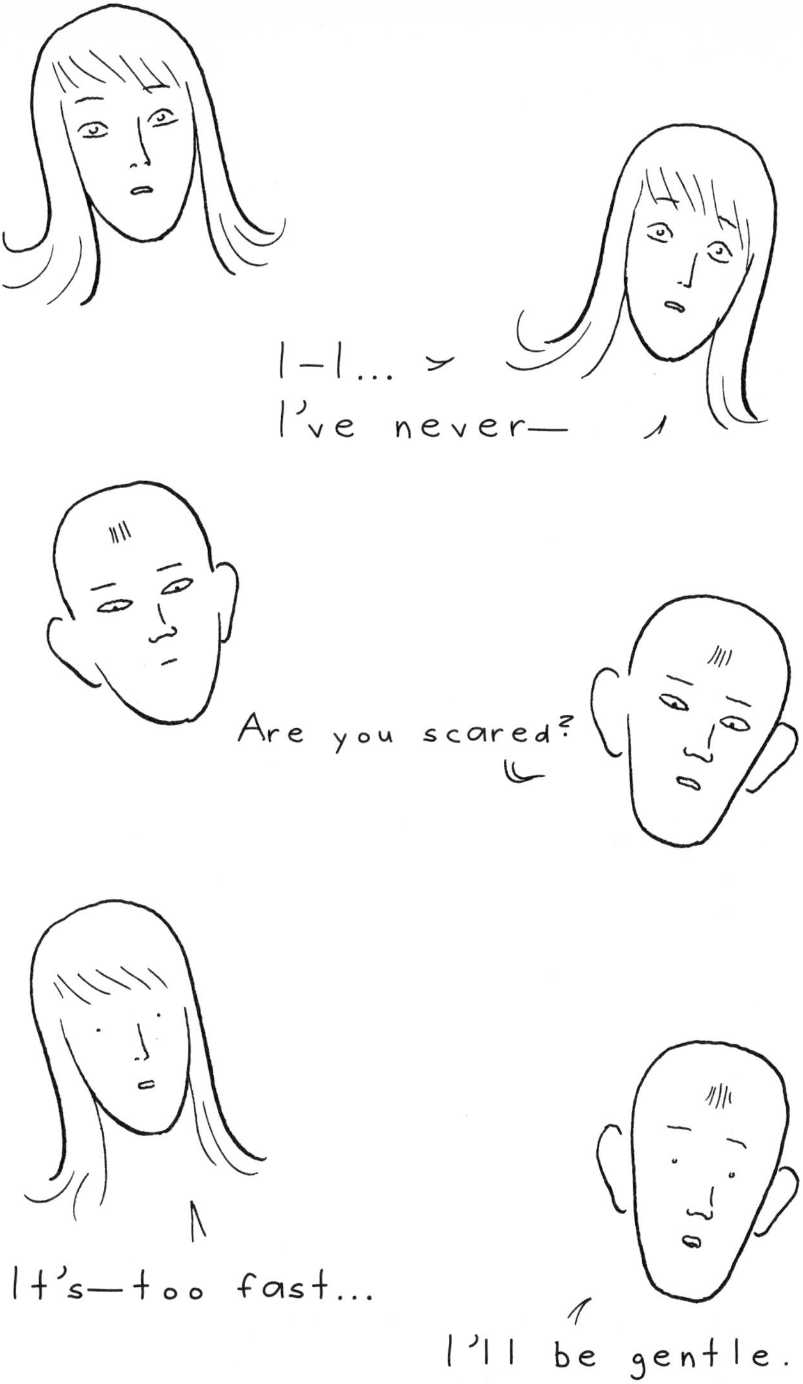
I–I...
I've never—
Are you scared?
It's—too fast...
I'll be gentle.

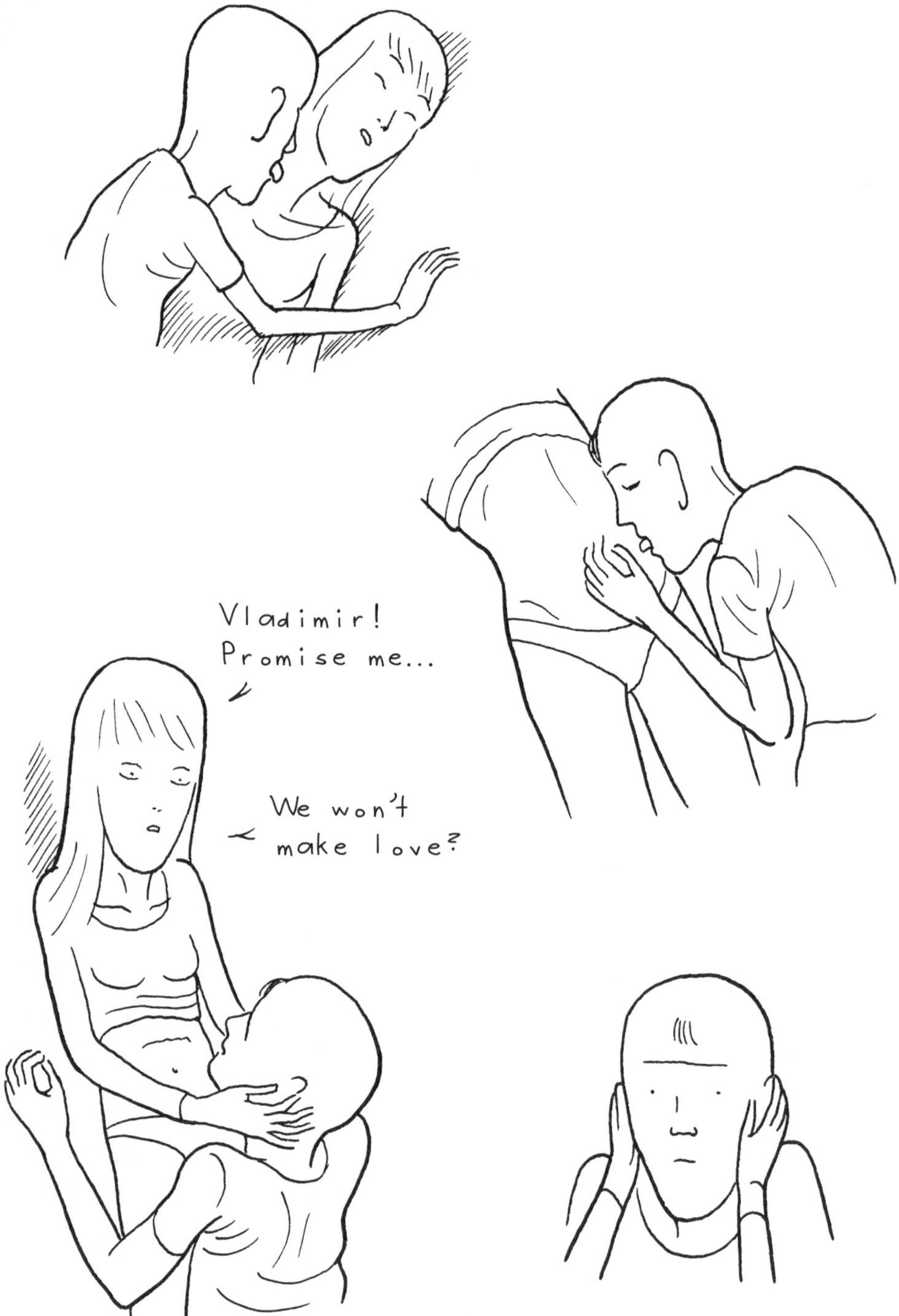
Vladimir! Promise me...
We won't make love?

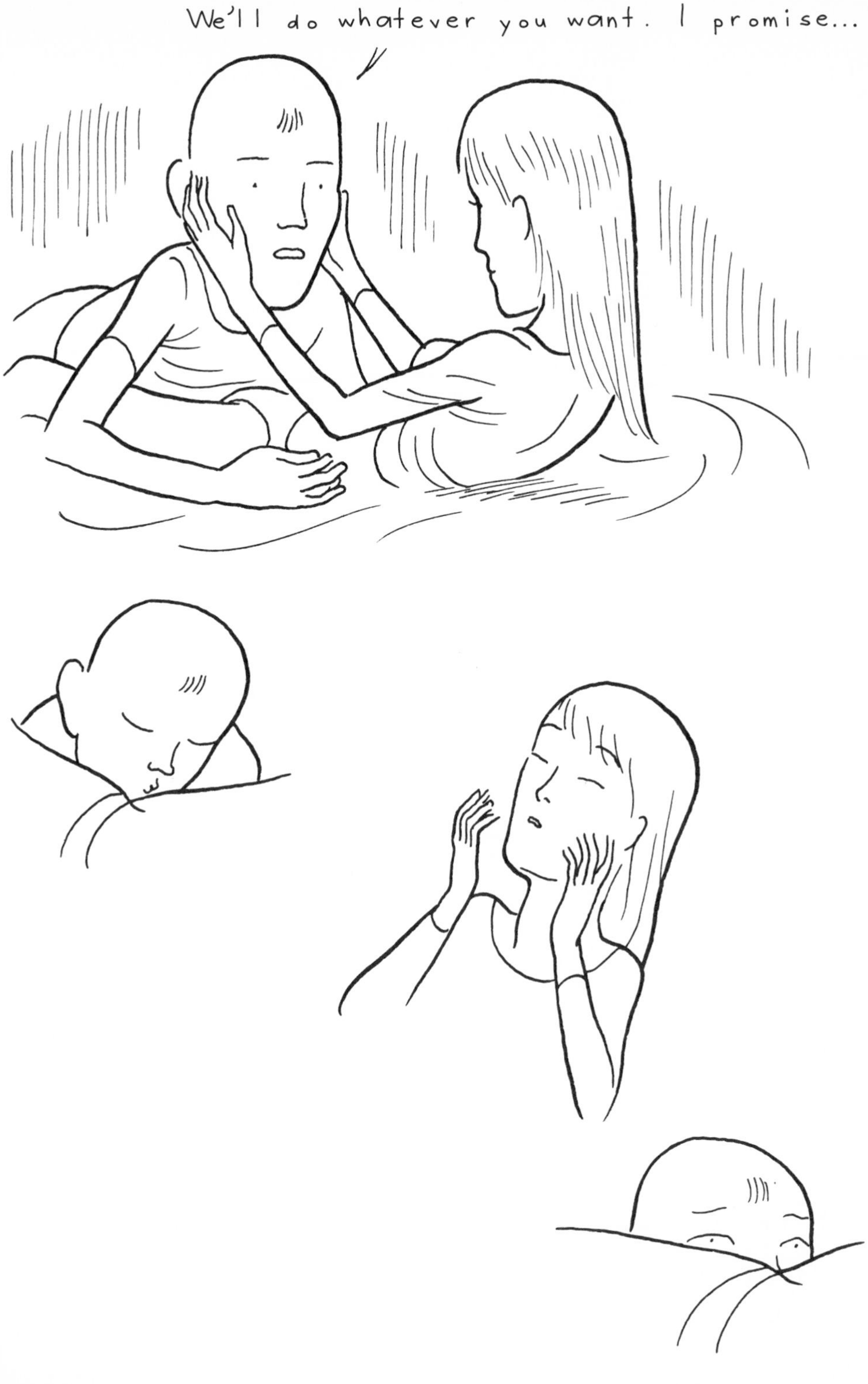
We'll do whatever you want. I promise...

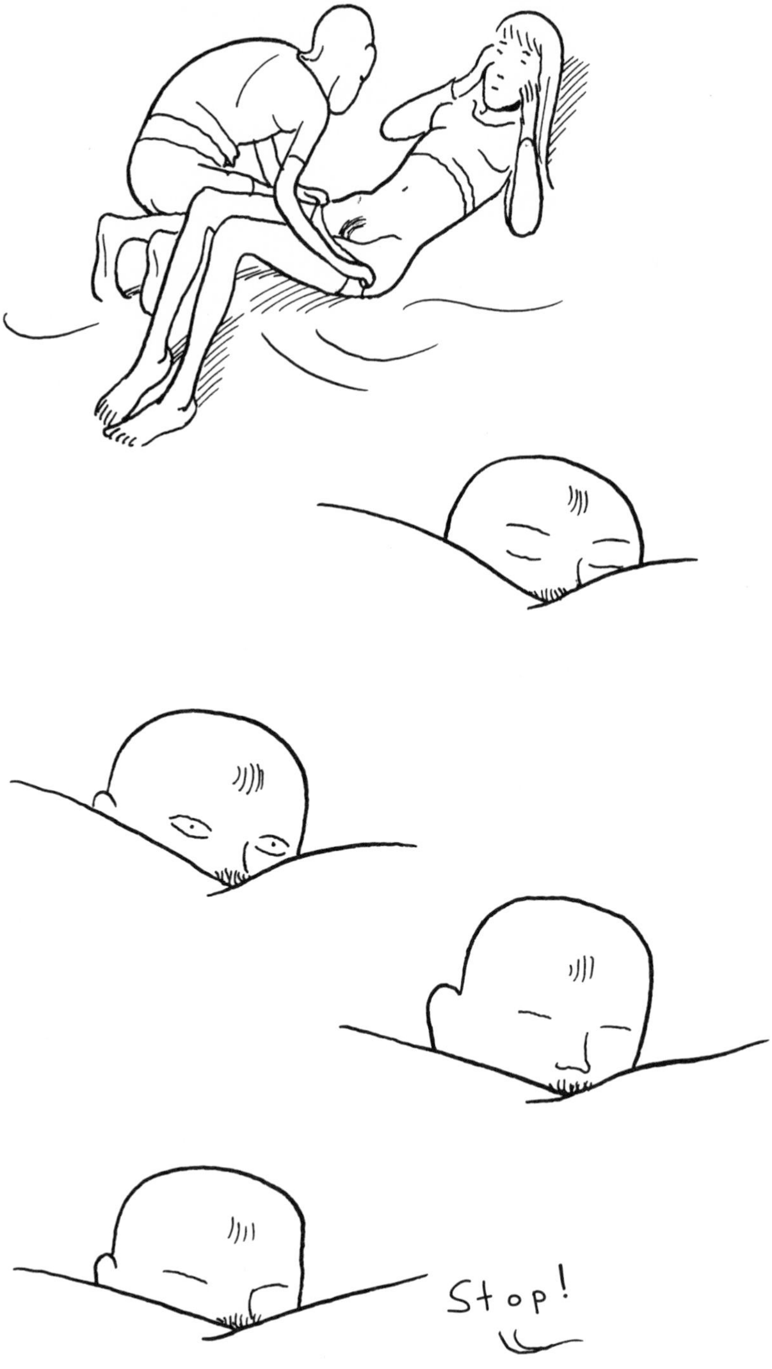
Stop!

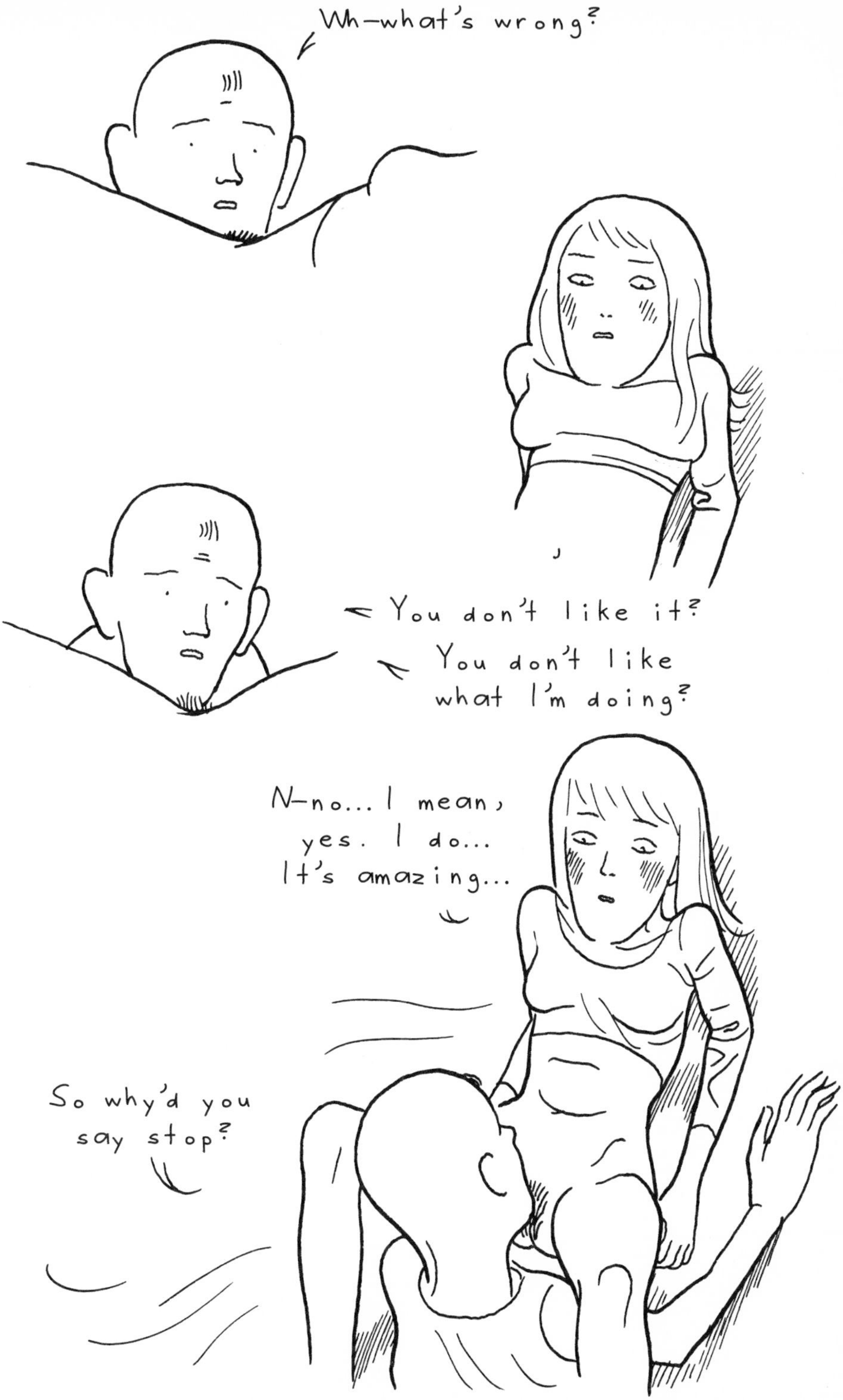
Wh-what's wrong?
You don't like it?
You don't like what I'm doing?
N-no... I mean, yes. I do... It's amazing...
So why'd you say stop?

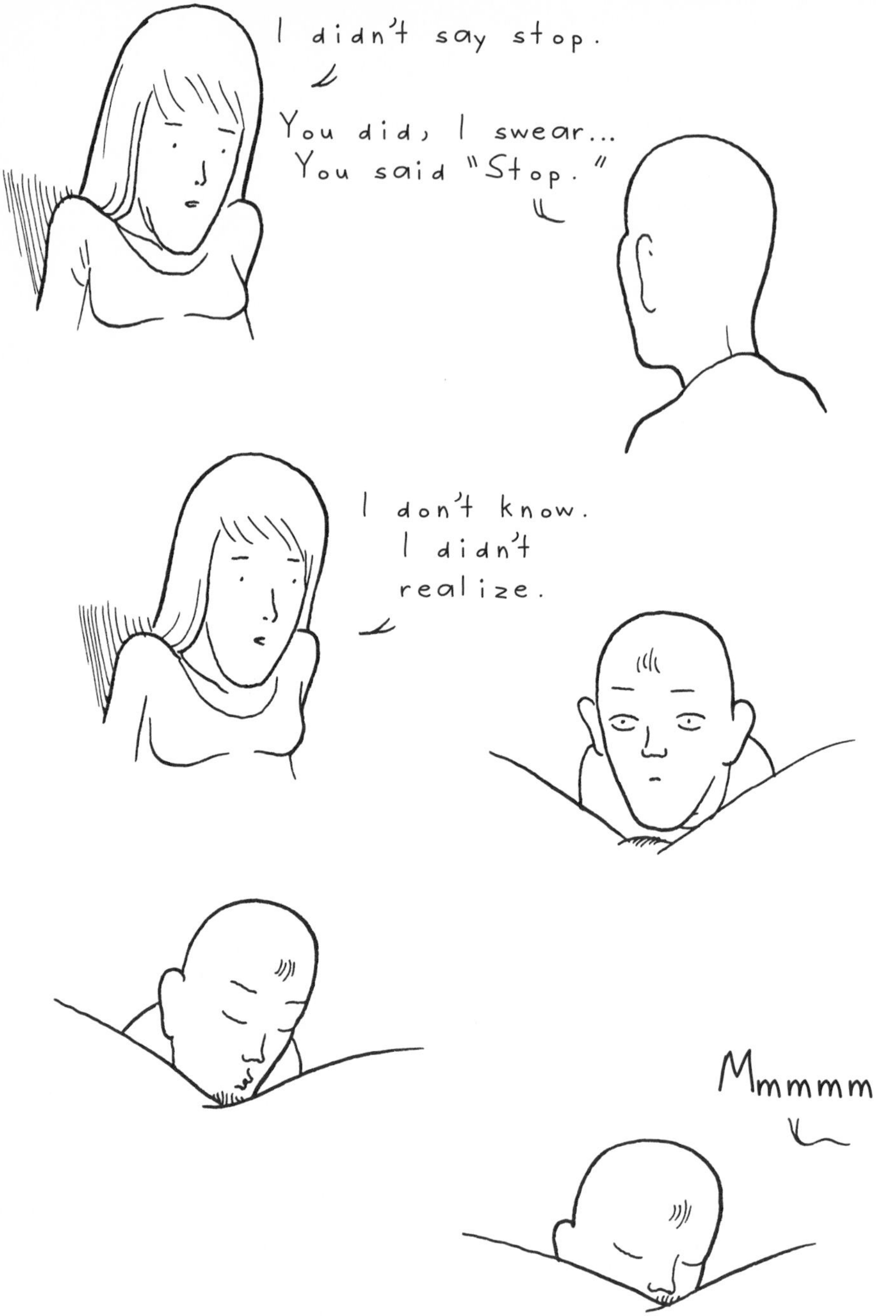

I didn't say stop.
You did, I swear... You said "Stop."
I don't know. I didn't realize.
Mmmmm

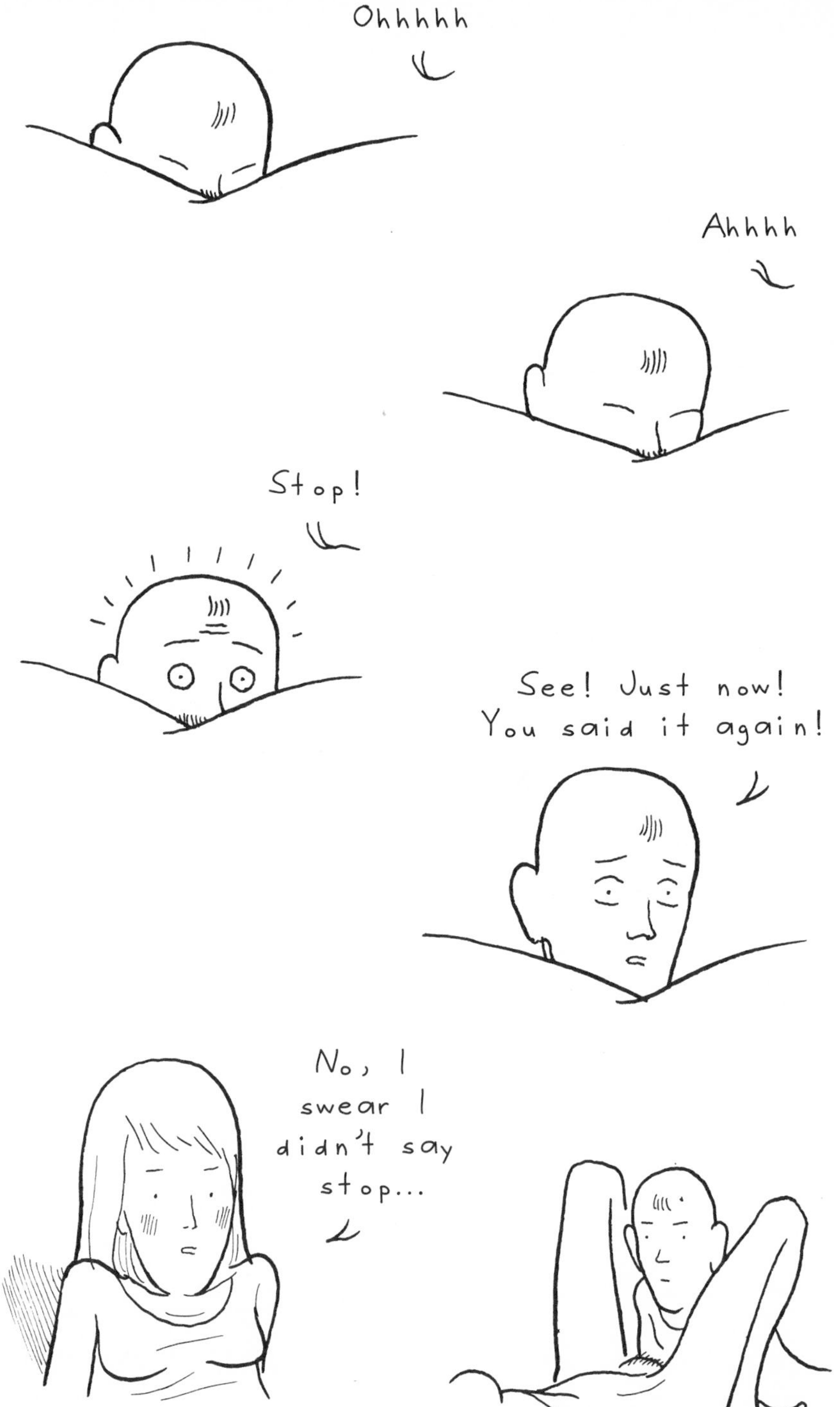
Ohhhhh
Ahhhh
Stop!
See! Just now! You said it again!
No, I swear I didn't say stop...

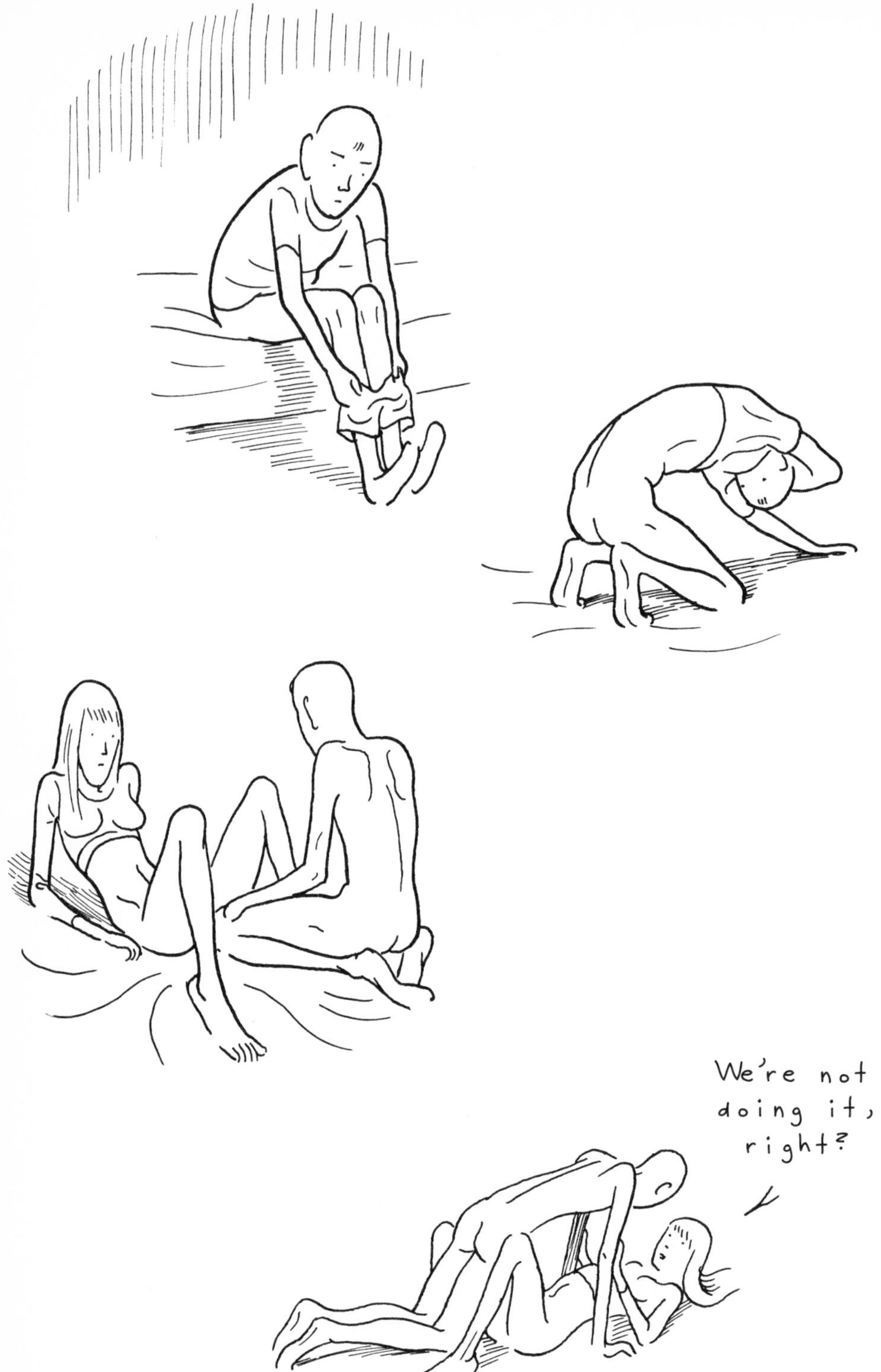
We're not doing it, right?

No, we're just—rubbing...

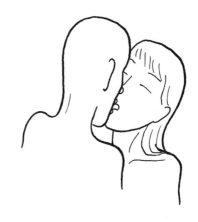

His prick presses against me! Right up against me...

There's nothing between us anymore. No more fabric...just skin.

I can almost catch him between my lips...

I've imagined this a thousand times. Here it is...now...

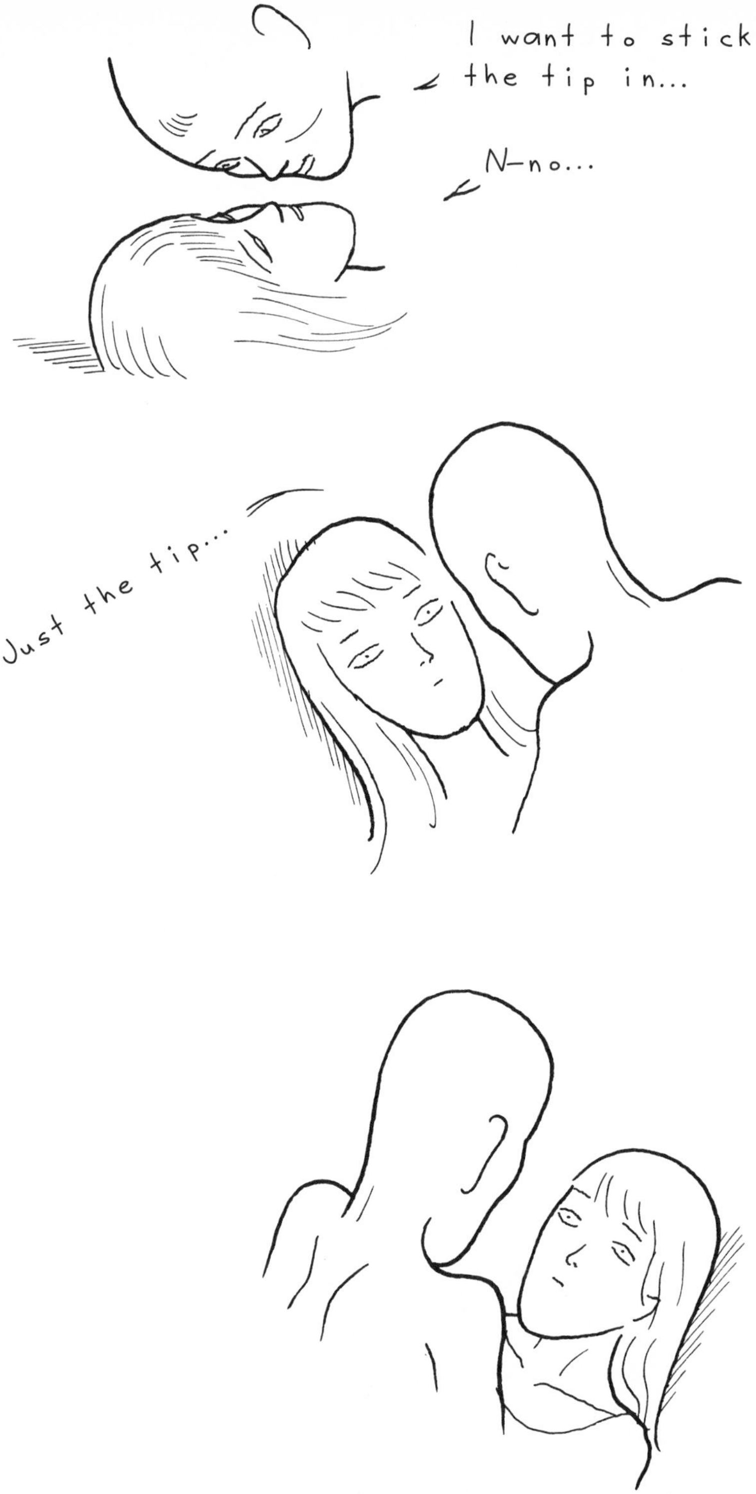
I want to stick the tip in...
N-no...
Just the tip...

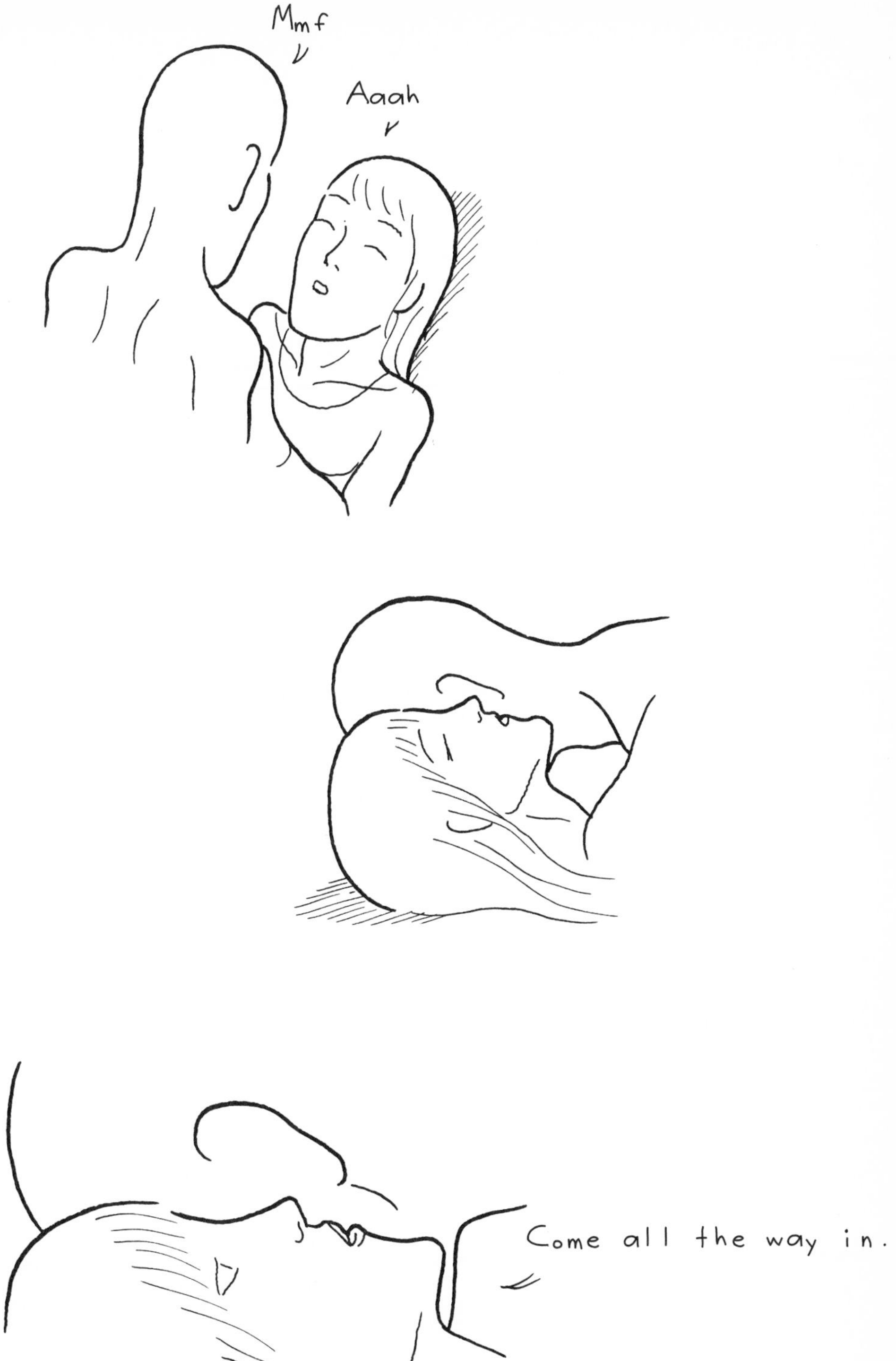
Mmf
Aaah
Come all the way in.

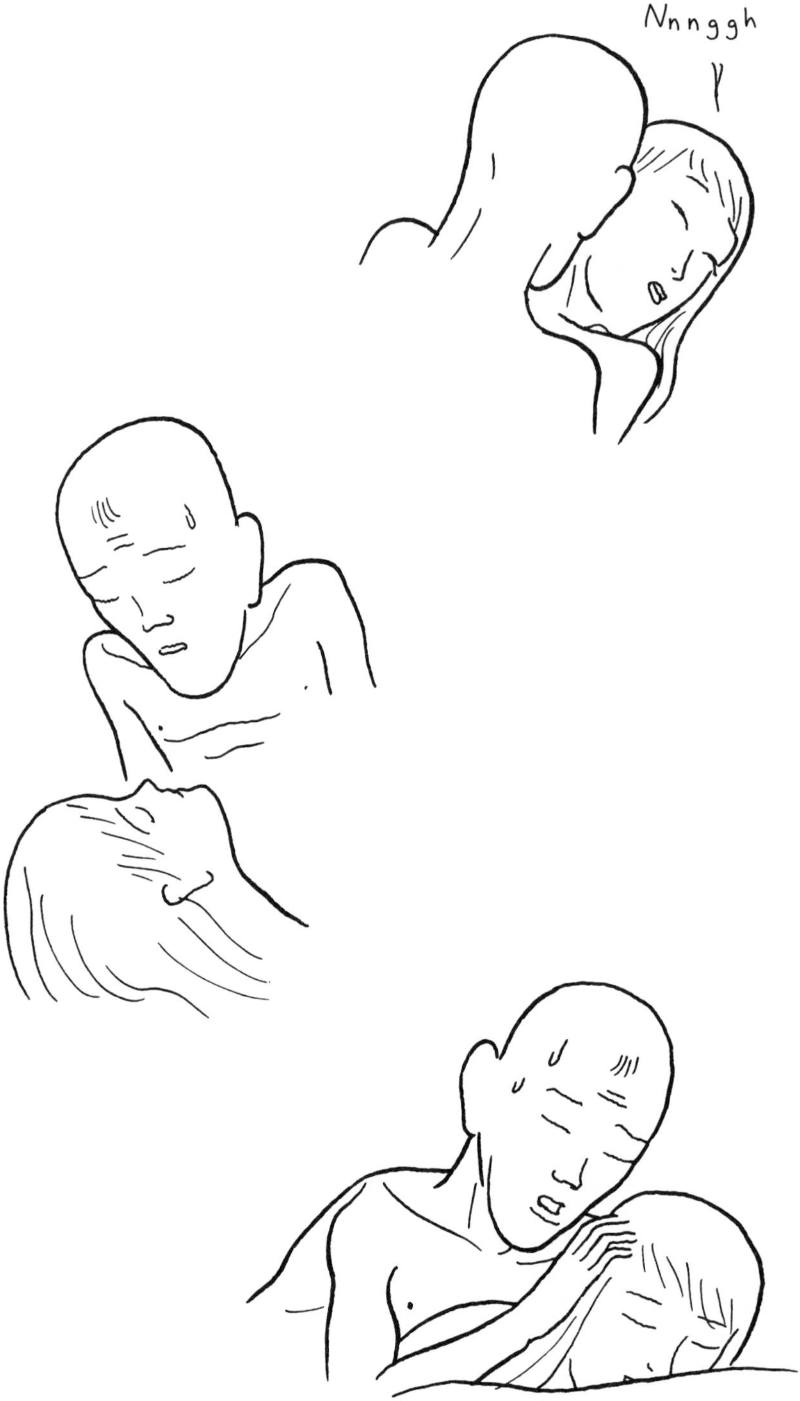
Nnnggh

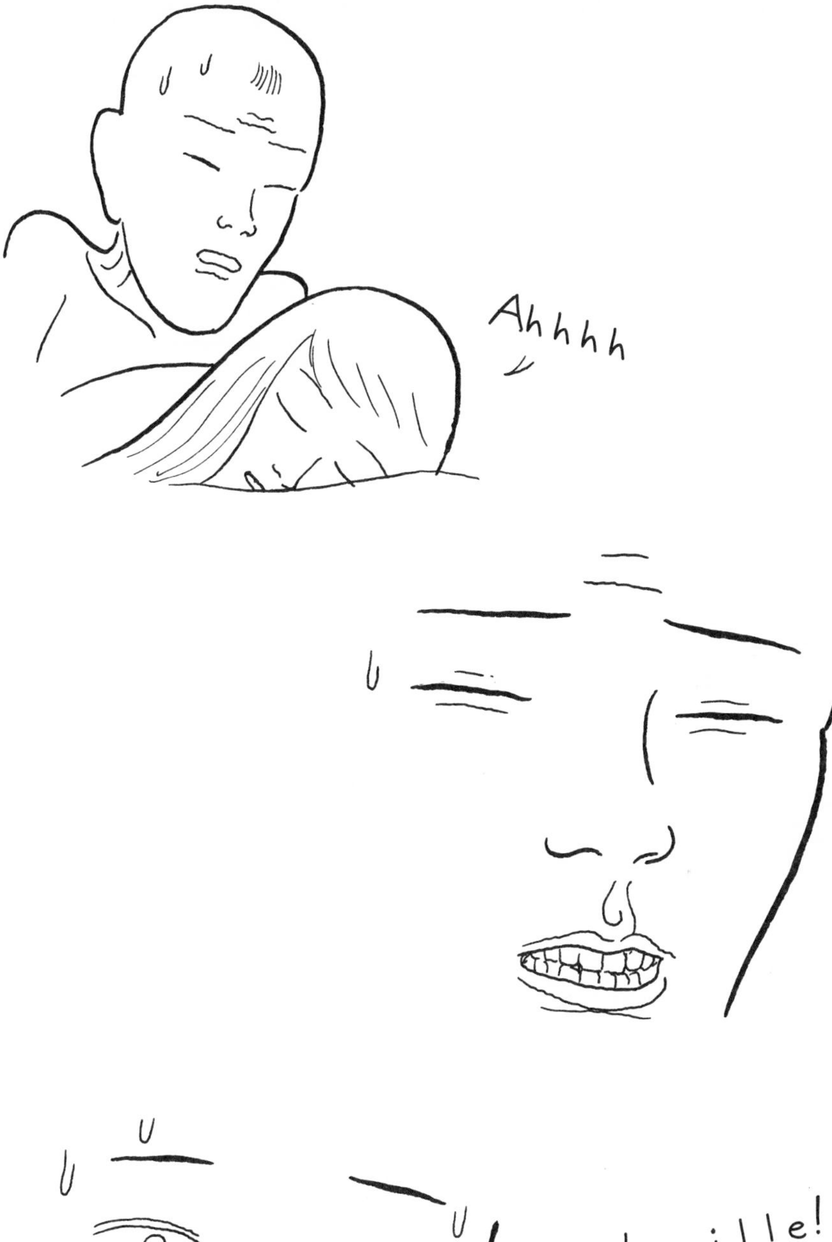
Ahhhh
Lucille!

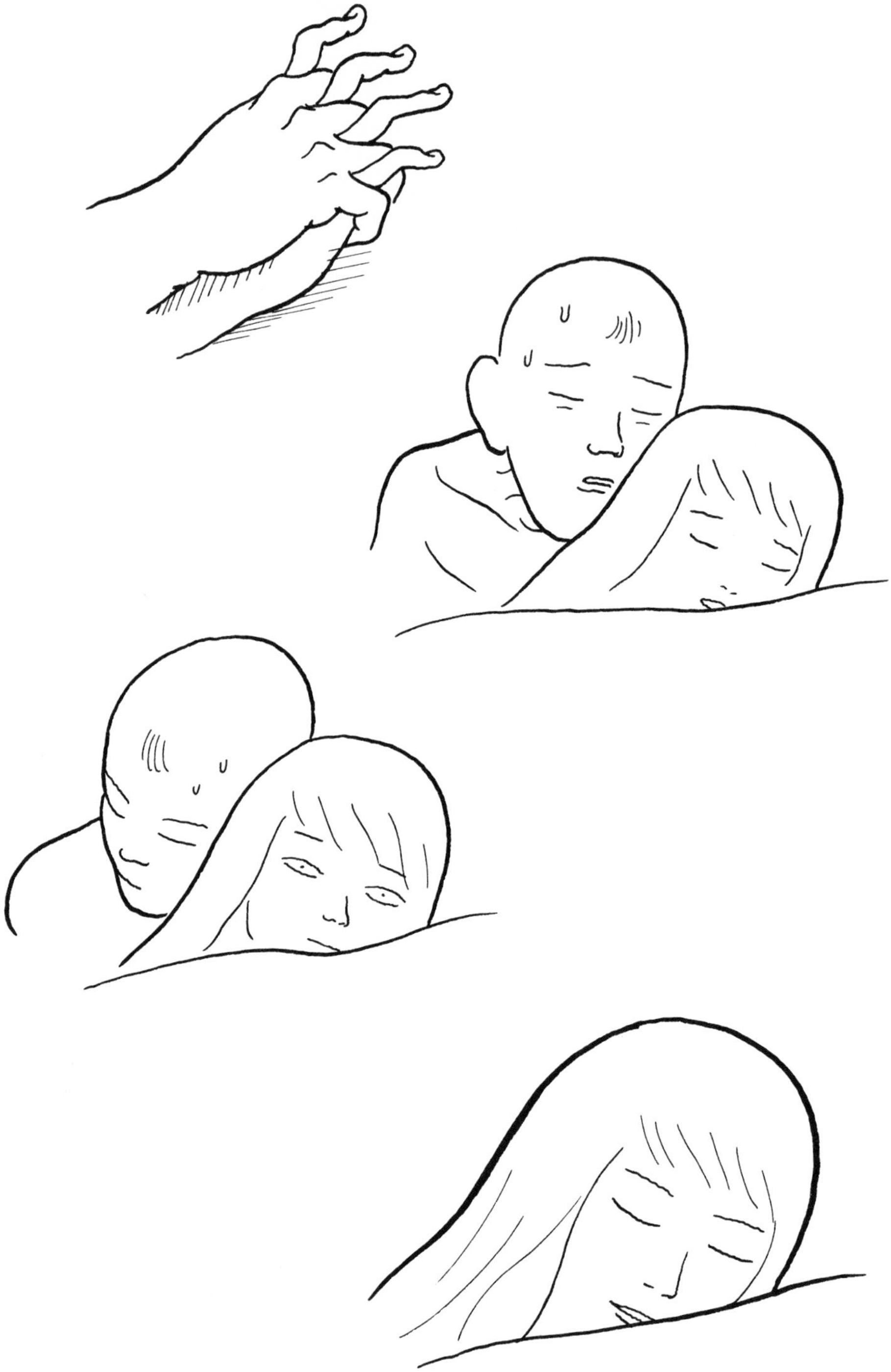

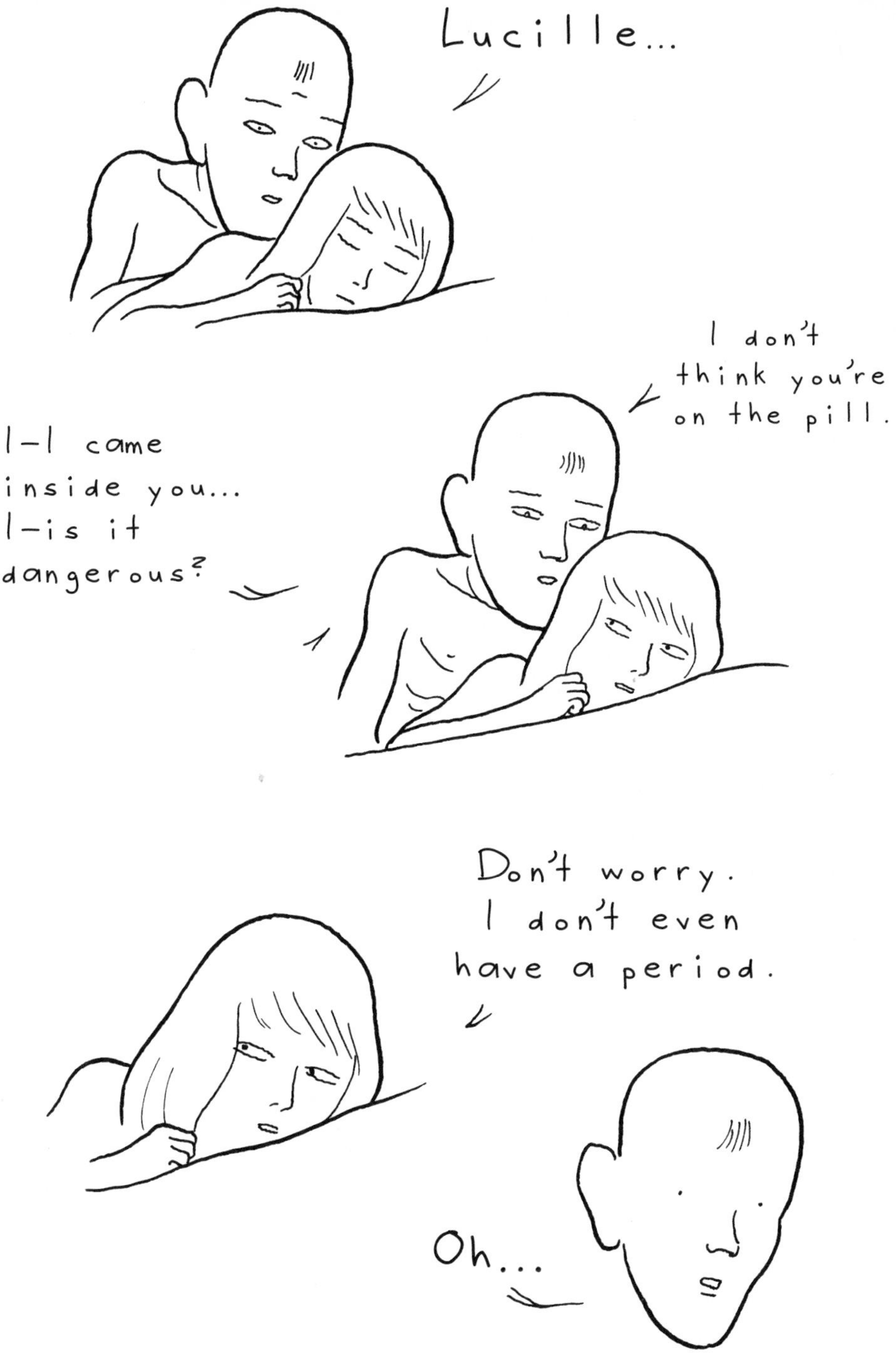
Lucille...
I don't think you're on the pill.
I-I came inside you... I-is it dangerous?
Don't worry. I don't even have a period.
Oh...

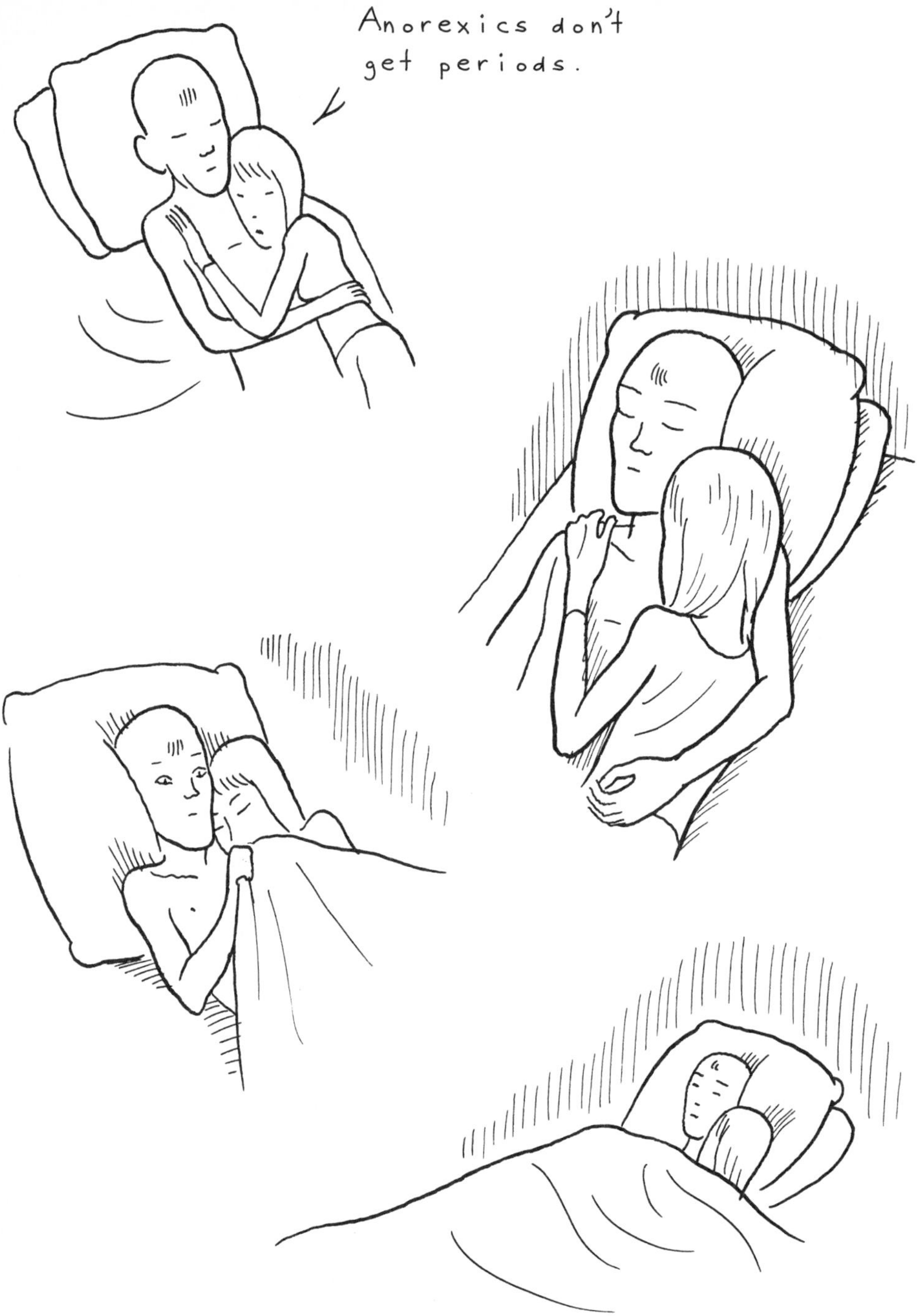
Anorexics don't get periods.

That Night...

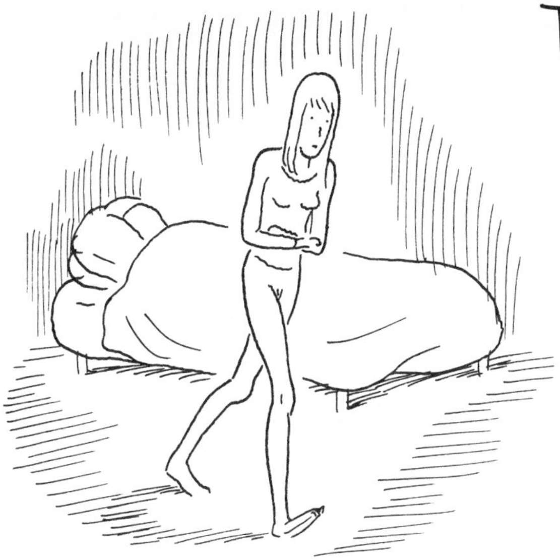

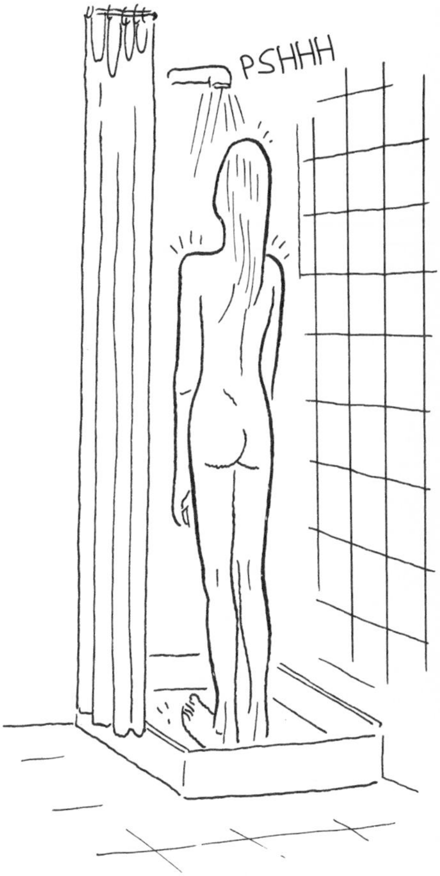
PSHHH

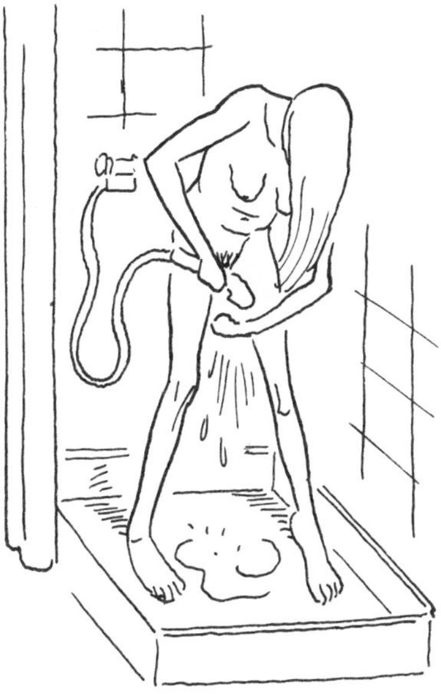

I showered for a long time...

I don't know if there's much left inside.

In the water was a mixture of sperm and blood.

This morning the owner called som important people in the area who often hire young people for the month.

Her husband will accompany us. It's on his delivery route.

These people are nice...

I miss my mother. I'm scared of causing her so much pain. I want to call her, even if I know Vladimir wouldn't want it.
He says that afterwards, they'd be able to find us.

TOSCANA

(Tuscany)

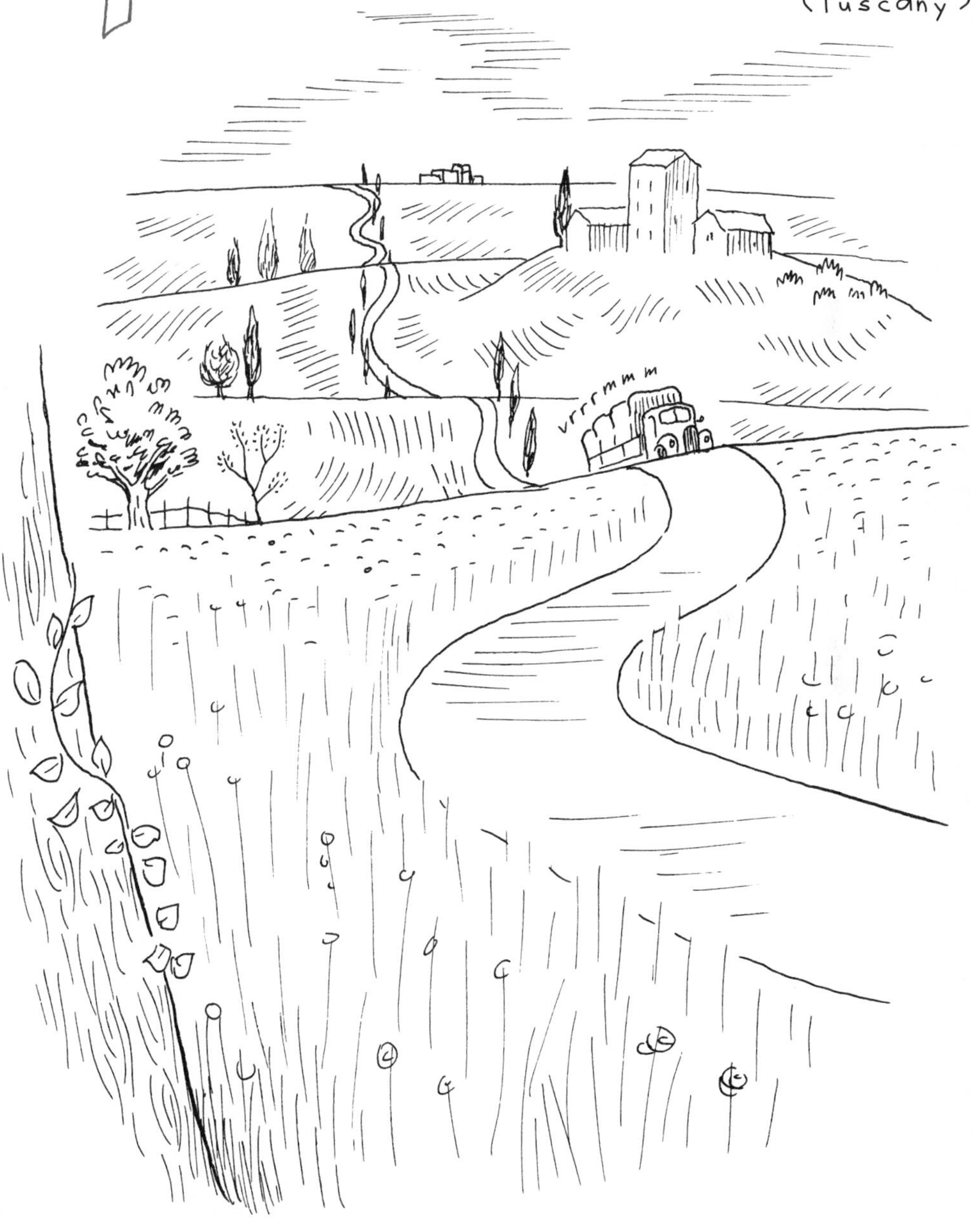

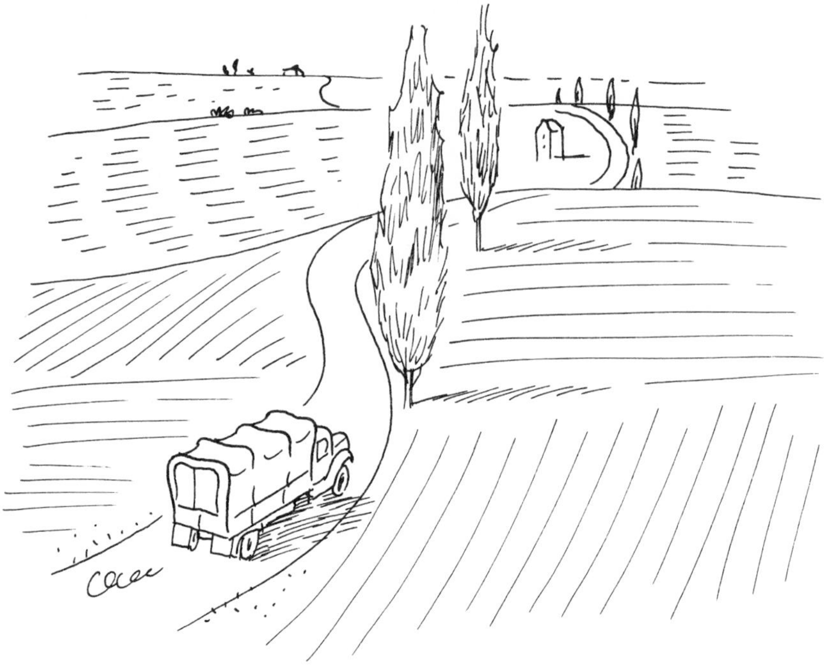

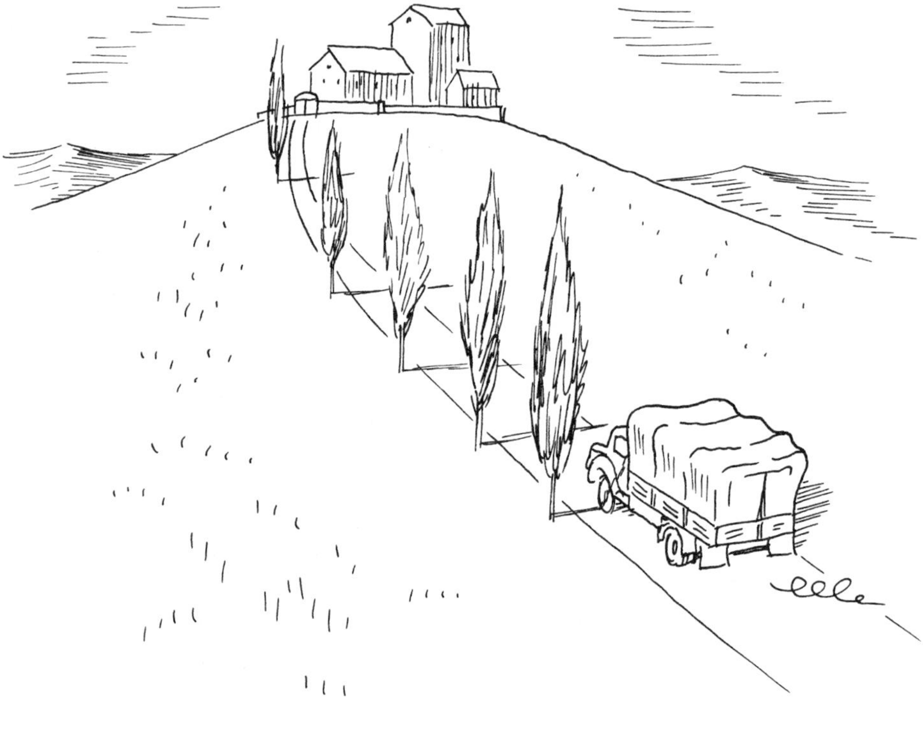

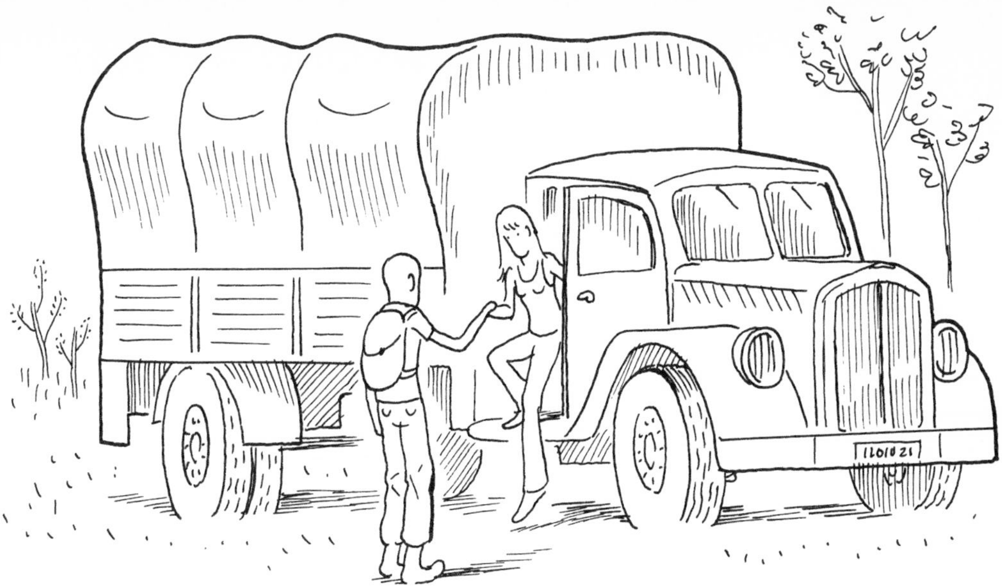

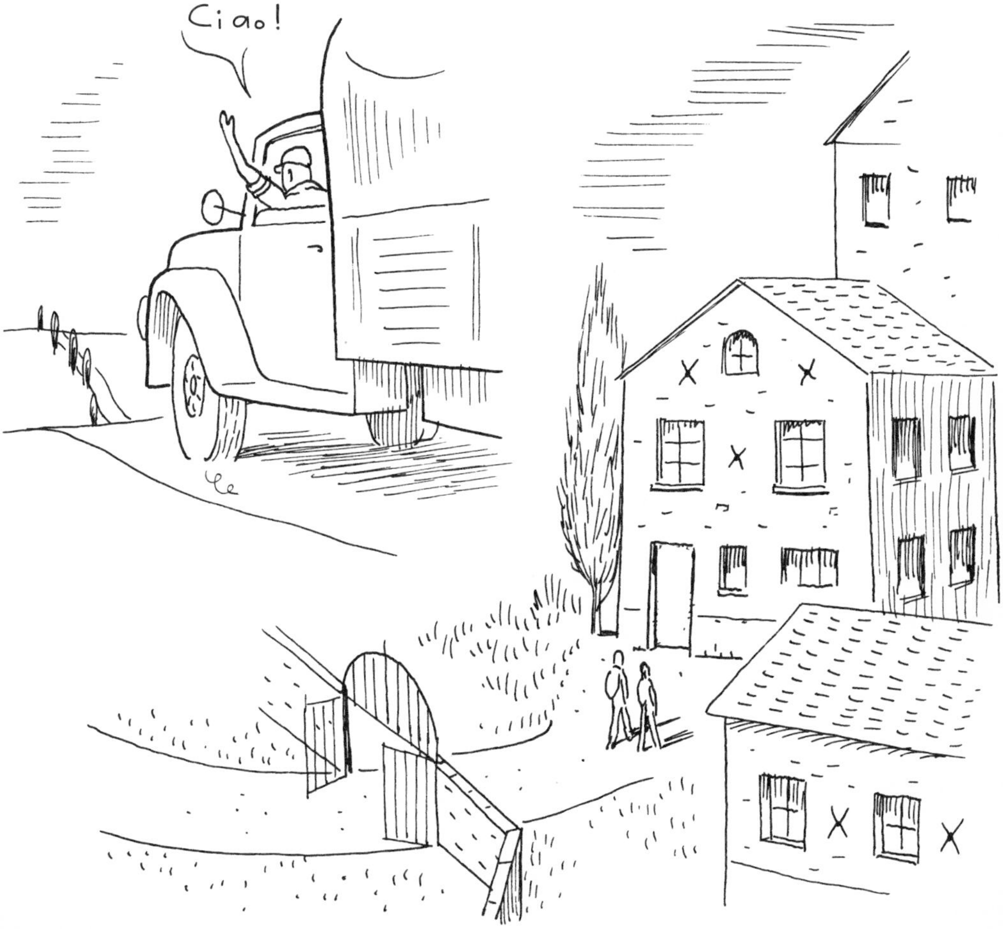
Ciao!

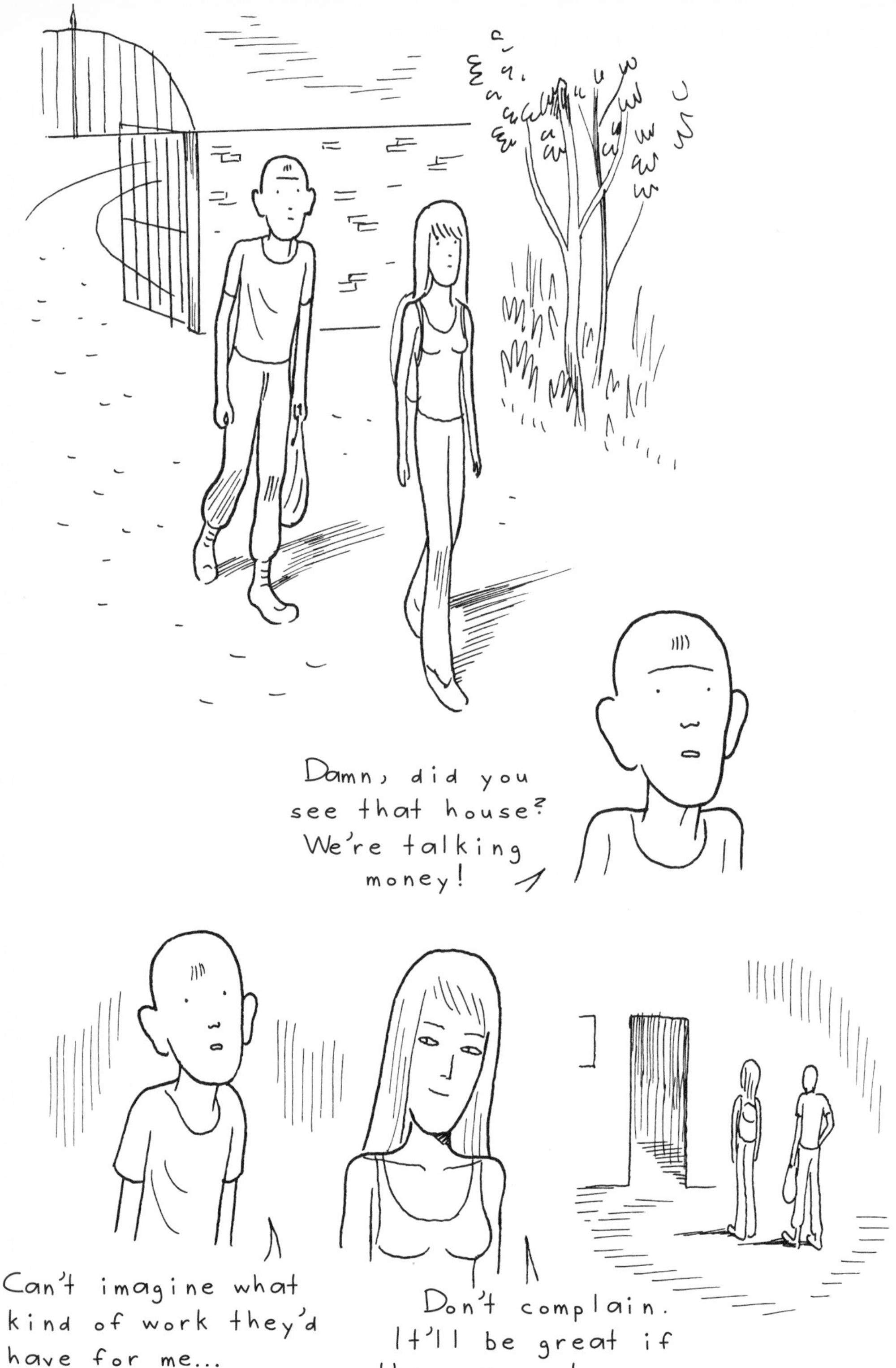
Damn, did you see that house? We're talking money!
Can't imagine what kind of work they'd have for me...
Don't complain. It'll be great if they can put us up.

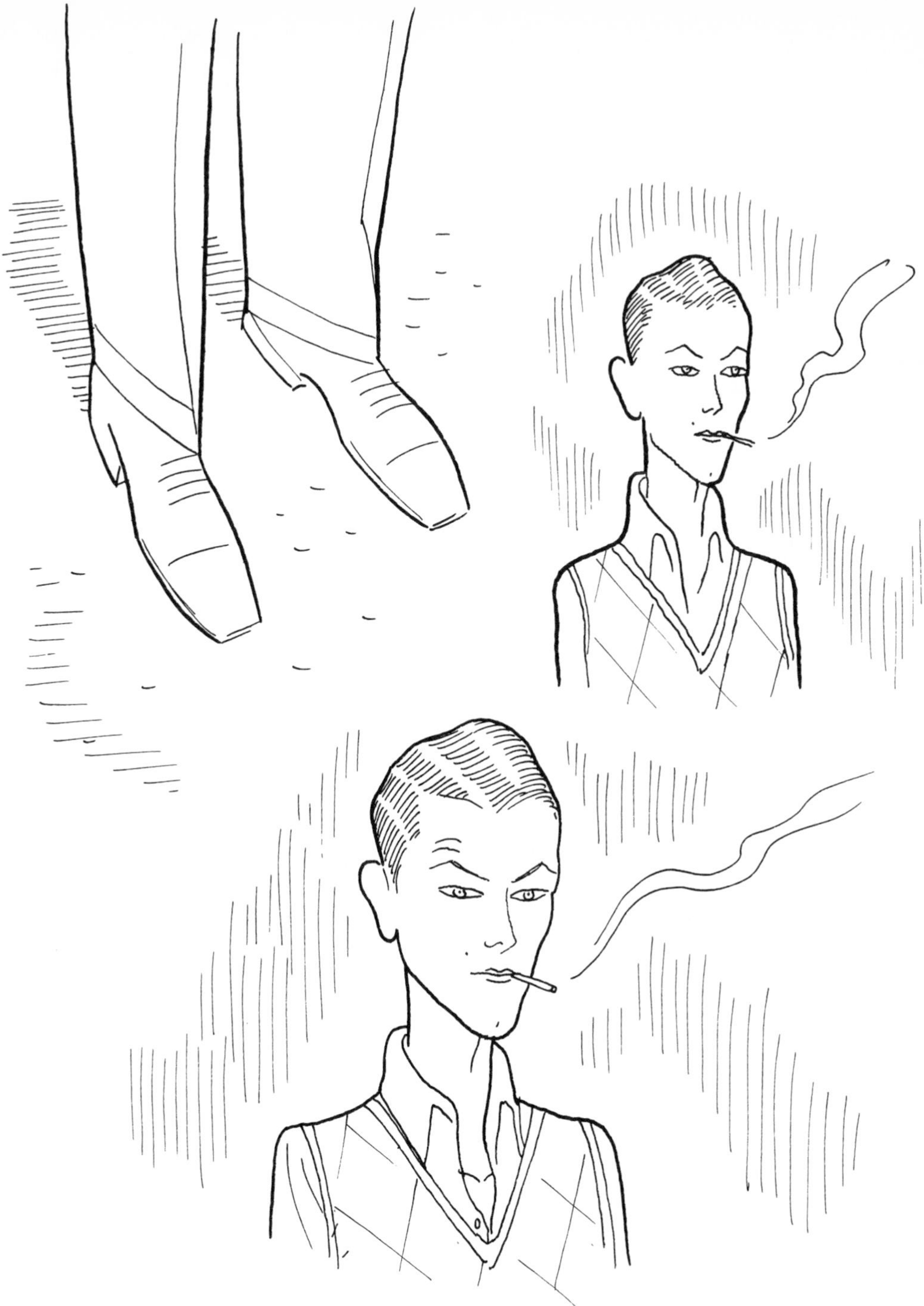

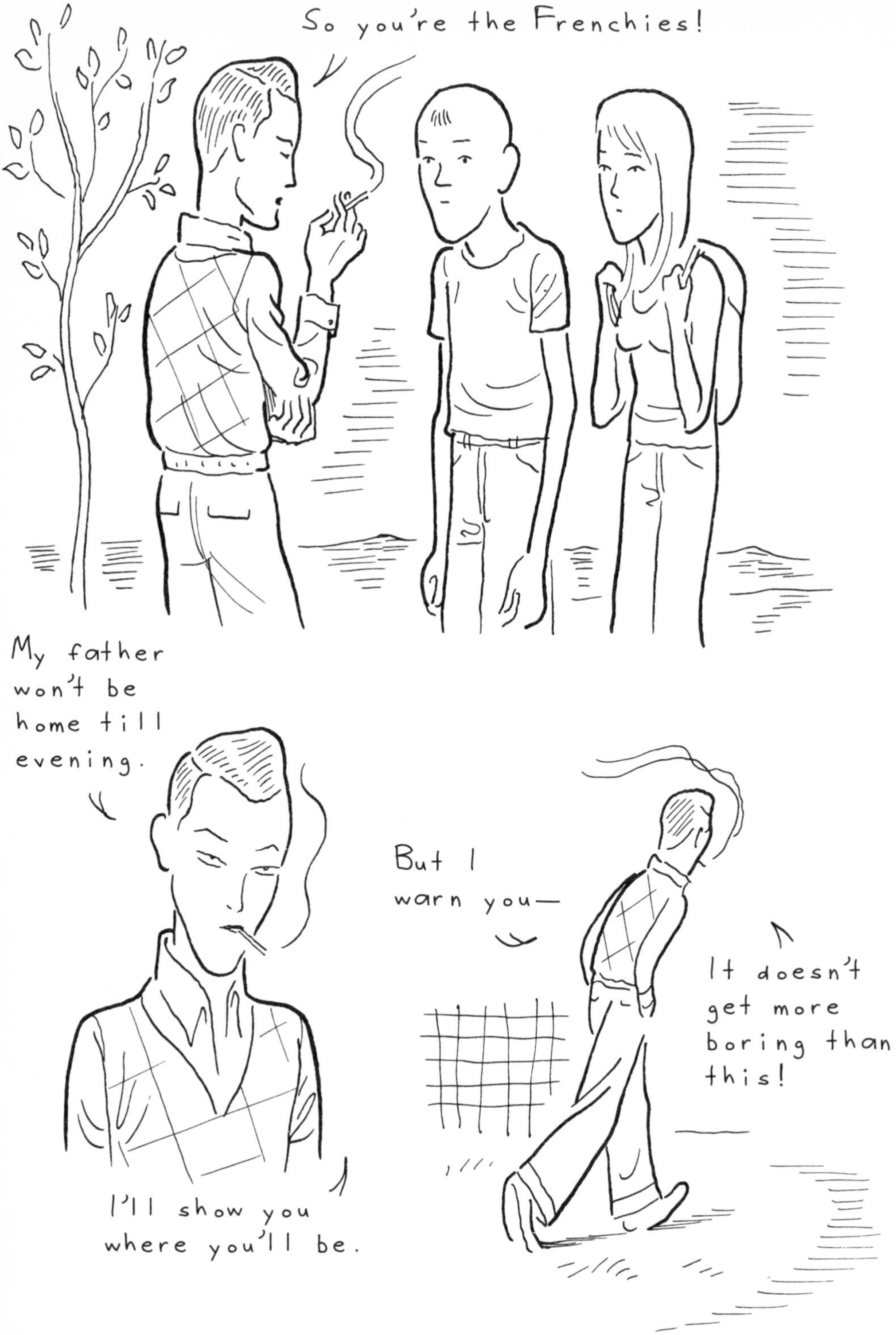
So you're the Frenchies!
My father won't be home till evening.
I'll show you where you'll be.
But I warn you—
It doesn't get more boring than this!

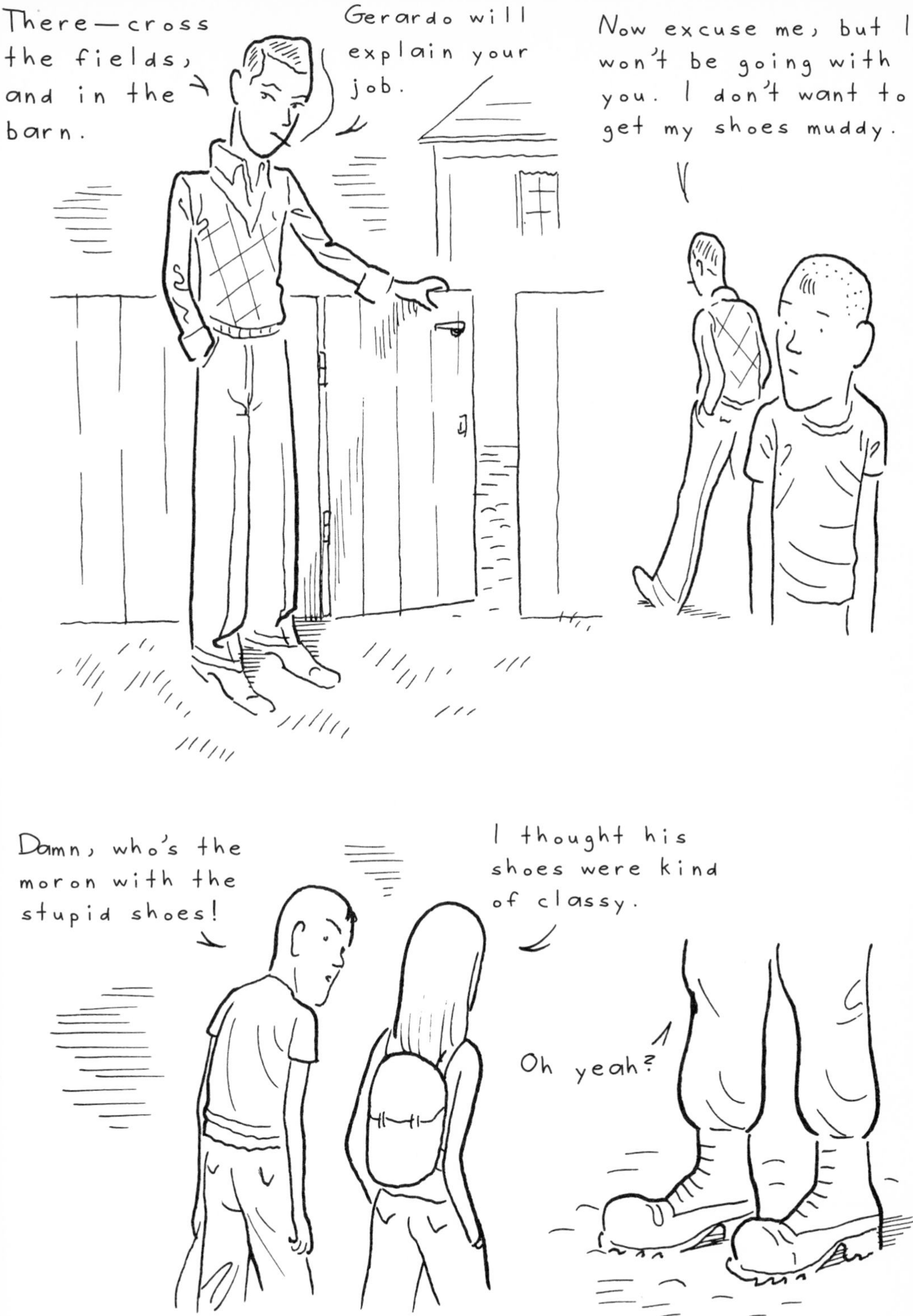
There—cross the fields, and in the barn.
Gerardo will explain your job.
Now excuse me, but I won't be going with you. I don't want to get my shoes muddy.
Damn, who's the moron with the stupid shoes!
I thought his shoes were kind of classy.
Oh yeah?

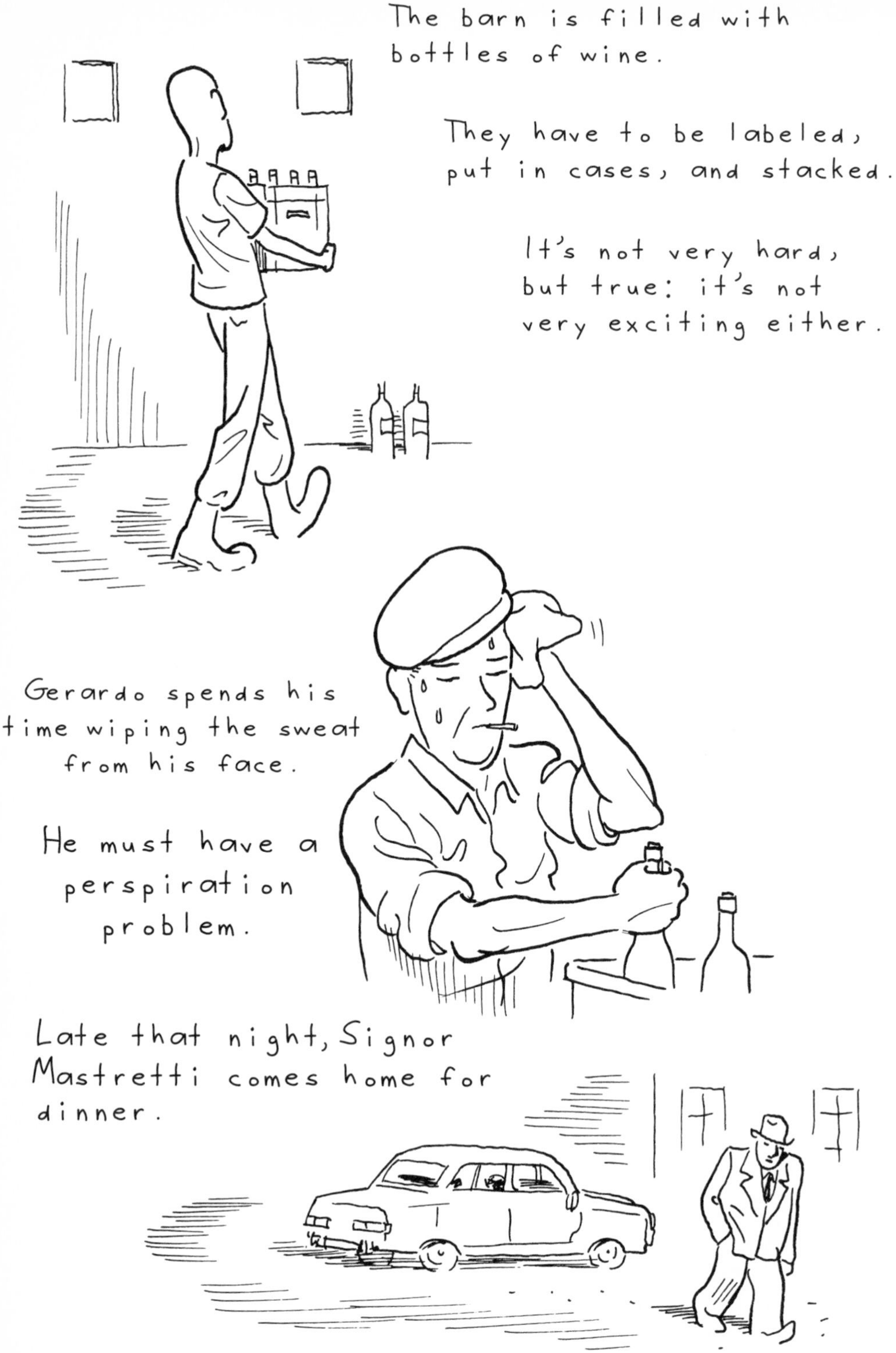
The barn is filled with bottles of wine.
They have to be labeled, put in cases, and stacked.
It's not very hard, but true: it's not very exciting either.
Gerardo spends his time wiping the sweat from his face.
He must have a perspiration problem.
Late that night, Signor Mastretti comes home for dinner.

We have to eat with everyone...I don't know how I'll manage. I'm frightened.

At the table are Adolpho—

But I gather he's rarely at dinner... Usually he goes out with his friends from the city.

There's Gerardo, who sweats in his soup like a piglet.

Clarissa, Adolpho's sister. She looks daggers at me whenever our gazes cross.

Signora Mastretti, who must be charged taxes for smiling...

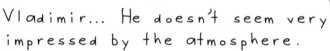

Vladimir... He doesn't seem very impressed by the atmosphere.

I think he's pretty used to Italian food now.

I've already managed to put half my meal in my napkin, under the table.

...and Signor Mastretti.

At one point, they start talking really loud and fast...

I'm not sure I caught it all. But I think Signor Mastretti wasn't happy at all to learn that his son—in addition to the theatre courses he's been taking for two years now—has decided to leave for France to study acting.

At the Cours Florent.

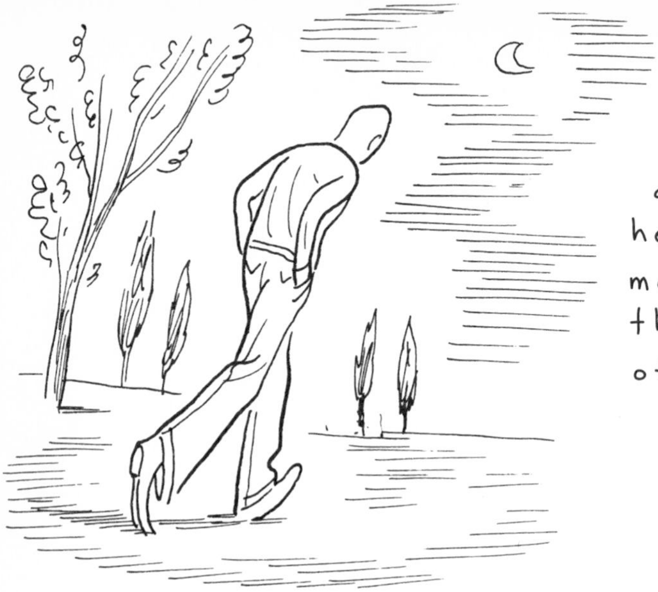

Adolpho left, slamming the door and saying he now had enough money saved up so that his old fart of a dad couldn't piss him off anymore.

Afterwards, Signora Mastretti started waving her hands around really fast while explaining to her husband that he was a peasant who'd never put up with the fact that his son had an artistic temperament...just like how he'd been with her. Her own sensitivity had long ago been trampled by her husband...

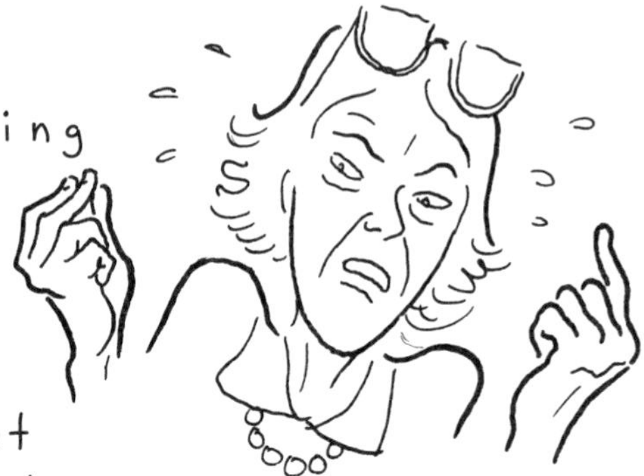

...she said.

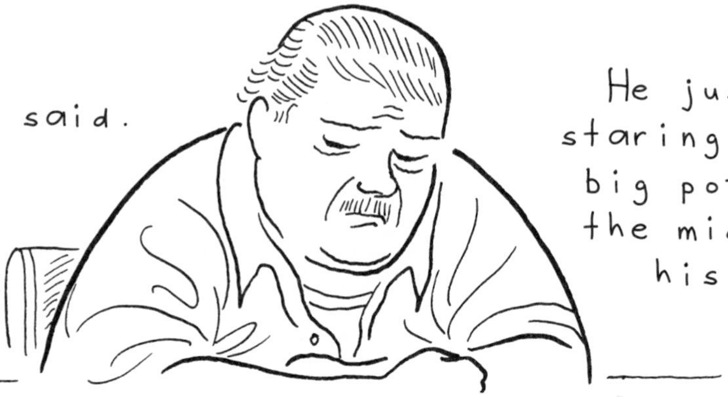

He just kept staring at the big potato in the middle of his plate.

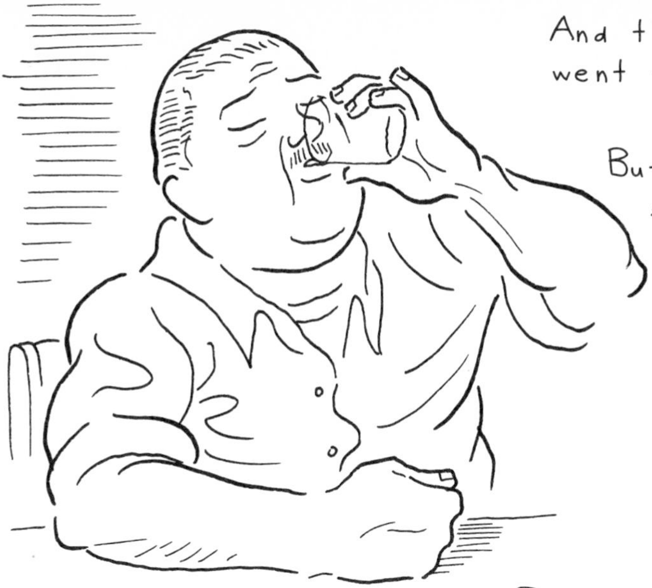

And then everyone went to bed.

But Signor Mastretti said he wanted to talk to us.

So we watched him down glass after glass.

He said we seemed like nice French kids, and that he liked Paris a lot.

That we shouldn't get the wrong idea... he had nothing against artists.

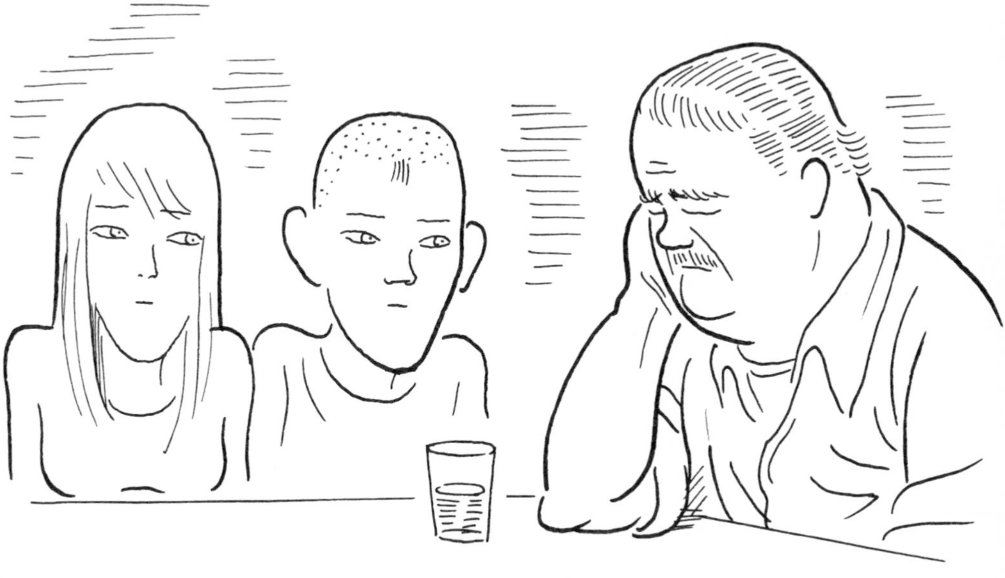

But that if his son became an actor, he'd have to sell his vineyard to a stranger when he grew too old.

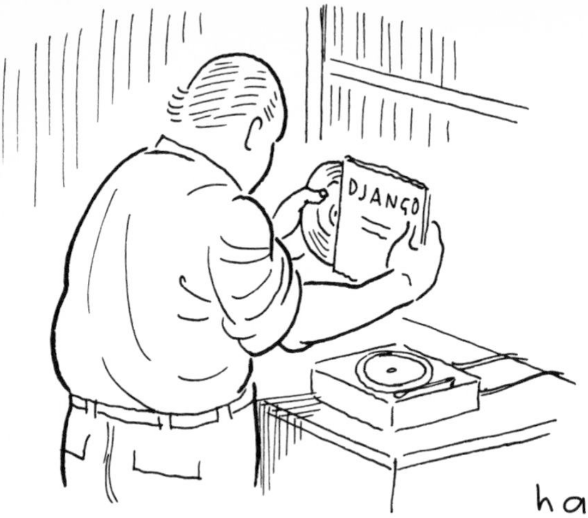
DJANGO

He also said he must have raised his son wrong, since he wasn't able to pass on a love of the vine.

And yet, the land had been handed down over so many generations...so that the blood of his ancestors was as much in the wine as the grapes.

After that, he put on a Django Reinhardt record.

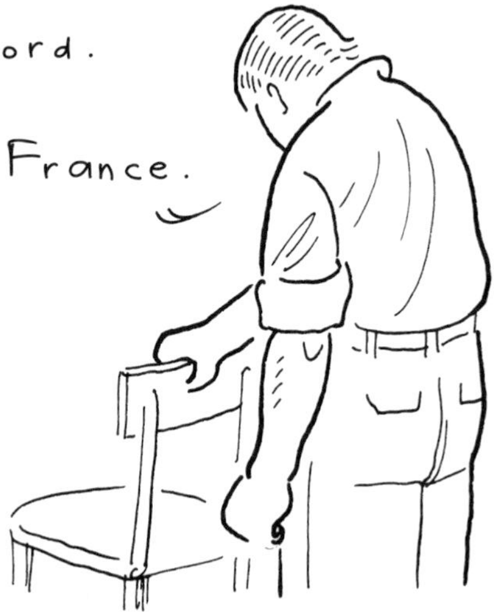
I love France.

Then he said his wife was a bitch and that we could go to bed.

We could see he was crying... but it was from the alcohol.

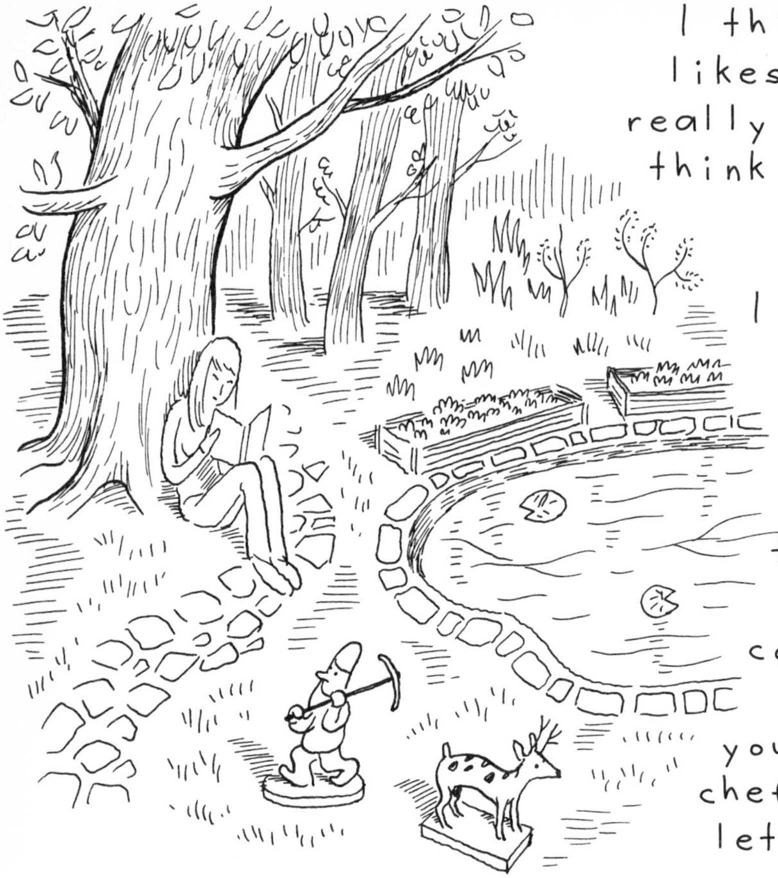

I think Vladimir likes me... I'm not really sure, but I think he likes me at least a little... I was reading a book of Italian recipes I found in the library. I like cookbooks and shows where you see famous chefs preparing lethal dishes...

I couldn't see much without my glasses, just that it was full of old yellowed photos, giving the impression that everything in the 70s had been made with curry.

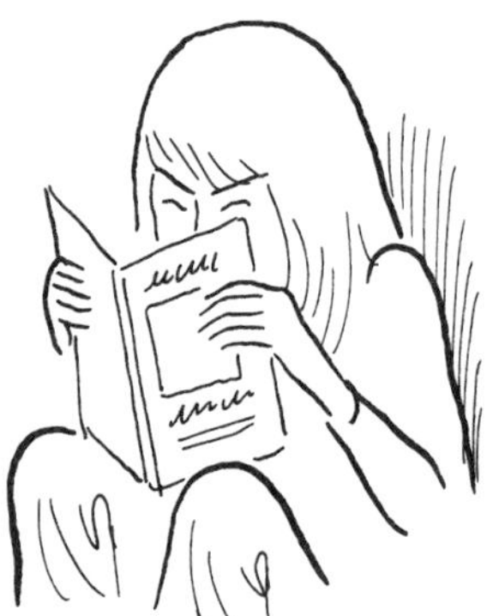

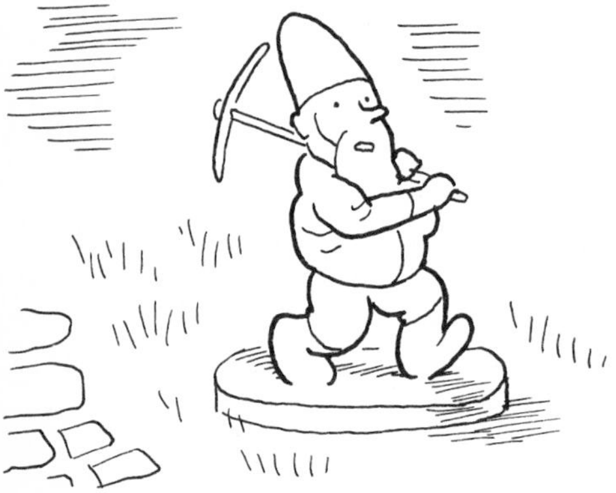

Vladimir had left on a delivery with Gerardo. I wanted to go, but Gerardo said he didn't have room. I think he's just a misogynist old virgin.

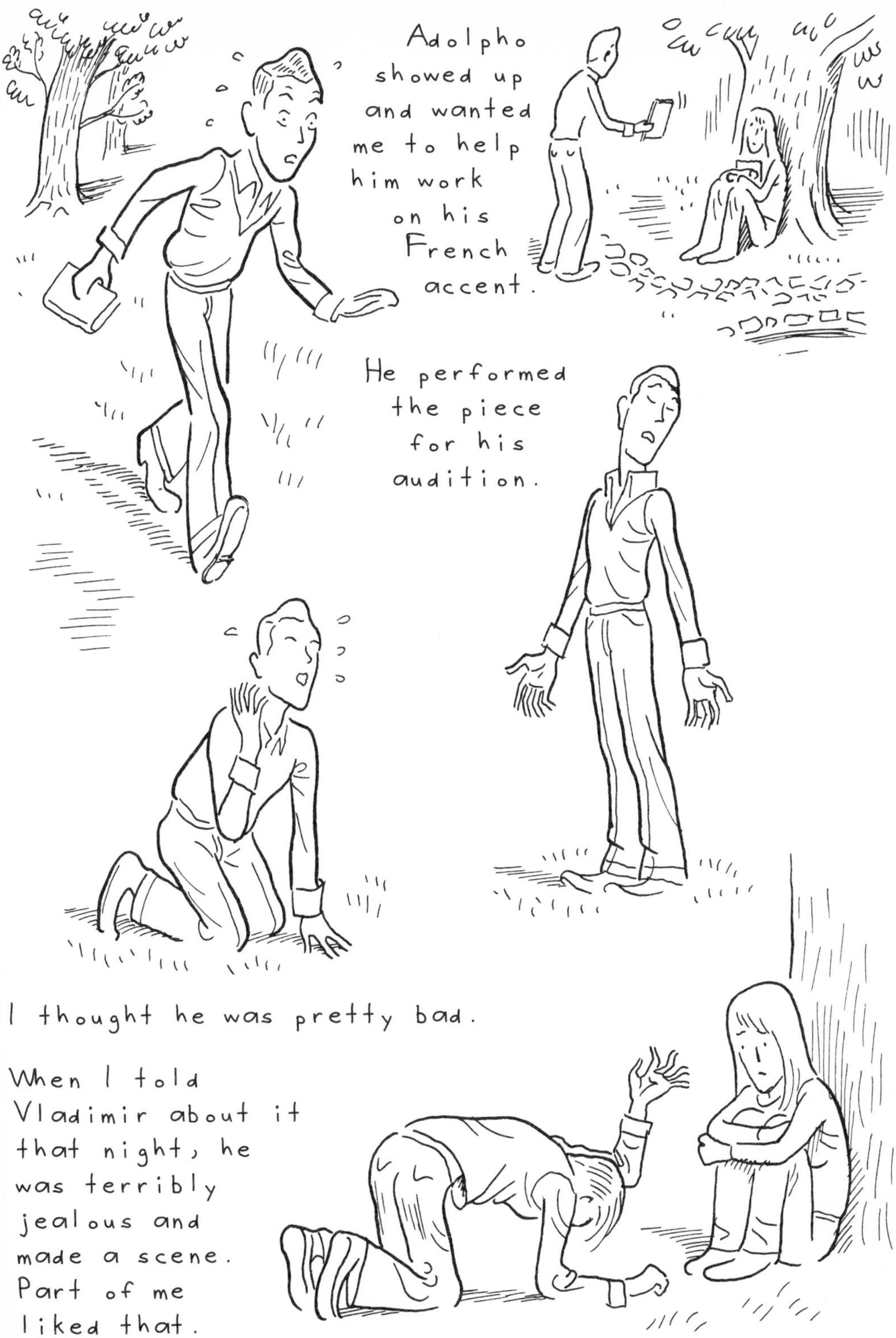
Adolpho showed up and wanted me to help him work on his French accent.
He performed the piece for his audition.
I thought he was pretty bad.
When I told Vladimir about it that night, he was terribly jealous and made a scene. Part of me liked that.

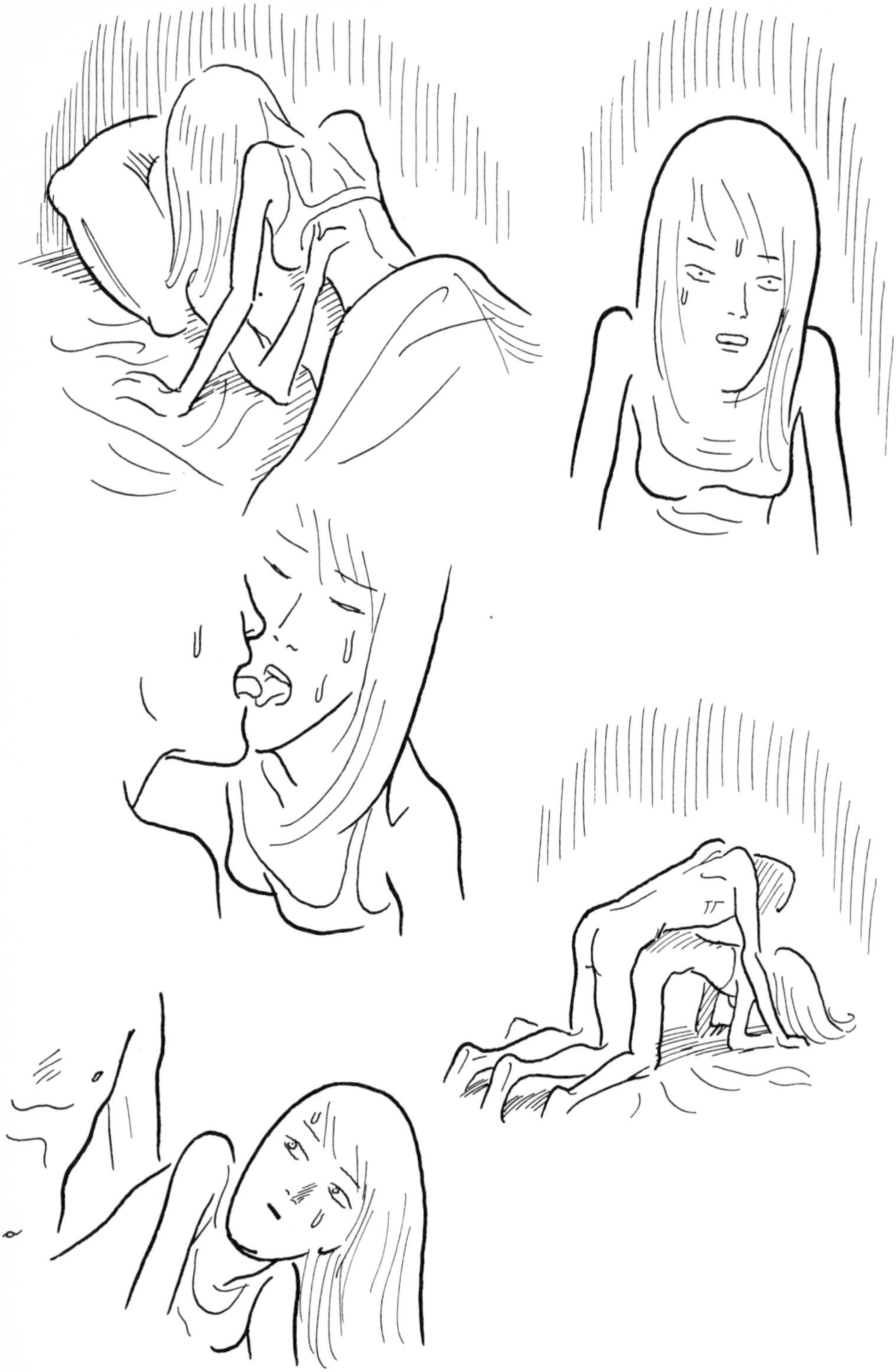

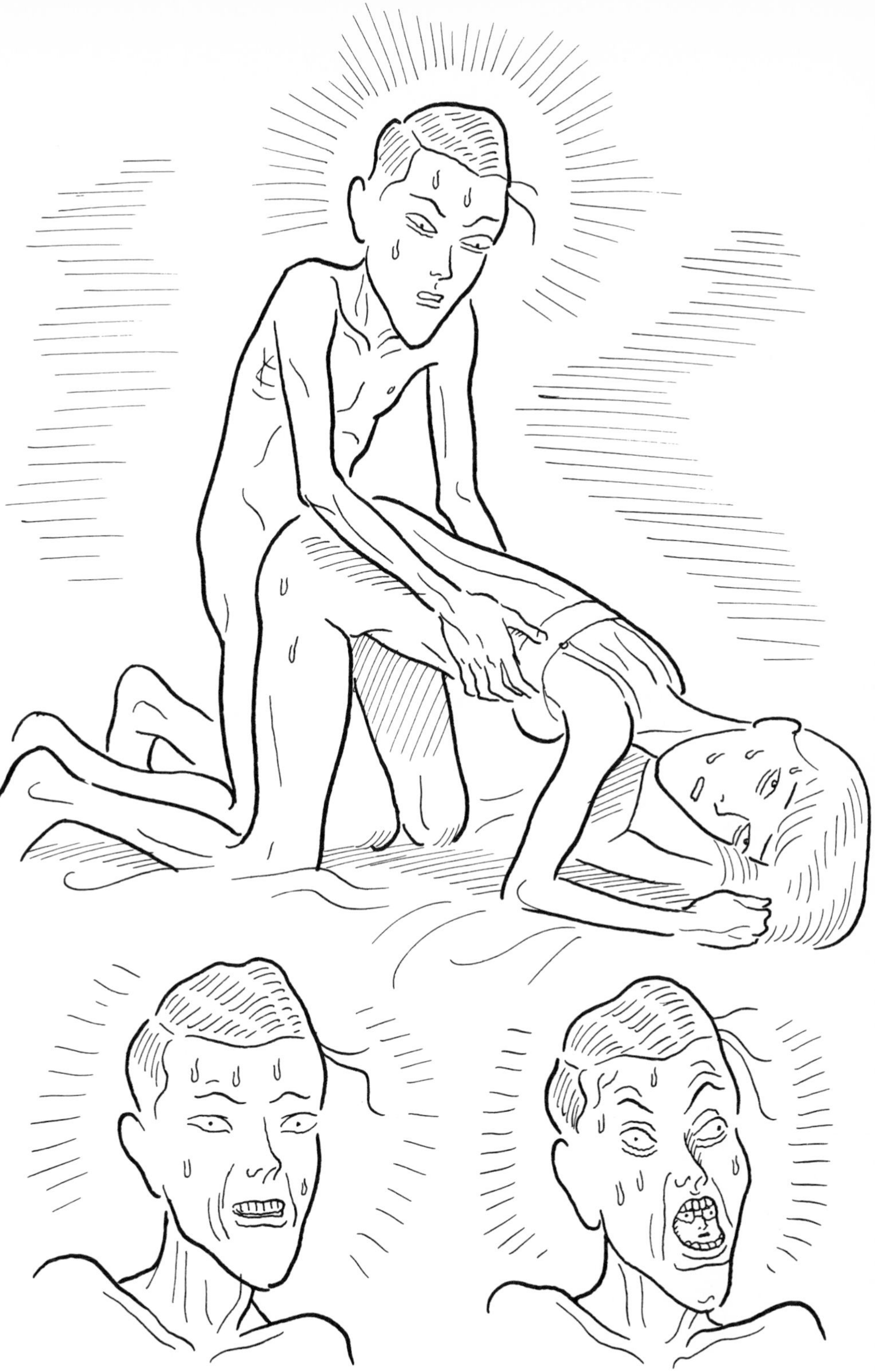

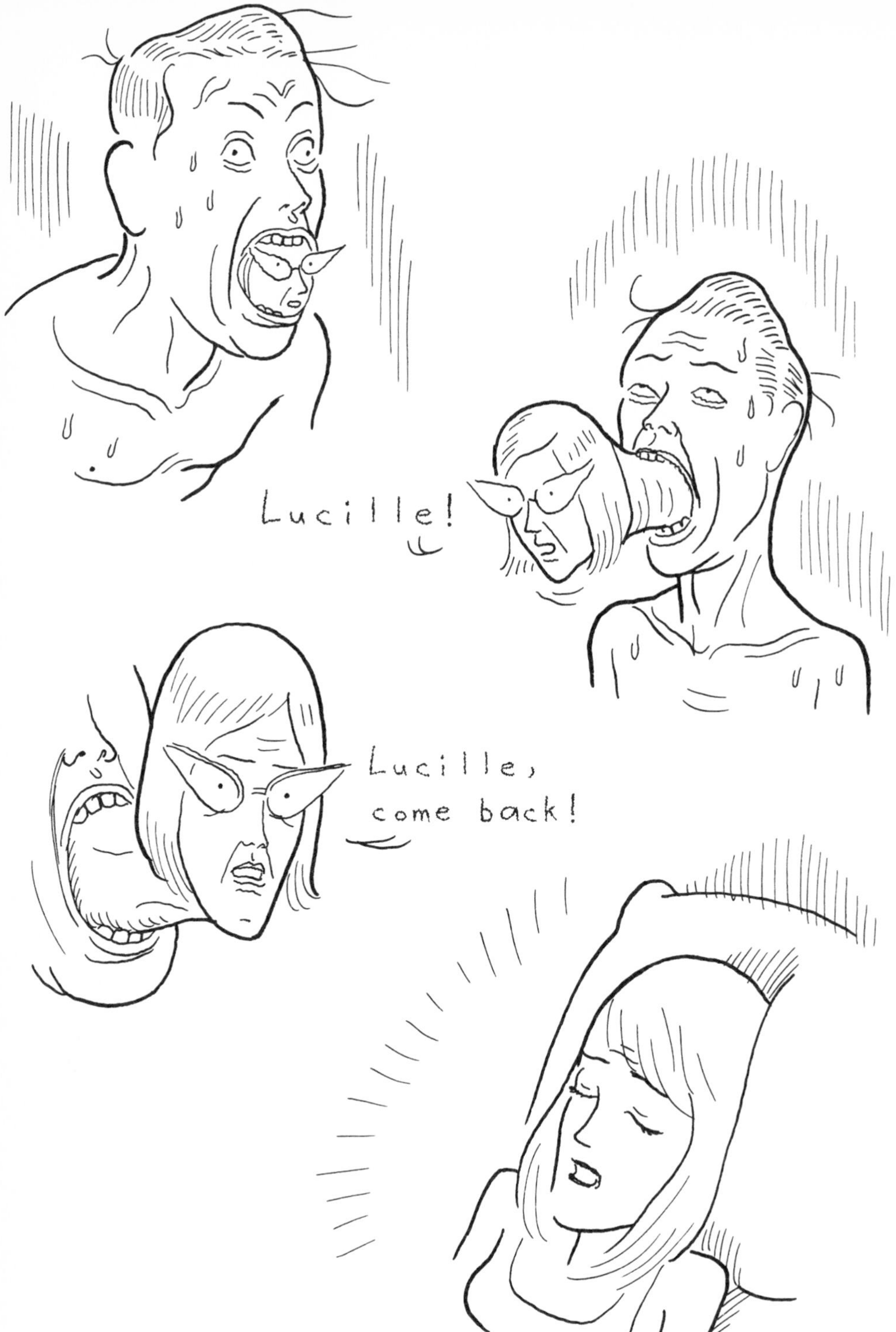
Lucille!
Lucille, come back!

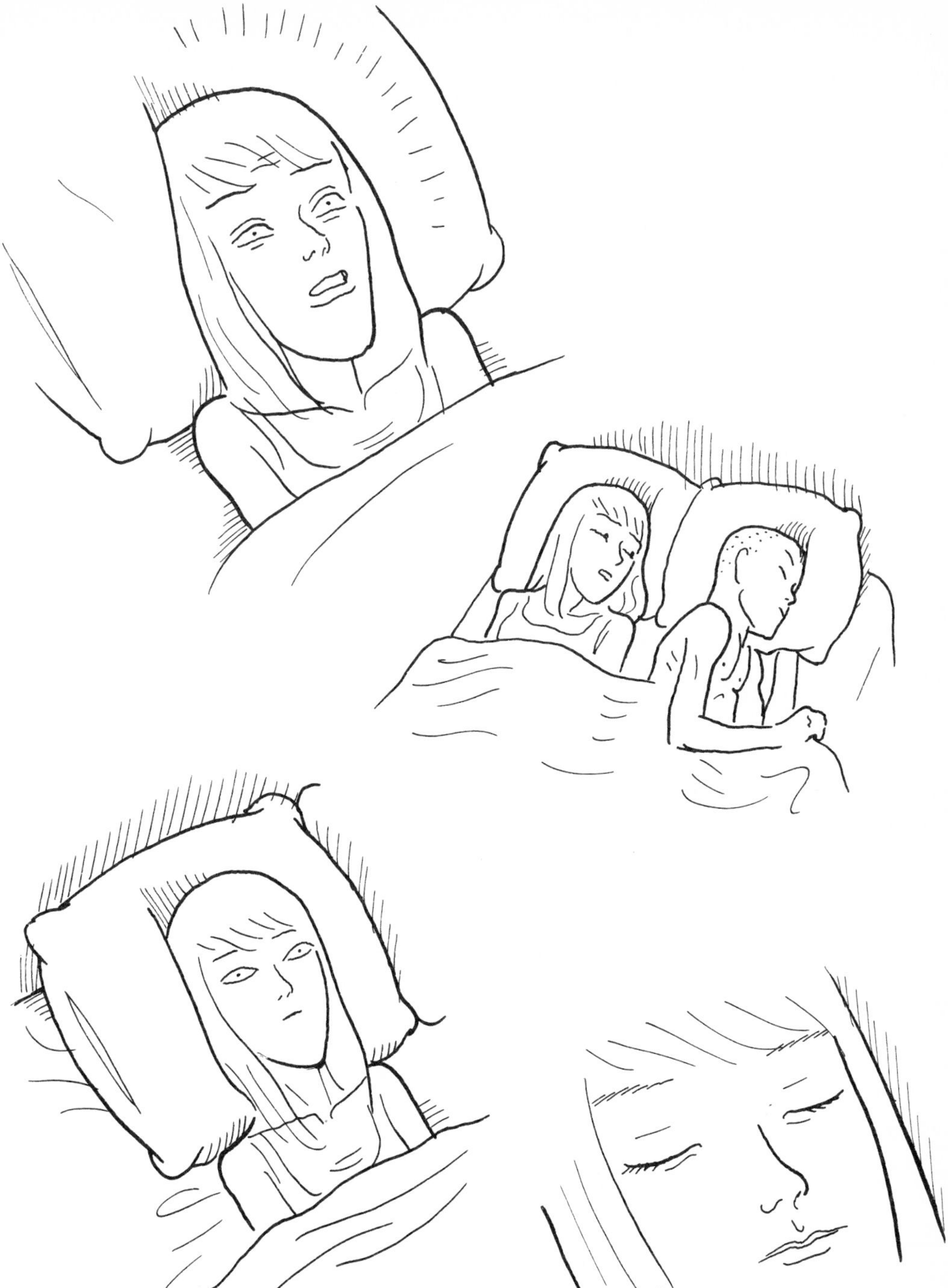

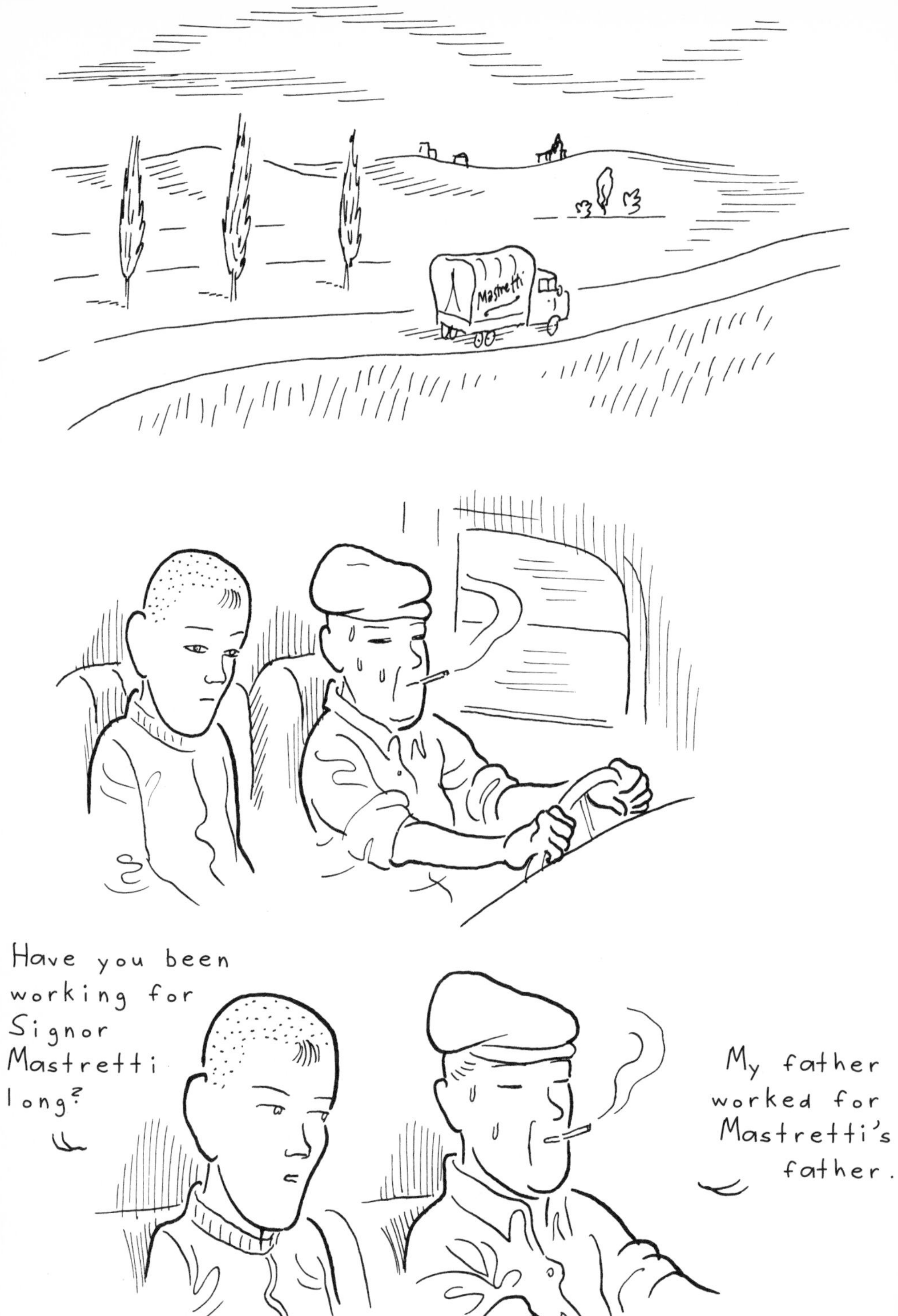
Mastretti
Have you been working for Signor Mastretti long?
My father worked for Mastretti's father.

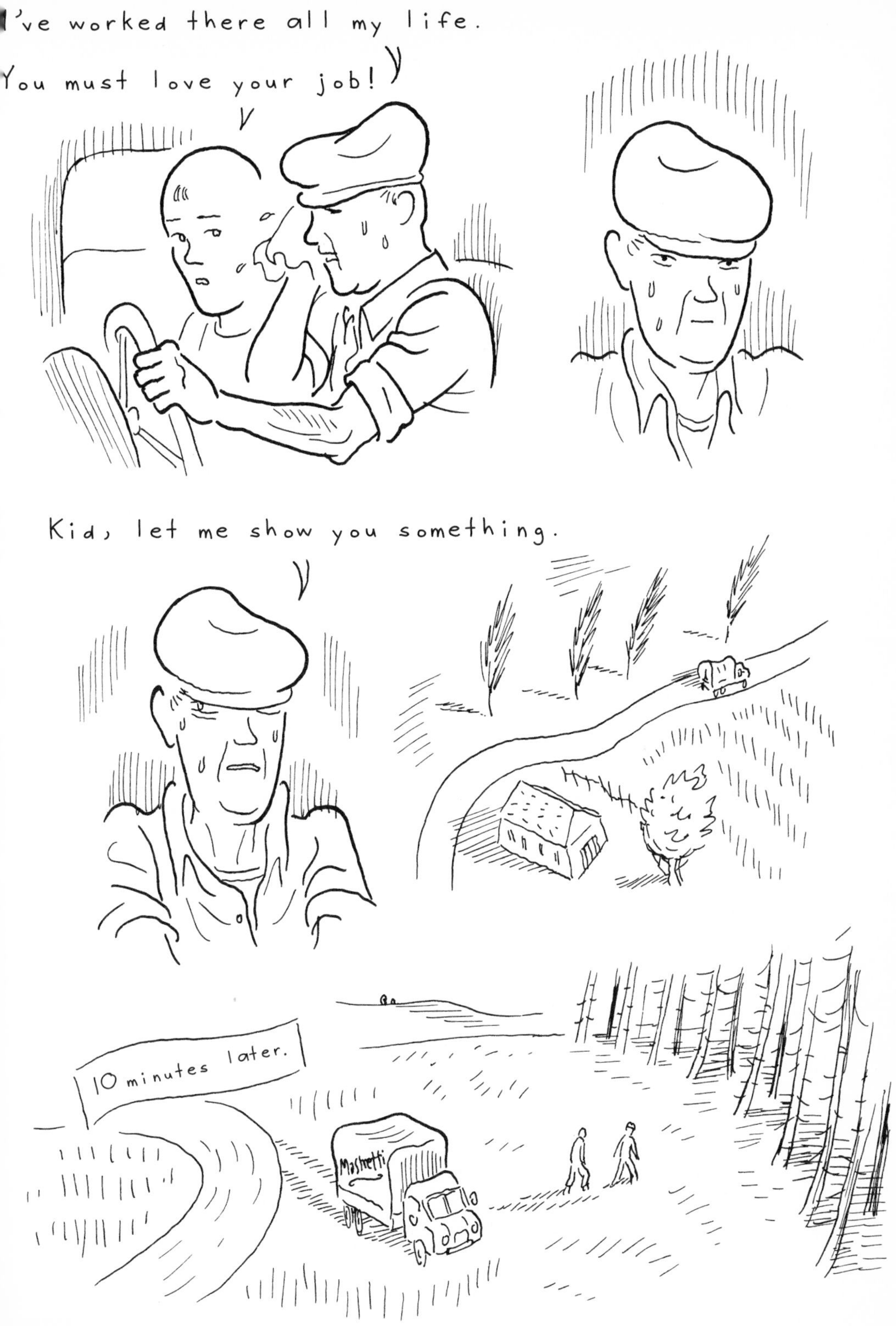
I've worked there all my life.
You must love your job!
Kid, let me show you something.
10 minutes later.
Mastretti

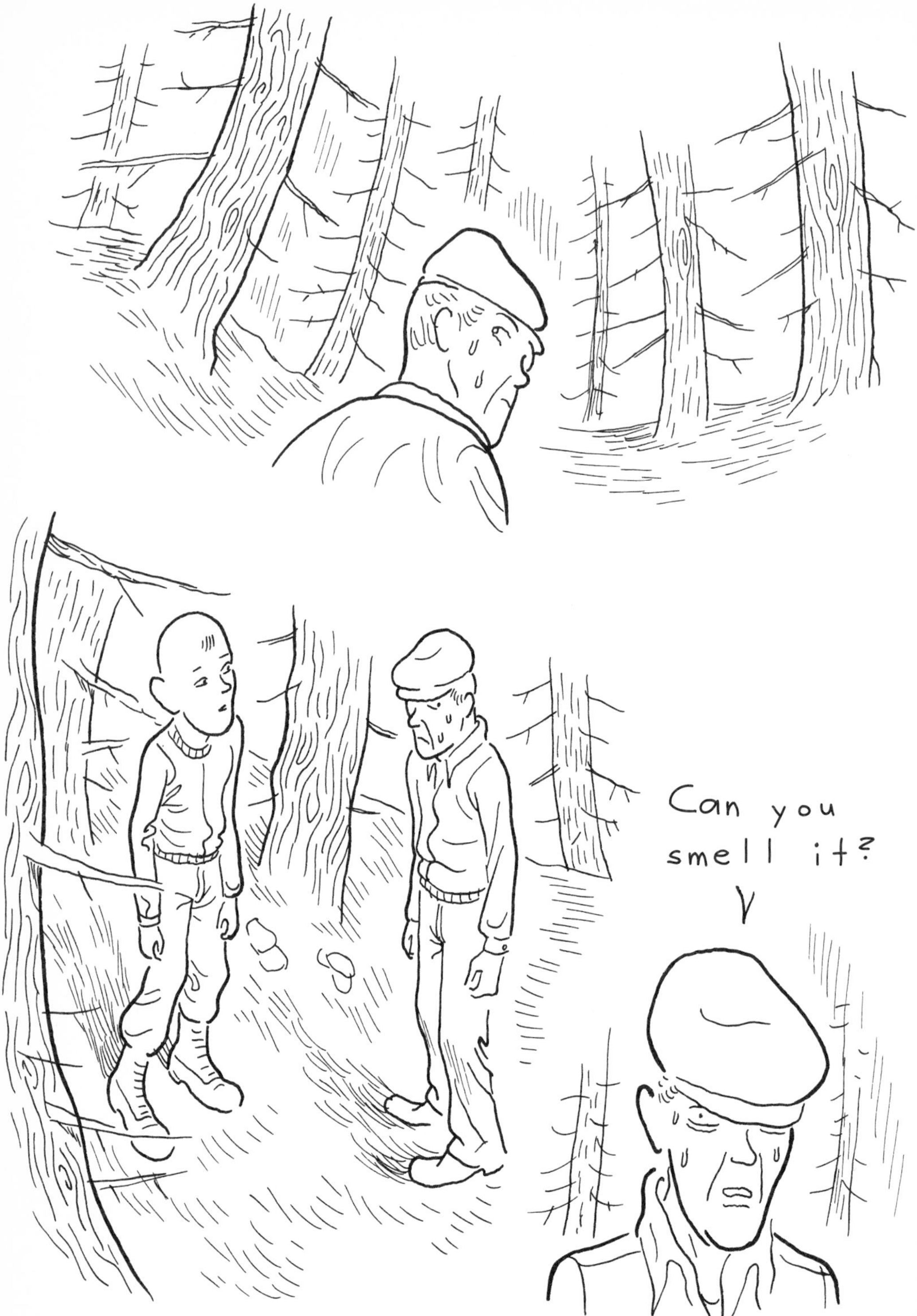
Can you smell it?

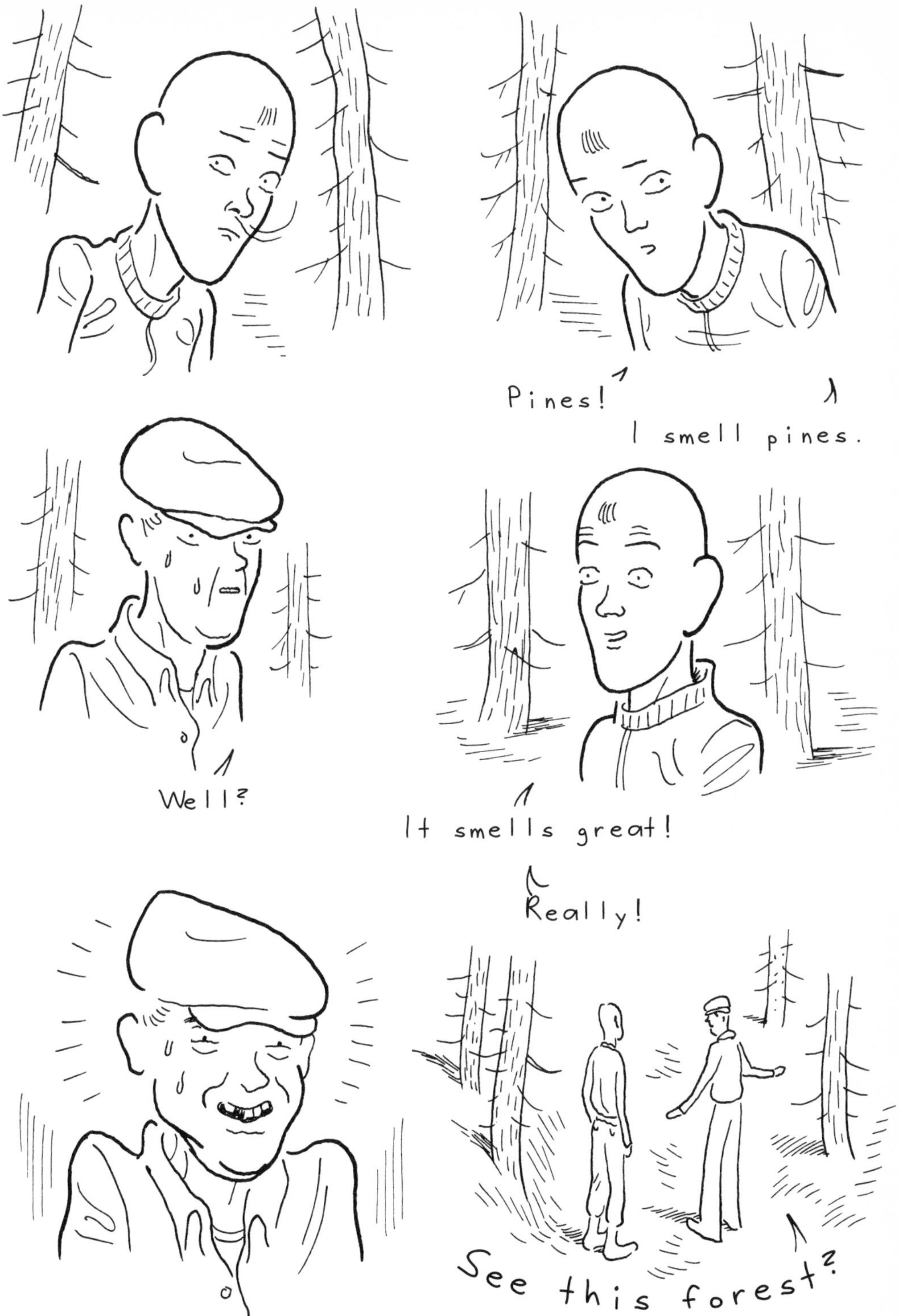
Pines!
I smell pines.
Well?
It smells great!
Really!
See this forest?

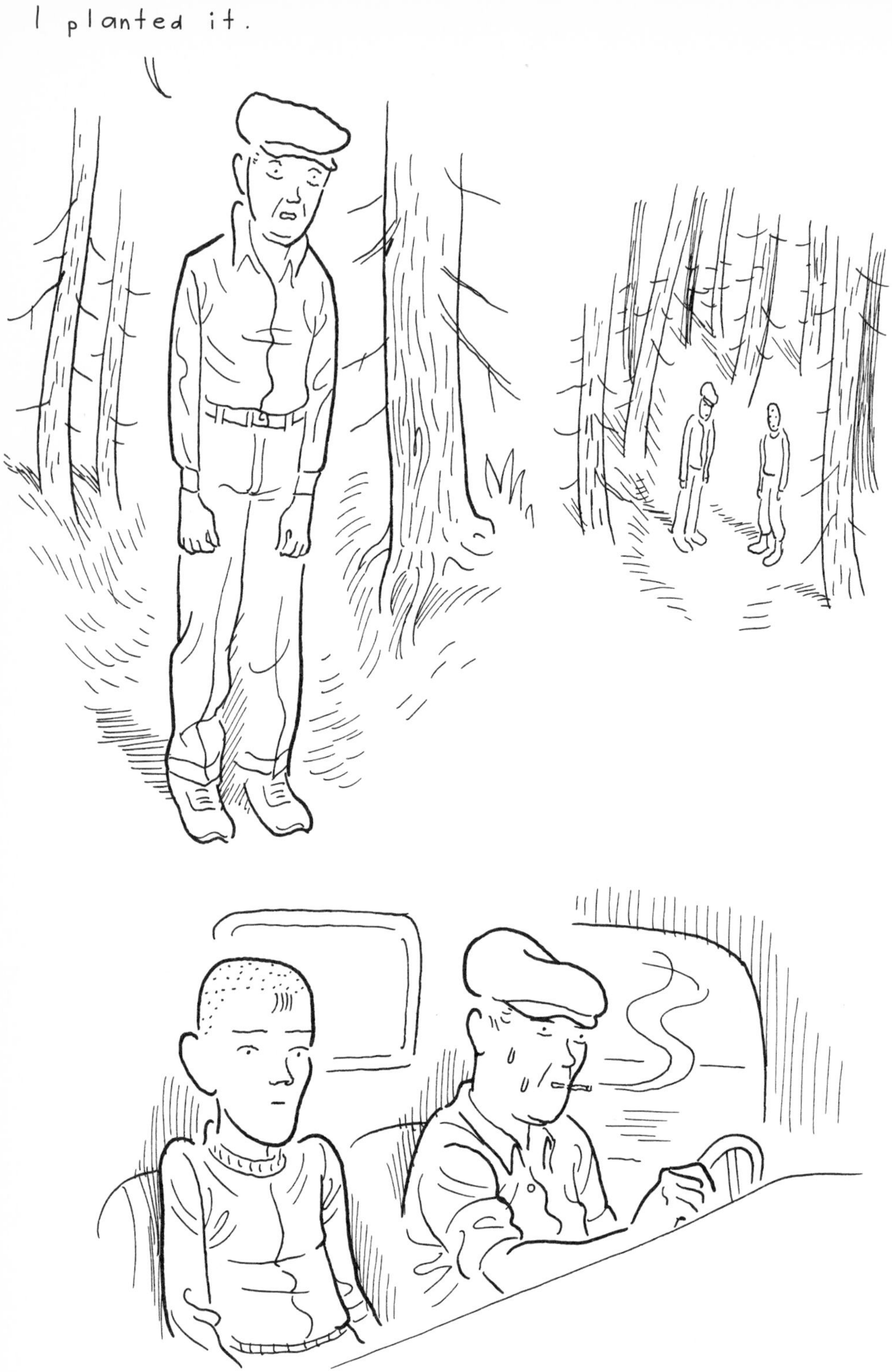
I planted it.

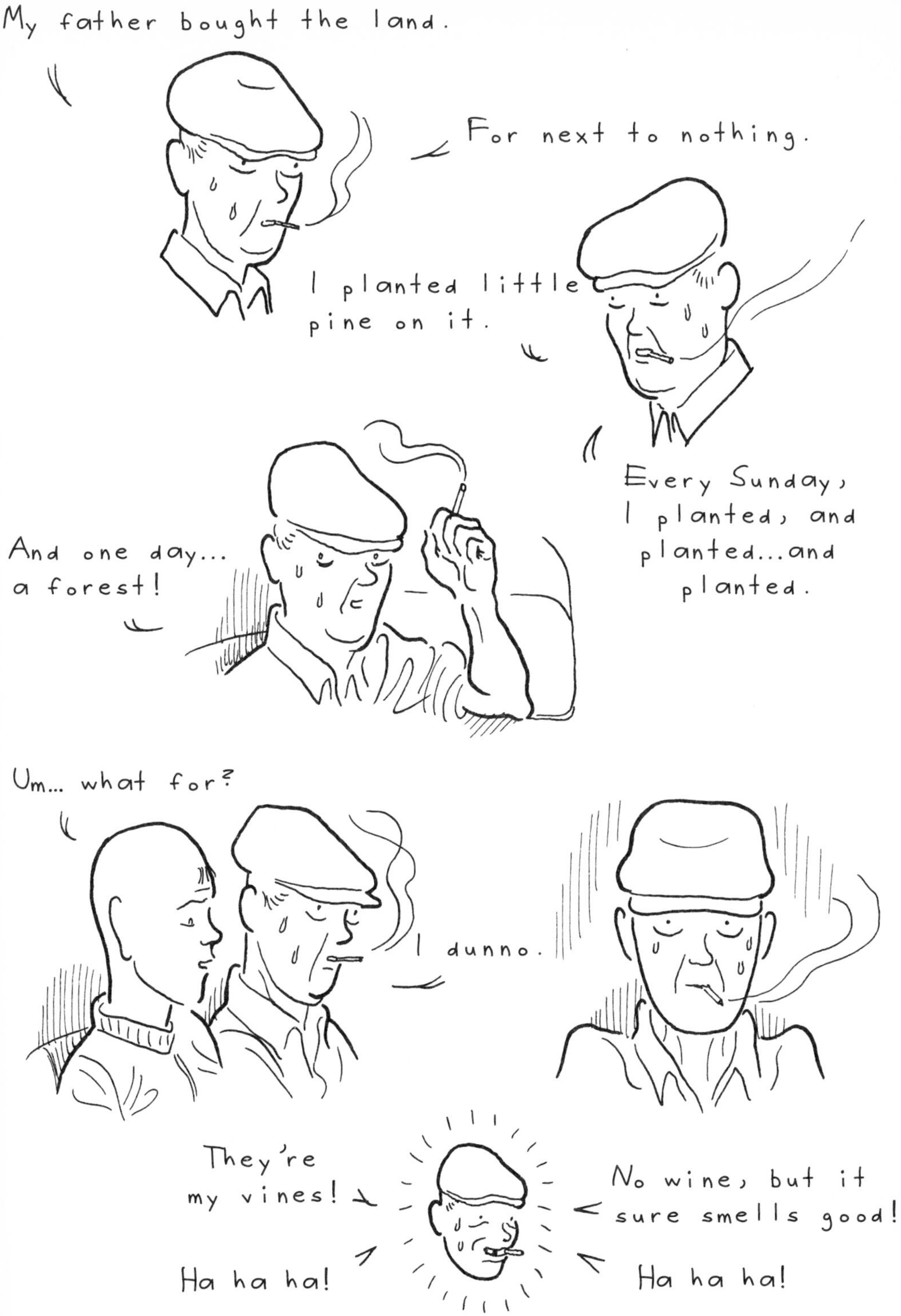

My father bought the land.
For next to nothing.
I planted little pine on it.
Every Sunday, I planted, and planted...and planted.
And one day... a forest!
Um... what for?
I dunno.
They're my vines!
No wine, but it sure smells good!
Ha ha ha!
Ha ha ha!

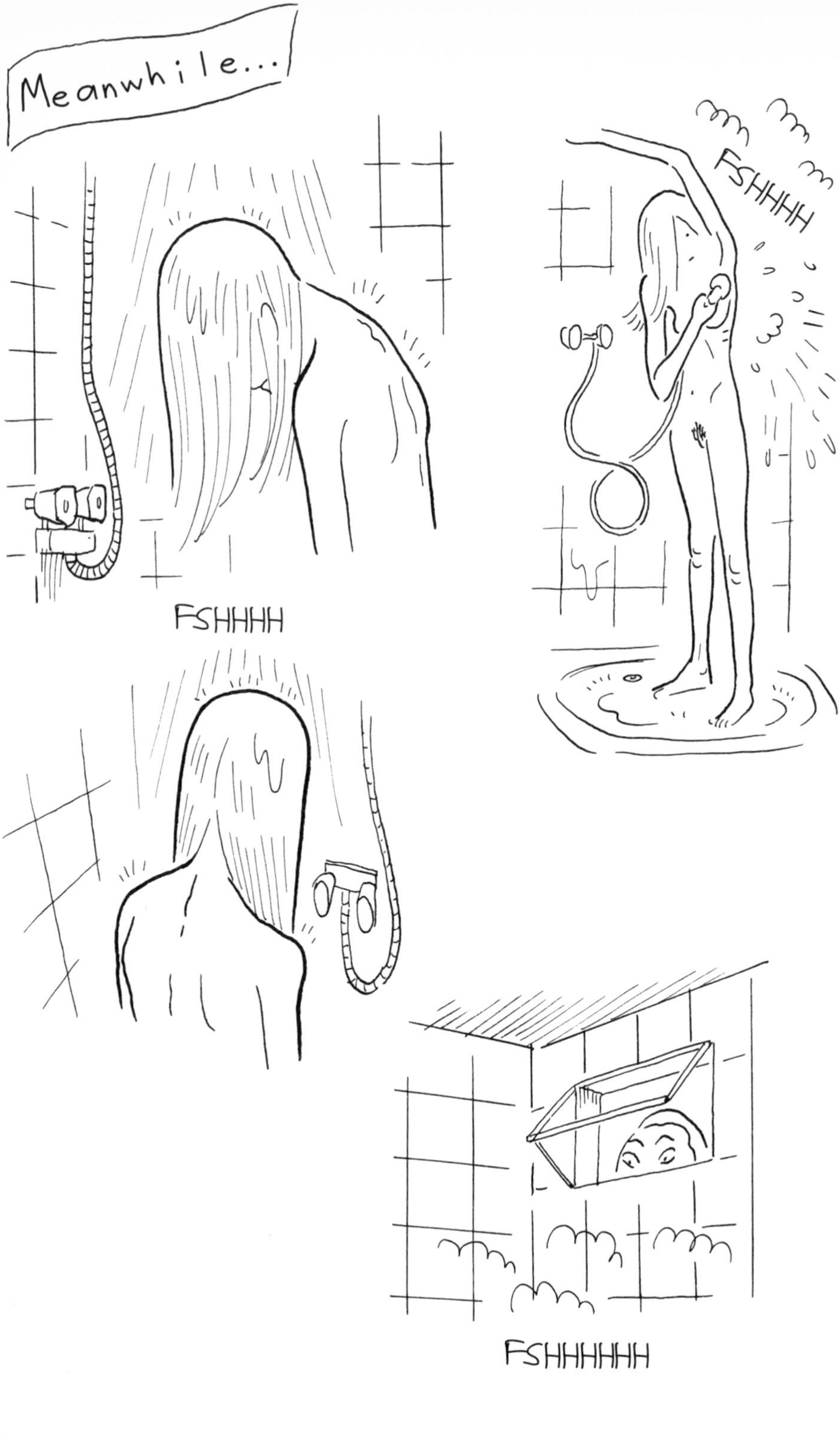
Meanwhile...
FSHHHH
FSHHHH
FSHHHHHH

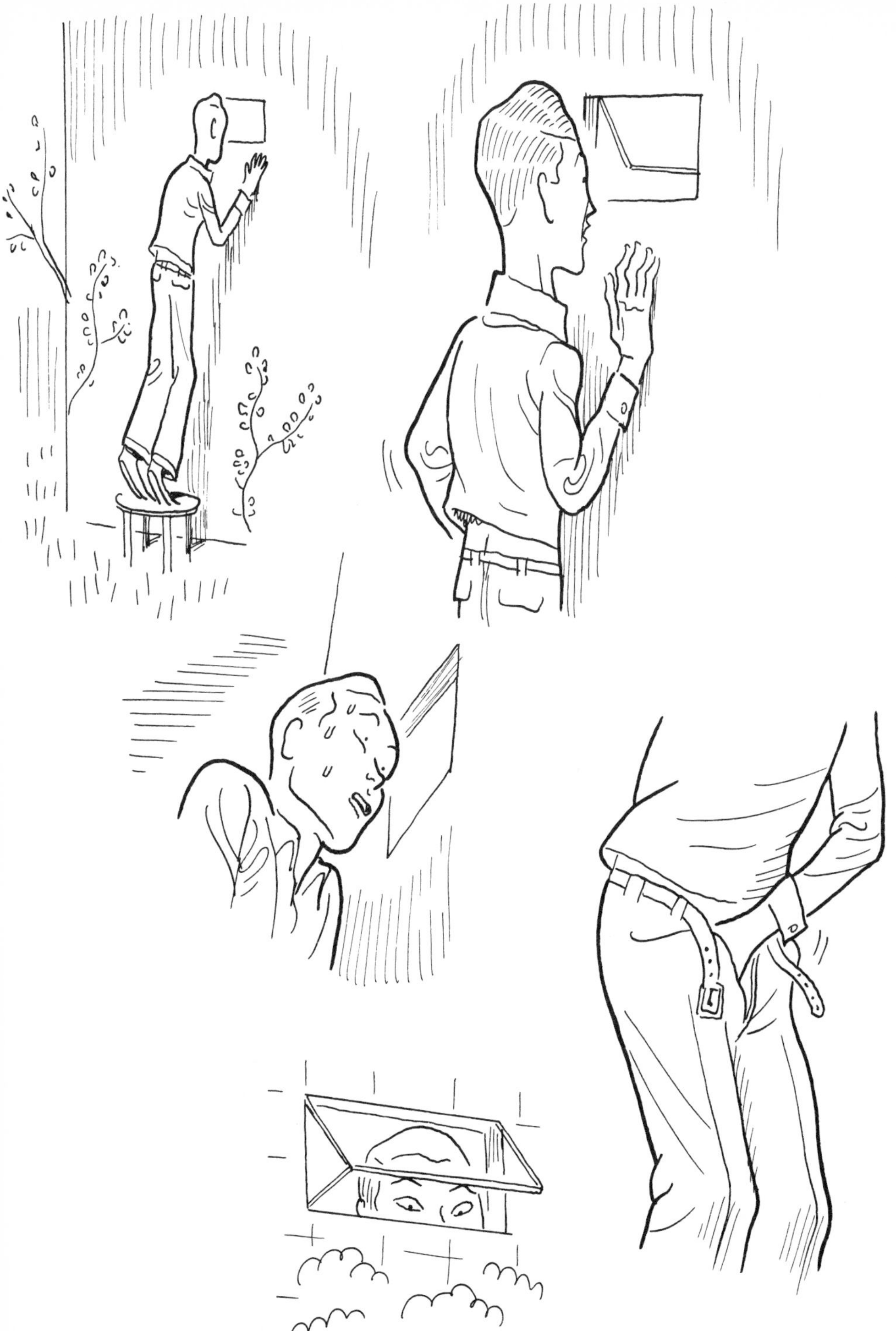
FSHHHH

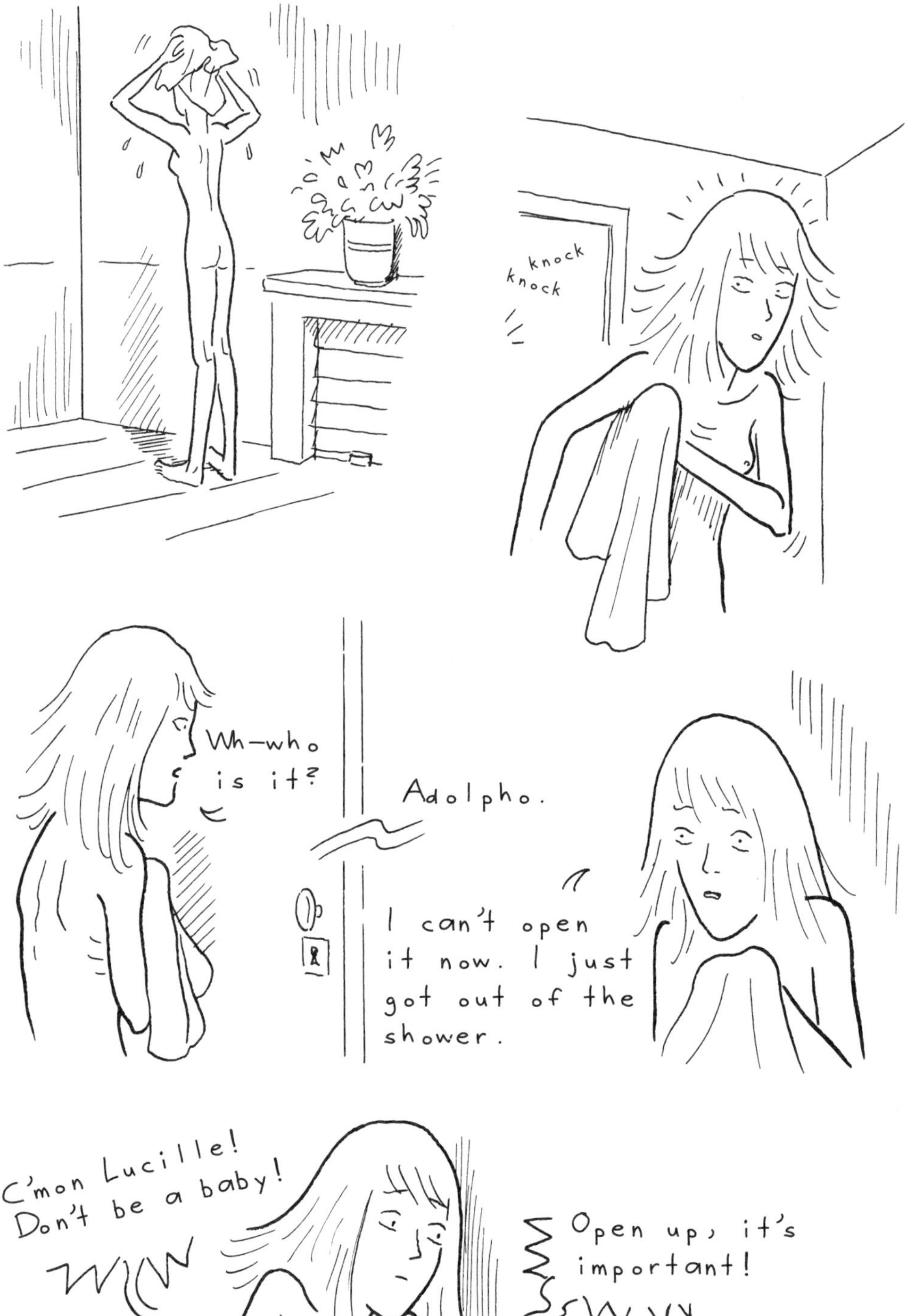
knock
knock
Wh-who is it?
Adolpho.
I can't open it now. I just got out of the shower.
C'mon Lucille! Don't be a baby!
Open up, it's important!

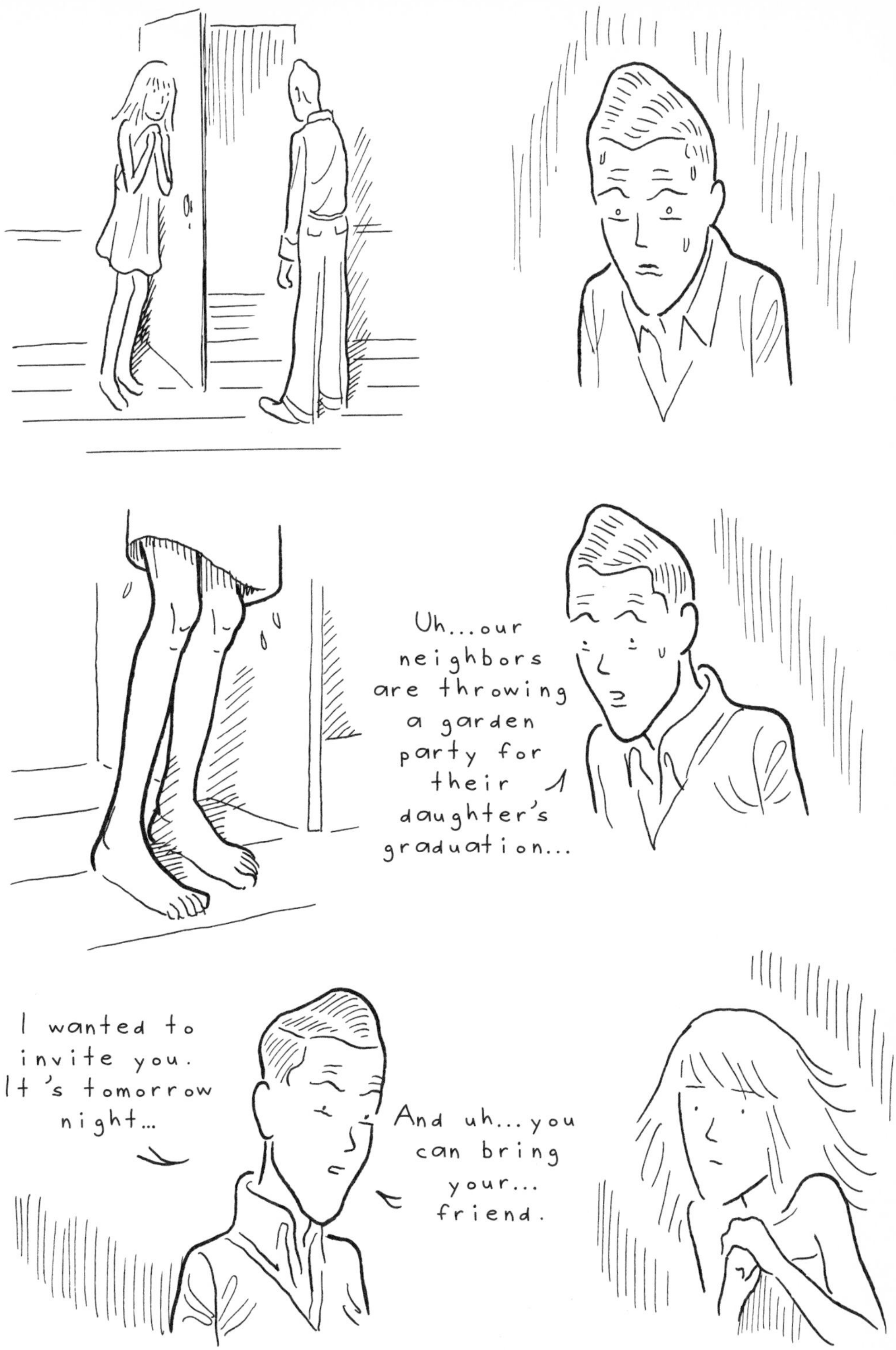
Uh...our neighbors are throwing a garden party for their daughter's graduation...
I wanted to invite you. It's tomorrow night...
And uh...you can bring your... friend.

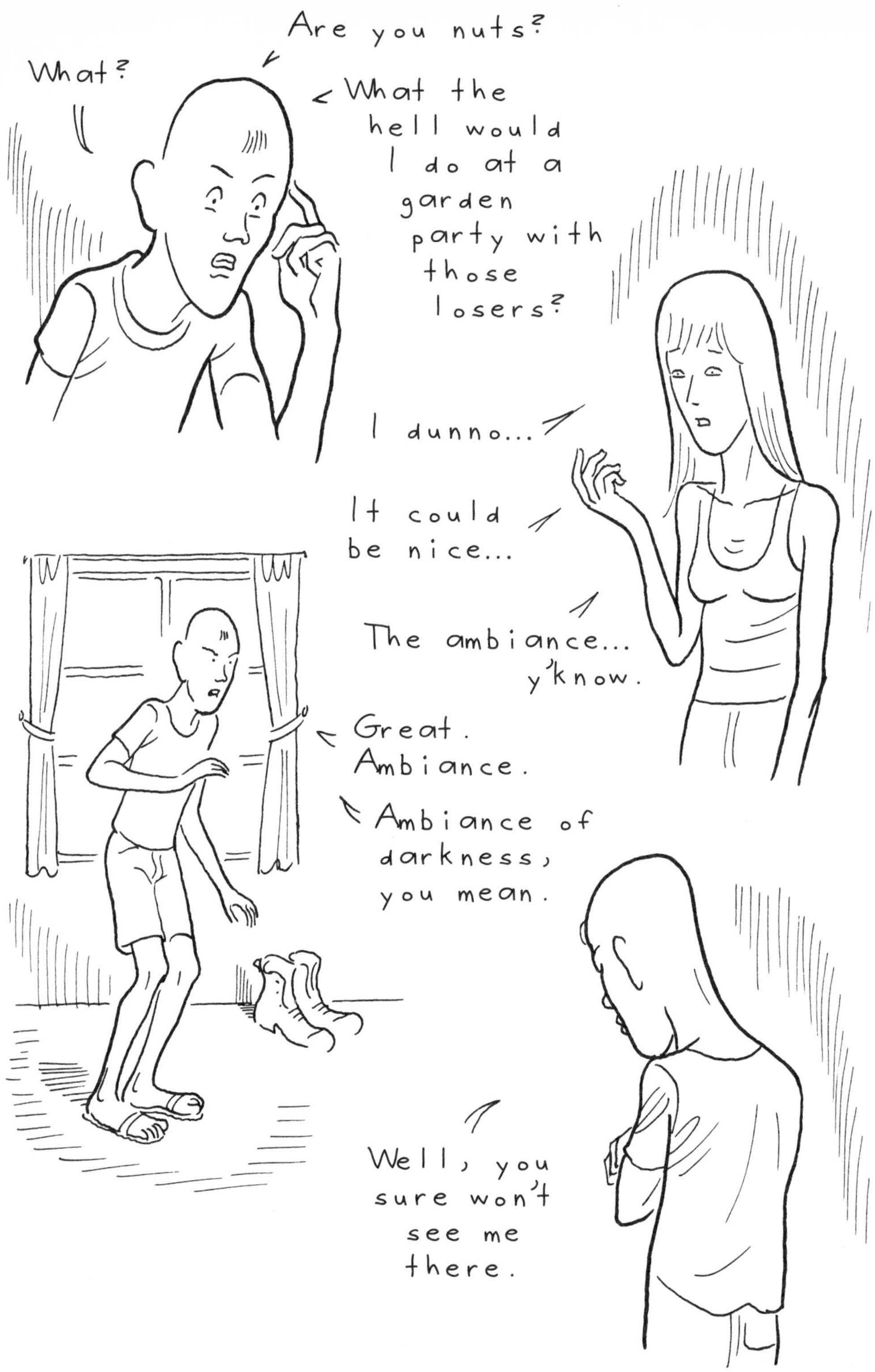
Are you nuts?
What?
What the hell would I do at a garden party with those losers?
I dunno...
It could be nice...
The ambiance... y'know.
Great. Ambiance.
Ambiance of darkness, you mean.
Well, you sure won't see me there.

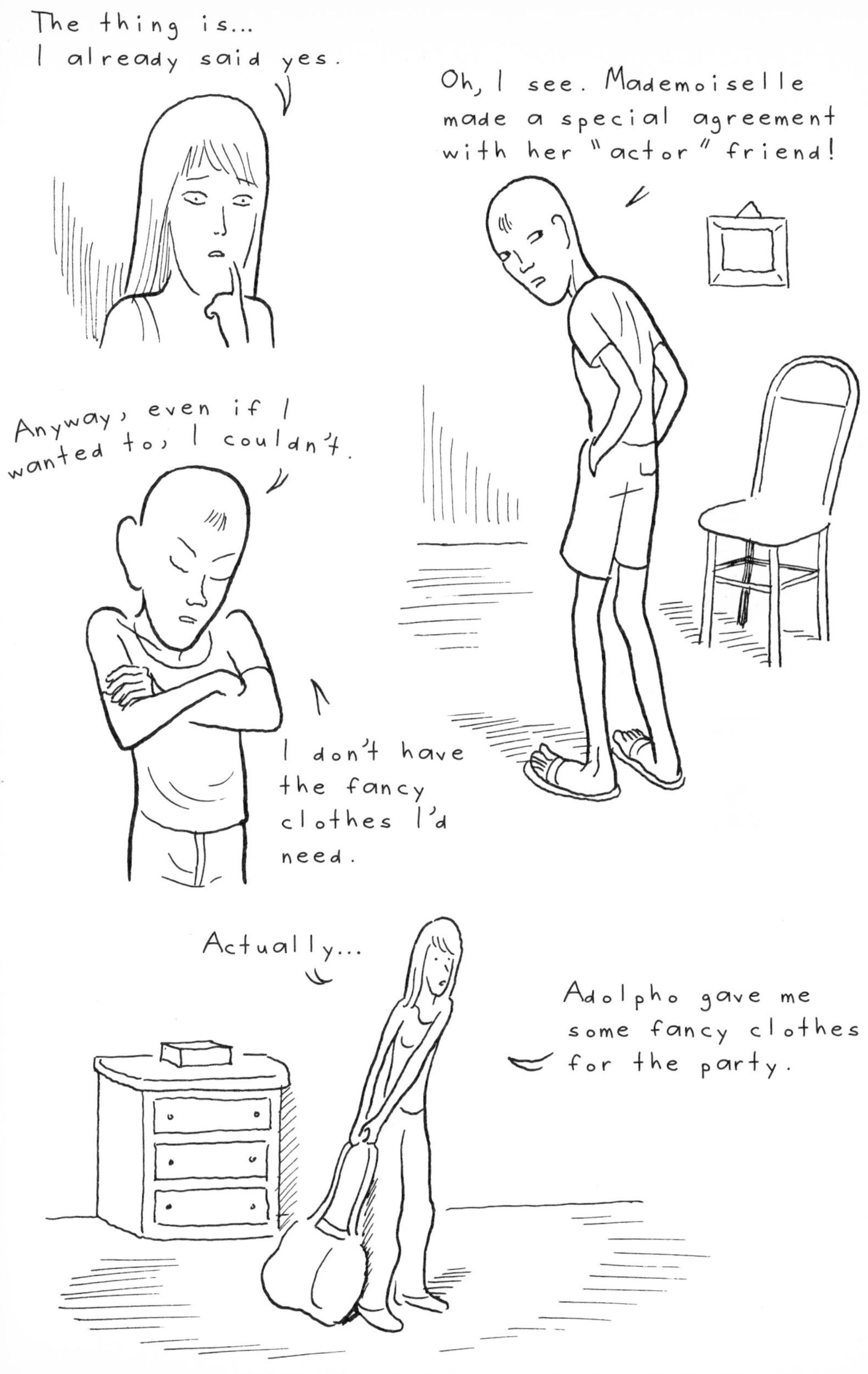
The thing is... I already said yes.
Oh, I see. Mademoiselle made a special agreement with her "actor" friend!
Anyway, even if I wanted to, I couldn't.
I don't have the fancy clothes I'd need.
Actually...
Adolpho gave me some fancy clothes for the party.

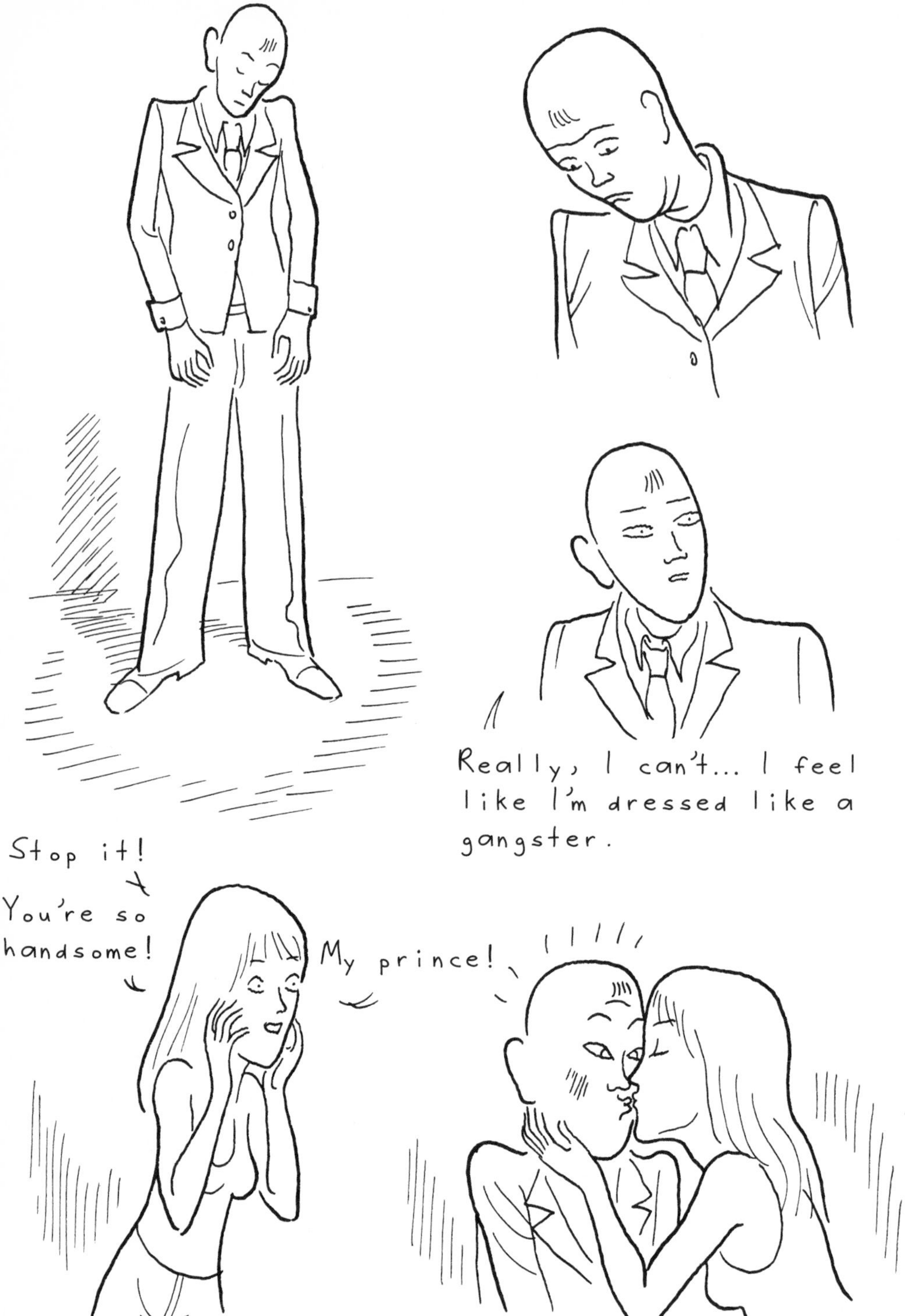
Really, I can't... I feel like I'm dressed like a gangster.
Stop it!
You're so handsome!
My prince!

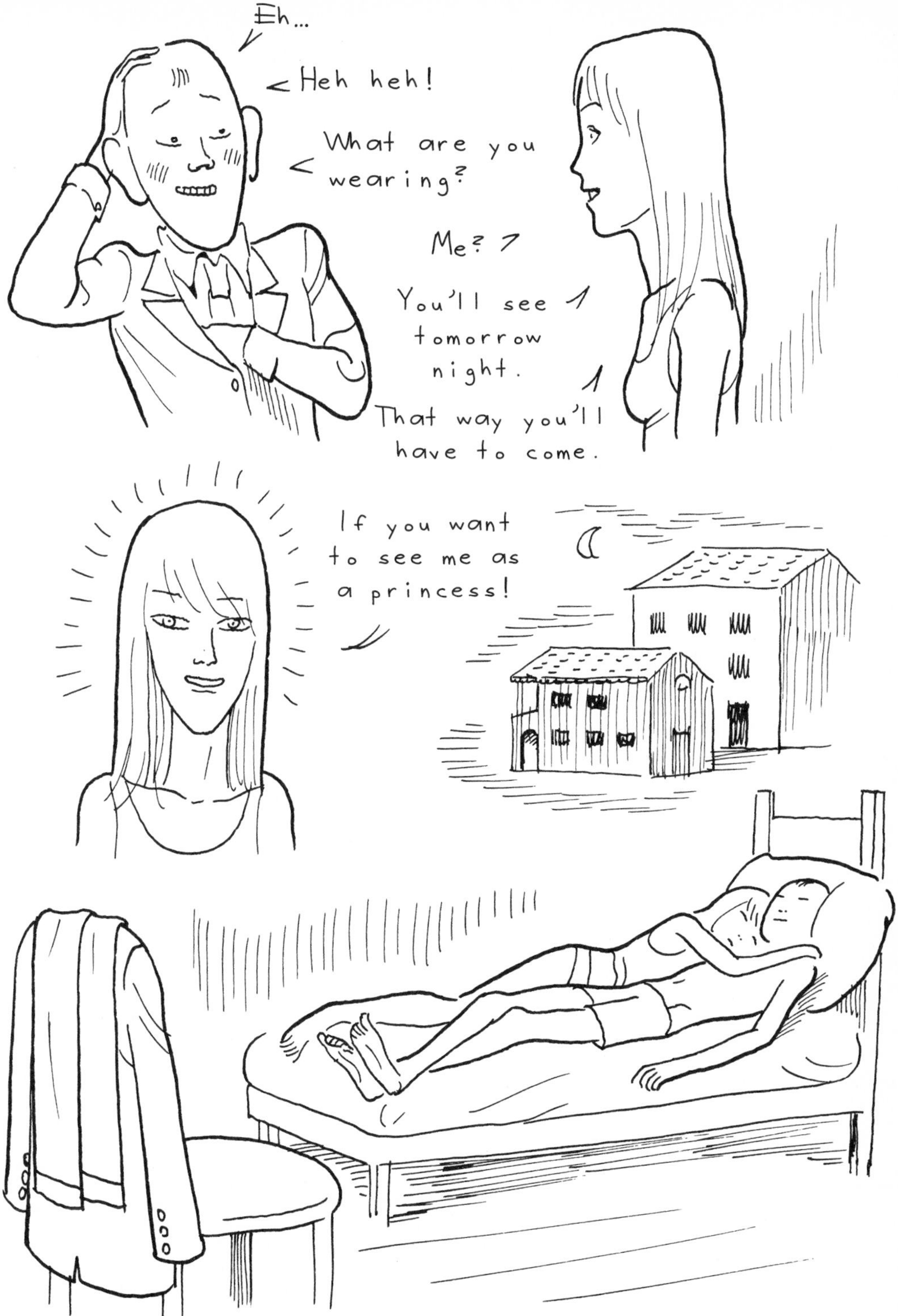
Eh...
Heh heh!
What are you wearing?
Me?
You'll see tomorrow night.
That way you'll have to come.
If you want to see me as a princess!

The Picard Sailor

Vladimir woke up in the night. He began touching me. I think he wanted to make love.

He asked me to suck him off... but I couldn't. He asked me if it was because it made me sick.

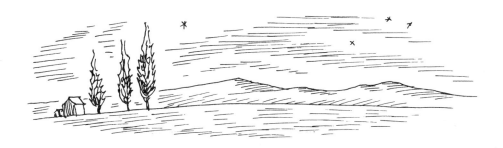

I don't think that's it... but it's a bit like with food. I'm afraid it'll fill me up.

I told him I wasn't the most normal girl he could've met.

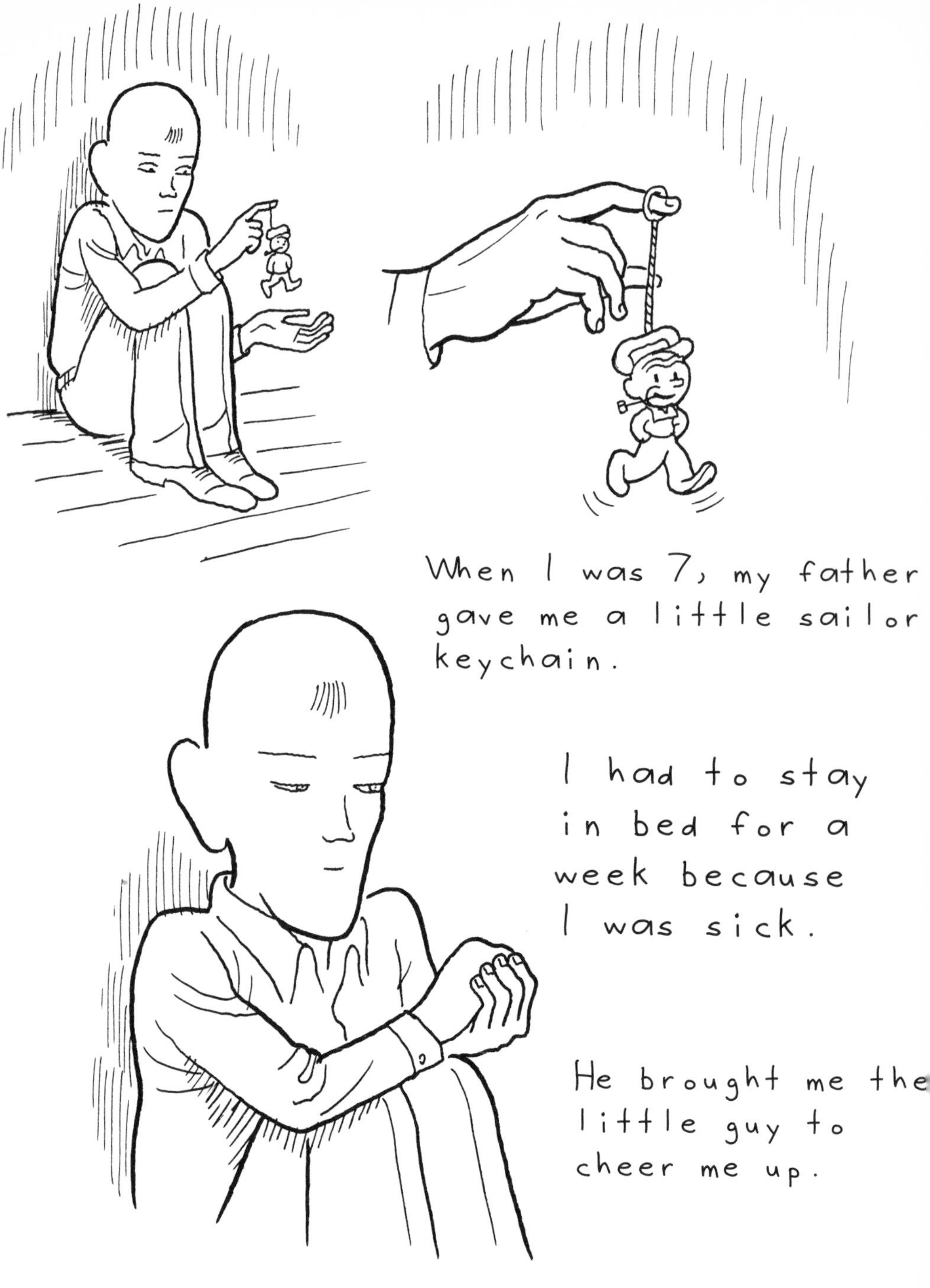
When I was 7, my father gave me a little sailor keychain.
I had to stay in bed for a week because I was sick.
He brought me the little guy to cheer me up.
I keep him with me all the time.

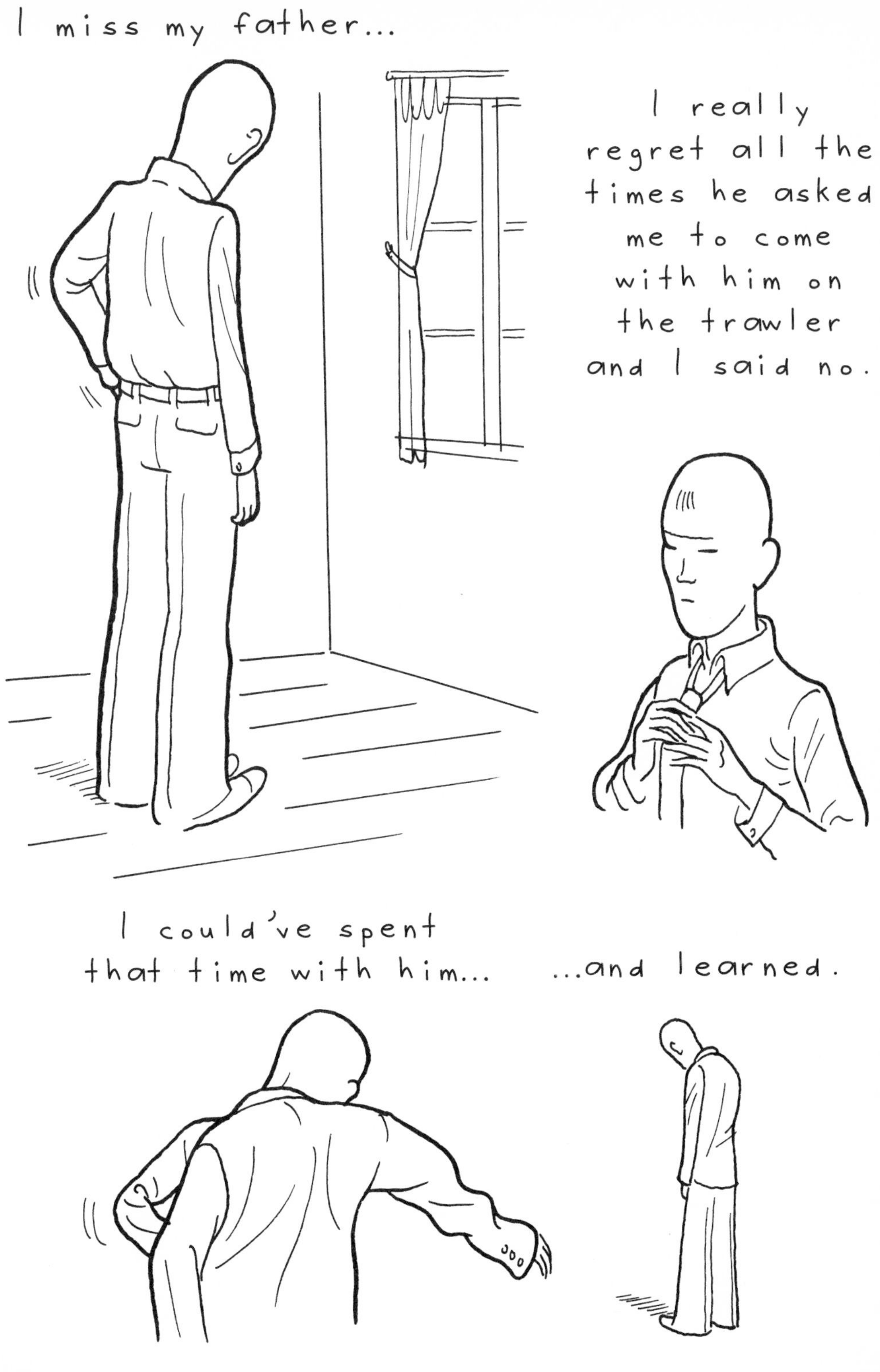
I miss my father...
I really regret all the times he asked me to come with him on the trawler and I said no.
I could've spent that time with him...
...and learned.

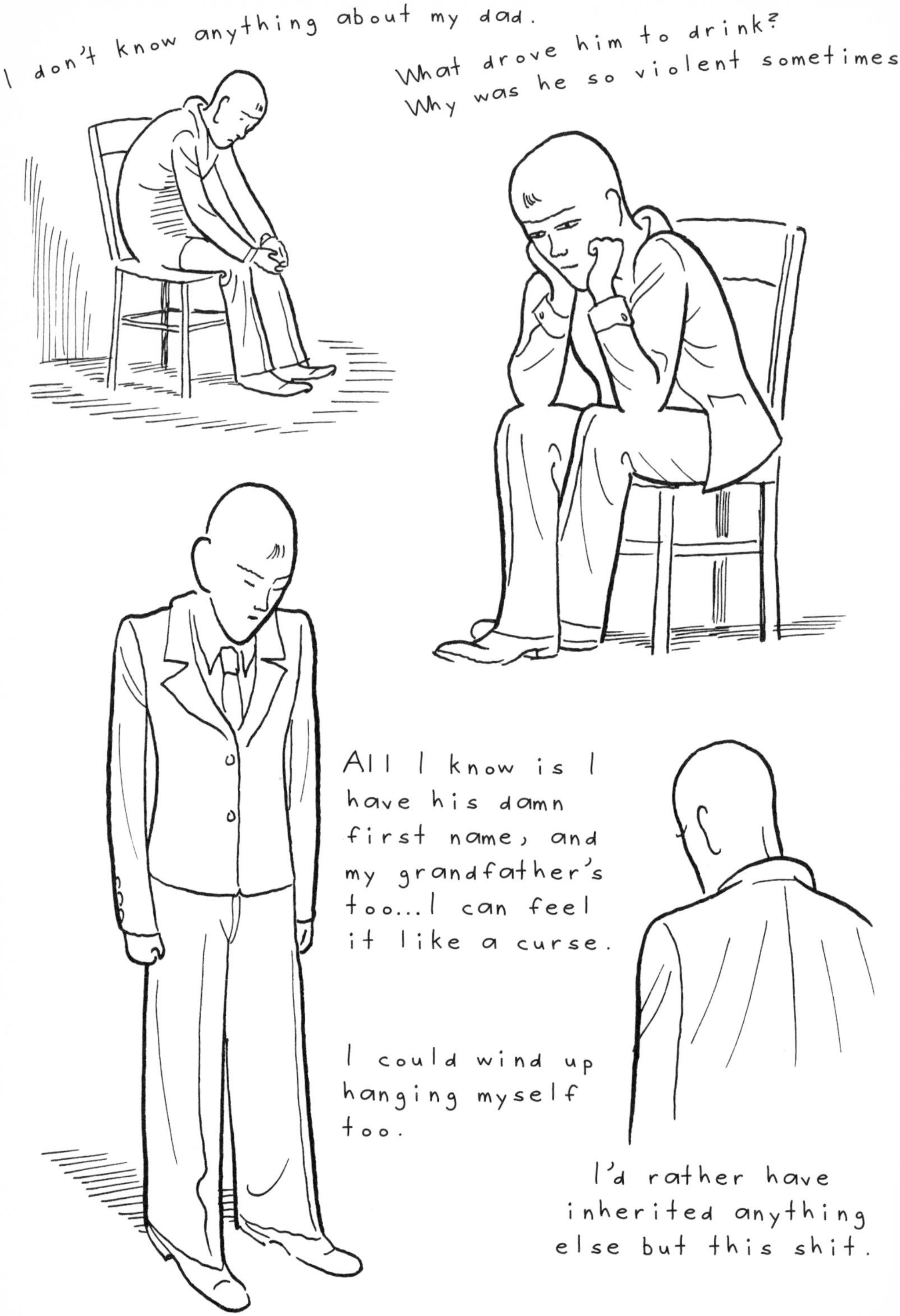
I don't know anything about my dad.
What drove him to drink? Why was he so violent sometimes
All I know is I have his damn first name, and my grandfather's too...I can feel it like a curse.
I could wind up hanging myself too.
I'd rather have inherited anything else but this shit.

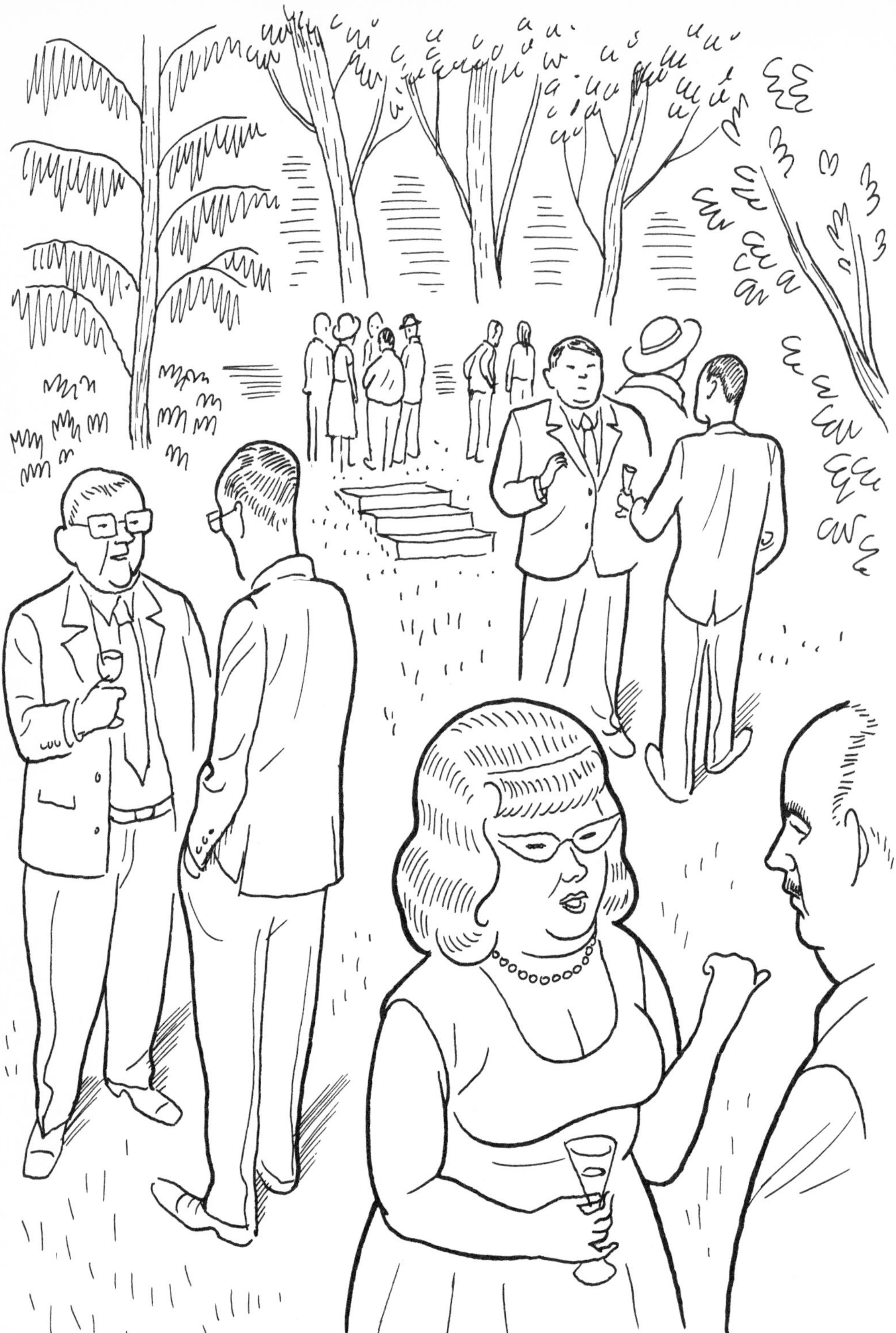

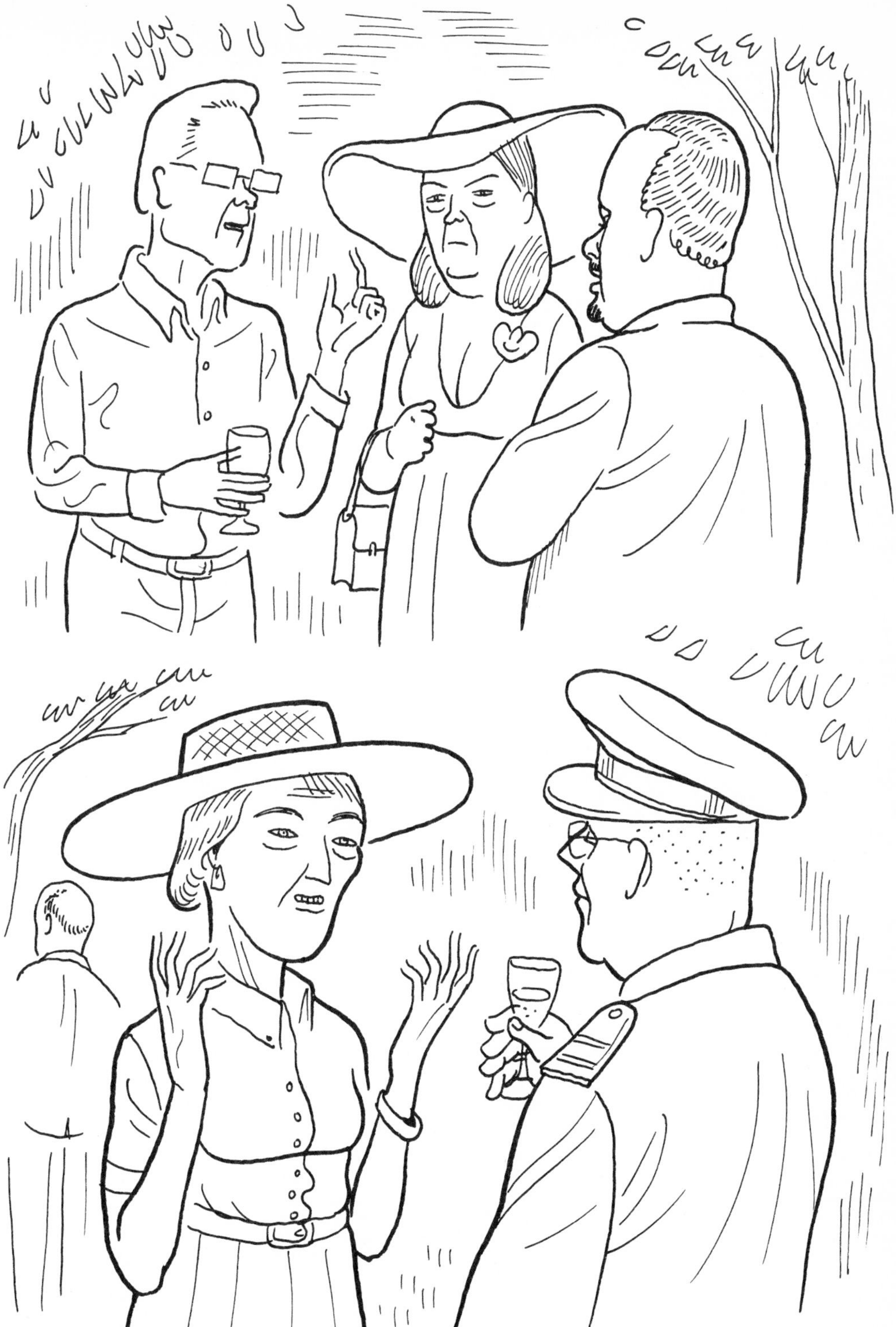

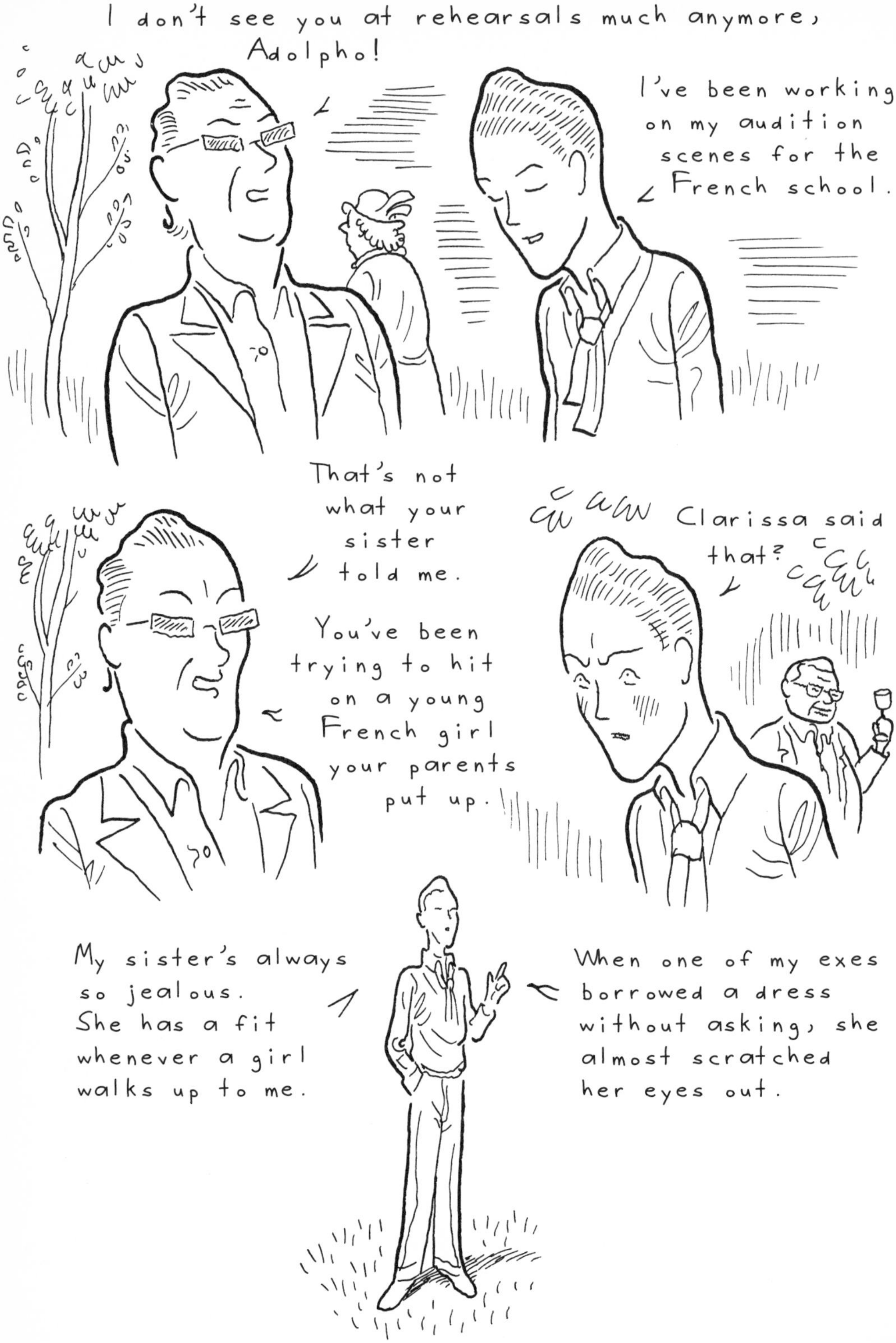
I don't see you at rehearsals much anymore, Adolpho!
I've been working on my audition scenes for the French school.
That's not what your sister told me.
You've been trying to hit on a young French girl your parents put up.
Clarissa said that?
My sister's always so jealous. She has a fit whenever a girl walks up to me.
When one of my exes borrowed a dress without asking, she almost scratched her eyes out.

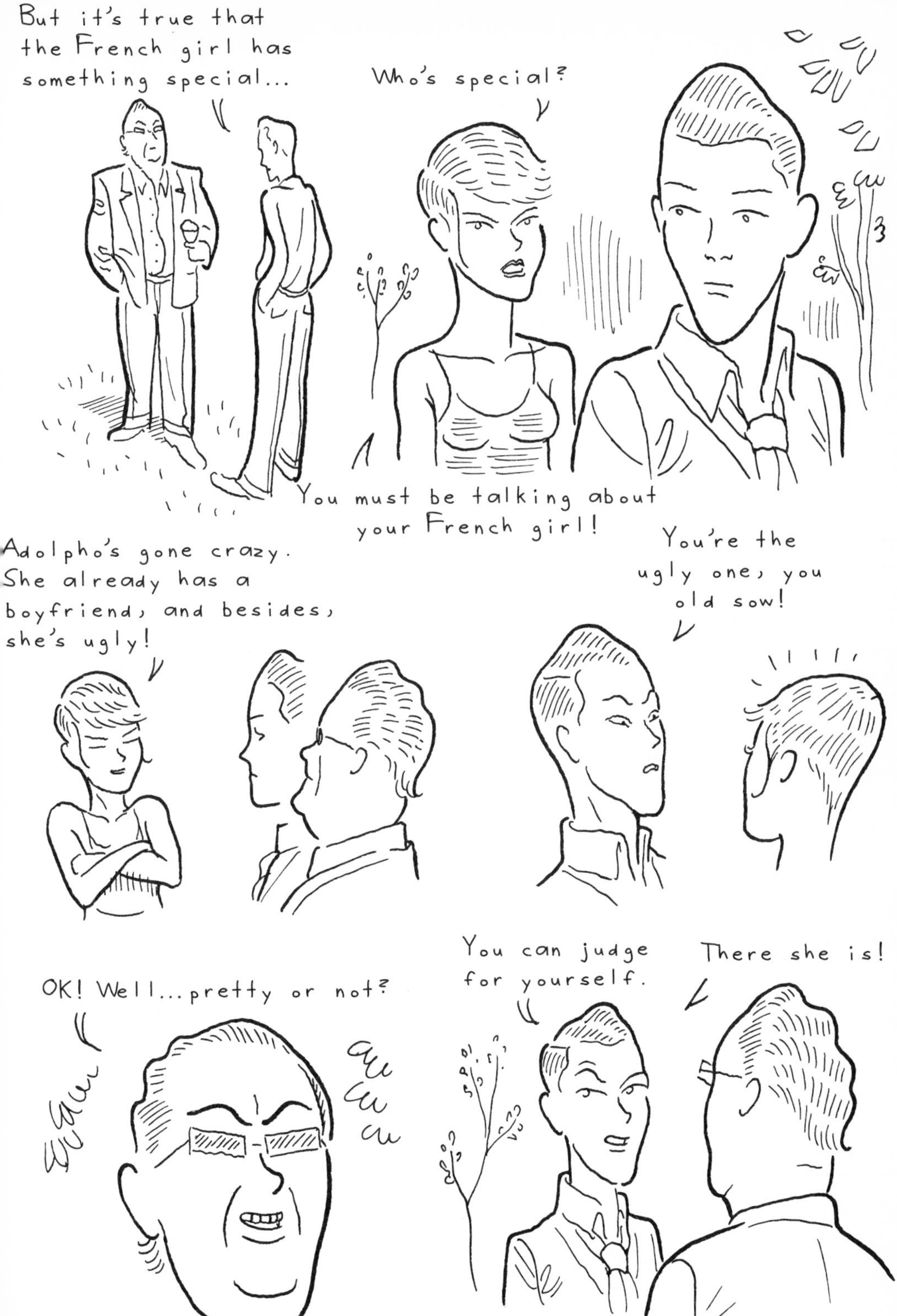
But it's true that the French girl has something special...
Who's special?
You must be talking about your French girl!
Adolpho's gone crazy. She already has a boyfriend, and besides, she's ugly!
You're the ugly one, you old sow!
OK! Well... pretty or not?
You can judge for yourself.
There she is!

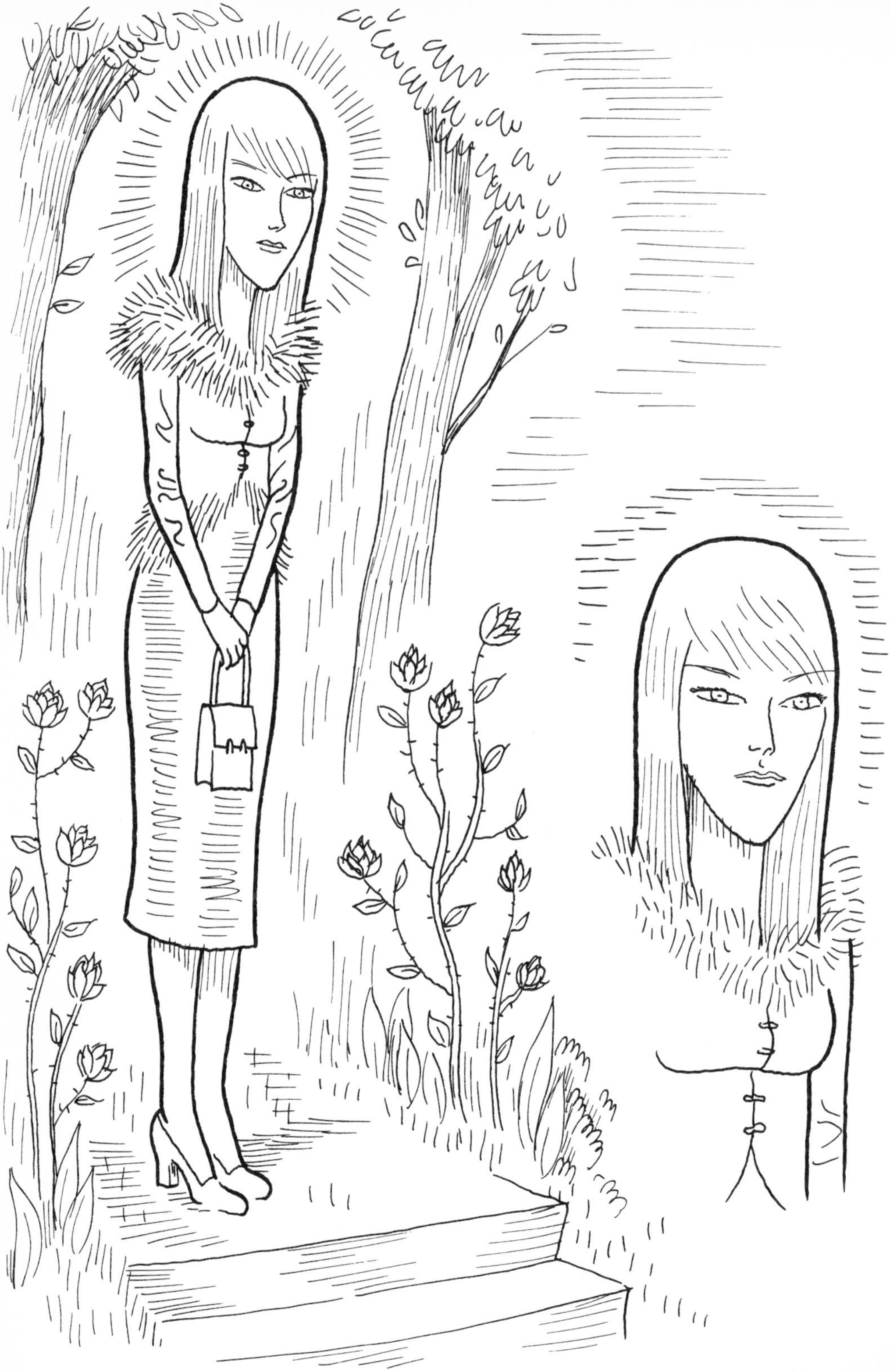

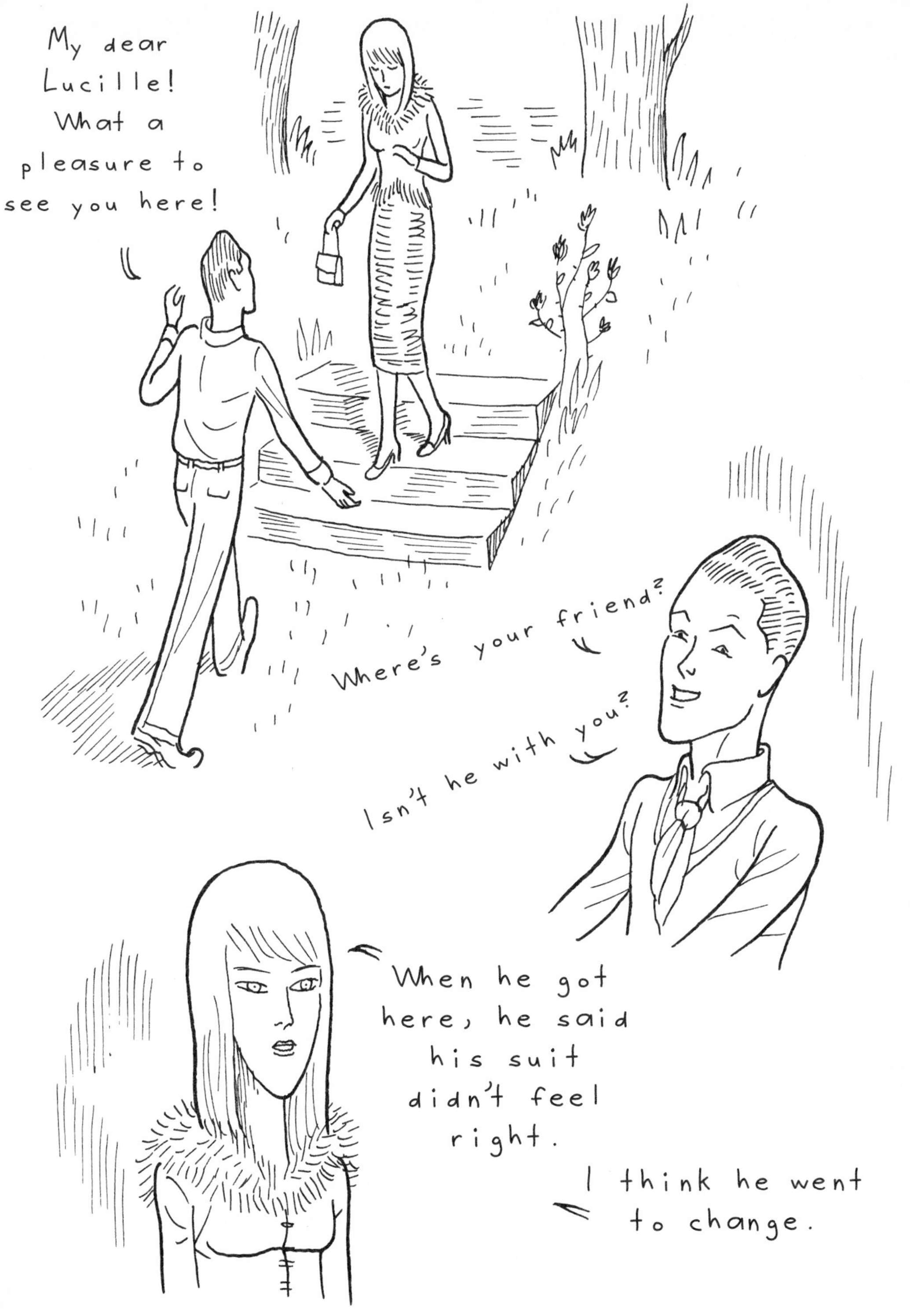
My dear Lucille! What a pleasure to see you here!
Where's your friend?
Isn't he with you?
When he got here, he said his suit didn't feel right.
I think he went to change.

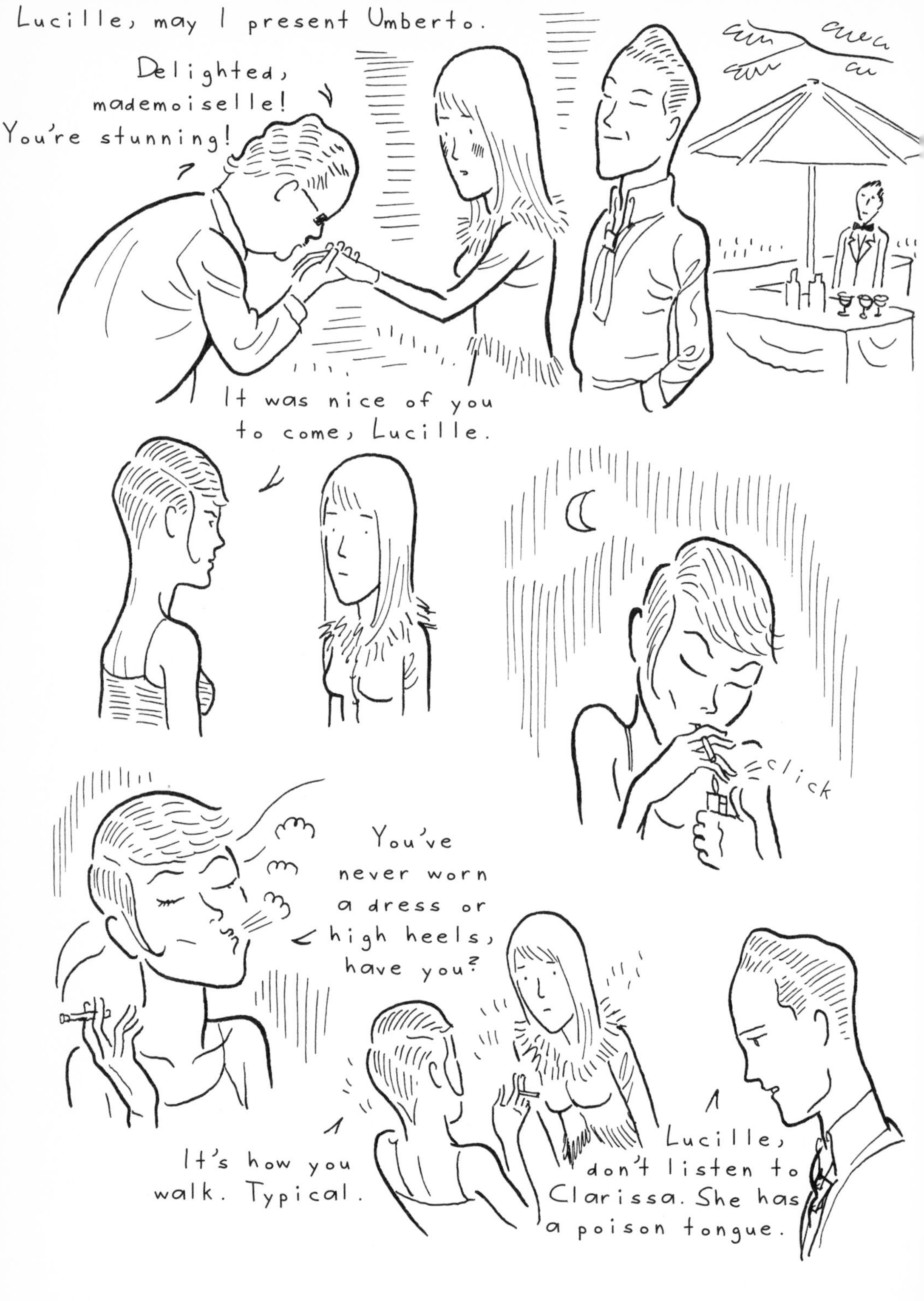
Lucille, may I present Umberto.
Delighted, mademoiselle! You're stunning!
It was nice of you to come, Lucille.
click
You've never worn a dress or high heels, have you?
It's how you walk. Typical.
Lucille, don't listen to Clarissa. She has a poison tongue.

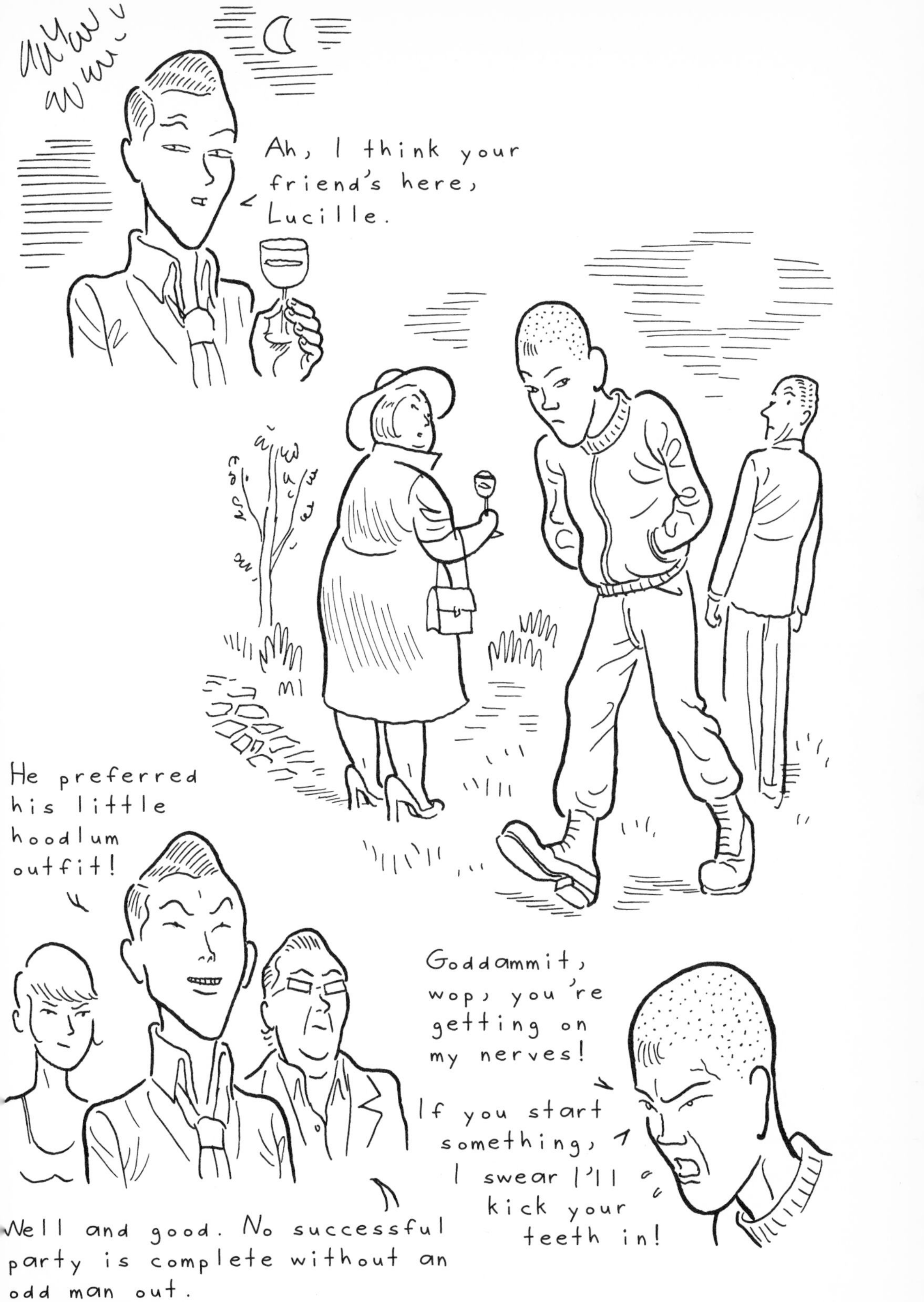
Ah, I think your friend's here, Lucille.
He preferred his little hoodlum outfit!
Well and good. No successful party is complete without an odd man out.
Goddammit, wop, you're getting on my nerves!
If you start something, I swear I'll kick your teeth in!

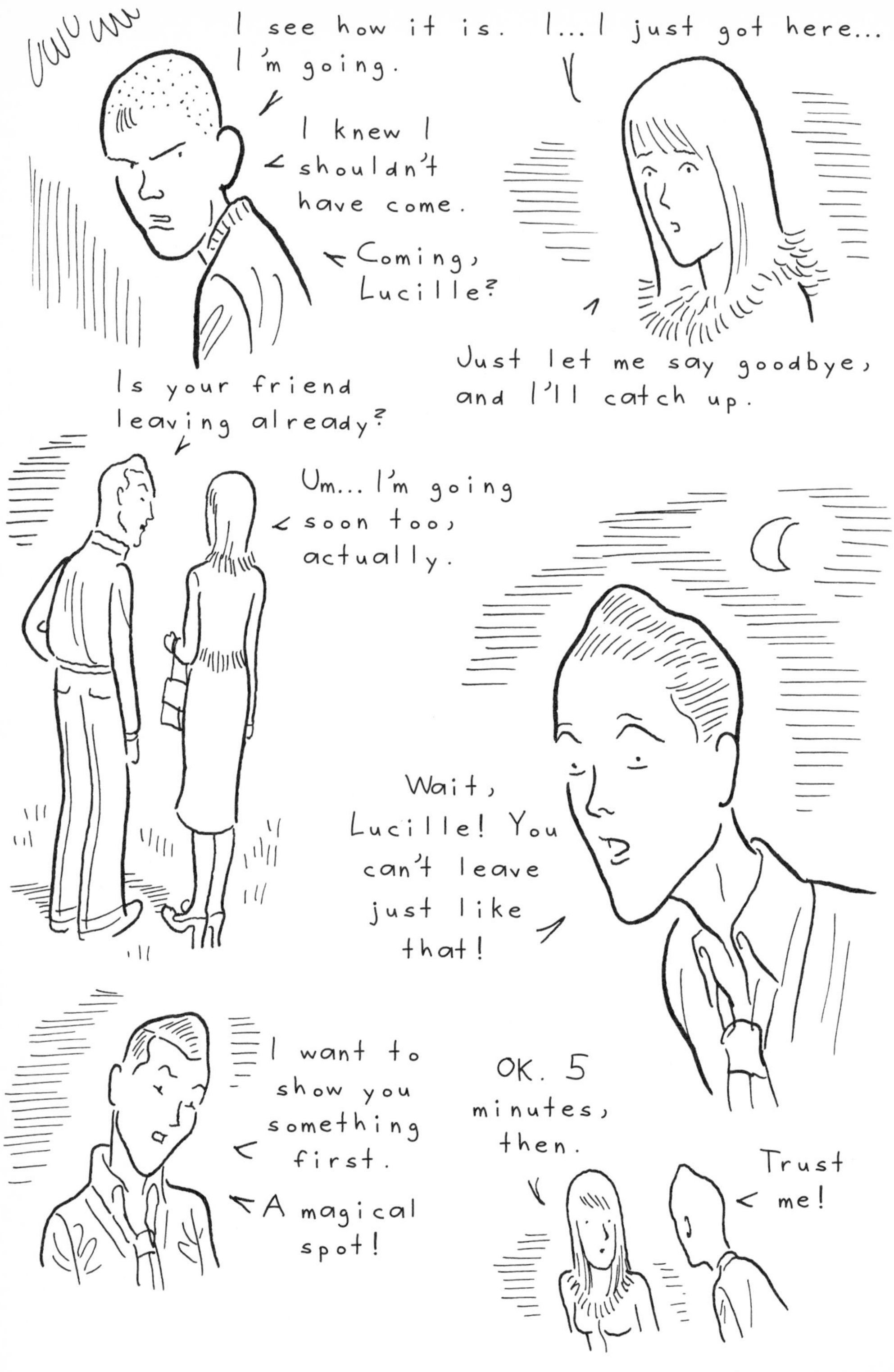
I see how it is. I'm going.
I knew I shouldn't have come.
Coming, Lucille?
I... I just got here...
Just let me say goodbye, and I'll catch up.
Is your friend leaving already?
Um... I'm going soon too, actually.
Wait, Lucille! You can't leave just like that!
I want to show you something first.
A magical spot!
OK. 5 minutes, then.
Trust me!

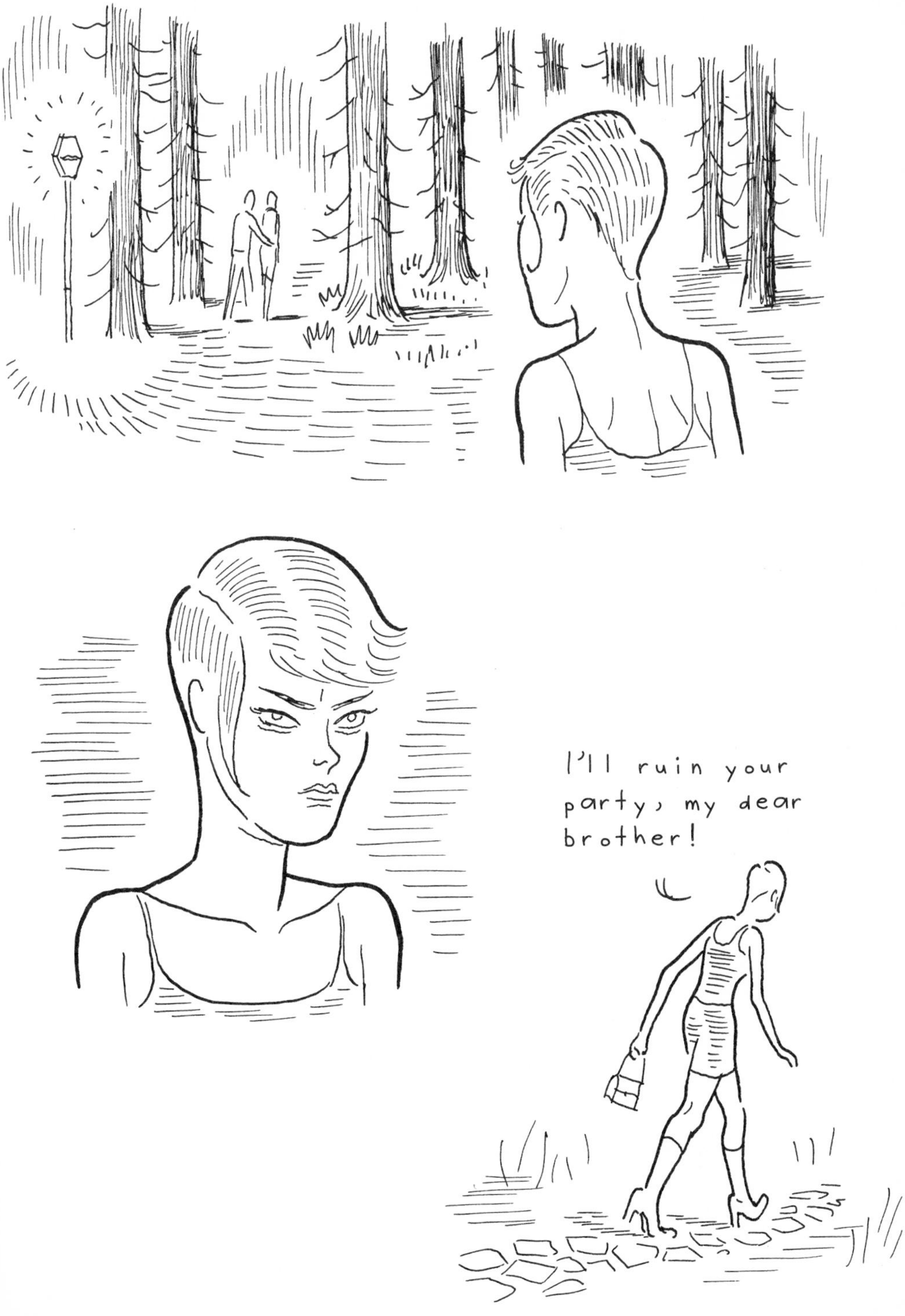
I'll ruin your party, my dear brother!

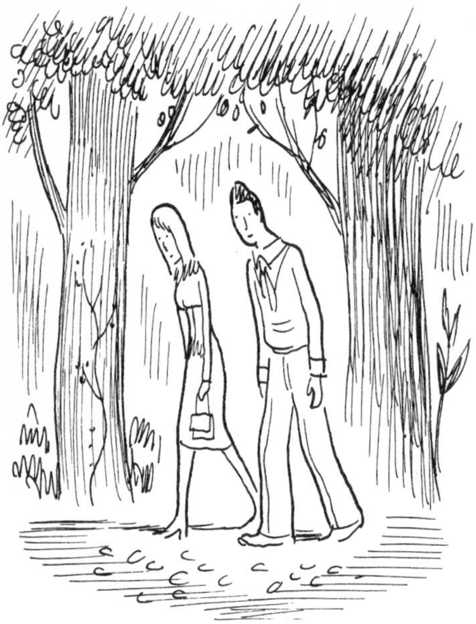

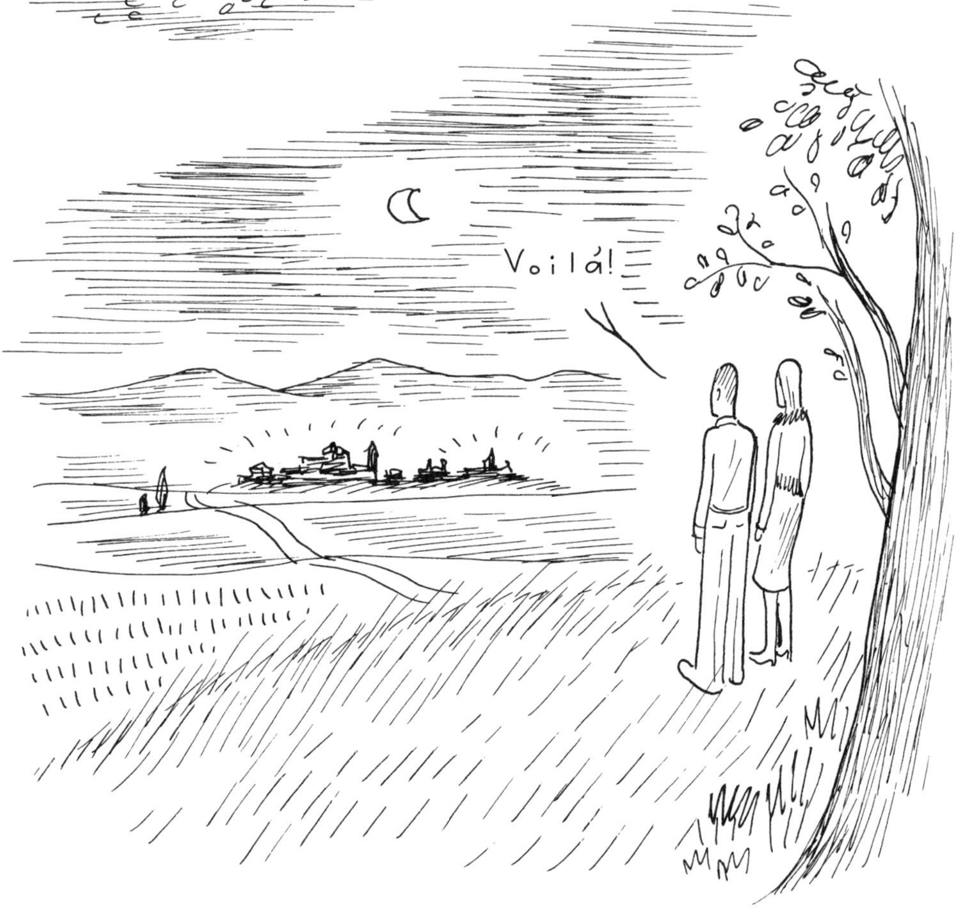
Voilá!

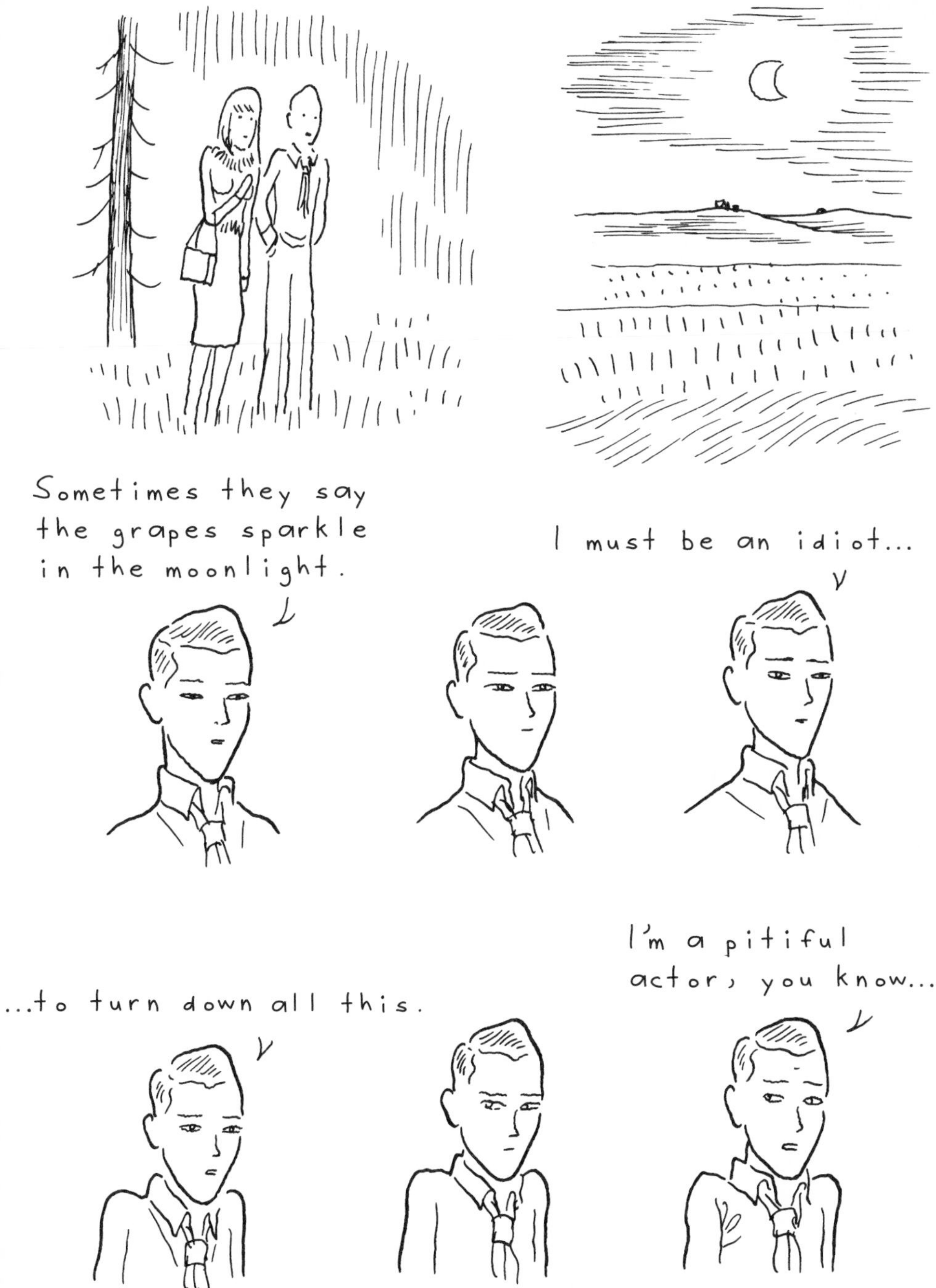
Sometimes they say the grapes sparkle in the moonlight.
I must be an idiot...
...to turn down all this.
I'm a pitiful actor, you know...

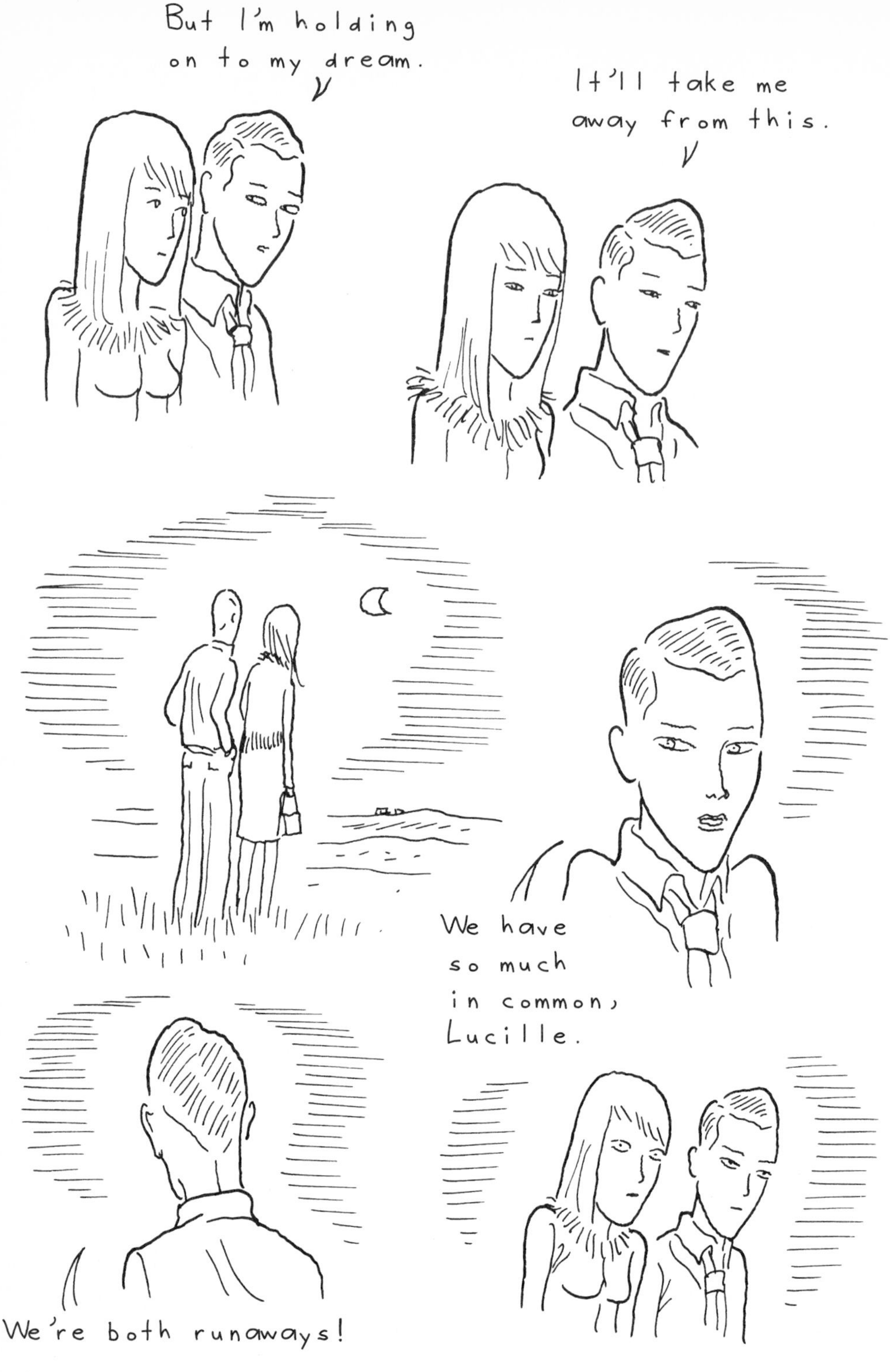
But I'm holding on to my dream.
It'll take me away from this.
We have so much in common, Lucille.
We're both runaways!

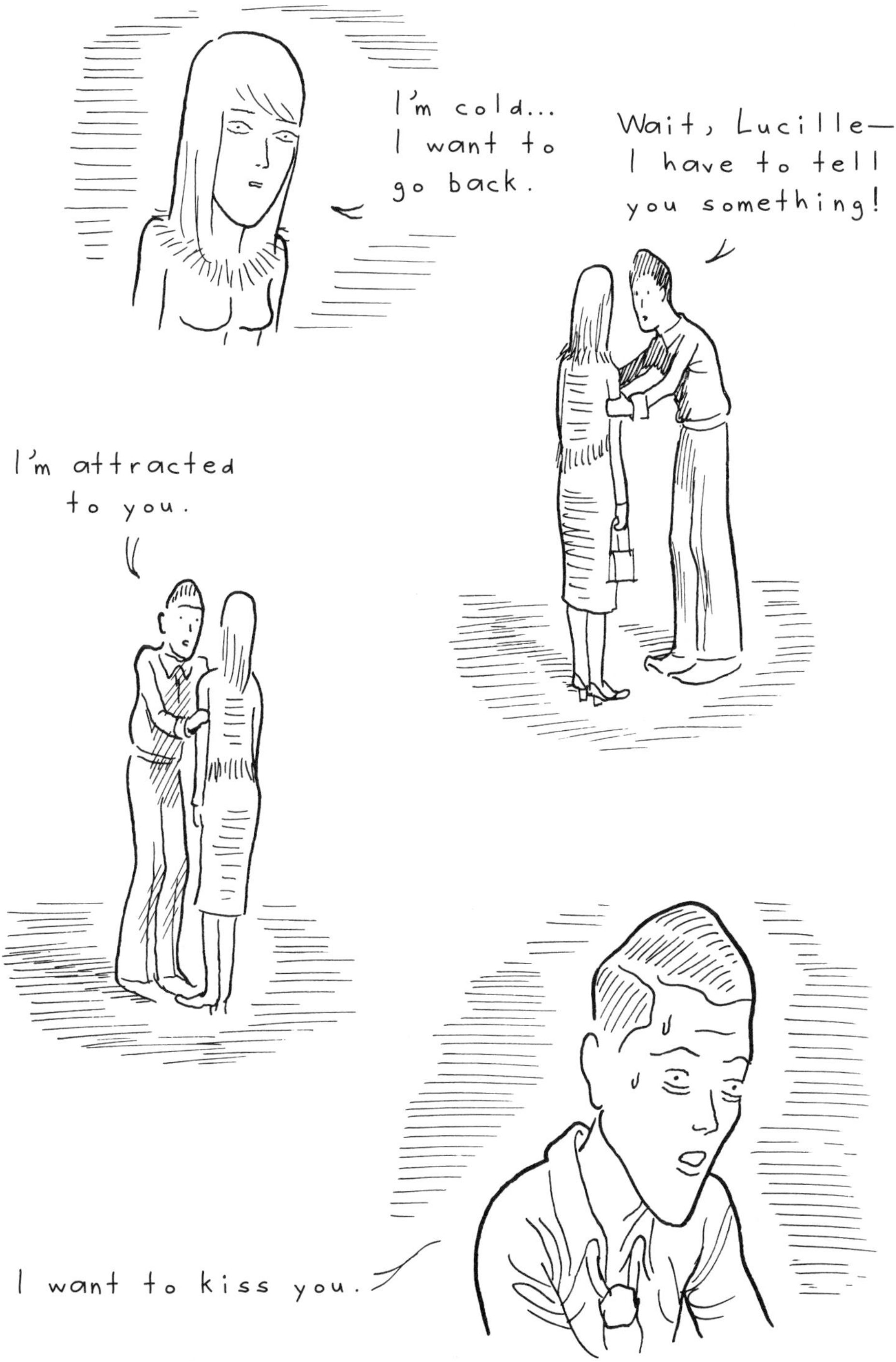
I'm cold... I want to go back.
Wait, Lucille— I have to tell you something!
I'm attracted to you.
I want to kiss you.

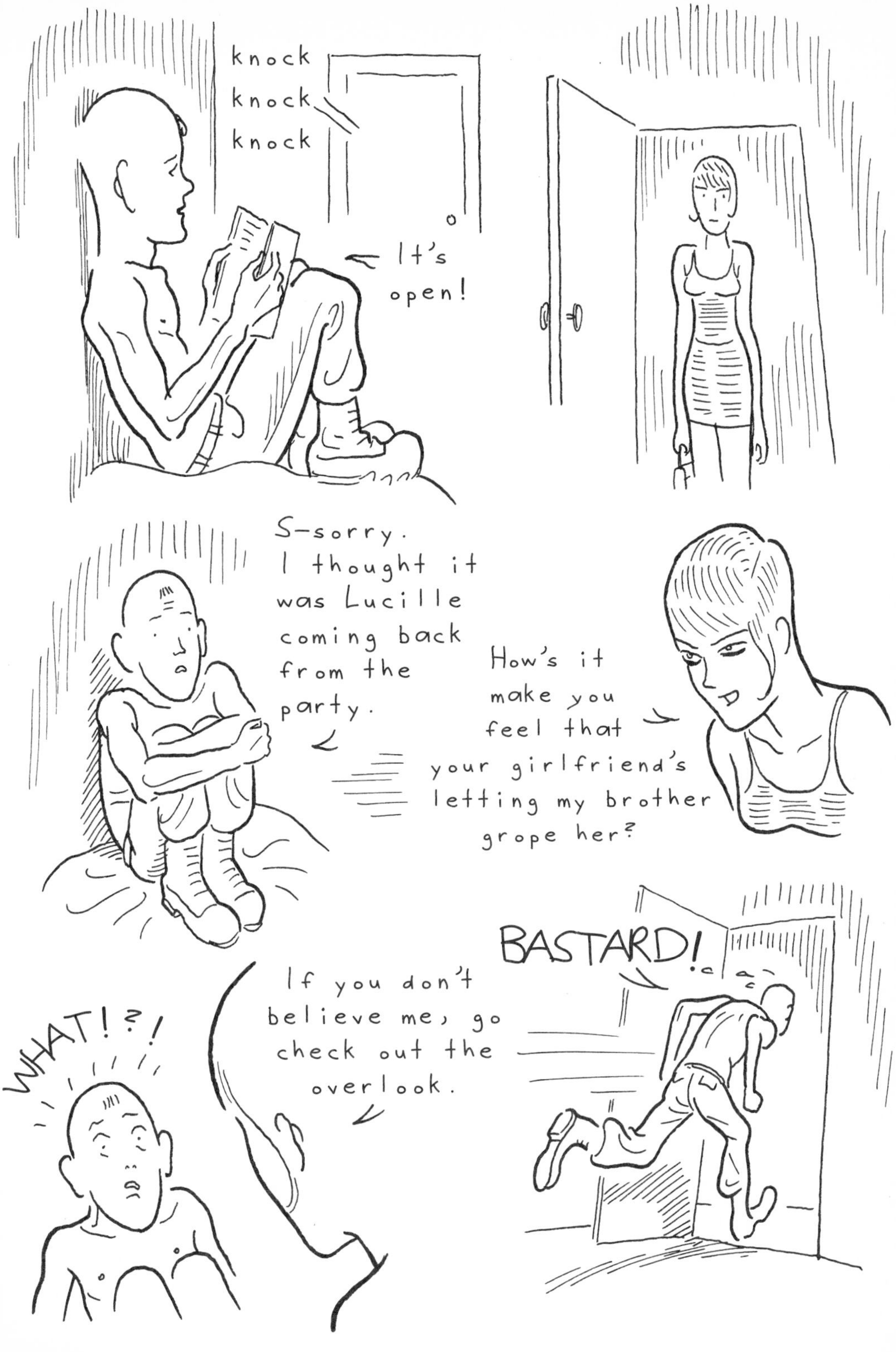
knock
knock
knock
It's open!
S-sorry. I thought it was Lucille coming back from the party.
How's it make you feel that your girlfriend's letting my brother grope her?
WHAT!?!
If you don't believe me, go check out the overlook.
BASTARD!

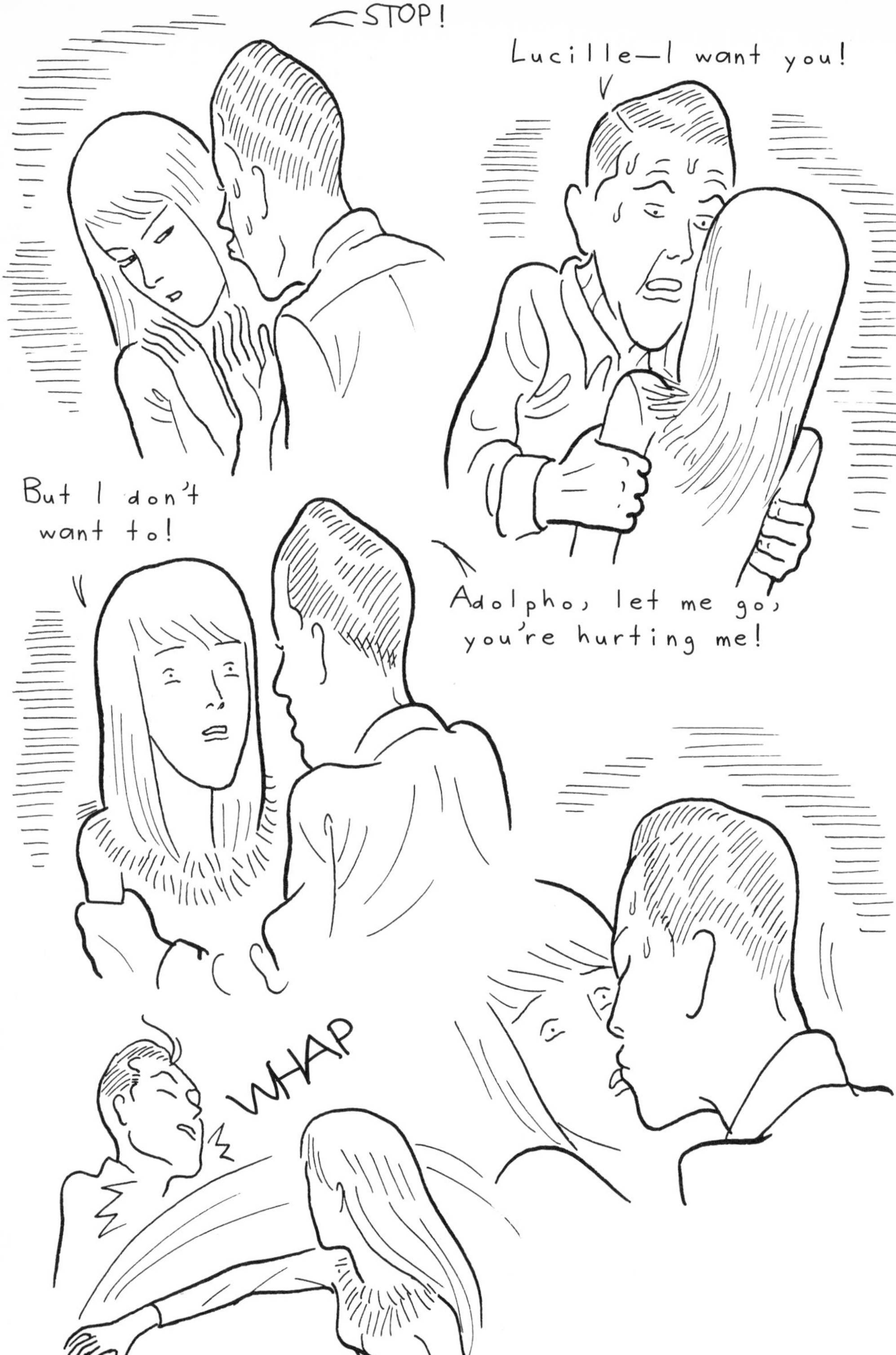
STOP!
Lucille—I want you!
But I don't want to!
Adolpho, let me go, you're hurting me!
WHAP

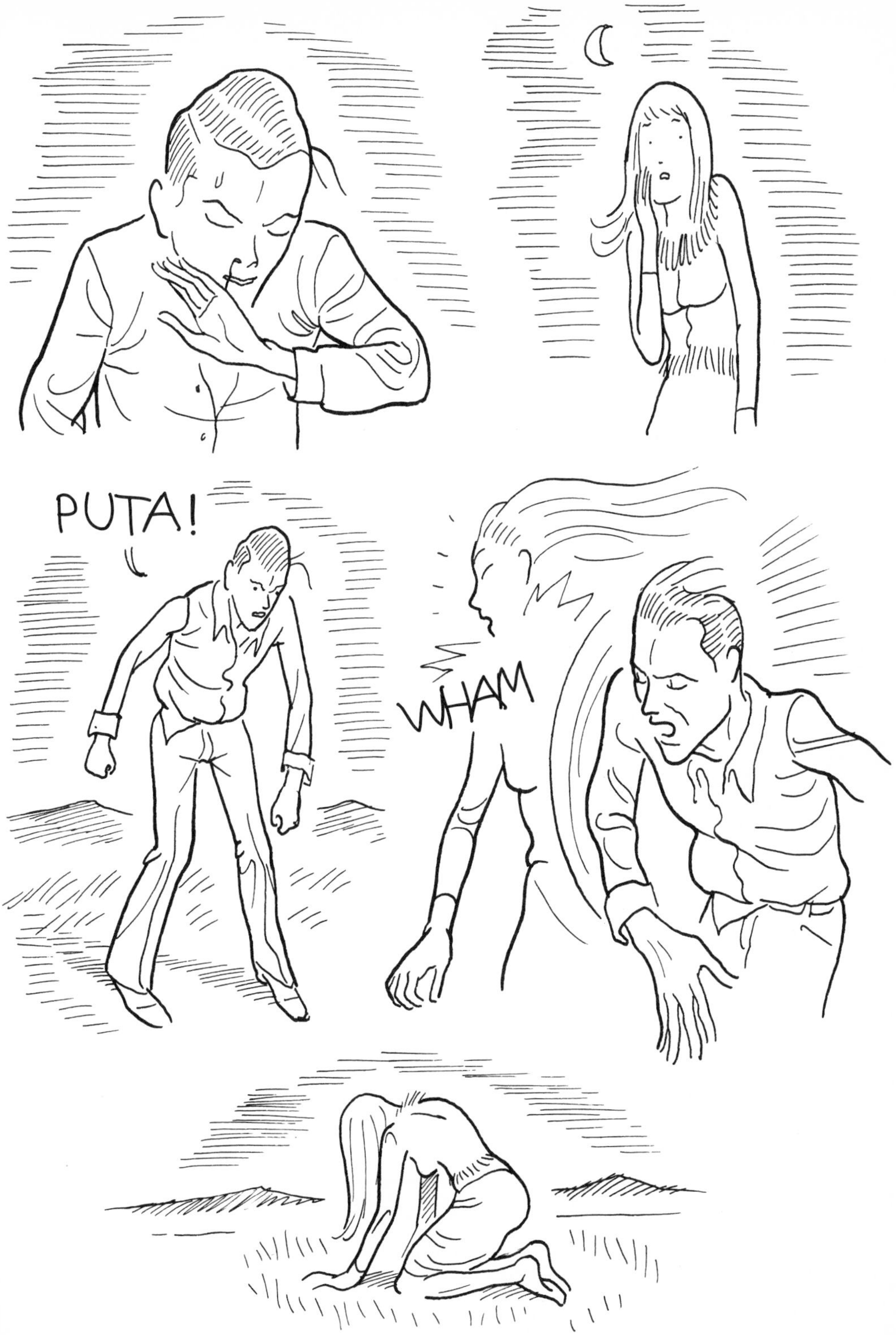
PUTA!
WHAM

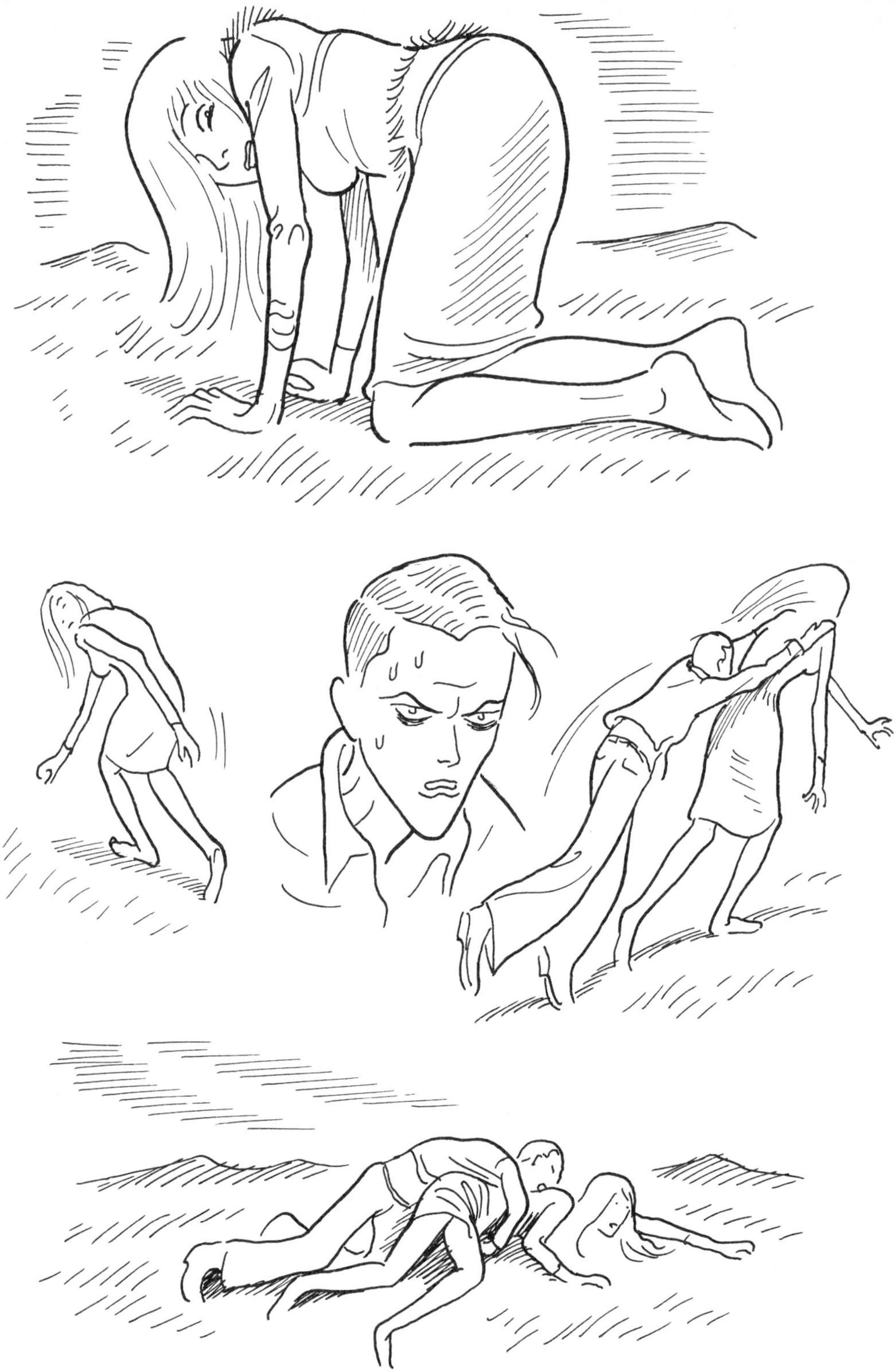

When a Sailor
meets another sailor

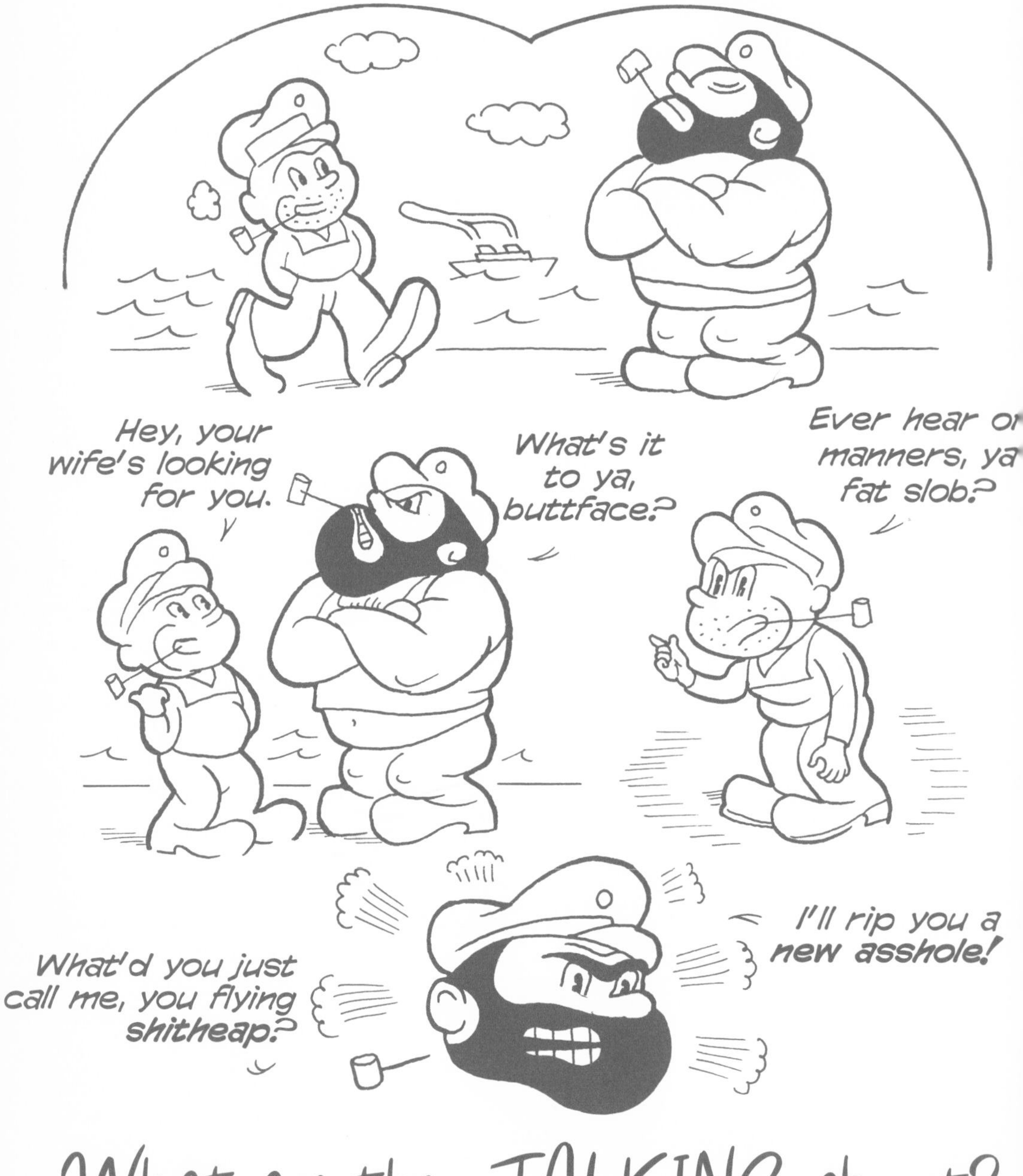
Hey, your wife's looking for you.
What's it to ya, buttface?
Ever hear o manners, ya fat slob?
What'd you just call me, you flying shitheap?
I'll rip you a new asshole!

What are they TALKING about?

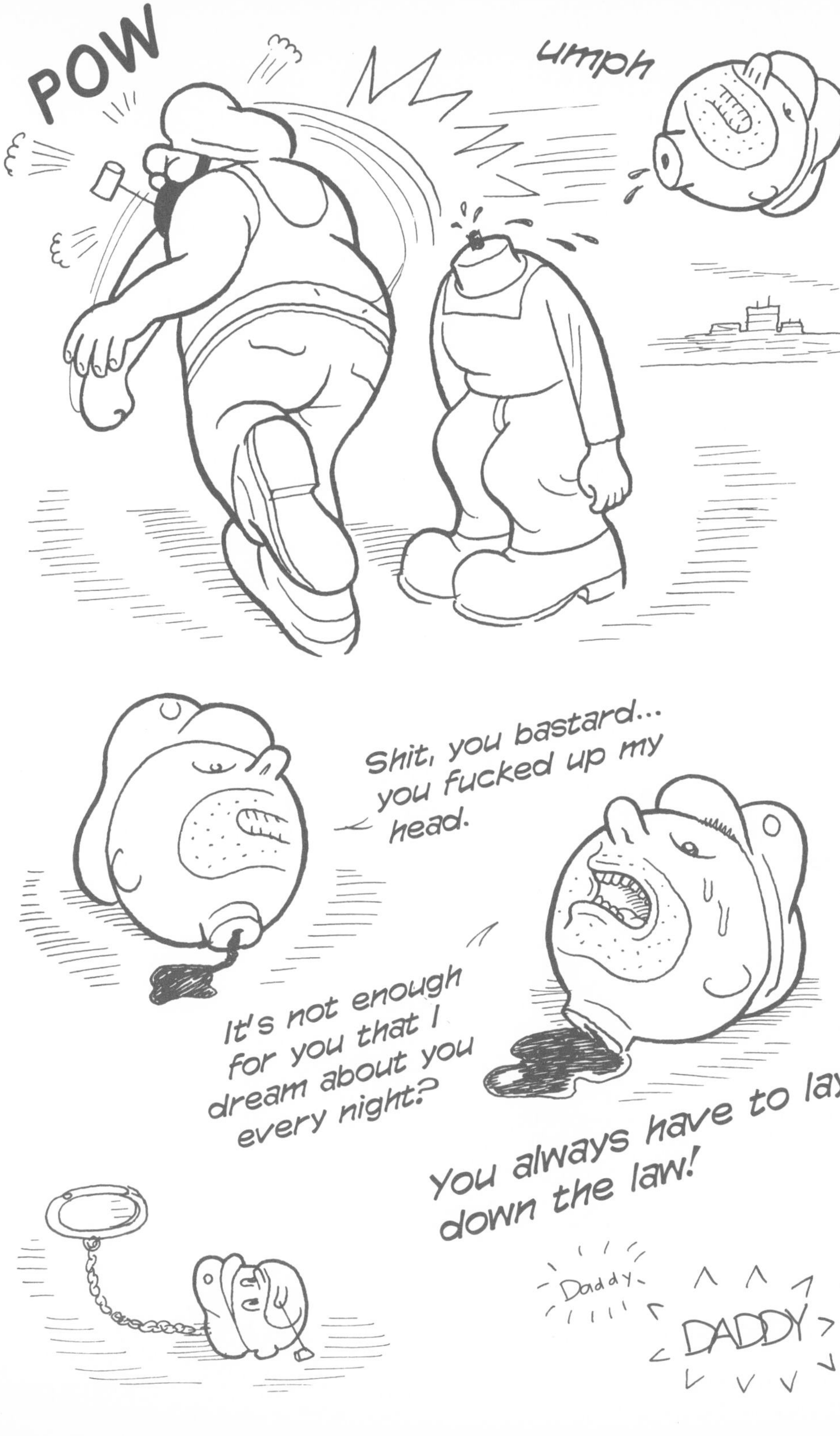
POW
umph
Shit, you bastard... you fucked up my head.
It's not enough for you that I dream about you every night?
You always have to lay down the law!
Daddy
DADDY

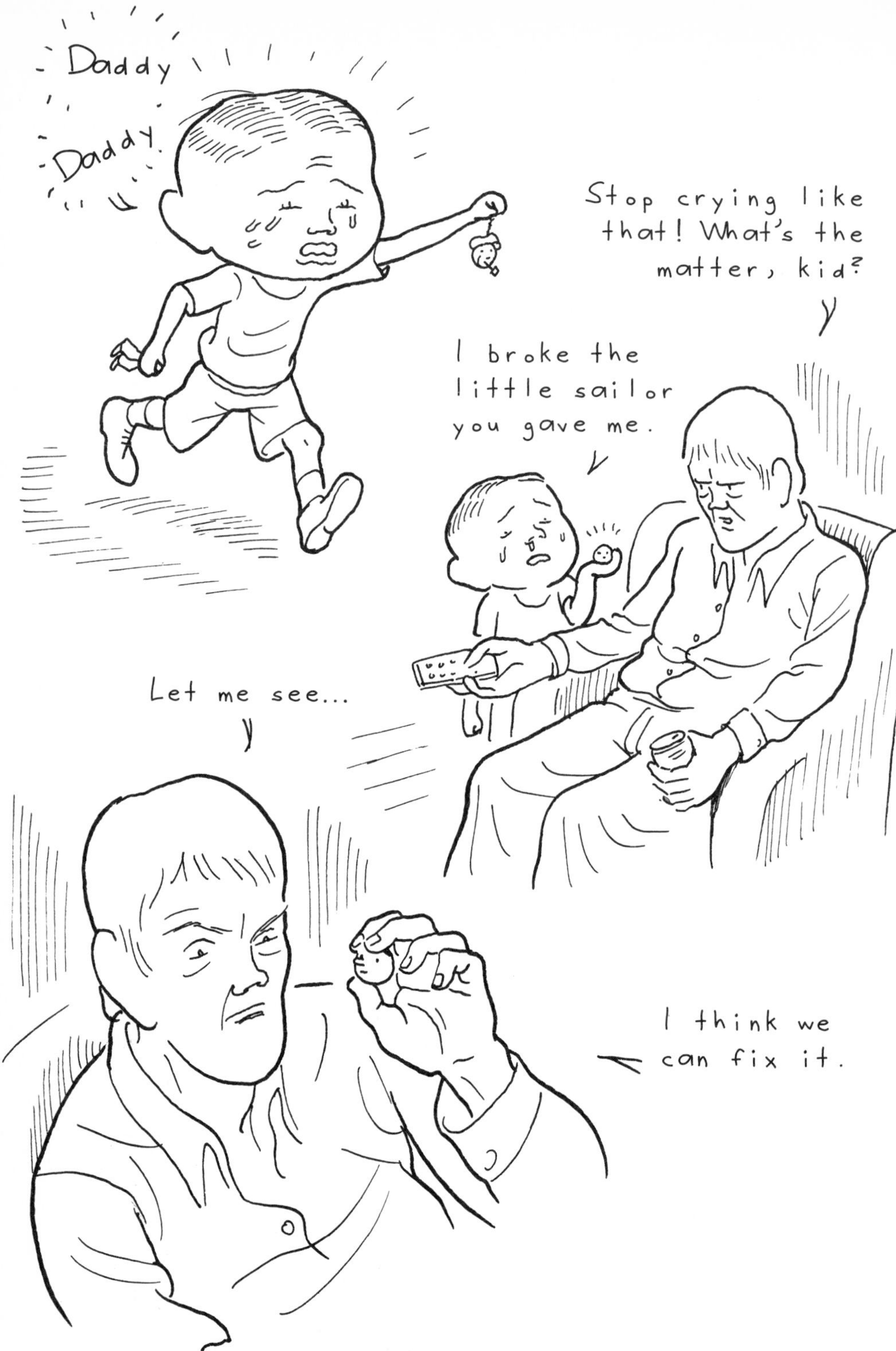
Daddy
Daddy
Stop crying like that! What's the matter, kid?
I broke the little sailor you gave me.
Let me see...
I think we can fix it.

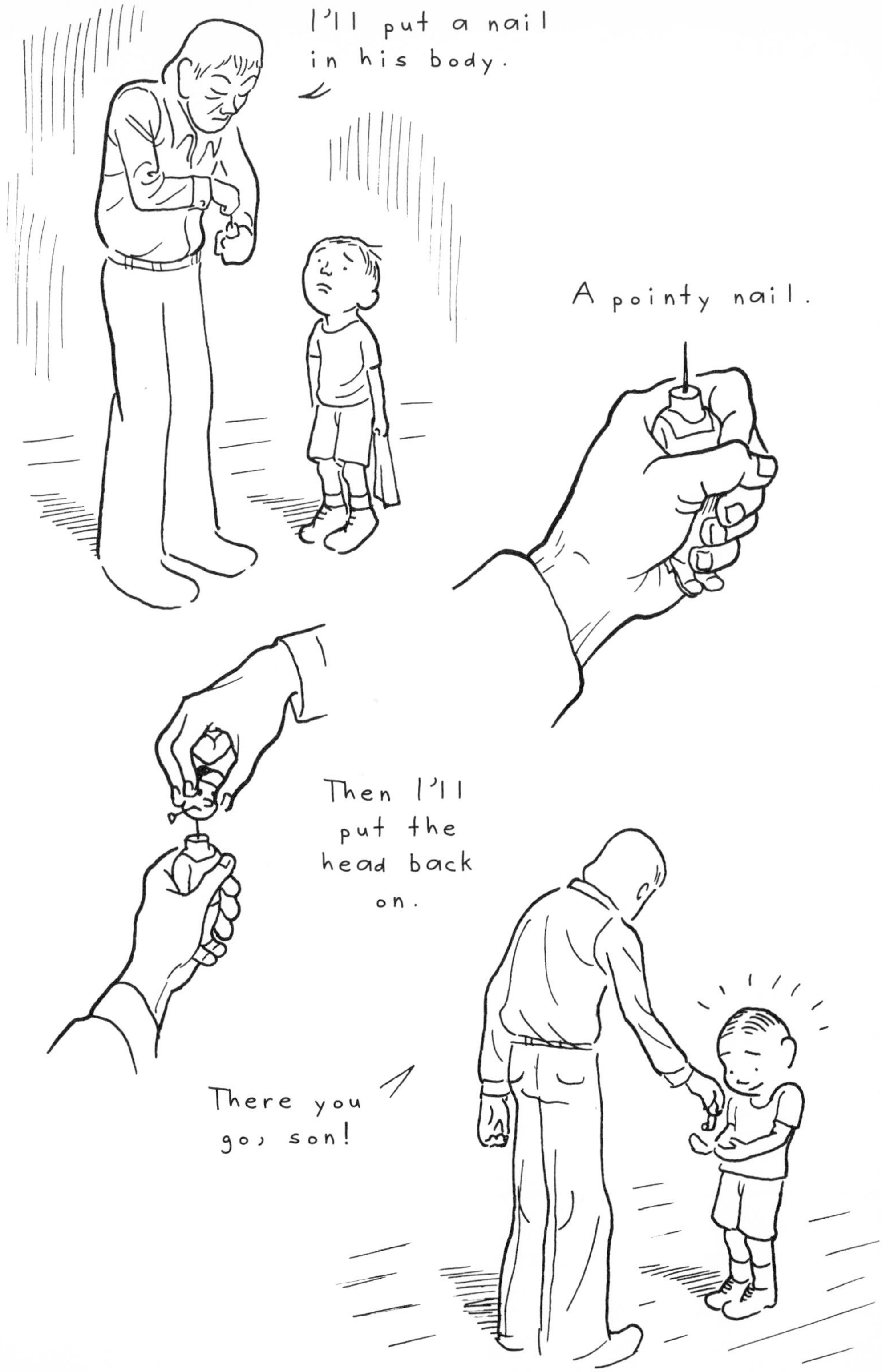
I'll put a nail in his body.
A pointy nail.
Then I'll put the head back on.
There you go, son!

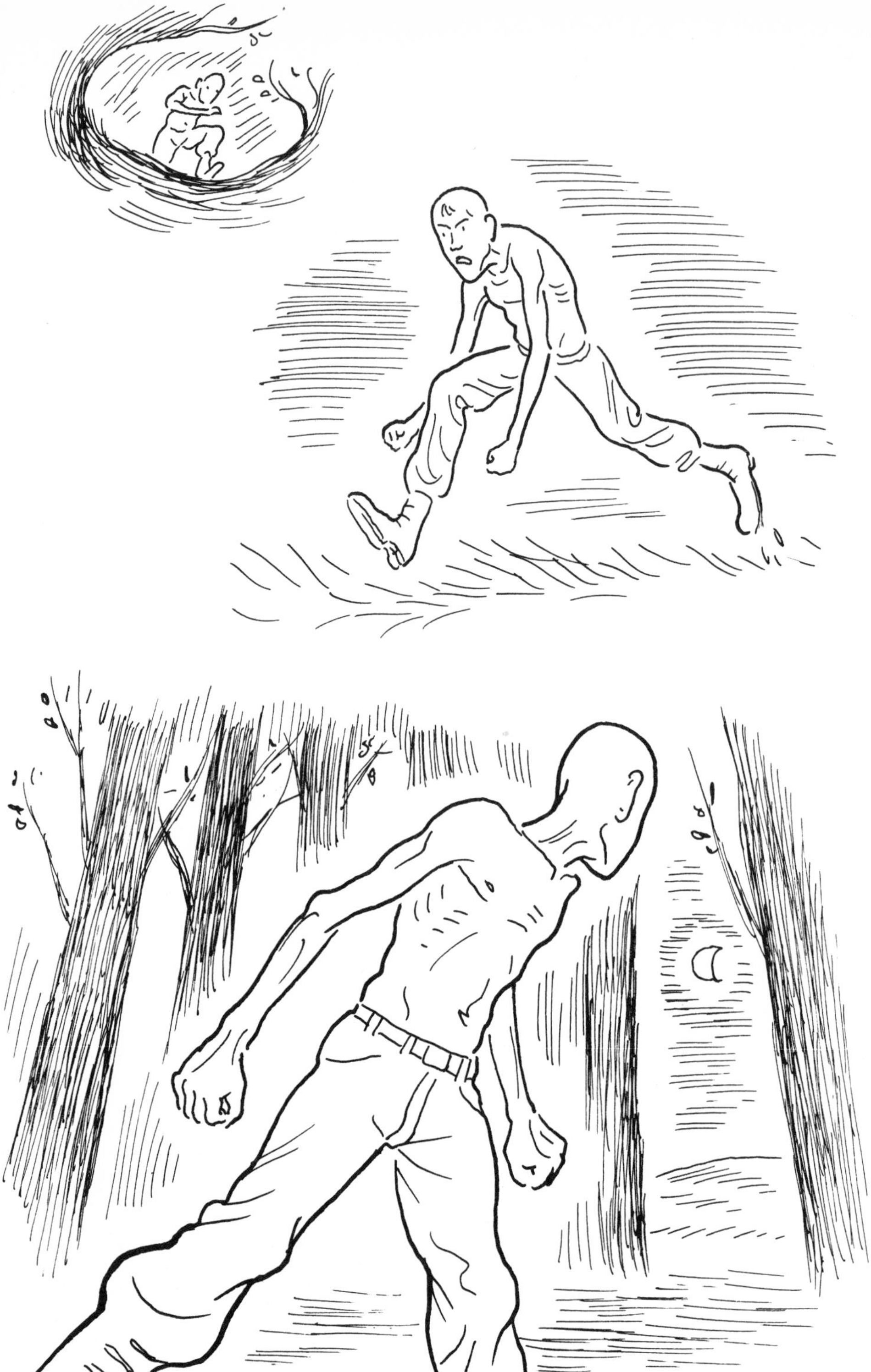

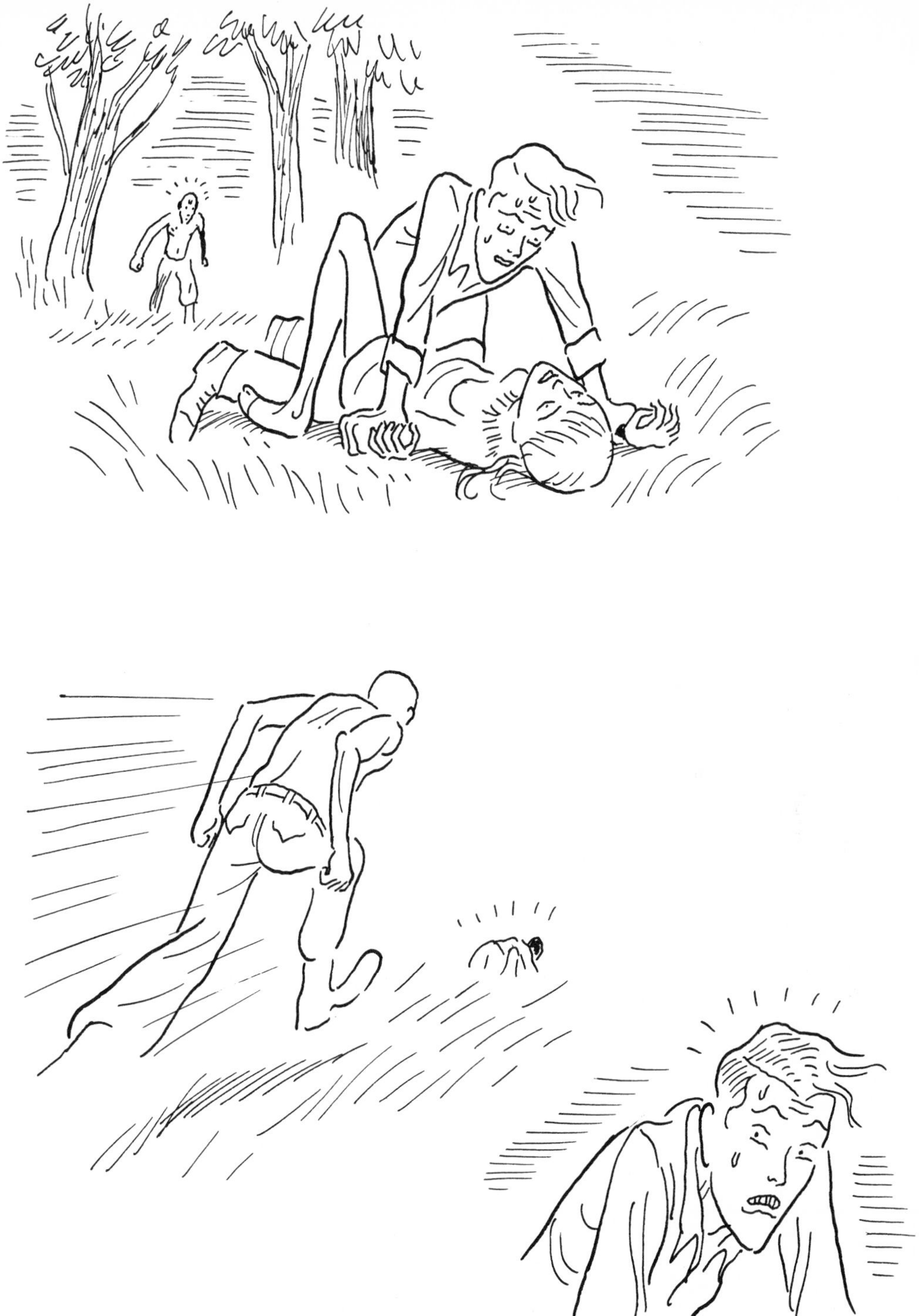

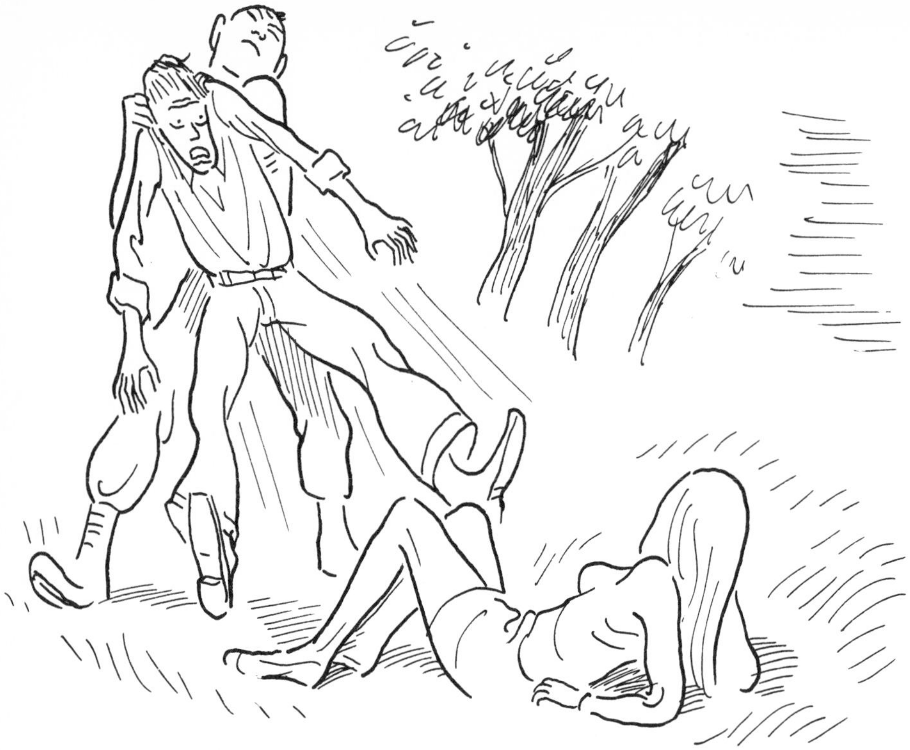

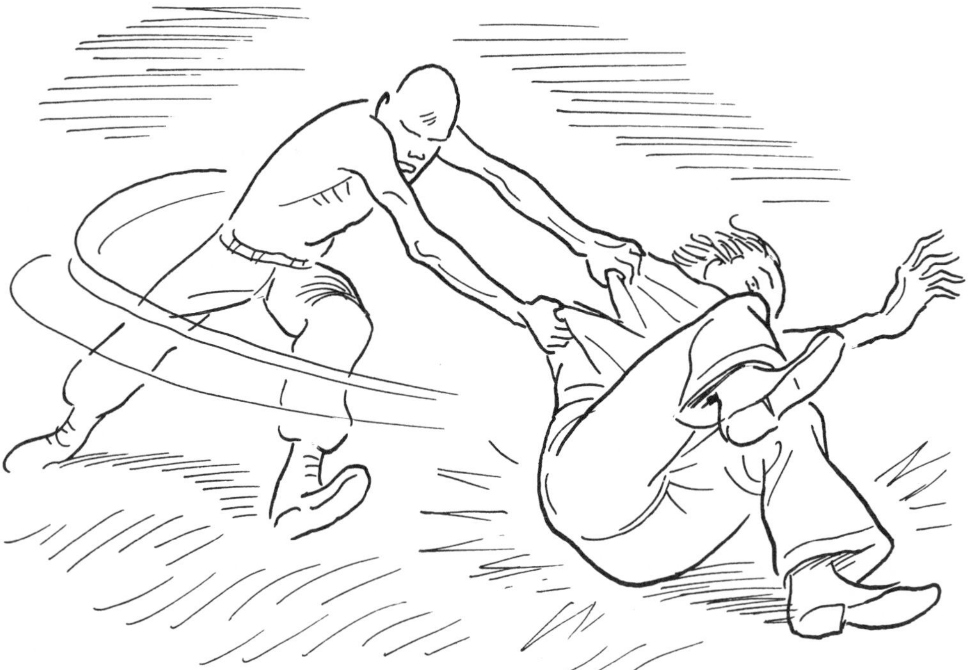

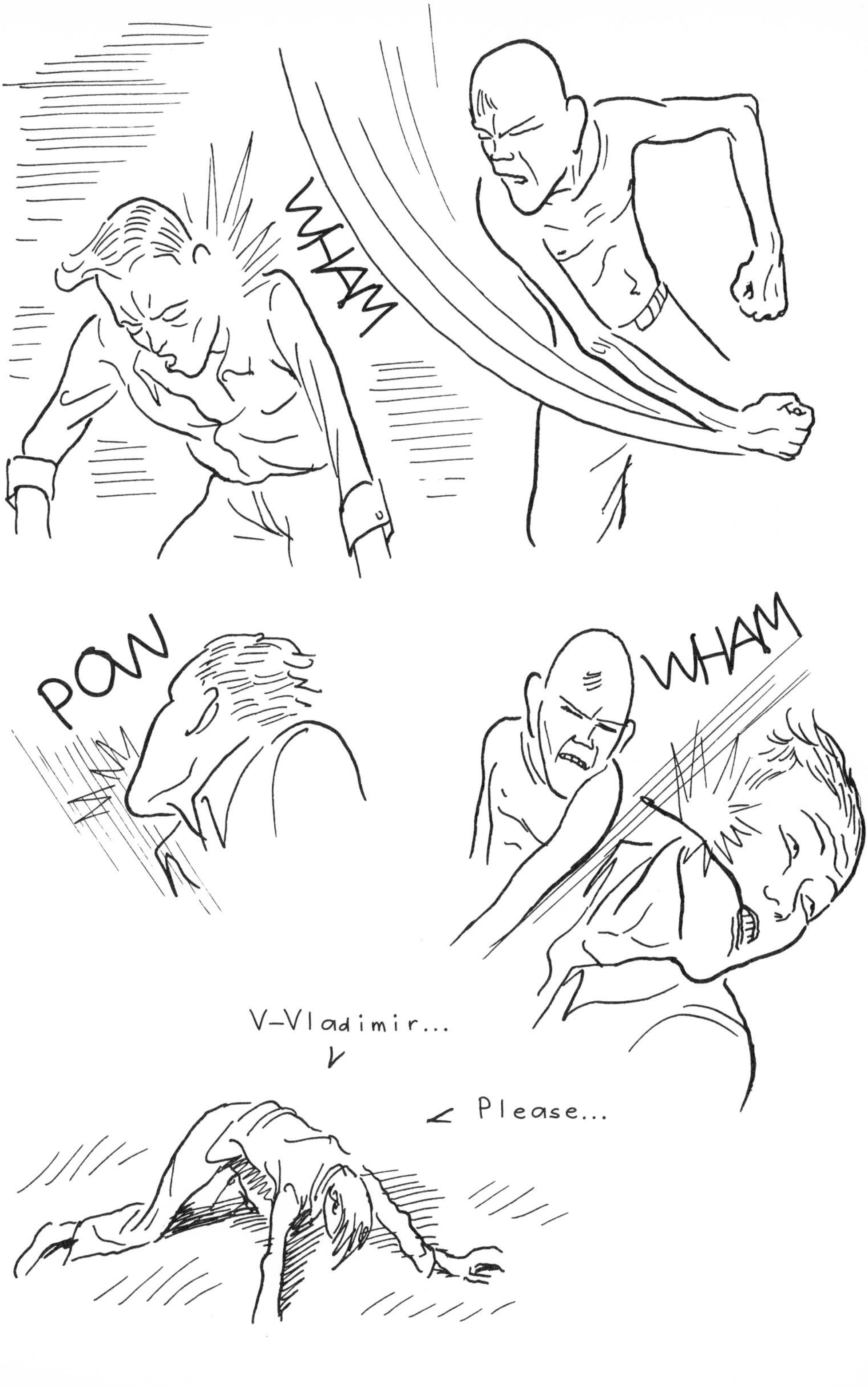
WHAM
POW
WHAM
V-Vladimir...
Please...

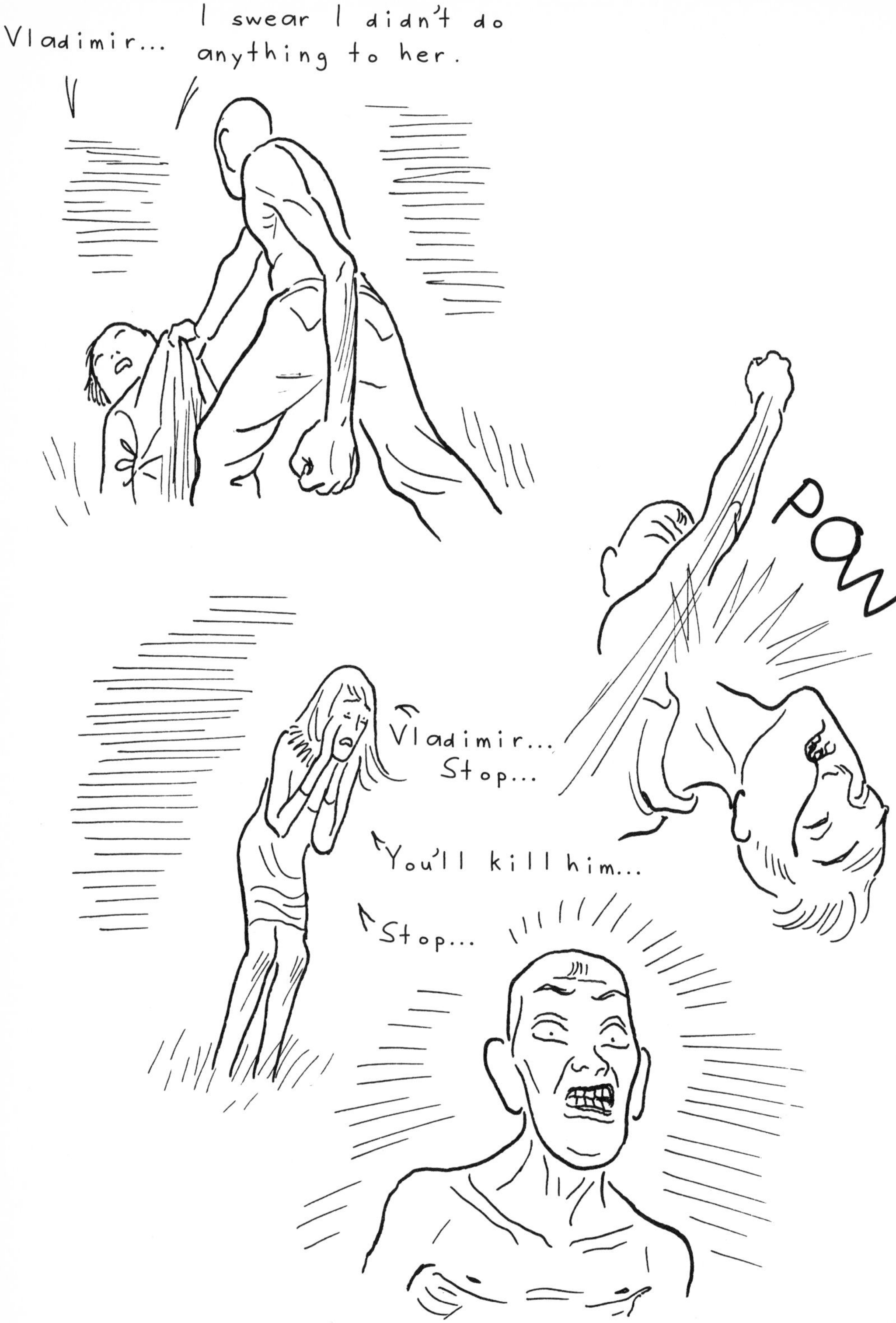
Vladimir...
I swear I didn't do anything to her.
POW
Vladimir... Stop...
You'll kill him...
Stop...

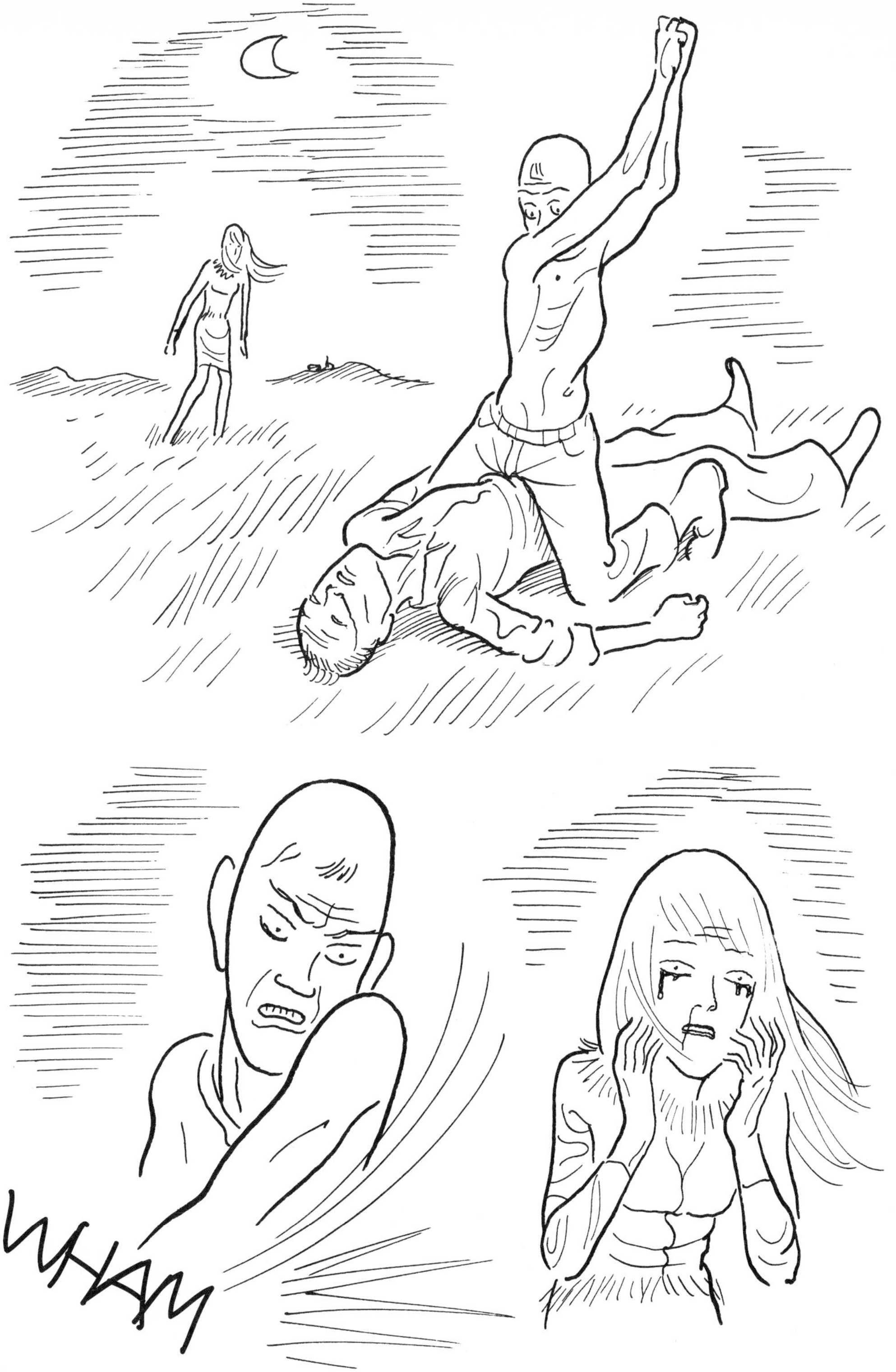
WHAM

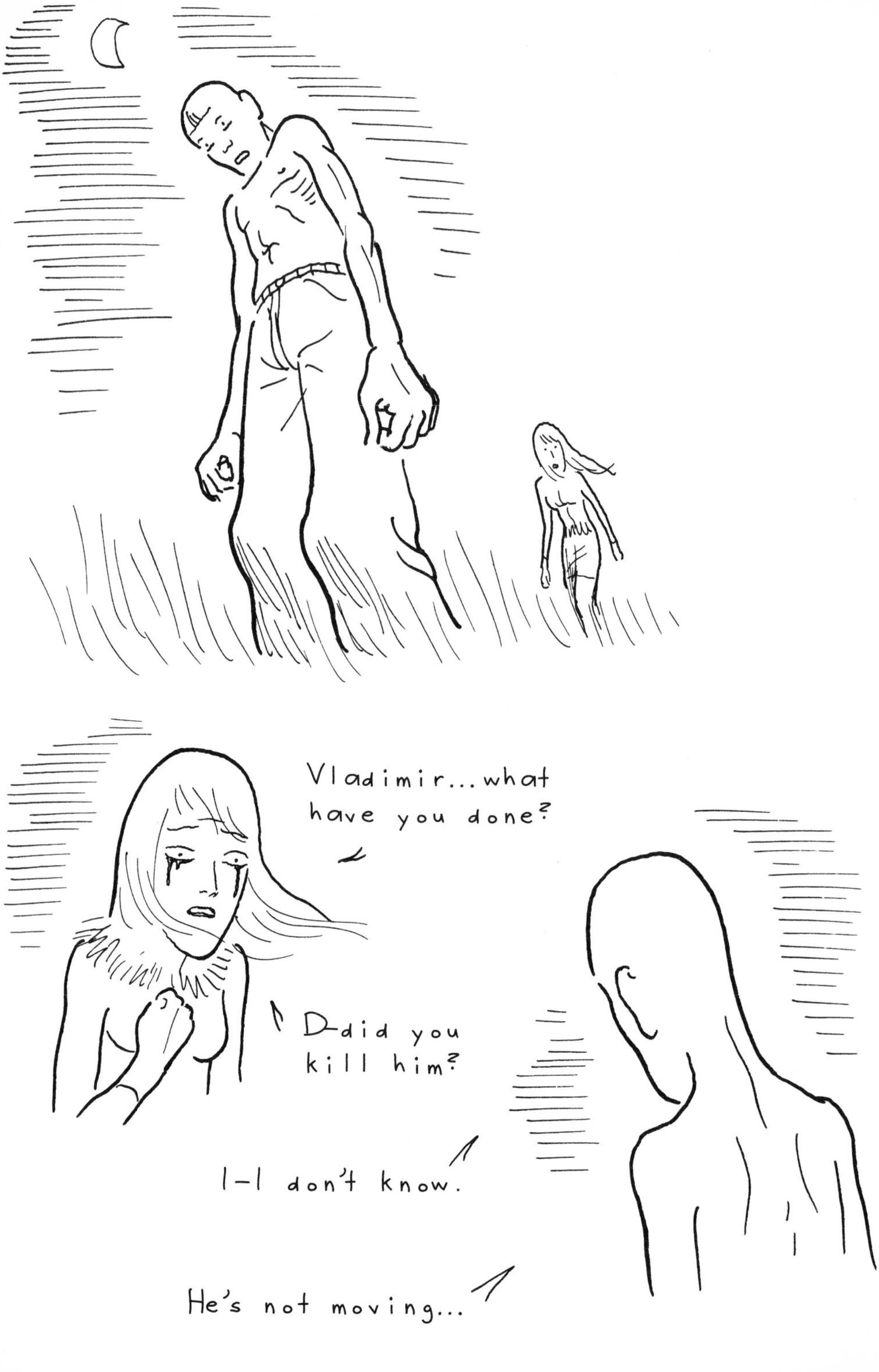
Vladimir...what have you done?
D-did you kill him?
I-I don't know.
He's not moving...

HYSTÉRÉSIS

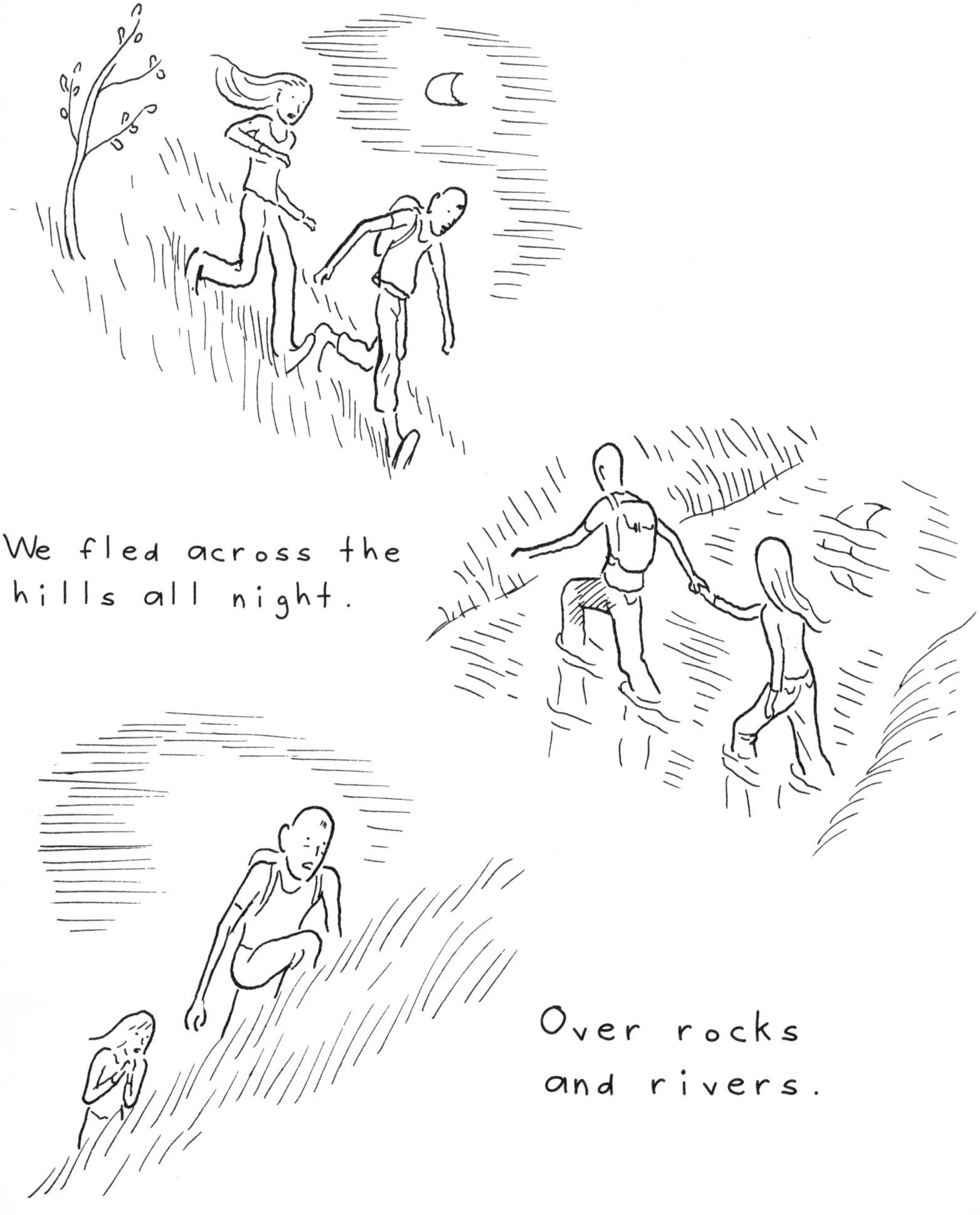
We fled across the hills all night.
Over rocks and rivers.

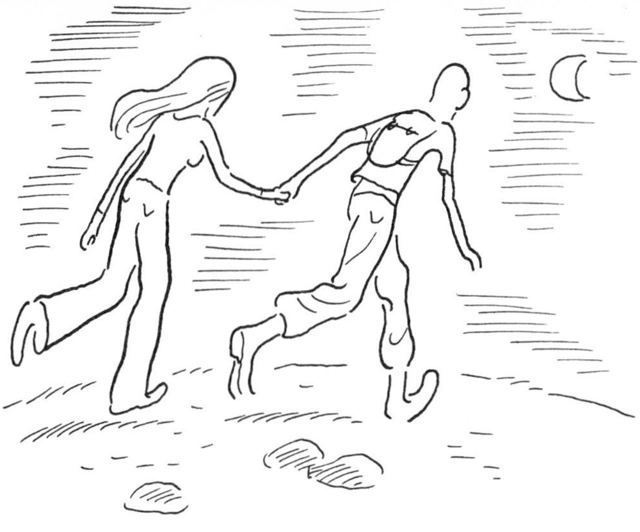

I heard Vladimir's voice,

louder and louder.

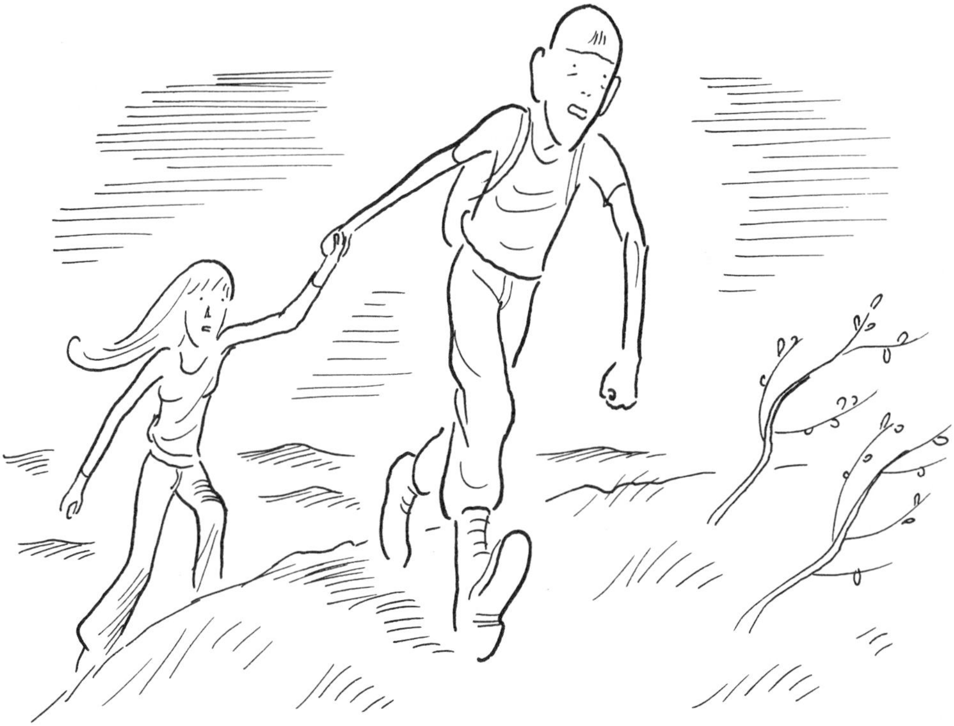

He was counting...

Counting his steps!

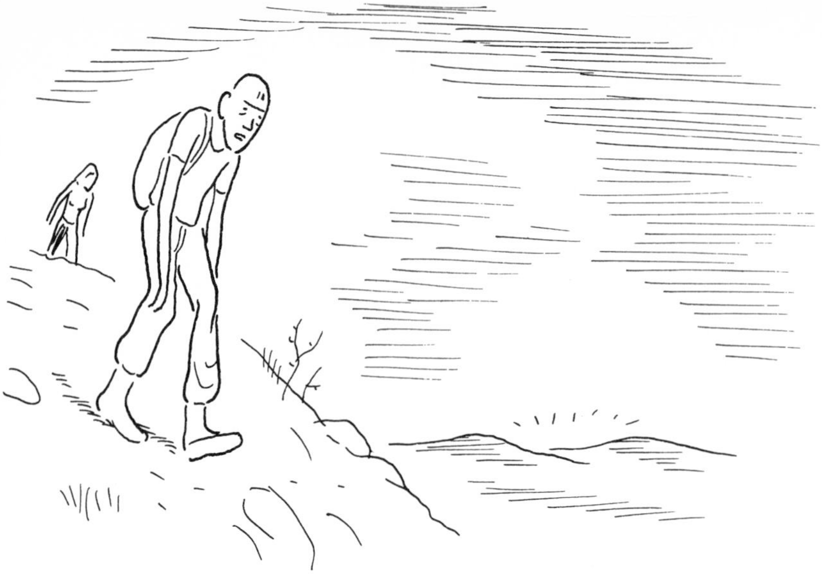

We reached a small hunting shelter just as day was breaking.

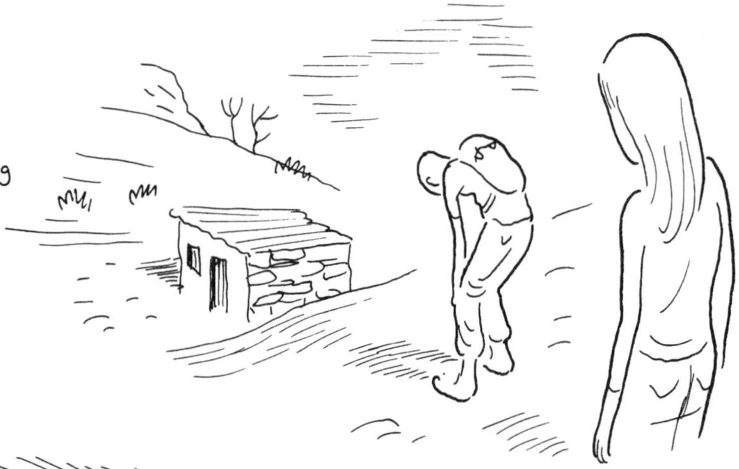

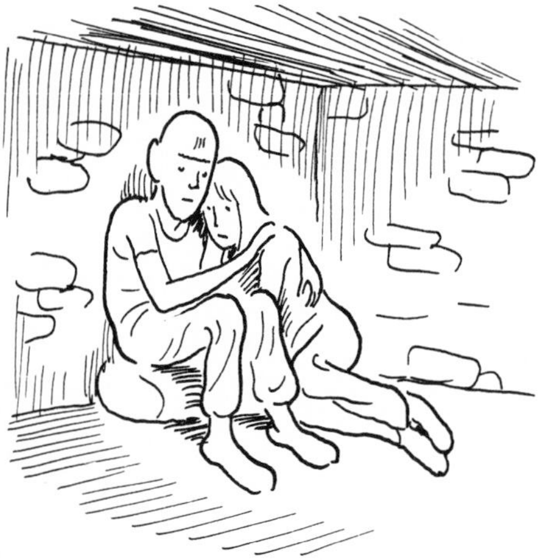

In a whisper, Vladimir kept repeating things I couldn't understand.

We lay down...

and made love...

weeping

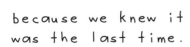

because we knew it
was the last time.

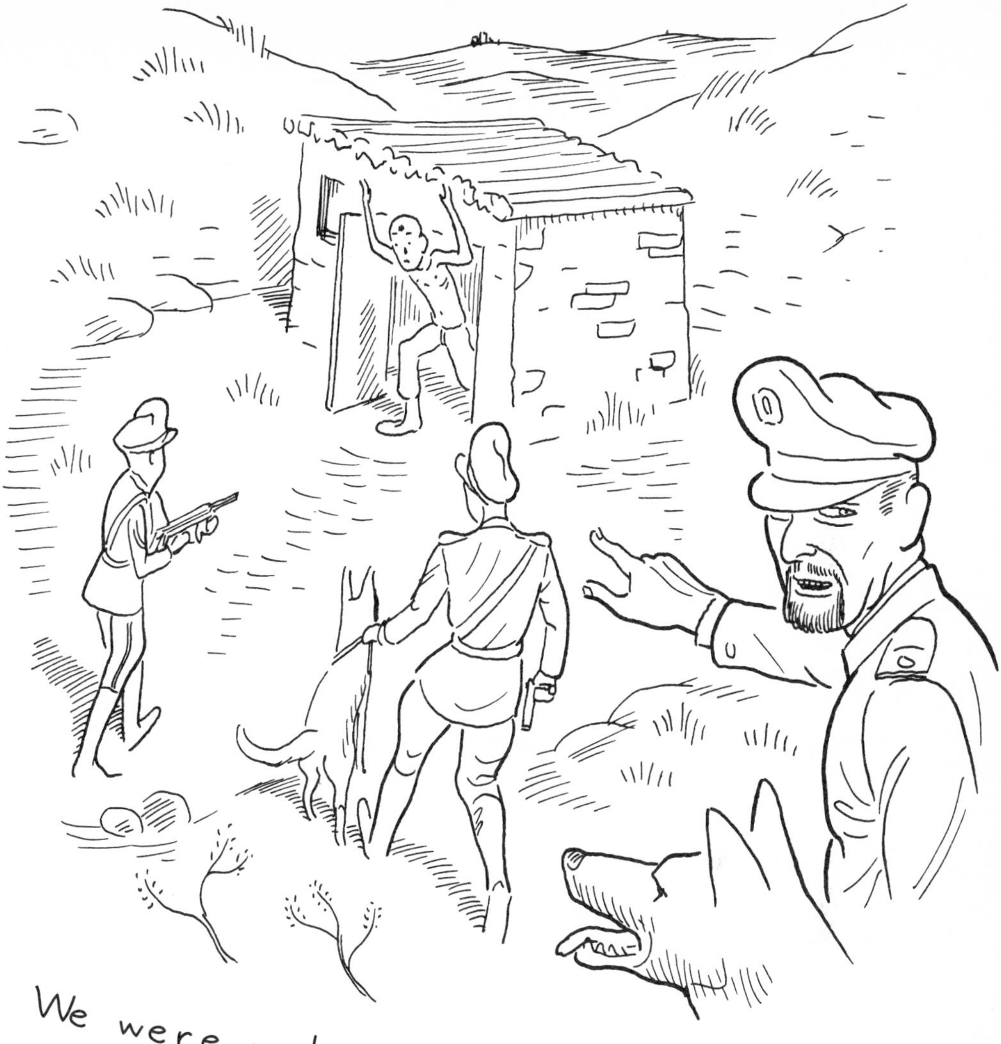

We were woken by barking.

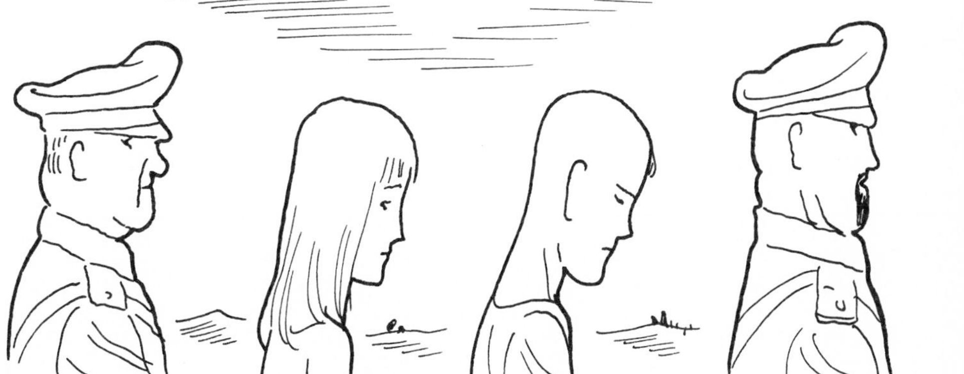

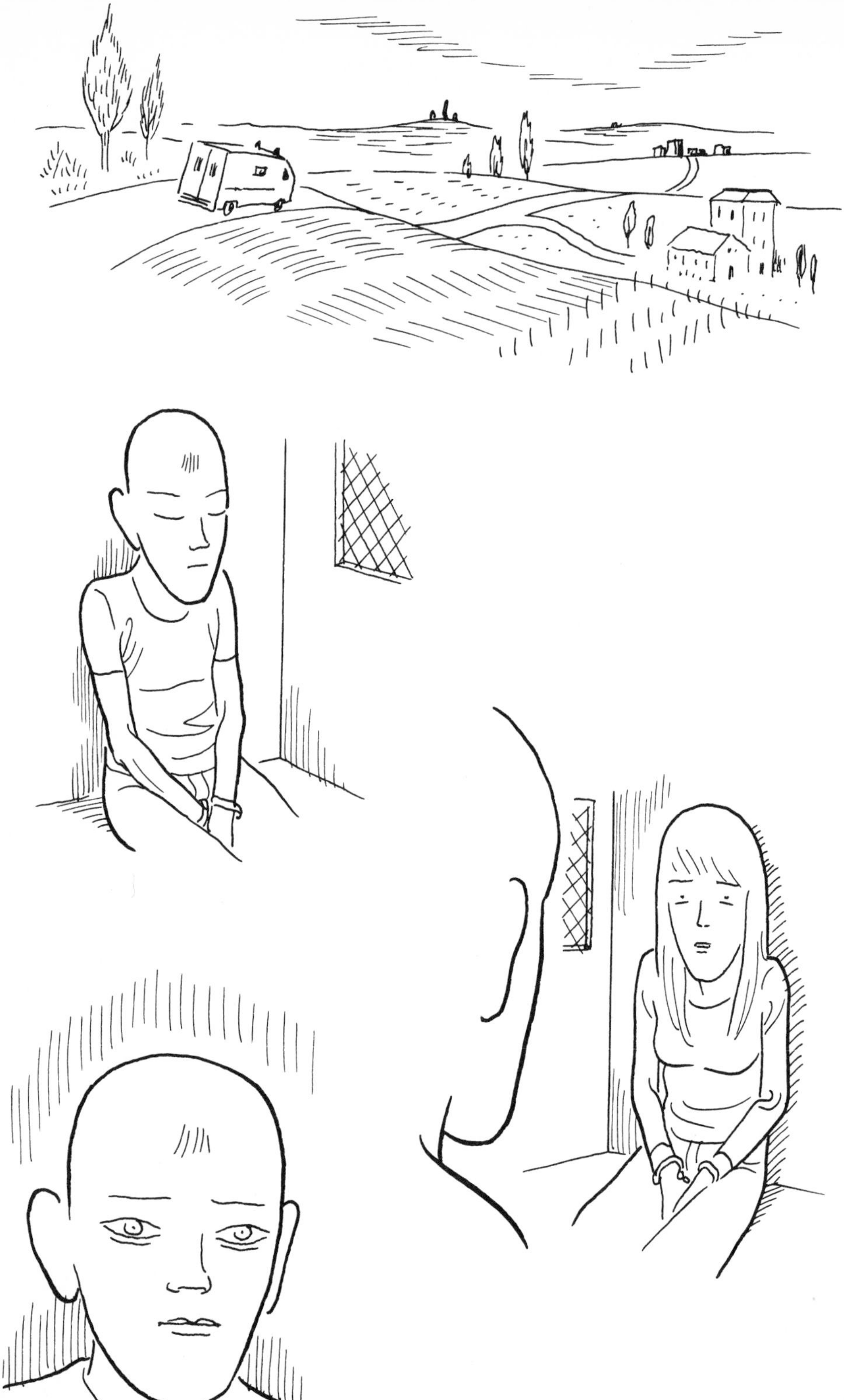

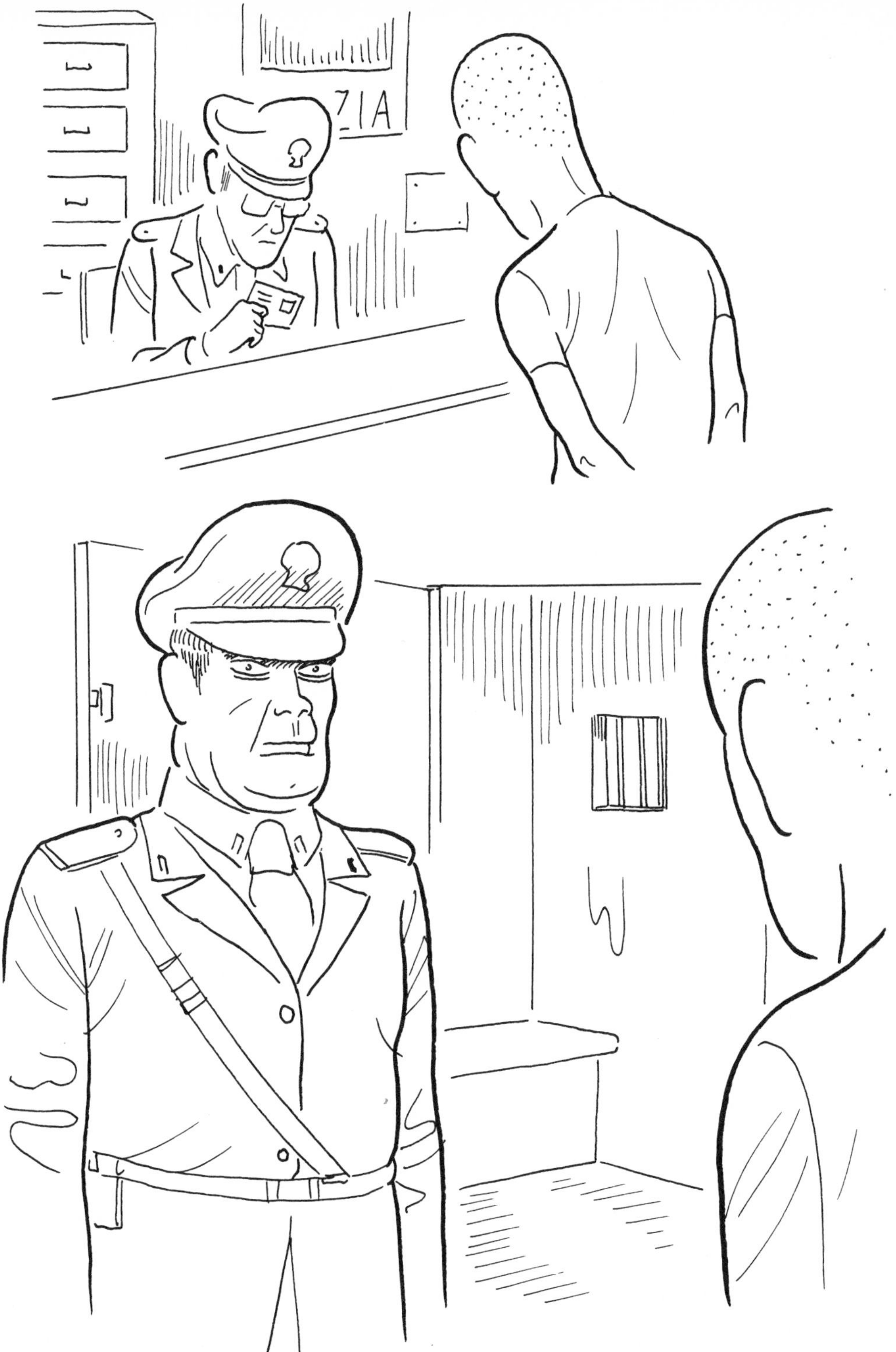
ZIA

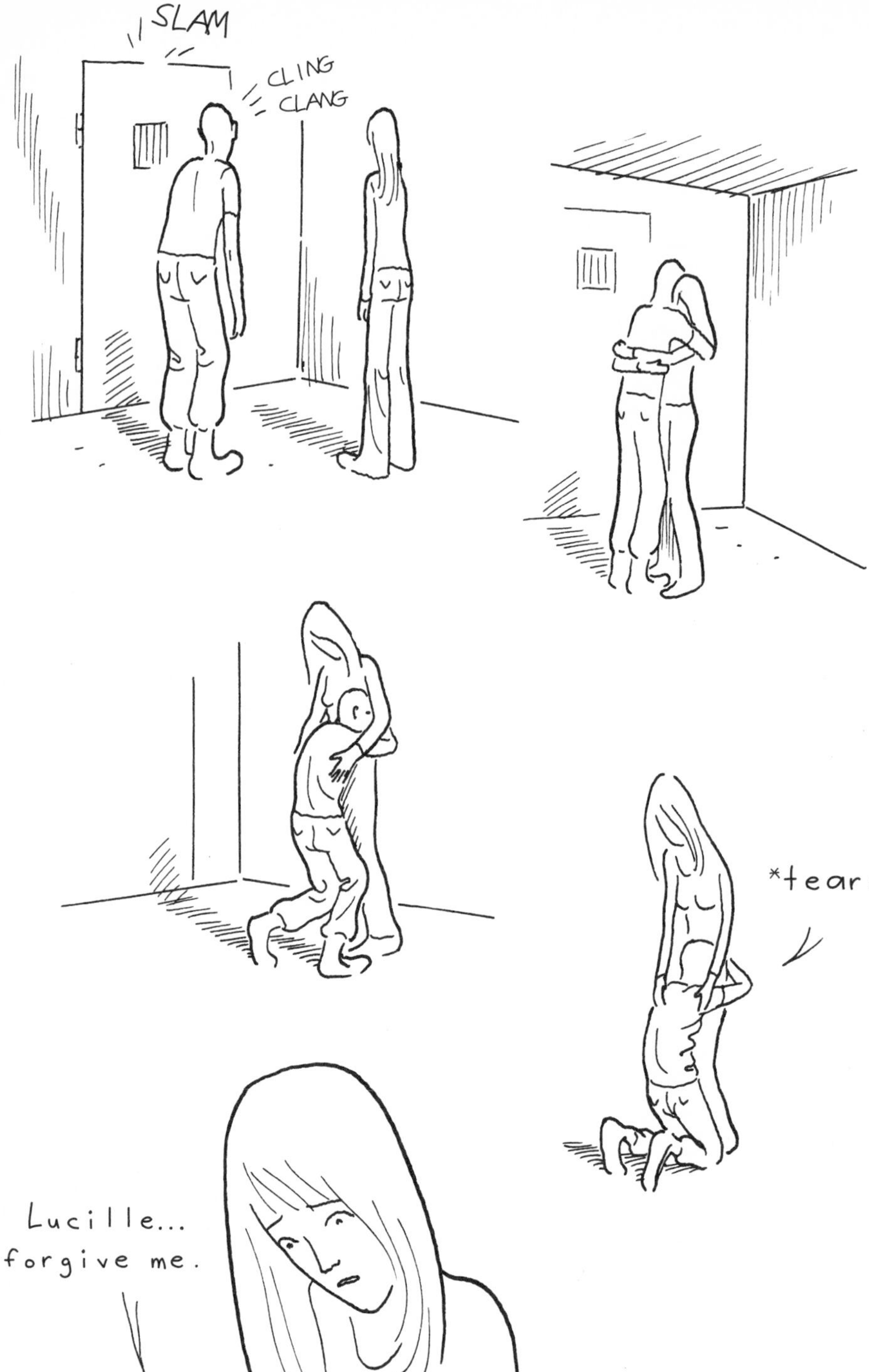
SLAM
CLING
CLANG
tears
Lucille...
forgive me.

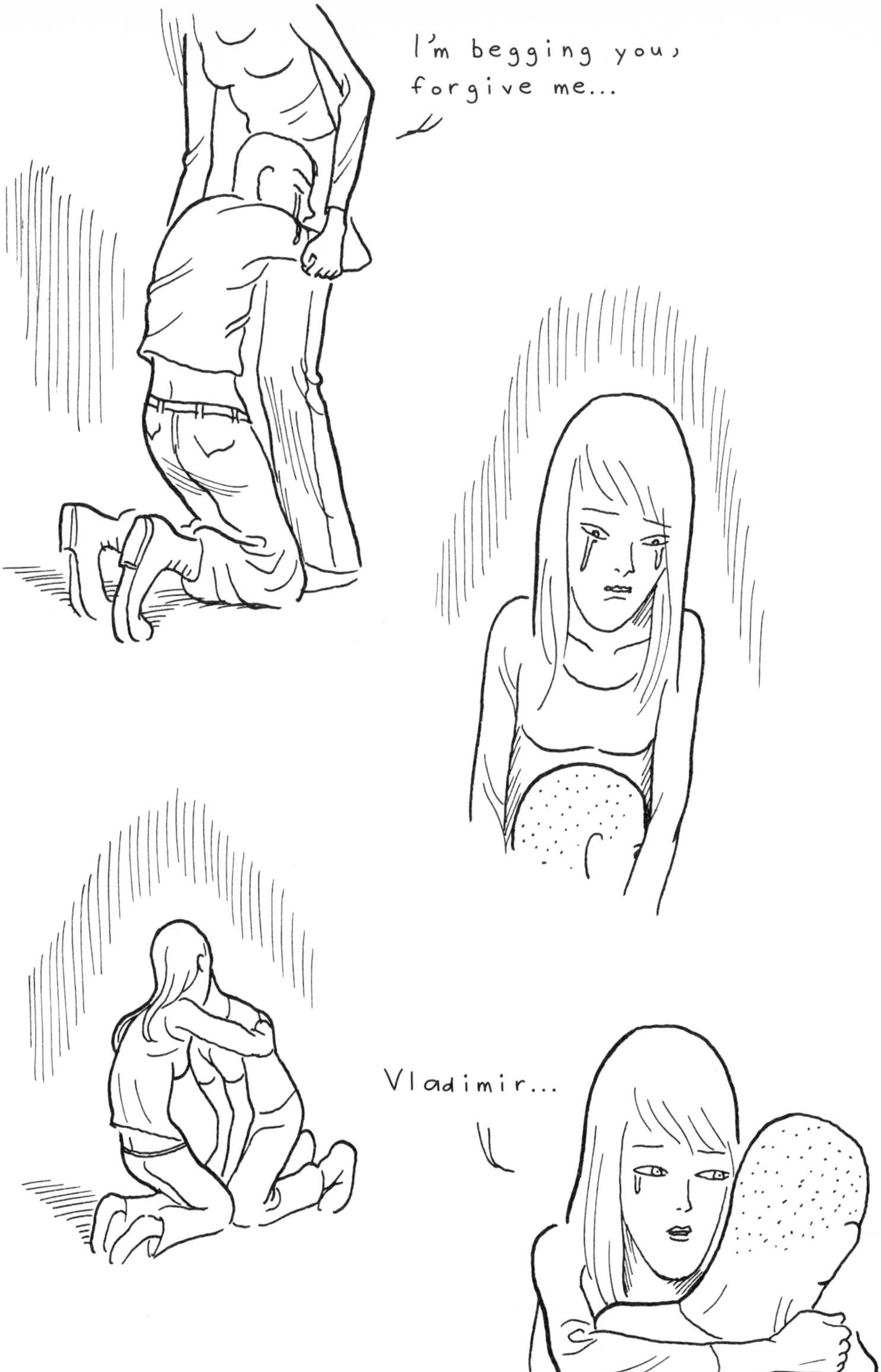
I'm begging you, forgive me...
Vladimir...

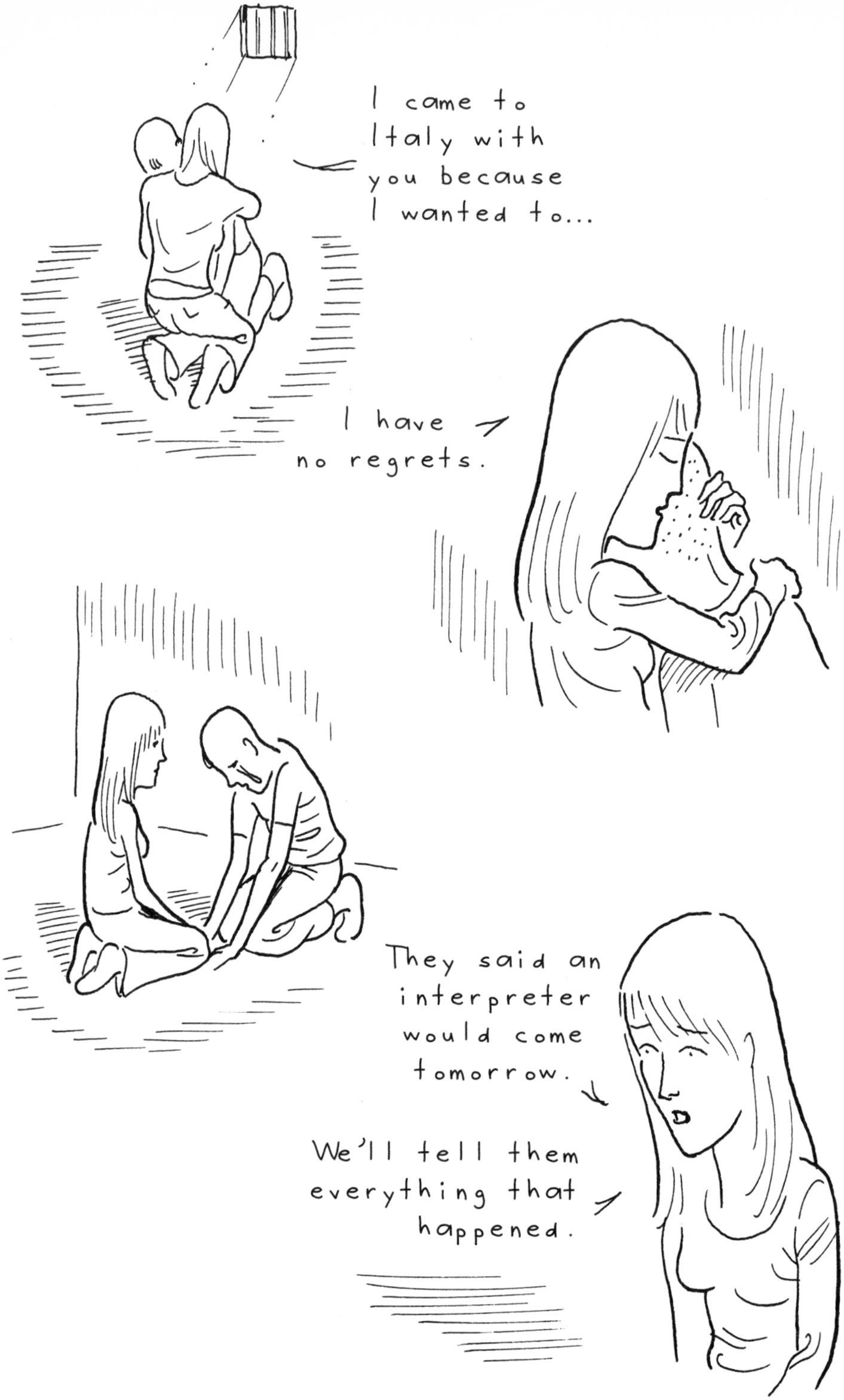
I came to Italy with you because I wanted to...
I have no regrets.
They said an interpreter would come tomorrow.
We'll tell them everything that happened.

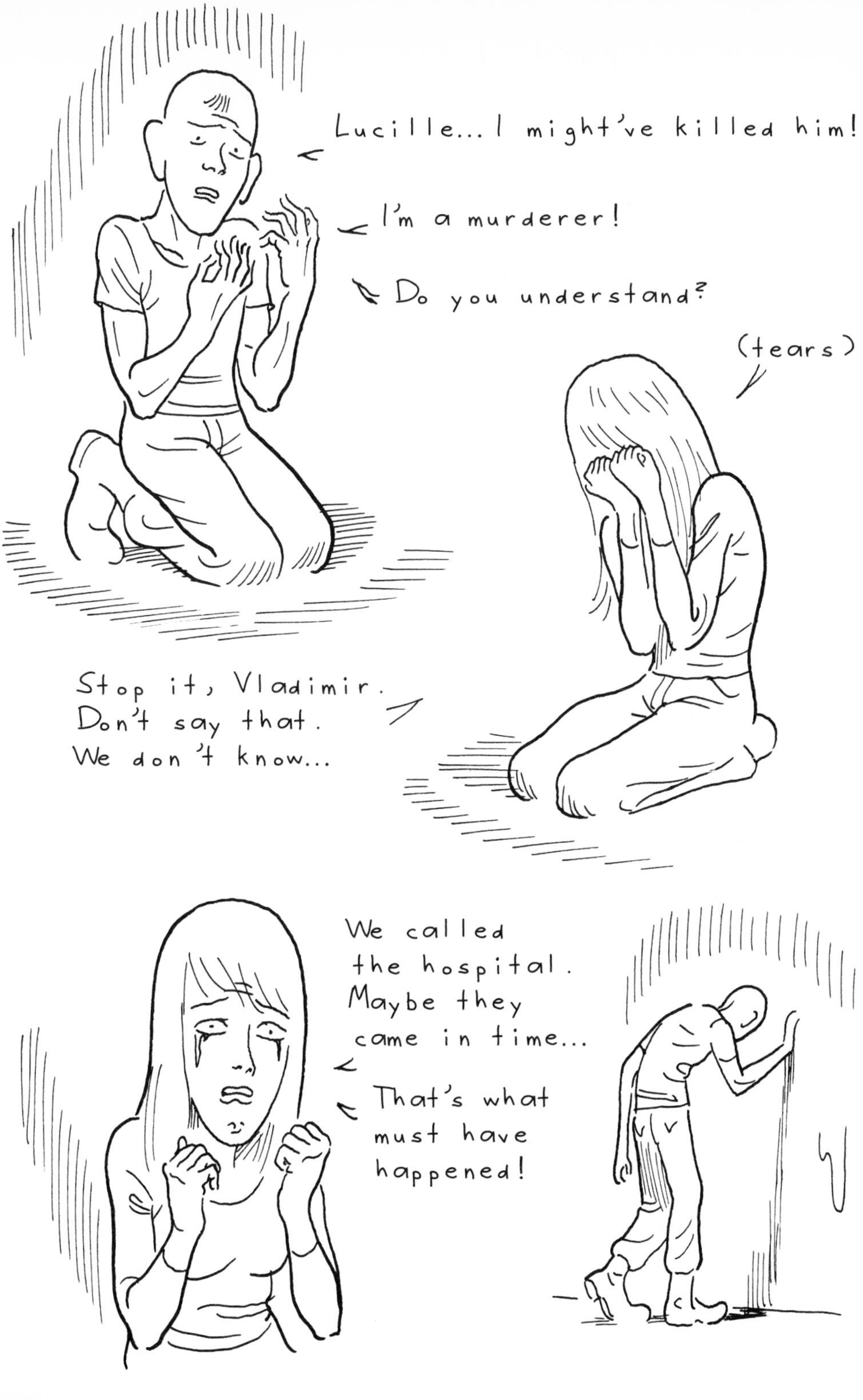
Lucille... I might've killed him!
I'm a murderer!
Do you understand?
(tears)
Stop it, Vladimir. Don't say that. We don't know...
We called the hospital. Maybe they came in time...
That's what must have happened!

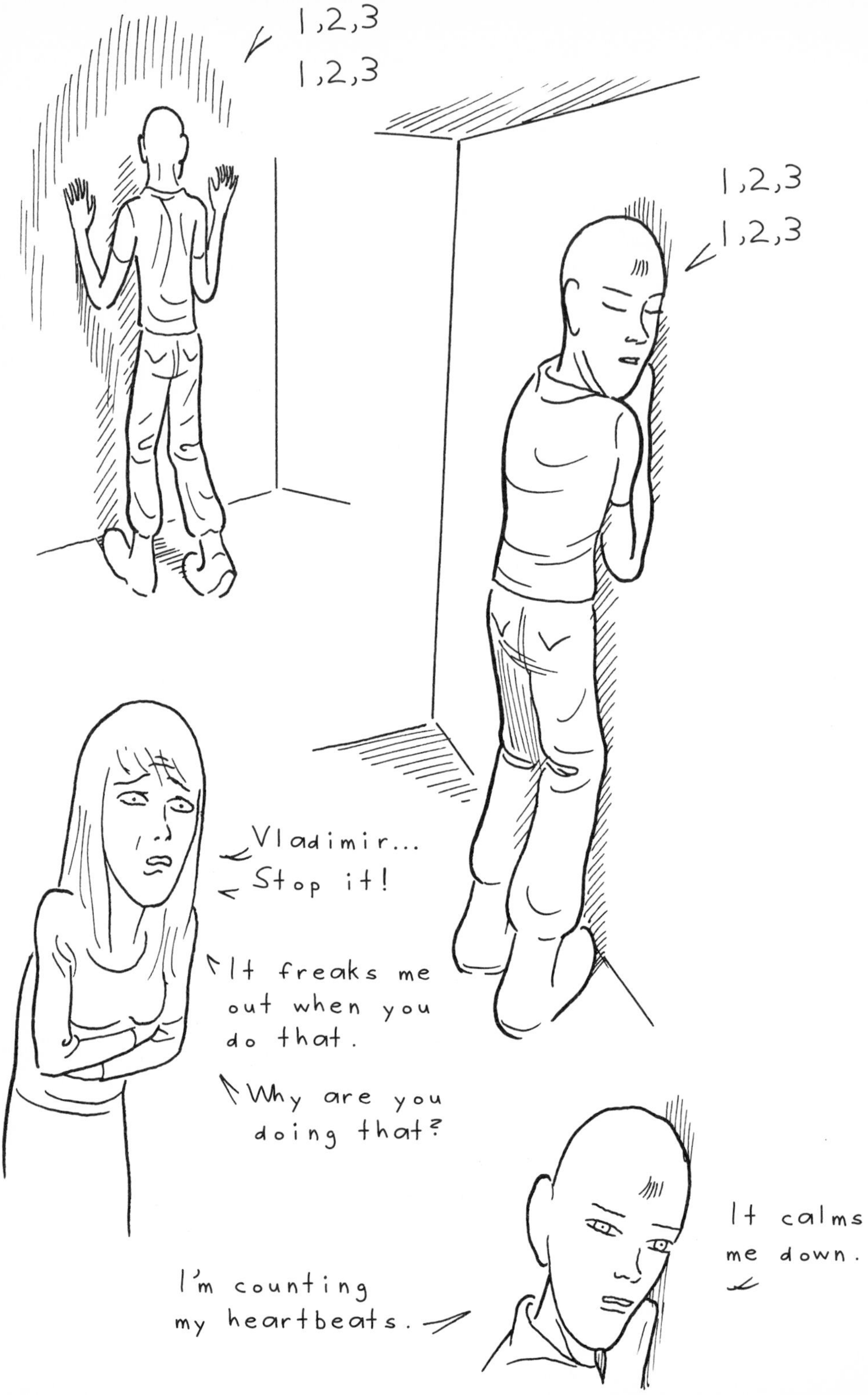
1,2,3
1,2,3
1,2,3
1,2,3
Vladimir...
Stop it!
It freaks me out when you do that.
Why are you doing that?
I'm counting my heartbeats.
It calms me down.

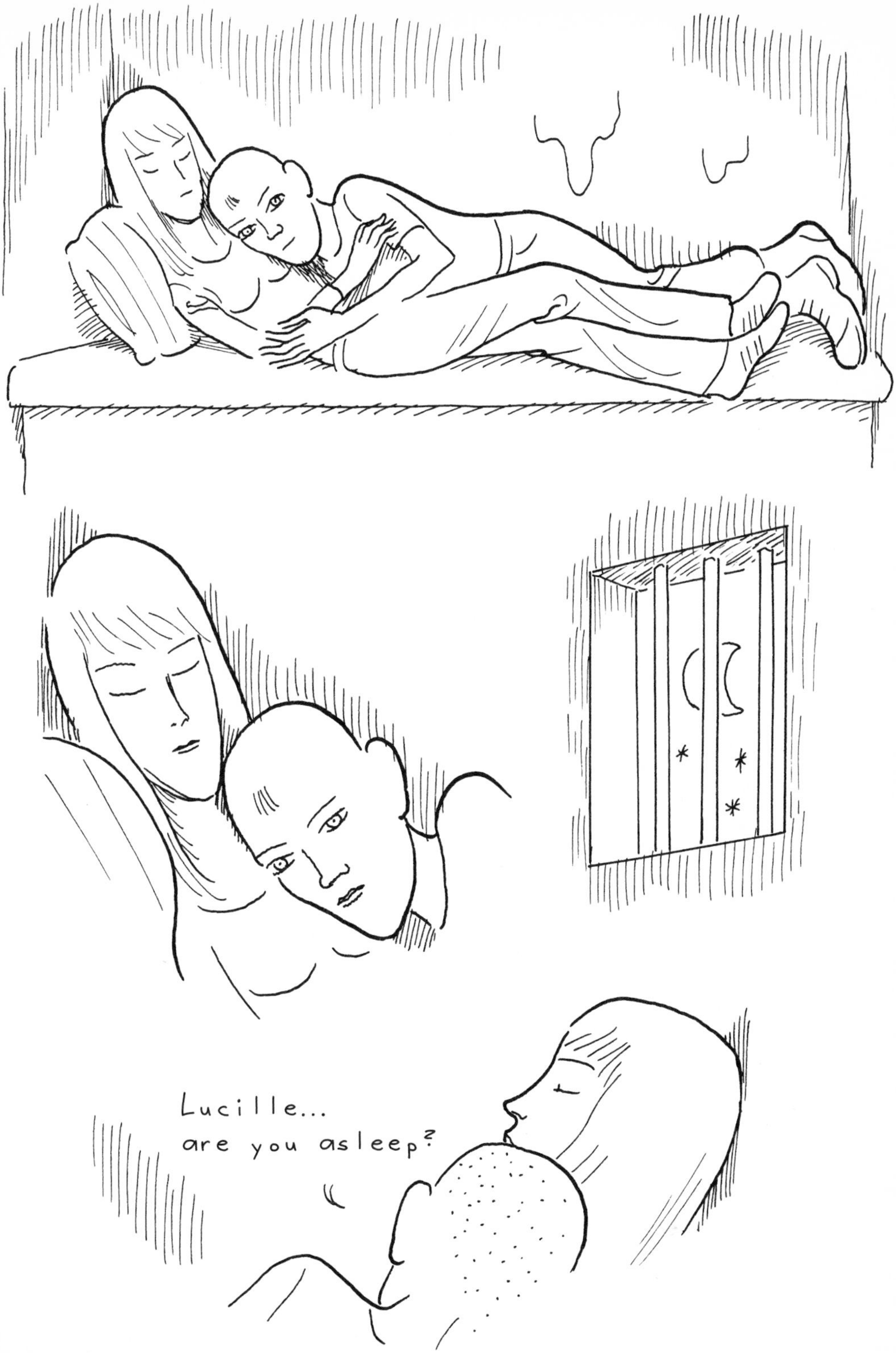
Lucille...
are you asleep?

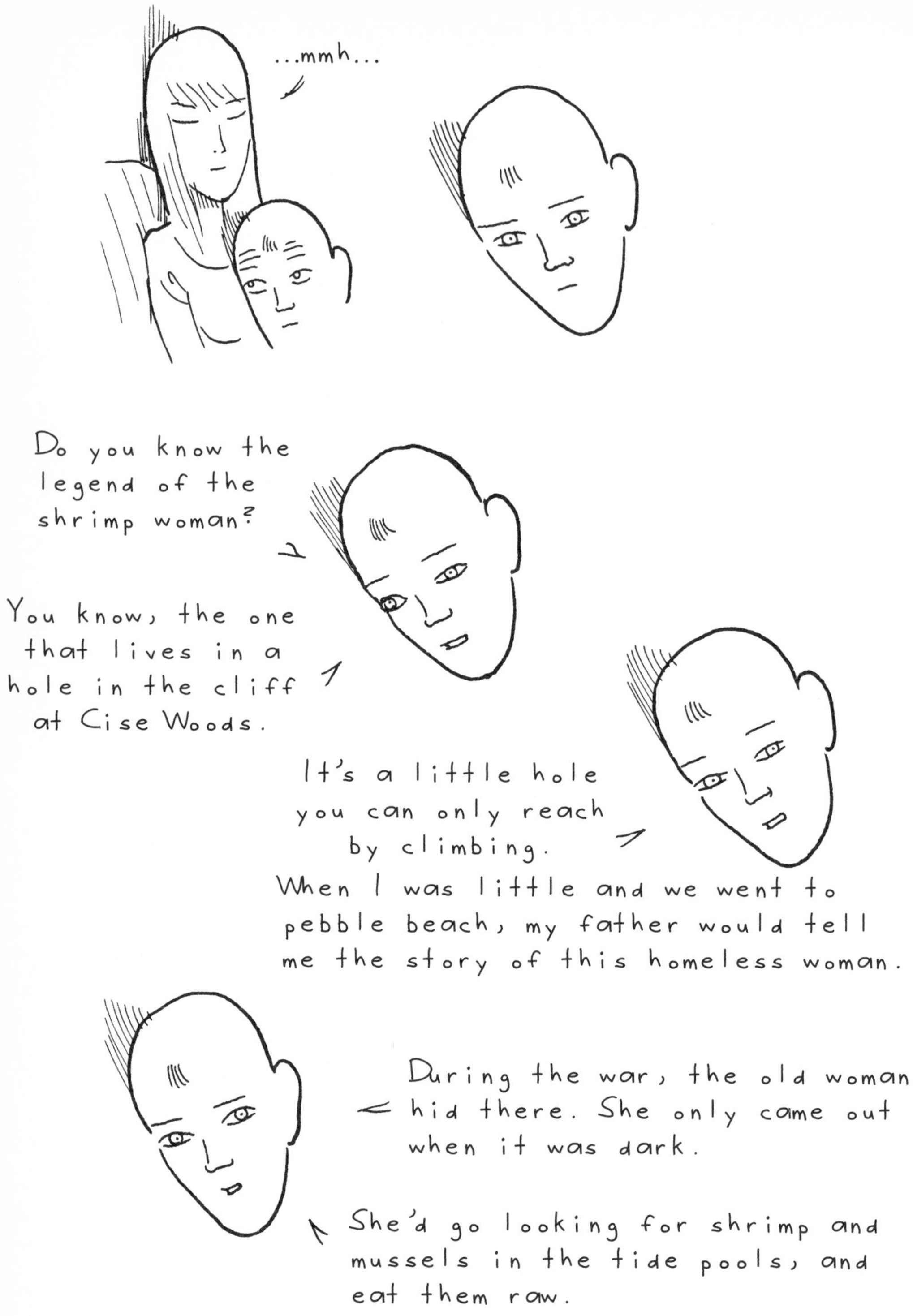

...mmh...

Do you know the
legend of the
legend of the
shrimp woman?

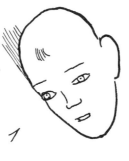

You know, the one
that lives in a
hole in the cliff
at Cise Woods.

It's a little hole
you can only reach
by climbing.

When I was little and we went to
pebble beach, my father would tell
me the story of this homeless woman.

During the war, the old woman
hid there. She only came out
when it was dark.

She'd go looking for shrimp and
mussels in the tide pools, and
eat them raw.

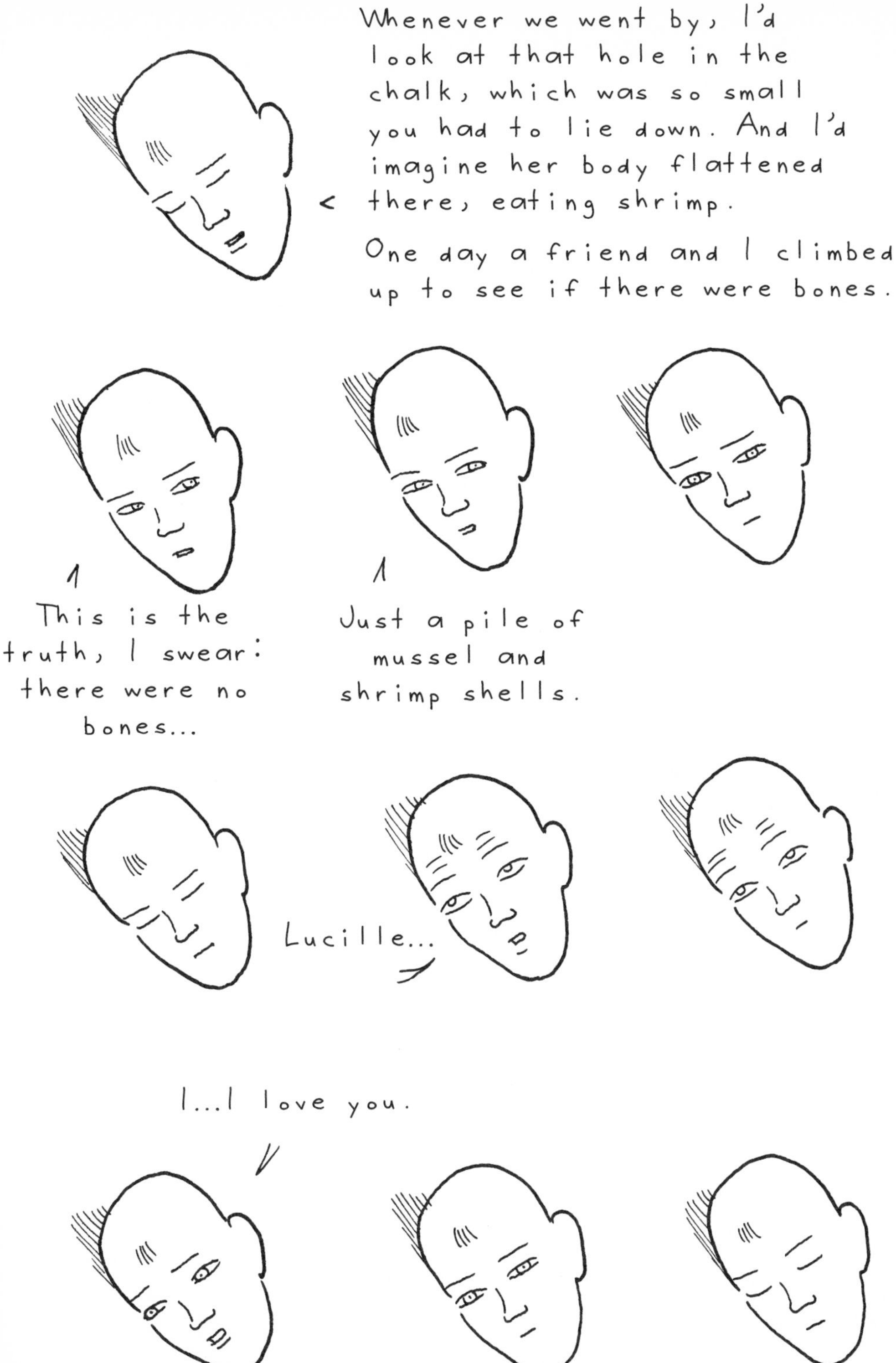
Whenever we went by, I'd look at that hole in the chalk, which was so small you had to lie down. And I'd imagine her body flattened there, eating shrimp.
One day a friend and I climbed up to see if there were bones.
This is the truth, I swear: there were no bones...
Just a pile of mussel and shrimp shells.
Lucille...
I...I love you.

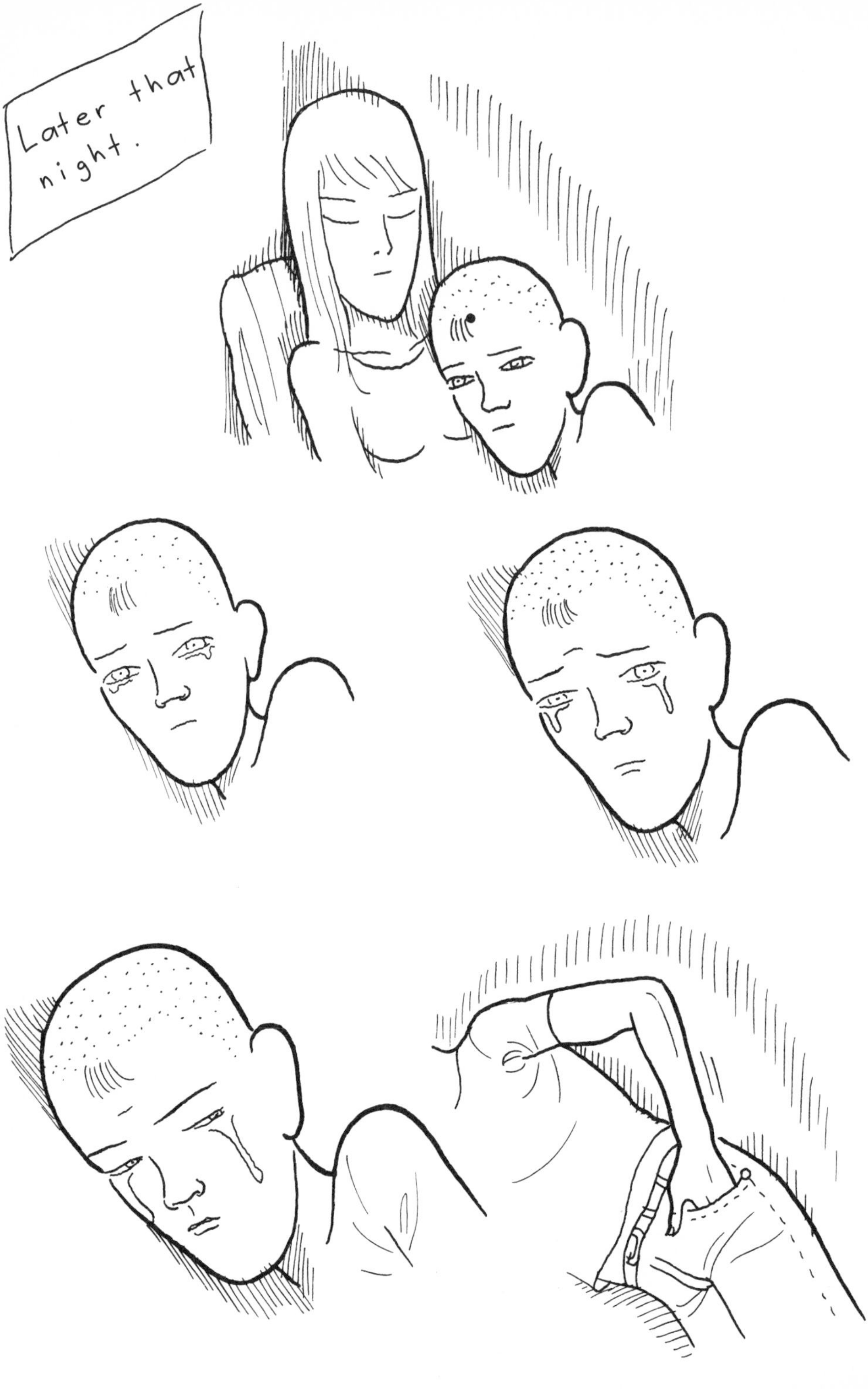
Later that night.

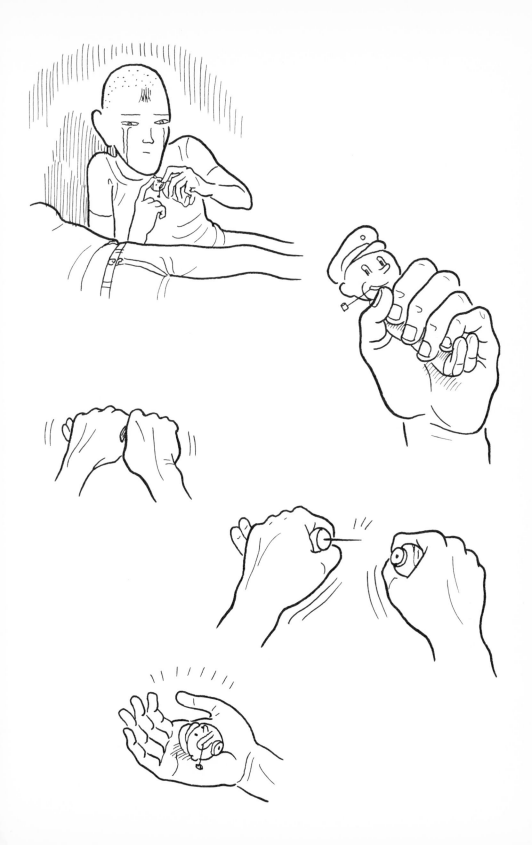

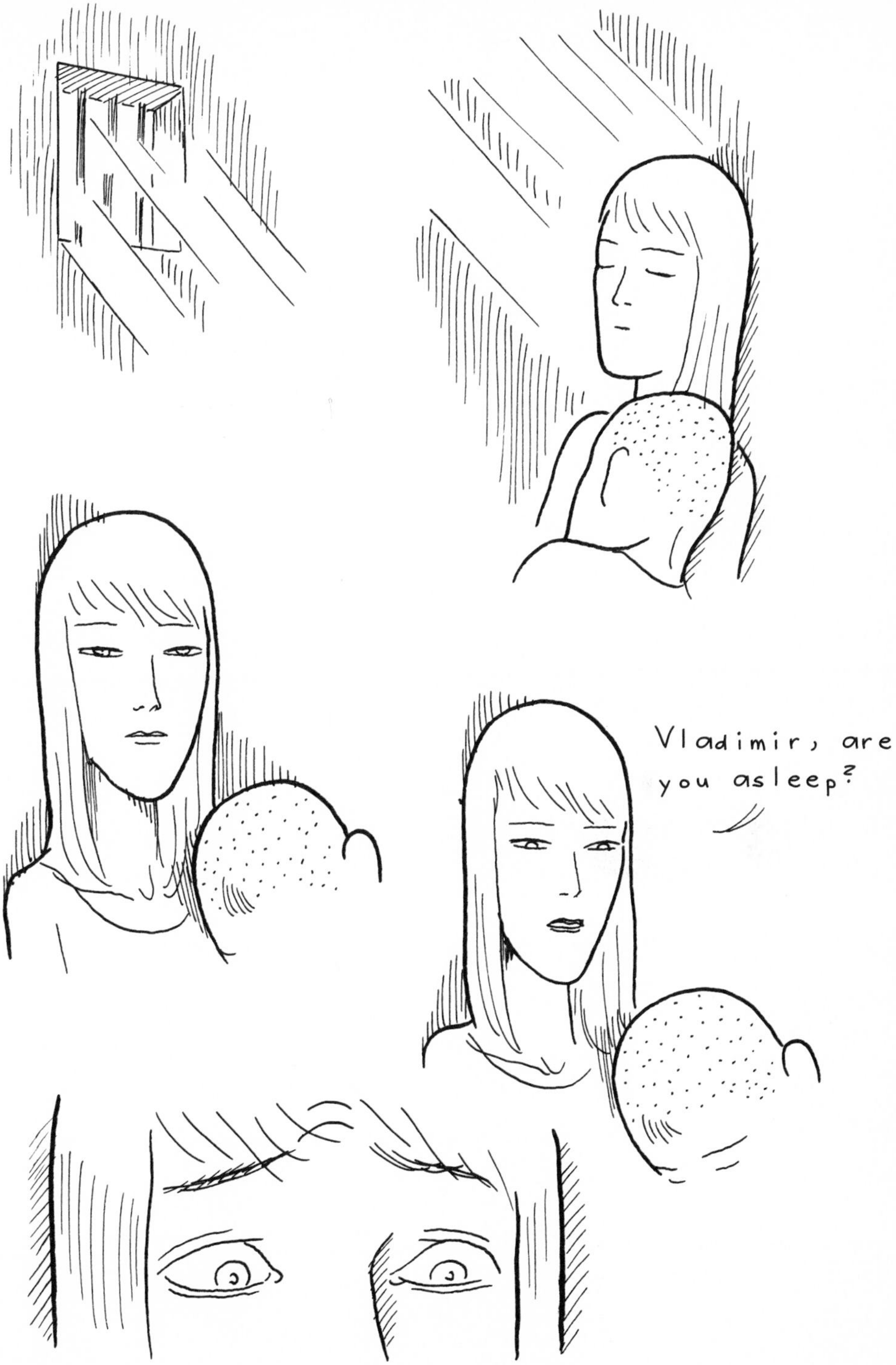
Vladimir, are you asleep?

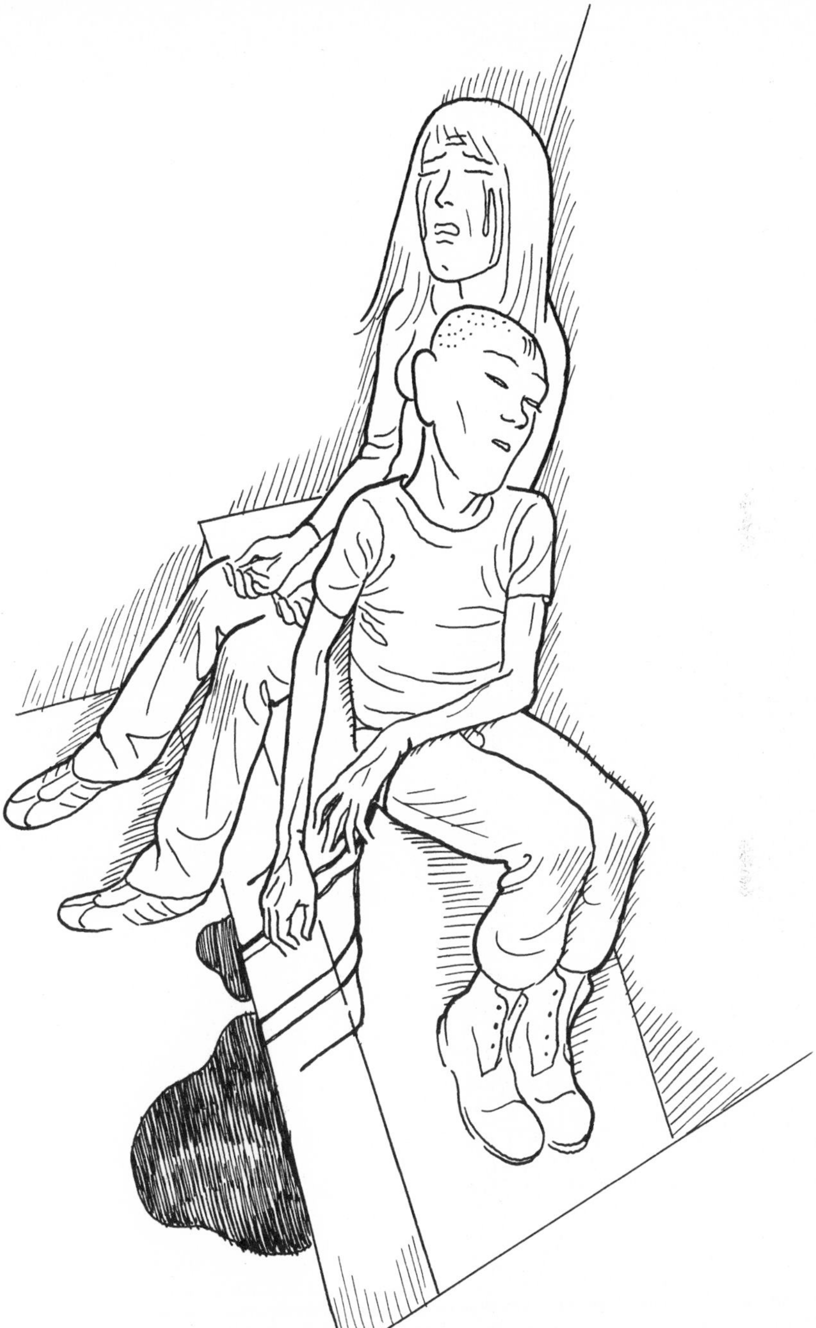

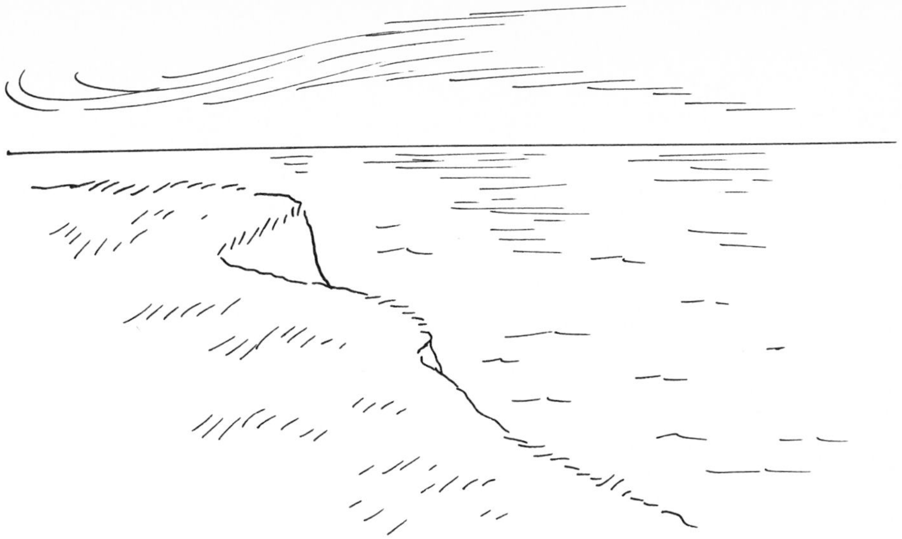

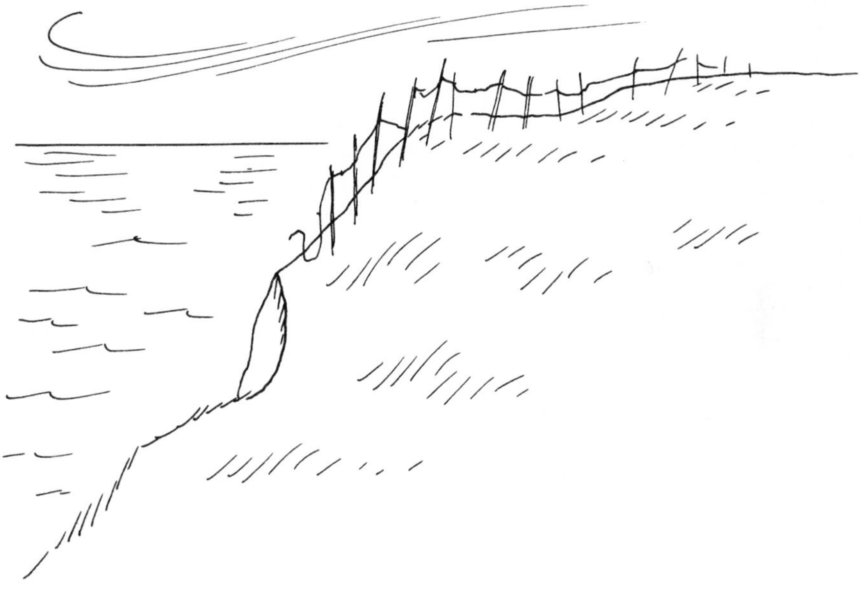

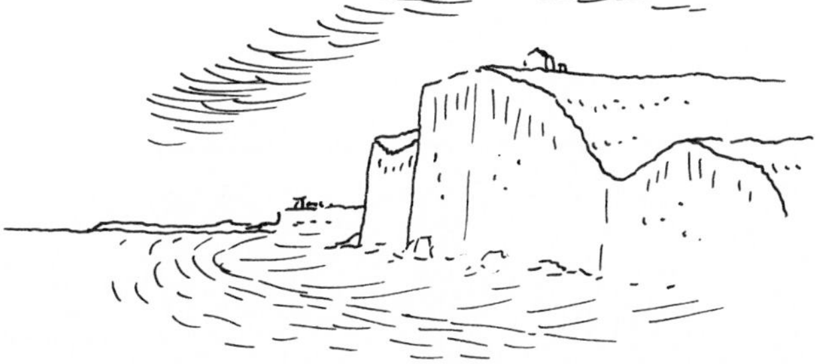

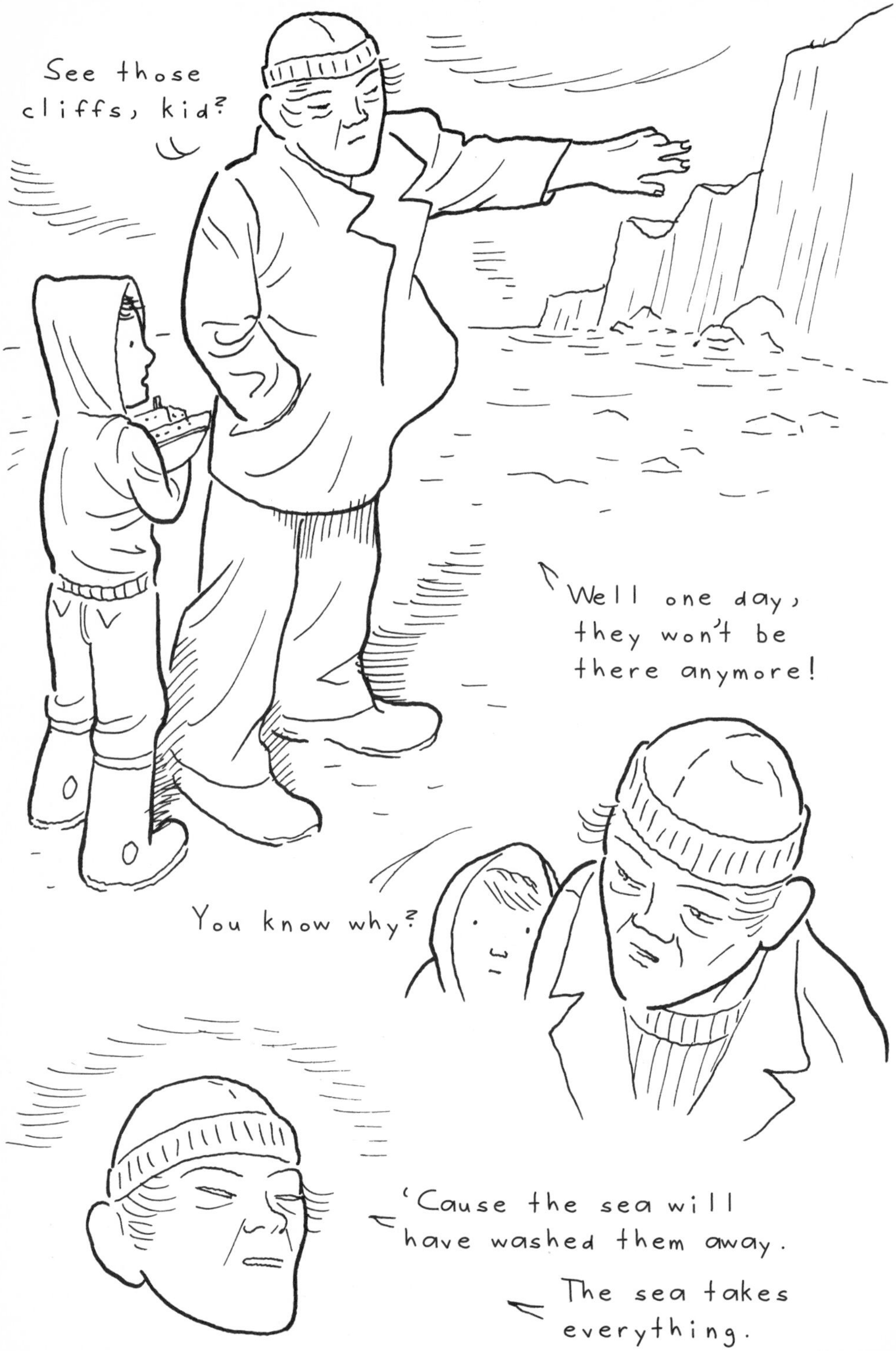
See those cliffs, kid?
Well one day, they won't be there anymore!
You know why?
'Cause the sea will have washed them away.
The sea takes everything.

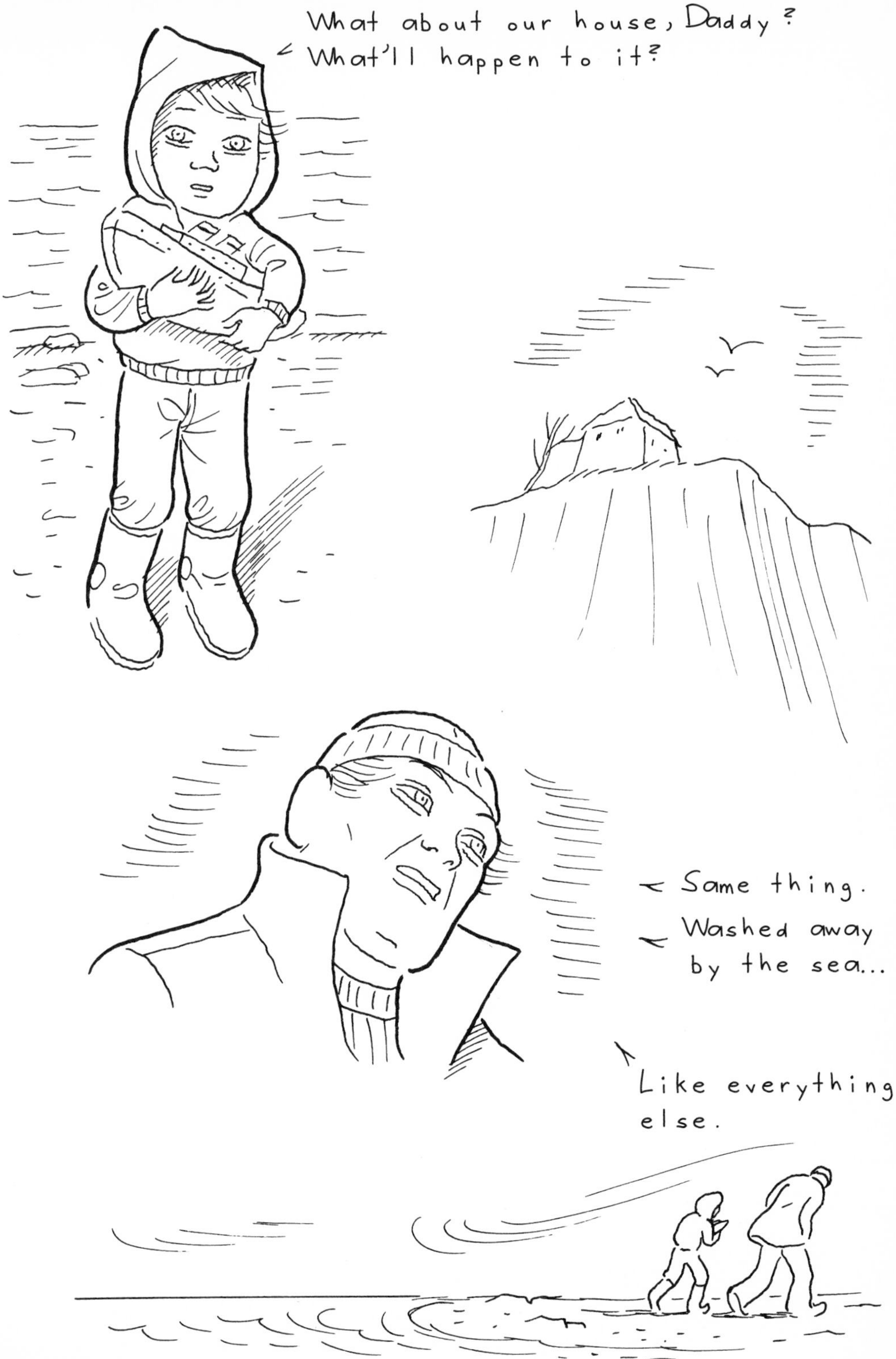
What about our house, Daddy? What'll happen to it?
Same thing.
Washed away by the sea...
Like everything else.

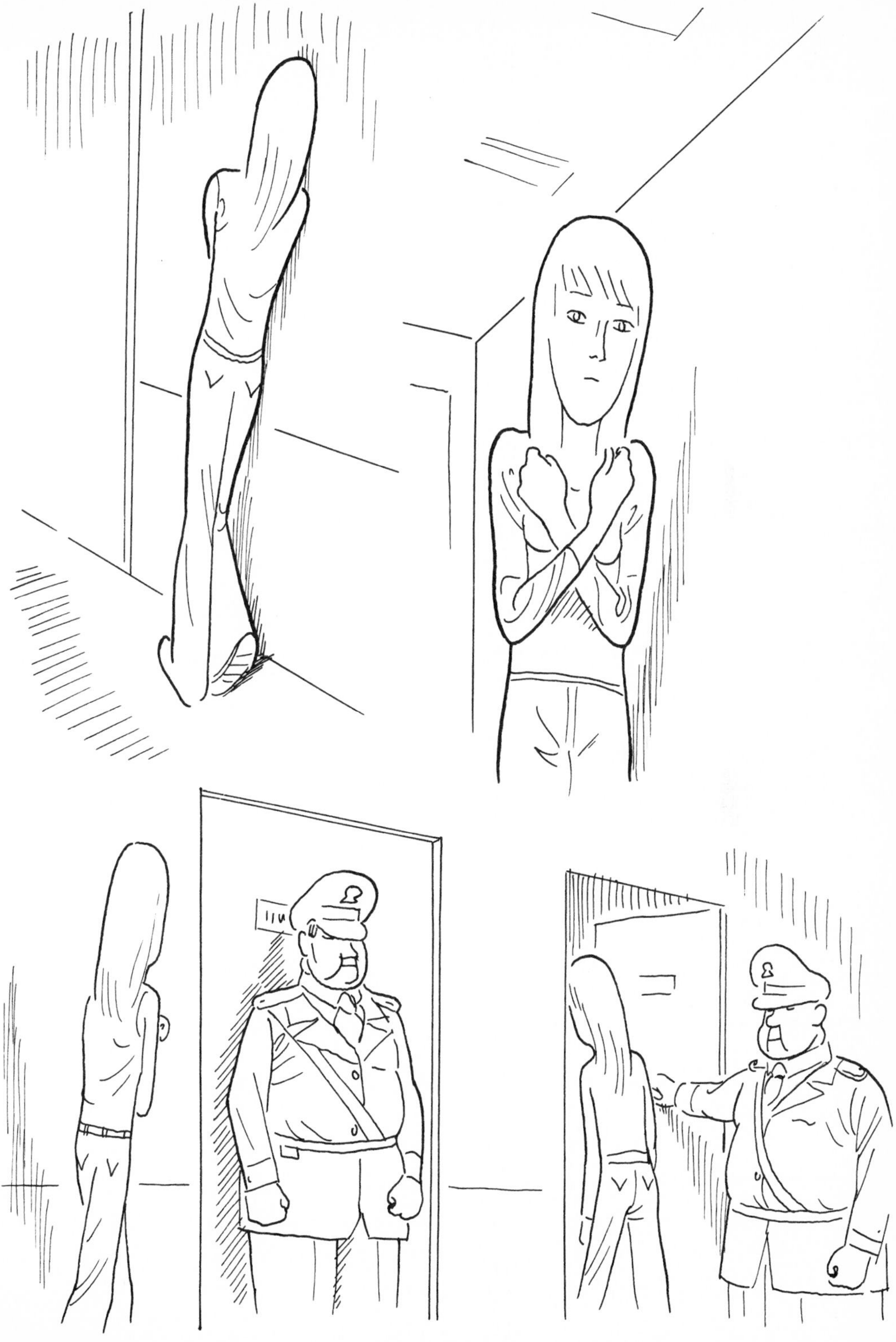

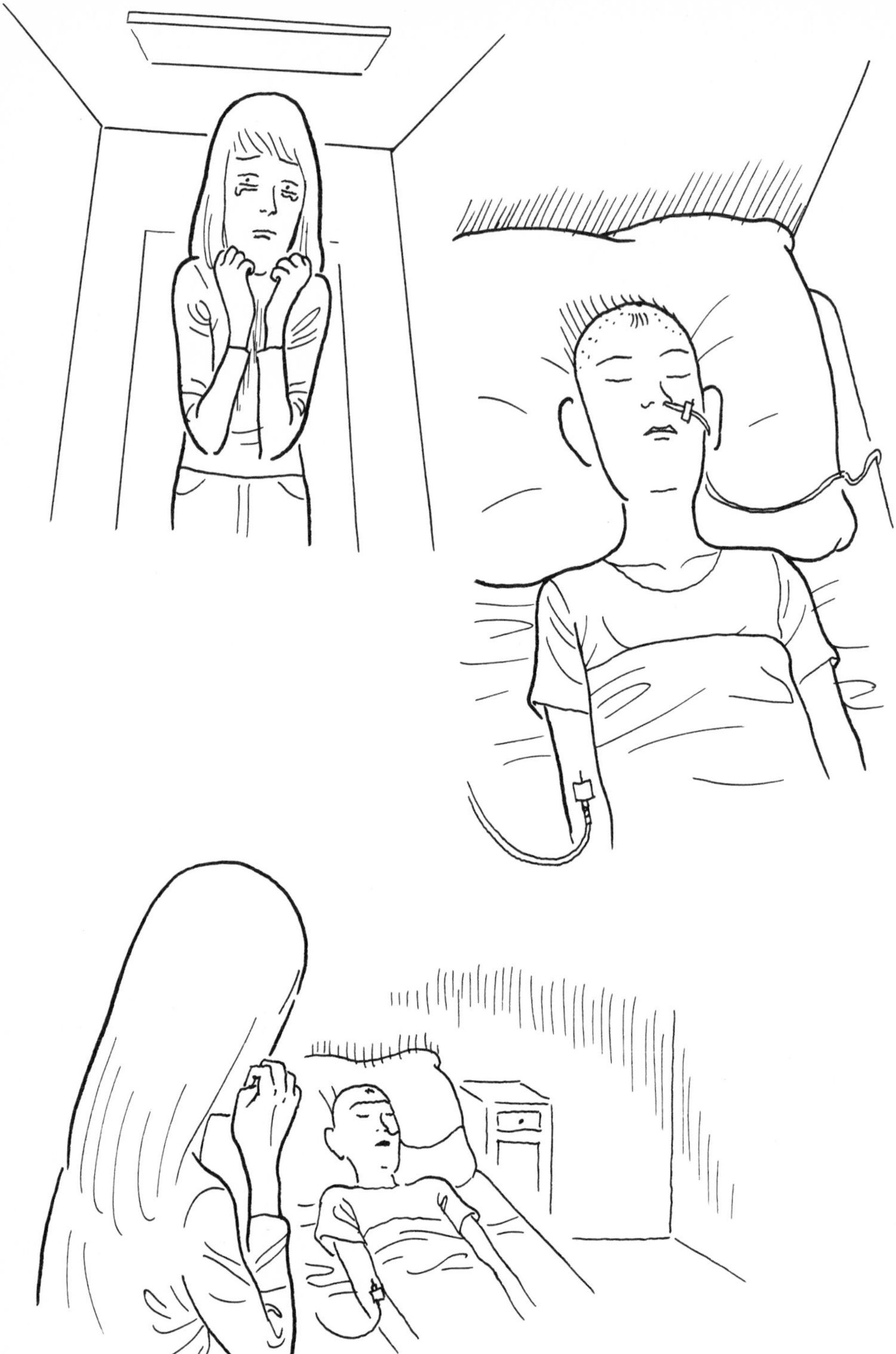

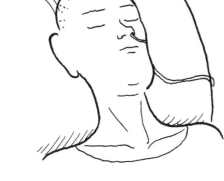

You're asleep...

It looks like
you're asleep.

It can't be anything else.

Do you remember what you
said to me?

You said you'd never
leave me.

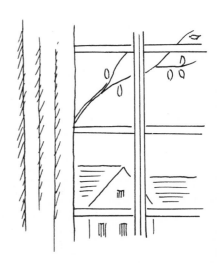

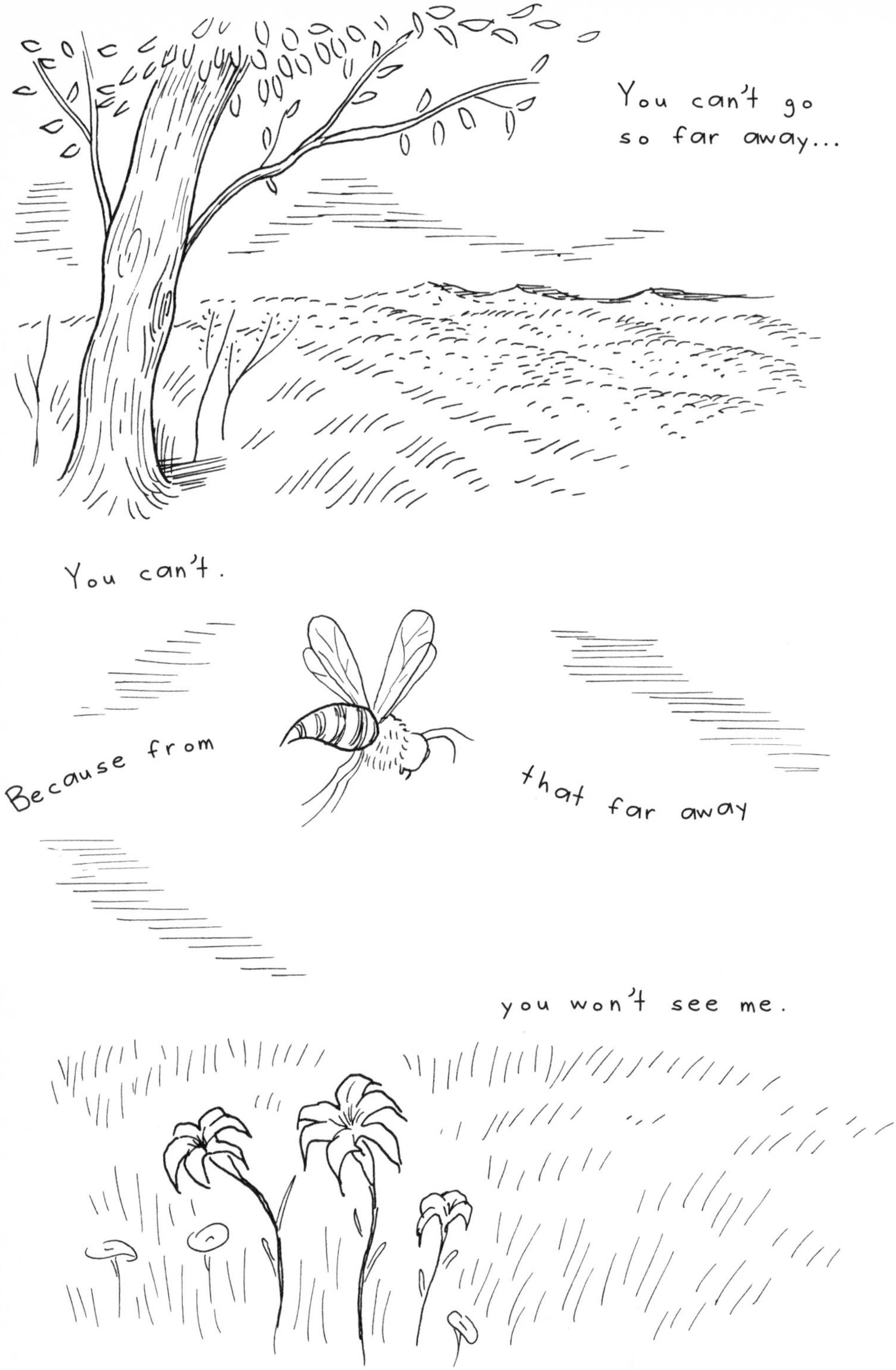
You can't go so far away...
You can't.
Because from
that far away
you won't see me.

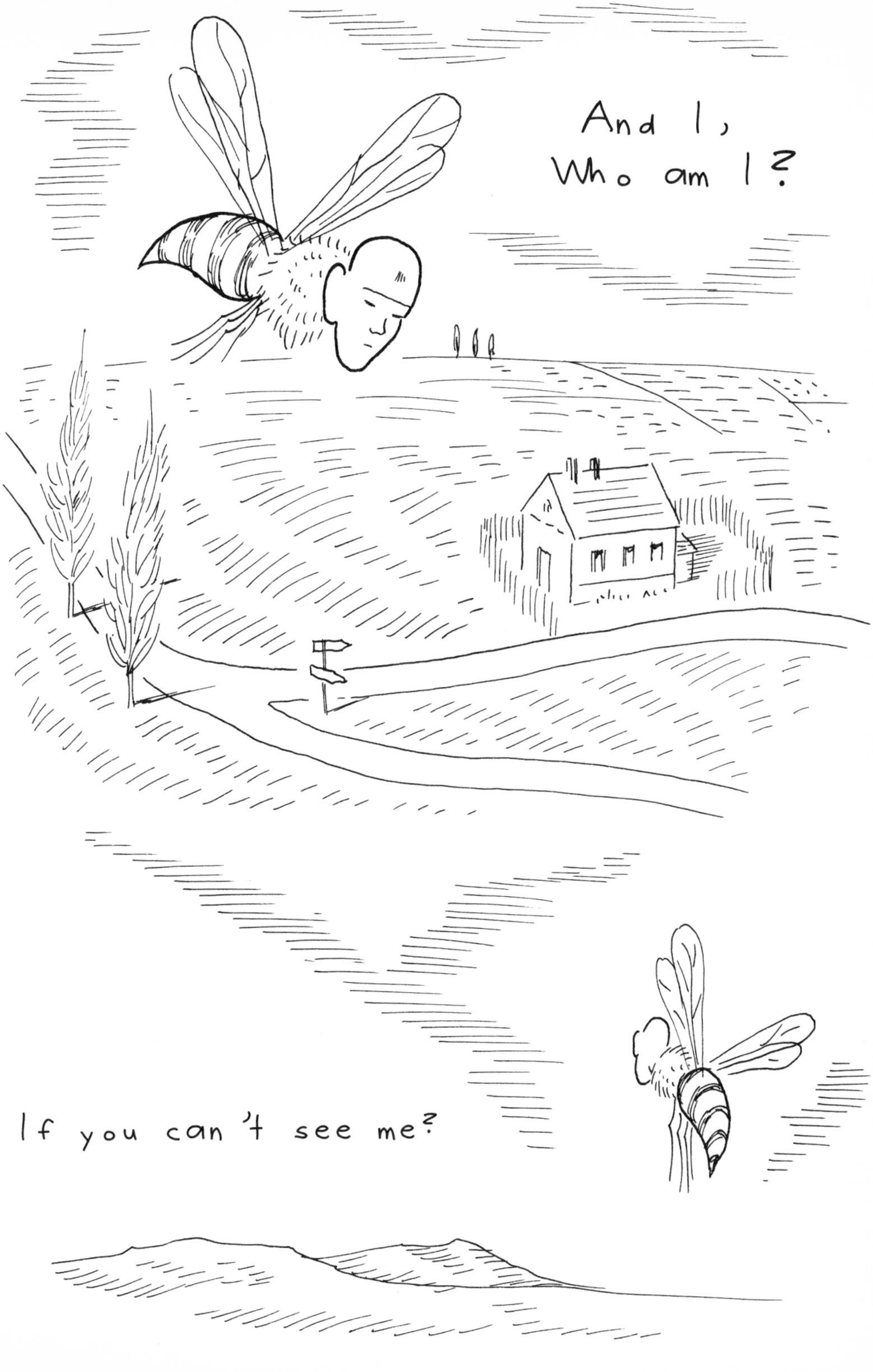
And I,
Who am I?
If you can't see me?

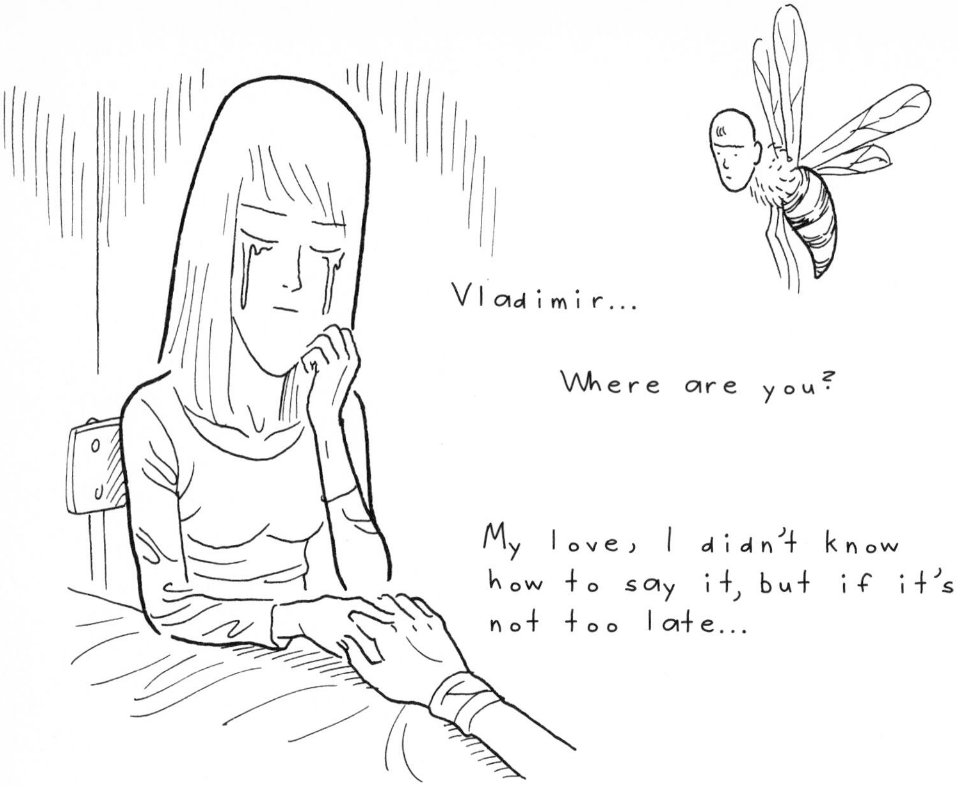
Vladimir...
Where are you?
My love, I didn't know how to say it, but if it's not too late...

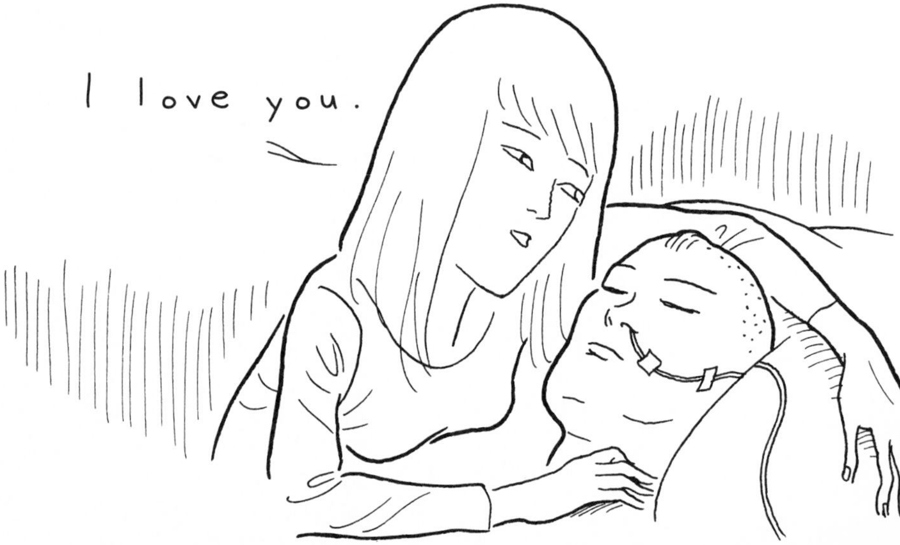
I love you.

REFLET

(Reflection)

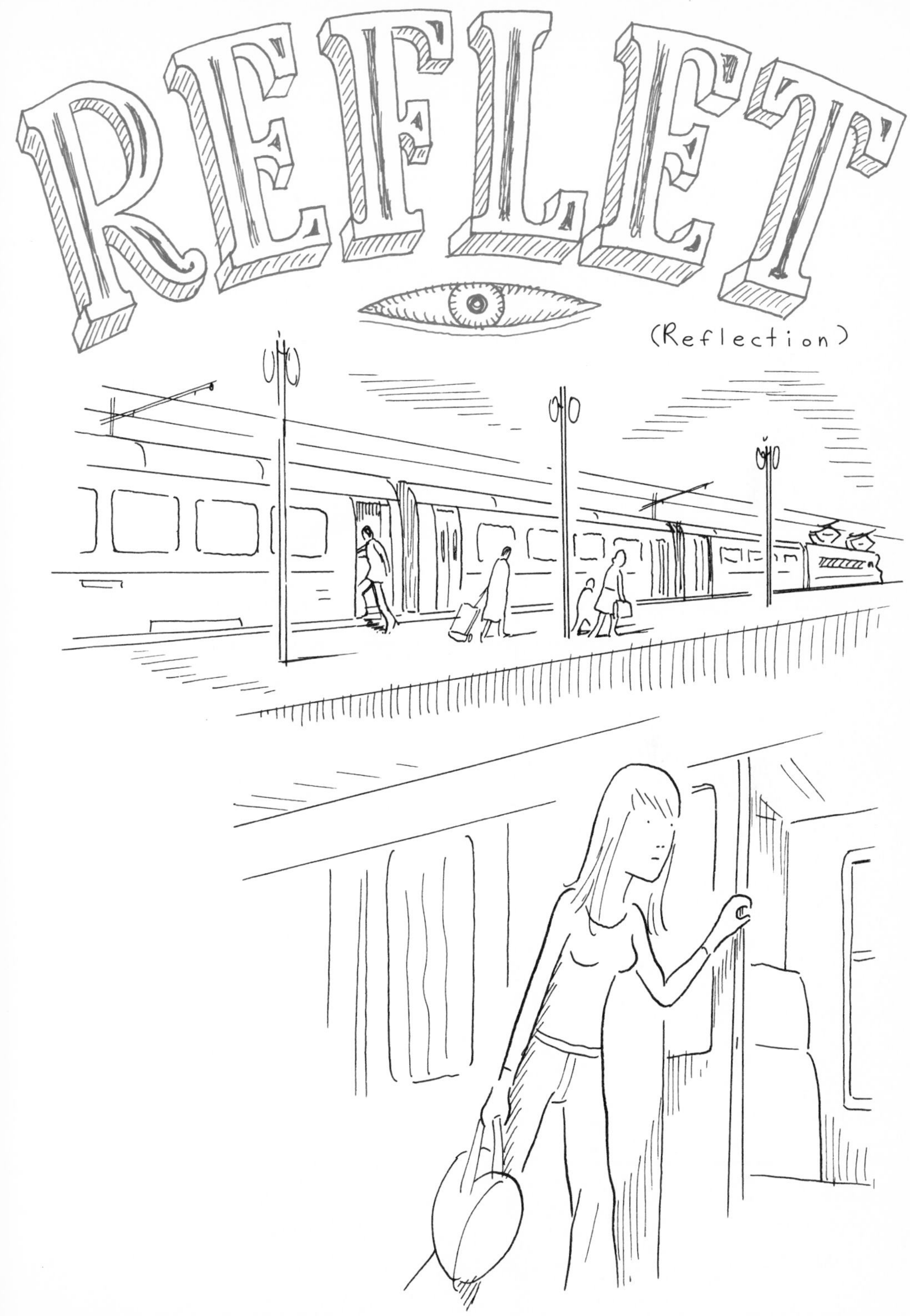

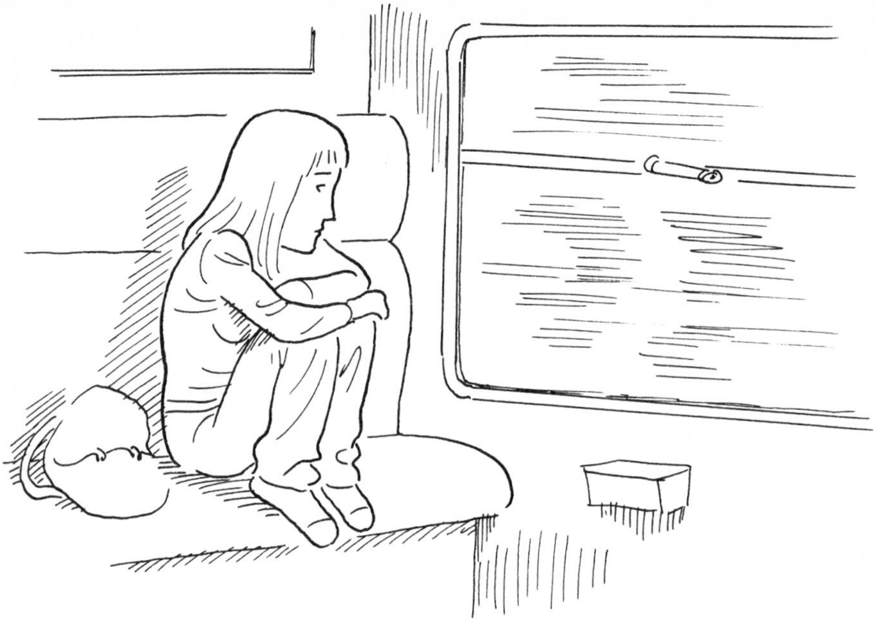
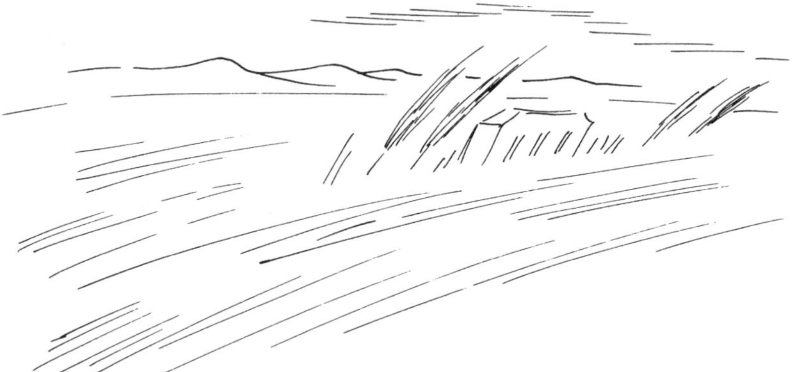
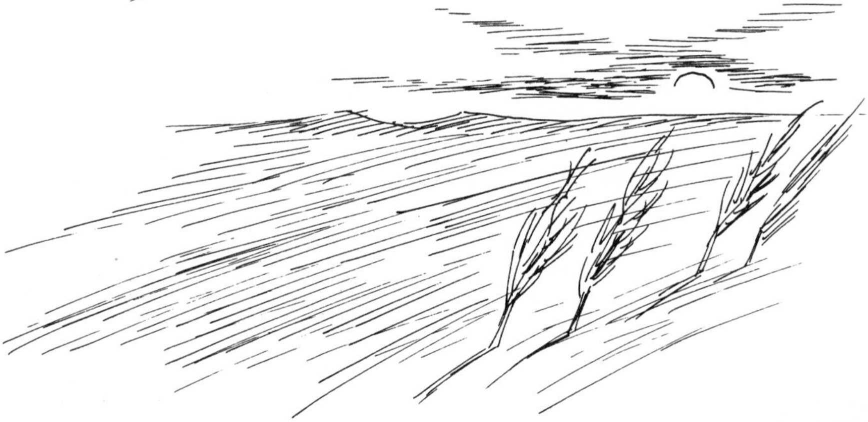

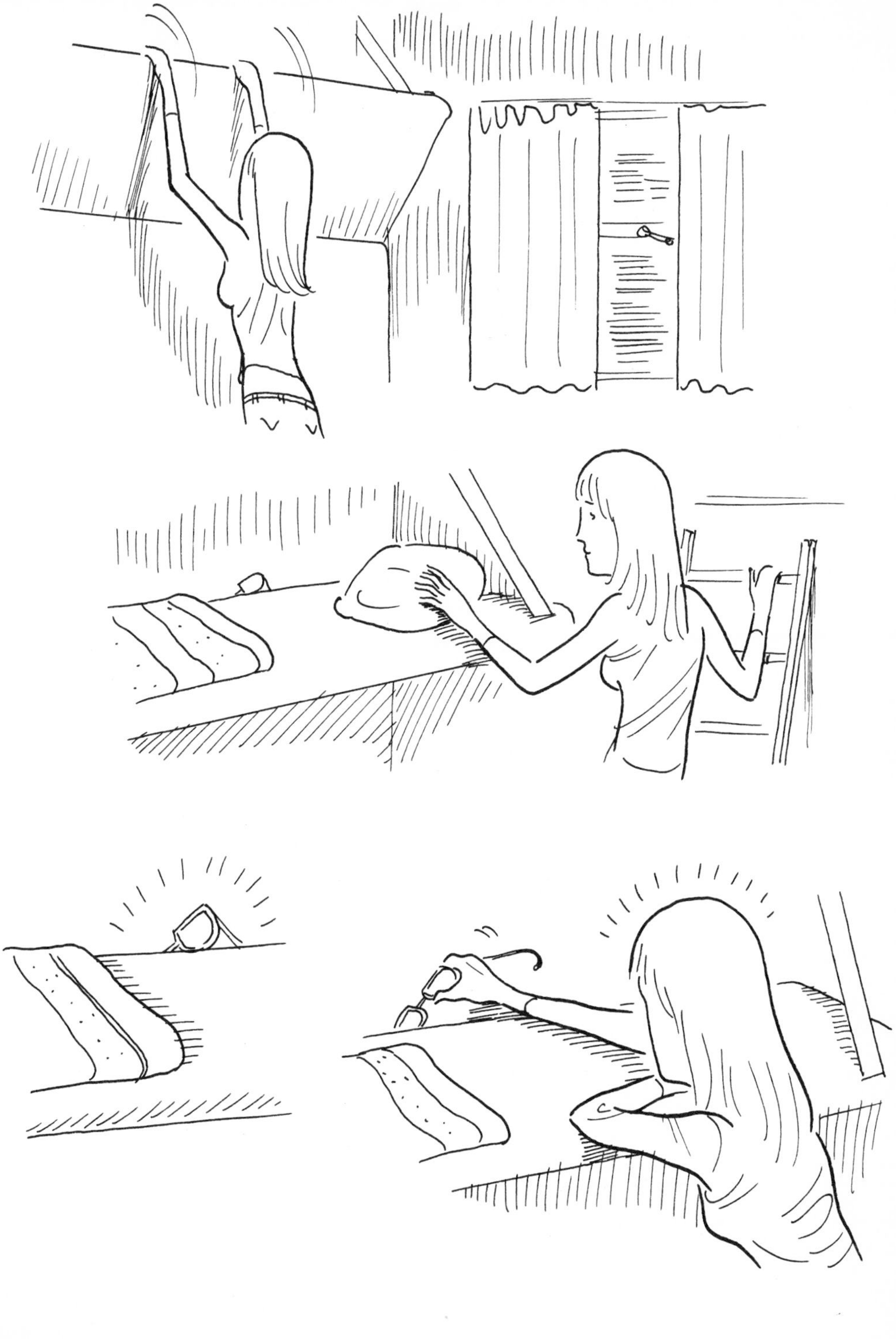

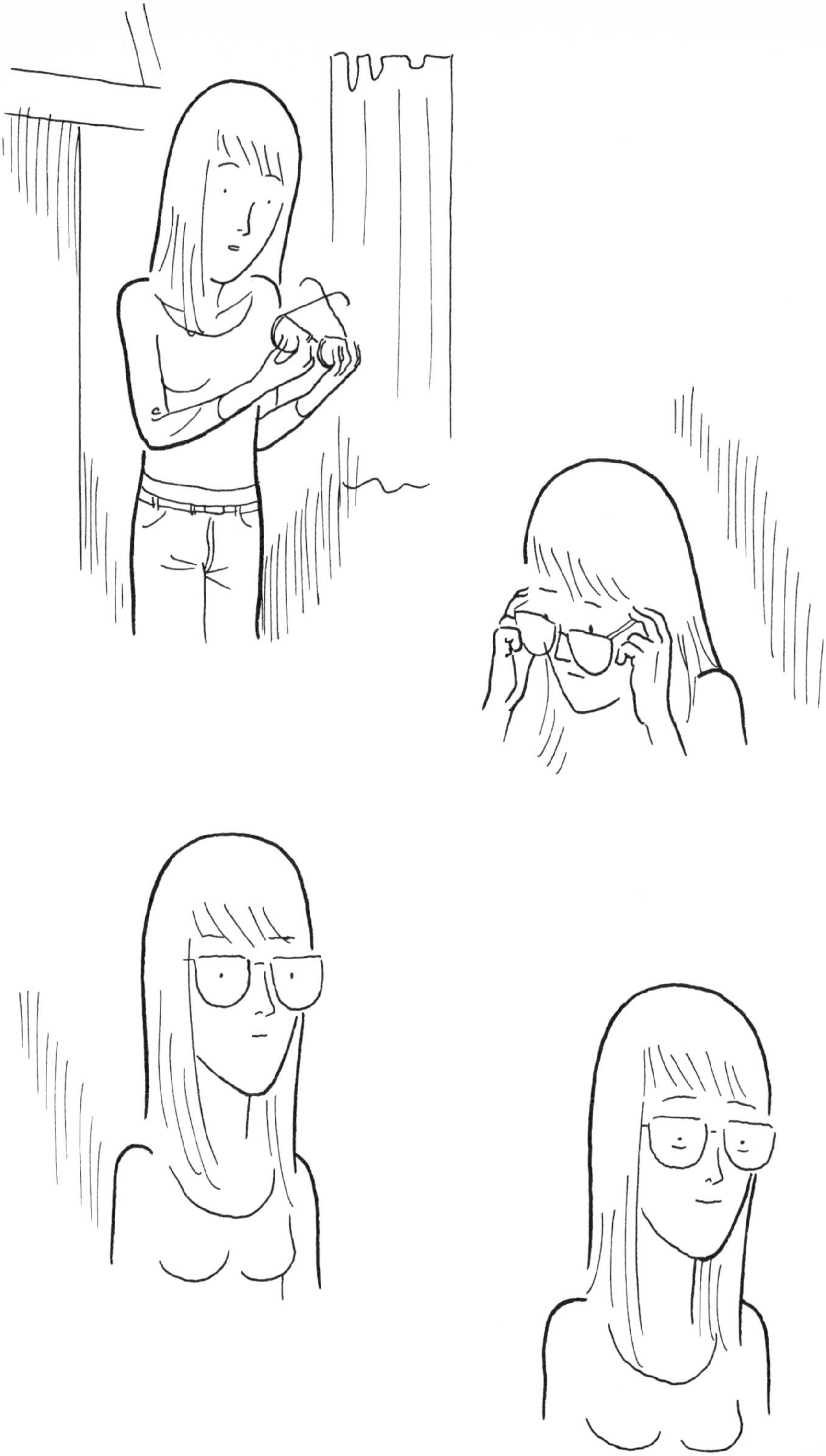

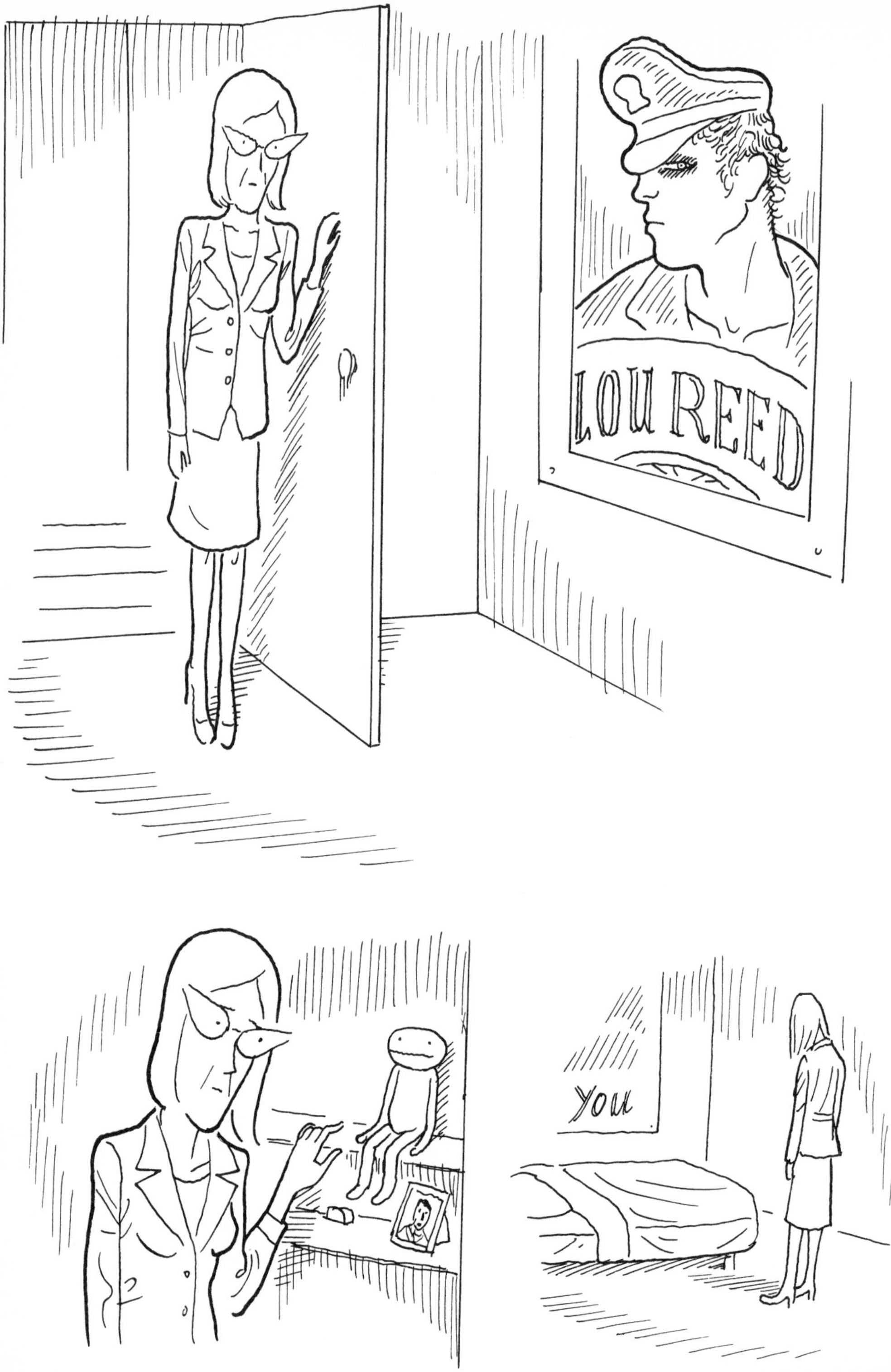
LOU REED
YOU

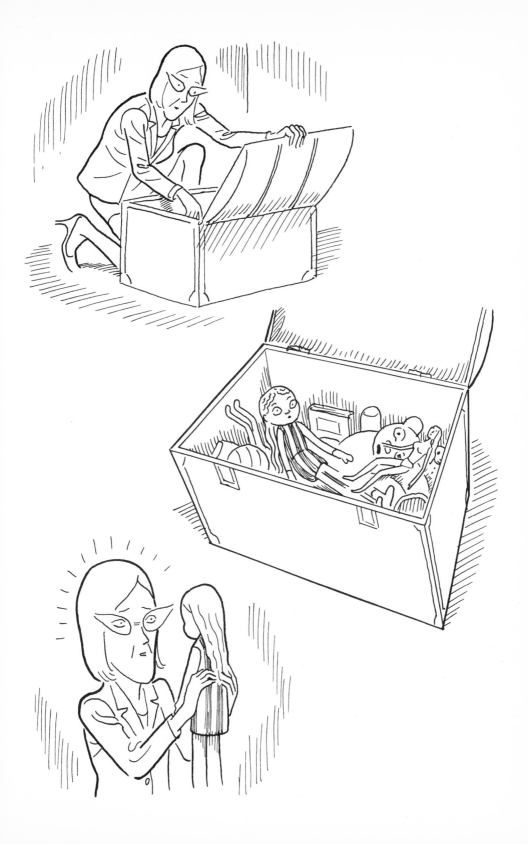

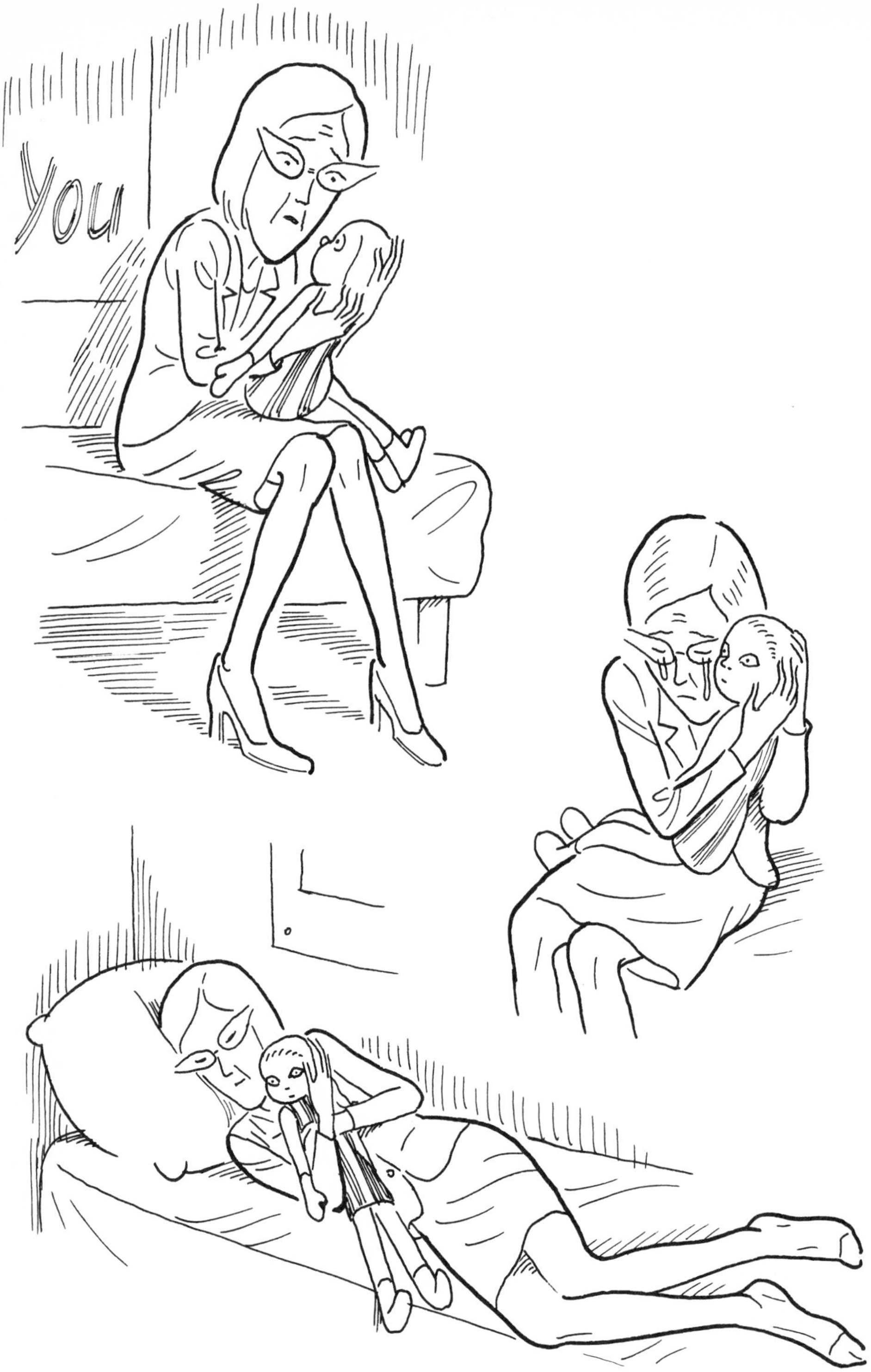
You

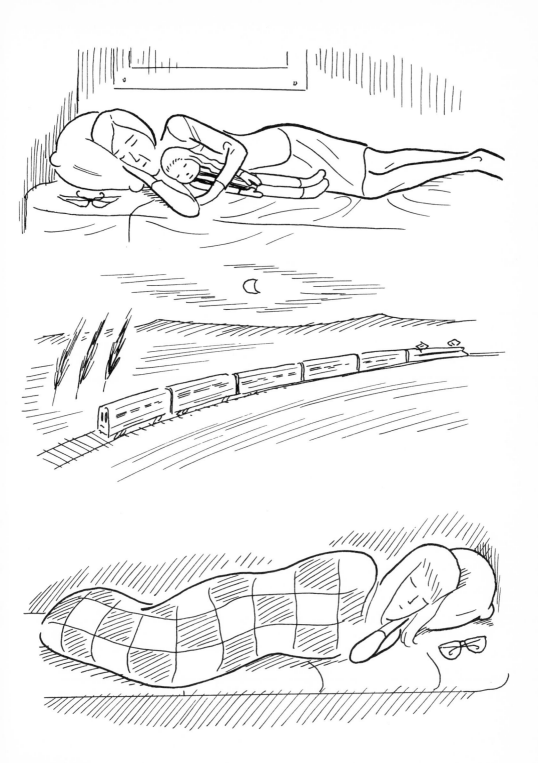

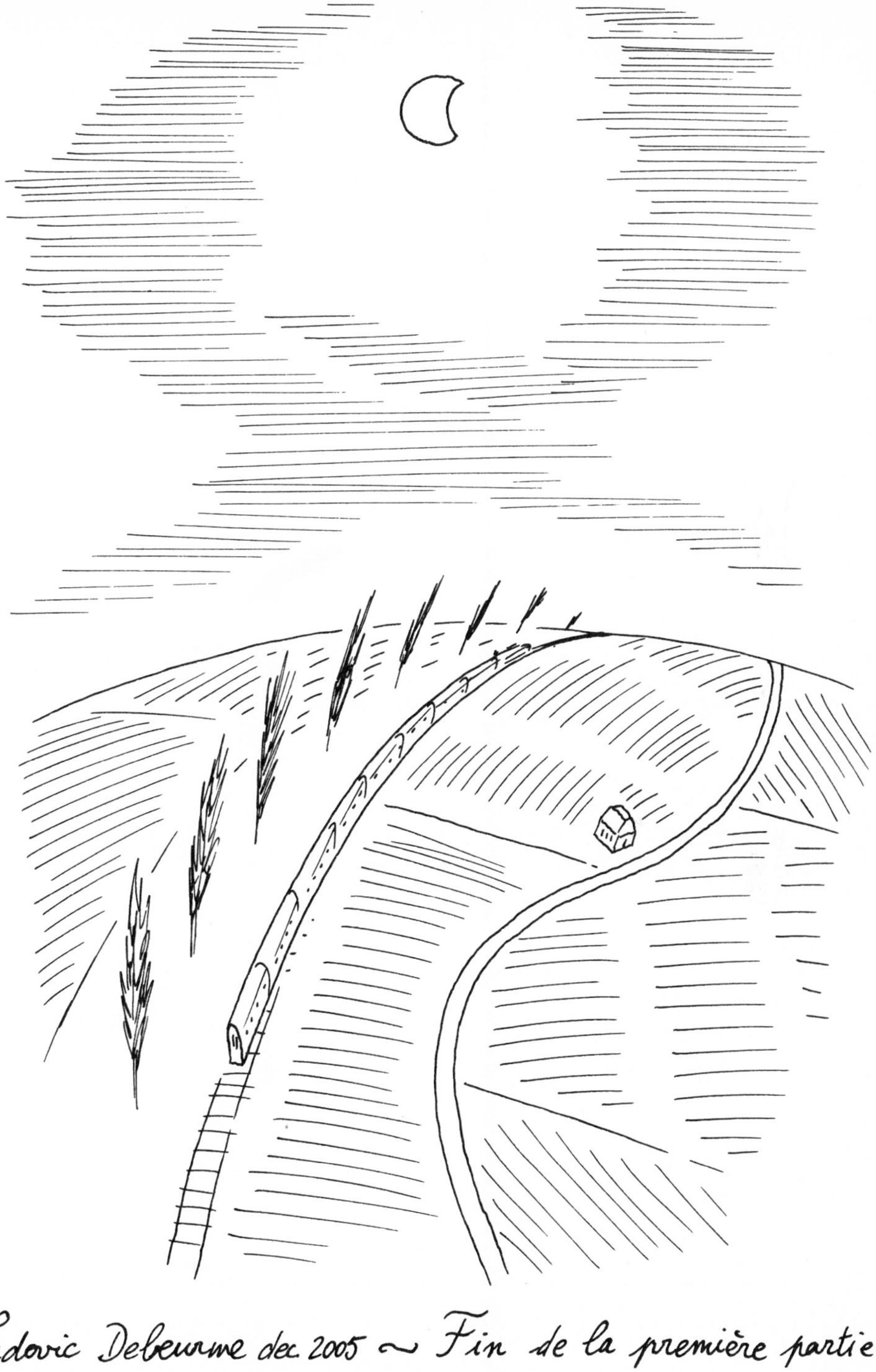

Ludovic Debeurme dec. 2005 ~ Fin de la première partie

End of Part I

Lucille by Ludovic Debeurme © 2006 Futuropolis (Paris, France)

First English-language edition published by
Top Shelf Productions
PO Box 1282
Marietta, GA 30061-1282, USA
Visit our online catalog at www.topshelfcomix.com

Publishers: Brett Warnock and Chris Staros
Translation: Edward Gauvin
Lettering and Design: Christopher Ross

First printing, April 2011

Printed in China